W9-BUR-254

NEW PERSPECTIVES ON POVERTY

Advisory Editor
Thomas M. Meenaghan, *New York University*

Related books of interest

Policy, Politics, and Ethics: A Critical Approach
Thomas M. Meenaghan, Keith M. Kilty, Dennis D. Long, and John G. McNutt

Advocacy Practice for Social Justice, Second Edition
Richard Hoefer

The Dynamics of Family Policy: Analysis and Advocacy
Alice K. Butterfield, Cynthia J. Rocha, and William H. Butterfield

Social Work with HIV and AIDS: A Case-Based Guide
Diana Rowan

The Costs of Courage: Combat Stress, Warriors, and Family Survival
Josephine G. Pryce, Col. David H. Pryce, and Kimberly K. Shackelford

Social Work Practice with Latinos: Key Issues and Emerging Themes
Rich Furman and Nalini Negi

Navigating Human Service Organizations, Third Edition
Rich Furman and Margaret Gibelman

Empowering Workers and Clients for Organizational Change
Marcia B. Cohen and Cheryl A. Hyde

Best Practices in Community Mental Health: A Pocket Guide
Vikki L. Vandiver

NEW PERSPECTIVES
ON POVERTY
POLICIES, PROGRAMS, AND PRACTICE

ELISSA D. GIFFORDS
Long Island University Post Campus

KAREN R. GARBER
Nassau County Department of Social Services

LYCEUM
BOOKS, INC.

Chicago, IL 60637

© 2014 by Lyceum Books, Inc.

Published by

LYCEUM BOOKS, INC.
5758 S. Blackstone Avenue
Chicago, Illinois 60637
773-643-1903 fax
773-643-1902 phone
lyceum@lyceumbooks.com
www.lyceumbooks.com

All rights reserved under International and Pan-American Copyright Conventions. No part of this publication may be reproduced, stored in a retrieval system, copied, or transmitted, in any form or by any means without written permission from the publisher.

6 5 4 3 2 1   14 15 16 17 18

ISBN 978-1-935871-52-1

Printed in the United States of America.

Library of Congress Cataloging-in-Publication Data

Giffords, Elissa D.
  New perspectives on poverty : policies, programs, and practice / Elissa D. Giffords, Long Island University Post Campus, Karen R. Garber, Nassau County Department of Social Services.
     pages cm
  Includes bibliographical references and index.
  ISBN 978-1-935871-52-1
  1. Poverty—United States. 2. Human services—United States. 3. United States—Social policy—21st century. I. Garber, Karen R. II. Title.
    HC110.P6G474   2014
    363.50973—dc23
                                                                          2014000034

Contents

Tables and Figures

Foreword

In *The Other America*, Michael Harrington's 1962 groundbreaking and seminal investigation into the "new" poverty of the United States, he wrote that

> it is a blow to reform and the political hopes of the poor that the middle class no longer understands that poverty exists. But, perhaps more important, the poor are losing their links with the great world. If statistics and sociology can measure a feeling as delicate as loneliness, . . . the other America is becoming increasingly populated by those who do not belong to anybody or anything. They are no longer participants in an ethnic culture from the old country; they are less and less religious; they do not belong to unions or clubs. They are not seen, and because of that they themselves cannot see. Their horizon has become more and more restricted; they see one another, and that means they see little reason to hope. (11)

In the fifty years since the publication of *The Other America*, what has really changed? Is there less poverty today? Have the billions spent on social support programs truly been effective in reaching the poorest of our peoples? And what of Harrington's 1962 middle class not even understanding that poverty even exists? Does twenty-first-century American society realize that poverty not only continues to exist, but its proliferation throughout more and more groups of society threatens the very fabric of our democracy and free society?

Thanks to the efforts of coeditors Elissa Giffords and Karen Garber, we are confronted with a stark new reality: that not only does poverty continue to exist at unimaginable levels in our society, but that there is a "new reality of poverty" where former middle and lower middle-class families now find themselves struggling to barely keep themselves out of poverty. And we now realize that poverty is no longer limited to any one group in society. The upward and seemingly unstoppable spiral of increased housing, energy, and food costs, coupled with historic levels of unemployment and underemployment, have not only brought the national tragedy of poverty to our attention, but in fact poverty has become an increasingly pervasive condition of living, if not survival for immigrants, veterans, senior citizens, the disabled, the mentally ill, and the homeless.

As Harrington (1962, p. 13) prophetically wrote, "When a recession comes, they [the poor] are pushed onto the relief rolls." And today we have reached unprecedentedly high levels of applications for local and state public assistance, including housing and homeless relief, Supplemental Nutrition Assistance Program (SNAP), child care, and the Home Energy Assistance Program.

If we subscribe to Mahatma Gandhi's belief that "a nation's greatness is measured by how it treats its weakest members," then we are indeed at a crossroad of conscience in determining and defining the true meaning of the American Spirit.

John E. Imhof, PhD
Commissioner, Nassau County Department of Social Services

Reference

Harrington, M. (1962). *The Other America: Poverty in the United States.* New York: Macmillan.

Preface

In 2006, the Nassau County Executive and county legislators with the approval from New York State appointed Dr. John Imhof as the new commissioner of the Department of Social Services. During Commissioner Imhof's first meeting with the Advisory Council's Executive Committee, he raised the question, *what is the Advisory Council doing to challenge the public's stereotypes and beliefs regarding the poor in Nassau County?* This book, *New Perspectives on Poverty: Policies, Programs, and Practice* is a product of that question, posed more than six years ago.

This book has been a labor of love. When we embarked on this journey, our goal was to educate our readers and challenge the old beliefs about people living in poverty. This book intends to answer the question, What is poverty? and to examine how it impacts various populations at risk, thereby increasing awareness among social workers, helping professionals, trained volunteers, and college students regarding how various factors such as employment policies contribute to economic inequality in the United States. It also provides targeted examinations into social welfare history, identifies key issues affecting vulnerable populations, and highlights government and community-based assistance programs. The text additionally offers discussions designed to get readers to think critically regarding social and economic justice and asks readers to consider fundamental issues related to individuals and families struggling with poverty in the United States. While we have incorporated major populations at risk, we regrettably acknowledge that there are other groups and we cannot cover all of them in a textbook. At the same time, we realize that poverty is a global issue although we deliberately kept the focus on the United States in order to bring attention to the new face of poverty in America—particularly because the poverty rate has surged to its highest levels since 1993. In this book, we also hope to challenge some of the stereotypes about the poor and educate readers about how our past plays a role in where we are today.

This book is unique in that it combines theoretical, empirical, and clinical knowledge in a jargon-free, reader-friendly manner to equip readers with current trends about the new reality of poverty in America, particularly since the Great Recession began in 2007, leaving many middle-class families in poverty or vulnerable to harsh economic conditions and a sluggish recovery. It attempts to present readers with balanced coverage regarding the multidimensional issues related to poverty and social inequity, while exploring issues related to social injustice and empowerment. Readers will also learn about the contemporary public and private sector approaches used to address poverty, and examine how value-based beliefs and political ideologies influence social welfare policies. We believe that social workers and other helping professionals must be aware of social welfare history as well as contemporary approaches used to address poverty in order to effect meaningful change. Knowledge in these areas is important as trends shift over time, and has a monumental impact on human service workers and people in need.

Throughout the book, we attempt to provide relevant information to readers that helps foster a better understanding of the salient issues facing people who live in poverty and to encourage professionals and students to challenge their thinking about this key social problem. The content primarily focuses on the misconceptions about people who are poor, what really constitutes poverty in America, and offers suggestions for challenging some of the myths about poverty. Accordingly, the first three chapters define poverty and social welfare in historical and contemporary contexts, explore various ideologies, address contemporary approaches to reducing poverty, and include an investigation into employment-related policies. Chapters 4–10 offer in-depth explorations of various populations at risk including people who are homeless, families and children, older adults, people with disabilities, immigrants and refugees, individuals with co-occurring disorders, and veterans and military families. While the book is intended to be read in its entirety, chapters can also be read separately. Most chapters contain relevant case studies, which are designed to enhance readers' critical thinking and provide examples of interventions at micro, mezzo, and macro levels of practice. Each case study also includes questions for consideration and discussion that can be used for personal reflection, or full class lectures or in small groups. Finally, the last chapter offers some concrete suggestions on how individuals and groups can change the face of poverty in their own communities through multilevel approaches such as advocacy, education, and policy development. Faculty may find this section useful for student assignments as it provides hands-on strategies geared toward education, advocacy, and effecting policy changes.

Helping must go beyond the initial desire to do something—to advocate successfully people need to have a deep understanding about the causes and effects of poverty and its effect on populations at risk. Only then can we truly challenge the myths about the poor in America and encourage readers to develop knowledge that is essential to addressing this serious social issue. It is our sincere hope that social workers, helping professionals, trained volunteers, and undergraduate and graduate students alike will find this material accessible and useful in their work. Together, we can proactively make positive, long-lasting changes that benefit vulnerable groups facing or experiencing poverty.

We want to express our gratitude to Lyceum Books for recognizing the importance of this book and for their commitment to bringing this project to fruition. There are also many people along the way who deserve acknowledgment. Special thanks go to Nassau County Department of Social Services Commissioner John Imhof for challenging the Advisory Council to educate the public. We are indebted to him for his refreshing belief that stereotypes can be challenged in meaningful ways. Thanks also go to the Advisory Council members for their support and subject matter expertise. Most importantly, the chapter authors receive our highest appreciation for their hard work and dedication to this project. We must additionally thank all the significant people in our lives and our colleagues for reviewing early chapters and helping to construct case studies. We would also be remiss if we did not mention the inspiration we obtained from the individuals and families who are at risk of becoming poor or who are already living in poverty. Surely, their struggles must serve to encourage students, professionals, and members of society to recognize and undertake actions that will promote a serious change in how we address unmet needs in America.

What Is Poverty?

Elissa D. Giffords

There are millions of individuals in the United States living in poverty. However, the precise number varies according to the defining factors and measurement tools used. This chapter introduces the term *poverty* and the method of calculating the *official poverty* measures in the United States. It also discusses alternate approaches to evaluating need. These mechanisms help answer the questions *Why are people poor? Who are the poor? How many people are poor? Why are some populations such as those of different races, ethnicities, gender, age, sexual orientation, or geographic location more at risk of living in poverty than other groups?* The chapter also provides a brief summary of historical and contemporary views of poverty in America and incorporates a discussion of social and economic justice. Finally, readers of this chapter will also explore the role of helping professionals to help meet human need.

What Is Poverty?

The term *poverty* is complex. It broadly and most traditionally refers to a lack of economic resources by which individuals can attain a minimal standard of living, but it can sometimes refer to "cultural, ethical, moral, spiritual and similar kinds of social poverty" as well (Lamale, 1965, p. 822). Research on poverty includes multiple perspectives. Dolgoff and Feldstein (2009) condense these into three useful categories: "(1) Poverty means a person or family has less than an objectively defined minimum; (2) they have less than others in society; or (3) they feel they do not have enough to get along" (pp. 162–163). These circumstances often exist disproportionately among different subgroups, which are referred to as populations-at-risk or vulnerable populations. Suppes and Wells (2009, p. 89) explain to some extent, that while everyone is at risk of being poor, not everyone experiences this risk equally. Members of populations at risk often experience poverty for reasons beyond their control, frequently because of prejudice and discrimination. This leads to social oppression, which limits individuals' free and full participation in society and hinders some people from gaining full meaningful employment and equal access to services that may enhance their well-being. Examples of these groups found in the United States include racial and ethnic minority groups, such as African Americans, Hispanics or Latinos, and Native Americans; families and children, including single parents, immigrants, and youth aging out of foster care; people with both physical and mental disabilities; and older adults. Each of these populations is at risk of experiencing poverty. Social workers and related health and human services professionals frequently work with these populations to meet the needs of individuals one on one (micro), to provide programs that support and enhance individuals, groups, and communities (mezzo), and to empower individuals, families, groups, organizations, and communities to effect change in policies to improve a social condition (macro). A more in-depth discussion of specific populations at risk is found throughout this book. The following discussion defines poverty and offers a glimpse into the historical trends and current figures.

Defining Poverty

There are essentially two distinct ways to define poverty in America. These are (1) absolute poverty and (2) relative poverty.

Absolute Poverty

Absolute poverty is a fixed measurement. In the United States, there are two slightly different versions of the federal poverty measure: these are the poverty thresholds, and the poverty guidelines. The threshold calculates the number of people in poverty for the previous year (U.S. Department of Health and Human Services [HHS], 2013). This type of measurement is commonly known as the "poverty line." It typically considers the number of people living below a certain income level and the number of household members in relation to their ability to afford certain basic goods and services, most typically food. Notably, the official United States poverty line does not currently consider expenses such as the cost of rent, transportation, child care, or home heating when calculating the number of people living in poverty. In the early 1960s, an economist named Mollie Orshansky from the Social Security Administration developed this version of the federal poverty measure. Fisher (1997, para. 2) explains that Orshansky based her poverty thresholds on the cheapest food plan developed by the Department of Agriculture needed to obtain a minimally adequate diet and was described as "designed for temporary or emergency use when funds are low." Alternately, the poverty guidelines are calculated by the HHS (2013) and are primarily used by federal and state programs to determine financial eligibility and/or calculate benefits for some programs such as the Supplemental Nutrition Assistance Program (SNAP, formerly called Food Stamps). See table 1.1 for key differences between thresholds and guidelines. The HHS poverty guidelines issued annually are in the *Federal Register*. Table 1.2 presents the 2013 HHS poverty guidelines from the Federal Register, 2013.

Relative Poverty

Relative poverty is also an important component to consider when describing poverty. This subjective type of definition of poverty may evolve over time and is the focus of frequent debate. Relative poverty considers the condition of individuals who possess significantly less income and wealth than others in the United States. While not classified as poor, according to an absolute definition, individuals may feel "relatively deprived" in comparison to the average American family. This view of poverty assumes that individuals are able to meet a certain minimal standard of living. In this sense, individuals often compare themselves to their neighbors, which is exemplified by the saying "keeping up with the Joneses." The notion of relative poverty is quite complex. For example, while a two-parent family may be working full-time at low-wage jobs that bring them above the absolute poverty line, the parents cannot afford holiday gifts for their children. The family is able to observe that other families in their neighborhood buy their young school-age children gifts. This may lead to the family feeling deprived. Yet, is a family who cannot afford to experience the holidays similar to their neighbors, poor? Consider, a single woman who receives Social Security Disability Insurance (SSDI) from the government because she has a chronic illness, which prevents her from working full-time. This woman uses her SSD check to pay her rent, electricity, and to purchase some food. She must rely on assistance from the local parish outreach for food and frequently skips her medication because there is not enough money left over to pay for her full prescription. The amount she receives from her SSD check causes her to be ineligible for Medicaid. Should this woman be considered impoverished?

Table 1.1. Key Differences between Thresholds and Guidelines

	Poverty Thresholds	Poverty Guidelines
Issuing Agency	Census Bureau	Department of Health and Human Services
Purpose/Use	Statistical—calculating the number of people in poverty	Administrative—determining financial eligibility for certain programs
Characteristics by Which They Vary	Detailed (48-cell) matrix of thresholds varies by family size, number of children, and, for 1- & 2-person units, whether or not elderly. Weighted average thresholds vary by family size and, for 1- & 2-person units, whether or not elderly. There is no geographic variation; the same figures are used for all 50 states and D.C.	Guidelines vary by family size. In addition, there is one set of figures for the 48 contiguous states and D.C.; one set for Alaska; and one set for Hawaii.
Timing of Annual Update	The Census Bureau issues preliminary poverty thresholds in January, and final poverty thresholds in September of the year *after* the year for which poverty is measured. The poverty thresholds are adjusted to the price level of the year for which poverty is measured. For example, the poverty thresholds for calendar year 2012 were issued in 2013 (preliminary in January, final in September), were used to measure poverty for calendar year 2012, and reflect the price level of calendar year 2012.	HHS issues poverty guidelines in late January of each year. Some programs make them effective on date of publication, others at a later date. For example, the 2013 poverty guidelines were issued in January 2013, calculated from the calendar year 2011 thresholds issued in September 2012, updated to reflect the price level of calendar year 2012. Therefore, the 2013 poverty guidelines are approximately equal to the poverty thresholds for 2012 (for most family sizes).
How Updated or Calculated	The *48-cell matrix* is updated each year from the 1978 threshold matrix using the CPI-U. The *preliminary weighted average thresholds* are updated from the previous year's *final* weighted average thresholds using the CPI-U. The *final weighted average thresholds* are calculated from the *current* year's 48-cell matrix using family weighting figures from the Current Population Survey's Annual Social and Economic Supplement.	Guidelines are updated from the latest *published* (final) *weighted average* poverty *thresholds* using the CPI-U. (Figures are rounded, and differences between adjacent-family-size figures are equalized.)
Rounding	Rounded to the nearest dollar	Rounded to various multiples of $10— may end only in zero.

Source: U.S. Department of Health and Human Services, http://aspe.hhs.gov/poverty/faq.shtml#differences.

Table 1.2. 2013 HHS Poverty Guidelines

Family size	48 Contiguous states and D.C.	Alaska	Hawaii
1	$11,490	$14,350	$13,230
2	15,510	19,380	17,850
3	19,530	24,410	22,470
4	23,550	29,440	27,090
5	27,570	34,470	31,710
6	31,590	39,500	36,330
7	35,610	44,530	40,950
8	39,630	49,560	45,570
More than 8 persons	Add $4,020 for each additional person	Add $5,030 for each additional person	Add $4,620 for each additional person

Source: Federal Register, vol. 78, no. 16, January 24, 2013, pp. 5182–5183, http://www.gpo.gov/fdsys/pkg/FR-2013-01-24/pdf/2013-01422.pdf.

Alternative Lenses to Understand Poverty

In recent years there have been ongoing discussions to identify ways to improve the way the United States measures poverty (for example, see Beverly, 2001; Citro & Michael, 1995; Garner & Short, 2008; Pimpare, 2009; Sandoval, Rank, & Hirschl, 2009). In 1995 the National Academy of Sciences (NAS) Panel on Poverty and Family Assistance released a report that evaluated poverty measures in the United States and made recommendations for improvement (Citro & Michael, 1995). The NAS Panel recommended several changes to reflect more accurately the state of economic well-being over time, among families and individuals, and to identify differences in poverty across population groups. The panel also suggested modifications to the poverty thresholds, and the definition of income or family resources (Citro & Michael, 1995; Short, 2001, 2005). Specially, recommendations include (but are not limited to) adjusting the poverty thresholds to reflect actual consumer expenditures; accounting for expenses such as child care and health insurance premiums; reflecting geographic regional differences in cost of living; and counting cash from income and noncash transfers from government benefits such as SNAP and the Home Energy Assistance Program (HEAP). The NAS Panel report concludes that without modification, the current poverty measure will be unable to provide the public or researchers and policymaking bodies with accurate information, particularly in the face of continuing socioeconomic and government policy change (Citro & Michael, 1995).

Since the NAS Panel released its report, there have been many alternate suggestions to reform poverty measures in the United States. Typically, these proposals reflect people's political ideologies. Briefly, Democrats for example, usually feel the poverty statistics grossly understate the numbers of people living in poverty for many reasons, including that the current mechanisms of measuring poverty do not take expenses such as housing costs, child care expenses, and out-of-pocket medical expenditures into account. Republicans, on the other hand, often believe the numbers are overstated for various reasons, including their belief that the current mechanism does not include noncash or government benefits. In general, it becomes clear that the way individuals define poverty and how they think it should be objectively measured is likely to reflect their own ideology or inherent beliefs about the poor.

As part of the NAS report, Citro and Michaels (1995) explain a related idea called poverty thresholds. Unlike the fixed state of absolute poverty, relative poverty thresholds compare the income or consumption of a family to that of other typical families. The relative approach, as such, designates a point in the distribution of income or expenditures. Relative thresholds, for example, might set the poverty threshold for a family at 50 percent of the median income and adjust it by family composition. Dolgoff and Feldstein (2009) state proponents of this approach argue this is a better indicator of who is poor because it is linked to a societal average income level. Opponents, however, suggest the cost of implementing this type of threshold is too costly.

People interested in studying poverty should be aware of two specific alternative measures frequently included in these types of discussions. The first is the Self-Sufficiency Standard, which defines the amount of income necessary to meet the basic needs of families in households where the adults are working full-time and includes the costs of basic needs (child care, food, health care, housing, miscellaneous items, and transportation). Additionally, it considers the impact of taxes and tax credits and assumes families are not receiving public assistance such as housing or Medicaid, or help from private or religious organizations or family (e.g., unpaid babysitting, food, or shared housing). This calculation also includes geographic specificity for each county in a state, and various family compositions such as a two-parent with one child or a single mother with three children (Pearce, 2010, p. 1).

Finally, the U.S. Census Bureau recently released a new supplemental poverty measure (SPM) in fall 2011 based on the NAS methodology, with some revisions. The Interagency Technical Working Group on Developing a Supplemental Poverty Measure (2010) explains that the SPM will not replace the official poverty measure; rather it was designed as an experimental measure that will define thresholds and resources in a manner different from the official poverty measure. This new tool will provide important information not traditionally available on the makeup and characteristics of the population living in poverty. The SPM is another macro-economic tool, which provides aggregate data on a national level or within sub-populations or areas to foster understanding of economic needs and trends. Like other measures of poverty, the SPM will need to be updated regularly, at the same time as the official poverty statistics, for example (Short, 2011).

Summary of Historical and Contemporary Views in America

Trattner (1999) reveals that the basic tenets and programs of social welfare systems reflect the values, customs, and past practices of their society. It is for this reason that it is crucial to have a fundamental understanding of the foundations on which the practice of helping people was built.

Colonial America

The mechanisms by which Americans began assisting others in the colonial era are rooted in Europe, especially England. Despite the portrayal of life in America as a land of opportunity, once they arrived, many new immigrants found themselves living in poverty and contending with the same social ills they thought they had left behind when they immigrated. Populations at risk including older adults, the blind, the physically disabled, mentally ill, widows, and other destitute people sometimes needed assistance. At the time there was no formalized system of care, and subsequently communities used mutual aid to assist those in need (Trattner, 1999). Mutual aid is a process wherein individuals or communities offer one another various types of help. For instance, in the colonial era if there was a barn fire, members of the community would come together to help the family rebuild their barn. Or if a widow with small children did not have many resources, community members might pay her to complete specifics tasks such as laundry or tailoring.

As the numbers of poor colonists grew, it became increasingly clear that they had to systematize poor-relief policies, especially around the mid-seventeenth century. Inevitably, the colonists in the original thirteen colonies and others as they entered the Union drew from English social and legal institutions, namely the English Poor Laws of 1601, to help the needy. Administration of these laws was through local church parishes and was rooted in the idea that poverty was an economic condition rather than a personal one. The laws, which remained for nearly 250 years, established the English government as responsible for meeting the needs of the poor. This system of assistance established three categories of dependents: (1) children, (2) able-bodied, and (3) the helpless, and it proposed measures of "indoor" (institutionalization) or "outdoor" (home) relief to address the needs of each group. Assistance included direct grants and institutional relief, apprenticeships for the young, and work relief for the able-bodied. How individuals were seen determined the relief efforts they received. Consequently, individuals viewed as worthy or deserving of assistance were provided with outdoor relief such as food, clothing, or other goods. Upon the conclusion that individuals were unworthy of outdoor relief, assistance policies mandated that recipients rely on indoor relief, which was often punitive, and administered through mechanisms such as poorhouses, where poor people were required to do backbreaking work with the intent of teaching them discipline and moral virtue (Trattner, 1999).

Akin to the Elizabethan legislation, the colonial policies established overseers of the poor in local parishes and provided officials with the authority to collect taxes for distribution to the needy. By the end of the seventeenth century, most localities established clear means of assistance that corresponded with how the community viewed the poor. Those believed to be poor through no fault of their own such as older widows or the ill would receive good treatment and support. However, the community dealt harshly with those thought to be able-bodied and lazy (Trattner, 1999).

The Aftermath of the Civil War

Following the Civil War (1861–1865) the Bureau of Refugees, Freedmen and Abandoned Land was established by an act in 1865 after an investigation into the conditions of freed slaves. Informally known as the Freemen's Bureau, it was set up amidst much political turmoil to meet the needs of newly freed slaves. At the onset, there was a bitter struggle between Congress and President Andrew Johnson, who vetoed the bill to establish the bureau, on the basis that it would help more African Americans than Caucasians and because he believed there should not be a federal system of support for indigent persons. Recovery from slavery, President Johnson believed, was the freed man's own responsibility. Congress however, overrode President Johnson's veto. The bureau, nevertheless, was instituted in such a manner and without adequate funding that it was not possible for it to meet its sweeping goal of developing meaningful social and economic programs to help the freemen. Implied by its placement under the War Department, the bureau was a temporary or wartime program rather than a permanent program, and it was terminated in 1872. During its brief existence, however, it did establish that the federal government could intervene on behalf of the needy when local efforts did not exist (Jansson, 2009; Trattner, 1999).

Scientific Charity

In the mid- to late nineteenth century many people began to look to the burgeoning realm of science to deal with the poor. Herbert Spencer and William Graham Sumner applied Charles Darwin's theory of evolution known as Social Darwinism to social conditions. This was merged with the economic philosophy called laissez-faire, a view rooted in the idea that the government should avoid any regulation of the economy, thereby enabling the market to regulate itself. Taking this belief one step further, the social scientists of the time applied these assumptions to society. The term "survival of the fittest," coined by Spencer, therefore characterizes the harsh belief of the time that individuals with limited resources should follow nature's evolutionary plan and be allowed to die out (Karger & Stoesz, 2014). This led to the general sense that the kindest approach to helping the poor was not to provide financial assistance per se, but to encourage self-reliance. Suppes and Wells (2009) assert that this philosophy overlooks the reality that people cannot truly survive without assistance and ask their readers to consider the example of infants to illustrate this point.

The philosophical arguments of that time are eerily similar to those previously discussed in earlier historical eras and to current-day ones as well. The conflicts in values still encroach upon the way society currently responds to people in need. There were two primary movements relevant to poverty affected by this conflict of values: the Charity Organization Society and the settlement house movement.

Charity Organization Society and the Settlement House Movement
Charity Organization Society

Early relief efforts started to change into a disciplined process in the latter part of the nineteenth century. Agencies, known as charity organization societies (COS), developed in many local jurisdictions. The first American COS created in 1877 in Buffalo, New York, by Stephen Humpreys Gurteen was patterned after the London Charity Organization Society to combat indiscriminate relief-giving and encouraging laziness and fraud (Trattner, 1999). These nongovernmental agencies initially sought to coordinate philanthropic giving—mostly to avoid duplication of assistance from two or more agencies, although eventually these agencies gave relief to destitute persons themselves. The early workers who were mostly women, called friendly visitors, learned to provide moral guidance and instruction to those under their care. As part of the process, friendly visitors were to conduct careful research of individuals and families in need and model acceptable behavior (e.g., hard work and thrift) throughout the helping process. They frequently turned away those who did not seem to live a moral life or those who did not strive toward achieving independence (Jansson, 2009). Like earlier points in history, the poor were viewed as "worthy" or "unworthy" of assistance. Josephine Shaw Lowell, a leader of the COS movement, echoed the thoughts of many when she declared:

> Human nature is so constituted that no [working] man can receive as a gift what he should earn by his own labor without moral deterioration. No human being . . . will work to provide the means of living for himself if he can get a living in any other manner agreeable to himself. (Josephine Shaw Lowell, 1884, in Trattner, 1999, p. 95)

Lowell and other leaders of COS drew from the conservative philosophies of Social Darwinism and the Protestant work ethic, a term originated by the sociologist Max Weber, that captured the value society placed on work during the seventeenth to nineteenth centuries. The Protestant work ethic proclaimed salvation was reached through hard work rather than through charity and was preordained by God. People of the time were judged based on the amount of wealth they acquired. If people were poor, it was believed to be the moral fault of the individual (Zastrow, 2010).

Eventually, society's beliefs shifted to recognize that morality did not always play a part in who was poor. There was also a growing view that workers required more training that focused on helping individuals adjust to society. Mary Richmond, another well-known American leader in the COS movement, taught in the first charity workers training school in 1898, the New York School of Philanthropy (now Columbia University). Soon many colleges and universities throughout the country offered similar curricula. These classes were early social work educational training programs (Suppes & Wells, 2009; Zastrow, 2010). Notably, social casework, a micro approach to helping individuals, developed from this movement.

Settlement House Movement

Settlement houses were formed around the late nineteenth century concurrently with the COS movement. In 1884, London's first settlement house, Toynbee Hall, emphasized the need for environmental reform—rather than the provision of moral guidance to assist the poor. Like previous methods for dealing with the poor, American cities looked to England for a model to address the ill effects of industrialization, urbanization, and immigration, which grew tremendously in the late nineteenth and early twentieth centuries. Stanton Coit opened Neighborhood Guild, America's first settlement house, in 1886, and Jane Addams, one of the movement's most famous leaders, established Hull House, the most famous settlement house, in 1889 (Trattner, 1999).

Settlement houses embodied the neighborhood ideal of establishing communities so that they could work to improve the neighborhood or to address collectively the social problems faced by various groups. Unlike COS, settlement workers, called residents, lived among the poor. This enabled them to understand the plight of the poor through direct observation and subsequently to work toward meeting their needs. In this role, residents were able to shed light on "the other half" of America. By living among the poor, they came to recognize what they considered the real causes of poverty and to address social issues such as industrialization through self-help and mutual aid (Trattner, 1999). The settlement house programs and services ranged from providing child care for working mothers, garbage collection for the community, and getting participants involved in the political process to advocate for social reform (Suppes & Wells, 2009). The social work methods of group work and community organization, mezzo and macro interventions, are associated with this movement. See exhibit 1.1 for more distinctions.

Exhibit 1.1. Charity Organization Society and Settlement House Movement Compared

Charity Organization Society	Settlement House Movement
Leader	
Mary Richmond	Jane Addams
Type of Worker	
"Friendly Visitors"	Volunteers Who Lived among Poor
Types of Aid Offered	
Central Registry of Poor Short-Term Charity Moral Uplift	Mutual Aid Self-Help Social and Political Action
Primary Level of Intervention	
Casework with Individuals and Families	Group Work; Work with Families, Organizations, and Communities

Source: Suppes & Wells, 2009, p. 107.

Merging Movements

By the early twentieth century, the settlement house and charity organization movements had merged. COS agents came to recognize that social and economic factors or other aspects within the environment contributed to poverty. Conversely, the settlement house workers acknowledged that personal frailties might contribute to poverty, though they did not feel that individuals should be held responsible for social and economic failings, which resulted in oppression. Thus, reformers sought preventative legislation and social insurance to reduce the need for charity (Trattner, 1999). Of course, as denoted throughout history, there remained two societal views of the poor: one with a belief that inherent personal defects or immorality caused individuals' poverty; and the second, which viewed poverty and dependency as a result of defects in the structure of society. Also notable is that at this time in history, no federal programs existed to assist the poor.

Progressive Era

The term *Progressive Era* roughly incorporates the time beginning with the turn of the twentieth century through the 1920s. This period in U.S. history reflects a time of change wherein Americans thought about and responded to poverty and related social conditions in a meaningful way. Before the Progressive Era, many discussions about the poor reflected the conservative philosophies of the post-Civil War period, where beliefs such as Social Darwinism were commonplace. This was the time also marked by the founding of the Charity Organization Society and the settlement house movement (Segal, Gerdes, & Steiner, 2010), when social problems were addressed differently (discussed above). There were challenges raised about the underlying assumptions about the poor and whether individuals were truly responsible for their plight during this time (Mink & O'Connor, 2004; Segal et al., 2010), and what if any role government had in addressing poverty and its related problems. This was also a time when U.S. workers changed from primarily earning their living from agriculture to one in which they worked in manufacturing, and the turn of the century was noted for rapid industrialization, immigration, and urbanization (Segal et al., 2010). During this time, Progressives believed that government should regulate or oversee "big business" (i.e., regulate manufacturing jobs) as a way to protect workers and the public's most vulnerable members of society. This time was particularly renowned for advocates' commitment to social justice and a distinct focus on social, economic, and political reforms. These ideas lasted until the 1920s, when the nation took on a more conservative tone again (Karger & Stoesz, 2014).

The Great Depression and the New Deal

The stock market crash in 1929 led to the Great Depression. The crash created a massive disruption in the financial markets of the country, drastically devalued capital stocks, greatly depressed levels of disposable income, and, by virtue of the high unemployment and rapid deflation it generated, so biased the already unequal distribution of purchasing power as to virtually eliminate consumer and investor confidence. Idle plants and unemployed workers dampened entrepreneurial spirit and depressed the rate of net investment. At the same time reduced investment lowered effective demand by lessening employment and thereby [further] idled plants and employees (Bemstein, 1987, p. 30 as cited in Hill, Hirschman, & Bauman, 1996, p. 264).

Hill et al. (1996) explain that within six months of the collapse of the stock market, the Great Depression exhausted individuals' small savings and other funds that buffered families from economic turmoil during difficult fiscal times. Renters fell behind in their payments, mortgages went unpaid, and unemployed families found themselves seeking charity from neighborhood churches and organizations. Unemployment rose to 25 percent of workers, and layoffs were commonplace (Jansson, 2009).

Before this devastating catastrophe, Americans generally believed in the notion of individualism. This means that people are the master of their individual fate and that if someone was in need it was because that person was lazy or morally corrupt. President Herbert Hoover (1929–1933) promoted a conservative philosophy and was a proponent of laissez-faire economics. Laissez-faire is "the theory that society works best when people freely advance their own material self-interest within an unimpeded private marketplace" (Gilbert & Terrell, 2002, p. 19). Hoover did not believe in governmental programs to help poverty-stricken Americans. Instead, he believed private agencies should address the needs of the poor and he "tended to favor budget cutting, tax reduction and trickle-down economics to cope with the depression" (Jansson, 2009, p. 219). Eventually, while Hoover did institute some minimal measures, they were few and underfunded. As the Great Depression deepened, American's confidence in Hoover and the role of government was dramatically shaken.

Franklin Delano Roosevelt (FDR) was president from 1933 to 1945. His overwhelming victory in the presidential election of 1932 served as a mandate for him "to lift the United States from the throes of its worst depression in history . . . [wherein] unemployment grew to over twenty-five percent of the nation's workforce, with more than twelve million Americans out of work" (Miller Center of Public Affairs, 2010, Domestic Affairs, para. 1). FDR's New Deal spent billions of dollars on food, clothing, and shelter and utilized public works projects to employ approximately 3.2 million individuals a month. In 1935, the Social Security Act, the foundation of the American social welfare system, became law. This legislation established the role of the federal government in helping to meet the social and economic needs of its citizens. No longer viewed as the fault of the individual, poverty affected millions of Americans throughout the country because of broad economic instability facing the nation (Dolgoff & Feldstein, 2009; Jansson, 2009; Karger & Stoesz, 2014). Thus, while there was wide acceptance of the environmental aspects of poverty (e.g., social rather than individual factors), there were primarily two approaches that reformers advocated to solve America's problems. One group (liberals) called for more government interventions, while the other (conservatives) wanted less, and while the federal government drastically enacted social insurance legislation, the initiatives reflected compromises.

The Role of the Welfare State

What if any should the role of government have in the day-to-day lives of its citizens? The current American social welfare system has its tenets firmly grounded in the past. Throughout history, there have been two primary views of how social welfare programs should function. One emphasizes self-reliance and avoiding dependency, while the second has more of an altruistic sense whereby community members collectively have responsibility for each other. In their seminal work, Wilensky and Lebeaux (1965) identified two concepts of social welfare in the United States that are in opposition to each other: the residual and the institutional.

Residual

According to Wilensky and Lebeaux (1965), under a residual view, social welfare institutions should come into play only when the normal structures of supply and demand, the family, and the market break down. Consequently, it is only after an individual exhausts all other assets, such as their family, community-based organizations, or religious institutions and other measures should the government step in and assist—temporarily—until the individual is able to become self-sufficient and independent again. This approach recognizes that things do happen and when this occurs "we" (society) should provide social and financial resources—but only as a last resort.

Institutional

Alternately, the institutional view suggests that social and financial programs should be "accepted as a proper, legitimate function[s] of modern industrial society in helping individuals achieve self-fulfillment" (Wilensky & Lebeaux, 1965, p. 139). This approach recognizes the environmental or societal aspects that may contribute to individuals' challenges, which are beyond their control. This view sees welfare services "as a normal first line function of modern society" (Wilensky

& Lebeaux, 1965, p. 138). This approach assists all socioeconomic groups rather than just those in poverty (residual). The institutional conception of social welfare therefore, is a universal approach, whereas the residual one is selective, which is also known as a safety net.

Universal versus Selective

Who shall benefit from assistance is often the subject of much debate. Gilbert and Terrell (2002) explain that the underlying criteria are referred to as social allocations. Like the institutional approach, under universalism benefits are provided to all citizens as a basic right. A popular example of a universal benefit is Social Security for older adults. In contrast, a selective approach is one based on needs and is subject to income and resource tests, known as means testing, to determine eligibility. Examples are the Supplemental Nutrition Assistance Program (SNAP) and public assistance. Given these types of programs have strict income and resource eligibility guidelines, only carefully targeted eligible beneficiaries receive assistance. Consequently, these allocations are in line with the residual view. This perspective tends to stigmatize those in need of assistance or charity, and assumes that recipients have failed in some way.

In succeeding chapters, readers will learn about various social welfare programs and explore their classification as universal benefit/institutional approach or in contrast if they are selective/residual programs. This material will be presented from a general perspective and then it will be followed by specific discussions for several targeted populations at risk. To understand the new realities of poverty among different people, it is first important to provide a depiction of the poor in the United States.

Current Demographics and Characteristics of Poverty in America
Income Inequality

The U.S. Census data from 2011 show that when aggregate household income is examined by quintiles that income declined for the middle and fourth quintiles. Yet, income increased 1.6 percent for the highest quintile. Also noteworthy is that the aggregate share of wealth of the top 5 percent increased 5.3 percent (from 21.0 to 22.1) (DeNavas-Walt, Proctor, & Smith, 2012). This gap in income is referred to as income inequality, which is when the wealthiest members of society possess the greatest concentration of income—in other words, the rich have more than the poor, and can be reflected in the saying "the haves and the have-nots." Between 2010 and 2011, there was an increase in income inequality (DeNavas-Walt et al., 2012), sometimes called the Great Divergence. Lowrey (2012) further purports that income inequality was at the highest levels since the Great Depression, with the top 1 percent of earners acquiring 93 percent of the income gains. This is a trend that advocates against poverty would like reversed. Another trend of concern is that the poverty rate has markedly increased during the last decade.

U.S. Official versus Alternate Measures of Poverty Estimates

The U.S. Census's official measure of poverty revealed that 46.2 million Americans lived below the poverty line in 2011, roughly comprising the same numbers as seen in 2010 (DeNavas-Walt et al., 2012). These numbers are the largest counted in the measure's recorded history, which goes back as far as 1959 (Gabe, 2012, p. 1). The 2011 poverty rate of 15 percent, statistically tied with 2010, is also the highest seen since 1993 (Gabe, 2012).

Readers should additionally review data from the supplemental poverty measure (SPM) discussed earlier in this chapter to get another picture of poverty in America. As explained previously, many believe that the "official measure" is outdated and inaccurate because as Gabe (2012) reminds us, it does not account for elements such as anti-poverty programs, geographic cost of living differences, taxes, work-related expenses (e.g., child care), medical costs, and changing family dynamics (e.g., cohabitation among unmarried couples).

With that in mind readers should consider that for 2011, the SPM yields a poverty rate of 16.1 percent and suggests there are nearly 50 million (49.7) Americans who are poor, compared to the 46.6 million under the official definition of poverty. Also notable is that for most demographic groups, SPM rates were also higher than official poverty rates (Short, 2012). (See figure 1.1.)

Characteristics of People Living in Poverty

The Institute for Research on Poverty (2013) explains the poverty rate "represents an average over the entire population, and does not really tell us who," in particular, "is well off, who is worse off." For that, it is necessary to examine poverty levels for particular groups. Most notably, for instance, "blacks and Hispanics have poverty rates that greatly exceed the average" (Institute for Research on Poverty, 2013, para. 3).

Figure 1.1. Poverty Rates Using Two Measures for Total Population and by Age Group: 2011

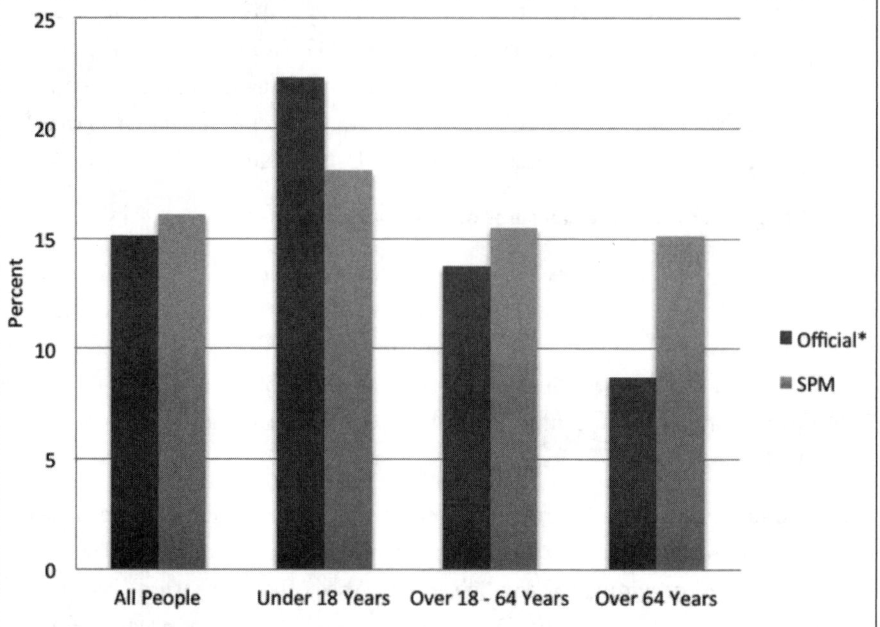

*Includes unrelated individuals under age 15.
Source: U.S. Census Bureau, Current Population Survey, 2012 Annual Social and Economic Supplement

Source: Short, K. (2012). The Research Supplemental Poverty Measure: 2010, p. 5. Retrieved from http://www.census.gov/prod/2012pubs/p60-244.pdf.

Race and Hispanic Origin

According to the U.S. Census Bureau (2012), the poverty rate for non-Hispanic Caucasians was lower in 2011 (9.8 percent) than it was for other racial groups. The 2011 poverty rate for blacks was 27.6 percent, for Asians it was 12.3 percent. Hispanics were the only group to see a decline in the poverty rate from 26.5 percent in 2010 to 25.3 percent in 2011 (DeNavas-Walt et al., 2012).

Nativity

The U.S. Census Bureau reveals the poverty rate for naturalized citizens went up between 2010 and 2011; among the foreign-born population, the poverty rate decreased (from 19.9 percent in 2010 to 19.0 percent in 2011). The 2011 poverty rates of native-born people were statistically unchanged from 2010 (14.4 percent) (DeNavas-Walt et al., 2012).

Gender

More females (16.3 percent) than males (13.6 percent) were in poverty in 2011, and while females did not show a statistically significant change, the male poverty rate decreased from 14.0 percent to 13.6 percent between 2010 and 2011. Most pronounced were gender differences in poverty rates for women aged 65 and older (10.7 percent), when compared to their male counterparts (6.2 percent) (DeNavas-Walt et al., 2012).

Age

In 2011, the poverty rates for children younger than age 18 (21.9 percent), adults 18 to 64 years of age (13.7 percent), and people over age 65 (8.7 percent) were not statistically different from their 2010 estimates (DeNavas-Walt et al., 2012). "Children represent 25 percent of the population. Yet, they comprise 36 percent of all people in poverty. Among children, 42 percent live in low-income families and approximately one in every five live in poor families" (Chau, Thampi, & Wight, 2010, p. 1).

Work Experience

When reviewing poverty rates and work experience, DeNavas-Walt et al. (2012) report that the poverty rates in 2011 were not statistically different from those in 2010. "7.2 percent of workers aged 18 to 64 were in poverty. The poverty rate for those who worked full time, year round was 2.8 percent, while the poverty rate for those working less than full time, year round was 16.3 percent" (p. 16). Sixty-one percent of people aged 18 to 64 who did not work were in poverty, compared with 25.4 percent of all people aged 18 to 64 in 2011 (DeNavas-Walt et al., 2012).

Other Categories

The U.S. Census Bureau also looks at other characteristics and their relationships to poverty. These include but are not limited to disability status, family composition, region, and residence (see table 1.3). Many of these characteristics are explored throughout this book.

Table 1.3. People in Poverty by Selected Characteristics: 2010 and 2011

Numbers in thousands, confidence intervals [C.I.] in thousands or percentage points as appropriate. People as of March of the following year. For information on confidentiality protection, sampling error, nonsampling error, and definitions, see www.census.gov/apsd/techdoc/cps/cpsmar12.pdf.

Characteristic	2010[1] Total	Below poverty Number	Below poverty 90 percent C.I.[2] (±)	Below poverty Percent	Below poverty Percent 90 percent C.I.[2] (±)	2011 Total	Below poverty Number	Below poverty 90 percent C.I.[2] (±)	Below poverty Percent	Below poverty Percent 90 percent C.I.[2] (±)	Change in poverty (2011 less 2010)[3] Number	Change in poverty (2011 less 2010)[3] Percent
PEOPLE **Total**	306,130	46,343	842	15.1	0.3	308,456	46,247	761	15.0	0.2	-96	-0.1
Family Status												
In families	250,200	33,120	728	13.2	0.3	252,316	33,126	729	13.1	0.3	6	-0.1
Householder	79,559	9,400	218	11.8	0.3	80,529	9,497	218	11.8	0.3	96	–
Related children under 18	72,581	15,598	364	21.5	0.5	72,568	15,539	377	21.4	0.5	-59	-0.1
Related children under 6	23,892	6,037	197	25.3	0.8	23,860	5,844	191	24.5	0.8	-193	-0.8
In unrelated subfamilies	1,680	774	115	46.1	4.8	1,623	705	109	43.4	4.5	-69	-2.6
Reference person	654	283	42	43.2	4.7	671	272	41	40.6	4.4	-10	-2.6
Children under 18	933	469	73	50.2	4.9	846	409	70	48.4	5.1	-60	-1.9
Unrelated individuals	54,250	12,449	369	22.9	0.6	54,517	12,416	347	22.8	0.5	-33	-0.2
Race[4] and Hispanic Origin												
White	239,982	31,083	675	13.0	0.3	241,334	30,849	646	12.8	0.3	-234	-0.2
White, not Hispanic	194,783	19,251	550	9.9	0.3	194,960	19,171	548	9.8	0.3	-80	–
Black	39,283	10,746	410	27.4	1.0	39,609	10,929	404	27.6	1.0	183	0.2
Asian	15,611	1,899	175	12.2	1.1	16,086	1,973	194	12.3	1.2	74	0.1
Hispanic (any race)	50,971	13,522	427	26.5	0.8	52,279	13,244	433	25.3	0.8	-278	* -1.2
Sex												
Male	149,737	20,893	469	14.0	0.3	150,990	20,501	369	13.6	0.2	-391	* -0.4
Female	156,394	25,451	473	16.3	0.3	157,466	25,746	492	16.3	0.3	295	0.1
Age												
Under 18 years	73,873	16,286	366	22.0	0.5	73,737	16,134	376	21.9	0.5	-152	-0.2
18 to 64 years	192,481	26,499	557	13.8	0.3	193,213	26,492	472	13.7	0.2	-6	-0.1
65 years and older	39,777	3,558	162	8.9	0.4	41,507	3,620	167	8.7	0.4	62	-0.2
Nativity												
Native born	266,723	38,485	796	14.4	0.3	268,490	38,661	681	14.4	0.3	176	–
Foreign born	39,407	7,858	297	19.9	0.7	39,966	7,586	311	19.0	0.7	-272	* -1.0
Naturalized citizen	17,344	1,954	120	11.3	0.7	17,934	2,233	152	12.5	0.8	*279	*1.2
Not a citizen	22,063	5,904	271	26.8	1.1	22,032	5,353	274	24.3	1.1	* -551	* -2.5

Region											
Northeast	54,710	7,038	325	12.9	0.6	54,977	7,208	319	13.1	0.6	170	0.2
Midwest	66,038	9,216	404	14.0	0.6	66,023	9,221	403	14.0	0.6	5	–
South	113,681	19,123	573	16.8	0.5	114,936	18,380	576	16.0	0.5	*–743	*–0.8
West	71,701	10,966	451	15.3	0.6	72,520	11,437	425	15.8	0.6	471	0.5
Residence											
Inside metropolitan statistical areas	258,366	38,466	925	14.9	0.3	261,155	38,202	848	14.6	0.3	–264	–0.3
Inside principal cities	98,816	19,532	584	19.8	0.5	100,183	20,007	659	20.0	0.6	475	0.2
Outside principal cities	159,550	18,933	741	11.9	0.4	160,973	18,195	625	11.3	0.3	*–739	*–0.6
Outside metropolitan statistical areas[5]	47,764	7,877	542	16.5	0.7	47,301	8,045	596	17.0	0.8	168	0.5
Work Experience											
Total, 18 to 64 years	192,481	26,499	557	13.8	0.3	193,213	26,492	472	13.7	0.2	–6	–0.1
All workers	143,687	10,462	280	7.3	0.2	144,163	10,345	257	7.2	0.2	–117	–0.1
Worked full-time, year-round	95,697	2,600	119	2.7	0.1	97,443	2,732	122	2.8	0.1	132	0.1
Less than full-time, year-round	47,991	7,862	245	16.4	0.5	46,720	7,614	230	16.3	0.5	–248	–0.1
Did not work at least 1 week	48,793	16,037	432	32.9	0.7	49,049	16,147	379	32.9	0.7	110	0.1
Disability Status[6]											
Total, 18 to 64 years	192,481	26,499	557	13.8	0.3	193,213	26,492	472	13.7	0.2	–6	–0.1
With a disability	14,974	4,196	194	28.0	1.0	14,968	4,313	175	28.8	1.0	117	0.8
With no disability	176,592	22,227	494	12.6	0.3	177,309	22,105	459	12.5	0.3	–122	–0.1

– Represents or rounds to zero.

* Statistically different from zero at the 90 percent confidence level.

[1] Consistent with 2011 data through implementation of Census 2010-based population controls.

[2] A 90 percent confidence interval is a measure of an estimate's variability. The larger the confidence interval in relation to the size of the estimate, the less reliable the estimate. Confidence intervals shown in this table are based on standard errors calculated using replicate weights instead of the generalized variance function used in the past. For more information see "Standard Errors and Their Use" at <www.census.gov/hhes/www/p60_243sa.pdf>.

[3] Details may not sum to totals because of rounding.

[4] Federal surveys now give respondents the option of reporting more than one race. Therefore, two basic ways of defining a race group are possible. A group such as Asian may be defined as those who reported Asian and no other race (the race-alone or single-race concept) or as those who reported Asian regardless of whether they also reported another race (the race-alone-or-in-combination concept). This table shows data using the first approach (race alone). The use of the single-race population does not imply that it is the preferred method of presenting or analyzing data. The Census Bureau uses a variety of approaches. Information on people who reported more than one race, such as White *and* American Indian and Alaska Native or Asian *and* Black or African American, is available from Census 2010 through American FactFinder. About 2.9 percent of people reported more than one race in Census 2010. Data for American Indians and Alaska Natives, Native Hawaiians and Other Pacific Islanders, and those reporting two or more races are not shown separately.

[5] The "Outside metropolitan statistical areas" category includes both micropolitan statistical areas and territory outside of metropolitan and micropolitan statistical areas. For more information, see "About Metropolitan and Micropolitan Statistical Areas" at <www.census.gov/population/metro>.

[6] The sum of those with and without a disability does not equal the total because disability status is not defined for individuals in the Armed Forces.

Source: U.S. Census Bureau, Current Population Survey, 2011 and 2012 Annual Social and Economic Supplements.

Source: DeNavas-Walt, C., Proctor, B. D., and Smith, J. C. (September 2012, p. 14), http://www.census.gov/prod/2012pubs/p60-243.pdf.

How Poverty Has Changed over Time

The National Poverty Center (2013) explains that from the late 1950s, the poverty rate for all Americans declined steadily throughout the 1960s, reaching a low of 11.1 percent, or 22.9 million individuals, in 1973. Since the mid-1970s, Waddan (2010) reveals there has been an acceleration in income and wealth inequality after 2001, particularly as the United States entered the Great Recession in 2008. He also notes while this inequality in the United States has been well documented, the role of public policy in either mitigating or exaggerating the uneven distributions produced by the market is worth emphasizing. "According to the Center on Budget and Policy Priorities the inflation-adjusted income of the top 1 percent of households grew more than *ten times faster* than the income of the bottom 90 percent of households" (Feller & Stone, 2009, p. 1 as cited in Waddan, 2010, pp. 246–247). Also notable, Waddan (2010) illustrates the distinctive severity of the current recession compared to other recent recessions by highlighting the extended nature of unemployment (Waddan 2010, p. 247).

Of those officially unemployed in March 2010, 6.5 million, or 44.1 percent, had been out of work for over 27 weeks (U.S. Bureau of Labor Statistics, 2010, para. 2). In late 2009, the average spell of unemployment lasted over six months, which was "the first time that has happened since 1948, when the Bureau of Labor Statistics started tracking that number" (Peck, 2010, para. 3).

In a report to members and committees of Congress, Gabe (2012) suggests poverty continued to grow exponentially over the last decade. He explains that while the United States enjoyed a strong economy during most of the 1990s, the poverty rate increased each year from 2001 through 2004 and did not recede before the Great Recession. Accordingly, unemployment continued to rise over most of 2009, reaching a high of 10.1 percent in October. From 2010 to 2011, the unemployment rate fell 9.4 percent to 8.5 percent (Gabe, 2012, p. 1). As noted in the previous section, the poverty rate of non-aged adults reached 13.7 percent in 2011 (DeNavas-Walt et al., 2012; Gabe, 2012). Gabe (2012, p. 1) states this rate is "the highest it has been since the early 1960s," explaining "the poverty rate for non-aged adults will need to fall to 10.8 percent to reach its 2006 pre-recession level."

Unemployment will be discussed in greater detail in chapter 3 and universal assistance programs such as Unemployment Insurance (UI) and selective programs such as SNAP food assistance and Temporary Assistance for Needy Families (TANF) will be addressed in chapter 2. Programs such as these are mechanisms to assist households that experience ongoing poverty and others who find that their living standards decreased as a direct result of the recession. First, however, it is important to explore the notion of social justice, a concept that reflects individuals' abilities to equally access or participate in the opportunities in society that ensure a basic quality of life.

Social Minimum, Human Rights, and Social Justice
Social Minimum

Inequality exists in contemporary America. Inequality is principally a multidimensional concept that Jansson (2009, p. 43) explains comprises "rights, life conditions, and opportunities" that can "be influenced by our religious beliefs, social status, and personal values" as well as political and cultural perspectives. The difficulties arise, however, because there is no definitive agreement regarding what constitutes inequality and how much inequity or disparity is acceptable. This idea is rooted in the concept of the social minimum. White explains that "when we speak of a 'social minimum' we mean to refer to *the bundle of resources that a person needs in order to lead a minimally decent life in their society*" (2008, section 1, para. 1). Of course, it is difficult to agree upon what a minimally decent life is. Based on an exploration by Nussbaum and others, Dolgoff and Feldstein (2009) argue the concept generally refers to "a life comprising full human functioning and whose human dignity is not violated by hunger fear, or the absence of opportunity" (p. 11). They also raise important questions regarding whether the idea of a social minimum should be permeable depending on the circumstances or general standards in the society. Building on the concepts of absolute and relative poverty, discussed earlier in this chapter, Dolgoff and Feldstein raise the question concerning what the increasing gap between rich and poor in America implies as it relates to poverty and/or inequality, given that people in poverty in the United States are better off than their counterparts in other parts of the world. Additionally, they ponder whether different populations at risk need more income and resources to live a life with minimum dignity. These are important inquiries for anyone interested in understanding poverty and developing strategies to reduce the numbers of impoverished individuals, groups, and communities, particularly when considering how inequality is interconnected to the ideas of social justice and human rights.

Social Justice

Why are millions of Americans unable to reach a social minimum? What makes some individuals or groups better able to reach or exceed this minimum? What can we learn by examining differences between those in the "mainstream" who have attained this standard and particular population groups such as children or people of color who are more at risk of living in poverty? An essential element paramount to this discussion is the concept of *social justice*, a concept rooted in the belief that some people do not have equal access to the same potential opportunities as others, which therein limits their free and full access to and involvement in society. Jansson (2009) suggests that when examining social and economic disparities, frequently significant differences are attributed to ideas most Americans deem unethical such as violations of civil rights, life conditions, and access to opportunities. More specifically he states, "violations of access to opportunities exist when members of specific vulnerable populations [or populations at risk] . . . receive substantially inferior educational, health, job training, transportation, child care, and preschool services in comparison with a mainstream population" (2009, p. 39). The reasons for this are complex and are explored throughout this book for specific population groups including families and children, people with disabilities, older adults, and veterans. Regarding these types of inequalities, Dolgoff and Feldstein (2009) assert that wealth, power, and status should be redistributed by government for the good of individuals, communities, and society to ensure that all citizens possess a basic quality of life or meet some social minimum. They also add that without this, members of society may experience shame, which directly impacts one's self-respect and dignity. Again, we can see how this view of helping to work toward social justice is rooted in specific political ideologies. For instance, those who believe in the institutional approach are typically those who believe that government should promote or intervene on behalf of the public good and are characterized as liberals. Conversely, those that believe in a more residual approach, wherein the view is that government should not intercede because the family or private sector (market) are the best places to meet the needs of individuals are characterized as conservatives. Accordingly, most social workers are frequently more in line with a liberal philosophy.

Human Rights

In 1948, the United Nations General Assembly adopted and proclaimed the Universal Declaration of Human Rights. There are thirty articles that seek to promote respect for human rights and related freedoms among all member nations (United

Nations, 1948). Poverty advocates often cite Article 25, particularly as it relates to civil and political rights, and social and economic justice. It reads:

(1) Everyone has the right to a standard of living adequate for the health and well-being of himself and of his family, including food, clothing, housing and medical care and necessary social services, and the right to security in the event of unemployment, sickness, disability, widowhood, old age or other lack of livelihood in circumstances beyond his control.

(2) Motherhood and childhood are entitled to special care and assistance. All children, whether born in or out of wedlock, shall enjoy the same social protection.

Pimpare (2009) asserts American organizations are using the Universal Declaration of Human Rights to evaluate U.S. well-being. He shares an example from the National Economic and Social Rights Initiative (2008, para. 4 as cited in Pimpare, 2009) that identifies what they refer to as an American "Human Rights Crisis":

Civil, political, economic, social and cultural rights have all been attacked and undermined in the courts, legislatures, workplaces and the streets. Economic and social rights in particular are virtually unrecognized in the U.S. The United States faces: the highest rate of child poverty among industrialized nations, over 45 million people without health insurance, over 36 million people suffering food insecurity, a shortfall of 5 million affordable housing units and 14% of households with critical housing needs, 20% of the population being functionally illiterate, the longest working hours in the industrialized world, and working families that cannot afford basic needs such as housing and health care.

The Office of the United Nations High Commissioner for Human Rights (OHCHR) affirms human rights are rights inherent to all irrespective of "nationality, place of residence, sex, national or ethnic origin, color, religion, language, or any other status" (n.d., para. 1). Still, it becomes complicated because like many concepts of this nature, there is little agreement on how to describe specifically what constitutes human rights. Zastrow (2010) maintains that most countries recognize the goal of striving for or safeguarding human rights for all citizens. He believes that with increased attention to this issue there will be a decrease in discrimination against populations at risk such as people of color, gays, lesbians, bisexuals and transgender, and people with disabilities. Reichert exclaimed that this focused concept however, has not yet received as much attention in the social work curriculum as the related vaguer ideal of social justice (Zastrow, 2010).

By examining the social and economic policies of the United States, social workers and other related professionals can promote awareness of injustice and disparities that directly place some population groups more at risk than other groups to experience living in poverty or not reaching the social minimum discussed earlier in this chapter. These individuals are not in their current predicament because they are lazy or failed in some way, but rather because of structural issues inherent in society, such as discrimination, they experience a deficit in opportunities and resources available for mainstream Americans. Social workers and others interested in advocating on behalf of the poor must discover and analyze those factors, which impede or promote reform, and plan accordingly to shape policy. But how?

The Role of Social Workers

In the Council of Social Work Education (CSWE), the organization that oversees and accredits social work programs, the Educational Policy and Accreditation Standards (EPAS) explain that

> the purpose of the social work profession is to promote human and community well-being. Guided by a person and environment construct, a global perspective, respect for human diversity, and knowledge based on scientific inquiry, social work's purpose is actualized through its quest for social and economic justice, the prevention of conditions that limit human rights, the elimination of poverty, and the enhancement of the quality of life for all persons. (2008, p. 1)

Furthermore, within Educational Policy 2.1.5—Advance human rights and social and economic justice, the CSWE (2008 p. 3) emphasizes that

> Each person, regardless of position in society, has basic human rights, such as freedom, safety, privacy, an adequate standard of living, health care, and education. Social workers recognize the global interconnections of oppression and are knowledgeable about theories of justice and strategies to promote human and civil rights. Social work incorporates social justice practices in organizations, institutions, and society to ensure that these basic human rights are distributed equitably and without prejudice. Social workers
>
> • understand the forms and mechanisms of oppression and discrimination;
>
> • advocate for human rights and social and economic justice; and
>
> • engage in practices that advance social and economic justice.

In addition, the National Association of Social Workers (NASW) strongly promotes the importance of social justice in its Code of Ethics, a document that is intended to serve as a guide for the professional conduct of its members. The primary mission of the social work profession, the document exclaims, "is to enhance human well-being and help meet the basic human needs of all people, with particular attention to the needs and empowerment of people who are vulnerable, oppressed, and living in poverty" (NASW, 1999, para. 1). They continue,

> Social workers promote social justice and social change with and on behalf of clients. "Clients" is used inclusively to refer to individuals, families, groups, organizations, and communities. Social workers are sensitive to cultural and ethnic diversity and strive to end discrimination, oppression, poverty, and other forms of social injustice. These activities may be in the form of direct practice, community organizing, supervision, consultation, administration, advocacy, social and political action, policy development and implementation, education, and research and evaluation. Social workers seek to enhance the capacity of people to address their own needs. Social workers also seek to promote the responsiveness of organizations, communities, and other social institutions to individuals' needs and social problems. (NASW, 1999, para. 2)

Generalist Social Work Practice

A generalist practitioner, typically a social worker, receives training to use a problem solving or planned change process to assess and intervene at multiple levels to accomplish targeted and meaningful change. CSWE (2008, pp. 7–8) defines generalist practice in the EPAS as follows:

> Generalist practice is grounded in the liberal arts and the person in environment construct. To promote human and social well-being, generalist practitioners use a range of prevention and intervention methods in their practice with individuals, families, groups, organizations, and communities. The generalist practitioner identifies with the social work profession and applies ethical principles and critical thinking in practice. Generalist practitioners incorporate diversity in their practice and advocate for human rights and social and economic justice. They recognize, support, and build on the strengths and resiliency of all human beings. They engage in research-informed practice and are proactive in responding to the impact of context on professional practice. BSW practice incorporates all of the core competencies.

This involves viewing a problem within a person-in-environment framework, which essentially means that clients are influenced by and interact with various systems (Suppes & Wells, 2009; Zastrow, 2010). Figure 1.2 depicts an example of how an individual interacts with different environmental systems. This idea is also applicable for other client levels such as families, groups, and communities that often necessitate intervention at various levels, referred to as micro, mezzo, and macro systems. They are discussed in further detail in the next section and throughout this book as it relates to various populations at risk of poverty.

Figure 1.2. Person-in-Environment Perspective

This figure illustrates the person-in-environment approach, which depicts how people in our society continually interact with and are affected by many systems, such as those identified here (adapted from Zastrow, 2010, p. 50).

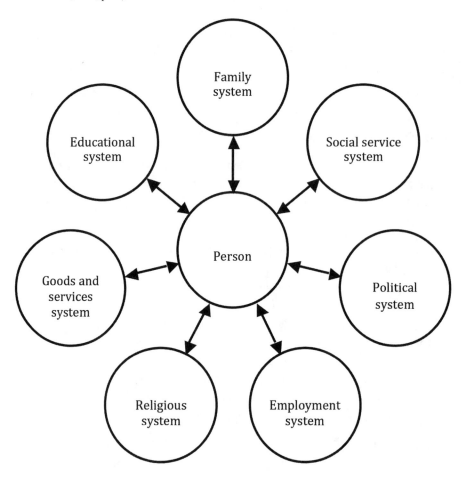

Levels of Intervention

Social workers and related helping professionals practice at micro (individuals), mezzo (families and small groups), and macro (organizations and communities) levels through specific helping activities.

Micro Intervention

Micro practice aims to intervene at the individual level on a one-on-one basis to help individuals to meet their needs with the goal of helping them adapt to or make changes in the environment to better meet their needs. Types of interventions as they relate to poverty may include social casework, wherein the social worker might link a person who is unemployed with job training programs, or case management to address the ongoing needs of individuals that are homeless by arranging or coordinating supportive services.

Mezzo Intervention

Intervening at the group level or working with families constitutes mezzo practice. This involves working with many individuals simultaneously through a group process rather than one-on-one. Social workers and related helping professionals facilitate many different types of groups designed to address social, emotional, or behavioral difficulties. At the mezzo level, practitioners may facilitate groups for individuals with co-occurring mental health and substance abuse problems that may struggle with wanting to continue being sober and maintaining employment, or alternatively, they may work with a group of children from low-income neighborhoods to help them develop strategies to increase their grades.

Macro Intervention

Community organization, administration of social agencies, and other related macro-level interventions seek to intervene on behalf of or with clients through changes in policies, planning, or administration. At the organizational level, practitioners may also intervene to make an agency more responsive to meeting the needs of clients by improving program objectives or developing new programs to meet community needs. At the community level, practitioners evaluate, plan, and coordinate change efforts, typically along with citizen or community participants.

Each of the descriptions above is simplistic and is only intended at this point in the reading to promote students' understanding that there are multiple intervention levels requiring change. Each chapter on various populations at risk provides multiple case studies to illustrate how practitioners intervene at all levels in order to promote meaningful change for people and the environments within which they interact.

Concluding Comments

The term *poverty* is complex. There are many definitions and conflicting views on what constitutes living in poverty and how we think about the poor. To help readers understand why some of these groups find themselves unable to meet their basic or relative needs, the chapter introduced the concept of poverty and its various definitions. It also introduced readers to historical and contemporary views of poverty in America, and presented data on individuals living in poverty and discusses the income and wealth gaps that exist in the United States. Chapter content also explored the notions of social minimum, social justice, and human rights—all key constructs in the discussion of poverty and reflecting individuals' abilities to equally access or participate in the opportunities in society that ensure a basic quality of life. Finally, the chapter describes social workers and other helping professionals' role as it relates to poverty and explores the various levels of interventions.

Internet Resources

The U.S. Census Bureau: http://www.census.gov/hhes/www/poverty/poverty.html

The Census Bureau reports poverty data from several major household surveys and programs. The Annual Social and Economic Supplement (ASEC) to the Current Population Survey (CPS) is the source of official national poverty estimates.

Institute for Research on Poverty (IRP): http://www.irp.wisc.edu/

The IRP is a center for interdisciplinary research into the causes and consequences of poverty and social inequality in the United States.

Self-Sufficiency Standard Project: http://www.selfsufficiencystandard.org/

The Center for Women's Welfare (CWW) researches income inequality and economic opportunity. It develops effective tools to measure poverty and income inadequacy by calculating the real cost of living.

National Poverty Center (NPC): http://www.npc.umich.edu/poverty/

The NPC conducts and promotes multidisciplinary, policy-relevant research on the causes and consequences of poverty and provides mentoring and training to young scholars.

The Urban Institute: http://www.urban.org/publications/412219.html

The Urban Institute gathers data, conducts research, evaluates programs, offers technical assistance overseas, and educates on social and economic issues.

National Center for Children in Poverty (NCCP): http://www.nccp.org/

The NCCP uses research to promote the economic security, health, and well-being of America's low-income families and children.

Southern Poverty Law Center: http://www.splcenter.org/

The Southern Poverty Law Center fights hate and bigotry, and seeks justice for the most vulnerable members of our society, using litigation, education, and other forms of advocacy.

National Coalition for the Homeless (NCH): http://www.nationalhomeless.org/

The NCH engages in public education, policy advocacy, and grassroots organizing. They primarily focus their work on housing justice, economic justice, health care justice, and civil rights.

Center on Budget and Policy Priorities: http://www.cbpp.org/

The CBPP works at the federal and state levels on fiscal policy and public programs that affect low- and moderate-income families and individuals.

Assistant Secretary for Planning and Evaluation (ASPE): http://aspe.hhs.gov/poverty/

The ASPE is the principal advisor to the secretary of the U.S. Department of Health and Human Services on policy development, and is responsible for major activities in policy coordination, legislation development, strategic planning, policy research, evaluation, and economic analysis.

Further Readings

Ehrenreich, B. (2002). *Nickel & dimed: On (not) getting by in America*. New York: Henry Holt & Company.

Goldberg, G. S., & Collins, S. D. (2001). *Washington's new Poor Law: Welfare "reform" and the roads not taken, 1935 to the present*. New York: Apex Press.

Iceland, J. (2006). *Poverty in America: A handbook* (2nd ed). Berkeley: University of California Press.

Newman, K. S. (2006). *Chutes and ladders: Navigating the low-wage labor market*. Cambridge, MA: Russell Sage Foundation and Harvard University Press.

Schwarz, J. E., & Volgy, T. J. (1992). *The forgotten Americans: Working hard and living poor in the land of opportunity.* New York: W.W. Norton.

Seccombe, K. (2011). *"So you think I drive a Cadillac?" Welfare recipients' perspectives on the system and its reform* (3rd ed.). Boston: Pearson/Allyn Bacon.

Shipler, D. K. (2005). *The working poor: Invisible in America.* New York: Random House/Vintage.

Steinbeck, J. (2006). *The grapes of wrath.* New York: Penguin Group.

References

Beverly, S. G. (2001). Measures of material hardship: Rationale and recommendations. *Journal of Poverty, 5*(1), 23–41.

Chau, M., Thampi, K., & Wight, V. R. (2010). *Basic facts about low-income children, 2009, Children under age 18.* National Center for Children in Poverty. Retrieved from http://www.nccp.org/publications/pdf/text_975.pdf.

Citro, C. F., & Michael, R. T., eds. (1995). *Measuring poverty: A new approach.* Washington, DC: National Academy Press. Retrieved from http://www.nap .edu/catalog.php?record_id=4759.

Council on Social Work Education. (2008). *Educational policy and accreditation standards.* Alexandria, VA. Retrieved from http://www.cswe.org/File.aspx?id= 13780.

DeNavas-Walt, C., Proctor, B. D., & Smith, J. C. (2012, September). *Income, poverty, and health insurance coverage in the United States: 2011* (Current Population Reports, P60-243). Washington, DC: U.S. Government Printing Office, 2012. Retrieved from http://www.census.gov/prod/2012pubs/p60-243.pdf.

Dolgoff, R., & Feldstein, D. (2009). *Understanding social welfare* (8th ed.). Boston: Pearson/Allyn and Bacon.

Fisher, G. M. (1997, Winter). The development and history of the U.S. poverty thresholds—a brief overview. *GSS/SSS Newsletter* [Newsletter of the Government Statistics Section and the Social Statistics Section of the American Statistical Association], 6–7. Retrieved from http://aspe.hhs.gov/poverty/ papershptgssiv.htm.

Gabe, T. (2012). *Poverty in the United States: 2011.* Congressional Research Service. Retrieved from http://www.fas.org/sgp/crs/misc/RL33069.pdf.

Garner, T., & Short, K. (2008). *Creating a consistent poverty measure over time using NAS procedures: 1996–2005.* U.S. Census Bureau, Working Paper Series, Poverty Thresholds. Retrieved from http://www.census.gov/hhes/www/ povmeas/papers/experimental_measures_96_05v7.p.

Gilbert, N., & Terrell, P. (2002). *Dimensions of social welfare policy* (5th ed.). Boston: Allyn and Bacon.

Hill, R., Hirschman, E. C., & Bauman, J. F. (1996). The birth of modern entitlement programs: Reports from the field and implications for welfare policy. *Journal of Public Policy & Marketing, 15*(2), 263–277.

HS Poverty Guidelines. *Federal Register, 78*(16), (January 24, 2013), 5182–5183. Retrieved from http://www.gpo.gov/fdsys/pkg/FR-2013-01-24/pdf/2013- 01422.pdf.

Institute for Research on Poverty. (2013). *Who is poor?* Retrieved from http://www.irp.wisc.edu/faqs/faq3.htm.

Interagency Technical Working Group on Developing a Supplemental Poverty Measure. (March 2010). Observations from the interagency technical working group on developing a supplemental poverty measure. *Supplemental Poverty Measure Federal Register Notice.* Retrieved from http://www.census .gov/hhes/www/poverty/SPM_TWGObservations.pdf.

Jansson, B. (2009). *The reluctant welfare state: Engaging history to advance social work practice in contemporary society.* Belmont, CA: Thomson Brooks/Cole.

Karger, H., & Stoesz, D. (2014). *American social welfare policy: A pluralist approach* (7th ed.). Boston: Pearson/Allyn and Bacon.

Lamale, H. (1965). Poverty: The world and the reality. *Monthly Labor Review, 88*(7), 822–827. Retrieved from SocINDEX with Full Text database.

Lowrey, A. (2012, October). Income inequality may take toll on growth. *The New York Times.* Retrieved from http://www.nytimes.com/2012/10/17/business/ economy/income-inequality-may-take-toll-on-growth.html?pagewanted= all&_r=0.

Miller Center of Public Affairs. (2010). *Franklin Delano Roosevelt: Domestic affairs.* American President: An Online Reference Resource. Retrieved from http://millercenter.org/president/fdroosevelt.

Mink, G., & O'Connor, A. (2004). *Poverty in the United States: An encyclopedia of history, politics, and policy.* ABC-CLIO. Retrieved from EBSCO*host.*

National Association of Social Workers. (1999). *Code of ethics of the National Association of Social Workers.* Retrieved from http://www.socialworkers.org/pubs/code/code.asp.

National Poverty Center. (2013). *Poverty in the United States: How has poverty changed over time?* Retrieved from http://npc.umich.edu/poverty/#3.

Office of the United Nations High Commissioner for Human Rights. (n.d.) *What are human rights?* Retrieved from http://www.ohchr.org/EN/Issues/Pages/WhatareHumanRights.aspx.

One version of the [U.S.] federal poverty measure. Retrieved from http://aspe.hhs.gov/poverty/13poverty.cfm#thresholds.

Pearce, D. (2010) *The self-sufficiency standard for New York state 2010.* Retrieved from http://www.hwcli.com/documents/news/1079.pdf.

Peck, D. (2010). How a new jobless era will transform America. *The Atlantic.* Retrieved from http://www.theatlantic.com/magazine/archive/2010/03/how-a-new-jobless-era-will-transform-america/307919/.

Pimpare, S. (2009). The failures of American poverty measures. *Journal of Sociology and Social Welfare, 36*(1), 103–122. Retrieved from Social Work Abstracts database.

Sandoval, D. A., Rank, M. R., & Hirschl, T. A. (2009). The increasing risk of poverty across the American life course. *Demography, 46*(4), 717–737.

Segal, E. A., Gerdes, K. E., & Steiner, S. (2010). *An introduction to the profession of social work: Becoming a change agent* (3rd ed.). Belmont, CA: Brooks Cole.

Short, K. (2001). *Experimental poverty measures: 1999.* U.S. Census Bureau, Current Population Reports, P 60-216. Washington, DC: U.S. Government Printing Office.

Short, K. (2005). Material and financial hardship and income-based poverty measures in the USA. *Journal of Social Policy, 34*(1), 21–38.

Short, K. (2011). *The research supplemental poverty measure: 2010.* U.S. Census Bureau, Current Population Reports. Retrieved from http://www.census.gov/prod/2011pubs/p60-241.pdf.

Short, K. (2012). *The research supplemental poverty measure: 2011.* U.S. Census Bureau, Current Population Reports. Retrieved from http://www.census.gov/prod/2012pubs/p60-244.pdf.

Suppes, M. A., & Wells, C. C. (2009). *The social work experience: An introduction to social work and social welfare.* Boston: Pearson/Allyn and Bacon.

Trattner, W. I. (1999). *From poor law to welfare state* (6th ed.). New York: Free Press.

United Nations. (1948). *Universal Declaration of Human Rights.* Adopted December 10, 1948. General Assembly resolution 217 A (III). Retrieved from http://www.un.org/en/documents/udhr/.

U.S. Bureau of Labor Statistics, Department of Labor. (2010). The Editor's Desk, *Unemployment in March 2010.* Retrieved from http://www.bls.gov/opub/ted/2010/ted_20100406.htm.

U.S. Department of Health and Human Services. (2013). *What are the differences between the poverty guidelines and the poverty thresholds?* Retrieved from http://aspe.hhs.gov/poverty/faq.cfm#differences.

Waddan, A. (2010). The U.S. safety net, inequality and the Great Recession. *Journal of Poverty & Social Justice, 18*(3), 243–254. Retrieved from EBSCOhost.

White, Stuart, "Social Minimum." *The Stanford encyclopedia of philosophy* (Fall 2008 edition), Edward N. Zalta, ed. Retrieved from http://plato.stanford.edu/archives/fall2008/entries/social-minimum/.

Wilensky, H. L., & Lebeaux, C. (1965). *Industrial society and social welfare: The impact of industrialization on the supply and organization of social welfare services in the United States.* New York: Free Press.

Zastrow, C. (2010). *Introduction to social work and social welfare: Empowering people.* Belmont, CA: Brooks/Cole.

2

Contemporary Responses to Poverty

Elissa D. Giffords and Karen R. Garber

Government and society's response to poverty has changed significantly throughout the history of the United States. Over the last fifty years, the shift has changed from a liberal perspective, which emphasizes that people are entitled to receive collective benefits and services as a right of citizenship, to an ideology that those in need should turn to government for benefits and services as a last resort. This chapter examines government's response to poverty from the 1960s to the present, and explores the impact changes have had on individuals and communities. Additionally, this chapter explains how mechanisms such as nonprofit social service agencies, faith-based organizations, and religious institutions strive to meet the needs of individuals and communities. It will begin by exploring contemporary approaches to address poverty.

Contemporary Perspectives to Delivering Social Welfare Benefits

As discussed in chapter 1, the term *poverty* incorporates multiple perspectives. Over the past several decades, there have been ideological shifts in how the United States views poverty and who is seen as deserving and undeserving of assistance. Accordingly, there has been much debate regarding what, if anything, we should do about poverty, and whether citizens have a right to social welfare benefits, and if so, under what circumstances. Overall, there is general agreement that poverty interventions require a multifaceted approach even if society cannot agree on what form assistance should take.

Entitlements versus Block Grants

Entitlements and block grants are important terms to know for those interested in combating poverty. Segal (2007) explains "*entitlement programs* are mandated by law to give aid to all who are eligible to receive aid regardless of the total cost involved in any given year or fiscal period" (p. 87). This means that no matter how many people apply for a specific benefit for which they are eligible, such as Social Security or veterans' benefits, the government must provide this assistance even if it means borrowing money to do so. Payment for entitlement programs differs from block-funded programs. *Block grants* equate to a specific sum of money provided to the states by the federal government.

Proponents of block grants explain that this approach encourages considerable discretion in how funds are spent, suggesting that the federal government is too far removed from the problems experienced by the individual states. Proponents also believe this approach allows for more creativity regarding program design. Alternately, opponents claim entitlement programs are a better mechanism to ensure that individuals in need have equal access to benefits. They also suggest that entitlements reduce the potential abuse of discretionary funding. Opponents also stress that once the block grants funds are gone, they are gone, because the dollar amounts are capped. This may leave some individuals in need without crucial assistance.

Typically, support for these approaches varies according to one's political belief system. To review, liberals who are often associated with the Democratic Party call for more government interventions, while the conservatives, often associated with the Republican Party, want less. Accordingly, liberals usually are in favor of government entitlement programs, while conservatives prefer block grants. Again, this comes back to the classic debate discussed in chapter 1. What role should government have in the lives of its citizens? Should the United States take an individualist perspective or a collective one? Gilbert and Terrell (2002, p. 19) remind us that predictably, the political beliefs of those on the right (conservatives) and left (liberals) are comprised of rival views with regard to the role that government should have in our society. Subsequently and not surprisingly, we can therefore observe the influence of different political philosophies and categorical approaches each side supports in an attempt to address poverty. This is not only apparent historically, but also seen in contemporary times as well.

Contemporary Welfare State

Central to a discussion about poverty and the contemporary welfare state is Wilensky and Lebeaux's (1965) residual versus institutional perspectives discussed in chapter 1. The residual approach is representative of the old poor laws, in which government assistance should be the last resort, and the institutional approach is seen as assisting all individuals regardless of poverty status. While we can observe that after the Great Depression the federal government enacted considerable social insurance legislation, it is also important to note that those initiatives reflected compromises, which were traditionally characteristic of America's social welfare history. Still, there are times when the United States is more focused on the individual causes of poverty, and other times when it is more aware of the influence of societal structures and is therefore more willing to assist populations at risk.

Social Reform: 1960s

Though the welfare state in America continued to evolve after the Great Depression, it expanded significantly during the 1960s under the leadership of Presidents Kennedy and Johnson. These advances followed the end of World War II, presumed to be a time of equal economic prosperity. The 1950s was a time wherein society once again came to see individuals living in poverty as causing their own misfortune, rather than concluding that poverty is a problem caused by something inherent in the larger social structure (Segal, 2007; Suppes & Wells, 2009). The social policy efforts of the 1960s focused on social responsibility and social reform. This time in United States history notably reflects a more institutional approach.

Michael Harrington's 1962 influential book *The Other America: Poverty in the United States* challenged the assumptions about America's affluence, describing an ongoing state of poverty, characterized by chronic subjection to inferior living standards and inadequate wages (Trattner, 1999). His book brought much-needed attention to this hidden American subculture and is credited with demonstrating that "poverty was one of the nation's gravest social problems, one that was not disappearing but growing worse, a way of life that had become permanent for some forty to fifty million Americans" (Trattner, 1999, p. 318).

Once the social causes of poverty were acknowledged, a flurry of liberal social welfare legislation was initiated to help populations at risk, including the poor, people with disabilities, and the aged. This decade also saw the passage of the Civil Rights Act in 1964 and many War on Poverty programs, a series of initiatives under the Economic Opportunity Act of 1964. While President Kennedy began assembling many antipoverty programs before his death, President Johnson is credited with declaring "an unconditional war on poverty in America" during his State of the

Union Address on January 8, 1964. In this speech, Johnson effectively brought poverty to the forefront of the national conversation, when he implored Americans to help replace individual despair with opportunity. This led to a series of legislation that created social programs that still exist today (Siegel, 2004). Examples include *Head Start* (a pre-school program that promotes school readiness for low-income children), *Food Stamps,* now referred to as *Supplemental Nutrition Assistance Program* (subsidies provide assistance to low-income households to afford food), *Women, Infants, and Children,* known as WIC (a supplemental food and nutrition education program for low-income pregnant, breast-feeding, and non-breast-feeding postpartum women, and to infants and children up to age five who are found to be at nutritional risk), and *Medicare* and *Medicaid* (programs that provide access to health care) (Gilbert & Terrell, 2002; Segal, 2007; Siegel, 2004; Suppes & Wells, 2009). (A discussion of these programs is found later in this chapter.)

The 1960s is often referred to as the Great Society in United States history because people felt a collective responsibility to help the most vulnerable members of our society. Johnson's unprecedented legislative success during 1964 into 1965 accounted "for passage of 84 of the 87 measures that he submitted to Congress, and into 1966 when 97 of 113 measures were enacted" (Califano as cited in Jansson, 2012, p. 272). Consequently, the welfare state expanded significantly. Programs included the ones identified above (e.g., Food Stamps, Medicare, and Medicaid) as well as many others such as Job Corps (job-training programs for impoverished youth), Peace Corps, Vista, and the Older Americans Act (Gilbert & Terrell, 2002; Segal, 2007).

The *Office of Economic Opportunity* (OEO) was established by the *Economic Opportunity Act* to coordinate Johnson's social and economic initiatives. Even with the promising outcomes expected from all these programs, there was criticism of President Johnson's commitment to the Great Society. Part of the condemnation of the War on Poverty programs stemmed from unrealistic expectations, poorly funded initiatives, strong political opponents, and services and training without income transfers and jobs (Jansson, 2012). While Johnson did increase spending for new social reforms, many programs did not receive adequate funding, which led to the accusation that they were ineffective. Much of the federal fiscal spending went to military costs. Johnson increased spending on military and related expenses by "almost three times as much as spending on education, training, employment, and social programs" (Jansson, 2012, p. 273). Still, many of the OEO programs were innovative and many of the programs still remain today providing improved services for many low-income individuals and families.

Retrenchment and Dismantling the Welfare State

By the mid-1960s through the mid-1970s, the anti-establishment movement, spurred on by the Vietnam War, inflation, and a new wave of conservatism, led to major efforts to dismantle the New Deal and Great Society programs. Conservatives argued that the programs were too costly and ineffective. They also wanted the states to have more control over policies and programs (Ambrosino, Heffernan, Shuttlesworth, & Ambrosino, 2001). Segal (2007) purports that many Americans were frustrated that individuals were still living in poverty despite the number of government-funded assistance programs. Trattner (1999) adds that by the end of the 1960s, Americans became resentful of the poor and minorities whom they felt received billions of federal dollars at the expense of "hard-working" middle-class citizens. This led to a backlash against what many perceived as endless spending on ineffective government social programs, which were complicated by a sluggish economy.

Republican Presidents Richard Nixon (1969–1974) and Gerald Ford (1974–1977) and Democratic President Jimmy Carter (1977–1981) made major attempts to reform the welfare state, most of which were not accepted by the United States Congress. Republican President Ronald Reagan (1981–1989) was elected with massive "right wing" conservative support, which some viewed as a public mandate to reduce taxes, lower inflation, and drastically reduce the federal expenditures for social welfare programs. This period of history is viewed as a residual one, in which public assistance was viewed as a temporary, last resort for those in need. This included eliminating welfare benefits for those viewed as the able-bodied and the working poor. For example, President Reagan signed the *Family Support Act* in 1988, a major bill designed to force mothers who received *Aid to Families with Dependent Children* (AFDC), previously known as Aid to Dependent Children (ADC), an assistance program for individuals and families with limited income, into the job market. (Note, this program will be discussed in more detail in chapter 5.) This bill also required all parents of children age three and over to work or enter job-training (Suppes &Wells, 2009). Republican President George H. W. Bush (1989–1993) essentially continued the conservative policies and agenda of President Reagan. However, notably, as described in more detail in the chapter on "People with Disabilities," President Bush signed the *Americans with Disabilities Act*

(ADA) on July 26, 1990. This important legislation regulates employment practices, programs, transportation, public accommodations, and other facilities.

The most drastic change came under Democratic President Bill Clinton (1993–2001), a "political centrist" who delivered on his campaign promise to change welfare as we know it. In 1994, following an overwhelming victory, the Republicans controlled both houses in Congress. It was the first time this had occurred in over forty years. It was during this time the Republicans introduced much legislation aimed at limiting the time people could receive welfare, restrict who could receive assistance, and require strict work conditions. President Clinton wanted to distance himself from the liberal Democrats. Especially disturbing to many members of the social work community was the Republicans' "Contract with America," a political pledge to decentralize control of welfare by decreasing the federal government's control of social welfare and giving more power to the state and local governments. Many of the conservatives of the time threatened to dismantle social programs from as far back as the New Deal initiatives of the 1930s. While many of the Republican proposals did not pass, the public called for change (Ambrosino et al., 2001; Segal, 2007; Trattner, 1999). In keeping with his centrist promise, President Clinton signed the controversial *Personal Responsibility and Work Opportunity Reconciliation Act* (PRWORA) in August 1996. Trattner (1999) explains this legislation either ended or reversed six decades of federal social welfare policy, which guaranteed a safety net for America's most vulnerable populations. The most notable change was the end of AFDC. In its stead is the program *Temporary Assistance for Needy Families* (TANF), explained in more detail later in this chapter. What is important to know as it relates to this discussion on dismantling the welfare state is that PRWORA essentially changed the way the United States had helped the poor for more than sixty years. Jansson (2012) explains this new legislation abolished the AFDC entitlement and replaced it with a system of decentralized block grants to the states. This means that TANF programs vary by state. TANF also requires adult recipients to participate in work or work-related activities and most drastic of all, this legislation imposes a five-year lifetime limit on cash assistance for families. Notable too is that TANF families were no longer entitled to other assistance programs such as Food Stamps and Medicaid.

Twenty-First Century

Changes to the American welfare state continued under Republican President George W. Bush (2000–2008), the son of former President George H. W. Bush.

Segal (2007) notes that following the attacks on the World Trade Center and Pentagon on September 11, 2001, President Bush, although a proponent of less government, instituted large-scale benefits to families, and provided the airline industry with loans and other economic support. Segal (2007) also highlights the war in Iraq, which began in March 2003, bringing attention to the financial and human costs of war and the impact that it had on the available resources to meet the need for American social services. In addition, many citizens expressed their disappointment and frustration with the federal and local governments' response to Hurricane Katrina in 2005, the strongest storm to hit the United States in 100 years. This disaster raised questions about the adequacy of American social policies and programs to meet the needs of the community (Segal 2007).

President Bush signed the *Medicare Modernization Act* (MMA) in 2003. Mays, Brenner, Neuman, Cubanski, and Claxton (2004) explain that MMA established an optional program that combines public and private options to help all 47 million older adults and people with disabilities pay for the high cost of prescription drugs. This new benefit, known as Part D, went into effect in 2006. All elderly and disabled beneficiaries have access to the Medicare drug benefit through private plans approved by the federal government. Under President Barack Obama (2008–present) the Affordable Care Act of 2010 changed some important features of the drug benefit in particular, phasing out the coverage gap by 2020 (this will be discussed in more detail in this chapter).

Taken together one can observe the changing attitude toward social welfare, ranging from liberal to conservative policies. Overall, from the 1930s to the 1960s the United States essentially had a collective and more institutional approach to social welfare, which reflected the value of a larger role of government in meeting the needs of its members. From the mid-1970s to the present day, however, the Republicans have touted the value of limited federal government, states' autonomy, tax cuts, and reduced social spending (Jansson, 2012). Goldberg (2002 as cited in Suppes & Wells, 2009) notes the recent trend in which social welfare provisions for the poor have continued to diminish. Assistance today is work-based and residual in its approach. This tactic forces many mothers to work outside the home at paltry wages. Most problematic has been that the federal government has not made meaningful attempts to develop employment opportunities.

The Budget Control Act of 2011, passed on August 2, 2011, was promoted as a compromise among Democrats, Republicans, and the White House when in truth the process was fraught with partisanship and divisiveness. The bill raises the American government's debt ceiling and cut trillions of dollars from its spending (U.S. House of Representatives Committee on the Budget, 2011). While it is still too early to determine the outcome of this legislation, what is clear from the tone of the debates is that the Republicans' goal was to maintain tax cuts and get as many spending cuts as possible. Alternately, the Democrats' goal was to prevent cuts to entitlement programs such as Social Security and Medicare, as well as other programs for beneficiaries with limited income (Pear, 2011; Steinhauer, 2011). While the long-term future of how the United States plans to address social welfare is unknown, it is clear that during this period of the "Great Recession," federal, state, and local government resources are shrinking.

Human Service Organizations

With shrinking government resources, community-based organizations (CBOs) are attempting to fill the gaps. This is in line with the residual approach typically seen in the United States. There are three primary types of CBOs or human service organizations, sometimes referred to as agencies, which strive to assist various populations, such as individuals, groups, and communities who are poor or at risk of living in poverty. These agencies are generally categorized as *private* entities or *public* (government) entities. Under the private type, there are typically two distinctions: *nonprofit* and *for-profit*, also referred to as proprietary organizations. While generally under the private umbrella other important terms are *self-help* (mutual aid) and *faith-based initiative*, wherein religious institutions use public funds to provide social services. Readers will find a discussion of these below.

The Private Sector: Nonprofit and Proprietary (For-Profit) Agencies

The private sector has a long history of providing services to individuals in need. This proviso is rooted in the nonprofit arena, but for-profit agencies have recently begun providing social services as well. Both are non-governmental entities, which are independent of government control, although they do receive government funds (Gibelman & Furman, 2008). Nonprofit organizations are governed by a voluntary board of directors and often have 501(c)(3) tax-exempt status given by Congress and the Internal Revenue Service (IRS) for charitable, educational, religious, scientific, or literary activities (Giffords, 2003). Nonprofit social agencies do not have an owner and any profits must be directed back into the agency. Typically, nonprofits seek to assist a specified client population with an identified social need; for example, the national organization the United Way reports that almost $65 billion in benefits go unclaimed by low-income working families each year. Accordingly, one of their goals is to "promote and connect low-income working families with all the available income supports for which they are eligible and work with community-based organizations and agencies to streamline enrollment processes" (United Way, 2011, para. 1–3). This agency is also illustrative of a non-sectarian organization, meaning it is without a religious affiliation or oriented toward a specified religious cohort. Conversely, sectarian or faith-based agencies are oriented toward providing services for a targeted religious group (Gibelman & Furman, 2008). Vidal (2001) explains that faith-based organizations comprise "(1) congregations; (2) national networks, which include national denominations, their social service arms (for example, Catholic Charities, Lutheran Social Services), and networks of related organizations (such as YMCA and YWCA); and (3) freestanding religious organizations, which are incorporated separately from congregations and national networks" (p. 1). Groups under these auspices are relevant to this discussion because of the growing role that these types of organizations have in the provision of social services. Suppes and Wells (2009) explain that "charitable choice" language contained in the PRWORA allowed public funding for religious-sponsored programs. In addition, faith-based initiatives supported by public funding have grown significantly since President George W. Bush announced a faith-based initiative and the creation of the White House Office of Faith-Based and Community Initiatives. Essentially President Bush's legislation allowed faith-based social service providers access to government grants and funds, enabling religious and secular social service organizations to compete for the same funding (Schuerger, 2002).

For-profits, also referred to as proprietary organizations, are under the auspices of the private sector; these are institutions or agencies governed by a paid board of directors, are investor-owned, and are designed to make a profit for their owners, investors, or stockholders. Gibelman and Furman (2008) explain in recent years that these types of organizations have grown substantially in human services. Settings such as nursing homes, adult and child day care, residential treatment centers, and home health care are examples of this type of organization. Many have expressed concern regarding what is thought to be the incompatibility between human services and a profit motive; however, others believe competition among businesses leads to the provision of more economical services. These philosophies are liberal and conservative, respectively.

A related intervention key to a discussion on the private sector is called mutual assistance, sometimes referred to as self-help. This approach to helping is often focused on social welfare activities and may be thought of as friends, neighbors, and peers helping each other. A classic example of a self-help group is Alcoholics Anonymous (AA); another is the National Alliance for the Mentally Ill (for families and friends of people with a serious mental illness). It is important to mention this because individuals often help friends and family living in poverty. For instance, someone may allow friends or family members to sleep on the couch or floor should they suddenly become homeless.

The Public Sector

Public agencies, also known as *governmental organizations,* or *government entities,* have oversight for the social welfare of their citizens. Their structure is defined by legislation and public policies. Funded by tax dollars, public organizations often determine how social welfare resources are allocated, and through what mechanisms they will be administered. For instance, at times, public benefits or services are given directly to citizens through programs such as the *Earned Income Tax Credit* (EITC, explained in more detail later in this chapter), or through specific departments such as the Department of Education, or Health and Human Services. Gilbert and Terrell (2002) explain that government is responsible for the welfare state and as such, must ensure economic prosperity and social stability for society. Accordingly, government must provide "minimum standards of health, education and housing, and protection against the contingencies of modern life that interfere with people's well-being" (Gilbert & Terrell, 2002, p. 12). Examples of public sector social service benefits (discussed in more detail in the next section of this chapter) include *Food Stamps* (recently renamed Supplemental Nutrition Assistance Program [SNAP]), *Social Security,* and *Medicare.* As discussed in chapter 1, historically there has been much debate over the role of government in society. The same is true in contemporary society. Many Americans cannot agree on how to meet public need. Presently however, there are federal programs that do exist, and to which people in poverty turn for assistance. The following section discusses the major antipoverty programs.

Government Antipoverty Programs

The United States government assists the most vulnerable members of society through cash assistance and in-kind benefits. Cash assistance, like the name reflects, provides recipients with money, while in-kind assistance is delivered in goods or services. In-kind services include health benefits, child care, and the Supplemental Nutrition Assistance Program (SNAP). Conservatives are not in favor of cash benefits, as they believe recipients will not spend the money wisely. Conversely, liberals believe people can be trusted to spend the money to meet their basic needs within the confines or rules of the program. Accordingly, government should not control or limit individuals' choices in how to spend this money, while conservatives believe cash benefits, especially those viewed as generous from safety-net programs, make things too easy for recipients, spurring laziness and removing the incentive to work. Liberals alternately believe it is a matter of social justice and view assistance, including cash assistance, as leveling the playing field and helping individuals to best meet their needs. Regardless of one's position, the amount of the grants has not kept up with the inflation rate, thereby resulting in less financial assistance than in previous decades (Jansson, 2012; Karger & Stoesz, 2010; Segal, 2007).

The following discussion will provide an overview of the major federal programs available to this vulnerable population. Discussions regarding specific populations will be addressed in detail in the subsequent chapters. It is important for readers to note that assistance programs fall into two categories: *social insurance* and *public assistance.* The first, social insurance, is a collectively funded federal program that covers workers and their dependents, provided individuals paid into the system while they worked. Alternatively, public assistance programs are not based on recipient contributions, are typically means-tested and considered temporary and thus less desirable (Segal, 2007). Since social insurance programs are linked to work and individual effort, recipients of these programs are considered deserving. Conversely, recipients of public assistance programs are thought to have failed in some way. Taken one step further using the knowledge learned in chapter 1, readers can observe that public assistance programs are residual while social insurance is more collective or institutional in nature.

Social Insurance
Social Security: Old Age, Survivors, and Disability Insurance (OASDI)

The traditional *Social Security* program falls under the umbrella of social insurance, and offers a federal system of benefits to qualified individuals. The number of people throughout the country receiving all types of Social Security benefits is staggering, making this the largest income program in the United States (Novak,

2009). As of June 2011, 52 million people were in receipt of Social Security benefits, an increase of 7.7 percent in 6 years (Social Security Administration, 2011a).

The Social Security Administration (SSA) also administers the Old Age, Survivors, and Disability Insurance (OASDI) programs. The most common and universally used program provides individuals with monthly income upon reaching retirement age. Like all social insurance programs, eligible recipients receive Social Security retirement benefits if they paid into the Social Security system while they were working and earned the required number of Social Security credits. Through federal taxes referred to as the Federal Insurance Contribution Act (FICA), money is deducted from employees' paychecks, which is put into the Social Security fund. People who are receiving Social Security now paid into the program previously. While they were working, their contributions were distributed to older generations. Today's workforce pays into Social Security and provides support for the current elderly population. The intention is for future generations to pay into the system to support the current workforce upon retirement. In 2012, the average monthly Social Security benefit was approximately $1,230 (SSA, 2013a). Benefits are provided in the form of a check and are categorized as cash assistance. Because individuals receive Social Security retirement benefits after paying into the system, and recipients are comprised of older adults, they are generally thought of as deserving this assistance.

Social Security Disability Insurance (SSDI)

Added to the Social Security Act in 1956, *Social Security Disability Insurance* (SSDI), another social insurance program administered by the Social Security Administration, is available to eligible individuals who cannot work due to a medical condition that is expected to last at least one year or result in death. Certain family members of workers with disabilities may also receive money from Social Security. Generally, to become eligible, individuals have paid Social Security taxes on their earned income for five of the past ten years. After two years of receiving Disability insurance, recipients are automatically eligible for Medicare coverage (SSA, 2011a). Akin to traditional Social Security, benefits are in the form of cash assistance. Because individuals receive this benefit after paying into the system, and recipients are comprised of people with disabilities, they are typically considered to be deserving of this assistance. According to the Social Security Administration, nearly 11 million disabled workers, spouses, and children of disabled workers were receiving SSDI benefits in June 2011 (SSA, 2013b, table 2).

Unemployment Insurance

Unemployment insurance (UI), another social insurance program, was enacted as part of the original 1935 Social Security Act. Benefits are in the form of cash and are available to individuals who worked, paid into the program, who are unemployed through no fault of their own, and who meet other eligibility requirements. Similar to Social Security, UI is a universal program. It provides sustainability, which benefits those individuals viewed as "deserving," because it is designed to protect only those workers who paid into the system from living in poverty (Boushey & Wenger, 2006). The U.S. Department of Labor (DOL) (2013a) explains that UI payments are intended to provide temporary financial assistance to unemployed workers. While the program is discussed in significant detail in chapter 3, it is important for readers to know that this assistance program targets those with a history of employment who are unsuccessful in locating other employment. Eligibility is measured by assessing the labor force participation (working the required time), and assessing the circumstances that led to unemployment (Boushey & Wenger, 2006). Typically, workers are ineligible for unemployment insurance if they quit their jobs voluntarily or if they were fired for cause. Similarly, part-time workers, even if laid off, or individuals who work inconsistently are also ineligible for this benefit. This suggests that those individuals employed full-time that work hard who get fired or laid off through no fault of their own are deserving of assistance, albeit temporarily. According to the U.S. Bureau of Labor Statistics, as of June 2013 there were 11.8 million individuals receiving unemployment insurance benefits with an unemployment rate at 7.6 percent (U.S. Department of Labor, 2013b). The important link between unemployment benefits and poverty is discussed in more detail in chapter 3.

Public Assistance

As described briefly above, social welfare assistance programs fall into either social insurance or public assistance categories. Much of this classification relates to the principles of universal vs. selective. Whereas in preceding discussions, readers learned that social insurance programs are universal, meaning benefits are available as a basic right to an entire population, selective programs are based on need and are means-tested (Gilbert & Terrell, 2002). Public assistance programs fall into this category. These programs are traditionally means-tested, a term that denotes eligibility requirements based on individuals' income and resources, and focus on those in the most need of assistance. These benefits are often restrictive and are explained in more detail below through a discussion of specific public assistance programs.

From Aid to Families with Dependent Children (AFDC) to Temporary Assistance to Needy Families (TANF)

Cash assistance has been the cornerstone of public welfare policies designed to reduce poverty among families since the mid-1930s (Washington, Sullivan, & Washington, 2006). From 1935 (the start of the Social Security Act) to 1996, Aid to Families with Dependent Children (AFDC) provided cash assistance to eligible families. This federally funded means-tested entitlement program has been sharply criticized over the years. During the 1960s, the number of women receiving welfare soared as women realized AFDC benefits entitled them to Medicaid, Food Stamps, day care, and work-related incentive payments (Jansson, 2012). Opponents of AFDC wanted to discourage dependence on welfare, as it was seen as encouraging parents to continue receiving welfare and discouraging them from working. As discussed previously, this ideology of seeking employment coincided with changing societal values as more and more women were choosing to enter the workforce. Segal (2007) explains that the recipients have changed dramatically since the inception of the program. Originally designed for impoverished widows and their children, today's recipients are mostly single women. The public perception is that "welfare recipients had it made" doing nothing but collecting a check from the government. The reality told a different story. Most recipients were single mothers who faced barriers to full employment.

Once an entitlement program, AFDC was replaced with *Temporary Assistance to Needy Families* (TANF) in 1996 (Segal 2007). The U.S. Department of Health and Human Services (HHS), Administration for Children and Families is the federal office that administers this program. HHS (2008a) explains that the Personal Responsibility and Work Opportunity Reconciliation Act (PRWORA) (Public Law 104-193) designed TANF as a block grant that decentralizes federal funds and gives the states control over services for needy families. Reauthorization of this program occurred in February 2006, under the Deficit Reduction Act of 2005 (HHS, 2008a). The enactment of PRWORA reflected the American mindset that individuals may receive government assistance, as long as benefits are temporary and time-limited. This residual program sends the message that government should provide assistance, however, only as a last resort while individuals work toward becoming self-sufficient.

While states are able to design their own programs, the program provides both cash and in-kind benefits on a temporary basis up to five years maximum. State and local municipalities can extend benefits, however, the money then comes out of state and local funds. Recipients of this program must engage in work-related activities, which involve either on-the-job training, paid employment, or preparing the individual for employment (Cohen, 2001). Work activities are defined by individual states and can include requiring recipients to obtain a high school diploma or its equivalent, completing drug treatment, engaging in a work experience program, on-the-job training, vocational education training, community service, or job search and job readiness (HHS, 2004). Additionally, TANF requires that people receiving assistance, particularly in the form of cash benefits, must seek full-time employment, and must comply with child support enforcement in order to remain eligible for benefits.

Proponents of TANF claimed that setting strict time limits would result in recipients seeking employment sooner. Opponents worried that ending AFDC and replacing it with a program such as TANF would lead to huge increases in poverty (Wadden, 2010). Moreover, pushing people into employment referred to as "work first" under TANF without providing them with basic skills or job training would not lead to economic independence (Washington et al., 2006). Statistically, welfare reform has increased work activities for welfare recipients, however, there are concerns that this population has now moved into the status of the *working poor* (Washington et al., 2006), a group described as living at or below the official poverty level.

For calendar year 2011, the total number of TANF recipients was 4,363,000. Of these, 1,845,638 were families, 955,984 of which were single-parent households and 97,497 were two-parent households. Also notable, 3,280,037 recipients were children (HHS, Office of Family Assistance, 2012).

Immigrants and PRWORA

United States sentiment toward immigrants has changed over the last several decades, which has impacted their rights to receive government assistance. Under welfare reform, PRWORA created two groups of immigrants, *qualified* and *unqualified*. Qualified immigrants, such as permanent residents and certain refugees, were granted welfare rights depending on their legal status as of August 22, 1996. Unqualified immigrants, who include undocumented and temporary immigrants on work or student visas, were ineligible for public benefits (Horn, 2006).

States, however, were afforded latitude regarding welfare benefits for immigrants. PRWORA authorized states to provide TANF and Medicaid to qualified immigrants who were granted legal status prior to August 22, 1996, and gave states discretion regarding qualified immigrants post August 1996 (chapter 9 offers an in-depth analysis regarding issues surrounding immigrants and poverty).

Food Stamps/Supplemental Nutrition Assistance Program (SNAP)

Enacted in 1964, the *Food Stamp program,* recently renamed the *Supplemental Nutrition Assistance Program* (SNAP), though still commonly referred to as food stamps, is another residual means-tested program viewed as a major success that "gave millions of impoverished families the resources to purchase food in quantities not possible with meager welfare checks" (Jansson, 2012, p. 272). The U.S. Department of Agriculture, Food and Nutrition Services oversees the program while state public assistance departments administer SNAP through their local offices. SNAP provides eligible individuals and families the finances to purchase nutritious food. For many decades, Food Stamp benefits were given in the form of a voucher, which looked like paper money. Presently, benefits are issued monthly through an electronic benefit card, similar to a debit card, and can be used like cash to select household food items such as breads and cereals; fruits and vegetables; meats, fish, and poultry; and dairy products. Recipients may also purchase seeds and plants, which produce food. The average monthly benefit in 2012 was $133.41 per person (U.S. Department of Agriculture, 2013, Supplemental Nutrition Assistance Program).

The U.S. Department of Agriculture reported that in May 2011, the number of SNAP recipients reached 45.8 million, a 12 percent increase from the previous year and a 34 percent increase from 2009 (Little, 2011). In March 2013, the number of recipients reached 47,724,596, which is a 2.8 percent increase from April 2012. The significant rise in benefits is indicative of the financial shape of the nation. This benefit is "an effective tool in helping both households that have suffered from sustained poverty and others whose living standards have fallen dramatically as a direct consequence of the recession" (Wadden, 2010, p. 249).

Earned Income Tax Credits (EITC)

Enacted by Congress in 1975, the *Earned Income Tax Credit* (EITC) is a refundable federal tax credit that is available to assist low- and moderate-income working individuals and families. It is the largest antipoverty program in the United States for non-elderly persons (Jansson, 2012) and only benefits those who work, further distinguishing those who work as deserving this assistance. Consequently, the general perception is that this benefit is not "a handout." Its popularity has increased, as EITC is a benefit that encourages employment and rewards individuals and families in the workforce. The amount of the credit depends on the taxpayers' income and the number of qualifying children, where applicable (Wadden, 2010). Additionally, wage subsidies increase with earnings (Chapman, 2004).

Nationwide in 2009, 27 million people received EITC, totaling $59.2 billion (Internal Revenue Service, 2013). While EITC has helped in reducing poverty and encouraging work, some advocates emphasize the program can do more to decrease the gaps between what families earn and what they need in order to make ends meet (Tax Credits for Working Families, n.d.).

Women, Infants, and Children (WIC)

Administered by the U.S. Department of Agriculture's (USDA's) Food and Nutrition Service, Women, Infants, and Children, commonly referred to as WIC, is a federal grant program that provides eligible pregnant women (including six weeks after birth), breast-feeding women, non-breast-feeding women (up to six months after delivery), infants (up to one years old), and children (up to their fifth birthday) with supplemental nutrition, education, counseling, screening, and appropriate health or social service referrals. Each year Congress authorizes money to fund WIC, which is a means-tested program. Applicants' gross income must fall at or below 185 percent of the United States Poverty Income Guidelines. Based on federal income eligibility guidelines, a family of four cannot earn more than $42,543 in order to qualify for WIC. States however, have the prerogative to set lower income limit standards. WIC is administered locally, usually through county health departments, hospitals, schools, public housing sites, and community centers. In 2012, the USDA reported approximately 8.9 million women, infants, and children were receiving WIC benefits. Of the 8.9 million, 4.75 million were children, 2.1 million were infants, and 2.1 million were women (USDA, 2013, Food and Nutrition Service).

Supplemental Security Income (SSI)

Eligibility for Supplemental Security Income (SSI) requires that recipients are 65 years of age or older, or that they are disabled, or blind at any age, with limited income and resources. Recipients must also be United States citizens (Social Security Administration, 2011a). There is no minimum age limit for adults and children with blindness or one or more disabilities. Enacted in 1974, SSI is authorized under Title XVI (Supplemental Security Income for the Aged, Blind, and Disabled) of the Social Security Act and is administered by the Social Security Administration (SSA, 2003). Unlike other SSA programs, SSI is labeled a needs-based welfare program that provides cash assistance to ensure a minimum level of income to qualified individuals. To qualify, individuals must have limited income and limited resources. SSI recipients may also be eligible for state benefits, which vary from state to state. What constitutes disabled has changed over the years. This is addressed in greater detail in the chapter on disabilities.

In May 2013, over 8.3 million people were in receipt of SSI. The average monthly benefit was $527.22 (SSA, 2013b, table b). This includes in January 2013 a 1.7 percent cost-of-living adjustment (COLA) increase. Notably, because of the downturn in the economy, there was no COLA increase in January 2010 or January 2011 for SSI recipients (SSA, 2012).

Public Housing Programs

Prior to the Housing Act of 1937, there was no national housing policy in the United States. In addition to the creation of the United States Housing Authority, this act provided financial assistance to states to "remedy the unsafe housing conditions and the acute shortage of decent and safe dwellings for low-income families" (U.S. Department of Housing and Urban Development, 1999, p. 5), reduce unemployment, and stimulate business. Since the 1930s, additional legislation has been enacted to address housing issues, such as urban redevelopment and creation of low-income housing units through the passage of the Housing Act of 1949. Furthermore in 1965, the United States created the Department of Housing and Urban Development, referred to as HUD, which has a number of programs designed to assist low-income individuals and families (HUD, 2011). Their largest and best-known program is the Housing Choice Voucher Program, also known as Section 8 Rental Assistance. This program provides vouchers to qualified people to obtain subsidized housing in preapproved apartments. As there are a finite number of Section 8 vouchers available in communities, frequently there is a waiting list for this program. In 2007, approximately 2 million low-income families received Section 8 vouchers, which covered $16 billion in rent subsidies (Karger & Stoesz, 2010).

As discussed previously, over the past several decades the federal government has decentralized many of its social welfare programs, thereby giving states greater latitude in creating and implementing programs. Congress passed the Cranston-Gonzalez National Affordable Housing Act in 1990, also referred to as the HOME Investment Partnerships Act, which provides housing-related block grants to state and local governments. This act allows states to design and administer their own housing programs, including partnering with nonprofit entities, facilitating home ownership for low-income people, and continuing to support federally subsidized housing units (Karger & Stoesz, 2010). Affordable adequate housing continues to be needed.

Health Care

The Social Security Amendments of 1965 created two health insurance programs, *Medicare* and *Medicaid*. Both public health care programs are critically important as they serve the elderly and the most vulnerable. According to Jansson (2012), without the Medicaid program, health care for people categorized as low-income "would have reached catastrophic proportions because local and state governments lacked the resources to address them" (p. 506). The Kaiser Family Foundation (KFF) reported that in 2011 nearly 48 million people were without health insurance (Kaiser Family Foundation, 2012). Individuals living below poverty comprised 38 percent of this population. Nine in ten of them were in low- or moderate-income families below the poverty line. More than 75 percent of the uninsured are in a working family without access to employer-sponsored insurance because they cannot afford the premiums or because it is not offered. In 2009, under President Obama, the Patient Protection and Affordable Care Act, sometimes referred to as the Affordable Care Act or Obamacare, was designed to target individuals without health insurance by broadening Medicaid eligibility and providing private coverage subsidies for eligible individuals with incomes up to 400 percent of the poverty level (for example, the 2013 poverty level for one individual is $11,490, so 400 percent of the poverty level is $45,960 for an individual) (Kaiser Family Foundation, 2012). Providing medical care promotes better health and ultimately helps to prevent poverty. Research shows people without health insurance "often face unaffordable medical bills when they do seek care. These bills can quickly translate into medical debt since most of the uninsured have low or moderate incomes and have little, if any, savings" (Kaiser Family Foundation, 2012, p. 6). The expanded coverage under health reform is also expected to protect against excessive out-of-pocket costs The following discussion describes some of the current public options for individuals in need of health care.

Medicare

Medicare is a federal health insurance program that provides medical coverage to individuals over 65 and people with disabilities who have contributed into the Social Security system and built up enough work credits. This social insurance program is for individuals who receive Social Security Retirement benefits or Social Security Disability. The U.S. Department of Health and Human Services manages the Centers for Medicare and Medicaid Assistance (CMS) and explains that Medicare is divided into 4 sections referred to as Parts A, B, C, and D (Health and Human Services, n.d.a). Part A provides hospital insurance that covers inpatient care, skilled nursing home care, hospice, and home health care; however, it only covers 80 percent of the costs. Recipients are expected to pay the remaining 20 percent on their own (Health and Human Services, n.d.b). Part B is supplemental medical insurance, which covers doctors' services, outpatient care, home health services, and some preventative services. The additional medical insurance coverage under Part B has a monthly standard premium (Health and Human Services, n.d.c). In 2013, the monthly fee for most people was nearly $105, however the premium ranged from $104.90 to $335.70 (Centers for Medicare & Medicaid Services, 2013). Part C, the Medicare Advantage plan, is available to people who receive Parts A and B. Under the Medicare Advantage plan, people can choose one approved provider to receive all of their health care services. An additional premium may be applied (Health and Human Services, n.d.d). Part D, which went into effect in 2006, is the Prescription Drug Coverage plan available to everyone who receives Part A, B, or C. This part has a monthly premium charge, which varies by plan, and covers prescription drugs (Health and Human Services, n.d.e). The average monthly premium in 2011 for Part D was $40.72. This is a 10 percent increase ($3.82) from the average monthly premium of $36.90 in 2010, and a 57 percent increase from $25.93 in 2006 (Hoadley, Cubanski, Hargrave, Summer, & Neuman, 2010). Notably, the Medicare premium varies by plan, and individuals with higher incomes pay an additional monthly fee. Because of the high cost of prescription drugs, many Medicare recipients have difficulty affording medication. While paying a premium for Part D coverage is an option, affordability can be the obstacle. Some states have a State Pharmaceutical Assistance Program (SPAP) that helps pay for drugs based on a person's financial need, age, or medical condition (Health and Human Services, n.d.f). According to the Centers for Medicare & Medicaid Services, as many as 2 million older adults in the United States could qualify for financial assistance with their prescription costs but do not take advantage of available programs (Uken, 2011).

Medicare is a critical health insurance program for older adults and people with disabilities. While some retirees have health benefits through their former employment, the majority of this population only has Medicare to cover their medical expenses. Older adults and people with disabilities often face greater health-related issues during the course of their life span. As such, medical care becomes critical in order to maintain and improve health. While Medicare meets many of their needs, the monthly premiums under Parts B and D can become impossible given the individuals' fixed income and poor to marginal living standards. After two years, Medicare is automatically provided for individuals who receive long-term disability (SSDI) or who have been diagnosed with a specific disease. It covers hospital and nursing home care, doctors' visits, and outpatient services. An exception exists for individuals suffering from end-stage renal failure. They are entitled to receive Parts A and B (Social Security Administration, 2011b).

Medicaid

Medicaid is a means-tested public assistance health care program designed and administered by each state, which provides medical coverage to low-income individuals and families. While states must comply with federal statutes in implementing this program as it is federally subsidized, each state establishes its own guidelines for eligibility and services. As guidelines for Medicaid differ from state to state, generally speaking, an individual or family is eligible for Medicaid if a person is pregnant, disabled, blind, or aged, has limited resources, and is a United States citizen or a lawfully admitted immigrant. When determining eligibility, low income, assets, and resources are evaluated. Medicaid typically covers doctors' visits, medications, hospitalizations, outpatient procedures, and mental health services.

According to the U.S. Department of Health and Human Services (2011), Medicaid expenses for medical care and mental health services totaled $241 billion in 2006. "Medicaid is the single largest payer for mental health services in the United States, providing services and supports for 58 million adults and children" (Health and Human Services, 2011, para. 1).

Some states have opted to enroll Medicaid recipients in managed care programs, which are less costly. The managed care provider receives a monthly premium, which is more cost-effective than paying for each doctor's visit separately. (Note that this does not mean this option is more efficient.) Some states offer dental coverage through managed care programs. The majority of the states provide for emergency dental care; however, less than half provide comprehensive dental services under Medicaid (Centers for Medicare & Medicaid Services, n.d). Informed consumers can shop around for a managed care program that best meets their needs. Medicaid consumers can also switch providers should the need arise.

Medicaid fraud, waste, and abuse are addressed through the U.S. Department of Health and Human Services' (Health and Human Services, 2011) initiative in reducing improper spending for this federal, state, and locally funded program. Each state Medicaid program is required to implement controls in order to protect the integrity of its program. Many state and local municipalities have developed sophisticated monitoring tools to identify Medicaid abuse. In one New York City suburb, for example, Medicaid fraud investigators began studying the number of prescriptions paid through Medicaid for Oxycontin (also known as Oxycodone), a controlled substance. The numbers were staggering. For the first three quarters in 2010 (January to September), Medicaid paid $2.4 million for this drug as compared to just over $1 million in 2008. With tighter controls, there was a 43 percent decrease in Medicaid expenditures for Oxycontin in the first half of 2011 (Strickler, 2010). While the majority of Medicaid recipients are legitimately obtaining medications and not defrauding the system, monitoring fraud and abuse are important components to cutting waste and keeping costs down.

State Children's Health Insurance Program (SCHIP)

Congress created the State Children's Health Insurance Program (SCHIP) as part of the Balanced Budget Act of 1997. This federal-state partnership apportioned $48 billion over 10 years to provide health coverage to children under 19 who are uninsured and ineligible for Medicaid. SCHIP allows states to insure children from working families who earn too much to qualify for Medicaid but earn too little to afford private health insurance (Karger & Stoesz, 2010). In February 2009, President Obama signed into law the Children's Health Insurance Program Reauthorization Act of 2009 (CHIPRA or Public Law 111-3), which reauthorized the Children's Health Insurance Program until the end of 2013. Currently the Centers for

Medicare and Medicaid Services (CMS) is reviewing recommended changes to the CHIPRA legislation, which is expected to be announced to the states and the public by January 2014 (Health and Human Services, 2013a). Financed by the federal and state governments, this program is designed and administered by the states. A summary issued by the Urban Institute and Robert Wood Johnson Foundation reported that in 2009, 4.9 million children nationwide were enrolled in the SCHIP program (Kenney, Lynch, Huntress, Haley, & Anderson, 2012).

Community Mental Health Centers

The Community Mental Health Centers Act of 1963 was signed into law by President John F. Kennedy. One goal of this legislation was to reduce inpatient hospitalizations for people with mental illness by providing federal funding for outpatient and preventive community-based services. Nearly fifty years later, some suggest that while this legislation never addressed all the needs of individuals with mental illnesses, it did lead to a national network of providers that delivered services to millions of people. Unfortunately, however, critics assert that the release of long-term inpatient psychiatric patients led to many members of this population residing in overcrowded single-room occupancies, or becoming homeless without a support system (Jansson, 2012; Segal, 2007).

The Affordable Care Act

Health care is a major issue facing our nation. In March 2010, the Affordable Care Act was signed into law by President Obama. Under this comprehensive health care reform, the intended primary beneficiaries were middle- and low-income individuals and families (Wadden, 2010). The act has many components, some of which have already been implemented. Currently in effect is the Patient's Bill of Rights, which prevents insurance companies from denying coverage to children with one or more preexisting conditions. Medicare recipients are now entitled to free preventive care, including screening. Under Medicare prescription drug coverage, also called Part D, there is a maximum amount of money covered for drugs. Recipients exceeding the allotted amount must pay out-of-pocket for their medication, referred to as the *donut hole*. Within the first year of implementing the Affordable Care Act, approximately 4 million seniors who fell into the Medicare Part D donut hole received $250 in rebates to help cover medication costs. Under this act, beginning in 2011, older adults who fall into the donut hole are eligible for a 50 percent deduction on all brand name prescription medication. Given that older adults frequently have more medical issues requiring additional medication, many seniors on fixed incomes would forfeit filling prescriptions rather than incur an additional expense. It is expected that by 2020, the donut hole will be completely eliminated. Also, as a result of this act, families who have health insurance can now keep their children on their plans until their children reach 26 years old. This is a dramatic change for many who only had their children covered to age 19. Additionally, small businesses and nonprofit organizations are now eligible for new tax credits to help them afford medical coverage for their employees. Many small business owners are also able to offer health insurance for their retirees (Health and Human Services, n.d.g).

One component of the Affordable Care Act, which took effect in March 2012, involves understanding and fighting health disparities by reviewing and analyzing data collected from various groups and communities (Health and Human Services, 2013b). As discussed in various chapters throughout the book, there is an imbalance in the delivery of services throughout the United States. People living in urban communities, for example, often have access to health care professionals, clinics, and hospitals that may not be readily available in rural areas. Likewise, wealthier communities often have a greater selection of specialists and treatment choices, resulting in better health outcomes. The act will look at race, ethnicity, and language in relation to health disparities and begin formulating recommendations to reduce health-related inequalities. Finally, increasing access to Medicaid and the initiation of new enrollment implemented in January 1, 2014, allow more individuals and families to be eligible for this program. Other components include making health care more affordable and providing more choices for coverage through the new Health Insurance Marketplaces (Health and Human Services, 2010; Kaiser Family Foundation, 2013).

The Working Poor

While significant changes to social insurance and public assistance programs have occurred over the last several decades, the debate continues regarding how much assistance should be given to welfare recipients in order to continue encouraging self-sufficiency and likewise encouraging those who work at low-wage jobs to continue working rather than seek government benefits. This debate has been around for several centuries. The principle of less eligibility, for example, first introduced through Britain's Poor Law Act of 1834, underscored the change in the government's response regarding who is and who is not deserving of assistance. The law permitted public relief to older adults, people with disabilities, and children living in poverty. However, paramount to this legislation was the notion that assistance to able-bodied individuals must be less than what the lowest paid worker earned. In other words, the non-working poor received less assistance than the working poor (Quigley, n.d.; Trattner, 1999). The intent of this doctrine was to ensure that life would be made so miserable that recipients would rather work than accept public aid. Careful analysis may lead some to conclude that similar punitive policies currently exist toward the able-bodied poor.

Today, the question remains, what happens to the working poor who make too much money to qualify for specific benefits but not enough to make ends meet? In order to receive government benefits, people must live substantially below the poverty line. Extreme poverty consists of households who fall below 50 percent of the official poverty level (Sandoval, Rank, & Hirschl, 2009).

According to Miller (2009), there is little support for the working poor who make slightly more than the recipients of government programs but certainly not enough to sustain themselves financially. For some, staying motivated to work when recipients of public assistance receive benefits for which they are ineligible is a struggle for many working poor, and is at the core of much debate. For many working poor, supportive services such as child care, food, and clothing are provided within their community. Additionally, some seek assistance from social networks including extended family, friends, neighbors, coworkers, and acquaintances (Wu & Eamon, 2007); however, not everyone in this category is fortunate to have this support. In addition, as discussed previously, immigrants, particularly Latinos, may be ineligible for government assistance based on their residency in the United States. As such, "working off-the-books" may be their only option (refer to the chapters on employment and immigrants for more detailed discussions). Private human service organizations historically picked up where the government left off; in other words, they provided necessary services that lessened the gap for the poor and working poor. Many nonprofit agencies and faith-based organizations, particularly those that rely on government grants and philanthropy, have faced significant cuts in recent years, yet there is still an expectation that they will continue to supplement public social services.

Current and Future Trends

The 1960s and 1990s contained the most significant changes in recent years with regard to how we address poverty in the United States. While in the 1960s, America developed many programs as part of President Johnson's antipoverty efforts, the 1990s saw many means-tested public assistance entitlement programs dismantled or transformed into temporary assistance, which mandates that recipients work to receive benefits. The United States is currently in the midst of what is sometimes referred to as "the Great Recession," a time when many Americans are finding themselves facing poverty for the first time in their lives. In recent decades, the trend toward retrenchment of social services along with the desire of conservatives to promote a smaller role for government led to the privatization of social services through grants and contracts to private agencies. Increasingly, however, these organizations, which have come to rely on government contracts for part of their funding, have found the mid- to late 2000s fraught with drastic cuts in their budgets, making it difficult to meet the needs of their clients and communities. While there are expectations that these organizations will meet the needs of more people with less money, it is becoming more challenging to do so in an era characterized by drastic cuts in federal funding for social service programs, particularly as the government works toward reducing the deficit through legislation such as the Budget Control Act of 2011.

Impact of Funding Cuts on Human Service Organizations

In recent years human service organizations, specifically private nonprofit agencies and some faith-based organizations, have seen their budgets reduced as many of these organizations rely heavily on state and federal grants to operate their programs. Both conservatives and liberals agree that if federal antipoverty programs encounter additional budget cuts, along with reductions in contracted services, those nonprofit social service agencies and religious organizations will have more unaided responsibility for meeting the basic needs of the poor and vulnerable in our society. Unfortunately, there is no sign of reversal in this trend for the near future. Consequently, in order to continue providing services, many public and private human service organizations are continuing to look toward reducing their costs while still providing effective services to their clients. In order to survive, many nonprofit human service agencies have had to modify the way they do business because the fiscal environment has forced them to change their organizational structure. This has led many of these organizations to engage in one or more of the following: mergers, consolidations, cost sharing, and collaboration.

Mergers

A merger is the coming together of two or more separate organizations into a single organization (Giffords & Dina, 2003). It has become an option that many nonprofit human service organizations have already undertaken or are in the midst of considering. La Piana (2010) explains the trend toward promoting mergers assumes that the nonprofit sector has too many organizations, and that because nonprofits are small, they are inefficient. The popular belief is that if agencies merge there will be a reduction in the intense competition for scarce funding and that merging helps to avoid duplication of services. La Piana also notes, however, that many of these assumptions are incorrect, explaining that several organizations doing similar work in a community suggests the community needs more services, not less. He provides an example of a neighborhood with five homeless shelters that have a combined capacity of 100 beds. However, there are nearly 500 homeless persons living in the area so that while these shelters may provide the same services, collectively they are only assisting one in five homeless individuals in their community. "The problem here is too few shelter beds, not too many" (La Piana, 2010, para. 13).

Still, the trend is for agencies to merge in an attempt to save money. Consider that each organization employs an executive director or president; there may be a chief operating officer, and director of fund-raising, human resources, budgeting, and accounting. In this instance, it may make sense for agencies to merge. In Mesa, Arizona, for example, the two largest nonprofit agencies merged in September 2010, thereby creating a "social-service mega agency." The merger of this mega agency has resulted in cost savings, and the agency can now service the community more effectively (Walsh, 2010). However, merging is not without its problems. Once a merger agreement has become legal, combining two distinctly autonomous organizations into one entity requires attention to a myriad of internal and external tasks (Giffords & Dina, 2003). It is important that administrators and staff continue to ensure they are meeting clients' needs throughout this process. Gibelman and Furman (2008) note that while it is beneficial for agencies to promote efficiency within their organizations, this change should not be at the expense of reduced levels of commitment and connection to the cause that led to the creation of the organization in the first place.

Consolidation and Cost Sharing

Like mergers, consolidations are increasingly becoming more common. Essentially "one side takes over the other side" in a merger, while through consolidation, the two organizations combine to become a new entity. Consolidation has also become more prevalent among government agencies as state and local dollars become increasingly scarce. In March 2011, for example, the governor of North Carolina declared that the state was embarking on an overhaul of state agencies with the goal of consolidating agencies that perform similar functions. Per the governor's office, combining departments is more efficient and streamlines services (State of North Carolina, 2011). Likewise, combining shared services such as human resources or information technology results in cost savings as it reduces redundancies.

Throughout the United States, agencies progressively are consolidating and sharing costs as a mechanism to continue providing services to clients. In many instances, consolidation can create unison, thereby improving efficiencies while working toward a common goal.

No Wrong Door is an alternative to consolidation, which likewise provides cost savings. States and local county government agencies that have implemented this service approach have realized cost savings (State of Maryland Department of Human Resources, 2011). Its purpose is to improve service delivery to individuals and families by streamlining government programs, removing duplication of services, and maximizing dollars. Many states provide a variety of health and human services to their residents that are managed by different departments such as Departments of Social Services, Health, Mental Health, Drug and Alcohol, Office of the Aging, Veterans Services, Office for Disabled, and the Youth Bureau. For example, the Department of Social Services provides financial benefits (TANF, Medicaid, SNAP) to eligible residents. Similarly, the Department of Health provides services such as WIC to eligible women, infants, and children. Frequently, recipients of both of these services need to go to different offices and are asked to provide the same information. Having all health and human services in one location eliminates duplication by centralizing these services and allowing recipients to provide required information one time. It is also financially advantageous to states as they can maximize funding streams. For instance, a homeless veteran coming to the Department of Social Services for housing may be entitled to a wider range of benefits, including permanent housing through the federal veterans' programs, thereby reducing costs at the state and local level.

Currently, there is no literature addressing the long-term impact of No Wrong Door, but initial observations show it has improved efficiencies in the delivery of health and human services. The Virginia Department for the Aging described their No Wrong Door system as changing the previous patchwork approach to service delivery and improving the coordination of care (Huffstetler, 2008). Furthermore, Lepler (2007) described a New York county's No Wrong Door program as breaking down the "silo nature of government" (p. 4). By creating a client-worker partnership, there is a greater opportunity to identify the multidimensional problems of the client and provide services in one location (Lepler, 2007).

Collaboration

Collaboration is another important trend evident among social service providers. It occurs when professionals from different autonomous organizations begin sharing information and identifying formalized ways in which they can work effectively together. Interagency collaboration can involve public, private, and faith-based organizations (Health and Human Services, 2008b). In the current economic climate, collaboration has become popular. Caseworkers and health and human service professionals, among others, frequently engage in collaboration to meet the needs of their clients and communities. This approach also includes mutual relationships between policy-makers and administrators who are responsible for organizational mandates, financing, and other management tasks. Notably, interagency collaboration is common in public, private, and faith-based organizations where each entity acts as a partner to accomplish various goals (National Technical Assistance and Evaluation Center, 2008).

Individuals struggling with job loss and who subsequently find themselves living in poverty may benefit from interagency collaboration. Take, for example, a community-based family-service type agency that increasingly sees clients in need. While this agency may offer job development skills and employment assistance, it may also help clients to complete their application for TANF and SNAP. The caseworker assigned to the family may need to work with the local department of social services to help the client secure proper documentation, or perhaps refer the client to another community-based agency with a food pantry or to a free health clinic, all of which have partnerships to better meet the needs of clients. From a financial perspective, evidence increasingly reveals that nonprofits that collaborate with multiple agencies are more likely to receive government funding, and also are likely to receive greater amounts of government funding if they join forces with other organizations (for example, see Suárez, 2011).

With the recession continuing, there is concern that the job market will further decline or not remain at its current anemic levels. Without strategic employment growth, there will be no new meaningful employment opportunities. Local social service departments report increases in the number of first-time applicants applying for government benefits. In many instances, individuals apply as a last resort, having exhausted their unemployment benefits and life savings. Regardless of how federal cuts impact social welfare programs, the number of applicants seeking government assistance is expected to rise. Given that funds are shrinking, other alternatives to assisting people in need must be explored. Additional mergers, consolidation, and collaboration among nonprofit agencies may strengthen programs, and ensure services are provided within communities. Agencies can also explore co-locating and sharing office space and staff, which further reduces overhead such as rent, insurance, electricity, and equipment.

Impact of Information Technology

Another trend in the provision of contemporary social service delivery systems is the current and ongoing development of technology. This tool plays a large part in administering social welfare programs and providing services to people in need. For basic casework or information gathering, the Internet, for instance, has transformed access to and the dissemination of information. It also enhances users' capacity for communication and geographic location (Giffords, 2009; Leiner et al., 2003). Professionals can access information through the World Wide Web, which provides a tremendous amount of information instantly. Additionally, many states have created data resource directories on the Web, making information to the community easy to access. One such site, 2-1-1, that is funded by the United Way, the Alliance for Information and Referral Systems, community support, and bipartisan legislation, provides information and referrals for food, housing, counseling, employment, and health care throughout the United States. 2-1-1 reports that it reaches approximately 246 million people (82 percent of the total U.S. population) in 47 states, the District of Columbia, and Puerto Rico. In 2010 it answered more than 16.4 million calls in the United States.

Other creative uses of technology have developed because of a mounting demand for the government to make services more accessible to the community. Accordingly, many states presently utilize web-based applications. Applications for SNAP, TANF, and Medicaid are now available online in several states and may be submitted electronically, thereby avoiding the need for potential recipients to come to the local social services office. Likewise, many federal government benefit programs such as Social Security Administration retirement, disability, and Medicare offer access to online applications, which further reduce the need for an office visit. Of course, this option is only beneficial for applicants who have access to a computer with an Internet connection and are computer-literate.

Greater reliance on technology for state and local governments is expected to increase. Florida, for instance, has installed an automated response system (referred to as My ACCESS Account) whereby people receiving public assistance can call in and access case information (Florida Department of Children & Families, 2012). Through the phone system, recipients can check their cases, recertify, and make minor changes without coming into the office. Being able to handle caseloads using technology saves money, as it is quicker and does not require manual data entry.

For the practitioner or agency administrator, the National Association of Social Workers and the Association of Social Work Boards (2005, p. 8) state "technology-based case management programs can generate reports, track personnel, automate billing, forecast budgets, and greatly assist service planning and delivery." They note that the roles for social workers (and other helping professionals) are changing and emphasize the importance of professional helpers to adjust accordingly. This indicates that in addition to maintaining knowledge about specific social welfare programs that will benefit clients, social workers need to be aware of and develop competent skills to use the new technology.

Online advocacy, sometimes referred to as cyber-activism, has also become popular in recent years. Advocates have recently used this electronic method of promoting or responding to public policy quite effectively, as a mechanism to promote change. This tool provides unprecedented access for advocates to reach a larger number of people and engage them in advocacy efforts such as online petitions, e-mails, and letter-writing campaigns. Nonprofit advocacy organizations have the potential to be more effective in promoting social and economic justice when using technology.

Given the current political environment, it is prudent for all social workers and other related professionals to foster the skills needed to use this technology successfully (Dunlop & Fawcett, 2008; Giffords, 2009; McNutt, 2008; McNutt & Menon, 2008).

Also notable is how technology is being used to target welfare fraud as part of the 1996 PRWORA. Presently, each state maintains its own welfare management system and is also responsible to protect itself against fraud. To prevent people from applying for benefits under assumed names, for example, a number of counties in California are checking recipients' fingerprints or hand images (Miller, 1995). Other jurisdictions across the country use sophisticated computer-based applications to detect both interstate and intrastate fraud. In addition to California, several states including New York and Texas instituted fingerprint-imaging programs as part of their welfare fraud control measures. These requirements have essentially applied to recipients of SNAP, TANF grants, and individuals who apply for other forms of cash aid. Sometimes photographs are also obtained through an electronic imaging system (Gustafson, 2009). Opponents to fingerprinting purport that in recent decades, government welfare policies at all levels of government—federal, state, and local—have unnecessarily treated people living in poverty as a criminal class. Fingerprinting serves to stigmatize low-income adults "in a way that equates poverty with criminality" (Gustafson, 2009, p. 676). With computerization in place, it would be quite difficult for people to engage in fraud today even if they used fake Social Security numbers. Computer checks on the numbers would likely reveal unreported earnings or assets associated with an individual's Social Security number (Gustafson, 2009). Yet, this policy continues as a mechanism to further stigmatize individuals that use welfare to meet their basic needs.

The Future of Social Security Programs

There is much debate regarding Social Security retirement benefits, specifically whether there will be enough money for younger generations when they are ready to retire. Some analysts believe the fund will not financially support the younger population as they age. This uncertainty creates unrest as people have come to rely on Social Security benefits for retirement, despite the fact that it was never intended as a full-retirement system; rather, it was intended to supplement pension plans, savings, and private insurance (Dolgoff & Feldstein, 2009).

The Social Security Administration (SSA) is currently working on developing a strategic plan that will outline the initiatives it plans to take through 2020. Key to this plan is the ongoing use of technology as the primary means for delivering services. For instance, it plans to automate routine work "without the need for human intervention" (Social Security Administration, 2011c, p. 5).

The SSA (2011c) also predicts that by 2020 the pool of all potential Old-Age and Survivors Insurance (OASI; retirement benefits), Disability, and SSI beneficiaries will be 344.7 million, an increase from 316.2 million (an 8.25 percent increase). Notably, however, Social Security was placed on the bargaining table during the August 2011 budget negotiations as one mechanism to reduce the debt ceiling. During these talks, the Republicans proposed cuts to mandatory programs, such as Social Security, while many Democrats were against tinkering with the program. It is likely that the nature of public insurance programs such as Social Security will change in upcoming years due in part to sustainability but only time will tell.

The Future of Public Benefits

Policy and governmental programs keep changing, making the future of public benefits uncertain. For people living at and below poverty levels, a strong economy is essential to self-sufficiency. Jobs that pay a livable wage are important to help people out of poverty and off public assistance rolls.

The future of all assistance programs in the United States is uncertain. The last several decades have been a time of retrenchment in public assistance programs. It appears this trend will continue, along with gradual cutbacks in social insurance programs. The debates surrounding these issues may be contentious given the future political and social climates. The policies that address the needs of the most vulnerable members of society are permeable, depending on which political party is in power.

Concluding Comments

There are many public assistance and social insurance programs used to assist members of society to meet their basic needs. This chapter introduced readers to several important concepts such as entitlements and block grants. Chapter content also explored various types of human service organizations, such as public, non-profit, proprietary, and faith-based agencies that assist people living below or near the poverty level. Organizational design, including how programs are structured, is crucial to the administration and funding of antipoverty efforts, and subsequently determines who receives assistance and how services are delivered. The chapter also introduced readers to the important distinction between social insurance and public assistance, and provided information on specific antipoverty programs currently implemented in the United States. Finally, the chapter described current and future trends including mergers, interagency collaboration, agencies' use of technology, and the Social Security program. Building on the information that readers learned in the present chapter about the working poor, the next chapter provides a detailed discussion of employment policies that affect this vulnerable population.

Internet Resources

2-1-1 Information and Referral Search: www.211.org

Provides information and referrals for food, housing, counseling, employment, and health care throughout the United States.

United Way of America: http://liveunited.org

United Way of America is a national and local organization dedicated to making an impact in the community.

Center on Budget and Policy Priorities (CBPP): http://www.cbpp.org

The CBPP is a nonpartisan research organization and policy institute that conducts research and analysis on government policies and programs that affect low- and moderate-income people.

Health Care Gov: http://www.healthcare.gov

Provides information on recent legislation related to health care.

United States Department of Health and Human Services (HHS): http://www.hhs.gov

HHS provides information related to families, prevention, and health programs.

Institute for Research on Poverty (IRP): http://www.irp.wisc.edu

The IRP is a center for interdisciplinary research into the causes and consequences of poverty and social inequality in the United States.

Official U.S. Site for Medicare: http://www.medicare.gov

Provides information about Medicare coverage.

Social Security Administration: http://www.socialsecurity.gov

The official website for the Social Security Administration provides information on retirement, disability, Medicare, SSI, and more. Federal forms are also available to download.

Further Readings

Albert, R., & Skolnik, L. (2006). *Social welfare programs: Narratives from hard times.* Belmont, CA: Thomson Brooks/Cole.

Cancian, M., & Danziger, S. (2009). *Changing poverty, changing policies (Institute for Research on Poverty Series on Poverty and Public Policy).* New York: Russell Sage Foundation.

Gibelman, M., & Furman, R. (2008). *Navigating human service organizations* (2nd ed.). Chicago: Lyceum.

Harrington, M. (1997). *The other America: Poverty in the United States.* New York: Scribner.

Iceland, J. (2006). *Poverty in America: A handbook* (2nd ed.). Berkeley: University of California Press.

Payne, R. K., Philip, E. D., & Terrie, D. S. (2001). *Bridges out of poverty: Strategies for professionals and communities.* Highlands, TX: Aha! Process Inc.

Rank, M. R. (2005) *One nation underprivileged: Why American poverty affects us all.* New York: Oxford University Press, 2004.

Segal, E. A. (2013*). Social welfare policies and social programs: A values perspective* (3rd ed.). Belmont, CA: Brooks/Cole.

Shipler, D. K. (2004). *The working poor: Invisible in America.* New York: Random House.

References

Ambrosino, R., Heffernan, J., Shuttlesworth, G., & Ambrosino, R. (2001). *Social work and social welfare: An introduction* (4th ed.). Belmont, CA: Wadsworth/Thompson Learning.

Boushey, H., & Wenger, J. B. (2006). Unemployment insurance eligibility before and after welfare reform. *Journal of Poverty, 10*(3), 23.

Centers for Medicare & Medicaid Services. (2013). *Part B costs.* Retrieved from http://www.medicare.gov/your-medicare-costs/part-b-costs/part-b-costs.html.

Centers for Medicare & Medicaid Services. (n.d.). *Dental care for Medicaid and CHIP enrollees.* Retrieved from http://www.medicaid.gov/Medicaid-CHIP-Program-Information/By-Topics/Benefits/Dental-Care.html/.

Chapman, J. (2004). *The minimum wage and Earned Income Tax Credit: Partners in making work pay.* Economic Policy Institute. Retrieved from http://www.epi.org/economic_snapshots/entry/webfeatures_snapshots_05052004/.

Cohen, M. (2001). *Mandatory work-related activities for welfare recipients: The next step in welfare reform.* Maryland School of Public Affairs, Welfare Reform Academy. Retrieved from http://www.welfareacademy.org/pubs/welfare/mandatorywork.pdf.

Dolgoff, R., & Feldstein, D. (2009). *Understanding social welfare* (8th ed.) Boston: Pearson/Allyn and Bacon.

Dunlop, J. M., & Fawcett, G. (2008). Technology-based approaches to social work and social justice. *Journal of Policy Practice, 7*(2/3), 140–154.

Florida Department of Children & Families. (2012). *ACCESS Florida.* Retrieved from http://www.myflfamilies.com/service-programs/access-florida-food-medical-assistance-cash.

Gibelman, M., & Furman, R. (2008). *Navigating human service organizations* (2nd ed.). Chicago, IL: Lyceum.

Giffords, E. D. (2003). An examination of organizational and professional commitment among public, not-for-profit, and proprietary social service employees. *Administration in Social Work, 27*(3), 5–23. Retrieved from ProQuest Social Science Journals. (Document ID: 521164891).

Giffords, E. D. (2009). The Internet and social work: The next generation. *Families in Society, 90*(4), 413–418. Retrieved from ProQuest Social Science Journals. (Document ID: 1881887531).

Giffords, E. D., & Dina, R. P. (2003). Changing organizational cultures: The challenge in forging successful mergers. *Administration in Social Work, 27*(1), 69–81. Retrieved from ProQuest Social Science Journals. (Document ID: 325571791).

Gilbert N., & Terrell, P. (2002). *Dimensions of social welfare policy* (5th ed.). Boston: Allyn and Bacon.

Gustafson, K. (2009). The criminalization of poverty. *Journal of Criminal Law & Criminology 99*(3), 643–716. Retrieved from http://www.law.northwestern .edu/journals/jclc/backissues/v99/n3/9903_643.Gustafson.pdf.

Hoadley, J., Cubanski, J., Hargrave, E., Summer, L., & Neuman, T. (2010). *Medicare Part D spotlight: Part D plan availability in 2011 and key changes since 2006.* Kaiser Family Foundation. Washington, DC. Retrieved from http://kaiserfamilyfoundation.files.wordpress.com/2013/01/8107.pdf.

Horn, W. F. (2006). *Benefits to immigrants under TANF.* Testimony before the Committee on Ways and Means, U.S. House of Representatives. Retrieved from http://www.hhs.gov/asl/testify/t060726.html.

Huffstetler, M. (2008). *No wrong door: Virginia's key strategic initiative for long-term care.* Virginia Center on Aging and Virginia Department for the Aging. *Age in Action, 23*(1), 1–19.

Internal Revenue Service. (2013). *Earned income tax credit.* Retrieved from http://www.eitc.irs.gov/central/eitcstats.

Jansson, B. (2012) *The reluctant welfare state: Engaging history to advance social work practice in. contemporary society.* Belmont, CA: Thomson Brooks/Cole.

Kaiser Family Foundation. (2012). *Five facts about the uninsured.* Retrieved from http://www.kff.org/uninsured/upload/7806-03.pdf.

Kaiser Family Foundation. (2013). *Getting into gear for 2014: Shifting new Medicaid eligibility and enrollment policies into drive.* Retrieved from http://kff.org/medicaid/report/getting-into-gear-for-2014-shifting-new-medicaid-eligibility-and-enrollment-policies-into-drive/.

Karger, H. J., & Stoesz, D. (2010). *American social welfare policy.* (6th ed.) Boston: Allyn and Bacon/Pearson.

Kenney, G., Lynch, V., Huntress, M., Haley, J., & Anderson, N. (2012). *Medicaid/ CHIP participation among children and parents: Timely analysis of immediate health policy issues.* The Urban Institute. Robert Wood Johnson Foundation. Retrieved from http://www.urban.org/UploadedPDF/412719-Medicaid-CHIP-Participation-Among-Children-and-Parents.pdf.

La Piana, D. (2010, Spring). Merging wisely. *Stanford Social Innovation Review.* Retrieved from http://www.ssireview.org/articles/entry/merging_wisely/.

Leiner, B. M., Cerf, V. G., Clark, D. D., Kahn, R. E., Kleinrock, L., Lynch, D. C., et al. (2003). *A brief history of the Internet, version 3.32.* Retrieved from the Internet Society website, http://www.isoc.org/internet/history/brief.shtml# Introduction.

Lepler, S. (2007), *Sharing promising system reform strategies; A resource manual describing Nassau County's no wrong door staff development initiative.* Retrieved from http://www.policyarchive.org/handle/10207/bitstreams/ 11079.pdf.

Little, L. (2011, August). Food Stamp nation: Alabama helps push U.S. program to all-time high. *ABC News/Money.* Retrieved from http/abcnews.go.com/ Business/surge-demand-food-stamps-united-states/story?id=14231657.

Mays, J., Brenner, M., Neuman, T., Cubanski, J., & Claxton, G. (2004). *Estimates of Medicare beneficiaries' out-of-pocket drug spending in 2006: Modeling the impact of the MMA.* Kaiser Family Foundation. Retrieved from http://kaiser familyfoundation.files.wordpress.com/2013/01/report-estimates-of-medicare-beneficiaries-out-of-pocket-drug-spending-in-2006-modeling-the-impact-of-the-mma.pdf.

McNutt, J. G. (2008). *Currents: New scholarship in the human services 7*(2), 1–16. Retrieved from http://currents.synergiesprairies.ca/currents/index.php/ currents/article/view/24/16.

McNutt, J. G., & Menon, G. M. (2008). The rise of cyberactivism: Implications for the future of advocacy in the human services. *Families in Society: The Journal of Contemporary Social Services, 89*(1), 33–38. Retrieved from EBSCO*host*.

Miller, B. (1995, April). Hand images help detect welfare fraud. *Government Technology.* Retrieved from http://www.govtech.com/magazines/gt/Hand-Images-Help-Detect-Welfare-Fraud.html.

Miller, M. L. (2009). Reward progress, reduce poverty: Most antipoverty programs fail to nurture the strengths of individuals and communities. *Stanford Social Innovation Review, 7*(3), 23–24.

National Association of Social Workers & Association of Social Work Boards. (2005). *NASW & ASWB standards for technology and social work practice* [electronic version]. Washington, DC: Authors. Retrieved from http://www .socialworkers.org/practice/standards/NASWTechnologyStandards.pdf.

National Technical Assistance and Evaluation Center. (2008, September). *A closer look: Interagency collaboration.* Retrieved from http://www.childwelfare.gov/ pubs/acloserlook/interagency/interagency.pdf.

Novak, M. (2009). *Issues of aging* (2nd ed.) New York: Pearson Higher Education.

Pear, R. (July 31, 2011). Congress must trim deficit to avoid broader cuts. *New York Times.* Retrieved from http://www.nytimes.com/2011/08/01/us/politics/ 01package.html?hp=&pagewanted=print.

Quigley, W. P. *Five hundred years of English Poor Laws, 1349–1834: Regulating the working and nonworking poor* (n.d.). Retrieved from http://www3.uakron .edu/lawrev/quigley.html.

Sandoval, D. A., Rank, M. R., & Hirschl, T. A. (2009). The increasing risk of poverty across the American life course. *Demography, 46*(4), 717–737.

Schuerger, K. (2002). *Information packet: Faith-based and community initiatives.* National Resource Center for Foster Care & Permanency Planning. Retrieved from http://www.hunter.cuny.edu/socwork/nrcfcpp/downloads/information_ packets/faith_based_and_community_initiatives-pkt.pdf.

Segal, E. A. (2007*). Social welfare policies and social programs: A values perspective.* Pacific Grove, CA: Brooks/Cole Cengage Learning.

Siegel, R. (2004). *Lyndon Johnson's War on Poverty weeks into office, LBJ turned nation's focus to the poor.* National Public Radio (NPR). Retrieved from http://www.npr.org/templates/story/story.php?storyId=1589660.

Social Security Administration. (2003). *What is the Supplemental Security Income (SSI) program?* Retrieved from http://ssa.gov/OP_Home/handbook/ handbook.21/handbook-2100.html.

Social Security Administration. (2011a). *Difference between Social Security disability and SSI disability*. Retrieved from http://ssa-custhelp.ssa.gov/app/answers/detail/a_id/245.

Social Security Administration. (2011b). *Compilation of Social Security Laws*. Retrieved from http://www.socialsecurity.gov/OP_Home/ssact/title18/1881.htm.

Social Security Administration. (2011c). *The Social Security Administration: A vision of the future: The first steps on the road to 2020*. Retrieved from http://www.ssab.gov/Publications/Miscellaneous/Vision2011.pdf.

Social Security Administration. (2012). *SSI Federal payment amounts for 2013*. Retrieved from http://www.ssa.gov/oact/cola/SSI.html.

Social Security Administration. (2013a). *Frequently asked questions*. Retrieved from http://ssa-custhelp.ssa.gov/app/answers/detail/a_id/13/~/average-monthly-social-security-benefit-for-a-retired-worker.

Social Security Administration. (2013b). *Master beneficiary record: Social Security benefits May 2013*. Retrieved from http://www.ssa.gov/policy/docs/quickfacts/stat_snapshot/2013-05.pdf.

State of Maryland Department of Human Resources. (2011). *Final report on the No Wrong Door project*. Retrieved from http://dlslibrary.state.md.us/publications/JCR/2010/2010_96(b).pdf.

State of North Carolina, Office of the Governor. (2011). *Gov. Perdue formally submits consolidation plan to General Assembly*. Retrieved from http://legislative.ncpublicschools.gov/resources-for-legislation/20110325-gov-lett-reorg.pdf.

Steinhauer, J. (August 2, 2011). Debt bill is signed, ending a fractious battle. *New York Times*. Retrieved from http://www.nytimes.com/2011/08/03/us/politics/03fiscal.html?ref=federalbudgetus&pagewanted=print.

Strickler, A. (October 21, 2010). Legal pill an Rx for concern: Medicaid prescriptions for OxyContin jump; Cops fear meds in wrong hands. *Newsday*, A2–3.

Suárez, D. F. (2011). Collaboration and professionalization: The contours of public sector funding for nonprofit organizations. *Journal of Public Administration Research & Theory*, 21(2), 307–326.

Suppes, M. A., & Wells, C. C. (2009). *The social work experience: An introduction to social work and social welfare.* Boston: Pearson/Allyn and Bacon.

Tax credits for working families. (n.d.). Retrieved from http://www.taxcreditsfor workingfamilies.org/earned-income-tax-credit/.

Trattner, W. I. (1999). *From poor law to welfare state* (6th ed.). New York: Free Press.

Uken, C. (2011). Medicare program helps low-income beneficiaries save on prescription drugs. *Billings Gazette.* Retrieved from http://billingsgazette.com/news/state-and-regional/montana/medicare-program-helps-low-income-beneficiaries-save-on-prescription-drugs/article_9cb85b47-01fc-57f1-90f3-5b3c2e5534f8.html.

U.S. Department of Agriculture, Food and Nutrition Service. (2013). *WIC program monthly data.* Retrieved from http://www.fns.usda.gov/pd/37WIC_Monthly.htm.

U.S. Department of Agriculture, Supplemental Nutrition Assistance Program. (2013). *Average monthly benefit per person.* Retrieved from http://www.fns.usda.gov/pd/18SNAPavg$PP.htm.

U.S. Department of Health and Human Services. (2010). *The Affordable Care Act becomes law.* Retrieved from http://www.healthcare.gov/law/timeline/index.html.

U.S. Department of Health and Human Services. (2011). *Combating fraud, waste, and abuse in Medicare and Medicaid.* Retrieved from http://www.hhs.gov/asl/testify/2009/05/t20090506d.html.

U.S. Department of Health and Human Services. (2013a). *Children's health insurance program reauthorization act (CHIPRA).* Retrieved from http://www.ahrq.gov/policymakers/chipra/index.html.

U.S. Department of Health and Human Services. (2013b). *What's changing and when.* Retrieved from http://www.healthcare.gov/law/timeline.

U.S. Department of Health and Human Services. (n.d.a). *Medicare Benefits.* Retrieved from http://www.medicare.gov/navigation/medicare-basics/medicare-benefits/medicare-benefits-overview.aspx.

U.S. Department of Health and Human Services. (n.d.b). *Medicare Part A.* Retrieved from http://www.medicare.gov/navigation/medicare-basics/ medicare-benefits/part-a.aspx.

U.S. Department of Health and Human Services. (n.d.c). *Medicare Part B.* Retrieved from http://www.medicare.gov/navigation/medicare-basics/ medicare-benefits/part-b.aspx.

U.S. Department of Health and Human Services (n.d.d). *Medicare Part C.* Retrieved from http://www.medicare.gov/navigation/medicare-basics/ medicare-benefits/part-c.aspx.

U.S. Department of Health and Human Services. (n.d.e). *Medicare Part D.* Retrieved from http://www.medicare.gov/navigation/medicare-basics/ medicare-benefits/part-d.aspx.

U.S. Department of Health and Human Services. (n.d.f). *State pharmaceutical assistance programs.* Retrieved from http://www.medicare.gov/pharmaceutical-assistance-program/state-programs.aspx.

U.S. Department of Health and Human Services. (n.d.g). *The Affordable Care Act: One year later.* Retrieved from http://www.healthcare.gov/law/introduction/ index.html.

U.S. Department of Health and Human Services, Office of Family Assistance. (2012). *Caseload data 2011.* Retrieved from http://www.acf.hhs.gov/ programs/ofa/resource/caseload2011.

U.S. Department of Health and Human Services, Administration for Children & Families. (2004). *Annual report on state TANF and MOE programs 2004 Connecticut.* Retrieved from http://archive.acf.hhs.gov/programs/ofa/data-reports/MOE-04/connect-04.htm.

U.S. Department of Health and Human Services, Children's Bureau, Administration for Children and Families. (2008a). Reauthorization of TANF final rule *Federal Register:* February 5, 2008, 45 CFR Parts 261, 262, 263, and 265. *Federal Register 73*(4) 6771–6828. Retrieved from http://www.acf.hhs.gov/sites/ default/files/ofa/tanf_final_rule.pdf.

U.S. Department of Health and Human Services, Children's Bureau, Administration for Children and Families. (2008b). *Interagency collaboration.* Retrieved from http://www.childwelfare.gov/pubs/acloserlook/interagency/interagency1.cfm.

U.S. Department of Housing and Urban Development. (1999). *United States Housing Act of 1937, P.L. 93-383.* Retrieved from http://www.hud.gov/offices/ogc/usha1937.pdf.

U.S. Department of Housing and Urban Development. (2011). *HUD history.* Retrieved from http://portal.hud.gov/hudportal/HUD?src=/about/hud_history.

U.S. Department of Labor, Employment and Training Administration. (2013a). *State unemployment insurance benefits.* Retrieved from http://www.workforce security.doleta.gov/unemploy/uifactsheet.asp.

U.S. Department of Labor, Bureau of Labor Statistics. (2013b). *Labor force statistics from the current population survey.* Retrieved from http://www.bls.gov/cps/.

U.S. House of Representatives Committee on the Budget. (2011). *Summary of the Budget Control Act of 2011: Overview.* Retrieved from http://democrats .budget.house.gov/sites/democrats.budget.house.gov/files/08.03.11%20 Budget%20Control%20Act%20summary.pdf.

United Way. (2011). *Income supports.* Retrieved from http://give.liveunited.org/our-work/income-supports/.

Vidal, A. (2001). *Faith-based organizations in community development.* Washington, DC: U.S. Department of Housing and Urban Development, 2001. Retrieved from http://www.huduser.org/portal/publications/faithbased.pdf.

Wadden, A. (2010). The US safety net, inequality and the Great Recession. *Journal of Poverty and Social Justice, 18*(3), 243–254.

Walsh, J. (2010). Mergers helping social service agencies survive. *The Arizona Republic.* Retrieved from http://lodestar.asu.edu/news-events/press-room/mergers-helping-social-service-agencies-survive.

Washington, G., Sullivan, M., & Washington, E. (2006). TANF policy: Past, present, and future directions. *Journal of Health & Social Policy, 21*(3), 1–16.

Wilensky, H. L., & Lebeaux, C. (1965). *Industrial society and social welfare: The impact of industrialization on the supply and organization of social welfare services in the United States.* New York: Free Press.

Wu, C., & Eamon, M. K. (2007). Public and private sources of assistance for low income households. *Journal of Sociology and Social Welfare, 34*(4), 121–149.

3

Employment, Poverty, and Social Welfare

Gertrude Schaffner Goldberg

The welfare state is the major means by which governments reduce poverty and inequality. Most frequently associated with the welfare state are benefits such as Social Security, public assistance, and social services. Less frequently regarded as a welfare state benefit, but perhaps more important, is full employment or the assurance of living-wage work for all who want it. Full employment policies are directed against unemployment and low wages, major sources of poverty and inequality that, in the absence of government intervention, inevitably arise in capitalist or free market economies.

William Beveridge, a British economist and one of the chief architects of the welfare state, considered the guarantee of employment an even more important benefit than income support. The latter, he wrote, could relieve the problem of "want" but not the problem of "idleness." According to Beveridge, full employment would result in more available jobs than job seekers, which would "ensure(s) to the people the first condition of happiness—the opportunity for useful service" (1945, p. 122). That so many Americans are denied that "first condition of happiness" must be considered a major failure of the U.S. welfare state and of a society that reveres the work ethic.

This chapter reviews employment policy in the United States from the Great Depression of the 1930s to the present. This history illustrates the paradox of a nation that pledges allegiance to the work ethic but too often fails to provide opportunities that enable individuals to adhere to that ethic—what Rev. Martin Luther King, Jr. called "the creed of . . . [our] society" (1967, p. 55). Indeed, unemployment is a chronic problem, afflicting millions of people, even in relatively "good" times, not only in periods like the Great Recession when it reaches mass proportions. This chapter will also explore current employment conditions and their consequences, particularly the severe labor market disadvantages facing certain population groups. The quality as well as quantity of jobs will be addressed, and the components of good or decent jobs identified. An analysis of these problems will be followed by strategies for alleviating or, more expansively, preventing them in the future. Finally, the chapter concludes with a discussion of how human service workers can help individuals and families to cope with unemployment as well as to move beyond micro practice with individuals through advocacy for full employment or for the right of all individuals who want them to obtain decent, living-wage jobs.

U.S. Employment Policy in Historical Perspective
Government Job Creation in the Great Depression

President Franklin D. Roosevelt (FDR) and Harry Hopkins, the gifted social worker who administered government relief programs during the Great Depression of the 1930s, preferred to provide work rather than welfare to able-bodied, unemployed persons. FDR disliked what he called "the dole" (welfare assistance); he held that continued dependence on relief "induces a spiritual and moral disintegration" (Roosevelt, 1935, para. 24). Thus, in proposing a massive government employment program in 1935, Roosevelt sought to "preserve not only the bodies of the unemployed from destitution but also their self-respect, their self-reliance and courage and determination" (Roosevelt, 1935, para. 29). This program was the Works Progress Administration (WPA), in which the federal government hired unemployed workers to build roads, bridges, airports, libraries, schools, parks, playgrounds and athletic fields; to make clothing and household goods for use by the needy; to record oral histories such as those of former slaves; to produce plays and concerts in remote areas of the country; and to create works of art such as murals, posters, and paintings.

The WPA was the largest and longest lasting of the New Deal work programs, but not the most innovative. This distinction belonged to the Civil Works Administration (CWA), an emergency measure created to provide work to millions of Americans during the severe winter of 1933–34. The CWA broke with tradition in several ways. It provided half of its jobs, not on the traditional basis of an income or a means test to determine whether an applicant was poor, but on unemployment alone. Further innovative was CWA's wage policy; instead of being equal to or somewhat lower than relief benefits, CWA pay was often higher than employers in certain regions or industries were accustomed to paying (Harvey, 2013; Schwartz, 1984).

Conceived by Harry Hopkins and his dynamic assistant Aubrey Williams, also a social worker, the CWA was the first of the New Deal programs to challenge the age-old belief that the unemployed were responsible for their condition (Harvey, 2012). It was a challenge carried forward into the WPA by Hopkins and Williams. Embodied in Title III of the Social Security Act of 1935, *unemployment compensation* was a policy that, in effect, acknowledged that the risk of involuntary unemployment is inherent in industrial labor markets and that insurance against such a hazard is a right rather than a matter of charity.

Although path-breaking in important respects, the New Deal work programs were flawed by racism and sexism as well as low wages. African Americans were believed to be accustomed to low wages and were required to accept lower-paying jobs than whites; they were classified as unskilled labor no matter what their skill levels (Rose, 2009). Because it was administered locally, finding WPA jobs for African Americans was hard, particularly in the South, but, "despite these hurdles, WPA made a major breakthrough in providing work opportunities for blacks in the North and at least opened the door in the South" (Bernstein, 1985, p. 134). While women were one-fourth of the labor force, only one-sixth of WPA jobs went to women (Rose, 2009). When women did get a slot in a work program, they were paid lower average wages than white men (Kessler-Harris, 1982).

As ambitious as work programs were, they employed on average between one-quarter and one-third of the unemployed (Burns & Williams, 1941). According to New Deal historian William Leuchtenburg, "by any standard . . . [the WPA] was an impressive achievement, [but] it never came close to meeting Roosevelt's goal of giving jobs to all who could work" (1963, p. 130). Consequently, the New Deal did not reduce unemployment below 14.6 percent until 1941, when it dipped slightly under 10 percent (still very high and comparable to the highest unemployment rate during the Great Recession) as a result of war production (for rates, Vangiezen & Schwenk, 2001; for war production, Ginsburg, 1983). Unemployment was high, though below peak levels in 1937 when the administration, motivated by a fear of inflation and deficit spending, made substantial cuts in federal expenditures. As a result, unemployment surged from 14 percent to 19 percent in the following year in what was called "the depression within the depression" (Ginsburg, 1983; Leuchtenburg, 1963). This is a grim reminder of what cutting expenditures can do during a severe recession or during a fragile recovery from such a downturn.

According to New Deal Labor Secretary Frances Perkins, who headed the committee that planned the Social Security Act, Roosevelt and Hopkins "had the idea of a permanent work-related program" (Perkins, 1946, pp. 188–189; see also Goldberg & Collins, 2001, pp. 58–61). Nonetheless, the only aid to the unemployed that found its way into permanent legislation was short-term unemployment compensation. This was the case even though Roosevelt's advisors, including Hopkins, believed that for years to come the economy would not be able to absorb all of the unemployed. Temporary and insufficient though they were, the work programs, in addition to employing millions of jobless people, left a permanent legacy for the nation's physical, social, and cultural resources—roads, bridges, schools, libraries, housing, parks, arts, cultural facilities, and much more.

Unexpectedly, massive government spending for World War II solved the problem of mass unemployment because the fear of deficit spending then gave way to the need to defend the nation against a foreign enemy. In the war years, unemployment fell to unprecedented depths, and the country enjoyed virtual full employment: 1.9 percent in 1943 and 1945 and 1.2 percent in 1944 (Ginsburg, 1983, table 1-1, p. 9). Instead of making peacetime products, millions of men and women were employed, either in the armed forces or in civilian industries serving the war effort. As economist Robert Lekachman observed, "It was World War II . . . that finally convinced the universe of the validity of Keynes' emphasis upon the symbiosis between employment and total spending" (1966, p. 259). Lekachman was referring to the great British economist John Maynard Keynes, whose advice that government spending must compensate for sagging private sector spending had not been sufficiently heeded during the Depression. Nor has it guided government policy in the Great Recession and its aftermath of continuing high unemployment.

Wartime full employment was very beneficial to all—except for those individuals who paid the price on the battlefield and the families who suffered their losses or disabilities. It was especially advantageous to African Americans and women who not only left the ranks of the unemployed but were often hired for higher skilled and better-paying jobs. It was probably these advantages and the recognition that full employment might be feasible in peacetime that led Roosevelt, near the close of the war, to frame an Economic or "Second Bill of Rights" that began with the right to "a useful and remunerative job" or living-wage employment (Roosevelt, 1944a; 1944b). Indeed, when FDR repeated the Economic Bill of Rights in his message to Congress in 1945, he held that "of these rights the most fundamental, and one on which the fulfillment of the others in large degree depends" is the right to a job (Roosevelt, 1945). The United Nations' Universal Declaration of Human Rights, essentially a bill of rights for the world, includes economic as well as civil and political rights and was inspired by Roosevelt's conceptualization of "freedom from want" or his view that "freedom without bread . . . has little meaning" (E. Roosevelt, 1990, 17, cited by Glendon, 2001, 43). The Universal Declaration that owed much to the leadership of FDR's widow, Eleanor Roosevelt, includes a broad conception of employment rights: "Everyone has the right to work, to free choice of employment, to just and favourable conditions of work and to protection against unemployment" (United Nations, 1948, Article 23; Glendon, 2001). The Universal Declaration of Human Rights is discussed in more detail in chapter 1.

The Postwar Experience

With the war ending, government leaders became concerned that demobilization and reduction of government spending could mean a return to high unemployment. Encouraged by the war's lesson that expansive fiscal policy or sufficient government spending could cure unemployment, progressive legislators drafted a full employment bill that passed the Senate in 1945 and was endorsed by President Harry Truman (1945–1953). However, the following year full employment was defeated in the House of Representatives. At that time, the House was a more conservative body than the Senate, but there were other reasons for the defeat of the full employment bill: unemployment was not mounting as much as expected and anti-labor sentiment, fueled by a wave of postwar strikes, had risen. In addition, despite public sentiment in favor of it, there was no large-scale movement to press for the enactment of full employment (Bailey, 1950; Ginsburg, 1983).

Although postwar unemployment rose above wartime levels, it was initially held in check by a combination of factors: pent-up consumer demand owing to limited incomes during the Depression and the limited availability of products during the war; the G.I. Bill of Rights that provided income support and education to many veterans who would otherwise have become part of an army of the unemployed; and the departure of many women from the labor market as a result of firings, pro-family propaganda, or their preference for the role of housewife. Even so, by 1949, unemployment was about triple the wartime lows. Shortly thereafter, however, the Korean War (1950–1953) reduced unemployment, and subsequent military spending for the Cold War helped to keep it in check, although nowhere near full employment. Readers, however, should bear in mind what will be discussed in greater detail subsequently: official unemployment rates greatly underestimate unemployment, and indeed are about half the number of jobless workers, either full- or part-time (see below). In the postwar period, the Keynesian prescription for conquering unemployment through expansive fiscal or taxing and spending policies was influential in the developed countries of Europe and North America.

Although it did not commit itself to full employment, the United States did adopt some Keynesian measures. Its brand leaned toward military Keynesianism as exemplified by its large Cold War defense expenditures. However, a big highway construction program during the presidency of Republican Dwight Eisenhower (1953–1960) has been seen as partly intended for job creation (H. Wilson, 2009), and spending for social insurance and public assistance increased, although not commensurate with rising need. Even with this increased defense and civilian spending, unemployment averaged 5.2 percent during the seven peacetime years of the Eisenhower presidency, and African American unemployment climbed to over twice the Caucasian rate, averaging 9.5 percent (Ginsburg, 1983, table 2.5, p. 40). African Americans lost ground because they were largely excluded from the white-collar occupations that accounted for nearly all of the postwar job growth. In 1961, when John F. Kennedy became president, the unemployment rate was 6.1 percent, and in some months that year, 7.1 percent (U.S. Bureau of Labor Statistics, 2011).

Unemployment fell in the 1960s. One reason was across-the-board tax cuts that, unlike recent ones targeted to upper-income groups, did stimulate consumer demand. Other contributors were increased domestic spending for the War on Poverty and stepped-up expenditures for the Vietnam war. From 1966 to 1969, unemployment averaged 3.7 percent (U.S. Bureau of Labor Statistics, 2013d). This was relatively low but hardly full employment, and like all such periods of low unemployment, it was not sustained.

Even with low overall unemployment, studies conducted by the Department of Labor and by a Senate subcommittee found that ghetto rates were much higher, and if various indices of sub-employment to which we have already alluded, such as involuntary part-time employment and poverty-level wages were included, the ghetto rates averaged around 30 percent (Ginsburg, 1975; Spring, Harrison, & Vietorisz, 1972).

Although both unemployment and poverty afflicted millions of Americans during the thirty years after World War II, there were signs of progress and a general view that rising national income would be a "shared prosperity." There were recessions but no depressions, a big change from the entire history of the United States prior to the 1930s. (There were depressions in 1837, 1857, 1873, 1893, 1907, and, of course, the Great Depression that began in 1929.)

In the three postwar decades, real wages rose steadily along with productivity. The shares of all income groups increased, but the bottom climbed faster than the top, and, at the end of the period, the grave political and civil inequalities of race and gender were being reduced through landmark civil rights measures. In addition, during the 1960s, there were government initiatives in health care, subsidized housing, food for the needy, and a large expansion of public assistance for single-mother families (Aid to Families with Dependent Children). For a time, there was some adherence to what earlier would have been considered an oxymoron, namely, "welfare rights" (West, 1981). According to liberal economist Robert Kuttner, the system "produced three decades of egalitarian economic growth" (2007, p. 64).

The U-Turn

A change of course or U-turn occurred in the mid-1970s. A number of economic changes had contributed to a "profit squeeze," a substantial drop in the after-tax profit rate of non-financial corporations between 1965 and the second half of the following decade. The response to these changes is important. Instead of capital investment or innovation to increase productivity and to make the U.S. economy more competitive with the resurgent industries of Western Europe and Japan, businesses adopted strategies that squeezed labor. These featured wage freezes and work arrangements that increased the flexibility with which workers could be hired, fired, and scheduled. Also damaging to labor, particularly in manufacturing, was globalization, or transferring U.S. capital and business operations to lower-wage areas of the world, a development encouraged by federal tax policies and later abetted by trade treaties like the North Atlantic Free Trade Agreement (NAFTA) that was promoted and signed by President Bill Clinton. Still another strategy was to abandon production for paper profits, which also led to loss of manufacturing jobs. Through an unprecedented political mobilization, the business community and its allies moved on the ideological front, attempting to re-legitimize an unregulated free market and discrediting the government policies of the postwar decades. Between the mid-1970s and the Great Recession, U.S. output per person grew 91 percent (U.S. Bureau of Labor Statistics, 2012a, table 1a). The nation became richer, but its prosperity was not shared.

Unemployment was a permanent feature of the U.S. economy, but it averaged 4.7 percent from 1947 to 1974, compared to 6.2 percent from 1974 to 2007 (U.S. Bureau of Labor Statistics, n.d.a). In the mid-1970s, unemployment rose to the highest level since the Great Depression, 8.5 percent in 1975 (U.S. Bureau of Labor Statistics, 2013b). In the early 1980s, the Federal Reserve Board raised interest rates in order to cope with inflation. When interest rates rise, the cost of purchasing cars, houses, and other products rises, and thus fewer consumers can afford to buy them. With declining sales, employers lay off workers. With higher unemployment, employers can lower wages and workplace benefits, and workers in such a labor market feel obliged to accept these losses in order to avoid unemployment. Thus, the result of raising interest rates was an even higher rate of unemployment than the previous post-Depression high of the mid-1970s. The unemployment rate was almost 10 percent (9.7 percent) in 1982 (U.S. Bureau of Labor Statistics, 2011). Once again, labor forcibly paid the penalty for problems in the economy, this time to fight inflation.

One response to high unemployment in the 1970s was a return to government job creation. The largest of these programs, the Comprehensive Employment and Training Administration (CETA), made it possible to extend the services of state public agencies as well as nonprofit social services, but CETA was much smaller in relation to total unemployment than the WPA (Ginsburg, 1983; Rose, 2009). The Ronald Reagan administration (1981–1989) repealed CETA in 1982, even though unemployment was nearly 10 percent. Another congressional response to unemployment was the Humphrey-Hawkins Full Employment and Balanced Growth Act of 1978 that set an interim target of 4 percent adult unemployment. However, the legislation was without teeth, and the average unemployment rate in the five years that followed was 8.0 percent, or double the interim target (U.S. Bureau of Labor Statistics, 2013d). Indeed, the nominal commitment to full employment did not stop the Federal Reserve from the previously mentioned policy of raising interest rates that led to higher unemployment.

Wages, like employment, changed course. Whereas real wages rose 75 percent between 1947 and 1973, they were stagnant between then and 2007, actually dropping 0.9 percent (Mishel, Bivens, Gould, & Shierholz, 2012, table 4.3). Due to congressional inaction or failure to raise the minimum raise in tandem with increases in the cost of living, its real value declined by 30 percent between 1968 and 2006. The poverty rate, which had been cut in half from 22.4 percent in 1959 to 11.1 percent in 1973, thereafter began to rise, reaching a high point of 15.2 percent in 1982. Although it approached the 1973 mark in the low unemployment year of 2000, the average from 1974 through 2007, just prior to the Great-Recession-induced steep rise in unemployment was 13.0 percent (U.S. Census Bureau, 2011, table 2). This was the U-turn: from relatively low unemployment rates, rising real wages, and falling poverty rates to rising unemployment, stagnant wages, and rising poverty. Despite the worsening conditions for workers, the Democratic administration of Bill Clinton tightened work requirements in public assistance in 1996 with the repeal of Aid to Families with Dependent Children, the entitlement to relief of poor women and their children (this is discussed in more detail in chapter 2). Indeed, Democrats as well as Republicans had taken the U-turn. The impact of these strict work requirements was softened by a reduction in unemployment in the next four years that, like similar previous periods, was short-lived. A brief recession began in 2001 and was followed by a "jobless recovery" that took much longer than in past recessions to regain a prior employment peak (Mishel, Bernstein, & Allegretto, 2007).

During most of the time since the Great Depression, labor market conditions have fluctuated between recessions, some mild and others more serious, and better times that were still fraught with job and income losses for millions of workers and their families. With recovery from the previous recession still incomplete, disaster struck. The financial meltdown of 2008 greatly exacerbated the recession that had already begun in the last month of the previous year. Unemployment doubled between December 2007 and October 2009 and was over 9 percent in all but one month until September 2011 (U.S. Bureau of Labor Statistics, 2013c). In December 2010, Federal Reserve Board Chairman Ben Bernanke warned that it could be four or five years until unemployment returned to a "normal" rate of 5–6 percent (Baranauckas, n.d.), a level that spells joblessness for millions of workers. Not only is unemployment high, much of it is long-term. By 2008, the proportion of the labor force unemployed for twenty-seven weeks or more had already reached its highest since the Bureau of Labor Statistics started keeping records of long-term unemployment in 1948, and it continued to climb (Rampell, 2010). The following section has a more detailed discussion of current and recent past labor market conditions.

Unemployment: Undercounted, Chronic, Disproportionate in Demographic Impact
Official and Hidden Unemployment

One important criterion for determining whether a social condition is serious enough to be considered a social problem is its size or magnitude (Manis, 1974). By underestimating the size of unemployment, official government data reduce the likelihood that unemployment will be taken seriously by the general public, particularly the chronic unemployment in relatively good times. The government conducts monthly sample surveys of the population and counts the unemployed as only those who during what is called a "reference week" did not work at all, were available for work, and were actively seeking work. What does "actively seeking work" mean? Sending a résumé to an employer would count as actively searching, but simply reading newspaper advertisements would not. Even if they want work and would take a job if it were available, those who are not working but not searching actively are considered out of the labor force and are not counted in the official employment rate. The official count thus omits people who fall into two categories of "hidden unemployment." First are those who are employed part-time or less than thirty-five hours a week, and want full-time work but are unable to get it. The Department of Labor refers to their status as "part-time for economic reasons" as compared with voluntary part-timers, but feminists point out that part-time work for a mother who cannot find or afford child care may be anything but voluntary. A second category of hidden unemployment is those who want jobs but are not looking, some of whom may have searched, not found a job, and become discouraged. If these "hidden unemployed" are included, then the numbers are at least double the official count (see table 3.1). These unemployment figures, large as they are, do not include the vast prison population (2.3 million in 2008) that is disproportionately comprised of young, unskilled minority men. If inmates were counted as unemployed, the official jobless rate would rise by about 1.5 percentage points (Ginsburg, Ayres, & Zaccone, 2010).

This underestimation of unemployment reflects indifference to the problem on the part of government officials and results in a lack of public concern. As labor economist Helen Lachs Ginsburg observes, "The implication of such undercounting is that policymakers aren't going to be thinking as big as they should be" (Gogoi, 2010, para. 7). The official poverty standard, which is based on an

Table 3.1. Official and hidden unemployment rates by race, ethnicity, sex, and age, June 2013 and June 2000

	June 2013	June 2000
Official Unemployment:	7.6	4.0
White	6.6	3.5
African American	13.7	7.6
Hispanic	9.1	5.7
Persons with a disability	14.2	[a]
Men 20 years and over	7.0	3.3
Women 20 years and over	6.8	3.6
Teen-agers (16-19 years)	24.0	13.1
Black teens	43.6	24.5
Total officially unemployed	11.8 million	5.7 million
Hidden Unemployment		
Working part-time because can't find a full-time job	8.2 million	3.2 million
Wanting jobs but not looking, so not counted in official statistics	6.6 million	4.4 million
Total Official and Hidden Unemployment	26.6 million	13.3 million

[a]Data on the disabled were not collected until 2008.
Source: U.S. Department of Labor, Bureau of Labor Statistics, 2000; 2013a.

emergency food budget and has not been updated for changes in the standard of living since it was devised more than forty years ago, is a comparable example of undercounting, underestimating, and giving insufficient attention to a serious social problem.

A quiz by the National Jobs for All Coalition (NJFAC), "Can You Count the Unemployed?" illustrates and humanizes the unemployment undercount (see figure 3.1). In fact, some of the workers who are afflicted by unemployment such as those who take jobs that are beneath their skill levels would not even be counted among the hidden unemployed.

Table 3.1 not only shows that the problem of unemployment is much greater than the official count but that unemployment is a chronic problem afflicting millions of people in relatively good times as well as bad. In 2000, unemployment was the lowest it had been in thirty years. Nonetheless, between five and six million people were officially counted as jobless. Including the "hidden unemployed," the number was more than twice that amount or 13.3 million people. This is almost as many people as live in the six states of New England. And this is unemployment in "good" times!

Figure 3.1. Can You Count the Unemployed? An NJFAC Quiz

1. Jack was laid off after seventeen years as a mechanic when his plant was relocated to Mexico. Unable to find a comparable job, Jack is working at Walmart at a fraction of his previous wage. *Answer:* Jack is a casualty of unemployment, but he is counted as employed, despite his downgrading.
2. Jill wants to work but stopped looking for a job because she can't afford child care for her daughter.
Answer: Once Jill stops looking for work she disappears from official statistics.
3. Jerry, eighteen years old, no longer attends school and has no job. After repeated but unsuccessful attempts to get a job, Jerry stopped looking for work and now hangs out with friends who are in the same boat.
Answer: Since Jerry is no longer looking for work, he isn't counted as unemployed.
4. John, sixty-two, lost his job last year. He continued to look for work long after exhausting his meager unemployment benefits. Then, as he watched his savings melt away, he despaired of finding another job because of illegal—but widespread—age discrimination. So he threw in the towel and now receives permanently reduced Social Security (early) retirement benefits. *Answer:* John is not counted as unemployed. He is no longer looking for work, and hence is out of the labor force.
5. Jane, a single mother, works full time, year round, at a minimum wage job that pays thousands of dollars less than what the government says is needed to support her and her two young children above the poverty level. She wonders if she will ever get a real job—one that pays a living wage.
Answer: Jane is treated as employed even though a job that pays so little is a form of underemployment.
6. Mary can't find a full-time job as a college teacher. She is forced to take a part-time position as an adjunct at a local college.
Answer: Mary is counted as employed even though she is forced to work part-time.

Source: National Jobs for All Coalition (NJFAC), n.d. http://www.njfac.org/quiz-unem.htm
http://www.bls.gov/cps/cpswom2008.pdf.

Populations at High Risk of Unemployment

Table 3.1 shows the different demographic impact of unemployment. African Americans have more than double the unemployment rate of whites in "good" and bad times. Hispanics also experience unemployment more frequently than whites, though not as severely as African Americans, but they are more likely to be in low-wage work. Teen workers have double-digit unemployment, even in "good" times, and in 2013, even with some improvement in unemployment rates since the low point of joblessness in 2009, about one in four of these youth is officially jobless. The high unemployment suffered by teen workers is deeply discouraging at the outset of their working lives, and words fail in describing the catastrophic scope of black teen unemployment. People with disabilities are among those most affected by unemployment, with a rate about as high as African Americans (see chapter 7 in this book for a full discussion of people with disabilities and poverty).

Since the early 1980s, men have had higher rates of unemployment than women during or immediately after recessions, but otherwise their rates were roughly similar. Men's higher unemployment was especially marked during and immediately after the Great Recession, 2007–2009 (U.S. Bureau of Labor Statistics, 2012b). From the start of the recovery to June 2013, women gained back nearly 90 percent of the jobs they lost in the recession, compared to only 64 percent for men. Cuts in public service employment, however, fall almost exclusively on women, who lost nearly one-fifth of their job gains as a result (National Women's Law Center, 2013). If the assault on public-sector jobs continues, women will continue to be vulnerable to job loss. As subsequent discussion will show, certain groups of women, particularly single mothers and all mothers with young children, have greater labor market disadvantages, including unemployment, than men with comparable age offspring.

Older workers, fifty-five and over, have somewhat lower unemployment than younger cohorts, although their joblessness increased sharply in the "Great Recession." Further, the average duration of their unemployment is higher than that of young and middle-aged workers (Sok, 2010). The labor force participation of older workers and their vulnerability to unemployment has risen in recent years for good and bad reasons. The former include a change in Social Security policy that made it pay to work between the ages of 65 and 70 because a portion of earnings was no longer deducted from benefits. On the downside, not only was there a collapse of financial markets and consequent declines in retirement savings, but also a related trend that increased in the 1990s—employers' replacement of defined-benefit retirement plans with riskier defined-contribution plans. In the former, employees are assured a specific benefit upon retirement whereas they are not, in the latter. As economist Teresa Ghilarducci has written, "older people are working more hours, postponing retirement, and going back to work after being retired, mainly because of the collapse of the pension system" (Ghilarducci, 2008, p. 41). Still another push into the labor market is rising out-of-pocket health costs and declining employer coverage of retiree health benefits. A mixed blessing, longer life expectancy also requires more retirement income. This decline in the economic security of older persons illustrates the importance of workplace benefits, a component of good or decent jobs that will be taken up subsequently in this chapter.

Good Jobs/Bad Jobs/No Jobs
No Jobs

Jobs Aren't Enough, the title of a book that emphasizes the problem of low wages and limited economic mobility, implies that unemployment is not the only labor market deficiency that must be overcome (Iverson & Armstrong, 2006). It is true that much contemporary work is fraught with social as well as economic indignity. The social critic Barbara Ehrenreich, worked at low-wage jobs and wrote movingly of its assaults. "What surprised and offended me most about the low-wage work place . . . was the extent to which one is required to surrender one's basic civil rights and—what boils down to the same thing—self-respect" (Ehrenreich, 2002, p. 208). Nonetheless, although it may say more about how badly the welfare system treated them, women who leave the Aid to Families with Dependent Children (AFDC) rolls, now Temporary Assistance for Needy Families (TANF), prefer even marginal employment to welfare and feel that work increases their self-esteem (Altman & Goldberg, 2007; Edin & Lein, 1997).

Those who viewed full employment as a key component of the welfare state held that the opportunity to work meant more than economic security for the individual. Sir William Beveridge's emphasis on work as an opportunity for useful service has already been noted. The Swedish welfare state, famous for generous welfare or income support, was, for many years, a full employment state, and that component was seen as more important than income support (Korpi, 1978, pp. 107–108). Swedish policymakers saw work as important to a normal life, a means of reducing isolation, loneliness, and alienation (Ginsburg, 1983, p. 123). In contemporary parlance, the approaches of Beveridge and the Swedish policymakers were directed against "social exclusion," a social as well as economic conception of impoverishment that implies, in addition to lack of income, "denial of access to employment, social benefits and services and other aspects of cultural and community life" (Kahn & Kamerman, 2002, p. 13; Paugam, 1996; Saraceno, 2002). Marginal work may not lead to social integration (Atkinson, 1998; Levitas 1996), nor is low-wage employment equivalent to "self-sufficiency," a catchword of welfare reformers in the 1990s. Nevertheless, unemployment certainly will not accomplish either of these goals. According to the Nobel laureate in economics, Amartya Sen, unemployment has "many far-reaching effects other than loss of income": "psychological harm, loss of work motivation, skill and self-confidence, increase in ailments and morbidity, and even mortality rates, disruptions of family relations and social life, hardening of social exclusion, and accentuation of racial tensions and gender asymmetries" (Sen, 1999, p. 94; see also Kieselbach, Winefield, Boyd, & Anderson, 2010). Soon after the Great Recession began, the devastating effects of unemployment were being felt. A New York Times/CBS News poll of unemployed adults found that being out of work was "causing major life changes, mental health issues and trouble maintaining even basic necessities" (Luo & Thee-Brenan, 2009, para. 3). In addition to its effect on unemployed workers and their families, unemployment means that the economy is wasting the goods and services that jobless workers could have produced (Ginsburg, 1995).

Particularly troubling are high levels of unemployment in the urban ghettos, a condition aptly captured by the title of William J. Wilson's book, *When Work Disappears* (1996). Wilson, in this and a later work (2009), distinguishes between social structural and cultural factors that contribute to joblessness, generally coming down on the side of structural factors such as employment opportunity instead of cultural attributes like education, skill, or attitudes. (The latter, it should be noted, often have their roots in such structural dimensions as racism and long-standing denial of economic opportunity.) Although Wilson's later work (2009) gives more weight to cultural factors, he nonetheless lays strong emphasis on the studies of Paul Jargowsky, who found very positive responses to economic booms among the ghetto poor. For example, the number of people living in neighborhoods where the poverty rate is 40 percent or higher declined by about one-fourth in the 1990s and over one-third among blacks (Jargowsky, 1997, 2003). This is particularly striking when one considers that the boom lasted only a few years in the last part of the decade.

Other evidence supporting a structural interpretation of unemployment among populations assumed to have cultural deficits comes from the work of economist Richard Freeman (1991). He showed that when employment opportunities expanded in local labor markets, the percentage of economically disadvantaged young men who were employed rose substantially and that employment of black youth was particularly sensitive to the state of local labor markets. Similarly, Paul Osterman, who studied the impact of full employment in Boston in the 1980s, concluded, "it is very clear that the poor did respond to economic opportunity when it was offered" (Osterman, 1991, p. 130).

Although structural factors—and most importantly the availability of jobs—are critical, personal traits related to one's socialization rise in importance during the more typical non-boom periods when jobs are less available. These cultural factors also bear some attention, particularly for persons who are providing help to unemployed individuals. There is mounting evidence that for jobs at the lower end of the hierarchy, employers are more likely to seek and retain workers who have positive attitudes, problem-solving ability, flexibility, and the ability to relate and communicate well with others (Handel, 2003; Holzer, 1996; Moy & Lam, 2004; Regenstein, Meyer, & Dickemper-Hicks, 1998). Ghetto socialization, as compared to that of higher-income areas, is less likely to produce such traits, and so intervention to increase the employability of disadvantaged workers might well attempt to improve these cultural deficits.

Before turning to a discussion of good jobs or job quality, it is important to recognize the relationship between unemployment and wages, the sine qua non of good jobs. Chronic loose labor markets or unemployment have contributed to wage stagnation, for when unemployment is high and there are many more job seekers than available jobs, employers can hire the workers they need without raising wages or providing other workplace benefits. Conversely, tighter labor markets lead to improvements in wages. As economist Robert Pollin (2007) points out, when unemployment fell slightly below 4 percent in the second half of the 1990s, wages and benefits rose, including those at the low end of the labor market. Jared Bernstein and Dean Baker provide data showing that for the years 1995–2000, when the average unemployment rate was just below 5 percent, males in the bottom 40 percent of the wage distribution made wage gains (annual hourly gains) between 2.2 percent and 2.9 percent, compared to –1.3 percent to 0.7 percent in the years from 1979 to 1994, when the average unemployment rate was 7.0 percent. They also found that gains for low-wage women workers followed a similar pattern (Bernstein & Baker, 2003, p. 43). Needless to say, some other workplace benefits depend on the level of wages and often go along with better-paying jobs. For example, all things being equal, pensions rise with income levels.

Good Jobs

What are the components of good jobs? These have been defined expansively to include not only living wages, good health and pension benefits, paid vacation, sick days, family leave, good working conditions, and job security (Mishel, Bernstein, & Shierholz, 2009). Affordable child care, job safety, a measure of autonomy or workplace democracy, collective bargaining rights, and reduced work time have also been included in the concept of good jobs or decent work (Bell, Ginsburg, Goldberg,

Harvey, & Zaccone, 2007). A more modest measure consisting of adequate pay, defined as at least the median male earnings in 1979, adjusted for inflation ($17 an hour in 2006), health insurance, and a retirement plan has been used to track good jobs in relation to growth in national wealth (Schmitt, 2007, table 1).

Although the period of lower unemployment in the late 1990s resulted in wage gains, many workers remained poor. In 2000, nearly 17 million people—more than the total of official and hidden unemployment—were working full-time, year-round but earning less than the official poverty level for a family of four (estimated from U.S. Census Bureau, 2001, table 11). That standard, as already pointed out, is a low one, only $17,603 in 2000.

Low wages fall heavily on women, especially minority women. In 2007, 31 percent of women workers earned less than the poverty level for a family of four; over a third of African American women and nearly half of Latinas were working poor. The rate for male workers is lower, 22 percent, itself a dismal record (Mishel et al., 2009, tables 3.8, 3.9, pp. 140–141). This is an indication that the male standard is not necessarily one to which women should aspire and that attention needs to be addressed to inequality of class as well as of gender and race/ethnicity. Class measures, as discussed later in this chapter, include full employment and increases in unionization, the minimum wage, and wage supplementation through the Earned Income Tax Credit (EITC).

A conventional comparison of women's and men's earnings is the ratio of women's to men's full-time, year-round earnings or the wage gap (actually misnamed since the difference should be the gap). In 2010, this was 77 percent, up from 61 percent in 1960 (U.S. Census Bureau, 2011, table p. 36). This full-time, year-round wage comparison underestimates women's inequality by omitting part-time employment in which women predominate and, more importantly, women's lesser continuity in the labor market. Women often take time out of the labor market for childbirth and child rearing. Thus, over a fifteen-year period from 1983 to 1998, women's earnings were only 38 percent of men's (Hartmann, Rose, & Lovell, 2006).

An important contributor to this continuity gap is insufficient, affordable child care. In the late 1990s, government child care subsidies were increased in response to strict work requirements in public assistance. Still, child care was far from an entitlement, with subsidies available to only 12–14 percent of income-eligible families

(Helburn & Bergmann, 2003). A survey by the National Women's Law Center in 2006 concluded that

> there are still far too many low-income families who are unable to qualify for child care assistance, remain trapped on waiting lists, strain to pay their co-payments even if they are receiving assistance, or cannot find good care for their children because state reimbursement rates are too low. (Schulman & Blank, 2006, p. 6)

There is a need for cultural change, in which fathers take a larger share of family responsibilities, thereby helping to diminish the continuity gap. Paid parental and sick leave would also be beneficial, since women are more likely to take time off for the nurturing of very young children and when they are ill.

Motherhood, Single Motherhood, and Labor Market Disadvantage

Women have been gaining some ground in the labor market, but motherhood generally and single motherhood, particularly, are substantial labor market penalties for many women. Perhaps as a result of employers' perception that their major responsibility for child care reduces their availability and productivity, mothers are much less likely to be hired than non-mothers with comparable credentials, and they are also more likely to have lower starting salaries (Correll & Bernard, 2007; Waldfogel, 1998).

Whereas the age of their children has virtually no impact on the labor force status of men, it bears a close relationship to women's employment (see table 3.2). The data in table 3.2 are from 2007, the year with the lowest unemployment rate in the new century and the one immediately preceding the financial crisis. Part-time employment, which means lower pay, often lower wage rates, less benefits, and less likelihood of mobility in the work force, is at least seven times higher for mothers than for fathers. Mothers' unemployment rate was considerably higher than fathers' regardless of the age of their children. While mothers' lower labor force participation is related to lack of suitable, affordable child care, and to the preferences of some to be full-time caregivers, the higher unemployment of those in the labor market who, by definition, are seeking employment but unable to find it, cannot be explained in this way. Rather, one is inclined to see mothers as more likely to be laid off because of lower seniority or the related factors of discrimination and employers' perception of them as less productive or reliable.

Table 3.2. Rates of labor force participation, full- and part-time employment, and unemployment by sex and age of children, 2007

	Labor Force Participation	Full-Time Employment	Part-Time Employment	Unemployment
With children under 18				
Women	71.0	75.7	24.3	4.6
Men	94.3	96.6	3.4	2.8
With children 6–17				
Women	77.2	77.8	22.2	3.8
Men	93.2	96.7	3.3	2.6
With children under 6				
Women	63.3	72.5	27.5	5.8
Men	95.7	96.4	3.6	3.0
With children under 3				
Women	59.2	70.7	29.3	6.4
Men	95.9	96.2	3.8	3.1

Source: Calculated from U.S. Bureau of Labor Statistics, unpublished data from the Current Population Survey, table 6.

Both the push of welfare reform and the pull of expanding employment contributed to the considerable increase in labor market participation of single mothers between 1994 and 2000. (See table 3.3.) Less likely than married mothers to be in the labor force prior to welfare reform, single mothers not only increased their participation but exceeded that of married mothers, and while their activity rate dipped after the peak employment year of 2000, it remained substantially above the 1994 rate, before the stiffening of work requirements in public assistance.

Table 3.3. Labor Market Status of Mothers and Fathers with Children under 18 by Marital Status, 1994–2007

	Single Mothers (%)			Married Mothers (%)			Married Fathers (%)		
	Labor Force[a]	Empl./ Pop.[b]	Unemploy- ment[c]	Labor Force[a]	Empl./ Pop.[b]	Unemploy- ment[c]	Labor Force[a]	Empl./ Pop.[b]	Unemploy- ment[c]
1994	67.2	59.3	8.0	69.6	66.4	4.5	94.5	91.0	3.8
2000	78.9	73.0	7.5	69.8	67.8	2.9	95.1	91.0	2.0
2007	76.5	70.4	8.0	68.8	66.7	3.0	94.8	92.4	2.5

Sources: Calculated from U.S. Bureau of Labor Statistics, n.d.b, tables 6 and 8.
[a] Percent of the population either employed or unemployed and looking for work.
[b] Percent of the population employed.
[c] Percent of the population unemployed and looking for work.

Although single mothers are more likely to be in the labor force than their married counterparts, single mothers were more than twice as likely to be unemployed in both 2000 and 2007. There are several reasons why single mothers are at high risk of unemployment. As lone parents, they may be more likely than married mothers to be absent from work when children are sick or day care arrangements fail, or, as mentioned in relation to partnered mothers as well, employers simply perceive them as more undependable. Race may also contribute to their high unemployment rates. In 2007, black women, who were 30 percent of single mothers, had an unemployment rate of 10.4 percent, compared to 7.0 percent for white single mothers (U.S. Bureau of Labor Statistics, n.d.b, table 6). Racism abets the other handicaps of black single mothers.

What Is to Be Done?

Policies for reducing, perhaps even virtually eliminating unemployment, underemployment, and low wages can intervene on the supply side of the labor market or the demand side. A prime example of the former is education, which is a favorite proposed remedy for labor market disadvantage and an oft-prescribed route to occupational success. Whereas education focuses on the characteristics of workers or on the supply side of the labor market (are there enough skilled workers to fill open positions), policies that expand the number of available jobs intervene on the demand side (are there enough jobs). Supply-side measures assume that it is primarily the characteristics of workers that determine labor market advantages whereas the premise of demand-side measures is that the labor market, if left alone, will chronically produce too few jobs at livable wages. A tighter labor market tends to improve, though not eliminate conditions such as low wages and discrimination based on race, ethnicity, and gender. Therefore, measures directed specifically to overcoming such barriers are also necessary.

Supply Side: Education

Education is often seen as a panacea for occupational mobility and for access to good jobs. It is true that for both men and women the higher the educational level, the higher the income. Yet, it is also true that in all educational categories, women's hourly wages are still lower than men's (Mishel et al., 2007, tables 3.18, 3.19). The greatest difference in earnings is between those with some college and those with a college degree, and that is the case for both genders.

Educational mobility is certainly a route to better wages and better jobs, but it is a difficult one. The barriers to higher education have become more formidable, particularly its steep cost, including study in the public universities. In reviewing the evidence on educational mobility, Mishel and colleagues (2007, pp. 97–101) find high correlations between children's educational attainments and their parents' incomes. Among children from high-income families, 74 percent of those who scored high on math tests in eighth grade finished college, compared to 29 percent of those from low-income families, a percentage about equal to college completion of children from high-income families who score low on these tests. Lower-scoring children from high-income families are ten times more likely to finish college than their achievement peers from low-income families.

Does this suggest the need to pursue an educational strategy? The answer is yes, but not because it will solve the big labor market problems that are discussed in this chapter. Educational attainment can be a promising individual strategy and a means to much more than economic rewards. However, a great increase in education might lead to an oversupply of applicants for good jobs that would tend to put downward pressure on earnings for some educated workers.

As it turns out, the demand for educated workers is not projected to increase in the near future. Calculations based on data from the Bureau of Labor Statistics found barely any increase in the number of jobs requiring a bachelor's degree or more (Dohm & Schniper, 2007). According to these projections, occupations that usually require only short- or moderate-term on-the-job training and little or no formal training will account for about half of all jobs in 2016. These include occupations such as retail salespersons, food preparation workers, and personal and home care aides (Dohm & Schniper, 2007). The workers who hold these jobs perform vital services in the economy. They are often our clients. Like all workers, they deserve living wages and other workplace benefits.

Demand-Side Measures: Job Creation

Tighter labor markets, as already noted, tend to raise wages, but have always been short-lived. Sustained full employment would do even more to increase the number of good jobs. When full employment legislation was under serious consideration in the 1940s, proponents predicted that it would increase the bargaining power of labor and consequently the quality, not only the quantity, of jobs:

> Our experience with periods of labor shortage indicates that its first effect is greatly to increase the bargaining power of labor, both individually and collectively. This results

in steady improvement of wages and working conditions, which means that employers must seek to make employment attractive, since the workers are no longer motivated by the fear of losing their jobs. A shift of workers from the less pleasant and remunerative occupations occur, so that standards are raised at the lower levels.

The status of labor will improve, since employers can no longer rely upon the discipline of discharge to enforce authority. The tendency will be for labor to have some participation in industrial and economic policy. (Eulau, Ezekiel, Hansen, Loeb, Jr., & Soule, 1945, p. 395)

Full employment, as this evaluation indicates, is "the worker's best friend." Employers would prosper from the expansion of consumer spending on the part of a well-paid and fully employed population, but the enhanced power of labor is quite another thing.

Insufficient jobs for all who want them can be dealt with through providing income support to unemployed workers or by measures to create more jobs. The former, typically met through unemployment insurance, is considered a passive labor market policy. Unemployment insurance benefits are vital for those who experience short-term unemployment. Benefits last twenty-six weeks or longer when state unemployment rises. With a vote of Congress, benefits can be extended in response to an increase in long-term unemployment, and that was the case during the Great Recession. However, during much of the period since 1990, the proportion of officially unemployed workers who got benefits was usually 40 percent or less (Stone, Greenstein, & Coven, 2007, figure 1). Unemployment insurance is the proper remedy for short-term unemployment and should be provided to *all* jobless persons who want to work, including those with no prior work experience.

An alternative to unemployment compensation for those workers who are unemployed for extended periods of time is to enact job creation programs modeled on those of the New Deal during the Great Depression. In contrast to unemployment benefits, this is an active labor market policy.

Plans for creating living-wage jobs that would reduce chronic unemployment and at the same time rebuild the nation's depleted and neglected physical and social infrastructure were devised before the economic meltdown. Direct job creation, though similar to the innovative work programs of the Great Depression, must avoid the deficiencies of the New Deal model that were already noted: racism, sexism, low wages, insufficient coverage of all the unemployed, and limited duration. The core approach is to employ jobless workers to renovate dilapidated housing; provide child and elder care; expand recreation and cultural activities; improve parks and other public spaces; undertake energy conservation measures; repair bridges, weak dams, and levees; improve public transportation, and so on (Baiman et al., 2009; Bell et al., 2007; Ginsburg & Goldberg, 2008; for a later proposal, see Darity, 2010).

After a short period on unemployment insurance, those who remain jobless would have the opportunity to earn a living, maintain the habit of working, and perhaps learn new skills by working on projects that would also serve and better the nation. Conceived before the Great Recession as a permanent program to eliminate chronic unemployment, direct job creation by government is needed even more to combat the mass unemployment brought on by the economic meltdown of 2008. If this was a permanent program, expanding and contracting in relation to the extent of unemployment and available to all of those who are without work beyond a short term, it would realize an important goal of both the Universal Declaration of Human Rights and Roosevelt's Economic Bill of Rights: the human right to a job at a livable wage.

The federal government's policy responses to our twenty-first-century crisis have helped to keep the economy from disaster but have done far too little to stem mass unemployment. It is estimated that without the government's interventions, especially the Obama job stimulus (American Recovery and Reinvestment Act, or ARRA) and the bank bailouts, unemployment would have climbed to 16 percent in 2010 rather than to just under 10 percent (Blinder & Zandi, 2010). Significantly, one of the economists who made this assessment, Alan Blinder, formerly vice chairman of the Federal Reserve Board, subsequently referred to the "jobs emergency" and called for New Deal-style hiring of workers onto public payrolls (Harwood, 2010).

A program of direct job creation like the New Deal work programs would have created many more jobs than the ARRA or Obama Stimulus and would have done so more quickly. Instead the ARRA took the indirect approach of stimulating private sector job growth through tax cuts and additional spending on health care, social welfare, and infrastructure. According to economist Philip Harvey (2011), the New Deal response to mass unemployment, inspired by the social workers who led it, was to provide unemployed workers with the jobs they needed in government programs like the WPA, rather than to require them to wait for jobs to reappear in the private sector. What the New Dealers did not realize, Harvey argues, is that in addition to providing temporary work for the unemployed, thereby meeting their immediate needs, their direct job creation strategy also provided exactly the same boost to the private sector's recovery that Keynesian economists seek to achieve through tax cuts and increased government spending on other things. When the direct job creation effect of these programs (the jobs created in the programs themselves) is added to their indirect job creation effect (the jobs created in the private sector by increasing demand via jobs program spending), the total job creation effect of the New Deal strategy far exceeds that of other types of stimulus spending. Indeed, Harvey estimates that if the $787 billion estimated cost of the Obama Stimulus had been spent instead on New Deal-style direct job creation programs, it would have created about 16 million jobs rather than the 3–4 million jobs the ARRA saved or created. Stated differently, the nation's unemployment rate could have been reduced to its pre-recession level of 4.5 percent immediately, while government spending on the jobs program would have generated more private sector job growth than did the ARRA.

Reduced Work Time

Another strategy to reduce unemployment is to reduce work time. This can be done by decreasing the length of the workday or increasing the number of vacation days. This strategy has been proposed as a means of dealing with chronic unemployment or reducing mass unemployment during a downturn such as the Great Recession. In the mid-1960s, when unemployment was relatively low by today's standards—5.7 percent in 1963 and 5.2 percent in 1964—the eminent manpower expert Sar Levitan evaluated reduced work time as a means of coping with what he referred to as "the persistent [*sic*] high level of unemployment which has prevailed for nearly seven years" (Levitan, 1964, p. 1).

In 2009, during the Great Recession, work sharing, made possible by a number of state unemployment insurance plans that paid benefits to workers whose hours were reduced, saved an estimated 166,000 jobs (National Association of State Workforce Agencies, cited by Schor, 2010). With official unemployment in the 14 million range and "hidden" unemployment taking a similar toll (table 3.1), the number of jobs saved by this means of work sharing seems minuscule. Nonetheless, the economist Juliet Schor (2010), a major current advocate of reduced work time who sees it as a means of dealing with a number of problems—overwork, environmental degradation, and unemployment—considers this a promising development, an "exit ramp" to a new and saner economy. This seems unduly optimistic.

Reduction of work time was a major demand of the labor movement. Over the years, the rationale for reduced work time has varied. In the nineteenth century, improving citizenship was one of the reasons given: that industrial workers would have the time to "improve themselves and consequently exercise their rights as citizens more effectively" (Levitan, 1964, p. 1). However, "the principal considerations in cutting the 60-hour workweek were social in nature. Health and fatigue factors and a desire for leisure were key considerations" (Levitan, 1964, p. 1). Reducing unemployment has also been a consistent rationale for shorter work time. Samuel Gompers, founder of the American Federation of Labor, put the case powerfully: "so long as there is one man who seeks employment and cannot obtain it, the hours of work are too long" (1887, cited by Schnapper, 1972, p. 250). In a similar vein, a century later, social worker and social policy professor David Gil, wrote that

> what we ought to do instead of arguing endlessly over job-creation, is to redistribute all presently undertaken work in a manner that assures everyone's inclusion by varying the legal length of the workday whenever necessary, so as to ensure a continuous match between the number of available workers and the changing scope of production. (Gil, 1983, p. 8)

Due in large part to workers' struggles, the workweek was dramatically reduced between 1860 and 1960—from 68 to 41 hours (Levitan, 1964). In the next decade or so, hours per week and the number of weeks worked per year fell somewhat. However, between 1973 and 2002, average weekly hours increased slightly and the number of weeks per year increased by a greater extent (over 7 percent) (Mishel, Bernstein, & Allegretto, 2005, table 2.2, p. 113). According to the U.S. Bureau of Labor Statistics, the average work week of full-time workers has ranged from 42.1 hours to 43.0 from 2003 to 2012 (2013a). In 1999 annual work hours were 4 percent higher than in 1980 and were higher than in any other industrialized country (Golden & Jorgensen, 2002; see also Gornick, 2010). Productivity growth or output per worker slowed after 1973, but in the next twenty years nonetheless grew significantly more than wages or compensation (Mishel et al., 2005). Productivity growth could have been used to reduce work time or increase workers' pay. Instead, wages fell and hours of work rose. The decline of the labor movement no doubt contributed to this reversal of a century-long process.

While the average workweek is 40 hours, many work more than that. A decade or so ago, almost one-third of the workforce regularly worked more than the standard

40-hour week, and one-fifth worked more than 50 hours (Golden & Jorgensen, 2002). The Fair Labor Standards Act of 1938, an important New Deal measure, penalizes overtime by requiring that workers covered by the act be paid an overtime premium of at least one-half the regular rate of pay for each hour exceeding the standard workweek. However, around the turn of this century about one-third of the workforce was not covered by this requirement (Golden & Jorgensen, 2002, citing Department of Labor estimates). Moreover, despite the penalty, many employers prefer to pay overtime rather than hire and train new workers. Another reason for eschewing new hires is that overtime does not increase the cost of some fringe benefits whereas these would have to be paid to new workers. Stiffer penalties and wider coverage of the law would seem an obvious means of reducing overtime. Further, the disincentive to shorter hours would be reduced by removing the cap on employers' payment for workers' benefits as well as shifting responsibility for benefits such as health care away from employers, for example to the government (Schor, 2005).

With more time on the job and particularly with the increase in two-worker families, many Americans are overworked. Although it means more money in the paycheck, overwork poses clear drawbacks for workers: stress, workplace accidents, sleep deprivation, less family time, including child care, and little left over for recreation, leisure, adult education, and community participation (Bianchi & Wight, 2010; Golden & Jorgensen, 2002; Schor, 1991). Thus, overwork creates many problems for individuals, families, and society. In the long run, workplace accidents, absenteeism, and workers' health and mental health problems are detrimental to employers, but nevertheless many favor the short-term advantages of overtime.

At the same time that some employed Americans are overworked, many others, as discussed earlier in this chapter, are unemployed, not only in bad times but in better ones as well. The sociologist Herbert Gans (2011, p. A35) has pointed out that the jobless "recovery" from the Great Recession is increasing the number of "superfluous" workers. Among other policies, Gans has called for work sharing: "reducing working time—perhaps to as low as 30 hours a week, with the lost income made up by unemployment compensation."

How effective is reduced work time in lowering unemployment? Several European countries have pursued the policy, and in general, it does create jobs but not in direct proportion to the amount of work time reduction (Askenazy, 2007; LaJeunesse, 2009). For example, if the 40-hour week were reduced to 35, a five-hour reduction for seven people would not make room for one full-time, 35-hour-a-week job. Based on review of an econometric analysis of the 7 percent reduction in work time in France between 1999 and 2001, economist Robert LaJeunesse concluded that "half of the 'job-creating' potential of work time reduction can be viewed as being offset by greater labor productivity" (2009, p. 216). Just as recent work-time reduction in the United States has been underwritten by public subsidy, that is, unemployment benefits, the French experience depended on contributions from the state. According to economist Philippe Askenazy (2007), the effort to achieve a 35-hour workweek in France was not carried out fully, and if it had been, the cost per job to the government would have been about the same as that of compensating a nurse or police officer. Askenazy asks whether the money would be better spent in developing public services—in other words, direct job creation. Insofar as public monies would be used, it may be preferable to choose what kinds of jobs to subsidize.

One might apply this reasoning to the assumed, yet unproven effects of reduced work time on the environment. Direct creation of jobs that would make residential and commercial buildings more energy efficient might be a more certain approach to sustainability. Job creation in the social infrastructure such as education and child, elder, and health care is compatible with sustainability. Moreover, work sharing might well preserve jobs that contribute to environmental degradation. Since there are compelling social reasons to reduce overwork, it seems important to pursue both work time reduction and direct job creation. Why not create 35-hour-a-week jobs? This, of course, is unlikely to occur without significant political change.

Reducing Workplace Discrimination

Earnings are low for the three-fifths of women who are employed in female-dominated occupations, even in "good" jobs such as supervisors in food service and retail work (Hartmann, Allen, & Owens, 1999), and the occupational segregation of minority workers, both women and men, is similarly disadvantaging. Thus, affirmative action that moves women and minorities into higher-paying, [white] male-dominated occupations is one form of redress. Pay equity that raises the wages in female- and minority-segregated occupations is another. However, affirmative action has suffered serious setbacks (Anderson, 2004; Kellough, 2006; Messer-Davidow, 2002). Pay equity improved some wages in unionized employment, but it never gained ground in the private sector and was limited in public jurisdictions as well (Figart & Hartmann, 2000). Subsidized child care, an income transfer, or social welfare benefit is an important means of reducing the inequality of women and the penalty of motherhood, including single motherhood.

With gender and race strategies in retreat and the white male standard less than it used to be, class strategies, as already noted, should also be pursued. While not addressed directly to gender or race, they nonetheless benefit women of all races and African American, Latino, and immigrant workers of both genders disproportionately. Full employment is par excellence a class strategy, but there are others. One study of the "collapse of low-skill wages" places responsibility not on decreases in workers' skills or the higher demands of technology but on the weakening of wage-setting institutions, especially unions and the minimum wage (Howell, 1998). Union density has declined precipitously since the mid-1950s, but unions are still boosters of good jobs. Unionized workers earn 14 percent more than nonunion workers, and the gains are especially high for minority men and new immigrants and for immigrant men who have been in the country more than ten years (Mishel et al., 2007, table 3.32). Union premiums (differences between union and nonunion workers) are substantial in coverage of health, retirement, and paid leaves (Mishel et al., 2007, table 3.33). Union organizers feel that without passage of the Employment Free Choice Act that presidential candidate Obama promised to support but which is no longer on the agenda, employees who attempt to organize fellow workers will continue to be at risk of firing and other harassment by their employers.

The minimum wage should be a living wage. An increase in the statutory minimum not only raises the wages of those whose earnings are below the new minimum (nearly 60 percent of whom are women) but also tends to spill over to workers with wages just above (Mishel et al., 2009). Another means of raising wages are living-wage campaigns that require employers who do business with city governments to pay their employees adequately. These ordinances have been enacted in many cities across the country but are sometimes not fully implemented because of government officials' reluctance to offend business (Luce, 2004). By definition, they are confined to government contractors but can have spillover effects to other employers who may, as a result, need to raise their wages in order to attract competent workers.

The Earned Income Tax Credit (EITC), which supplements the wages of low-income workers with children, is an important antipoverty program. When Aid to Families with Dependent Children (AFDC) was repealed, the federal government was already spending somewhat more on the EITC than AFDC, and federal spending for the EITC was projected to exceed combined AFDC and TANF expenditures by nearly 50 percent in fiscal year 1997 (Goldberg & Collins, 2001, 408, note 150). The EITC can raise the income of a family with two or more children about 40 percent if the worker's income falls within the range of the poverty level, and many states and some cities supplement the credit. It is a refundable tax credit that is granted regardless of whether the worker pays federal income taxes, and most recipients do not, making the EITC essentially public assistance. However, since it is for the working poor and administered through a universal agency, the Internal Revenue Service, it is not stigmatized. Unlike traditional public assistance, benefits are lower for very low-paid workers than for those near and within the range of the poverty line, and unlike wages, EITC benefits are not included in calculating unemployment insurance or Social Security (Cherry & Goldberg, 2000; Gitterman, 2010; Goldberg, 2010). The EITC provides only minimal benefits for workers who do not support children but could be expanded to provide them with higher supplements.

Not surprisingly, the EITC is popular, expanding even during hard times for other entitlements. Why would employers not like a measure that pays part of their wage bill, and which they think holds down pressure on wages (Perez-Peña, 1998, p. B24)? Regardless of whether it does, the rise of the EITC has been accompanied by a decline in the value of the minimum wage. The 2006 value of the minimum wage plus the EITC for a family of three with two children was only 94 percent of the three-person poverty standard. Even with the rise in the minimum wage in 2007, its value plus the EITC is still below the 1968 value of the minimum wage alone, which was equivalent to 120 percent of that three-person standard (Goldberg, 2010). The EITC subsidizes any low-wage job, whereas direct government job creation uses public funds to create jobs that simultaneously invest in human and physical resources.

What Can Social Workers and Helping Professionals Do?
Helping Individuals and Families

Helping individuals and families, referred to as "micro practice," addresses the many problems that stem from unemployment, underemployment, low wages, and blocked mobility. Such practice should be guided by recognition of the systemic roots of many individual and family problems. Human service workers with a systemic perspective would, for example, avoid the confusion abetted by welfare reform ideology of equating any job at all, regardless of the wage, with "self-sufficiency." By calculating the costs of "necessities"—food, shelter, transportation, health and child care—in various areas of the country, social worker Diana Pearce and her colleagues have done much to show that most jobs taken by former welfare recipients fall far short of the wages necessary for "self-sufficiency" (Center for Women's Welfare, n.d.).

Individual or group work that addresses the guilt or self-blame as well as shame or the actual or anticipated loss of social respect from unemployment is an important part of practice with this population. Workers can help reduce debilitating self-blame through what is, in effect, political socialization; that is, helping clients to reframe their problems in terms of systemic dysfunction. Such work not only counters disempowerment and the "slings and arrows" of their class position but prepares clients for empowering involvement in social reform. The next step is for human service workers to refer and facilitate clients' involvement in organizations that are attempting to raise wages, expand workplace benefits, and advocate for fuller employment. Also important are organizations that champion women's and minority rights, providing that their efforts to improve the conditions of their constituents emphasize workplace discrimination, occupational segregation, and other forms of labor market inequities as well as limited access to affordable child care. Referral to resources such as these are an important part of individual work with labor market problems, and it is important that human service workers add these resources to the more traditional ones that facilitate their direct-service goals.

The families of unemployed, underemployed, and poorly paid workers suffer the economic and social disadvantages of their breadwinners' positions in the labor market. Children and spouses may well resent and blame their family breadwinners for consequent economic deprivation. Human service workers may reduce some of these family tensions by helping the dependents of marginal workers to understand the roots of the problem, here again engaging in some political socialization.

Although part of the usual repertoire of referrals for individual and family problems, social agencies specializing in vocational training and guidance as well as those that provide information and case advocacy in relation to workers' benefits such as unemployment insurance are especially important for practice with employment problems. Practitioners, of course, need to be thoroughly informed about eligibility and access to the major income support programs that increase the incomes of workers afflicted by one or more labor market inadequacy, especially the Supplemental Nutrition Assistance Program (SNAP, formerly Food Stamps), EITC, unemployment compensation, Disability Insurance, workers' compensation, and Temporary Assistance for Needy Families (TANF) (discussed in chapter 2). In addition, they need to be prepared to advocate for their clients when they are denied benefits to which they are entitled as well as to collaborate with organizations that specialize in such advocacy.

There are, of course, instances where problems in the workplace are not primarily systemic in origin although they may well be exacerbated by some of its indignities and inequities or more generally by the assaults of class, gender, and racial or ethnic inequality. The workplace problems of some employees may well be consequences of both structural and cultural factors. One approach is for human service workers to develop individual and group interventions geared to the development of the types of workplace skills that employers are seeking, or they may refer those they help to agencies that specialize in such services, always making quite certain that the focus is on such skill development. Also important, where clients clearly manifest behavior that is problematic in the workplace like alcohol and drug abuse, interventions would draw on practice with populations exhibiting such interpersonal problems and would also make use of appropriate referrals to agencies specializing in these problems. Where appropriate, counseling should, of course, encourage and facilitate occupational mobility through education and training, here again making use of appropriate referrals.

An attempt to spell out these interventions brings to mind the lack of a well-defined practice in relation to labor market deficiencies in the field of social work. This is a reflection of the profession's greater interest in welfare than in work. The social work profession—direct practitioners, researchers, and educators—needs to devote more resources to the development and evaluation of innovative practice directed to employment problems and to the enhancement of services that are potentially needed by millions of individuals and families.

Social Change Practice

Social workers are obligated by their Code of Ethics to engage in social change on behalf of oppressed individuals and groups. The code specifies unemployment as one of the forms of social injustice on which social action should focus (National Association of Social Workers, 2008). In the broadest terms, social workers should take part in organized efforts to reduce the labor market disadvantages that beset so many of their clients. Although not obligated by this Code of Ethics, other human service workers are equally likely to recognize the extent to which injustice accounts for many of the problems of their clients. Consequently, they will feel obligated to engage in the efforts to change social conditions discussed in this section, even though some of the discussion is directed specifically to social workers.

Human services workers should take action to ensure that the organizations to which they belong such as the National Association of Social Workers (NASW) make employment issues a priority, and not only during severe economic downturns. Indeed, clients often fall into the group that suffers from the chronic failure of the labor market to provide enough jobs, much less good ones, and whose plight is often submerged beneath a general prosperity that they certainly do not share. Human service workers should be aware of whether organizations promoting the rights of women give more than "lip service" to the public subsidy of child care for all who need it. If they belong to trade unions, they should press them to pay attention to the problems of the working class as a whole, not simply their members. Even though a tight labor market is a strength at the bargaining table, the U.S. labor movement, surprisingly, has not been a strong champion of full employment and has done little to mobilize workers on behalf of that goal. Human service workers can also take part in the social change organizations to which they refer their clients that are dedicated to the resolution of the various labor market problems that have been identified, such as extension and improvement of unemployment benefits, living-wage campaigns, and advocacy of job creation.

Practice with individuals can prepare human service workers to bear witness to the harsh realities of the labor market and the resultant burdens that so many of their clients experience. Public education is an important ingredient of efforts to change social conditions, and workers' firsthand knowledge of these problems should position them to assume this role. They can also groom their clients to bear witness effectively to the impact of unemployment, low wages, and workplace indignities. Human service workers should add to their knowledge of the consequences of these problems an understanding of their causes and of desirable and feasible solutions like government job creation that can both aid the victims of the labor market and enrich the nation's social and physical infrastructure. In doing so, these workers can move from case to cause, that is, from individual advocacy on behalf of clients to efforts to change conditions that harm a whole group of clients.

Some social workers have shown leadership in the pursuit of social justice in the labor market. They have been among the leaders in the founding of the National Jobs for All Coalition, the only national organization whose primary goal is to secure the right to living-wage jobs for all (for more information, see www.njfac.org and www.jobscampaign.org). The Coalition for Human Needs is a social work-led organization that has successfully defended low-income social programs and has increasingly taken action on employment issues (for more information, see www.chn.org).

Labor market problems afflict a large swath of the population but especially the very populations to which social workers and human service workers have a special obligation. Unemployment is a drain on the economy, reducing the tax base and wasting the goods and services that jobless workers could have produced. Social workers and human service professionals, generally, should be dedicating more individual and community interventions to reduce the scourge of unemployment and the many workplace deficiencies associated with it. Is it too much to hope that we will once again rise to the occasion of mass unemployment and show leadership, if not commensurate, then at least worthy of those social workers who inspired and led the stirring employment programs of the New Deal?

Concluding Comments

The assurance of decent, living-wage jobs, this chapter has argued, is a critical component of the welfare state because it reduces poverty and economic inequality, not only boosting income but providing an opportunity for useful service and social inclusion. A brief history of employment conditions since the Great Depression demonstrated that the U.S. welfare state falls far short of providing decent work to all who want it; indeed, even in relatively good times, millions suffer various forms of unemployment and low wages. Readers learned how the government defines unemployment and how this official undercount both reflects and exacerbates public indifference and failure to recognize the seriousness of this social problem and to address it effectively. Unemployment, it was shown, disproportionately afflicts certain population groups: both partnered and single mothers, minorities, the young, the elderly, and the disabled. Many of those who work, moreover have low pay and few, if any workplace benefits such as pensions or paid parental or sick pay; in short, they lack what were referred to as decent or good jobs.

Measures that benefit the unemployed as well as improve the conditions of disadvantaged workers and contribute to decent work were identified: increase in the minimum wage and wage supplementation through the earned income tax; strengthening collective bargaining rights; increasing subsidized child care; and enacting or upholding anti-discrimination laws and affirmative action. Unemployment insurance, usually available to only a minority of officially unemployed workers, should cover all who experience short-term joblessness. Preferable to this passive labor market policy for those who remain jobless for extended periods of time, are active labor market policies—job creation by the federal government that would not only provide the opportunity to work but improve the nation's neglected physical and social infrastructures.

Finally, examples of micro, mezzo, and macro practice will be presented. Micro interventions are those that help individuals and families to cope with the consequences of unemployment. Mezzo and macro measures include advocacy to benefit the unemployed but more importantly to reduce unemployment, increase the quality of jobs, and secure the economic human right to decent work.

Case Studies
Micro Level

Ms. Sanchez, overwhelmed with multiple stressors, referred herself to a community-based preventive program to receive supportive services, advocacy, and linkage within the entitlement systems. Ms. Sanchez is a 46-year-old Hispanic woman, the mother of three boys, ages 17, 8, and 7. She has been a victim of domestic violence and is currently in the United States under a U non-immigrant-status visa (referred to as a "U visa"), which offers protection for victims of crimes who help law enforcement and government officials in prosecuting or investigating the crime. Ms. Sanchez is employed earning minimal wages and experiencing major housing and financial difficulties.

Ms. Sanchez has been in the United States over twelve years; her eldest son, José, is also in the United States on a U Visa. Both mother and child fled a domestic abusive relationship in El Salvador, where to date José's father remains. The two younger children were born in the United States and have the same father.

Ms. Sanchez was a victim of domestic violence in both of these marital relationships and has sought services from the Coalition Against Domestic Violence. The whereabouts of these fathers are unknown, and efforts to file for child support have been unsuccessful.

Although the children are meeting developmental milestones, there are many unresolved issues that should be addressed. All have witnessed domestic violence and would benefit from counseling and tutorial services, and these are being explored.

Ms. Sanchez earns approximately $700 a month as a house cleaner. Her salary varies each week depending upon new clients and cancellations. With the assistance of the preventive program, she now receives $268 worth of food stamps per month and $299 in public assistance. Due to her reported income increase of $100 last month, Ms. Sanchez has been advised that her public assistance will now be terminated because her income is over the federal eligibility limits. The family resides in a crowded two-bedroom apartment on a busy street, over a deli. Their rent is $1,200 a month, electricity is $70, and gas is $40. Last month, the local church assisted the Sanchez family in paying their rent. The month before, Ms. Sanchez took in friends of friends for three weeks, to help pay expenses. Although adequate and with no safety hazards, the apartment is small and minimally maintained by the landlord. It is not ideal for a single parent raising three children, but it is a place to call home.

Affordable housing in the county where the family resides is very difficult to obtain. Ms. Sanchez has searched for more affordable housing, and has been unsuccessful. She would move out of the county, but is fearful she will not secure employment.

Ms. Sanchez is a wonderful mother to her three children and works hard to meet her family's needs. The realities of her financial struggles impact the overall functioning of this mother as well as her children. Lack of stability and fear of homelessness dominate their minds daily.

Questions
1. Ms. Sanchez's public benefits have been cut since she is earning an extra $100 per month. What is the incentive for Ms. Sanchez to earn the extra money?

2. If you were working with Ms. Sanchez, would you encourage her to continue working despite her benefits being reduced? Why or why not? If yes, how would you encourage her?

3. What services could be provided to Ms. Sanchez's oldest son (age 17) to prepare him for education or vocational training after high school?

4. Are there any additional services in your community that could be offered to Ms. Sanchez to help her with her family?

5. What is the benefit for Ms. Sanchez if the fathers of her three children were located and paid child support?

Mezzo Level

In accordance with the Personal Responsibility Work Opportunity Reconciliation Act (PRWORA) (explained in detail in chapter 2), clients who are eligible for financial assistance and are deemed employable are required to actively seek employment in order to continue receiving benefits. Clients must provide their local Department of Social Services (DSS) with documentation on a regular basis that they are actively seeking work.

DSS clients with criminal histories have particular difficulty securing employment. Many employers do not want to hire someone who has been incarcerated. In order to address issues such as this, local Reentry Task Forces have been created. These task forces engage individuals prior to their release from prison or jail in order to make the transition from incarceration into the community easier. Prisons notify local reentry task force personnel with the dates of release, particularly when individuals have limited resources in the community. Prior to release, the task force personnel reach out to these individuals to obtain additional information, including living arrangements, if any, and previous work history. In cases where a person is released without housing, the task force notifies the local DSS office and advises of the person's discharge date and that they are homeless.

Given the difficulties associated with reentry into the community, groups have been established to assist people who are newly released from prison. The groups focus on common issues such as employment and housing as these interventions can reduce recidivism.

During employment-related meetings, the participants are split into two groups in order to role-play a job interview. Half the group plays the role of the interviewer and the other half the role of the interviewee. Through role-playing, the participants learn how to conduct themselves during job interviews by accentuating strengths and answering questions about gaps in work history due to incarceration.

These strategies assist this population in building their confidence during interviews, making them stronger candidates in the job market.

Similarly, the task force educates potential employers about the rehabilitation many individuals undergo while incarcerated in order to reduce the stereotypes associated with this population. In response education and advocacy, some employers have hired individuals who had been incarcerated and have found them to be hard-working and dedicated employees.

Questions

1. Should prior incarceration matter to a potential employer?

2. If no one will hire individuals due to a previous incarceration, should they be entitled to receive benefits from DSS regardless of PRWORA regulations?

3. What other interventions could a reentry task force do to help this population (with issues such as securing housing and employment)?

4. If you are an employer, would you consider hiring someone who had been incarcerated?

5. How does society judge individuals who have been incarcerated? Does the type of crime matter?

6. If you are a helping professional working with this population, how might you prevent them from feeling discouraged in seeking employment?

Macro Level

An interdisciplinary group of social activists and academics, including veterans of the national struggle for full employment in the 1970s, became concerned about this latent social problem of unemployment, latent in the sense of being at odds with current interests and values but not recognized as such by the general public (Merton, 1976). Social work academics were prominent in this group of initiators, remaining in leadership positions throughout its history. Based in New York City, this group, first called New Initiatives for Full Employment (NIFE), began to meet regularly, study the problem, consider solutions, write position papers and policy proposals, and organize conferences in which the problem was addressed by leading social scientists and social reformers.

By the mid-1990s, the NIFE initiators had defined the problem and developed a plan of action in the form of a manifesto that they circulated widely in search of endorsements. They used this document to convene a conference at a New York City university. Attending this conference were interested people with a range of backgrounds—a future Nobel laureate in economics and other distinguished social scientists and educators, trade unionists, clergy, and grassroots organizers. The conference participants decided to form the National Jobs for All Coalition (NJFAC) that would raise consciousness of the issue through publications, public speaking and the like and, in time, engage in political action on behalf of full employment.

The name of the new organization, National Jobs for All Coalition, seemed more descriptive of its goals than "full employment" and less dated than the latter term. NJFAC later published the manifesto as a book, *Jobs for All: A Plan for the Revitalization of America* (Collins, Ginsburg, & Goldberg, 1994). NJFAC is the only national organization that has as its primary goal a living wage, or decent work for all who want it.

The NJFAC had no funds at the time but soon after was provided with space and part-time staff in the Urban Ministries unit of the National Council of Churches. One task of staff and a volunteer executive committee was to recruit an advisory board of distinguished scholars, public officials (including two past secretaries of labor), religious and labor leaders, and entertainers. The NJFAC executive committee consisted of the volunteers who had founded the organization, some of them giving near full-time to the cause. NJFAC began *Uncommon Sense,* a series of popular educational publications, organized "Full Employment Weeks" (small demonstrations and teach-ins at universities), solicited members throughout the country, secured small grants for special projects, raised money through appeals to members, and lobbied successfully for a demonstration Job Vacancy Survey in the Department of Labor that required a small authorization of federal funds.

With a nation still uninterested in unemployment—despite the fact that millions were unemployed, underemployed, and working poor even in "good" times—the group used the strategy of tying joblessness to issues that were on the mind of the public and on the political agenda. For example, in the case of Social Security, NJFAC gathered information to refute the program's alleged financial shortfall, emphasizing at the same time that the best *insurance* for Social Security is full employment or more people working and paying taxes and less therefore requiring public income support, not only unemployment insurance but disability benefits when, particularly as older workers, they lose hope of becoming reemployed. In time the organization's website became a valuable resource visited by many, including academics, public officials, and activists seeking information on employment, unemployment, and related issues.

One of the most visited sections of the NJFAC website is its full report of monthly unemployment statistics, which includes the numbers of hidden unemployed and the working poor. It attempts to arouse public interest and involvement by showing that the problem is of far greater magnitude than the official unemployment figures lead us to believe. NJFAC's various publications also emphasize that unemployment is a primary problem resulting in poverty, social exclusion, and a host of mental and physical ills. The organization also points out that unemployment is literally throwing away the national product or potential goods and services—those that the unemployed could have produced had they been working.

When unemployment reached crisis proportions in the past decade, NJFAC proposed that those who were jobless beyond the usual time limit for receipt of unemployment benefits should be provided with work in the service of the nation. During the crisis NJFAC has maintained that direct job creation by the federal government is the most efficient and effective way of reducing mass unemployment and at the same time improving the quality of life in the United States. In fact, it has maintained that had the $787 billion stimulus enacted early in 2009 been used in this way, it would have provided jobs for all officially unemployed workers. That would have been a lower rate of unemployment than the nation has ever reached in peacetime.

In the wake of the financial collapse of 2008, NJFAC took the lead in organizing a National Conference to Create Living-Wage Jobs, Meet Human Needs, and Sustain the Environment (New York City, November 2009) that was attended by activists from a number of states and cosponsored by labor and faith-based organizations, advocacy groups, academic departments, and so on. NJFAC and its part-time organizer, based in Ohio, have sparked "First Friday" events, observances in a number of cities on the day the Department of Labor announces the unemployment statistics of the preceding month. Among the organizations that have joined these "First Friday" events are women's organizations that have seen the liabilities for women, particularly in the cutbacks of public service workers. These and the national conference have enabled NJFAC to build ties with a wide range of organizations concerned with reducing unemployment, extending unemployment benefits, advocating government job creation, and a human right to employment.

Through a national clearinghouse for economic justice on one of its websites, NJFAC hopes to coordinate actions on behalf of the unemployed and job creation and to provide ideas for action and knowledge of pending legislation and other proposals to reduce unemployment. NJFAC has also worked with the office of Representative John Conyers (D-MI) in framing the Humphrey-Hawkins Full Employment and Training Act (H.R1000 in the 113th Congress), a comprehensive and innovative federal and local government job creation and training bill that would create millions of new jobs for the nation's unemployed. Although passage of the bill is extremely unlikely in the near future, this legislation is an important means of increasing public knowledge and support for job creation that would not only aid the unemployed but the nation as a whole.

NJFAC, like any other advocacy group, requires the knowledge of experts and the skills of organizers. It has drawn on interdisciplinary expertise in economics, political science, and social policy. Throughout its history, NJFAC has benefited from the leadership of social workers who have contributed their knowledge of social policy and of the effects of unemployment on individuals and families as well as their skills in advocacy and community organization.

Questions

1. What are the significant issues connected to unemployment?

2. What are some of the advantages and disadvantages of forming an organization such as NJFAC?

3. What other methods for addressing the effects of unemployment on individuals and families could NJFAC try?

4. How does interdisciplinary collaboration benefit the change effort?

5. What types of knowledge and skills are needed to influence policy at the macro level?

6. In times when the public and/or public officials are unreceptive to the reforms proposed by an organization like NJFAC, what strategies should NJFAC adopt?

Internet Resources

Economic Policy Institute: http://www.epi.org/

Research on jobs, wages, living standards, and retirement.

National Jobs for All Coalition: www.njfac.org

Research and information on unemployment, employment, strategies for achieving full employment.

National Employment Law Project: http://www.nelp.org/

Research on policies to enforce workers' rights and create good jobs.

Chicago Political Economy Group: http://www.cpegonline.org/

Research on federal job creation paid for by a financial transaction tax.

Center on Economic and Policy Research: http://www.cepr.net/

Research on jobs, minimum wage, social security, and retirement.

Institute for Women's Policy Research: http://www.iwpr.org/

Research on women's employment, pay equity, discrimination, family leave, social security.

U.S. Bureau of Labor Statistics: http://bls.gov/

Current and historical data on employment, unemployment, working conditions, foreign nations. For data on specific states, see http://www.bls.gov/regions/news_release_finder.htm.

U.S. Bureau of the Census: http://www.census.gov/

Current and historical data on characteristics of the U.S. population—income, poverty, health care.

Further Readings

Beveridge, W. (1945). *Full employment in a free society.* New York: W. W. Norton.

Collins, S. D., Ginsburg, H. L., & Goldberg, G. S. (1994). *Jobs for all: A Plan for the revitalization of America.* New York: Apex Press.

Ginsburg, H. L., & Goldberg, G. S. (2008). Decent work and public investment: A proposal. *New Labor Forum, 17*(1), 123–132.

Hartmann, H., Rose, S. J., & Lovell, V. (2006). How much progress in closing the long-term earnings gap? In F.D. Blau, M. C. Brinton, & D. B. Grusky (eds.), *The declining significance of gender?* (pp. 125–155). New York: Russell Sage.

Harvey, P. (1989). *Securing the right to full employment: Social welfare policy and the unemployed in the United States.* Princeton, NJ: Princeton University Press.

Kurban, H., & Green, R., eds. (2012). Special issue on jobs and the future of the U.S. economy. *Review of Black Political Economy 29* (March).

Luce, S. (2004). *Fighting for a living wage.* New York: ILR Press.

Mishel, L., Bernstein, J., & Allegretto, S. (2005). *The state of working America 2004/2005.* Ithaca, NY: ILR Press.

Mishel, L., Bernstein, J., & Allegretto, S. (2008). The state of working America 2006/2007. Ithaca, NY: ILR Press.

Mishel, L., Bernstein, J., & Shierholz, H. (2009). *The state of working America 2008/2009.* Ithaca, NY: ILR Press.

Roosevelt, F. D. (1944a). *Second Bill of Rights,* January 11, 1944. http://en.wiki pedia.org/wiki/Second_Bill_of_Rights.

Rose, N. E. (2009). *Put to work: The WPA and public employment in the Great Depression* (2nd ed.). New York: Monthly Review Press.

Saraceno. C. (2002). Social exclusion: Cultural roots and variations on a popular concept. In *Beyond childhood poverty: The social exclusion of children,* ed. A. J. Kahn & S. B. Kamerman (pp. 37–76). New York: The Institute for Child and Family Policy at Columbia University.

Wilson, W. J. (2009). *More than just poor: Being black and poor in the inner city.* New York: Norton.

References

Altman, J. C., & Goldberg, G. S. (2007). The quality of life paradox: A study of former public assistance recipients. *Journal of Poverty, 11,* 71–90.

Anderson, T. H. (2004). *The pursuit of fairness: A history of affirmative action.* New York: Oxford University Press.

Askenazy, P. (2007). France's 35-hour workweek: Myths and realities. *Dissent, 54*(4), 29–35.

Atkinson, A. B. (1998). Social exclusion, poverty and unemployment. In *Exclusion, employment and opportunity,* ed. A. B. Atkinson & J. Hills. CASEpaper/ CASE4, London School of Economics. Retrieved from http://eprints.lse.ac .uk/5489/1/exclusion_employment_and_opportunity.PDF.

Bailey, S. K. (1950). *Congress makes a law: The story behind the Employment Act of 1946.* New York: Columbia University Press.

Baiman, R., Barclay, B., Hollander, S., Persky, J., Redmond, E., & Rothenberg, M. (2009). *A permanent jobs program for the U.S.: Economic restructuring to meet human needs.* Chicago: Chicago Political Economy Group. Retrieved from http://www.cpegonline.org/reports/jobs.pdf.

Baranauckas, D. (n.d.). Fed chairman says jobless rate could remain high for years. *Politics Daily.* Retrieved from http://www.politicsdaily.com/2010/12/06/ fed-chairman-says-jobless-rate-could-remain-high-for-years/.

Bell, C., Ginsburg, H. L., Goldberg, G. S., Harvey, P., & Zaccone, J. (2007). *Shared prosperity and the drive for decent work.* New York: National Jobs for All Coalition. Retrieved from http://www.njfac.org/sharedpros.pdf.

Bernstein, I. (1985). *A caring society: The New Deal, the worker, and the Great Depression.* Boston: Houghton, Mifflin.

Bernstein, J., & Baker, D. (2003). *The benefits of full employment: When markets work for people.* Washington, DC: Economic Policy Institute.

Beveridge, W. (1945). *Full employment in a free society.* New York: W. W. Norton.

Bianchi, S., & Wight, V. R. (2010). The long reach of the job: Employment and time for family life. In *Workplace flexibility: Realigning jobs for a 21st century workforce,* ed. K. Christensen & B. Schneider (pp.17–42). Ithaca, NY: ILR Press.

Blinder, A., & Zande, M. (2010). *How the Great Recession was brought to an end.* Retrieved from http://www.economy.com/mark-zandi/documents/End-of-Great-Recession.pdf.

Burns, A. E., & Williams, E. A. (1941). *Federal works, security and relief programs.* Research Monograph XXIV, Federal Works Agency and Works Progress Administration. Washington, DC: U.S. Government Printing Office.

Center for Women's Welfare. (n.d.). *The self-sufficiency standard: What a difference a measure makes.* Seattle, Washington, School of Social Work, University of Washington. Retrieved from http://www.selfsufficiencystandard.org/docs/SSS%20FAQs_061909.pdf.

Cherry, R., & Goldberg, G. S. (2000). The Earned Income Tax Credit: What it does and doesn't do. *Political economy and contemporary capitalism: Radical perspectives on economic theory and policy,* ed. R. Baiman, H. Boushey, & D. Saunders. (pp. 294–301). Armonk, NY: M. E. Sharpe.

Collins, S. D., Ginsburg, H. L., & Goldberg, G. S. (1994). *Jobs for all: A plan for the revitalization of America.* New York: Apex Press.

Correll, S. J., & Bernard, S. (2007). Getting a job: Is there a motherhood penalty? *American Journal of Sociology, 112*(5), 1297–1338.

Darity, W. (2010). A direct route to full employment. *Review of Black Political Economy, 37*(3/4), 179–181.

Dohm, A., & Schniper, L. (2007). Occupational employment projections to 2016. *Monthly Labor Review, 130*(11), 86–125.

Edin, K., & Lein, L. (1997). *Making ends meet: How single mothers survive welfare and low-wage work.* New York: Russell Sage.

Ehrenreich, B. (2002). *Nickled and dimed: On (not) getting by in America.* New York: Henry Holt.

Eulau, H., Ezekiel, M., Hansen, A. H., Loeb, J., Jr. & Soule, G. (1945). The road to freedom: Full employment. *New Republic,* Special Section, September 24, 395–415.

Figart, D. M., & Hartmann, H. I. (2000). Broadening the concept of pay equity. In *Political economy and contemporary capitalism: Radical perspectives on economic theory and policy,* ed. R. Baiman, H. Boushy, & D. Saunders (pp. 285–293). Armonk, NY: M. E. Sharpe.

Freeman, R. B. (1991). Employment and earnings of disadvantaged young men in a labor shortage economy. In *The urban underclass,* ed. C. Jencks & P. E. Peterson (pp. 103–121). Washington, DC: Brookings Institution.

Gans, H. J. (2011, November 24). The age of the superfluous worker. *New York Times*, p. A35.

Ghilarducci, T. (2008). *When I'm sixty-four: The plot against pensions and the plan to save them.* Princeton, NJ: Princeton University Press.

Gil, D. (1983). 100 × 8 = 1143 × 7 or how to lick unemployment. *The Humanist Sociologist, 8*(2), 8–9.

Ginsburg, H. (1975). *Unemployment, subemployment, and public policy.* New York: Center for Income Maintenance Policy, New York University School of Social Work.

Ginsburg, H. (1983). *Full employment and public policy: The United States and Europe:* Lexington, MA: Lexington Books.

Ginsburg, H. L. (1995). Unemployment means lost output and human deficits. *Uncommon Sense* 2. New York: National Jobs for All Coalition. Retrieved from http://www.njfac.org/us2.htm.

Ginsburg, H. L., Ayres, B., & Zaccone, J. (2010). Unemployment statistics: Let's tell the whole story. *Uncommon Sense* 4, rev. New York: National Jobs for All Coalition. Retrieved from http://www.njfac.org/us4.html.

Ginsburg, H. L., & Goldberg, G. S. (2008). Decent work and public investment: A proposal. *New Labor Forum, 17*(1), 123–132.

Gitterman, D. P. (2010). *Boosting paychecks: The politics of supporting America's working poor.* Washington, DC: Brookings Institution Press.

Glendon, M. E. (2001). *A world made new: Eleanor Roosevelt and the Universal Declaration of Human Rights.* New York: Random House.

Gogoi, P. (2010). The jobless effect: Is the real unemployment rate 16.5%, 22%, or. . .? *Daily Finance*, July 16. Retrieved from http://www.dailyfinance.com/story/careers/what-is-the-real-unemployment-rate/19556146/.

Goldberg, G. S. (2010). Feminization of poverty in the United States: Any surprises? In *Poor women in rich countries: The feminization of poverty over the life course,* ed. G. S. Goldberg (pp. 230–265). New York: Oxford University Press.

Goldberg, G. S., & Collins, S. D. (2001). *Washington's new poor law: Welfare "reform" and the roads not taken, 1935 to the present.* New York: Apex Press.

Golden, L., & Jorgensen, H. (2002). *Time after time: Mandatory overtime in the U.S. economy.* Washington, DC: Economic Policy Institute. Retrieved from http://www.epi.org/publication/briefingpapers_bp120/.

Gornick, J. C. (2010). Limiting working time and supporting flexibility for employees: Public policy lessons from Europe. In *Workplace flexibility: Realigning jobs for a 21st century workforce,* ed. K Christensen & B. Schneider (pp. 223–244). Ithaca, NY: ILR Press.

Handel, M. (2003). Skills mismatch in the labor market. *Annual Review of Sociology,* 29, 135–165.

Hartmann, H., Allen, K., & Owens, D. (1999). *Equal pay for working families.* IWPR Publication #344. Washington, DC: Institute for Women's Policy Research.

Hartmann, H., Rose, S. J., & Lovell, V. (2006). How much progress in closing the long-term earnings gap? In *The declining significance of gender?* ed. F. D. Blau, M. C. Brinton, & D. B. Grusky (pp. 125–155). New York: Russell Sage.

Harvey, P. (2011). *Back to work: A public jobs proposal for economic recovery.* New York: Demos. Retrieved from http://www.demos.org/publication/back-work-policy-brief-public-jobs-proposal-economic-recovery.

Harvey, P. (2012). Why is the right to work and income security so hard to secure? In *The state of economic and social rights,* ed. A. Minkler & K. Libal. Cambridge, Eng.: Cambridge University Press.

Harvey, P. (2013). The New Deal's direct job-creation strategy: Providing job assurance for American workers. In *When government helped: Learning from the successes and failures of the New Deal,* ed. S. D. Collins & G. S. Goldberg (pp. 146–179). New York: Oxford University Press.

Harwood, J. (July 19, 2010). Where did the jobs go? *The Politics and Government Blog of the Times.* Retrieved from http://thecaucus.blogs.nytimes.com/2010/07/19/mystery-for-white-house-where-did-the-jobs-go/.

Helburn, S. W., & Bergmann, B. (2003). *America's child care problem: The way out.* New York: Palgrave Macmillan.

Holzer, H. J. (1996). *What employers want: Job prospects for less-educated workers.* New York: Russell Sage.

Howell, D. R. (1998). The collapse of low-skill wages: Technological change or institutional failure? *Uncommon Sense* 13. New York: National Jobs for All Coalition. Retrieved from http://www.njfac.org/us13.htm.

Iverson, R. R., & Armstrong, A. L. (2006). *Jobs aren't enough: Towards a new economic mobility for low-income families.* Philadelphia: Temple University Press.

Jargowsky, P. A. (1997). *Poverty and place: Ghettos, barrios, and the American city.* New York: Russell Sage.

Jargowsky, P. A. (2003). *Stunning progress, hidden problems: The dramatic decline in concentrated poverty in the 1990s.* Washington, DC: Brookings Institution.

Kahn, A. J., & Kamerman, S. B. (2002). Social exclusion: A better way to think about childhood deprivation? In *Beyond childhood poverty: The social exclusion of children,* ed. A. J. Kahn & S. B. Kamerman (pp. 13–36). New York: Institute for Child and Family Policy at Columbia University.

Kellough, J. E. (2006). *Understanding affirmative action: Politics, discrimination, and the search for justice.* Washington, DC: Georgetown University Press.

Kessler-Harris, A. (1982). *Out to work: A history of wage-earning women in the United States.* New York: Oxford University Press.

King, M. L., Jr. (1967). *The trumpet of conscience.* New York: Harper and Row.

Kieselbach, T., Winefield, A. H., Boyd, C., & Anderson, S., eds. (2010). *Unemployment and health: International and interdisciplinary perspectives.* Sydney: Australian Academic Press.

Korpi, W. (1978). *The working class in welfare capitalism: Work, unions and politics in Sweden.* London: Routledge & Kegan Paul.

Kuttner, R. (2007). *The squandering of America: How the failure of our politics undermines our prosperity.* New York: Alfred A. Knopf.

LaJeunesse, R. M. (2009). *Work time regulations as a sustainable full employment strategy: The social effort bargain.* London: Routledge.

Lekachman, R. (1966). *The age of Keynes.* New York: Random House.

Leuchtenburg, W. E. (1963). *Franklin D. Roosevelt and the New Deal: 1932–1940.* New York: Harper Torchbooks.

Levitan, S. A. (1964). *Reducing worktime as a means to combat unemployment.* Kalamazoo, MI: W.E. Upjohn Institute for Employment Research.

Levitas, R. (February 1996). The concept of social exclusion and the new Durkheimian hegemony. *Critical Social Policy, 16,* pp. 5–20.

Luce, S. (2004). *Fighting for a living wage.* New York: ILR Press.

Luo, M., & Thee-Brenan, M. (2009). Poll reveals trauma of joblessness in U.S. *New York Times,* December 15, A1. Retrieved from http://www.nytimes.com/2009/12/15/us/15poll.html?_r=1.

Manis, J. G. (1974). Assessing the seriousness of social problems. *Social Problems, 22*(1), 1–12.

Merton, R. K. (1976). Introduction: The sociology of social problems. In *Contemporary social problems* (4th ed.), ed. R. K. Merton & R. A. Nisbet (pp. 5–43). New York: Harcourt Brace Jovanovich.

Messer-Davidow, E. (2002). *Disciplining feminism: From social activism to academic discourse.* Durham, NC: Duke University Press.

Mishel, L., Bernstein, J., & Allegretto, S. (2005). *The state of working America 2004/2005.* Ithaca, NY: ILR Press.

Mishel, L., Bernstein, J., & Allegretto, S. (2007). *The state of working America 2006/2007.* Ithaca, NY: ILR Press.

Mishel, L., Bernstein, J., & Shierholz, H. (2009). *The state of working America 2008/2009.* Ithaca, NY: ILR Press.

Mishel, L., Bivens, J., Gould, E., & Shierholz, H. (2012). *In working America,* 12th ed. Washington, DC: Economic Policy Institute. Retrieved from http://stateofworkingamerica.org/files/book/Chapter4-Wages.pdf.

Moy, J. W., & Lam, K. F. (2004). Selection criteria and the impact of personality on getting hired. *Personnel Review, 33*(5/6), 521–535.

National Association of Social Workers. (2008). *Code of ethics of the National Association of Social Workers.* Washington, DC: Author. Retrieved from http://www.naswdc.org/pubs/code/code.asp.

National Jobs for All Coalition. (n.d.). *Can you count the unemployed? An NJFAC quiz.* New York: National Jobs for All Coalition. Retrieved from http://www.njfac.org/quiz-unem.htm.

National Resources Planning Board. (1943). *National resources development report for 1943, Part I. Post-war plan and program.* Washington, DC: U.S. Government Printing Office.

National Women's Law Center. (2013). *Stronger jobs recovery reaching women.* Washington, DC: Author. Retrieved from http://www.nwlc.org/resource/stronger-jobs-recovery-reaching-women.

Osterman, P. (1991). Gains from growth? The impact of full employment on poverty in Boston. In C. Jencks & P. E. Peterson (Eds.), *The urban underclass,* ed. C. Jencks & P. E. Peterson (pp. 122–134). Washington, DC: Brookings Institution.

Paugam, S. (1996). Poverty and social disqualification: A comparative analysis of cumulative social disadvantage in Europe. *Journal of European Social Policy, 6,* 287–304.

Perez-Peña, R. (1998). Tax credit urged for poor in New York. *New York Times,* March 2, p. B24.

Perkins, F. (1946). *The Roosevelt I knew.* New York: Harper and Row, 1946/1964.

Pollin, R. (2007). A people's economy is possible. *New Labor Forum, 16*(3 and 4), 8–17.

Rampell, C. (July 2, 2010). Bleak outlook for long-term unemployed. *New York Times, Economix.* Retrieved from http://economix.blogs.nytimes.com/2010/07/02/bleak-outlook-for-long-term-unemployed/#more-71685.

Regenstein, M., Meyer, J. A., & Dickemper-Hicks, J. (1998). *Job prospects for welfare recipients: Employers speak out.* Washington, DC: Urban Institute. Retrieved from http://www.urban.org/publications/308016.html.

Roosevelt, F. D. (1935). Annual Message to Congress, January 4, 1935. Retrieved from http://www.presidency.ucsb.edu/ws/index.php?pid=14890.

Roosevelt, F. D. (1944a). Second Bill of Rights, January 11, 1944. Retrieved from http://en.wikipedia.org/wiki/Second_Bill_of_Rights.

Roosevelt, F. D. (1944b). State of the Union Address, January 11, 1944. Retrieved from http://teachingamericanhistory.org/library/index.asp?document=463.

Roosevelt, F. D. (1945). State of the Union Address, January 6, 1945. Retrieved from http://www.presidency.ucsb.edu/ws/index.php?pid=16595.

Rose, N. E. (2009). *Put to work: The WPA and public employment in the Great Depression,* (2nd ed.). New York: Monthly Review Press.

Saraceno. C. (2002). Social exclusion: Cultural roots and variations on a popular concept. In *Beyond childhood poverty: The social exclusion of children,* ed. A. J. Kahn & S. B. Kamerman (pp. 37–76). New York: Institute for Child and Family Policy at Columbia University.

Schmitt, J. (2007). *The good, the bad and the ugly: Job quality in the United States over the three most recent business cycles.* Center for Economic and Policy Research. Washington, DC. Retrieved from http://www.cepr.net/documents/publications/goodjobscycles.pdf.

Schnapper, W. B. (1972). *American labor: A pictorial history.* Washington, DC: Public Affairs Press.

Schor, J. B. (1991). *The overworked American: The unexpected decline of leisure.* New York: Basic Books.

Schor, J. B. (2005). Sustainable consumption and worktime reduction. *Journal of Industrial Ecology, 9*(1–2), 37–50.

Schor, J. B. (2010). The work-sharing boom: Exit ramp to a new economy? *Yes! Magazine.* August 9. Retrieved from http://www.yesmagazine.org/new-economy/the-work-sharing-boom-exit-ramp-to-a-new-economy.

Schulman, K., & Blank, H. (2006). *State child care assistance policies 2006: Gaps remain, with new challenges ahead.* National Women's Law Center. Washington DC. Retrieved from http://www.nwlc.org/sites/default/files/pdfs/statechildcareassistancepolicies2006.pdf.

Schwartz, B. F. (1984). *The Civil Works Administration, 1932-1934: The business of emergency employment in the New Deal.* Princeton, NJ: Princeton University Press.

Sen, A. (1999). *Development as freedom.* New York: Knopf.

Sok, E. (2010). Record unemployment among older workers does not keep them out of the job market. *U.S. Bureau of Labor Statistics, Summary* 10-04, March 2010. Retrieved from http://www.bls.gov/opub/ils/summary_10_04/older_workers.htm.

Spring, W., Harrison, B., & Vietorisz, T. (1972). Crisis of the underemployed: In much of the inner city 60% don't earn enough for a decent standard of living. *New York Times Magazine,* November, 44, 46ff.

Stone, C., Greenstein, R., & Coven, M. (2007). *Addressing longstanding gaps in unemployment insurance compensation.* Washington, DC: Center on Budget and Policy Priorities. Retrieved from http://www.cbpp.org/cms/?fa=view&id=517.

United Nations. (1948). *The Universal Declaration of Human Rights.* New York: Author. Retrieved from http://www.un.org/en/documents/udhr/index.shtml.

U.S. Bureau of Labor Statistics. (2000). *The employment situation: June 2000.* USDL 80-194. Washington, DC: Author. Retrieved from http://www.bls.gov/news.release/history/empsit_07072000.txt.

U.S. Bureau of Labor Statistics. (2011). Household data, annual averages. Washington, DC: Author. Retrieved from http://www.bls.gov/cps/cpsa2011.pdf.

U.S. Bureau of Labor Statistics. (2012a). *International comparisons of GDP per capita and per hour, 1960–2011.* Washington, DC: Author. Retrieved from http://www.bls.gov/fls/#GDP.

U.S. Bureau of Labor Statistics. (2012b). *The recession of 2007–2009.* Washington, DC: Author. Retrieved from http://www.bls.gov/spotlight/2012/recession/pdf/recession_bls_spotlight.pdf.

U.S. Bureau of Labor Statistics. (2013a). *Average hours, persons who usually work full time, all industries,* Series Id: LNS12505054. Washington, DC: Author. Retrieved from http://data.bls.gov/timeseries/LNS12505054.

U.S. Bureau of Labor Statistics. (2013b). *The employment situation–June 2013,* USDL-13-1284. Washington, DC: Author. Retrieved from http://www.bls .gov/news.release/pdf/empsit.pdf.

U.S. Bureau of Labor Statistics. (2013c). *Labor force statistics from the Current Population Survey, unemployment rate, monthly.* Washington, DC: Author. Retrieved from http://research.stlouisfed.org/fred2/data/UNRATE.txt.

U.S. Bureau of Labor Statistics. (2013d). *Labor force statistics from the Current Population Survey, unemployment rate, yearly.* Washington, DC: Author. Retrieved from http://data.bls.gov/timeseries/LNU04000000?years_option= all_years&periods_option=specific_periods&periods=Annual+Data.

U.S. Bureau of Labor Statistics. (n.d.a). Databases, tabulators, and calculators by subject, labor force statistics from the Current Population Survey, unemployment rate, Series Id: LNU04000000.

U.S. Bureau of Labor Statistics. (n.d.b). Employment status of persons by presence and age of own children, sex, race, Hispanic or Latino ethnicity, and marital status, annual average. Unpublished data from the Current Population Survey.

U.S. Census Bureau. (2001). *Current Population Survey: Income 2000.* Current Population Survey. Washington, DC: Author. Retrieved from http://www .census.gov/hhes/www/income/data/incpovhlth/2000/inctab11.html.

U.S. Census Bureau. (2011). *Historical Poverty Data–People.* Washington, DC: Author. Retrieved from http://www.census.gov/hhes/www/poverty/data/ historical/people.html.

Vangiezen, R., & Schwenk, A. E. (2001). Compensation from before World War I through the Great Depression. *Compensation and Working Conditions,* Fall, 17–23. Retrieved from http://www.bls.gov/opub/cwc/archive/fall2001art3.pdf.

Waldfogel, J. (1998). Understanding the "family gap" in pay for women with children. *Journal of Economic Perspectives, 12*(1), 137–156.

West, G. (1981). *The national welfare rights movement: The social protest of poor women.* New York: Praeger.

Wilson, H. (2009). President Eisenhower and the development of active labor market policy in the United States: A revisionist view. *Presidential Studies Quarterly, 39*(3), 519–554.

Wilson, W. J. (1996). *When work disappears: The world of the new urban poor.* New York: Knopf.

Wilson, W. J. (2009). *More than just poor: Being black and poor in the inner city.* New York: Norton.

4

People Experiencing Homelessness
Carolyn J. Hanesworth

For the average middle-class American, 2008 was a difficult year. The looming economic downturn placed an additional burden on the working class. Following the initial turmoil, it became evident that the crisis would have a devastating financial impact. The housing crisis became a common topic in the news, as economists warned that many homeowners could go into foreclosure. For over a century, however, housing issues already existed in the United States, which typically affected large groups of individuals and families in lower income levels, leaving many finding themselves facing homelessness. This group, often stigmatized by society as weak or lazy, is thought to have failed in some way, or is to blame for their plight—irrespective of the current economic environment. What is becoming clear is that a home can be lost in spite of the owner or tenant's status as a hard-working, tax-paying person. While many hard-working low-income people were already intimately familiar with this reality, the new threat of home loss has also reached the middle class, most notably, families with young children.

This chapter seeks to enlighten readers about the new face of homelessness, and to recognize that reducing homelessness is possible. This chapter presents homelessness as it exists and in the context of history. The information shared is both retrospective and current. Additionally, the chapter addresses the demographics of homelessness, giving readers an opportunity to grasp the breadth and scope of this crisis. It also includes examples of homelessness and explores the social injustice associated with this societal problem. Readers will additionally learn about micro, mezzo, and macro interventions that may be used to address housing challenges.

Demographics and Characteristics

The word *homeless* is a deeply stigmatized label in our society. For many, this evokes a picture of a person who is assumed to be poor, dirty, without family, friends, or any sort of meaningful purpose in life. However, a person from any social or economic group can experience a loss of housing. Consider, for example, a runaway from an upper-income home, a newly arrived but highly educated immigrant, or a middle-class woman escaping domestic violence—all are likely to be without resources for housing, but are not identified with the more stereotypical picture of the "homeless."

Understanding the Label of Homelessness

So, "who" are the homeless? According to the U.S Department of Housing and Urban Development (HUD) (2010c), homelessness is defined as (1) an individual who lacks a fixed, regular, and adequate nighttime residence; and (2) an individual who has a primary nighttime residence that is (a) a supervised publicly or privately operated shelter designed to provide temporary living accommodations, (b) a facility that provides a temporary residence for individuals needing to be institutionalized; or (c) a public or private place not designed for, or ordinarily used as, a regular sleeping accommodation for human beings. This definition covers those in shelters and those living on the street, but leaves out individuals and families living in tight quarters with family or friends. This situation is commonly referred to as "doubled up" or "precariously housed." The term *doubled-up* refers to friends or family members sharing living accommodations because of inadequate access to affordable housing. Examples include individuals who need a place to stay because of unemployment, low income, illness, or disability. Technically, individuals who are "doubled-up" are considered homeless (Campbell, Forrest, Moore, & Taylor, 2008). When this occurs, another family, sometimes relatives, often host individuals in their residence. Unfortunately, their situations are frequently unstable, as they are usually in rental properties, which limit the number of people living in a residence. The families fortunate enough to find housing themselves often end up becoming hosts for another family, thus placing themselves at risk of homelessness again (Campbell et al., 2008; Glasser & Bridgman, 1999). The U.S. Department of Education uses a different definition of homelessness, which includes children living in "doubled up" homes, thus affording them equal access to educational resources available to children living in stable housing. Under the requirements of the federal law called the McKinney-Vento Act, public schools must ensure that "homeless children and youth have equal access to the same free public education, including a public preschool education, as is provided to other children and youth"

(HUD, 2007). There is some widespread belief among homeless advocates that HUD's resistance to adopt the expanded definition (which includes doubled-ups) is partially due to the fear that an increase in reported numbers will overwhelm HUD homeless assistance programs, rendering them unable to meet the current need. For instance, the 2007 report from the Homeless Research Institute of the National Alliance to End Homelessness estimates that the current homeless numbers would nearly triple if doubled ups were included in the data.

Difficulties in Counting

The most recent attempts to collect nationwide data come from HUD's *2009 Annual Homeless Assessment Report to Congress* (HUD, 2010c), and includes information gathered from two sources: the first from service providers through a tool called Homeless Management Information Systems (HMIS), and the second from point in time (also known as point prevalence) counts, which involves a count of the homeless on one night. HMIS is an electronic database intended to capture unduplicated numbers of people utilizing shelters and transitional housing programs. A related term, *unduplicated,* describes data in which people counted are only counted once, even though they may have used services more than once over a period of time. These self-reported data are collected directly from individuals who are homeless, usually during their admission or intake when they present for shelter.

The second source of data, point prevalence, involves individual service providers, volunteers, and the homeless themselves, who scour the streets, campsites, makeshift tent cities, and other hidden spots, attempting to take a count on one night each January of the unsheltered homeless, meaning they are living in a place not fit for human habitation. While point prevalence is the most commonly used source of data, this method impedes the ability of researchers and advocates to capture an accurate accounting of the number of people who are homeless, as people frequently move in and out of homelessness. In addition, these individuals may not be visible at the time the count is taken, resulting in skewed numbers. Many studies have analyzed the problems inherent with these methods (Baumohl, 1996; Burt, 1995; Hopper, 2003).

An accurate count is important to federal and local policymakers who provide funding intended to address this social problem, yet there is consensus among homeless advocates that a reliable method, which truly measures and describes the population has not yet been employed (Gould & Williams, 2010). The authors of the most recent HUD report repeatedly emphasize interpretation of data only be viewed as approximations. Baumohl (1996) notes that different data sets are useful to various groups according to their particular needs: for instance, the service provider who needs to know the number of beds in demand on any given night or the soup kitchen that is preparing meals for the "street homeless." Similarly, the federal government provides funding through HUD for emergency and supportive housing, and therefore is interested in how many people use these services. Their counts depend heavily on reports of shelter usage, but a flaw in this approach emerges with the reality that not everyone who is homeless utilizes the shelters. Some choose not to, others are turned away (due to overcrowding), or there may not be one available, as is the case in many rural areas. HUD also counts individuals living in "places not meant for human beings," or street homeless, yet even these data would not include the chronically homeless, a group of individuals who often find themselves moving, over long periods of time from the street to emergency rooms, state psychiatric hospitals, and jail (Hopper, 2003).

Current Picture Nationwide

Gould and Williams (2010) describe three paths in which people travel into homelessness: (1) the single adult who lives a lifetime of chronic, unstable housing (approximately 20 percent), (2) those who experience "episodic" homelessness but eventually either find housing or join the chronic homeless (approximately 35 percent), and (3) the remaining approximately 45 percent who have a single event of homelessness but eventually secure permanent housing. In January 2009, on one night across the nation, (point prevalence) 643,067 people were found to be homeless—including both sheltered and unsheltered. Approximately 40 percent were unsheltered, in "places not meant for human habitation," such as a park, or under a bridge, or a car. The remaining approximate 60 percent were sheltered. Among sheltered individuals, the report found that 75 percent of them are over the age of 30; 63 percent are male, 62 percent are members of minority groups, and 40 percent have a disability. African Americans are largely overrepresented, making up 39 percent of the sheltered population. In 2009, 170,000 families were sheltered, compared to 130,000 in 2008, representing a 30 percent increase (HUD, 2010a). Possible reasons for this increase are examined later in this chapter. The following discussion describes the various subgroups, which may challenge readers' preconceived notions of what constitutes a homeless individual. (See table 4.1.)

Table 4.1. (HUD 2009 Report, p. 23). Demographic Characteristics of Sheltered Homeless Persons in 2009 Compared to the 2008 U.S. and Poverty Populations

Characteristic	% of All Sheltered Homeless Persons, 2009	% of the 2008 U.S. Poverty Population	% of the 2008 U.S. Population
Gender of Adults			
Male	63.7%	40.5%	48.7%
Female	36.3%	59.5%	51.3%
Ethnicity			
Non-Hispanic/ Non-Latino	80.5%	75.1%	84.6%
Hispanic/Latino	19.5%	24.9%	15.4%
Race			
White, Non-Hispanic	38.1%	46.2%	65.4%
White Hispanic	11.6%	15.0%	9.6%
Black or African American	38.7%	22.1%	12.4%
Other Single Race	4.7%	13.8%	10.3%
Multiple Races	7.0%	2.9%	2.3%
Age (α)			
Under age 18	22.2%	33.9%	24.3%
18 to 30	22.3%	23.8%	18.2%
31 to 50	38.3%	21.9%	28.2%
51 to 61	14.4%	9.2%	13.9%
62 and older	2.8%	11.3%	15.4%
Household Size (β)			
1 person	64.1%	16.6%	13.0%
2 people	10.0%	18.4%	25.6%
3 people	10.2%	17.1%	18.9%
4 people	7.9%	18.5%	20.9%
5 or more people	7.9%	29.4%	21.6%
Special Populations			
Veteran (adults only) (Ç)	11.1%	5.2%	9.7%
Disabled (adults only) (Ç)	37.8%	26.2%	15.5%

(α) Age is calculated based on a person's first time in shelter during the one-year reporting period.
(β) If a person is part of more than one household or the household size changed during the reporting period, the household size reflects the size of the first household in which the person presented during the one-year reporting period. For all population types, past reports counted each person in a multi-adult or multi-child household as an individual household composed of one person. In this report, persons in these households are counted as one household composed of multiple people. For example, a household composed of two adults with no children is counted as one household with a household size equal to two, rather than two households with each household size equal to 1.
(Ç) Veteran and disability status are recorded only for adults in HMIS. The percentage calculations shown indicate the percent of homeless adults with this characteristic. Some records were missing information on disability status (10.5 percent) and veteran status (5.3 percent) in 2009. The percentage calculations are for those whose disability and veteran status was known.
Sources: Homeless Management Information System data, 2009; 2008 American Community Survey

Characteristics: Subpopulations

HUD gathers data about specific subpopulations of the sheltered homeless, including the chronically homeless, people with severe mental illness and/or addictions, veterans, unaccompanied youth, and people living with HIV and AIDS. Figure 4.1 illustrates the various populations facing homelessness. A person could be in two or more categories, such as a veteran who is also a substance abuser or a youth with HIV. The data do not include unsheltered individuals.

The following section examines three subpopulation groups of interest: unaccompanied youth, families with children, and veterans.

Unaccompanied Youth

Despite the efforts made by HUD to account for all of the homeless, some groups are not accurately represented in their report. According to HUD (2010c), 1.5 percent of the 643,067 sheltered homeless counted were unaccompanied minors. This group consists of youth under the age of eighteen who have left home as runaways or been forced to leave by their caregiver. HUD estimates there are approximately 6,000 homeless youth nationwide, which is considerably lower than what most researchers of homeless youth believe to be accurate.

Figure 4.1. (HUD 2009, p. 17): Trends in Sheltered Homeless Populations 2006–2008

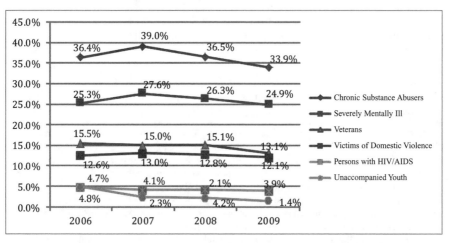

Source: 2006 through 2008 Continuum of Care Application: Exhibit 1, CoC Point-in-Time Homeless Population and Subpopulations Charts as cited in U.S. Department of Housing and Urban Development Office of Community Planning and Development (2009). *The 2008 Annual Homeless Assessment Report,* retrieved from http://www.huduser.org/portal/publications/4thHomelessAssessmentReport.pdf

In her 2007 testimony to the U.S. Congress, noted scholar Martha Burt estimated the number of homeless youth between the ages of 12 and 17 to be between 1.6 and 1.7 million a year, accounting for 7–8 percent of all U.S. youth (Hammer, Finkelhor, & Sedlak, 2002, as cited in Burt, 2007; Ringwalt, Greene, Robertson, & McPheeters, 1998). The vast majority of these youth are likely to be unsheltered, living on the street or with family or friends. Numbers are dependent on definitions, and "homeless youth" has an expanded meaning to include runaways or "throw aways," a term that refers to youth who have been forced out of their homes, but may be living with others. It is easy to understand why unaccompanied youth living on the street would be difficult to count, as their detection by authorities would likely result in foster care placement, or their return to home.

Of sheltered youth, males and female numbers tend to be equal, and their race/ethnicity is reflective of the general population in the community. Most notable in the characteristics of this subpopulation is the prevalence of gay, lesbian, bisexual, and transgender (GLBT) youth, who may represent 20 percent of the homeless youth population (Whitbeck, Chen, Hoyt, Tyler, & Johnson, 2004). Burt (2007) notes, "sexual minority status is a powerful risk factor for youth homelessness, as disclosure to a parent or parent's discovery of that status may lead to being thrown out or running away" (p. 3).

Homeless youth are also three times as likely as other youth to be pregnant (Burt, 2007), abuse substances, and report double the amount of overall drug use than housed youth (Lawrenson, 1997; Mallett, Rosenthal, & Keys, 2004, as cited in Thompson, Bender, Windsor, Cook, & Williams, 2010). A history of foster care and involvement with child welfare may also be a significant contributing factor to subsequent loss of housing (Park, Metraux, Brodbar, & Culhane, 2004).

Families with Children

According to HUD (2010a), 34 percent of the people who utilized shelters in 2009 were in families, excluding those who were doubled up in other households. This is a rise of 30 percent from the previous year. Estimates from advocacy groups such as the National Alliance to End Homelessness are substantially higher at 41 percent, and the National Coalition for the Homeless reports that families with children are the fastest growing segment of the homeless population. The U.S. Conference of Mayors (2008) reported that all twenty-seven participating cities expect a substantial increase in the numbers of homeless families, and this was prior to the "Great Recession" (2007–2009). A look at the numbers in New York City as of

March 2010 finds that of the record 38,187 number of those in shelters, close to 30,000, or 79 percent, are individuals in families. This is more than double what was reported on the national level two years prior. Children in those families make up 40 percent of the total homeless population in New York City. Nationwide, the children in homeless families are quite young, with over 50 percent being under the age of six. This population will be discussed in more significant detail in chapter 5.

Veterans

Since the American Civil War and the era of tramping and hobos, men who have fought on behalf of this country have encountered enormous obstacles in their attempts to reenter civilian life. Returning soldiers struggle with high rates of traumatic brain injury, post-traumatic stress disorder, substance abuse, and mental illness, resulting in a decreased ability to cope with the demands of work and family. Oftentimes, they are unable to return to a job because of a change in their physical ability, thus leaving them vulnerable to economic stress, a sense of incompetence (particularly painful for a trained soldier), and subsequent depression (Franklin, 2009).

According to the National Coalition for the Homeless (2009c), America's homeless veterans have served in World War II, Korean War, Vietnam War, Grenada, Panama, Lebanon, Afghanistan, Iraq, and the military's anti-drug cultivation efforts in South America. Of the approximately 200,000 veterans who are currently homeless, another 600,000 are experiencing rental burdens, which place them at risk for housing loss. Notably too, 23 percent of the homeless population are veterans, 47 percent of these having served in the Vietnam War, with 67 percent of them serving three or more years in combat and 89 percent receiving an honorable discharge. It is thus far unknown what the true impact of the wars in Afghanistan and Iraq will have on the numbers of veterans entering homelessness. In comparison to previous wars, however, soldiers found themselves deployed to Iraq and Afghanistan for longer periods with fewer breaks between deployments and considerably more exposure to combat (Jaycox & Tanielian 2008 as cited in Franklin, 2009). The mental and physical difficulties faced by modern-day veterans suggest their presence among the ranks of the homeless may continue, if not increase substantially due to the stresses faced by this population. Homelessness among veterans and their families will be discussed in more detail in chapter 10.

Historical Perspectives
Colonial Times

Americans have experienced homelessness since colonial times. It is likely that war was the cause for people being displaced from their farms and homes during this period. Kusmer (2003) describes a time during the mid-eighteenth century in which repeated battles during the French and Indian War uprooted whole families, who were left to wander and were treated as outcasts for their "idleness"—a sin in the eyes of a predominately Puritan society that placed a high value on hard work and independence. Yet it was also the nature of early American religious culture to care for the poor, and the homeless were taken in by extended family or the church, and sometimes supported by public funds. Hopper (2003, p. 27) notes "religious duty and outpost solidarity made it unthinkable that one's neighbors should go begging." The tradition of the times indicated that those in need were cared for, and it was common for most homes to include boarding residents—some of whom were subsidized by the government.

The Crime of Vagrancy: Historical Origins and the Impact of Slavery

The charity that characterized the colonial era eventually gave way to fear and suspicion of those individuals without homes and "purpose." Tolerance began to wane as numbers increased, and the first formal institutions to house the poor were erected. In 1734, New York City built its first such public building to house the poor on the grounds of present-day City Hall (Hopper, 2003). Reflecting the general perception of those in need, it was called the "House of Corrections, Workhouse and Poorhouse," which signaled the beginning of a long history of equating the status of "poor" with that of a "criminal." An idle person was suspect since there was ample opportunity for labor, if one was willing and able.

During the late seventeenth century in Virginia, there was much concern about what to do about runaway slaves and former indentured servants, many of whom were angry for not receiving land or monies promised to them at the beginning of their tenure. English vagrancy laws were enacted in the wake of rising fears that vengeance-induced crime would threaten the stability of the colony. The language of English laws was extremely broad: "any person of bad character who prowls about, apparently for an unlawful purpose, is likely to be treated as a rogue and a vagabond" (Hall, 1902, p. 400). The term *vagrant* emerged to identify the wandering poor—and harsh laws were created to control their behaviors and movements—especially those of African Americans (Kusmer, 2003). In general, a vagrant was a person without income who refused to work. Kusmer (2003) makes a connection between the emergence of vagrancy laws and the increase in "masterless" slaves during this period. These laws were established after Bacon's Rebellion of 1676, an uprising that united various angry lower-class whites, runaway slaves, and property owners in a hostile attempt to oust the leadership in Jamestown, Virginia (Kusmer 2003). Although these various factions had differing reasons to be angry with the colony leadership, their collective numbers posed a real threat, which presumably led the government to enact legislation to contain and repress individuals that might oppose the government. These fears naturally combined with societal views, which condemned those thought to be "lazy," and justified their actions in criminalizing all those who were found to be idle, disconnected, without work or home. In the South, these laws were rarely enforced if the offender was white, yet still left room to prosecute the white vagrant who might aid or join forces with runaway slaves of African descent. Those of African descent were always severely punished.

Additional factors contributed to the perception of the wandering poor, including slavery and the post-Civil War era. In the post-Civil War era, vagrancy laws took aim at former slaves through the "black codes." These codes, written in Southern states, with the intention of controlling the movement and behavior of freed slaves, included detailed rules about work relationships, housing, recreation, and above all, free time. Oberholtzer (1917, p. 129) described South Carolina's codes:

> On farms the hours of labor would be from sunrise to sunset daily, except on Sunday. The negroes were to get out of bed at dawn. Absentees on Sunday must return to the plantation by sunset. House servants were to be at call at all hours of the day and night on all days of the week.

Furthermore, the vagrancy laws were enforced to "keep the negroes from roaming the roads and living the lives of beggars and thieves" (Oberholtzer, 1917, p. 129).

These black codes were established to provide "protective measures against [the black's] ignorance and his childishness" and were duplicated in states such as Georgia, who defined vagrants as those "persons strolling about in idleness who are able to work and who have no property to support them," and Alabama where a vagrant was defined as "a laborer or servant who loiters away his time or refuses to comply with any contract for a term of service without just cause" (Olberholtzer, 1917, p. 129).

Vagrancy law in the United States has included such vague and broad language as "beggars," "players at dice," "gypsies," and "minstrels" but in general refers to someone who is able to work, but prefers instead to live idly, begging for aid from others (Novak, 1996). Historically, punishment for vagrancy could be harsh and people found wandering into town with no work to do, particularly single women and people of color, were subject to extreme physical punishment. Today's vagrancy laws are rarely enforced and much subdued. This is due to the realization that the law is in conflict with the due process clause of the Fourteenth Amendment, which protects individuals from being arrested simply because they are considered "suspicious." Currently, there are local laws in place that prohibit panhandling, which is the act of stopping people on the street to ask for food or money. These laws are controversial, and rarely enforced. A later section of this chapter will explore the ways in which homelessness has continued to attract legal persecution in the form of modern day "sit-lie" ordinances, which are historical descendants of the vagrancy law.

Nineteenth Century: The Impact of Industrialization and the Civil War

The nineteenth century proved to be a time of great transition with regard to both the movements of the poor and the government's response to their needs. This was the era of industrialization, a time when America was transitioning from an agricultural society to an economy based on manufacturing. Many young Americans left their farms and small towns in search of excitement and work opportunity in the country's expanding urban centers. This mobilization also reduced the proximity of kin, which for those in transition had previously served as a stopgap measure during times of economic trouble. The nineteenth century also included a massive influx of immigrants looking to escape hardship in their home countries, bringing more than 5 million people to the United States between 1820 and 1860 (Baum & Burnes, 1993). With expansion of infrastructure came the railroads, and with the ability for wandering poor to move quickly from one town to the next, "tramps" emerged.

Americans have always been fascinated by tramps. They are romanticized in books and movies, such as Jack Kerouac's *On the Road*, which portrays the main character's father as a tramp who is a rogue adventurer and icon of the American West. Tramps are nostalgically thought of in literature and film as fiercely independent, rebellious, and free. In reality, their lives were fraught with danger and struggle. Kusmer (2003) concluded that much of the postwar "tramping" was in fact parallel in behavior to the traveling soldier of the Civil War. Soldiers were transported via box and cattle cars, "herded together much like the animals for which the conveyances has been designed" (Kusmer, 2003, p. 36). This, along with the soldiers' need to forage and pilfer for food along their journey, are considered the antecedents for the decades-long tradition of "riding the rails" by the homeless poor in the latter half of the nineteenth century.

Many former soldiers turned to "tramping" after the war, likely due to the struggling economy of the 1870s and their postwar trauma, for which there was neither treatment nor sympathy from civilian society. Undeniably, they were drawn, like many others, to "the promise of cheap land, work on the railroads, and jobs as cowboys in the cattle industry" (Baum & Burnes, 1993, p. 105). The numbers of those without permanent dwellings during this period swelled considerably due to the depression and subsequent high unemployment of 1873, and larger cities began to shift their approach to housing the poor. In 1886, the Department of Charities and Corrections was established in New York City, officially blending those in need with those who broke the law. Interestingly, the notion that poor men did not want to work was dispelled by efforts to recruit soldiers for World War I. This effort virtually emptied out public shelters as men readily volunteered both at home and abroad. This somewhat disproved their classification as "vagrants" (Hopper, 2003). As the 1920s approached, the era of tramping declined. Just as the rise of tramping followed the rise of industrialization, its decline aligned with a growing corporate era and the emergence of a welfare state for the poor (Monkkonen, 1984).

Twentieth Century: The Great Depression and the Beginnings of Federal Aid

The Great Depression that began in 1929 brought a massive increase in the numbers of people that were homeless, including women and children who up until this time had relied mostly on kinship networks for emergency housing. According to figures kept by the National Committee on Care of the Transient and Homeless, there were 1.2 million persons without permanent housing in 1933 (Cromley, 2010). Across the nation, various versions of makeshift housing emerged, such as the "Hooverville, a name chosen in part to depict the blame Americans placed on Herbert Hoover for his role in the Great Depression" (Kusmer, 2003). Other versions included the infamous Bowery of New York City, and the Tenderloin district of San Francisco known as "skid row," a term originally used to describe the living environments of unemployed men who took occasional work "skidding logs" down tracks for the sawmills of the Northeast. These shantytowns and patched-together dwellings housed a core group of unskilled workers who were replaced by machines, and lived together with others who were aged, addicted, or otherwise disaffiliated with productive, working-class America (Baumohl, 1996). In response to this disturbing visual landscape, the federal government became involved in addressing the problem of the houseless poor after World War II, beginning with President Harry Truman's Fair Deal legislation, described in a later section of this chapter.

World War II to the Present

In their book *A Nation in Denial: The Truth about Homelessness*, Baum and Burnes (1993) describe the years immediately following World War II as a time when prosperity reigned, the economy expanded, and unemployment was virtually eradicated. Despite this boom and America's subsequent optimism, "the growing prosperity, however, stood in stark contrast to the lingering and persistent poverty in America, and this contrast forces Americans to examine the disparity between the rich and the poor" (Baum & Burnes, 1993, p. 105). Clearly, the postwar economic boom was not felt by all, a theme that was to emerge again in the coming years.

Kim Hopper (2003), for example, describes the homeless as the "spoilers" of the decadent and economically prosperous 1980s. The numbers of homeless increased tremendously during this time, their economic circumstances further devastated by an influx of crack cocaine and the HIV/AIDS pandemic. Individuals with HIV, its related illnesses, or full blown AIDS in the 1980s faced extraordinary stigma, discrimination, and rejection by a society that did not fully understand its transmission and held deep prejudices against the gay population, who were amongst the first to contract the disease. Invariably, a person with HIV became ill, their illness became known, and they probably faced job loss and social isolation. This left these populations at greater risk of homelessness.

By the mid-1980s the numbers of individuals that were homeless returned to those seen during the Great Depression (Hopper, 2003). In 1986 the federal government passed landmark legislation, the Stewart B. McKinney Homeless Assistance Act (PL100-77). President Clinton added Vento to the name in 2000, after the death of one of its key supporters, Representative Bruce Vento (HUD, 2007). Known as the McKinney-Vento Act, this legislation requires states to provide shelter and programs to the homeless, with a particular emphasis on children, elderly, veterans, and Native Americans. The act acknowledges that "there is no single, simple solution to the reasons for homelessness, and the different needs of the homeless individuals." Furthermore, the act states that the "federal government has a clear responsibility" and needs "to fulfill a more effective and responsible role to meet the basic needs and to engender respect for the human dignity of the homeless" (McKinney-Vento Homeless Assistance Act, 1987).

Beginning in 1949, and continuing to the present, several government programs were developed in an attempt to address the growing numbers of homeless. These programs are discussed in detail in the "Government Policies and Programs" section in this chapter.

Key Issues

Over the past several years, over 300 communities have created ten-year plans to "end homelessness." These plans come at the urging of the U.S. Interagency Council on Homelessness, which emphasizes the importance of identifying the root causes of homelessness and developing services and programs to address this social problem. This attempt, although seemingly audacious in scope, brings awareness to the structural, political, and economic issues at the heart of homelessness. As communities grapple with these plans, more understanding of the environmental influences causing homelessness is emerging.

The Causes Below the Surface

As for the personal difficulties that some homeless individuals face, they do not account for the steadily increasing numbers of homeless over the past several decades. If they did, then the mental health, substance abuse treatment, and job readiness services created in the 1990s should have helped reduce the numbers of individuals seeking shelter (Burt, 2001). Culhane and Metraux (2008) argue that these services, largely created as a result of HUD's Continuum of Care policy, have created the institutionalization of shelters, with interventions focused on a lack of shelters, rather than a more prevention-oriented perspective. To truly understand root causes, we must address the question, what leads to imminent housing loss? Shinn, Baumohl, and Hopper (2001) suggest that "homeless prevention be reoriented from efforts to work with identified people 'at risk' to projects aimed at increasing the supply of affordable housing and sustainable sources of livelihood" (p. 96).

Access to affordable housing and, as discussed in chapter 3, the opportunity to earn a living wage are widely identified environmental causes of homelessness. For instance, one predictor of homelessness is a person living in what is called extreme poverty, or who has an income that falls at less than half the poverty level (Burt, 2001). It follows that if there was more affordable housing, coupled with higher-wage jobs, a person may be able to avoid a bout of homelessness. The homeless services industry has developed enormous capacity in serving the presently homeless, yet until now, not much has been done to address the cause or focus on prevention. Many researchers feel that if "ending homelessness" is ever to be realized, a shift in paradigm toward prevention must be realized on a political and policy level (Burt, 2001; Shinn, Baumohl, & Hopper, 2001).

Affordable Housing

According to the Department of Housing and Urban Development (HUD), close to 13 million low-income people spent more than half of their monthly income on rent and/or lived in substandard housing in 2007. Substandard housing refers to housing that does not meet local health or building codes. In a report to Congress, these were deemed "worst case housing needs" and their numbers were found to have significantly increased by nearly 1 million between 2001 and 2007 (Sullivan, 2010). HUD tracks these cases because they are the households most likely to eventually lose their housing and present for emergency shelter. These 13 million people reside in 5.91 million households, and of these, 2.19 million are families with children, and 1.21 million have an elderly member. Between 2007 and 2009, there was a 20 percent increase to 7.1 million people, which cut across all regions and demographics in the country (Steffen et al., 2009). Simultaneously, a shortage of affordable housing units exists as a result of a lack of available rental properties, causing some to be pushed out of the housing market. While the urban areas continue to have higher rental costs, the rural and suburban areas are reported to have the highest number of "burdened renters," or those spending more than half their income on rent. This is due to the lessened availability of government assistance in rural areas. The following examples illustrate the affordable housing crisis from two different parts of the country.

For every family or individual that struggles to maintain housing, there are a different set of circumstances that lead to homelessness. Death or sudden illness, loss of a job, substance abuse relapse, divorce, fires, or other natural disasters can all create financial burdens, which contribute to homelessness. From an economic point of view, these households lack the resources to manage financially.

Affordable housing is also closely connected to homelessness. New York City, for instance, offers an extreme example of housing crisis, as Manhattan is deemed among the most expensive urban areas to live in the United States. The Center for an Urban Future reports "in the third quarter of 2008, only 10.6 % of all housing in New York City was affordable to people earning the median income for the area" (Bowles, Kotkin, & Giles, 2009, p. 7). While New York City has always been known as a difficult place to live for the poor, it is now seeing large numbers of middle-class residents leave for more affordable locales. Simultaneously, the wages of middle-class workers in New York have flattened, showing no substantial increase in recent years, and the numbers of working poor have jumped from 29 percent living below the poverty line in 1990 to 46 percent in 2005. According to the center's report, the average monthly rent in New York City during the fourth quarter of 2008 was $2,801.00. If one were to stay within the standard HUD guideline of spending no more than 30 percent of one's income on rent, this would only be affordable for a person or family that earns a net income of $100,836 per year. It is easy to conclude that millions of New York City's residents fall within the "worst case housing needs" subset defined by HUD. This new reality of the professional middle class who are college educated and struggling to maintain housing does not fall within society's stereotypical image of a poor, ill homeless person. Although a housed but struggling person is not yet considered "homeless," these "worst cases" are at considerable risk, and certainly could contribute steadily to the next wave of first-time shelter seekers.

On the other side of the country, in Tooele County, Utah, there is a different problem; the demand for affordable housing is exceeding the supply. Tooele County is a rural/suburban area in the northwest section of Utah with a population of approximately 58,200 people. The population is predominately white (90 percent), with a median income of $56,053 (U.S. Census Bureau, 2011). In 2010, there was a shortage of 1,200 housing units for those making 50 percent or less of the area median income. For families in a very low-income bracket making $19,680 or less, there was a shortage of 1,500 units (Wood, 2011). The problem, unlike New York City, is not the cost of housing as the median monthly rental is $685. Rather, there is a shortage of units. More people across the country are now falling into the category of "worst case housing needs," and there are only so many low-cost units available. Whether it is due to stagnant wages, high rental cost, or a lack of units, many Americans are at risk of losing their homes.

The New Homeless: The Impact of Foreclosures

Amidst the more typical stories of chronically poor individuals and families cycling in and out of homelessness is a new wave of first-time shelter seekers, homeowners experiencing mortgage foreclosure. Foreclosure is an action taken by a lender to take possession of a property after an owner fails to repay their loan. At the time of press, firm data had not yet been published on the numbers of those in foreclosure having to resort to shelters, although advocacy groups and city officials have begun to sound an alarm. In December 2008, the U.S. Conference of Mayors indicated that 12 of the 25 cities attending reported an increase in homelessness due to foreclosure, with 6 other cities lacking enough data to be certain. The National Coalition for the Homeless (2009a) reported that low and extremely low-income households were going to bear the greatest impact of mortgage foreclosure, and noted a 32 percent jump in foreclosures between April 2008 and April 2009.

Prior to the housing crisis, Howard Jacob Karger (2008), a recognized author and educator, wrote about the impending disaster facing low-income families and individuals who were fortunate to have finally achieved home ownership through low-cost financing, yet were significantly at risk of foreclosure due to the riskiness of subprime lending. The term *subprime lending* refers to the manner in which banks loan money to individuals who do not have the income or capital to repay their loans. The working poor were targets for "predatory" lenders who ultimately repackaged these loans with high interest rates and sold them to other banks, thereby acquiring lucrative front-end fees without being burdened by the long-term risk of lending to low-income buyers. Stagnant wages, job losses, and the rising price of fuel and food in the summer of 2008 resulted in many homeowners having less to spend on housing. Mortgage payments were missed and the bottom fell out of the housing market, meaning the value of the homes were no longer worth the price paid for them. As courts across the country have a backlog of foreclosure cases, some families have been able to stay in their homes for over a year since their last mortgage payment, thus the full impact of the foreclosure displacement has not been realized (Streitfeld, 2010).

Government Policies and Programs

The federal government has made many attempts to address the issue of homelessness over the past fifty years. As part of the sweeping domestic policy outlined in Harry Truman's Fair Deal legislation, the Housing Act of 1949 committed federal resources to the production of public housing and urban renewal. This led to large federal housing "projects" characterized by large buildings, which became permanent fixtures on the landscapes of urban America. Although hailed at the time as a step forward in addressing the housing needs of the poor, the "urban renewal" effort was explicitly meant to reduce or "clear" the slums, hence this was the beginning of federal housing policy aimed at removing or hiding the effects of poverty without efforts to understand or address the root causes. The War on Poverty programs enacted during the presidency of Lyndon B. Johnson were a set of policies created as an attempt to resolve and prevent poverty. Cromley (2010) indicates that leaders involved in Johnson's War on Poverty were active in structural reform, which attempted to improve living conditions and access to prosperity for traditionally disenfranchised populations. The following discussion highlights various programs designed to respond to or prevent homelessness.

The Community Mental Health Centers Act

Signed in October 1963, this act, the first of the War on Poverty programs, led to the release of thousands of individuals with mental illnesses from inpatient psychiatric facilities. This was known as the "deinstitutionalization" of the mentally ill, and has since been referred to as one of the leading causes of increased homelessness during the 1960s and 1970s. This effort failed to produce promised community-based mental health care, and over time contributed to the increase in the homeless population. Barak (1992) is careful to point out that the impact of deinstitutionalization peaked in the 1970s, and although undeniably a notable cause of homelessness then, it should not overshadow the structural economic factors that contribute to housing loss today.

Housing Choice Voucher Program

The Housing Choice Voucher Program is part of the Housing and Community Development Act of 1974, otherwise known as Section 8 Housing. In response to the government recognizing that the housing crisis was the result of a lack of affordable housing for low-income earners rather than a surge of substandard housing, Section 8 vouchers became available to subsidize a portion of the rent for qualified tenants. In the years since this program was enacted, Section 8 allocations increase or decrease, depending on the political climate in Washington and federal budget limitations.

McKinney-Vento Act

Many larger cities have used McKinney-Vento funding to maintain "emergency shelters," which provide temporary housing until housing benefits or employment could be obtained. The use of emergency shelters continues with the additional shift toward supportive or transitional housing models, designed to provide more time and support during the transition from homelessness to independent living.

Veterans Affairs Supportive Housing (HUD-VASH)

In response to the needs of veterans, the federal government established the HUD-VASH program, which stands for Veterans Affairs Supportive Housing. In 2008, $75 million was set aside for this program, which combines supportive housing, case management, and clinical services through the Veterans Administration. In 2009, another $1.5 billion was set aside under the American Recovery and Reinvestment Act to aid in preventing homelessness by rapidly rehousing individuals and families following housing loss (another program, which is explained immediately below). As these funds relate to veterans, however, it is important for readers to note that portions of these funds are also being used to help eligible HUD-VASH participants secure housing by providing security or utility deposits (HUD, 2010b).

Homeless Prevention and Rapid Re-Housing Program (HPRP)

The Homeless Prevention and Rapid Re-Housing Program (HPRP) is a federally sponsored program made possible through the American Recovery and Reinvestment Act of 2009. This program is intended to provide funding to newly displaced families in order that they re-secure housing immediately, thereby reducing long-term shelter costs and preventing homelessness.

Homeless Emergency Assistance and Rapid Transition to Housing Act (HEARTH)

In June of 2009 and as part of the Homeless Emergency Assistance and Rapid Transition to Housing Act (HEARTH), President Barack Obama asked the United States Interagency Council on Homelessness (USICH) to create a national, comprehensive plan to end homelessness (United States Interagency Council on Homelessness [USICH], 2010). The report, entitled *Opening Doors: Federal Strategic Plan to End Homelessness* was released in June 2010 and incorporates lessons learned on the regional level from the over 300 ten-year plans to prevent, reduce, and end homelessness implemented in the past decade. These ten-year plans were encouraged by the federal government so that the eventual federal response could "harness the public resources and build on innovations that have been demonstrated at the local level and in cities nationwide" (USICH, 2010, para. 1). The plan focuses heavily on partnerships, with the federal government acknowledging that the process of ending homelessness will depend on an integrated effort between public and private entities. The goal of the plan is to end homelessness among veterans and the chronically homeless by 2015, and among children, family, and youth by 2020. Development of the plan involved stakeholders at all levels, including researchers in the field, homeless service providers, and invited general public comment on the agency's website.

Key aspects of the 74-page document appear to reflect the best practices developed at the local level in recent years, such as a priority focus on housing stability and rapid rehousing. One noteworthy strategy is the involvement of the U.S. Department of Education as a partner to HUD in locating and targeting children at risk of homelessness for intervention. This suggestion comes at a time when social workers are being laid off in local school districts due to severe budgetary cutbacks, bringing to mind the general question of how the plan will be funded and implemented amidst the current economic conditions. The plan's 6 goals, 10 objectives, and 52 strategies are extraordinarily comprehensive in scope and suggest a massive shift that will necessitate substantial funding for the creation of affordable housing. The plan highlights the $2 billion already in place as a result of the American Recovery and Reinvestment Act of 2009, which created additional supportive housing in communities. Moreover, $3.79 billion was set aside for the nineteen different collaborating agencies in 2010. Beyond 2010, funding is uncertain, and will likely depend on results achieved in the first two years, and subsequent funding approved by Congress.

Individuals and families who are homeless may be eligible for other government-funded programs that are discussed in chapter 2. These include but are not limited to temporary assistance to needy families, the supplemental nutrition assistance program, and Medicaid.

Social Justice

The stereotypical image of homelessness is that of a human being lying on a cold sidewalk, dirty and malnourished, and dressed in tattered clothing. This is disturbing for most of society, especially in urban centers so visibly saturated with wealth and resources. Although it is fair to say that many people are upset by this image, it is also true that their reasons for being disturbed vary considerably. Some may look upon such an individual as lazy, or generally inferior in their ability to work, care for themselves, and cope. These individuals may feel resentful for their dependence on those that can, and do care for themselves. Others may feel compassion, wondering about their past and the particular events or misfortunes that led them to such a poor state of life. In general, both groups likely feel uncomfortable, and wish the scene did not exist. Nobody wants to "see" the homeless. Perhaps it reflects people's greatest fears that they too could be without basic needs, suffering and alone. Efforts to make the homeless "go away" have resulted in social injustices across a spectrum from a community attempting to "relocate" street homeless to a place less populated by economy-boosting tourism and business, to the policing and criminalization of the homeless, and the extreme injustice of hate crimes.

Unwelcome Spaces

San Francisco has long been known as a progressive city in which various lifestyles and manners of expression are not only tolerated, they are welcomed. This tolerance may have reached its limit in early 2010, when the city's government proposed a law that would make it illegal for people to sit or lie on the city's public sidewalks during the day (McKinley, 2010). The implication is that a person doing nothing other than sitting can be charged with a crime. While sidewalks are for walking, it unfortunately does not address the need for a "place" in which people without homes can be during the day. Depriving people of the ability to freely sit on public sidewalks has caused advocates to question if these laws are violating a person's human rights. Most city shelters close for the day, leaving the homeless no place to go. Many of these individuals are unable to work due to mental or physical illness, or disability. Street-bound homeless are in no position to pay fines when they are in violation of public ordinances, and this type of legal burden can serve to create an increased barrier to work or housing. The National Law Center on Homelessness and Poverty (NLCHP) is one group that has challenged the constitutionality of these laws.

NLCHP is an advocacy group whose aim is to "prevent and end homelessness by serving as the legal arm of the nationwide movement" (National Law Center on Homelessness and Poverty, 2010). NLCHP has actively sought to challenge the legality of sit-lie ordinances, panhandling laws, and laws that in general prohibit activities that homeless people do in public such as sleep or sit. This, according to their lawyers, is the "criminalizing" of a life circumstance, and not of behaviors that are threatening or harmful to society. The NLCHP released a study in 2006, together with the National Coalition for the Homeless, which surveyed 224 cities. Of these, 27 percent prohibited sitting and lying in public areas and 43 percent prohibited begging in certain public places. Based on the recent news in San Francisco, these numbers are on the rise.

Even without new laws designed to reduce the presence of the homeless, there are ways in which existing laws are unfairly enforced to achieve the same end. In June 2010 in New York City, a group called "Picture the Homeless" gathered outside police headquarters to protest the arrest of homeless individuals for vague disorderly conduct charges, including "being near a bottle in the park," and "putting a package on an empty subway seat." These arrests can cause the loss of a shelter bed, a job, or eligibility for subsidized housing. The activists found an ally in former police officer and Senator Eric Adams, who stated, "The police must never threaten, coerce, or violate the civil rights of a New Yorker with a vague disorderly conduct charge merely because he or she is homeless" (Zhu, 2010, para. 4).

The consensus amongst advocates is that such laws really do nothing to address the causes of homelessness, and simply serve to make the problem worse. The homeless can "move along," but to where? Since there are not enough shelters with daytime access, the homeless invariably shift into the criminal justice system, state hospitals, and emergency medical services. Many advocates see this as an additional burden to city systems, and the "criminalization" of the homeless. They argue that while it may be possible to remove the homeless from sight, they cannot be "removed" from the landscape of our economy. If the root causes are not addressed, and they are removed from the street, they will be "sheltered" in places vastly more expensive than daytime city drop-in centers. For the mentally ill or actively substance-abusing homeless, an altercation with the police can easily result in either a trip to jail or an ambulance ride to the psychiatric department of the nearest emergency room.

Hate Crimes

If laws prohibiting sitting and lying were to be considered a means of formally controlling the behavior and presence of the homeless, hate crimes could be categorized as a more informal, albeit vicious, means of social control (Wachholz, 2005). The term *hate crimes* brings to mind criminal activity, including that which is directed against groups simply because of their identity. The National Coalition for the Homeless (NCH) has been tracking hate crimes since 1999, and espouses the view that laws that criminalize the homeless encourage hate crimes by encouraging the belief that the homeless are unworthy, and less than human (NCH, 2009b). According to their data covering 1999 to 2010, 880 acts of violence have been committed, resulting in the deaths of 244 homeless individuals. In 2006 alone, hate crimes increased 65 percent from the year before. The crimes themselves are often extremely violent, as evidenced by headlines depicting street-dwelling homeless being beaten to death by bats, harassed with chainsaws, and set on fire. In a radio interview, David Pirtle reflected on the motives behind the physical attacks he suffered while living on the streets of New York in 2004. He stated, "You know, I don't think that people are going out to attack homeless people specifically because they hate homeless people. It's just that we're there, and they don't really think of us as real people, kind of part of the scenery. They attack us just like they vandalize a stop sign, basically" (Pirtle, 2009, as cited in Davidson, 2009, para. 21). Currently the homeless are not considered a "protected class" under the current federal hate crime laws, although advocates are trying to change this, which would require the Department of Justice to monitor data gathered by law enforcement about crimes against the homeless.

Violent crimes are what make the headlines, but a more common, yet unpublicized form of hate crimes against the homeless come from individuals passing by, and not necessarily from a premeditated or organized effort to harm. Levin and McDevitt (2001) conclude that "crimes motivated by bigotry usually arise not out of the pathological rantings and ravings of a few deviant types in organized hate groups, but out of the very mainstream of society" (p. xi). These incidents include the verbal and physical assaults that the homeless incur as a part of their everyday life.

Wachholz (2005) conducted a study intended to collect data on the types of hate crimes experienced by thirty homeless people in one New England city. The crimes documented included having food and objects thrown at them while panhandling, verbal assaults usually reflecting disdain for their lack of work, and outright physical attacks. One homeless man in the study described an incident that occurred while he was panhandling: "a man got out of his car, pushed me with his chest and called me a 'worthless piece of shit' and smacked me right in the face . . . closed fist punch–wham" (Wachholz, 2005, p. 150).

For the struggling working person, the picture of a seemingly "able-bodied" person asking for money can cause anger and frustration. The reasons for individuals reaching the point where they must ask for handouts are varied, complex, and certainly unlikely to be known to the passersby. It would be easy to point out the fact that many such homeless cannot work due to disability or illness, or that they are young people escaping a violent home life. Yet this leads to the argument that has dominated poverty debates for decades: the deserving vs. the undeserving poor. This idea reflects the belief that some deserve the burden of poverty due to poor choices they have made, whereas the "deserving" poor (such as children) are viewed as having done nothing to cause their poverty.

The Rights of the Homeless

Due to the diligence of advocates and the homeless individuals themselves, homeless have rights. The National Coalition for the Homeless has embarked on a nationwide community organizing effort to promote voter registration by the homeless, promoted by their slogan "You Do Not Need a Home to Vote" (National Coalition for the Homeless, 2010). Although legislation to ensure their right to vote occurred in 1984, the struggle continues to remove barriers to registration and voting for the low income and homeless. Some states require identification to vote, which many homeless do not have. Obstacles include a lack of access to information about candidates, the location of polls, and procedures for voting.

Other legal measures in place to ensure the rights of the homeless include the landmark 1979 legislation affording the Right to Shelter (emergency housing) for indigent men in New York City. This legislation was later ratified to address the quality of emergency housing, setting minimal standards of decency, which led to efforts across the nation to secure similar standards for families, children, and people with HIV/AIDS (Hopper, 2003). These efforts were helpful in addressing short-term housing solutions, but did little to resolve the problems at the root of housing loss. Recent struggles for change have shifted to address long-term solutions, yet Hopper (2003) warns that "short term efforts must contend with the legacy of a decade which saw visible misery burgeon in the streets and contempt for the poor lose its shame" (p. 184). Although Kim Hopper was referring to the 1980s when he wrote this, it seems that little has changed in the thirty years that followed. While the fight evolves toward a long-term resolution to the problem of homelessness, the shame and stigma persist. While efforts are being made toward ending homelessness, the problems are multifaceted and thus require a variety of interventions and strategies that respond to the needs of the various populations.

Interventions

Over the years, there have been different approaches to helping individuals struggling with homelessness. It has been recognized over the past ten years that the most effective intervention is *housing*. This realization only came after years of addressing what service providers and policy makers felt were the root causes such as mental illness, substance abuse, lack of education or job readiness, which led to their housing loss. While services have been useful in reducing poverty, they have not eliminated homelessness. The numbers of families entering shelters is at an all-time high. In January 2013, there were 50,135 people, including 21,034 children, sleeping in municipal shelters, the worst year since New York City began keeping data twenty-seven years ago (Markee, 2013). It is evident, however, that there has been a slight decrease in the numbers of chronically homeless single adults, and this may be due in part to a massive policy shift around this group, which has been steadily gaining ground in the past ten years. This section will examine the characteristics of homeless individuals and families, as well as explore best practices at the micro, mezzo, and macro level.

Micro Interventions

Micro interventions for the homeless are those services directed toward resolving homelessness for a particular individual or family. The main intervention for all individuals experiencing homelessness is to secure shelter. Once people are safely placed, other more specific interventions are usually offered to promote permanent housing. These services may differ depending on individuals' or families' needs, but are normally offered within a case management model at a shelter or transitional housing. The term *shelter* is used to describe a wide array of emergency housing and may include the warehouse-type dwellings meant to house many people, or buildings that have small, private dormitory-style rooms. Transitional housing refers to temporary residences that serve as a bridge between emergency shelter and permanent living arrangements. The consensus among researchers seem to indicate that the most successful programs are those that combine housing and supportive services, and do so in coordination with nearby providers in order to maximize funding and streamline services (Green, 2005). Culhane, Metraux, and Hadley (2001, in Green, 2005) conclude that the marriage of supportive services and housing results in "marked reductions in shelter use, hospitalizations (regardless of type), length of stay per hospitalization, and time incarcerated" (p. 1). The evidence supporting these interventions has made its way into the highest level of policy and now forms long-term strategic plans to permanently end homelessness in the United States. For single adults living on the streets, an effort to "reach out" must first be initiated, as many are unwilling to access shelter voluntarily. Families with children may more readily present themselves for shelter, yet bring to the shelter the added complexities of parenting, and family relationships. The micro interventions called for in these cases are detailed in the following section.

Supportive Services

For all populations who experience homelessness, the Continuum of Care model has been standard for the past thirty years. This term refers to the offering of a spectrum of services available to the homeless, from emergency to supportive housing, along with the accompanying mental health treatment, substance abuse treatment, and job training services that often come with it. Green (2005) explores a particularly effective type of homeless service delivery under the Continuum of Care model, which allows providers to act as a single system by which they can coordinate and, ideally, co-locate services. The co-location of services is helpful as people can access several different supports at one time, or in "one stop." This might include financial and legal counseling, mental health counseling or referral, a food pantry, and job readiness courses. A recent best practice developed on this premise is Project Homeless Connect (PHC). Now offered in several cities, PHC began in San Francisco in 2004 as an initiative by Mayor Gavin Newsom to create a one-day, one-stop event in which all homeless individuals and families can access a broad array of resources and services (Project Homeless Connect, 2010). These include everything from health care, dentistry, and haircuts to state identification cards, massages, shoes, clothing, and crisis counseling. The biannual (or more often) events draw on resources and volunteers throughout the business and non-profit communities, and engender a spirit of welcome and acceptance. One of the key principles in PHC is that the homeless be welcome guests, treated with dignity and respect, and a firm belief that nobody should wait in line.

Although it is clear that housing and supportive services have been the main micro interventions for all, some distinctions can be further made between the types of supportive micro interventions for single adults vs. families with children. These are detailed in the two subsections below.

Micro Interventions: Single Adults

Chronically homeless adults are defined by HUD (2003) as "an unaccompanied homeless individual with a disabling condition who has either been continuously homeless a year or more or has had at least four episodes of homelessness in the past three years" (p. 4019). Based on the point in time counts, which are conducted annually by HUD (2010c), 36 percent of sheltered individuals suffer from chronic substance abuse and 26 percent are severely mentally ill. These numbers are not entirely reflective of the chronically homeless population as they only cover those in shelter, and do not include 63 percent of the chronic homeless who are unsheltered. The term *chronic* brings some controversy as many advocates feel the term has a stigmatizing effect, emphasizing the perception that one's personal failings have caused repeated bouts of housing loss (Meschede, 2010). For the purposes here, the term is meant to convey a person's experience over time, and recognizes the lack of intervention strategies to end homelessness.

"Outreach" has its beginnings in working with the chronically homeless, as the word literally means going out into the streets, parks, alleys, and woods to reach the homeless population. Traditionally outreach aims to bring the street homeless into shelters and to provide case management in an effort to move them toward sobriety, mental wellness, and self-sufficiency. It is fair to say that some understandably do not want to be in shelter. Without discounting the good intentions of most shelter providers, the typical city shelter atmosphere is institutional, depressing, cold, and chaotic. Kryda and Compton (2009) found that the homeless resisted the services of outreach workers in part because they felt that there were no long-term solutions being offered them, but rather just a free trip to a shelter. The consensus among them was that shelters were no better than jails, and infused with an environment of violence, theft, and drugs. In addition, shelters are sometimes crowded with people, and it is not hard to imagine that years of life on the streets could create some personal discomfort for individuals living in a communal, physically close space. Consequently, some chronically homeless living on the street do not want to go into a shelter. Shelters, while offering a place to retreat from the elements, bring a whole new set of difficulties to a person who is not ready to stop using substances, take psychiatric medication, or who feels overwhelmed by the often heavily regulated and monitored environment of shelter living. For these reasons, and for the purpose of preparing a person for independent living, psychiatric services, addiction counseling, and regular meetings with a mental health professional are offered. In the Housing First model, which is explained in the mezzo section, housing is now offered with supportive services but does not mandate these services.

Once in a shelter, a case manager along with the client begins working on a plan toward permanent, self-supported housing. This plan incorporates a systems approach, which takes into account the psychological, social, biological, and spiritual needs of clients. Steps are taken to increase access to resources, maximize strengths, and improve a person's ability to function independently in the shelter. This type of approach is also utilized with families, designed to focus on the challenges unique to them.

Supportive Services: Families and Children

As the numbers of families entering homelessness reaches an all-time high, homeless community advocates are developing strategies to intervene effectively with this population. In the past three decades, services to families have followed the continuum of care model, providing case management, mental health counseling, parenting, addictions treatment, and job readiness training at the forefront. Despite the relief families feel being off the street, the initial entry into shelter is a traumatic event. Families who present for shelter often do so after a long battle with finances and housing. They have bounced from one family or friends' residence to another, parenting under difficult circumstances, while watching the impact of constant change and uncertainty on their children's health, behavior, and emotional well-being. Often their own health understandably declines, and job loss, if it has not already happened, is sometimes inevitable. Regardless of what came first, the housing loss or the deterioration of their personal well-being, many homeless families would benefit from mental health services. Although housing may be the priority, it is rarely the only service offered. Some researchers believe that housing for families without supportive mental health services cannot on its own resolve homelessness (Buckner, Bassuk, & Zima, 1993).

It has long been known that homelessness can have a negative impact on the emotional, physical, and mental well-being of children (Bassuk & Ruben, 1987). Usually by the time a child actually reaches a shelter, the deleterious effects of homelessness have already emerged. These include separation from family members through divorce, abandonment, and incarceration or due to the gender guidelines of emergency housing. A father, for instance, may be unable to accompany a mother and child to shelter. While it is hard to separate out the impact of non-housing variables on the well-being of children, Menke (1998) found that 57 percent of the homeless school-aged children in her study showed evidence of high depression scores on the Child Behavior Checklist, a scale used to measure depression in children. Access to education can also be disrupted, as children are often moved away from their home school. According to the Institute for Children in Poverty (1999), homeless children are nine times more likely to repeat a grade, four times more likely to drop out of school, and three times more likely to be placed in a special education program. Health issues are also of concern, with homeless children having an asthma rate of 40 percent (Grant et al., 2007), and although one study found no significant difference in cognitive abilities between housed and homeless children, it did find that homeless children fare much worse on tests of academic performance than their housed peers (Ruben et al., 1996).

For these reasons, agencies that have the resources often provide micro interventions such as play therapy, developmental therapy, and family therapy to homeless families. One such agency is the Vogel Alcove, in Dallas, Texas. The "Alcove" as it is known, opened in 1987 as a child care facility for children living in area shelters. The center operates just as other child care centers, with parents dropping their children off in the morning and picking them up in the evening, while also providing necessities such as diapers, formula, and meals. This free service allows homeless parents to job search, work, or attend school. Shortly after opening, the Vogel Alcove founders, a group of dedicated members of the Dallas Jewish community, added on-site social and medical services to address the mental and developmental health needs of the children (Vogel Alcove, 2011).

Interventions are guided by models, such as the Continuum of Care, or Housing First models, mentioned previously in this chapter. Best practice models continue to evolve as evidence-based research gains momentum. The following section explores practice at the mezzo level.

Mezzo Practice: Housing First, An Intervention Model

The Housing First model is premised on the idea that in order for people to achieve sobriety or psychiatric wellness, they *first* must be housed. Housing First removes the mandates that individuals must be sober or even agree to receive treatment as a prerequisite to housing. The creators of Housing First utilize scattered-site housing, which consists of subsidized apartment units that are integrated into standard multi-unit residences, thereby providing the sense of a "normal" home environment. Additionally, "wrap around" services are provided that support a person's psychiatric wellness, employment, education, and sobriety without force, and only by way of consent with the resident (Pathways to Housing, 2013).

Research investigating the effectiveness of this model has shown that compared to people in treatment first services, Housing First participants were housed sooner, stable longer, and showed no difference in the rate of substance use than those in treatment-mandated housing (Gulcer, Tsembaris, & Padgett, 2006; Tsembaris, Gulcer, & Nakae, 2004). It also seems clear that if housing is not made a central piece of intervention, any gains made in short-term treatment programs may be lost as individuals usually return to the street following completion of service (Meschede, 2010). Tsembaris and Eisenberg (2000) found that 88 percent of tenants in a Housing First program remained housed versus 47 percent from a similar population housed in a "linear residential program," or Continuum of Care model. Cost effectiveness and evidence of success in housing retention have led to Housing First becoming a recognized "best practice" by the Interagency Council on Homelessness and is now being replicated in cities throughout the United States.

Supportive services, which include comprehensive mental health treatment, are critical for many to maintain their housing and thus remain a vital component in both the Continuum of Care and Housing First models, with the difference being in how, and at what point services are offered. When services are combined with housing, it is referred to as "Supportive Housing," a model that in the city of Portland, Maine has resulted in 77 percent fewer inpatient hospitalizations, 62 percent fewer emergency room visits, and 62 percent fewer days in jail (Mondello, Gass, & McLaughlin, 2001 as cited in Green, 2005). Many providers that have not fully adopted Housing First refer to their programs as supportive housing.

There has been opposition to Housing First. In its beginning stages, advocates felt that the movement was taking valuable attention and resources away from families and children, since the model was initially aimed at single adults. That has since changed, as the success of Housing First has enabled its expansion to all those without housing. There is still some resistance among those who feel that providing housing to people first is akin to rewarding the "undeserving," and there are some in the service realm who simply feel that a mentally ill person or someone actively struggling with addiction is not ready to be a responsible tenant (Finn, as cited in Schroeder, 2010).

The Role of Faith-Based Organizations

No discussion of service models would be complete without mention of faith-based organizations (FBOs). FBOs are owned and operated by religious organizations that may provide services to those in need. Organizations such as Catholic Charities and Salvation Army have long been providing services to the homeless, following federal guidelines that require them to keep their religious ideology separate from the services they provide. As of 1996, FBOs can receive public funds to provide services centered on a spiritual or religious philosophy, including but not limited to programs run by various churches and synagogues. This shift occurred via a provision in the Personal Responsibility and Work Opportunity and Reconciliation Act, otherwise referred to as "welfare reform." The little known provision is known as "Charitable Choice" and served to remove barriers in providing government funds to FBOs for human services. Prior to this act, FBOs had to follow strict rules when receiving public funds, including the removal of any and all religious symbols or icons from the service environment. With the passage of Charitable Choice, FBOs do not have to do so, and are permitted to use their religious views as a means to promote positive outcomes. Despite these freedoms, they must also provide non-religious services to those who request it, and recipients of services can always refuse to receive service in FBOs (Cnaan & Boddie, 2002).

Politicians of both parties have supported FBOs' strong presence in the homeless services arena. In 1999 Al Gore suggested that FBOs provide the spiritual motivation—in the form of "inner discipline and courage"—that is often necessary for a person to make significant life changes (Cnaan & Boddie, 2002). President George W. Bush, just prior to creating a White House Office of Faith Based and Community Initiatives, said that "some needs and hurts are so deep they will only respond to a mentor's touch or a pastor's prayer. Church and charity, synagogue and mosque lend our communities their humanity, and they will have an honored place in our plans and in our laws" (White House, 2001). President Barack Obama redefined this initiative when he took office, calling it the White House Office of Faith-Based and Neighborhood Partnerships. Despite their increasing popularity and prevalence, researchers have yet to reveal the effectiveness of FBOs, but not for lack of trying. An extensive study looking at dozens of FBOs across the nation in 2002 revealed that measurements of effectiveness were either not in place or not reliable (Flanelly, Weaver, & Tannenbaum, 2005). This will likely change as all organizations compete for funding that demands evidence-based practice.

Macro Interventions:

Interventions at the macro level are those that serve to provide broad change for large numbers of people. Macro efforts to address homelessness include federal and state policies, and private sector initiatives, such as community organizing, legal advocacy, and research. Public sector interventions were discussed in depth in the previous section entitled "Government Policies and Programs." Public and private sector efforts often go hand in hand, as many of these policies are informed by independent research conducted by academic institutions, private nonprofit organizations such as the Coalition for the Homeless and the National Law Center on Homelessness and Poverty, or public entities such as the U.S. Department of Housing and Urban Development. The most visible of macro interventions from the private sector is community organizing.

Community Organizing

As characteristic of this approach (discussed in chapter 1), the National Coalition for the Homeless actively reaches out to the homeless themselves to become advocates, offering them opportunities to engage in voter registration drives, join speaker bureaus, or engage directly in community organizing as volunteers. Community organizing efforts have achieved powerful changes in how the homeless are treated in society. One example of this type of macro intervention is a movement that occurred in San Francisco, out of a need to provide daytime services to the neighborhood's poor. Some shelters require residents to leave the facility early in the morning, and allow reentry only in the evening. These individuals, along with those who remain on the street at night, are often without a place to stay during the day. In San Francisco's Mission District, a group of community advocates organized in 1999 around the need for a comprehensive drop-in center to serve the neighborhood's vulnerable population (Wenger, Leadbetter, Guzman, & Kral,

2007). The Mission Neighborhood Resource Center (MNRC) was only fully realized after countless conversations with community residents to address concerns related to the impact the center would have on their neighborhood. Although funds had been secured, organizers needed to convince local citizens that the presence of the center would not cause additional problems in the area. As an example of this negotiation, the MNRC built a second-floor open air smoking facility in response to the residents' concerns about loitering on the street. MNRC continues to retain its grassroots focus by making community organizing a central activity and enlisting those served in activities to raise awareness and self-advocate.

Although community organizing in and of itself is a powerful intervention, the addition of legal action has been used to protect the rights of the homeless, as well as alter the public's perception of them.

Legal Advocacy

Several of the most sweeping advances in homeless advocacy were a direct result of legal action. Due to their lack of financial resources, the homeless are unable to hire lawyers, therefore organizations such as the National Coalition for the Homeless will take action on their behalf. The landmark case *Callahan v. Carey* in 1979 (mentioned earlier in this chapter) was brought by a lawyer on behalf of six homeless men in New York City. A victory in the case secured the right to shelter, based on a statute in the state constitution (Barak, 1992). This resolution continues to protect thousands of homeless today, as the law mandates that those who are proven to be in need of emergency shelter must be granted it. Legal advocacy in the 1990s focused more on resisting laws that denied the homeless rights in terms of occupying public spaces, vagrancy, and panhandling (Hafetz, 2003). These types of cases, as were detailed in the section on "Social Justice," continue to the present day.

Lawyers can also bring action on behalf of one individual or family, such as in cases of impending eviction, which is often used as a means for preventing homelessness. The addition of good case management can serve to promote smooth resolution in legal cases, as legal advocacy is most effective when coupled with services that address the non-legal issues also hindering a person's stability (Hafetz, 2003), such as mental illness. It is challenging for a person living in shelter, or on the street, to meet the requirements of the court with regard to scheduling, or appearing. Social workers can work together with lawyers to both identify the need for advocacy and assist individuals in their participation.

Research

Research on the homeless is an area of macro intervention that has improved in recent decades. Research conducted in the last 20–30 years has provided a deeper understanding of the causes and consequences of homelessness, along with specific information about the individuals who experience it. Data collected in the 1990s made the vast diversity of the homeless population clear (Toro & Warren, 1999). Research has also served to help us understand the course of homelessness over time (longitudinal data) and allowed for better analysis of its root causes. Along with the profession of social work, disciplines such as anthropology, law, public policy, and public health have contributed to the knowledge base, and helped to ensure that data gathered are used to inform programs and policies.

Research has to be shared in order to make its way into practice, and one avenue for this is through national conferences, such as the National Conference on Ending Homelessness, held by the National Alliance to End Homelessness. The focus of this conference and others is to raise awareness and promote strategic planning around current best practices, such as rapid rehousing. Best practices are those that are informed by evidenced-based research. Participants gather to share ideas and learn methods that have been proven to create results.

Concluding Comments

Those who work with and on behalf of the homeless do not like the word *homeless*. What this word indicates to most of society does not define the individuals they know who have faced this problem. It is a common feeling among the advocates of this group that the homeless give back much more than they take. Their strength and resilience in the face of enormous adversity is inspiring and humbling to those who witness it, and reminds us all that people are capable of overcoming the greatest of obstacles. This chapter has aimed to provide the reader a beginning foundation for understanding the history and demographics of the problem, along with causes and interventions. To work on behalf of people who are homeless is to engage in social justice every day. This is something readers hopefully concluded after learning about the daily ongoing obstacles for those without homes. Twenty years ago, there was very little research on the homeless. Now, because of the committed efforts of many, several of whom are cited in this chapter, the reality of housing those living in poverty is recognized and is addressed at the micro, mezzo, and macro levels. There is certainly more that needs to be done, but interventions that benefit this population are increasing.

Case Studies
Micro Level: Working-Class Family in Rural Texas

Kathy and Michael Johnson were a couple in their late twenties living in New Orleans in 2005, raising their two daughters and son, when they suddenly got the news that Hurricane Katrina was headed their way. They loaded their belongings into their van, hitched a trailer to it with furniture, artwork, and clothes and headed back to Bastrop, Texas, Michael's hometown, for what they hoped would be a short visit before returning to Louisiana. Until the hurricane, Michael worked as a furniture maker, creating custom tables, chairs, and dressers out of old reclaimed wood. His clientele included upscale stores catering to those eager to furnish their expensive homes with unique pieces. Kathy worked part-time cleaning homes and producing her own works of art, paintings that occasionally sold in local gift shops. Life for this working-class family had its struggles, but in general, they were stable, happy, and felt fortunate that they could sustain their family through the artwork they created.

While waiting out the storm and its aftermath, the Johnsons stayed with Michael's aging father and stepmother, in an overcrowded farmhouse on a few acres of land. News came that the Johnsons' rental home had been completely destroyed by the floods of Katrina. The family decided to stay in Bastrop and attempted to rebuild their lives while waiting for the renter's insurance claim to be processed. Michael was unable to successfully replicate his business in the small Texas town as it seemed people were not interested or could not afford handmade furniture. Kathy cleaned homes again, this time full-time, as Michael's elderly parents took over child care responsibilities. Over time, tensions mounted in the small, crowded home and the Johnsons were eager to move out as soon as they could.

The Johnsons were relieved to finally receive a check from the insurance company in 2006 for $15,000. By this time, Michael had secured work as a carpenter working in new home construction. Michael learned from his boss that despite their meager income, they could qualify for a new home. They decided to stay in Bastrop in order to be close to Michael's parents, who still helped with the children, and using their insurance claim money as a down payment, began building and owning their first home. Their life stabilized for the next two years, and feeling their troubles were behind them, the couple decided to leverage the equity in their home to rebuild Michael's furniture-making business, investing money in a workshop, materials, truck, and trailer.

In the fall of 2008, the family received a notice that the mortgage payment on their home had increased by $300 a month to reflect an adjustment in their interest rate. This was unexpected, and created financial stress that was compounded by the fact that Kathy's house-cleaning customers had almost all canceled her services, citing their own financial stresses. Michael's father died that year, and his stepmother sold their home and land to pay for her new assisted living housing. Shortly thereafter Michael was laid off from his job due to a drastic decrease in new home construction. Although he had built some furniture, he could not take it to the shops in nearby Austin because he did not have the almost $40 per trip in gas money needed to get there and back. The couple decided that their only recourse was to sell their home and move into a small apartment. When they met with a realtor in the spring of 2009, they were told that the value of their home had decreased by 30 percent and that even at the lowered price, the chances of finding a buyer were unlikely. Additionally with the home equity loan, they now owed more than the home was worth.

With no income to cover the mortgage, they fell into foreclosure and within six months received an eviction notice. During this time, the couple sold off most of their possessions, except their van. With no other options, they again loaded their children and what little they had left, and headed for Austin to enter a homeless shelter. Once there, Michael and Kathy learned that there were only a few spaces allotted in the homeless system for families, and that they were all full. If they were to access shelter, the family would have to split up, with Michael going to a shelter for men, and Kathy to one for women and children. Michael refused, and the family lived in their van for three weeks before a shelter space for families finally became available.

Questions

1. What are the systemic issues that led to the Johnsons' loss of housing? Consider the economic environment in particular.

2. Do you think society in general would view the Johnsons as deserving or undeserving of their sudden poverty? How would you view them, and what factors inform your opinion?

3. Sometimes a stable family can become homeless as a result of a series of events. What events led to the Johnsons' housing loss, and could they have been avoided? How?

4. What are the social justice issues in this family's situation? Some areas to consider are how they were perhaps misadvised in their purchase of a home, and the difficulties they had in finding emergency shelter for the whole family.

5. Although it wasn't mentioned in the case example, discuss the impact this experience had on the mental health and relationships of the family members. If you were their caseworker at the shelter, what information would help you in determining what services might be useful? Consider the numerous losses and transitions and eventual separations the family endured.

Mezzo Level: Transgender Youth: New York City

Rita is a nineteen-year-old young transgender woman of biracial descent: her mother was white and her father, Puerto Rican. She was born in New York City and raised for her first nine years by her parents in Spanish Harlem. Her mother left the family, moving back to her hometown in Florida due to the physical violence she endured at the hands of Rita's father, who was an alcoholic. Rita stayed with her father for one year before she was removed by the Administration for Children Services due to parental neglect. Rita revealed to her teachers that her father often left her alone for several days at a time, and it was apparent to them that her basic needs for food, clothing, and safety were not being met in the home. Rita was placed in the kinship care of her paternal grandmother, a 72-year-old, religiously devout woman who although strict, was also loving and protective of Rita.

In the eighth grade, Rita began to express outwardly what she had always believed about herself internally, that she was female. Her style of clothing and mannerisms began to reflect this and she ultimately suffered from intense bullying and isolation from peers at school. Rita turned to marijuana to ease her emotional pain, thus beginning a downward spiral in which her grades dropped and the relationship with her grandmother deteriorated. Although Rita's grandmother continued to care for her, she made it clear that her transgender identity was unacceptable to her, and their evenings often ended in heated arguments. Rita knew her grandmother would never fully accept her as she was, and she could not bear the pain of her rejection any longer. At the age of sixteen, Rita decided to leave home and seek out acceptance among the transgender and gay/lesbian youth she had met in bars in

Manhattan. These youth were mostly runaways and like her, had left or been forced to leave homes in which their identity was not accepted. Many had suffered trauma much worse than Rita, including sexual and physical abuse, abandonment, and long stretches of time living and surviving on the streets.

Rita was drawn into this world out of a need to belong and be accepted. Despite the dangers, she thrived on the sense of community and a feeling that she was among people who understood and shared her experiences. She had friends, yet for eighteen months, Rita struggled to survive and was constantly in danger. Securing employment was impossible. Rita was homeless, uneducated, and her transgender identity meant that in addition to discrimination, she was at risk of violent hate crimes. She engaged in sex work as a means to feed herself and pay for the occasional hotel room where she could rest and take a shower. At the age of seventeen, she came to the attention of the local social services department after being taken to the emergency room following a physical attack by a man soliciting sex from her. Rita was taken into custody by the state, but caseworkers could not locate a foster family willing to take her. She lived in a state-run group home for a year, where she suffered bullying similar to what she experienced in high school. At age eighteen, she signed herself out of foster care and through the help of a social worker, located a small shelter taking in lesbian, gay, bisexual, and transgender (LGBT) youth between the ages of 18 and 24. This LGBT shelter provided group counseling to the residents, which were facilitated by a former resident who is a social worker.

Rita now has what she desperately yearned for all along—a friendly community, and a safe environment. She has enrolled in a GED class, is taking art classes at a community college, and working full-time at a coffee shop. With the help of group and individual counseling she has begun to heal from the trauma she experienced nearly all her life. She hopes to finish her college degree in art education, and become a teacher. The shelter will allow her to stay there until she is twenty-four, so she currently is guaranteed a safe place to stay at night.

Questions

1. What cultural issues are apparent in this case, and why are these important to be aware of?

2. What type of intervention might have prevented Rita from leaving her grandmother's care? Consider the strain in their relationship just prior to Rita leaving home.

3. How critical was the shelter to Rita, and what might have occurred had she not been allowed to live there?

4. Discuss how discrimination can lead to the economic oppression of whole groups. How was this illustrated in this case?

5. How can social workers achieve a better understanding and respect for the transgender community in society?

Macro Level: The Development of an Urban Homeless Prevention Program

The "Family Resource Center" (FRC), a private, nonprofit organization, received a notice from the city requesting grant proposals for a new program intended to prevent homelessness. The organization thought this would be a good opportunity to create a program to reach out to those at risk of losing their housing in order to prevent an episode of homelessness. The services offered by the grant could potentially include cash assistance for rental or utility arrears, mediation or legal advocacy to resolve tenancy disputes, job training, and assistance in acquiring welfare benefits such as disability insurance or Food Stamps. FRC is located in a high-poverty neighborhood, with many families at risk for homelessness. The director, a social worker named Maria, felt a homeless program would help the community and she and her team began the task of gathering information and supportive documentation in order to prepare a grant proposal.

Home visits with local residents, for example, enabled caseworkers to document that many residents were living in substandard housing, with leaky plumbing, pest infestations, and lead paint. Simultaneously, Maria began making appointments with key community leaders including the community board president and members, church leaders, school principals, shelter staff, police, fire department staff, homeowners, and tenants to assess additional needs and enable her to determine what services were already available within the community. During these meetings, the community expressed mixed feelings about more homeless services coming to their neighborhood. The local pastor, in particular, felt that the neighborhood had become a blend of shelters and service organizations, and was resistant to welcoming a new program. Maria explained that this service, if successful, would reduce the need for shelters and work to transform and improve the living conditions of neighborhood residents. Other stakeholders, including police, felt that the program would help bring stability to the community by offering a resource for those at risk of eviction, or in need of tenant-landlord mediation. Shelter staff confirmed for Maria that no service of this kind currently existed in their neighborhood and expressed their belief that such a program would help to reduce the number of people seeking emergency housing.

During one of her visits with the local community board, the local city councilman agreed to write a letter of support for Maria to include with her grant proposal. With his help, Maria determined that an advisory board made up of community representatives, including residents, should be organized to inform the process of program development and to provide ongoing evaluation and guidance to the agency after the program was implemented. Additionally, Maria's team decided to further brainstorm ways to incorporate legal advocacy for residents' housing problems into their grant proposal.

Months later, the grant was funded and the real work of program implementation, operations, and evaluation began. Maria was pleased to see that the pastor who was initially resistant to the program joined the advisory board and offered ideas and guidance on how to reach families in need of services. In turn, Maria's staff joined forces with the pastor to promote the development of a farmer's market in the neighborhood with the intent of increasing the availability of fresh produce to residents.

Questions

1. What are the root causes of homelessness? Do you think Maria's new program will have long-term success in preventing homelessness? Why or why not?

2. The local pastor is initially resistant to this new program because he believes it promotes an atmosphere of "need" as opposed to prosperity in his neighborhood. What do you think are the implications of placing numerous social service programs in one geographical area? What would you do to address the pastor's concerns?

3. How important is it to obtain the "buy in" of various stakeholders when considering a new program? What would be the challenges and benefits in doing this?

4. How do you think programs like this are impacted by state and city budget cuts? Is it ultimately more expensive or cost-effective to eliminate programs such as this?

5. Why would a farmer's market be important to a low-income community? Why do you think there is a lack of sources for healthy, fresh produce in poor neighborhoods?

Internet Resources

United States Interagency Council on Homelessness: http://www.ich.gov/

This is a federal agency in charge of coordinating the government's response to homelessness.

National Coalition for the Homeless: http://www.nationalhomeless.org/

The site includes information on efforts to educate the public, and advocate legally and within the political realm.

National Law Center on Homelessness and Poverty: http://www.nlchp.org/

This website includes recent press releases, and alerts the public to emerging legal, human, and civil rights issues related to homelessness.

U.S. Department of Housing and Urban Development: http://www.hud.gov

This site is the official portal for information related to government policy, programs, and activities conducted within HUD.

Coalition for the Homeless–New York City: http://www.coalitionforthehomeless.org/

This site is an example of a local organization's efforts to end homelessness.

National Policy and Advocacy Council on Homelessness (NPACH): http://www.npach.org/

This site publishes research and raises awareness about technical assistance to homeless service providers.

The National Alliance to End Homelessness: http://www.endhomelessness.org/

This is a private, nonprofit, and nonpartisan organization that utilizes data to inform policy at the local and national levels.

National Association for the Education of Homeless Youth and Children (NAEHYC): http://www.naehyc.org/

The NAEHYC focuses on the needs of children and youth facing homelessness.

National Association for Homeless Veterans: http://www.nchv.org/

This website publishes research, policy analysis, and general information for those helping homeless veterans, including veterans themselves.

Hennepin County, Minnesota: 10-Year Initiative to End Homelessness: http://www.headinghomeminnesota.org/hennepin/

This website describes one local community's effort to implement a ten-year plan to end homelessness.

Center for an Urban Future: http://www.nycfuture.org/

This is a local, private, nonprofit "think tank" that publishes research and policy briefs concerning the homeless.

Project Homeless Connect: http://www.projecthomelessconnect.com/about/

This is an agency in San Francisco providing a single location for multiple medical and social services for the homeless.

Further Readings

Bassuk, E. L. (2010). Ending child homelessness in America. *American Journal of Orthopsychiatry, 80*(4), 496–504.

Cunninghan, M. J., & Diversi, M. (2012). Aging out: Youths' perspectives on foster care and the transition to independence. *Qualitative Social Work, 12*(5), 587–602.

Davis-Berman, J. (2011). Older women in the homeless shelter: Personal perspectives and practice ideas. *Journal of Women & Aging, 23*(4), 360–374.

Davis-Berman, J. (2011). Older men in the homeless shelter: In-depth conversations lead to practice implications. *Journal of Gerontological Social Work, 54*(5), 456–474.

Erickson, J., & Wilhelm, C. (2012). *Housing the homeless*. Rutgers University Center for Urban Policy Research.

Fantuzzo, J. W., LeBoeuf, W. A., Chen, C. C., Rouse, H. L., & Culhane, D. P. (2012). The unique and combined effects of homelessness and school mobility on the educational outcomes of young children. *Educational Researcher, 41*(9), 393–402.

Fargo, J., Metraux, S., Byrne, T., Munley, E., Montgomery, A. E., Jones, H., & Culhane, D. P. (2012). Prevalence and risk of homelessness among US veterans. *Preventing Chronic Disease: Public Health Research, Practice and Policy, 9*(110–112), 1–9. Retrieved from http://www.cdc.gov/pcd/issues/2012/pdf/11_0112.pdf.

Murphy, J. F., & Tobin, K. J. (2011). Homelessness comes to school: How homeless children and youths can succeed. *Phi Delta Kappan, 93*(3), 32–37.

Shepard, J. (2010). *Kicked out*. S. Lowrey & J. C. Burke, eds. Homofactus Press.

Wasserman, J. A., & Clair, J. M. (2010). *At home on the street: People, poverty, and a hidden culture of homelessness*. Lynne Rienner Publishers.

References

Barak, G. (1992). *Gimme shelter: A social history of homelessness in America*. New York: Cengage.

Bassuk, E. L., & Ruben, L. (1987). Homeless children: A neglected population. *American Journal of Orthopsychiatry, 57*(2), 279–286.

Baum, A. S., & Burnes, D. W. (1993). *A nation in denial: The truth about homelessness*. Boulder, CO: Westview Press.

Baumohl, J., ed. (1996). *Homelessness in America*. Phoenix: Oryx Press.

Bowles, J., Kotkin, J., & Giles, D. (2009). *Reviving the city of aspiration: A study of the challenges facing New York City's middle class*. Center for an Urban Future. Retrieved from http://www.nycfuture.org/content/articles/article_view.cfm?article_id=1233&article_type=0.

Buckner, J. C., Bassuk, E. L., & Zima, B. T. (1993). Mental health issues affecting homeless women: Implications for intervention. *American Journal of Orthopsychiatry, 63*(3), 385–399.

Burt, M. (1995). Critical factors in counting the homeless: An invited commentary. *American Journal of Orthopsychiatry, 65*(3), 334–339.

Burt, M. (2001). *What will it take to end homelessness?* Briefing retrieved from http://www.urban.org/publications/310305.html.

Burt, M. (2007). Understanding homeless youth: Numbers, characteristics, multisystem involvement, and intervention options. In testimony to the U.S. House Committee on Ways and Means, Subcommittee on Income Security and Family Support. June 19, 2007. Retrieved from http://www.urban.org/publications/901087.html.

Campbell, T., Forrest, K., Moore, B., & Taylor, H. (2008). *"Doubled up" housing survey*. Retrieved from http://www.unitedwayuc.org/continuumofcare/docs/DOUBLED_UP_Study_2008.pdf.

Cnaan, R. A., & Boddie, S. C. (2002). Charitable choice and faith-based welfare: A call for social work. *Social Work, 47*(3), 224–235.

Cromley, C. (2010*).* Unraveling the social construction of homelessness. *Journal of Human Behavior in the Social Environment, 29*(2), 319–333.

Culhane, D., & Metraux, S. (2008). Rearranging the deck chairs or reallocating the lifeboats? *Journal of the American Planning Association, 74*(1), 111–121.

Davidson, K. (2009, October 18). Debating homeless hate crimes. *National Public Radio.* Retrieved from http://www.npr.org/templates/story/story.php?storyId=113916951.

Flanelly, K. J., Weaver, A. J., & Tannenbaum, H. P. (2005). What do we know about the effectiveness of faith-based health programs? *Southern Medical Journal, 98*(12), 1243–1244.

Franklin, E. (2009). The emerging needs of veterans: A call to action for the social work profession. *Health and Social Work, 34*(3), 163–167.

Glasser, I., & Bridgman, R. (1999). *Braving the street: The anthropology of homelessness*. New York: Berghahn Books.

Gould, T. E., & Williams, A. R. (2010). Family homelessness: An intervention of structural effects. *Journal of Human Behavior in the Social Environment, 20,* 170–192.

Grant, R., Bowen, S., McLean, D. E., Berman, D., Redlener, K., & Redlener, I. (2007). Asthma among homeless children in New York City: An update. *American Journal of Public Health, 97*(3), 448–450.

Green, D. (2005). History, discussion and review of best practices model for service delivery for the homeless. *Social Work in Mental Health, 3*(4), 1–16.

Gulcer, L., Tsembaris, S., & Padgett, D. K. (2006). *Housing first services for people who are homeless with co-occuring serious mental illness and substance abuse.* Retrieved from http://www.pathwaystohousing.org/.

Hafetz, J. L. (2003). Homeless legal advocacy: New challenges and directions for the future. *Fordham Urban Law Journal, 30*(3), 1215–1265.

Hall, A. C. (1902). *Crime in its relations to social progress.* New York: Columbia University Press.

Homeless Research Institute of the National Alliance to End Homelessness. (2007). *Data snapshot—Doubled up in the United States.* Retrieved from http://www.endhomelessness.org/library/entry/data-snapshot-doubled-up-in-the-united-states.

Hopper, K. (2003). *Reckoning with homelessness.* Ithaca, NY: Cornell University Press.

Institute for Children in Poverty. (1999). *Access to success: Meeting the educational needs of homeless children and families.* Retrieved from http://www.icphusa.org/PDF/reports/AccesstoSuccess.pdf.

Karger, H. J. (2008). America's fringe housing market. *Journal of Policy Practice, 6*(3), 25–42.

Kryda, A. D., & Compton, M. T. (2009). Mistrust of outreach workers and lack of confidence in available services among individuals who are chronically street homeless. *Community Mental Health Journal, 45,* 144–150.

Kusmer, K. L. (2003). *Down and out, on the road: The homeless in American history.* New York: Oxford University Press.

Lawrenson, F. (1997). Runaway children: Whose problem? A history of running away should be taken seriously: It may indicate abuse. *British Medical Journal, 314*(7087), 1064.

Levin, J., & McDevitt, J. (2001). *Hate crimes: The rising tide of bigotry and bloodshed.* Boulder, CO: Westview Press.

Markee, P. (2013). State of the homeless 2013. *Coalition for the Homeless.* Retrieved from http://www.coalitionforthehomeless.org/pages/state-of-the-homeless-2013.

McKinley, J. (2010, May 21). Debating whether it's a crime to rest on San Francisco's sidewalks. *New York Times.* Retrieved from http://www.nytimes.com/2010/05/22/us/22sit.html?scp=1&sq=debating%20whether%20its%20a%20crime&st=cse.

McKinney-Vento Homeless Assistance Act of 1987, 42 U.S.C. § 11301 (1987).

Menke, E. M. (1998) The mental health of homeless school-age children. *Journal of Child and Adolescent Psychiatric Nursing, 11*(3), 87–98.

Meschede, T. (2010). Accessing housing: Exploring the impact of medical and substance abuse services on housing attainment for chronically homeless street dwellers. *Journal of Human Behavior in the Social Environment, 20,* 153–169.

Monkkonen, E. H., ed. (1984). *Walking to work: tramps in America, 1790–1935.* Lincoln, NE: University of Nebraska Press.

National Coalition for the Homeless. (2009a, June). *Foreclosure to homelessness: The forgotten victims of the subprime crisis* (fact sheet). Retrieved from http://www.nationalhomeless.org/factsheets/foreclosure.html.

National Coalition for the Homeless. (2009b, August). *Hate crimes and violence against people experiencing homelessness.* Retrieved from http://www.nationalhomeless.org/factsheets/hatecrimes.html.

National Coalition for the Homeless. (2009c, September). *Homeless veterans* (fact sheet). Retrieved from http://www.nationalhomeless.org/factsheets/veterans.html.

National Coalition for the Homeless. (2010). *You Don't Need a Home to Vote project.* Retrieved from http://www.nationalhomeless.org/projects/vote/index.html.

National Law Center on Homelessness and Poverty. (2010). Retrieved from http://www.nlchp.org/program.cfm?prog=5.

Novak, W. (1996). *The people's welfare: Law and regulation in nineteenth-century America*. Chapel Hill, NC: University of North Carolina Press.

Oberholtzer, E. P. (1917). *A history of the United States since the Civil War*. Vol. 1. New York: Macmillan.

Park, J. M., Metraux, S., Brodbar, G., & Culhane, D. P. (2004). Child welfare involvement among children in homeless families. *Child Welfare 83*(5), 423–436.

Pathways to Housing. (2013). *Our model*. Retrieved from http://pathwaysto housing.org/.

Project Homeless Connect. (2010). *History of PCH*. Retrieved from http://www .projecthomelessconnect.com/mission.

Ringwalt, C., Greene, J. M., Robertson, M., & McPheeters, M. (1998). "The prevalence of homelessness among adolescents in the United States. *American Journal of Public Health, 88*(9), 1325–1329.

Ruben, D. H., Erickson, C. J., San Agustin, M., Cleary, S. D., Allen, J. K., & Cohen, P. (1996). Cognitive and academic functioning of homeless children compared with housed children. *Pediatrics, 97*(3), 289–294.

Schroeder, A. (2010). Joe Finn on the housing first movement and long term solutions to homelessness. *New Prosperity*. Retrieved from www.thenew prosperity.org.

Shinn, M. B., Baumohl, J., & Hopper, K. (2001). The prevention of homelessness revisited. *Analysis of Social Issues and Public Policy, 95*(1), 95–127.

Steffen, B. L., Fudge, K., Martin, M., Souza, M. T., Vandenbroucke, D. A., & Yao, Y. G. D. (2009). *Worst case housing needs 2009: Report to Congress*. U.S. Department of Housing and Urban Development and the Office of Policy Development and Research. Retrieved from http://www.huduser.org/ publications/pdf/worstcase_HsgNeeds09.pdf.

Streitfeld, D. (2010, May 21). Owners stop paying mortgages and stop fretting. *New York Times*.

Sullivan, B. (2010, May 25). HUD releases "worst case housing needs" report to Congress. Press release. Retrieved from http://portal.hud.gov/hudportal/HUD?src=/press/press_releases_media_advisories/2010/HUDNo.10-107.

Thompson, S. J., Bender, K., Windsor, L., Cook, M., & Williams, T. (2010). Homeless youth: Characteristics, contributing factors, and service options. *Journal of Human Behavior in the Social Environment, 20,* 193–217.

Toro, P. A., & Warren, M. G. (1999). Homelessness in the United States: Policy considerations. *Journal of Community Psychology, 27*(2), 119–136.

Tsembaris, S., & Eisenberg, R. F. (2000). Pathways to housing: Supported housing for street dwelling homeless individuals with psychiatric disabilities. *Psychiatric Services, 51,* 487–493.

Tsembaris, S., Gulcur, L., & Nakae, M. (2004). Housing first, consumer choice, and harm reduction for homeless individuals with a dual diagnosis. *American Journal of Public Health, 94*(4), 651–656.

U.S. Census Bureau. (2011). *State and county quick facts: Tooele County, Utah.* Retrieved from http://quickfacts.census.gov/qfd/states/49/49045.html.

U.S. Conference of Mayors. (2008). Press release: Mayors examine causes of hunger, homelessness. Retrieved from http://www.usmayors.org/press releases/documents/hungerhomelessness_121208.pdf.

U.S. Department of Housing and Urban Development. (2003, January 27). Notice of funding availability for the collaborative initiative to help end chronic homelessness. *Federal Register, 68*(17), 4019.

U.S. Department of Housing and Urban Development. (2007). *McKinney-Vento Act.* Retrieved from http://portal.hud.gov/hudportal/HUD?src=/program_offices/comm_planning/homeless/lawsandregs/mckv.

U.S. Department of Housing and Urban Development, Office of Community Planning and Development. (2009). *The 2008 annual homeless assessment report.*

U.S. Department of Housing and Urban Development. (2010a, June 19). *HUD to help nearly 1300 homeless veterans find permanent homes* (press release). Retrieved from http://portal.hud.gov/hudportal/HUD?src=/press/press_releases_media_advisories/2010/HUDNo.10-124.

U.S. Department of Housing and Urban Development. (2010b). *HUD-VASH vouchers, overview.* Retrieved from http://www.hud.gov/offices/pih/ programs/hcv/vash/.

U.S. Department of Housing and Urban Development. (2010c). *The 2009 annual homeless assessment.* Retrieved from www.HUD.gov.

U.S. Interagency Council on Homelessness. (2010). *Overview of plan, and opening doors: Federal strategic plan to prevent and end homelessness.* Retrieved from http://www.usich.gov/PDF/OpeningDoors_2010_FSP PreventEndHomeless.pdf.

Van Wormer, R., & Van Wormer, K. (2009). Non abstinence-based supportive housing for persons with co-occurring disorders: A human rights perspective. *Journal of Progressive Human Services, 20,* 152–165.

Vogel Alcove. (2011). *History.* Retrieved from http://www.vogelalcove.org.

Wachholz, S. (2005). Hate crimes against the homeless: Warning-out New England style. *Journal of Sociology and Social Welfare, 32,* 142–163.

Wenger, L. D., Leadbetter, J., Guzman, L., & Kral, A. (2007). The making of a resource center for homeless people in San Francisco's mission district: A community collaboration. *Health and Social Work, 32*(4), 309–314.

Whitbeck, L. B., Chen, X., Hoyt, D. R., Tyler, K. A., & Johnson, K. D. (2004). Mental disorder, subsistence strategies and victimization among gay, lesbian and bisexual homeless and runaway adolescents. *Journal of Sex Research, 41*(4), 329–342.

White House. (2001). Transcript of President Bush's inaugural address. Retrieved from http://whitehouse.georgewbush.org/news/2001/012001.asp.

Wood, J. (2011). *Tooele County housing needs assessment.* Retrieved from http://www.tooeleeconomicdevelopment.com/PDF/housingneeds.pdf.

Zhu, H. (2010, June 16). NYC homeless accuse NYPD of harassment. *Epoch Times.* Retrieved from http://www.theepochtimes.com/n2/content/view/37484/.

5

Families, Women, and Children
Kathryn Krase

When thinking about families and children living in poverty in the United States, some envision the Great Depression, or maybe black-and-white photographs of sullen mothers holding malnourished children outside a shack without running water. However, family and child poverty in the United States is not that simple. Approximately 16 percent of families and more than 22 percent of children in the United States currently live in poverty (U.S. Census Bureau, 2012). After reading this chapter, students will better understand the experiences of families and children living in poverty in the United States, and be able to identify what efforts can and are being done to address this epidemic.

Demographics and Characteristics

Not all children living in the United States have the same experiences. The overwhelming majority of children in this country are raised by their own parent(s). Approximately 89 percent are raised in a household with at least one legal parent Additionally, millions of children are raised by others (see figure 5.1). Grandparents are raising over 7 percent of American children, and almost another 3 percent of children are raised by other family members. Less than 2 percent of children in the United States are living in foster care, or under the care of non-family members (U.S. Census Bureau, 2012).

Even when children live with a parent, the family unit varies (see figure 5.2). Twenty-six percent of children live with a single mother. Approximately 7 percent live in a household led by a single father (U.S. Census Bureau, 2012).

Over the past 40 years, births to single mothers have increased, while the divorce rate has also increased, resulting in the growth of single mother-headed households (U.S. Census Bureau, 2012). The growth of families headed by single mothers is often attributed to a growth in teenage parenting. However, there has been a

Figure 5.1. Who's Raising Children in America: Parents or Non-Parents?

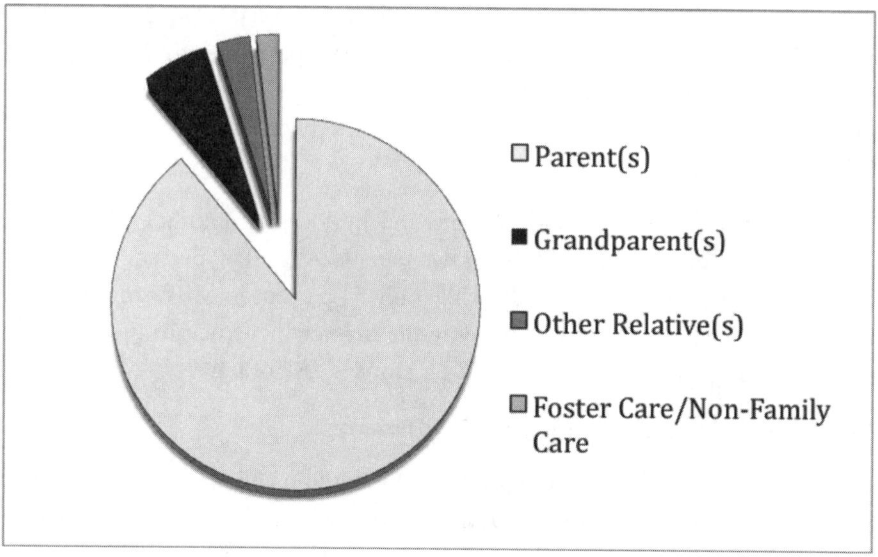

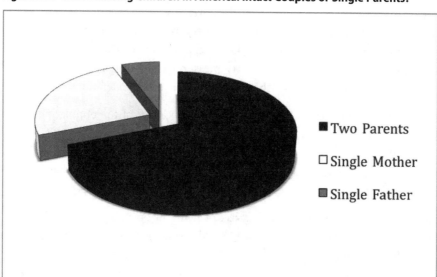

☐ Parent(s)

■ Grandparent(s)

■ Other Relative(s)

■ Foster Care/Non-Family Care

Source: Data from U.S. Census Bureau, American Community Survey (2012), retrieved from http://www.census.gov/acs/www/.

Figure 5.2. Who's Raising Children in America: Intact Couples or Single Parents?

■ Two Parents

☐ Single Mother

■ Single Father

Source: Data from U.S. Census Bureau, American Community Survey (2012), retrieved from http://www.census.gov/acs/www/.

decline in the rate of births to teenage unmarried mothers in the past twenty years. Births to teenage mothers peaked at over 61 births for every 1,000 teenage girls in 1991 (Guttmacher, 2010). In 2008, this number was approximately 41 such births for every 1,000 teenage girls. More than half of all single mothers were previously married, though a growing proportion of single mothers have never been married (U.S. Census Bureau, 2012).

Trends in family structure vary by state and by local communities. Nationally almost 66 percent of children live with two parents. Almost 80 percent of children in Utah live in a two-parent family, while only 54 percent in Mississippi do (U.S. Census Bureau, 2012). As noted further in the chapter, the structure and composition of the family unit has implications on families' risk of poverty.

Measuring Poverty: Family Poverty and Child Poverty

In order to understand poverty experienced by children and families in the United States, it is important to define poverty. There are two different measures of poverty: family poverty and child poverty. The U.S. Census Bureau provides statistics on the prevalence of poverty among family households, differentiating between family households with or without children present. For the purposes of this chapter, family poverty will refer to family households where children *are* present and household income falls below the poverty line. In the family poverty measure the entire family unit is measured once regardless of the number of children residing in the household, whereas the child poverty measure counts each child separately. Therefore, the child poverty measure is often higher than the family poverty measure because more than one child may reside in a family.

Family and child poverty affect a significant proportion of the population of the United States. Fifteen percent of families with children, and 22 percent of all children in the United States, live below the poverty line (U.S. Census Bureau, 2012). However, where a family resides, who heads the household, and how many people make up the family unit can greatly influence the risk of living in poverty.

Families with children are at higher risk of living in poverty than other types of households. Adults between the ages of 18 and 64 and older adults (65 and older) are almost half as likely as children to live in poverty (U.S. Census Bureau, 2000). Children are expensive. They have to be housed, fed, and clothed yet they do not contribute financially to the household. They need medical care and require substantial supervision. Child care is prohibitively expensive for low-wage earners. Some parents prefer to care for their children themselves, and do not work, while others may choose to work part-time, thus substantially reducing household earnings.

The stereotype that poor families are led by single mothers capable but unwilling to work is not the norm. Nor is family poverty fraught with unemployed, lazy, or chemically dependent parents. In reality, most child and family poverty is experienced transiently, not chronically. The vast majority of poor families have parents with jobs (U.S. Census Bureau, 2010). Periods of poverty are often caused by inadequate wages, underemployment, family disruption, employment instability, or medical emergency.

The United States is often considered one of the wealthiest countries in the world. However, the comparative economic well-being of our nation's children is not to be envied. Compared to twenty-four of the other richest countries in the world, children in the United States are more likely to live in poverty (measured by the U.S. poverty threshold) than children from almost half of the other rich countries, including Canada, Germany, France, and Taiwan. Using international measures of poverty, the United States ranks second to Russia for the worst child poverty rates among twenty-five of the richest nations (Bradbury & Jantti, 1999).

Child poverty rates in the United States declined significantly in the middle of the twentieth century, from more than 25 percent in 1960 to less than 15 percent by the end of the decade (U.S. Census Bureau, 2000). There was a rapid rise in child poverty in the late 1970s and early 1980s, followed by a modest decline in the mid-1980s, only to rise again to 23 percent during the late 1980s and early 1990s. The economic boom of the 1990s led to a significant decline in child poverty through the early 2000s to levels not seen since the early 1970s. Since the recession that began in 2008, child poverty rates are increasing again (U.S. Census Bureau, 2012). (See figure 5.3.) The increase is attributed to the economic insecurity caused by the current recession (Foundation for Child Development, 2010).

Geographic Location and Poverty

The poverty rate varies significantly across the United States. Ten percent of families and 12 percent of children in New Hampshire live in poverty, while 26 percent of families and 32 percent of children in Mississippi fall below the poverty line (U.S. Census Bureau, 2012). Map 5.1 reveals the breakdown of child poverty by

Figure 5.3. Poverty Rates by Age: 1959 to 2009

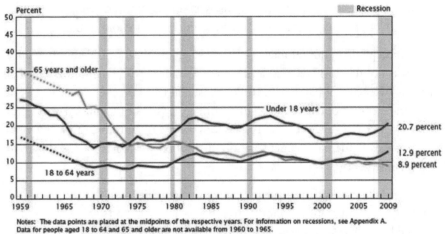

Notes: The data points are placed at the midpoints of the respective years. For information on recessions, see Appendix A.
Data for people aged 18 to 64 and 65 and older are not available from 1960 to 1965.
Source: U.S. Census Bureau, Current Population Survey, 1960 to 2010 Annual Social and Economic Supplements.

Source: U.S. Census Bureau, retrieved from http://www.census.gov/hhes/www/poverty/data/incpovhlth/
2009/pov09fig05.pdf.

state. Child poverty is clustered geographically, with the highest levels of child poverty occurring in the central South, and lowest levels in the Northeast, Alaska, Hawaii, and parts of the northern Midwest. Differences are largely attributed to urban and non-urban areas, family structure, and economic opportunity, but other factors may apply.

There are significant differences in the experiences of children living in urban, suburban, and rural areas in the United States. Children living in rural areas are more likely to live in poverty than their metropolitan counterparts (Churilla, 2008). Approximately 20 percent of children in rural areas live in poverty, compared to 15 percent of children from metropolitan areas (U.S. Census Bureau, 2010). When metropolitan areas are divided into cities and suburbs and compared to rural communities, it becomes evident that children in cities are most likely to live in poverty. Alternately, suburban children are the least likely. Additionally, if one considers the raw numbers, many more children from large urban centers are categorized as poor than are children from rural and suburban areas (Churilla, 2008).

Map 5.1. Percentage of Children Living in Poverty, by State, 2011

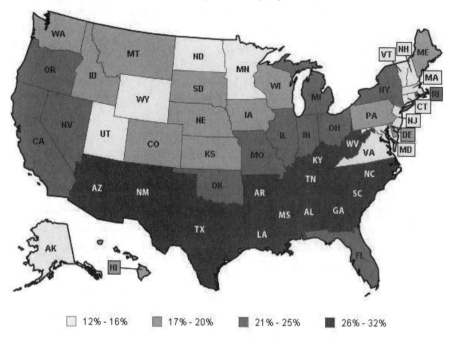

| | 12% - 16% | | 17% - 20% | | 21% - 25% | | 26% - 32% |

Source: KIDS COUNT Data Center, www.kidscount.org/datacenter.

Differences in child poverty across urban, suburban, and rural areas are related to differences in job opportunities, including the availability of transportation and child care, amongst other economic and social factors. As stated previously, the economic boom of the 1990s helped decrease the child poverty rate for all children, but children from urban and suburban areas benefited more than those from rural areas. This boom in urban areas was largely a result of a rise in wealth in the banking and technology industries, while rural areas experienced losses in agriculture and manufacturing (Rogers & Dagata, 2000).

Family Structure and Poverty

Family structure is a major contributor to family and child poverty. Single-parent families are more likely to live in poverty than families headed by two parents

(Mather, 2010). Two-parent households often have the advantage of two wage earners and in cases where one of the parents does not work, for example, the stay-at-home parent can provide child care, thereby reducing household expenses. For both single-parent and two-parent families, however, the availability of affordable child care as well as the paucity of family-friendly employment policies are major issues that impact the employment prospects. Almost 9 percent of two-parent families live in poverty, whereas more than 37 percent of families headed by single-mothers live in poverty (U.S. Census Bureau, 2012).

The majority of children in poverty are living in single mother-headed families (U.S. Census Bureau, 2012). Although approximately three-fourths of single mothers are employed, this group is more likely than mothers in two-parent families to be unemployed. Compared to other working mothers, employed single mothers are more likely to work in low-wage earning positions in retail, service, and administrative sectors. Jobs in these sectors are less likely to carry benefits, including health care coverage (Mather, 2010).

Children living in households headed by single mothers are more likely to live in poverty than children living in households headed by single fathers. Families led by single fathers have a poverty rate of almost half of that of families headed by single mothers (U.S. Census Bureau, 2012). Single mothers are at a disadvantage over single fathers, in that women on average earn less than men for the same work, a result of lost work experience to child bearing and child rearing as well as gender discrimination in the workplace (U.S. Government Accountability Office [GAO], 2003).

How Race Impacts Families and Children in Poverty

Contrary to popular beliefs and media depictions that suggest most poor children in America are African American, numerically, non-Hispanic white/Caucasian children make up the largest group of poor children in the United States. In fact, more than a third of all children living in poverty in the United States are white (U.S. Census Bureau, 2012). However, there is an important intersection between race and child poverty that needs to be examined.

Non-white children are disproportionately poor, meaning that these children have a higher likelihood of being poor than white children. Approximately 39 percent of black children in the United States live in poverty, whereas 34 percent of Hispanic children, 14 percent of Asian-American children, and 14 percent of white children live in poverty (U.S. Census Bureau, 2012).

Higher poverty rates among black and Hispanic children are largely due to the higher prevalence of poverty risk factors in these populations. One of the main contributors to higher rates of poverty among these children is the respectively higher proportion of black and Hispanic children who live in single mother-headed households (U.S. Census Bureau, 2012). As discussed previously, single mother-headed households are more likely to live in poverty than other types of families. Additionally, parents in black and Hispanic families have generally lower educational attainment than parents in white and Asian-American families (U.S. Census Bureau, 2010), which impacts their employment and financial prospects.

Structural and pervasive racial and ethnic bias in education, housing, and employment sectors also contribute to differential poverty rates for black and Hispanic children in the United States. Black families in particular suffered systematic discrimination in the design of public school systems, housing, and employment opportunities through much of the twentieth century.

Historical Perspectives

From colonial times through the turn of the twentieth century, the United States has made drastic changes in how family and child poverty are addressed. In the early years of this country, responsibility for caring for poor families and children largely rested on the individual family unit. As a last resort, religious institutions and local government stepped in to assist the family in limited ways (Trattner, 1999).

Through the Civil War, the needs of impoverished families and children were largely ignored by the federal government. The federal government disclaimed responsibility for the welfare of the poor, citing local, if not personal responsibility. Further limiting assistance to the needy, most local private and governmental entities only provided support to white children and families established in the area, excluding black children and families, as well as newcomers (Trattner, 1999).

An exception to these limitations was the establishment of widow's pension programs, to support women and children whose husbands were killed fighting for their country (Trattner, 1999). Widow's pension programs eventually expanded to families whose husbands died outside of war and then to single mothers in general, in a trajectory of policy that eventually leads to our current Temporary Assistance for Needy Families (TANF) program administered by the federal government. By 1931, forty-eight states, with the exceptions of Georgia and South

Carolina, supported 200,000 American children through mother's pension programs (Katz, 1986).

With the industrial revolution, growth of inner cities, and exploding immigration and population growth, the end of the nineteenth century saw increased private response to families and children in need. Driven mostly by private philanthropy and the volunteer work of the privileged class, charitable organization societies and settlement houses sought to eradicate poverty by solving the ills of the poor and improving their living conditions, respectively (Katz, 1986; Trattner, 1999).

Not coincidentally, the growth in coordinated response to family and child poverty parallels the introduction and expansion of the social work profession and related human services. In fact, the training programs to prepare workers for charitable organization society (COS) and settlement houses were the basis for early social work education. These early training programs eventually moved from agency to academia, being taught in colleges and universities (Katz, 1986; Trattner, 1999). From Jane Addams's Hull House to Mary Richmond and the COS, social work practice was integral to shaping society's response to the plight of impoverished families and children.

COS and settlement houses were not the only efforts aimed at improving the lives of families and children living in poverty. In 1853 Charles Loring Brace founded the Children's Aid Society in New York City to address the plight of poor children (Children's Aid Society, 2010). The Children's Aid Society provided housing for street children and created industrial schools to teach young boys and girls useful trade skills (Katz, 1986).

Charles Loring Brace also spearheaded the Orphan Train movement, which sent tens of thousands of inner-city children to live with farming families in the Midwest (Children's Aid Society, 2010). Supporters of the Orphan Train movement highlight the effort's success at removing children from chaotic and neglectful homes in overcrowded urban areas. Critics of the movement point to the fact that many of the "orphans" were not such, and were actually separated, perhaps through coercion, from living parents, siblings, and extended families. After placement on farms far from the city, there was little oversight to guarantee that children were cared for appropriately (Trattner, 1999). Orphan Train programs ceased in the late 1920s and early 1930s, as local and state governments became more involved in efforts to ensure the welfare of children (Whitelaw Downs, Moore, & McFadden, 2009).

After the Great Depression of the 1930s devastated millions of families, it was no longer politically possible for federal and state governments to refuse to provide for the social welfare of poor families and their children. Emergency aid for those affected by the Great Depression, generally in the form of jobs programs, mainly benefited white men, with very few women gaining employment through these programs and limited access to people of color. In fact, the Civilian Conservation Corps, a New Deal program that sent thousands of young men to work camps in mainly rural areas, officially limited enrollment of African American young men to 10 percent of the program's capacity and limited their assignments to areas with a high concentration of African American people (Trattner, 1999).

Another New Deal program ushered in the era of federal entitlement programs for children and families. Through the Social Security Act of 1935, the Aid to Dependent Children (ADC) program was created and largely replaced widow's/mother's pension programs (Katz, 1986). Through ADC, the federal government provided financial assistance to the states to provide income to poor households with children (Blau & Abramovitz, 2010). ADC was designed to meet the financial needs of families where a father was no longer able to work, due to death or disability (Katz, 1986; Trattner, 1999).

World War II catapulted the country out of depression and started a period of growth and prosperity that would lift many families and children out of poverty over the next thirty years (Trattner, 1999). As men were sent off to war across the oceans, women were called into the workforce to keep the economy moving. In support of women working in the factories, the Lanham Act of 1943 was passed by the federal government. The Lanham Act provided government funding for on-site child care in factories across the country, in order that women could work without concern for the welfare of their children, or the expenditure associated with paying for child care. When the war was over and men returned to the United States in search of work, 2.7 million women were removed from their positions, and the Lanham Act was repealed (Blau & Abramovitz, 2010).

Postwar America is largely seen as a prosperous time when all Americans rose with the tide of wealth. However, this tide largely ignored the needs of many of the most impoverished in our society. Families and children of color were systematically excluded from many of the benefits that government provided, such as free and appropriate education and federal cash assistance (Trattner, 1999). The Civil Rights era raised awareness and responded to this deprivation.

The Civil Rights and Voter Rights Acts passed into law by a divided Congress brought attention to racial disparities in access to government services (Blau & Abramovitz, 2010; Katz, 1986; Trattner, 1999). Additionally, the expansion of federal social welfare programs to include health insurance (Medicaid) and food security (Food Stamps and Women, Infants, and Children) is credited in part for the decline in child and family poverty for all families, regardless of race, through the 1960s and 1970s (Trattner, 1999).

In 1962, ADC changed names to Aid to Families with Dependent Children (AFDC), in recognition that not just children in these families were receiving benefits under the program (Popple & Leighninger, 2011). Not much substance to the program was altered when the name changed (Katz, 1986; Trattner, 1999). When first implemented in the mid-1930s, most families served by ADC were headed by white widows with young children (Trattner, 1999). By the 1960s, a growing number of AFDC recipients were never-married African American single mothers. This statistic troubled many policy makers, and contributed to the criticisms of the program for decades.

The 1980s and 1990s saw a rapid decline in support for government programs for poor children and families, and a resulting increase in the poverty rate for these populations. Large-scale public sentiment against "welfare dependency" and a push for "personal responsibility" led to the "end of welfare as we know it" and the end of federal entitlements under AFDC (Trattner, 1999). In 1996, the Temporary Assistance for Needy Families (TANF) program replaced the entitlement program of AFDC as part of the Personal Responsibility Work Opportunity Reconciliation Act (PRWORA). Among its requirements, TANF established a time limit to receive federal benefits and created more stringent work requirements in order to qualify for cash benefits (Blau & Abramovitz, 2010).

The poverty rate for children has steadily increased since the turn of the twenty-first century (U.S. Census Bureau, 2012). Unemployment, lack of affordable child care, and inadequate access to quality education continue to be among the biggest problems facing the growing population of families and children in need in the United States today.

At the same time as the government's role in providing a safety net has evolved, so has the role of government intervention in the family. Prior to 1873, parents could expect little or no interference with how they treated their children (Lau, Krase, & Morse, 2008). Child abuse and neglect were outside of the government's purview until 1873, when an early social worker seeking protection for Mary Ellen Wilson, an abused child whom she found in the course of her work, prompted the creation of the first child welfare agency in the world, the New York Society for the Prevention of Cruelty to Children (NYSPCC, 2000). NYSPCC was a private organization that took on the role of investigating and prosecuting child abuse cases in New York City for over seventy-five years. The U.S. government became involved in child protective services in the middle of the twentieth century when medical research confirmed an alarming prevalence of child abuse, and society responded by demanding a coordinated governmental response to protect children (Lau et al., 2008).

Since the 1960s, individual states, with considerable financial support from the federal government, offer child protective services, allowing for the reporting, investigation, and response to allegations of suspected child abuse and neglect (Whitelaw Downs et al., 2009). As discussed in greater detail later in this chapter, child abuse and neglect are correlated with poverty. Children who are abused or who witness the intimidation of partners or domestic abuse are also more at risk.

As explained in chapter 1, there are key socioeconomic issues that often lead to populations experiencing poverty for reasons beyond their control. The following section will discuss key issues related to families and children's at-risk status.

Key Issues

Already disadvantaged by economic insecurity, today's families and children living in poverty are also affected by the following socio-environmental factors that exacerbate family stress.

Poor Outcomes for Children in Poverty

Growing up impoverished greatly impacts children's well-being, affecting them into and throughout their adulthood. Children who live in poverty have worse health (Aligne, Auinger, Byrd, & Weitzman, 2000; Centers for Disease Control and Prevention [CDC], 1995; CDC, 2009), lower educational attainment (Swanson, 2004), more criminal system involvement (Office of Juvenile Justice and Delinquency Prevention [OJJDP], 2008), and end up with less favorable employment prospects than children from more affluent families.

Children's Health

Children born to poor families fare far worse in health-related indicators than children with more family income security. The infant mortality rate for mothers living in poverty is more than 60 percent higher than mothers with family income above the poverty level (CDC, 1995). Mississippi and Louisiana, the states with the highest child poverty rates, have the highest infant mortality rates (U.S. Census Bureau, 2005). Children born into poverty are twice as likely to die before they reach their first birthday than children born into families above the poverty level (CDC, 1995). Making matters worse, poor children are half as likely to have health insurance as compared to non-poor children (U.S. Census Bureau, 2010), though they suffer more health complications.

Childhood Asthma

Childhood asthma is a growing epidemic that affects poor children, often in inner-city environments, more than other children (Aligne et al., 2000). Children living in poverty in inner cities are exposed to respiratory irritants both inside and outside their homes. Bad air quality and indoor pathogens (like cockroach and dust mite feces) in low-quality, low-income housing contribute to the incidence of asthma in these communities (Fleg, 2008). Disproportionate exposure to irritants with inadequate access to affordable medical treatments places inner-city children living in poverty at higher risk for asthma than their counterparts in other areas.

Childhood asthma disproportionately affects black children. However, studies that control for income and physical environment have found that family income and the child's environment play the most significant role in determining racial disparity in asthma prevalence and not race itself (Aligne et al., 2000).

Childhood Obesity and Striving for Healthier Family Food Options

Throughout history, children living in poverty suffered from malnutrition that resulted in low body weight. Even today, we see images of emaciated children in impoverished developing countries in Africa (Domb Sadof, 2010). However, the opposite phenomenon, childhood obesity, is more closely related to childhood poverty in the United States in the twenty-first century. Children living in poverty are more likely to be overweight than children living in economically secure households in this country. Childhood obesity is the result of a combination of poor diet and lack of exercise (CDC, 2009).

Poor families often have limited access to fresh fruits and vegetables. There is a lack of full-service supermarkets in low-income areas. The food stores in these areas often have poor selections of fresh or frozen produce, and charge more for all items. In order to access markets with better selection and prices, families without cars have to pay for transportation in the form of taxi service, or use public transportation that further limits the amount of food that a family can carry comfortably through a transit system. As a result, parents with a limited food budget are often faced with choosing more inexpensive food items that tend to be high in fat and calories, and low in nutritional value (Bolen & Hecht, 2003). These parents are meeting the caloric needs of their children, but their children are not receiving nutritious food.

Poor food options in combination with insufficient physical activity contribute to the growth of childhood obesity in the United States. Poor communities lack adequate access to parks, playgrounds, and organized physical activities due to a lack of funding (Powell, Ambardekar, & Sheehan, 2005). Recent trends in public education find that public schools have reduced time spent on physical activity (Podulka Coe, Pivarnik, Womack, Reeves, & Malina, 2006). The prevalence of childhood obesity is not uniform across the United States. Childhood obesity varies regionally. Children in rural areas are more likely to be overweight or obese than children in cities and urban areas. Additionally, the highest concentrations of childhood obesity are found among the Southern states of the United States, which also happen to have the highest rates of family and child poverty. Children in West Virginia have the highest risk of obesity in the country. More than 20 percent of all children in West Virginia are obese compared to 17 percent of all American children (CDC, 2009).

The medical costs associated with childhood obesity are rising with the incidence of obesity among children. In the past thirty years, childhood obesity has doubled for children ages 2 to 5, tripled for children ages 6 to 11, and quadrupled for adolescents 12 to 19. Overweight and obese children have a higher incidence of medical conditions, including type 2 diabetes and hypertension, conditions more commonly associated with overweight older adults. Obese children are more likely to be hospitalized, diagnosed with a joint disorder, and suffer with a mental health disorder than children of healthy weight. Obesity also complicates other disorders and diseases, like asthma, which poor children are already disproportionately affected by (CDC, 2009).

In an effort to combat obesity, and improve overall health, communities are embracing healthier food options, as exemplified through the astounding growth in farmers' markets across the country. Farmers' markets are community-based marketplaces where local farmers, bakers, and other small-scale food producers can sell their goods. Farmers' markets provide an excellent source of healthy food options (Brown, 2002). Farmers' markets are found in urban, suburban, and rural communities. The number of community farmers' markets in the United States has increased by 263 percent since 2005 (U.S. Department of Agriculture [USDA], 2012c). In order to ensure access of low-income families to this healthy food source, the federal government is partnering with farmers' markets across the country to accept Supplemental Nutrition Assistance Program (SNAP) redemptions (formerly known as Food Stamps) (USDA, 2013c).

Awareness of childhood obesity is increasing, but the problem is still growing. More attention and efforts at the individual, family, and community level need to be aimed at addressing this problem.

Mental Health

Poverty is not just related to poor outcomes in a child's physical condition, but has implications for a child's mental and emotional condition as well. Approximately one in every ten American children suffers from a mental illness that impairs their functioning (Burns et al., 1995; Shaffer et al., 1996). Children with mental health disorders suffer more school interruptions (including suspensions and expulsions) and are less likely to graduate from high school than their counterparts (Kapphahn, Morreale, Rickert, & Walker, 2006). As a result, they enter adulthood underprepared.

Mentally ill children are increasingly medicated with psychotropic medications (Olfson, Marcus, Weissman, & Jensen, 2002). There is growing concern as to the physical and emotional consequences of medicating children. Increased suicidal ideations have been linked to adolescent use of certain anti-depressants, drugs intended to improve a child's mood, not worsen it (National Institute of Mental Health, 2010). Poor children are more likely to be medicated with psychotropic drugs than non-poor children. One of the reasons suspected for this disparity relates to health insurance coverage. Poor children are less likely to have access to behavioral health coverage that would pay for psychotherapeutic treatment, so medication may be the more accessible and cheaper option to treat mental illness in children (Wilson, 2009).

Children and adults living in poverty are at increased risk for mental health disorders. More than one-fifth of poor children are diagnosed with a mental health disorder, twice as likely as other children (Howell, 2004). Furthermore, poor children with mental health issues are disadvantaged due to inferior access to appropriate services, including mental health programs (Chow, Jaffee, & Snowden, 2003). Additionally, poor children often lack transportation appropriate to access services outside their communities (Pumariega, Glover, Holzer, & Nguyen, 1998).

Researchers and policy makers are puzzled by the conundrum, does poverty cause mental illness or does mental illness cause poverty? Research does not provide a conclusive answer. There is also concern that poor children may be unjustly labeled as "mentally ill" because of professional judgment based on their family's situation (Wilson, 2009). Because of the many unresolved questions, efforts to address the problem should be targeted at antipoverty initiatives, as well as improved access and quality of mental health services for low-income communities.

Education

Access to quality education and educational attainment are important to prevent and respond to poverty. Parental education and poverty are closely linked. The more educated the parent, the less likely their child will live in poverty (National Center for Children in Poverty [NCCP], 2007). Poor children do worse in school than non-poor children (Dahl & Lochner, 2005). Children living in poverty are more likely to drop out of school before earning a high school diploma (Kaufman & Chapman, 2004). They are also less likely to attend college (Advisory Committee on Student Financial Assistance [ACSFA], 2010), and those that do are less likely to complete college (ACSFA, 2010) than their economically secure counterparts. All of these statistics further increase the likelihood of children of poor parents continuing the cycle of poverty, since educational attainment is linked to future income (De Gregorio & Lee, 2003).

Additionally, children's educational attainment is closely linked to parental participation in their schooling. Studies consistently show that increased parental involvement in schooling leads to better grades for children and more advanced levels of attainment. Research also finds that parents with low income are less likely to be involved in their children's schooling. Parents with low income may feel they have less to contribute to their child's schooling because they are not likely to be highly educated. Purposefully or not, schools and teachers may be less likely to encourage low-income parents to be more involved in their child's education. Whatever the reason for disparities in parental involvement, efforts are being made to increase such involvement in school districts across the country (Lee & Bowen, 2006).

Children in impoverished communities also suffer disadvantages of substandard school systems and educational services. Per pupil expenditures in low-income communities are substantially lower than in wealthy communities. Therefore, children in poor communities are more likely to receive lower quality educational opportunities (Carey, 2002; Luebchow, 2009). Inferior school systems, coupled with familial stress due to income insecurity, may contribute to decreased educational attainment for poor children.

Children of color are disproportionately disadvantaged by inferior schools. In 1954 the U.S. Supreme Court decision in *Brown v. Board of Education* achieved the doctrine of equal educational opportunity for all, yet it has arguably not been achieved. Generations of African Americans educated after the Brown decision have still experienced inferior education throughout public education systems across the country (Collins, 2009).

In response to the Brown decision that required public schools to integrate by race, white policy makers in segregated school districts took measures to delay or defy school integration mandates. A number of southern counties actually *closed* their public school systems for years, instead of allowing African American children to be educated alongside white children. Prince Edward County in Virginia, one of the school system defendants in the *Brown v. Board of Education* case, shuttered its public schools for five years. White families that remained in Prince Edward County sent their children to all-white private and parochial schools. Many of these schools received state and local government financial support. African American families with the financial ability or family support moved north, or sent their children to live in areas where they could be educated. Poor families, especially those of color who could not afford these options, tried to educate their children at home. Thousands of already marginalized poor children of color were further disenfranchised through the denial of their right to a free and appropriate public education due to the color of their skin (Payseur & Raja, 2009).

Although it is illegal in the United States to segregate schools by race, the reality is that school systems today are far from racially integrated (Patterson, 2010). Almost 40 percent of African American and Latino children attend schools that are almost entirely African American or Latino. Statistically, schoolchildren of color are more segregated from white schoolchildren than they were in the 1960s (Orfield & Yun, 1999). Even charter schools, which received a lot of recent attention and praise by educational systems reformists, are highly segregated by race. In fact, research suggests that many charter schools are more racially segregated than the public schools in the communities they serve (Frankenberg, Siegel-Hawley, & Wang, 2010).

Racial segregation in schools is largely due to residential segregation patterns. Schools are segregated by race because the residential communities they serve are racially segregated (Patterson, 2010). Much of this segregation is due to economics; areas that are more affluent have higher concentrations of white people. However, affluent areas also have better public school systems. In 2009, for example, West-chester County, New York, entered an agreement wherein it must make strides to desegregate communities through financially supporting the creation of affordable housing units in affluent communities within better school districts. Westchester County entered into this settlement agreement to avoid litigation that accused the county of using federal funding targeted for affordable housing in a manner that furthered residential segregation, contrary to the mandate of receiving the funding (Roberts, 2009).

Private foundations have dedicated substantial resources to improve educational opportunities for children. For example, the Bill and Melinda Gates Foundation funds programs that aim to improve access to early childhood education, developmental education, prepare students for post-secondary study, and prepare effective teachers. Since 2000 they have funded over $4 billion in their educational initiatives. They target these funds to communities, schools, and children who are economically disadvantaged (Bill and Melinda Gates Foundation, 2009).

The educational differences between poor and non-poor are numerous and stark. Although policy and programs are already targeted toward mitigating these differences, the problems still exist at record levels. New and innovative efforts are needed to address these long-standing issues.

Criminal Activity

Children who grow up in poverty are more likely to be involved in criminal activity than other children. However, poverty itself is not necessarily the cause. Research has found that family disruption and family structure have a stronger effect on criminal behavior than family income. Children who experience family disruption in the form of parental separation and divorce are at increased likelihood of criminal involvement. Children living in families headed by single parents are also more likely to be involved in criminal activity than children in families headed by two parents. Educational failure, including dropping out of high school and academic difficulties, is linked to increased likelihood of juvenile criminal behavior as well (OJJDP, 2008).

Intimate Partner Violence/Domestic Violence

Intimate partner violence (IPV) or domestic violence (DV) refers to the "willful intimidation, physical assault, battery, sexual assault, and/or other abusive behavior perpetrated by an intimate partner against another" (National Coalition Against Domestic Violence [NCADV], 2010, para. 1). IPV affects people in every community across the United States, regardless of age, gender, sexual orientation, race, religion, and income (Domestic Violence Resource Center, 2010). Risk factors for IPV perpetration and victimization include drug and alcohol use, childhood victimization, witnessing violence in the home as a child, and increased stress, often due to financial instability (CDC, 2012).

Poverty and domestic violence are deeply interwoven issues. Poor families are at increased risk of experiencing domestic violence (Davies, n.d.). Research involving women receiving public assistance has found reported incidences of domestic violence as high as 50 percent (Tolman & Raphael, 2000). Poverty also creates additional barriers to finding safety from domestic violence. Victims of domestic violence are often financially dependent on their violent partner, and thus attempting to separate from a violent relationship is complicated. Accessing the legal system to challenge abusers is both financially and structurally difficult. Legal mechanisms such as separation and divorce are prohibitively expensive for poor families. Seeking court intervention means physically appearing at court, which can be difficult due to child care responsibilities, unforgiving work situations, or controlling partners (Davies, n.d.).

Although IPV affects both men and women, 85 percent of cases involve violence against women. More than 1.3 million women are victimized by their partners every year. More than half of these assaults go unreported to the authorities (Domestic Violence Resource Center, 2010).

Grassroots efforts born out of the women's rights movement of the 1970s created a network of privately run services for victims of IPV. Through the efforts of the IPV advocates across the country, the past twenty years have seen a growth in targeted services to this population. Shelters, crisis hotlines, and specialized legal services programs are among the most common IPV services available (Jackson, 2007).

On a single day in September 2009, over 65,000 victims of intimate partner violence were provided services, as measured by the National Census of Domestic Violence Services of the National Network to End Domestic Violence [NNEDV] (2009). More than 30,000 victims found refuge in a domestic violence shelter. An additional 30,000 or more adults and children benefited from individual counseling, support groups, and legal assistance, provided through an extensive network of intimate partner violence organizations across the country. Nearly 10,000 additional victims were turned away from services in this single day, due to lack of funding (NNEDV, 2009).

Child Abuse and Neglect

Child abuse and neglect is defined as the act or omission of a parent or other person legally responsible for a child that results in harm to a child, or contributes to the risk of such harm to a child (Lau et al., 2008). More than 3 million reports of suspected child abuse and neglect are made in the United States per year (U.S. Department of Health and Human Services, 2007). Poverty is a risk factor for child maltreatment (Garbarino & Collins, 1999; Sedlak & Broadhurst, 1996). Research on the incidence and prevalence of child abuse and neglect consistently find children living in poverty are at the highest risk for most forms of maltreatment (Garbarino & Collins, 1999).

Currently, there is much attention in child welfare policy to the overrepresentation of African American children in the child protection system (Child Welfare Information Gateway, 2010). In fact, African American children are disproportionately *overrepresented* in all parts of the child welfare system. This is known as "disproportionate minority representation," or DMR. African American children make up 25 percent of reports made to Child Protective Services (U.S. Department of Health and Human Services, 2004); 26 percent of children placed in foster care (Hill, 2007); and almost 30 percent of children in foster care at a given time (Hill, 2006). Yet, African American children only make up 15 percent of the U.S. child population. The federal and state governments are addressing the disproportionate representation of minority children in the child protection system through research, policy, and training efforts (Center for Juvenile Justice Reform & Chapin Hall Center for Children, 2009; Roberts, 2002).

African American children are more likely to be abused or neglected than children of most other races, but research has found that race alone does not explain the difference. The National Incidence Survey (NIS) found that the risk of child maltreatment does not differ by race, when socioeconomic factors were controlled for (Ards, Chung, & Myers, 1998). Data from NIS (NIS-4), however, did find that the maltreatment rate was higher for African American children than for white children in certain maltreatment categories even when socioeconomic factors were controlled for. Among families with low socioeconomic status, differences in maltreatment by race were not significant. However, children from African American families who were not associated with low socioeconomic status were two times more likely than their white counterparts to be at risk of physical abuse (Sedlak, McPherson, & Das, 2010).

Immediate injuries resulting from child abuse and neglect, such as cuts and bruises, are obvious, but the long-term consequences are more difficult to observe and measure. Child abuse and neglect lead to physical health, mental health, behavioral, and societal consequences for victims in their childhood and adulthood. Abused and neglected children may suffer from impaired brain development and general poor physical health as a result of maltreatment (Dallam, 2001; U.S. Department of Health and Human Services, 2007). Children who are the victims of child abuse or neglect are more likely to have mental or emotional health problems as well as cognitive and social difficulties (Child Welfare Information Gateway, 2010).

A history of child abuse victimization increases a child's likelihood of delinquent behavior (Smith & Thornberry, 1995). Such a history also increases a child's likelihood of adult criminal behavior by 28 percent and violent crime involvement by 30 percent (Maxfield & Widom, 1996). Additionally, maltreated children are more likely to become abusers themselves (Wang & Holton, 2007). All of these issues related to child abuse victimization contribute to the increased likelihood that such children will grow up to be adults living in poverty.

Preventive Services

Also part of the child protective system are state-sponsored preventive service programs that aim to prevent child maltreatment and to reduce the risk of foster care placement. Preventive programs are often found in low-income communities that experience increased reporting rates of child abuse and neglect. Families at risk for child abuse or neglect can receive family support services or counseling in an effort to prevent the occurrence or reoccurrence of child abuse and neglect (Whitelaw Downs et al., 2009). In many states, preventive services are mandated and require that the parent(s) and children engage with a preventive worker. Families and children who engage in preventive services often have better outcomes than those who do not as they are better equipped to handle life's stressors.

Foster Care

When children are deemed unsafe, child protective services petition Family Court to remove children from their homes and place them in substitute care, also known as foster care (Whitelaw Downs et al., 2009). In 2008, there were over 450,000 children living in foster care in the United States (U.S. Department of Health and Human Services, 2009). The majority of children in out-of-home care are placed with foster families. Older children and those with special medical or mental health needs are often placed in institutions referred to as residential treatment facilities or centers (Whitelaw Downs et al., 2009).

In recent years, attention has been paid to the experiences of older children and young adults who exit the foster care system into independence. This process is called "aging out." Over 20,000 young adults age out of foster care in the United States each year. Recent studies of young adults who have aged out of foster care have found that they are at high risk of poverty, are more likely to be homeless, have lower educational attainment, and less income security than other young adults. The federal and state governments are responding by improving programs designed to prepare these youths for independent living, as well as providing more income and educational support prior to and shortly after discharge from foster care (Gardner, 2008).

Lead Poisoning

Lead poisoning is a major environmental health problem in the United States affecting approximately half a million children ages 1–5. It occurs when lead enters the body, usually through ingestion or respiration (CDC, 2013). Prior to 1978, before the federal government banned consumer use of lead in household and industrial paints, children were frequently at risk of exposure. Even now, children can be exposed to lead if they spend time in pre-1978 built structures (CDC, 2013; U.S. Environmental Protection Agency [EPA], 2013). The risks of lead poisoning include exposure to lead from paint, including lead-contaminated dust that may be on surfaces from chipped paint on ceilings, walls, and windows (CDC, 2013; EPA, 2013). Children are more likely to ingest dust because they put their hands and other objects in their mouth more often than adults. Lead is more dangerous to children than adults as it interferes with brain and nervous system functioning and can lead to growth impairment, cognitive impairment, hearing problems, neurological disorders, and behavioral problems (CDC, 2013).

Lead poisoning disproportionately affects families and children living in poverty. There are also ethnic and racial differences in the incidence of lead poisoning. Poor children, especially children of color, are at greatest risk of lead exposure due to their increased likelihood of living in substandard and older housing (CDC, 2013). Compared to non-Hispanic white children, African American children are more than twice as likely, and Mexican American children are 75 percent more likely, to be exposed to dangerous levels of lead (CDC, 2005). Given the number of children affected by lead poisoning throughout the United States, lead testing has become part of routine pediatric examinations so that lead exposure can be addressed before becoming problematic (CDC, 2013).

More recently, attention has been paid to the use of lead paint in toys and jewelry, usually manufactured overseas in countries like China. Children playing with those toys or wearing that jewelry were found to have elevated lead levels. Although much attention has been paid to recalls of lead-painted toys, most dangerous lead exposure occurs in and around children's homes (CDC, 2013).

Government Policies and Programs

Over the past century, federal, state, and local governments have responded to the needs of families and children in poverty by creating programs and services. These programs provide needs-based and universal cash and in-kind assistance to millions of families and children every year.

Cash Assistance

Cash assistance is available to many low-income families with children in the United States. Temporary Assistance to Needy Families (TANF), public assistance, and safety net assistance all refer to cash benefit programs administered by state and local governments, and supported by a federal block grant program. In order to be eligible for cash assistance, a family must make less than the income threshold for their family size in their state, and participate in mandatory work programs. States have the authority to determine the qualifications and requirements of their programs, including exemptions from work requirements for caretakers of young children (Blau & Abramovitz, 2009).

The TANF income threshold varies greatly across states, from just over $3,000 per year in Alabama to almost $20,000 per year in Hawaii, for a single parent-headed household of three. Benefit levels differ across states as well, from $204 per month in Arkansas to over $700 per month in California for a single parent-headed family of three (NCCP, 2010b). Federal TANF funds are used to reimburse states for a portion of their expenditures to families receiving cash assistance for the first sixty months. After that, states can continue to provide cash assistance to families; however, with few exceptions, states will not receive federal reimbursement (Blau & Abramovitz, 2010).

Food and Nutrition Programs

Federal programs designed to address child and family food insecurity have greatly reduced the percentage of hungry children in the United States (Blau & Abramovitz, 2010). Food Stamps, renamed Supplemental Nutrition Assistance Program (SNAP) in October 2008, was initially started as an experimental program to address Depression-era hunger while supporting the commodity-distributing systems of the Midwest. Food stamps were generally purchased by families and then traded for certain foods, but were only available in specific areas. The program grew into the national food assistance program through the Food Stamps Act of

1964 (USDA, 2013d). The number of SNAP recipients has dramatically increased since the start of the recession in 2008. A record number of recipients (approximately 44 million) were receiving SNAP benefits throughout the United States in 2011, more than a 70 percent increase in recipients since May 2007 (Congressional Budget Office [CBO], 2012).

SNAP is administered by the U.S. Department of Agriculture (USDA) and is fully funded by the federal government. As a result, the benefit calculations are almost the same across the country. Current recipients receive an electronic benefit card, similar to a debit card that allows them to use credits to purchase food items (excluding alcohol, pet food, and prepared foods) (CBO, 2012). In 2013, a family of three earning less than $2,069 per month, which is 130 percent of the poverty level, may be eligible for SNAP depending on the household's income and resources. The income limits and benefit levels are higher in Alaska and Hawaii, and some people must adhere to work requirements (USDA, 2013c).

The Special Supplemental Nutrition Program for Women, Infants, and Children (WIC) was established nationally in 1972. WIC is designed to target income-eligible (household income at or below 185 percent of the poverty level) pregnant women and children up to five years of age, to guarantee access to nutritional support at a critical juncture in their lives (Colman et al., 2012). WIC provides for specific quantities of particular foods to be redeemed, as opposed to SNAP, which provides a dollar amount to spend on an electronic benefit card. WIC participants are also given health and nutritional information, and referrals to related services. WIC is also federally administered through the United States Department of Agriculture (USDA, 2012b).

Analysis of the WIC program has found that women in the program have lower levels of fetal mortality and fewer premature births than similar women who did not participate in the WIC program (Colman et al., 2012). The federal Government Accountability Office (GAO) estimates that every dollar spent on WIC saves more than three dollars by avoiding costly medical conditions (GAO, 1992). In order to be eligible, the household income cannot be more than 185 percent of the federal poverty threshold, or $42,643 for a family of four (higher in Alaska and Hawaii) (USDA, 2012b).

The National School Lunch Program is comprised of several federally assisted meal programs, which provide breakfast, lunch, and even snacks to millions of children every year at state and local public and private organizations (USDA, 2012a; n.d.). Gunderson (2013) explains that school lunch programs began as a private agency initiative during the later part of the nineteenth century, when it was recognized that hunger interfered with a child's ability to learn and function in the school environment. Initiatives began with local and state government support and later, through the Depression era and World War II, the federal government began subsidizing state and local school meal programs. In 1946 the federal government established the National School Lunch Act, providing states with reimbursements for expenditures for school lunch programs (Gunderson, 2013). Presently, children with household income below 130 percent of the poverty level are eligible for free meals through the school meals program. Children with household income between 130 and 185 percent of the poverty level are eligible for reduced-cost meals. Children from households whose income exceeds the income limits can still purchase the meal for a reasonable cost due to governmental subsidies (USDA, 2012a).

The 1960s saw an expansion of the federal school meals program to include a pilot breakfast program. The 1970s brought an extension of school meals through the summer months. More recently, snack programs were added to the list of programs funded by the federal government (Gunderson, 2013).

School meal programs are currently under criticism for not providing healthy food options for children, thus contributing to problems like childhood obesity. Schools often purchase highly processed, high-fat, high-calorie, inexpensive food options that are easier to prepare, and arguably easier to get picky kids to eat (Ralston, Newman, Clauson, Guthrie, & Buzby, 2008). Recently, First Lady Michelle Obama and television food personalities such as Emeril Lagasse, Rachael Ray, and Jamie Oliver have brought attention to these issues, which has helped prompt changes to local, state, and federal legislation. Subsequently, federal and state governments are addressing concerns with the quality of school food programs through policy. These policy initiatives have increased awareness of healthier food options, improved access to high-quality, low-cost food, as well as emphasized the importance of physical activity.

In 2010 the federal government passed into law the Healthy, Hunger-Free Kids Act. This reauthorization of the Child Nutrition Act that funds school meal programs, and other initiatives, is aimed at reducing childhood obesity. The act increased per meal reimbursement rates so that schools can afford to buy healthier foods and provides additional financing for schools that choose healthier options on their menu. This new law authorizes oversight by a regulatory body to monitor the quality of food offered in school meals, with the purpose of decreasing the fat and sugar content of food provided to schoolchildren. Thirty-three states have established programs to directly address childhood obesity through revitalizing their school nutrition programs or increasing the opportunity for children to be physically active during the school day (USDA, 2013a).

Health Insurance and Medical Care

Families and children living in poverty are at increased risk for medical and mental health conditions (as outlined above). Many of these families are uninsured or underinsured through employer-provided health insurance coverage. Eleven percent of all children, and over 18 percent of children from families with low income, are uninsured (U.S. Census Bureau, 2010). Children from low-income families are often eligible for state-administered, federally and state-funded Medicaid programs, or State Child Health Insurance Programs (SCHIP).

Medicaid was established as a federal program in 1965 as an amendment to the Social Security Act. Medicaid covers hospital stays, primary care, and specialist visits. Federal law requires states to provide dental coverage for individuals under twenty-one years of age, but providing such coverage for other adults is optional. Vision care coverage is also optional; individual states can determine if they want to provide vision care coverage, how much, and to whom. Medicaid is the largest provider of mental health services coverage for low-income people (U.S. Department of Health and Human Services, Centers for Medicare and Medicaid Services [DHHS CMS], 2010).

Medicaid is available to children of families whose income falls below a state-set threshold, as well as to low-income adults and the disabled (DHHS CMS, 2010). Over 31 million children were served by Medicaid in 2010 (Kaiser Family Foundation, 2012). More than half of all Medicaid enrollees in the United States are children, yet less than 20 percent of Medicaid expenditures are for services to children (DHHS CMS, Statistical Enrollment Data System [SEDS], 2009). State Child Health Insurance Programs (SCHIPs) are state-administered, federally supported health coverage designed to ensure that all American children have access to appropriate medical care through the provision of government-subsidized health insurance. Recognizing the importance of preventive care and addressing child health concerns early as to prevent long-term consequences, states began to develop their own child health insurance programs (Blau & Abramovitz, 2010). Close to 8 million children are covered by SCHIP programs across the country (Kaiser Family Foundation, 2013).

These programs are not limited to low-income children, but are aimed at filling the gap in insurance coverage for children of all incomes (Blau & Abramovitz, 2010). The poorest children qualify for free coverage. As family income increases, families are required to contribute for the coverage, but the government subsidizes the coverage to make it affordable (DHHS CMS, 2010). In an effort to encourage state development of such programs, the federal government began to subsidize SCHIP programs in 1997, passing legislation under the sponsorship of the late Senator Edward Kennedy of Massachusetts.

Growth in Medicaid and SCHIP expanded the access of poor children to medical care in the late 1990s and early 2000s. However, since 2003, access to medical care for children in low-income families decreased, especially for children with the lowest family income. This change is most likely explained by a reduction in employer-sponsored health coverage (Cunningham & Felland, 2008).

Health reform legislation, entitled the Affordable Care Act, was passed by Congress in March 2010 and signed into law by President Barack Obama on March 23, 2010. This comprehensive legislation seeks to reduce rising health care costs, hold insurance companies accountable, insulate individuals from insurmountable financial hardship due to illness, increase coverage, and ultimately enhance the quality of care for all Americans. Among the provisions relevant to poor families and children, the Affordable Care Act expands eligibility of Medicaid to families with income higher than the current eligibility thresholds. The act also provides for young adults to continue receiving benefits under their parents' insurance coverage until they turn twenty-six. To improve child health outcomes, the act also provides increased funding for home visiting programs, targeting at improving outcomes for low-income families with young children (U.S. Department of Health and Human Services, 2010).

Family Medical Leave Act (FMLA)

Some western European nations provide paid leave to mothers and fathers for months to years after a child's birth (Austrian Institute for Family Studies, n.d.). Alternately, the United States Family Medical Leave Act (FMLA) of 1993 provides job security for up to twelve weeks for workers in certain positions. FMLA does not provide *paid* leave. FMLA simply requires certain employers to guarantee a worker their job back if they take qualified leave from employment to care for a new child, or ill family member (U.S. Department of Labor, 2009). Some states have policies requiring job security for an additional time for such unpaid leave. California and New Jersey are two of the largest states that guarantee paid leave (National Conference of State Legislatures, 2008). Notably, poor families are disproportionately disadvantaged by the lack of paid family leave in most of the country.

Tax Credits for Low-Income Families

Government programs that aim to assist poor families and children living in poverty come in various forms. Financial relief in the form of tax credits are a popular option for policy makers who want to encourage work among the poor, but understand that families facing poverty need more economic assistance. Tax credits provide a reduction in taxes for families who work on-the-books. The Earned Income Tax Credit (EITC), a federal program, lifts millions of children out of poverty every year. EITC, originally enacted in 1975, supplements the wages of low-income workers. In the 2012 tax year, for example, depending on marital status and the number of dependent children, working families that have annual incomes below $36,900 to $50,300 may be eligible for this benefit. Families with two parents have a higher income limit. Families receive a bigger credit for having a second or a third child, but no larger credit for having more than three children. Households without children can qualify for the EITC, but will receive a substantially lower credit. Given the benefits of this program, a number of states and the District of Columbia have instituted similar programs for state and local taxes (Center on Budget and Policy Priorities, 2013).

A tax credit that assists families and children of all income groups is the Child and Dependent Care Credit. This credit is a proportion of the amount of money spent on child care in calculation with the family's adjusted gross income. Unfortunately, families with a larger income get a larger credit. In order to qualify for this credit, the child care provider's identifying information has to be reported on the tax return (National Center for Children in Poverty, 2010a).

Child Support Enforcement

As part of the Personal Responsibility Work Opportunity Reconciliation Act (PRWORA), a federal child support enforcement program was created. The federal government provides funding to states to assist families in collecting child support from absent parents through the Office of Child Support Enforcement (OCSE). Single parents of all incomes are eligible to receive OCSE services. However, participation in OCSE is mandatory for low-income, single-parent families seeking assistance through many government benefit programs, including TANF. OCSE provides assistance in locating non-custodial parents, establishing paternity, establishing and enforcing child support orders, and collecting child support. Child support payments from non-custodial parents of children receiving cash assistance (TANF) are submitted to the government to offset government cash expenditures to their children (National Center for Children in Poverty, 2010c).

Over the years OCSE has been credited with removing many children from the Temporary Assistance for Needy Families program or federal foster care maintenance payments (under Title IV-E) rolls by holding non-custodial parents accountable. However, due to the economic downturn, assistance cases involving families receiving cash assistance increased by 0.9 percent since 2009 and by 7.3 percent since 2008. Still, notably, in 2010, the program collected $26.6 billion for 17.5 million children in its caseload, which helps to provide financial support to families (U.S. Department of Health and Human Services [US DHHS], OCSE, 2013).

Child Care

For many families with parents who work outside the home, child care is a necessity, but can create additional stress. Working families need child care in order to guarantee the safety of young children, but the service can be prohibitively expensive and difficult to secure. This situation is dire for low-income families, for whom child care can absorb more than one-third of their income. Federal, state, and local governments sponsor some subsidized child care programs, but many more are needed to meet the demand for these services (Blau & Abramovitz, 2010).

Through the Child Care and Development Block Grant (CCDBG), TANF, and the Social Services Block Grant (SSBG), the federal government provides limited programs to subsidize child care for children of low-income families. In 2007, approximately 2.7 million children received child care assistance from these programs. However, many more children, in high-demand areas, remain on waiting lists awaiting the availability of services (Children's Defense Fund, 2008).

The recession that began in 2008 has resulted in states cutting back on ancillary services, including subsidized child care. These cuts have made it more difficult for low-income families to remain working during these tough economic times (Johnson, 2010).

Head Start

The government has long acknowledged that education is necessary to prevent poverty. In the 1960s, the federal government, under President Lyndon B. Johnson, began Project Head Start. Head Start is an initiative to provide early childhood learning opportunities for children from low-income families. This federally subsidized, locally run program has served more than 27 million children since 1965, with over 900,000 children being served in 2009 alone. Families with income below the poverty level are eligible for Head Start. Poor families with income above the poverty threshold may be eligible for Head Start, depending on the policy of their local program (U.S. Department of Health and Human Services, Office of Head Start [OHS], 2010).

Head Start programs are designed to improve the socio-emotional and cognitive functioning of young children living in poverty and to better prepare them for their future educational pursuits. Head Start provides educational, health, nutritional, social, and other services to low-income children and their families. Most programs require children to be at least three years of age, but not yet eligible for kindergarten. Some programs, called Early Head Start, serve children younger than three years old (OHS, 2010).

Head Start has been criticized for not delivering the benefits promised from its inception in 1965. Research shows that Head Start participation has large beneficial impacts on children's cognitive and socio-emotional functioning in the short term, but differences between Head Start children and other children mostly disappear in the early years of elementary school (Haskins & Sawhill, 2003). Other studies have found Head Start participants are more likely to graduate from high school and less likely to repeat grade levels than non-participants (Barnett, 2002).

Early Intervention

Early intervention services were designed to enhance the development of disabled infants and toddlers, with the aim of reducing the need for long-term support services. Early intervention refers to a series of services targeted to children under the age of three who are developmentally delayed. These services include physical, occupational, and speech therapies, as well as special instruction for the child and caretaker (National Dissemination Center for Children with Disabilities [NICHNY], 2010).

Early intervention programs are locally run, usually by private entities, however they are funded by federal and state government sources. When children reach age three, if they still exhibit developmental delays, they may continue to receive services through state and locally funded preschool special education services (NICHNY, 2010). Children ages 5 to 21 with developmental delays receive services through the Committee on Special Education (CSE), which is provided by local school districts. Services are universally available to children regardless of family income. However, poor children are disproportionately recipients of early intervention services (Hebbeler, Spiker, Mallik, Scarborough, & Simeonessen, 2004).

Public Education

States are responsible for running public education systems. The federal government provides assistance to states through supplemental financial support (U.S. Department of Education, 2010a). As a result, most school systems are largely financed by local and state taxes. Local communities that wish to spend more money on their educational systems can levy taxes that increase the school budget. Communities with a high concentration of low-income families are unable to levy such a tax, because their residents cannot afford the expense. As a result, per pupil expenditures in affluent communities are dramatically higher than such spending in poor communities (Downs & Figlio, 1997).

State governments have made efforts over the years to address disparities in educational spending across school districts. In 1948, New York State created the Boards of Cooperative Educational Services (BOCES) to provide the mechanism for school districts to share the costs of education-related services. The BOCES network is made up of all school districts *not* located in the major five cities of the state: New York City, Rochester, Yonkers, Buffalo, and Syracuse. BOCES programs most often include career and technical education programs, and English as a second language instruction. Over $2.5 billion of state tax money is spent on BOCES programs, reducing the demand on local school districts to shoulder the costs. By sharing the cost of related services, school districts save money while providing more services to children and families (BOCES, 2010). However, disparities continue to exist in New York, and other states.

Recognition of these disparities resulted in court action in states, such as New York and New Jersey. In the *Robinson v. Cahill* court decision in 1973, the New Jersey Supreme Court found that the financing structure for New Jersey's public schools relied too heavily on property taxes, discriminated against low-income school districts, and resulted in educational disparities. After the state failed to address these inequities, the *Abbott v. Burke* case was filed in 1981, again alleging discrimination against low-income, mainly urban, school districts (*Abbott v. Burke*, 1985). Though the state has implemented policy changes and increased spending in a variety of troubled school districts, a series of court decisions continues to find New Jersey's financing structure discriminatory, and New Jersey continually fails to meet the educational needs of low-income youth (Education Law Center, 2010).

New York State was sued by the Campaign for Fiscal Equity (CFE) for similar problems. In 1993, a group of concerned parents from New York City sued New York State, alleging that New York City public schools did not get a fair share of state expenditures for education. After thirteen years of litigation, New York's highest court found that all children in the state have a right to a sound basic education through high school, and that the children of New York City were not getting their fair share of state education dollars. The New York State legislature has since passed a law codifying the court's decision. The parents of CFE continue to advocate with policy makers and educators to guarantee equality in educational opportunities (CFE, 2010).

Federal legislative efforts have been made to address educational inequities. The 2001 reauthorization of the Elementary and Secondary Education Act of 1965 is more commonly known as the No Child Left Behind Act (NCLB). This act, signed into law by President George W. Bush, aims to hold schools accountable for adequately preparing children academically and provide parents with flexibility in school choice. NCLB embodies a response to the realities that many public schools fail to prepare children for further educational and employment pursuits, and that parents without the financial means to move to a better school district or pay for private education have no choice but to send their children to low-performing schools (U.S. Department of Education, 2010a). Criticisms of NCLB are that it abandons public schools and focuses on privatizing education, as well as displeasure with the emphasis on standardized testing to assess school performance (Meier & Wood, 2004).

In response to the criticisms of NCLB, the federal Department of Education under the Obama administration recently financed the $4 billion "Race to the Top" program. States compete for grants to finance ambitious yet achievable plans for implementing coherent, compelling, and comprehensive education reform. States with the best plans for improving achievement in their lowest-performing school districts, that adopt standards and assessment processes to best prepare students for higher education and employment, plan for recruiting and training the best new teachers, and build data systems that can appropriately evaluate their progress will be rewarded with the financial support of the federal government (U.S. Department of Education, 2010b).

In addition to "Race to the Top," recent local, state, and federal policy efforts have targeted school districts in low-income areas to improve their services to give poor children a better chance of escaping poverty. The 21st Century Community Learning Center initiative is funded through the U.S. Department of Education. Grants through this program support academic enrichment opportunities for children and their families during non-school hours in community-based organizations and schools. Since 2003, more than $4 billion has gone into this program in all fifty states (U.S. Department of Education, 2010c).

Social Justice

Income inequality is a growing problem in the United States. The median income of the richest fifth of American households is fifteen times more than the median income of the poorest fifth (U.S. Census Bureau, 2010). This income gap is growing rapidly. From 2002 to 2007, the average income of the richest 1 percent of American households grew more than ten times as fast as the bottom 90 percent of American households (Center on Budget and Policy Priorities, 2009).

While struggling with financial challenges, families and children living in poverty also face structural and personal discrimination. Families living in poverty tend to reside in areas with less access to services and lower quality of available services than families with more income. When services are available, poor families often cannot afford to purchase high-quality services (Dyer, 2007). These structural hindrances discriminate against low-income families by providing them no choice but to accept low-quality or no services.

The largest concentrations of poor people reside in urban areas where access to public transportation is central. In recent years, substantial increases in the cost of public transportation have drastically impacted the finances of low-income families in these areas (Glaeser, Kahn, & Rappaport, 2008). For families in rural areas, transportation is also a constant challenge. Automobiles are costly. The initial cost of purchasing a vehicle is compounded by insurance payments, high gasoline prices, and maintenance costs. However, without access to automobiles in most of these areas, families are isolated and unable to work at all (Pruitt, 2007).

Structural discrimination that hinders the success of poor children is most obvious in the public education system. State and federal laws ensure that all children in the United States have access to free and appropriate education. Yet the financing and delivery systems of the public education system disadvantage poor children, especially children of color.

Living in poverty puts children at higher risk for social, emotional, and economic uncertainty. As a society, there needs to be a proactive response to poverty in order to secure a healthy and safe future for children and families. Whether through professional service, community activism, or court or legislative advocacy, there are many ways for social workers and other human services personnel to participate in efforts to equalize opportunities for families and children living in poverty.

Interventions

Social work and related human services have developed a myriad of programs and services at the micro, mezzo, and macro levels of practice to address poverty among families and children.

Micro Interventions

Micro-level interventions involve practice with individuals and families (Kirst-Ashman & Hull, 2009). Psychotherapy in the form of individual, couples, and family counseling is one way to assist families and children living in poverty to process their emotional and behavioral responses to stress. Psychotherapy is not just appropriate for people with mental disorders, but can be helpful for anyone who could benefit from support during a difficult period in their lives (Whitelaw Downs et al., 2009).

Social service agencies may provide support groups for families and children living in poverty or facing related issues. Support groups have numerous purposes. Support groups provide individuals facing similar situations the opportunity to share valuable information with each other. Participants learn from each other about resources and the degree to which they find them helpful. Additionally, group members share coping mechanisms. Support group participants often appreciate knowing that they are not alone in facing a particular problem, and that others have successfully addressed similar issues. Support groups are used widely in mental health, domestic violence, and child protective services (Whitelaw Downs et al., 2009).

Preventive programs are aimed at serving at-risk individuals and families before harmful conditions take place. Prevention-oriented programs in community-based social service agencies are designed to avert such conditions as teenage pregnancy, child maltreatment, foster care placement, and substance abuse. These programs may use a variety of methods of service, including casework, support groups, and psycho-educational programs (Whitelaw Downs et al., 2009).

Key to the success of any micro-level intervention is cultural awareness on the part of the service provider. The United States has a diverse population, and service providers may not be aware of cultural differences between themselves and their clients. Failure to appreciate these cultural differences can lead to distrust of social services in particular communities. Improving cultural competency in social work practice has been a goal of the National Association of Social Workers (NASW). The result of their efforts is their "Standards of Cultural Competence in Social Work Practice." This document provides guidance for social workers and other human services professionals to understand and educate themselves about the communities they serve so that they can provide appropriate and beneficial services (NASW, 2001).

Mezzo Interventions

Mezzo-level intervention is practice with small groups. These small groups can be made of unrelated individuals or families, among other types of groups, though families are sometimes referred to as a micro-level unit (Kirst-Ashman & Hull, 2009).

Psycho-educational programs are one form of mezzo-level intervention. These programs offer participants helpful information and provide attendees the opportunity to ask questions and relate the information to their own situation. These programs provide information and counseling in one package. Psycho-educational programs can be individual, family, or group-based programs. Research shows that they are particularly useful in helping the families of mentally ill and chronically ill patients understand their disorders and address their own emotional reactions to stressful situations. Psycho-educational programs are particularly useful for parents of children with a mental illness or chronic illness (Parry, 1997).

Family support services can combine psychotherapy, support groups, psycho-educational programs, and other services to holistically serve families and children in poverty (Whitelaw Downs et al., 2009). Family support services are designed to help meet the needs of families as they face life stressors.

Training and education for practitioners and program staff who work with families and children in poverty can improve the provision of services in low-income communities. Training that highlights theories that explain poverty, and particularly debunking theories that suggest poor families are inferior to others, will prepare staff to not just serve, but also empower clients.

Macro Interventions

Macro-level interventions involve social work practice with larger systems. Social work practice with communities and organizations is most often considered macro-level practice (Kirst-Ashman & Hull, 2009).

Community organization involves the coordination of people in a community to address issues or problems that affect the group as a whole. Community organizing can be particularly effective in low-income communities where individual voices are not heard by powerful players, such as local politicians. Organizing the community around concerns such as crime, drug use, inadequate housing, and the need for educational system improvement has been particularly effective across the country.

History has proven that policies at the federal, state, and local levels can greatly impact the incidence of poverty. The combination of Old Age, Survivors, and Disability Insurance and Medicare programs, for instance, led to a two-third reduction in poverty of older adults (Englehardt & Gruber, 2004). Innovative and effective policy efforts aimed at family and child poverty can be just as successful. Large-scale advocacy efforts are needed to effectuate such widespread change.

A particularly exciting macro-level, policy advocacy intervention is the New England Consortium (NEC, 2010). A young regional initiative, largely funded by grants from the Annie E. Casey Foundation and Voices of America's Children, NEC is made up of researchers, policy makers, and social service providers in six states: Connecticut, Maine, Massachusetts, New Hampshire, Rhode Island, and Vermont. The consortium recognizes that regionally, some urban centers have the highest poverty rates among children and families in the country, and these rates are growing. Their goal is to take proactive steps to reverse family and children poverty in the region through coordinated federal, state, and local policy advocacy.

NEC utilizes its partner agencies from various states and communities to band together to advocate with members of Congress for federal policies that support their goals and objectives. They are actively involved in early education and early intervention initiatives, as well as the Healthy, Hunger-Free Children Act of 2010. They were vocal advocates for the health reform legislation of 2010. They are also active on the state policy level, advocating for policy and programs that support their goals.

Concluding Comments

Poverty for families and children is not a new problem in the United States, but it is one that can no longer be ignored. Millions of families and children live in poverty every year, and the consequences go far beyond the simple financial implications. Immediate attention needs to be paid to improving policy, programs, and services for this population, so that future generations do not suffer.

Case Studies
Micro Level: Jack

Jack is a fifteen-year-old African American young man who lives with his single mother and two younger sisters in a rural area with a high concentration of low-income families. Jack's father, though local to the area, is unemployed and does not contribute to the family. Jack has sought part-time employment to help support his mother and sisters, but work is hard to come by in the area and generally reserved for adults.

The students in the public school system in this area repeatedly fail to meet state and national standards upon testing. Jack would like to finish high school and go to community college, or alternatively, he would like to study to become a car mechanic. However, he is faced with the decision whether to stay in school, or seek full-time employment farther away from his home.

Questions

1. What key issues are affecting Jack?

2. What government programs/policies can assist Jack?

3. What are the greatest concerns for Jack?

4. What issues are concerning in the community?

5. How can a social worker assist Jack?

Mezzo Level/Family: Charlene

Charlene is the 26-year-old single mother of 3 children, ages 4, 6, and 10. They live in government-subsidized housing in a large urban area with a high concentration of low-income families. The apartment is adequate for their family size, but in deteriorating condition. Charlene's two older children attend the local public elementary school, and her youngest child just started in a local Head Start program. The family's main source of income is public assistance, and they receive SNAP, and qualify for Medicaid. Now that her youngest child is entering school, Charlene wants to become gainfully employed. She always wanted to be a veterinarian because she loves working with animals, but she dropped out of high school before completing the eleventh grade.

Charlene contacted her DSS worker regarding the work experience program (WEP). Her worker thought this was a great idea and encouraged her to participate in an employment-training group that would enable Charlene to gain marketable skills. Charlene began her work group at a local community-based agency on the following Monday. She role-played with other group members to practice her interviewing skills and learned about job-seeking strategies. The following week, she was placed in an office to gain hands-on experience providing entry-level skills. Charlene continued to participate in the group to discuss her experiences with other members, who were in similar situations. She looked forward to meeting with her peers to talk about her feelings about her new work. After a few meetings, Charlene realized that half of the group members felt as if they were gaining valuable skills through the program, while the other half expressed their frustration that they believed they were working for meager welfare benefits rather than an honest wage.

Questions

1. What key issues are affecting Charlene's family?

2. What government programs/policies can assist this family?

3. What are the greatest concerns for Charlene?

4. What issues are concerning in the community?

5. As the worker assigned to this group, how would you address the members' feelings that they were being taken advantage of by the system?

6. Is it the responsibility of the group worker to make sure that everyone believes that the goal of the WEP assignment is valuable?

Macro Level: Highbridge, Bronx, NY

The Highbridge section of the Bronx, New York, had seen better days. At the turn of the twenty-first century, most of the country was benefiting from high rates of income growth and low unemployment, but Highbridge was stuck in a funk. Ranked the least healthy neighborhood in New York City with double-digit adult illiteracy rates, some of the poorest performing schools in the country, and the lowest-income congressional district in the country, the residents of Highbridge had little to be proud of. Intergenerational poverty was the norm in the community, and the local, state, and federal governments did not seem too eager to infuse the community with funding for badly needed services. Instead, they pulled out lifeline services, like police and fire stations.

The Highbridge Community Life Center, a neighborhood social services agency since 1979, did not give up. Working in conjunction with state and city government officials, they created a series of coalitions with other social service providers and community members to improve access to health care, revitalize their schools, increase local employment opportunities, and reduce incidents of child abuse and neglect.

Now receiving support from private and government entities, their budget has nearly doubled since 2000. In the past year alone, over 200 children advanced their educational attainment through after-school tutoring and peer mentoring programs, 250 youth participated in recreational and summer camp activities, over 500 individuals were served through psychotherapeutic offerings, and over 1,500 students completed literacy, GED, and English as a Second Language courses.

Questions

1. What key issues does the Highbridge Community Life Center face?

2. What government policies/programs could assist this community and the Highbridge Community Life Center itself?

3. From which federal programs would Highbridge Community Life Center be likely to receive funding?

4. What other role(s) could a social worker undertake to help improve and empower the community?

Internet Resources

Child Trends: http://www.childtrends.org

Nonpartisan research center that provides research to program providers, the policy community, researchers and educators, and the media.

Children's Defense Fund: http://www.childrensdefense.org

Nonprofit child advocacy organization that works to eliminate child poverty and protect children from maltreatment.

Kids Count Initiative of the Annie E. Casey Foundation: http://datacenter.kids count.org/

Nonprofit initiative to compile statistics relevant to the well-being of children.

Institute for Children and Poverty: http://www.icphusa.org/

Research institute that compiles data and writes reports on issues affecting children in poverty.

Institute for Research on Poverty: University of Wisconsin-Madison, http://www.urp.wisc.edu

Research institute that compiles data and writes reports on issues affecting those in poverty.

Centers for Disease Control and Prevention: http://www.cdc.gov

Federal government research and policy institute aimed at improving the health of Americans.

National Center for Children in Poverty, Columbia University, Mailman School of Public Health: http://nccp.org

Research institute that compiles data and writes reports on issues affecting children in poverty.

National Poverty Center, Gerald R. Ford School of Public Policy, University of Michigan: http://www.npc.umich.edu

Research institute that compiles data and writes reports on issues affecting those in poverty.

New England Consortium: Advancing Policies to Reduce Poverty and Build Opportunities for Children and Families: http://www.endpovertynewengland.org

Consortium of social service agencies and government agencies aimed at reducing poverty and improving communities.

Orphan Trains movement: http://www.orphantraindepot.com/OrphanTrainHistory.html; http://www.childrensaidsociety.org/about/history/orphan-trains

Historical information on the Orphan Train movement of the nineteenth and twentieth centuries.

Robert Wood Johnson Center to Prevent Childhood Obesity: http://www.reversechildhoodobesity.org

Nonprofit, nonpartisan effort to use research and evidence-based practice to prevent and respond to childhood obesity.

Further Readings

DeParle, J., & Gebeloff, R. M. (2010). The safety net: Living on nothing but Food Stamps. *New York Times*, January 3, 2010, A1.

Jensen, E. (2009). *Teaching with poverty in mind: What being poor does to kids' brains and what schools can do about it.* Alexandria: ASCD.

Journal of Children and Poverty. (1995–). New York: Institute for Children and Poverty. http://www.icphusa.org/jcp/.

Lau, K., Morse, R., & Krase, K. (2009). *Mandated reporting of child abuse and neglect: A practical guide for social workers.* New York: Springer Publishing Company.

Lindsey, D. (2008). *Child poverty and inequality: Securing a better future for America's children.* New York: Oxford University Press.

References

Abbott v. Burke, 119 NJ 287 (1985).

Advisory Committee on Student Financial Assistance. (2010). *The rising price of inequality.* Report to Congress and the Secretary of Education, June 2010. Retrieved from https://www2.ed.gov/about/bdscomm/list/acsfa/rpijunea.pdf.

Aligne, C. A., Auinger, P., Byrd, R. S., & Weitzman, M. (2000). Risk factors for pediatric asthma: Contributions of poverty, race and urban residence. *American Journal of Critical Care and Respiratory Medicine, 162*(3), 873–877.

Ards, S., Chung, C., & Myers, Jr., S. L. (1998). The effects of sample selection bias on racial differences in child abuse reporting. *Child Abuse & Neglect, 22*(2), 103–115.

Austrian Institute for Family Studies. (n.d.). Parental leave in Europe.

Barnett, W. S. (2002). *The battle over Head Start: What the research shows.* Presentation at a Science and Public Policy Briefing sponsored by the Federation of Behavioral, Psychological, and Cognitive Sciences. Retrieved from http://www.plan4preschool.org/documents/battle-over-hs.pdf.

Bill and Melinda Gates Foundation. (2009). *Annual report: 2008.* Retrieved from http://www.gatesfoundation.org/Who-We-Are/Resources-and-Media/Annual-Reports.

Blau, J., & Abramovitz, M. (2010). *The dynamics of social welfare policy* (3rd ed.). Oxford: Oxford University Press.

Boards of Cooperative Educational Services. (2010). *What Is BOCES?* Boards of Cooperative Educational Services of New York State. Retrieved from http://www.boces.org/wps/portal/BOCESofNYS/!ut/p/c1/04_SB8K8xLLM9 MSSzPy8xBz9CP0os3gLA1dXN4NgfwsLE3dzS18XU0cXAwjQ9_PIz03VL8h2 VAQAlA10Mg!!/dl2/d1/L2dJQSEvUUt3QS9ZQnB3LzZfODBFRUYwU084O DRHNzlNREFBRDAwMDAwMDA!/.

Bolen, E., & Hecht, K. (2003). *Neighborhood groceries: New access to health food in low-income communities.* California Food Policy Advocates. Retrieved from http://www.cfpa.net/Grocery.PDF.

Bradbury, B., & Jantti, M. (1999). *Child poverty across industrialized nations.* UNICEF. Retrieved from http://www.unicef-irc.org/cgi-bin/unicef/Lunga .sql?ProductID=186.

Brown, A. (2002). Farmers' market research 1940–2000: An inventory and review. *American Journal of Alternative Agriculture, 17,* 167–176.

Brown v. Board of Education, 347 U.S. 483 (1954).

Burns, B. J., Costello, E. J., Angold, A., Tweed, D., Stangl, D., Farmer, E. M. Z., & Erkanli, A. (1995). DataWatch: Children's Mental Health Service Use Across Service Sectors. *Health Affair, 14*(3), 147–159.

Campaign for Fiscal Equity. (2010). *A brief history of the lawsuit.* Retrieved from http://www.cfequity.org/static.php?page=historyoflawsuit&category=resources.

Carey, K. (2002). *Education funding and low income children: A review of current research.* Center on Budget and Policy Priorities. Retrieved from http://www .cbpp.org/archiveSite/11-7-02sfp3.pdf.

Center for Juvenile Justice Reform. Washington, DC. Retrieved from http://ocfs .ny.gov/main/recc/cjjr_ch_final-1.pdf.

Center for Juvenile Justice Reform & Chapin Hall Center for Children. (2009). *Racial and ethnic disparity and disproportionality in child welfare and juvenile justice: A compendium.* Washington, DC: Center for Juvenile Justice Reform. Retrieved from http://ocfs.ny.gov/main/recc/cjjr_ch_final-1.pdf.

Center on Budget and Policy Priorities. (2009). Figure 1. *The Top Decile Income Share, 1917–2007.* Retrieved from http://elsa.berkeley.edu/~saez/TabFig 2007.xls.

Center on Budget and Policy Priorities. (2013). *Earned Income Tax Credit.* Retrieved from http://www.cbpp.org/cms/?fa=view&id=2505.

Centers for Disease Control and Prevention. (1995, December). Poverty and infant mortality in the United States 1988. *Morbidity and Mortality Weekly Report* (MMWR) 44(49), 923–27. Retrieved from http://www.cdc.gov/ mmwr/preview/mmwrhtml/00039818.htm.

Centers for Disease Control and Prevention. (2005). Blood lead levels: United States, 1999–2002. *Morbidity and Mortality Report,* Table 1. Retrieved from http://www.cdc.gov/mmwr/preview/mmwrhtml/mm5420a5.htm#tab1.

Centers for Disease Control and Prevention. (2009). Obesity prevalence among low-income, preschool-aged children: United States 1998–2008. *Morbidity and Mortality Report.* Retrieved from http://www.cdc.gov/mmwr/preview/ mmwrhtml/mm5828a1.htm.

Centers for Disease Control and Prevention. (2012). *Understanding intimate partner violence fact sheet.* Retrieved from http://www.cdc.gov/violence prevention/pdf/ipv_factsheet2012-a.pdf.

Centers for Disease Control and Prevention. (2013). *Lead.* Retrieved from http://www.cdc.gov/nceh/lead/.

Child Welfare Information Gateway. (2010). *Recent works on racial disproportion-ality in the child welfare system, May 2010.* Retrieved from http://www.hunter .cuny.edu/socwork/nrcfcpp/info_services/Disproportionality%20bibliography .final.pdf.

Children's Aid Society. (2010). *History.* Retrieved from http://www.childrensaid society.org/about/history.

Children's Defense Fund. (2008). *Child poverty in America.* Retrieved from http://www.childrensdefense.org/child-research-data-publications/data/child-poverty-in-america.pdf.

Chow, J. C., Jaffee, K., & Snowden, L. (2003). Racial/ethnic disparities in the use of mental health services in poverty areas. *American Journal of Public Health, 93*(5), 792–797.

Churilla, A. (2008). Urban and rural children experience similar rates of low-income and poverty. *Carsey Institute, Issue Brief,* 2, Summer 2008. Retrieved from http://www.carseyinstitute.unh.edu/publications/IB_UrbanRural Children08.pdf.

Collins, P. H. (2009). *Another kind of public education: Race, schools, the media, and democratic possibilities.* Boston: Beacon Press.

Colman, S., Nichols-Barrer, I. P., Redline, J. E., Devaney, B. L., Ansell, S. V., & Joyce, T. (2012). *Effects of the special supplemental nutrition program for women, infants, and children: A review of recent research.* United States Department of Agriculture, Food and Nutrition Service, Office of Research and Analysis. Report WIC-12-WM. Alexandria, VA. Retrieved from http://www.fns.usda .gov/ora/MENU/Published/WIC/FILES/WICMedicaidLitRev.pdf.

Congressional Budget Office. (2012). *Supplemental Nutrition Assistance Program.* Retrieved from http://www.cbo.gov/sites/default/files/cbofiles/attachments/04-19-SNAP.pdf.

Cunningham, P. J., & Felland, L. E. (2008) *Falling behind: Americans' access to medical care deteriorates.* Tracking Report No 19. Center for Studying Health System Change. Retrieved from http://www.hschange.com/CONTENT/993/#ib4.

Dahl, G., & Lochner, L. (2005). *The impact of family income on child achievement.* Institute for research on poverty discussion paper no. 1305-05. Retrieved from http://www.irp.wisc.edu/publications/dps/pdfs/dp130505.pdf.

Dallam, S. J. (2001). The long-term medical consequences of childhood maltreatment. In *The cost of child maltreatment: Who pays? We all do,* ed. K. Franey, R. Geffner, and R. Falconer. San Diego, CA: Family Violence and Sexual Assault Institute.

Davies, J. (n.d.). *Policy blueprint on domestic violence and poverty.* National Resource Center on Domestic Violence, University of Iowa School of Social Work, and Greater Hartford Legal Assistance. Building comprehensive solutions to domestic violence, Publication #15. Retrieved from http://new.vawnet.org/Assoc_Files_VAWnet/BCS15_BP.pdf/.

De Gregorio, J., & Lee, J.-W. (2003). Education and income equality: New data from cross-county data. *Review of Income and Wealth, 48*(3), 395–416.

Domb Sadof, K. (2010). *Unsung allies battle starvation in Africa.* Retrieved from http://lens.blogs.nytimes.com/2010/07/09/showcase-184/.

Domestic Violence Resource Center. (2010). *Resources.* Retrieved from http://www.dvrc-or.org/domestic/violence/resources/C76/.

Downs, T. A., & Figlio, D. N. (1997) *School finance reforms, tax limits, and student performance: Do reforms level up or dumb down?* Institute for Research on Poverty, Discussion Paper # 1142-97. Retrieved from http://www.irp.wisc.edu/publications/dps/pdfs/dp114297.pdf.

Dyer, E. (2007). Lack of access to services taxing for poor, study finds. *Pittsburgh Post-Gazette,* Thursday, March 15, 2007.

Education Law Center. (2010). *Abbott v. Burke: Education justice for all.* Education Law Center. Retrieved from http://www.edlawcenter.org/ELCPublic/AbbottvBurke/AboutAbbott.htm.

Englehardt, G. V., & Gruber, J. (2004). *Social security and the evolution of elderly poverty.* National Bureau of Economic Research. Working Paper 10466. Retrieved from http://urbanpolicy.berkeley.edu/pdf/Ch6SocialEG0404.pdf.

Fleg, A. (2008). Childhood asthma. In Zhang, Y. (Ed.). *Encyclopedia of Global Health,* pp. 180–181. Thousand Oaks, CA: Sage Publications, Inc.

Foundation for Child Development. (2010). *New report: Impact of recession on children to reach new lows in 2010.* Press Release: June 8, 2010. Retrieved from http://fcd-us.org/sites/default/files/FINAL%20Press%20Release.pdf.

Frankenberg, E., Siegel-Hawley, G., & Wang, J. (2010). *Choice without equity: Charter school segregation and the need for civil rights standards.* The Civil

Rights Project, University of California: Los Angeles. Retrieved from http://civilrightsproject.ucla.edu/research/k-12-education/integration-and-diversity/choice-without-equity-2009-report/frankenberg-choices-without-equity-2010.pdf.

Garbarino, J., & Collins, C. C. (1999). Child neglect: The family with a hole in the middle. In *Neglected Children: Research, Practice and Policy,* ed. H. Dubowitz, pp. 1–23. Thousand Oaks, CA: Sage Publications.

Gardner, D. (2008). *Youth aging out of foster care: Identifying strategies and best practices.* Research Division of National Association of Counties' County Services Department. Retrieved from http://www.naco.org/Content/ContentGroups/Issue_Briefs/IB-YouthAgingoutofFoster-2008.pdf.

Glaeser, E. L., Kahn, M. E., & Rappaport, J. (2008). Why do the poor live in cities? The role of public transportation. *Journal of Urban Economics, 63*(1), 1–24.

Gunderson, G. W. (2013). *The National School Lunch Program Background and Development.* United States Department of Agriculture Food and Nutrition Service. Retrieved from http://www.fns.usda.gov/cnd/Lunch/AboutLunch/ProgramHistory.htm.

Guttmacher Institute. (2010). *U.S. teenage pregnancies, births and abortions: National and state trends by race and ethnicity.* Retrieved from http://www.guttmacher.org/pubs/USTPtrends.pdf.

Haskins, R., & Sawhill, I. (2003). *The future of Head Start.* Brookings Institute Policy Brief: Welfare and Beyond # 27, July 2003. Retrieved from http://www.brookings.edu/~/media/Files/rc/papers/2003/07children families_haskins/pb27.pdf.

Hebbeler, K., Spiker, D., Mallik, S., Scarborough, A., & Simeonessen, R. (2004, November). *National early intervention longitudinal study: Demographic characteristics of children and families entering early intervention, Executive Summary.* NEILS Data Report No. 3, November 2004.

Hill, R. B. (2006). *Synthesis of research on disproportionality in child welfare: An update.* Casey Family Programs. Casey-CSSP Alliance for Racial Equity in Child Welfare.

Hill, R. B. (2007). *An analysis of racial/ethnic disproportionality and disparity at the national, state and county levels.* Casey Family Programs. Casey-CSSP Alliance for Racial Equity in Child Welfare.

Howell, E. (2004). *Access to children's mental health services under Medicaid and SCHIP.* Washington, DC: Urban Institute. Retrieved from http://www.urban .org/uploadedPDF/311053_B-60.pdf.

Jackson, N. A. (2007). *Encyclopedia of domestic violence.* New York: Routledge.

Johnson, A. (2010). *Recession squeezes day care from both sides.* Kids and Parenting on MSNBC. Retrieved from http://www.msnbc.msn.com/id/29882470/.

Kaiser Family Foundation. (2012). *Health coverage of children: The role of Medicaid and CHIP.* Publication 7698-06. Retrieved from http://www.kff.org/ uninsured/upload/7698-04.pdf.

Kaiser Family Foundation. (2013). *Medicaid: A Primer.* Retrieved from http://kaiserfamilyfoundation.files.wordpress.com/2010/06/7334-05.pdf.

Kapphahn, C., Morreale, M., Rickert, V., & Walker, L. (2006). Financing mental health services for adolescents: A position paper of the society for adolescent medicine. *Journal of Adolescent Health, 39*, 456–458.

Katz, M. B. (1986). *In the shadow of the poorhouse: A social history of welfare in America.* New York: Basic Books Inc.

Kaufman, P., & Chapman, C. (2004). *Dropout rates in the United States: 2001* (NCES 2004–057), table A-1. Data from U.S. Department of Commerce, Bureau of the Census, Current Population Survey (CPS), October Supplement, 1972–2001.

Kirst-Ashman, K. K., & Hull, G. H. (2009). *Generalist practice with organizations and communities* (4th ed). Belmont, CA: Brooks/Cole Cengage Learning.

Lau, K., Krase, K., & Morse, R. (2008). *Mandated reporting of child abuse and neglect: A practical guide for social workers.* New York: Springer Publishing Company.

Lee, J.-S., & Bowen, N. K. (2006). Parent involvement, cultural capital, and the achievement gap among elementary school children. *American Educational Research Journal, 43*(2), 193–218.

Luebchow, L. (2009). *Equitable resources in low income schools: Teacher equity and the federal Title I comparability requirement.* Retrieved from http://www.new america.net/files/Equitable_Resources_in_Low_Income_Schools.pdf.

Mather, M. (2010) *Children in single-mother families.* Population Reference Bureau. Retrieved from http://www.prb.org/pdf10/single-motherfamilies.pdf.

Maxfield, M. G., & Widom, C. S. (1996). The cycle of violence: Revisited 6 years later. *Archives of Pediatric and Adolescent Medicine, 150* (April), 390–395.

Meir, D., & Wood, G. (2004). *Many children left behind: How the No Child Left Behind act is damaging our children and our schools.* Boston: Beacon Press.

National Association of Social Workers. (2001). *Standards of cultural competence in social work practice.* Washington, DC: NASW. Retrieved from http://www.naswdc.org/practice/standards/NASWCulturalStandards.pdf.

National Center for Children in Poverty. (2007). *Parents' low education leads to low income, despite full-time employment.* Retrieved from http://nccp.org/publications/pdf/text_786.pdf.

National Center for Children in Poverty. (2010a). *Federal child and dependent care credit.* Retrieved from http://www.nccp.org/profiles/extended_35.html.

National Center for Children in Poverty. (2010b). *50-state policy wizard.* Retrieved from http://www.nccp.org/tools/policy/.

National Center for Children in Poverty. (2010c). *State child support enforcement.* Retrieved from http://www.nccp.org/publications/pub_539.html.

National Coalition Against Domestic Violence. (2010). *Domestic violence fact sheet.* Retrieved from http://www.ncadv.org/.

National Conference of State Legislatures. (2008). *State family and medical leave laws that differ from the federal FMLA.* September 2008. Retrieved from http://www.ncsl.org/Portals/1/documents/employ/fam-medleave.pdf.

National Dissemination Center for Children with Disabilities. (2010). *Overview of early intervention.* Retrieved from http://nichcy.org/babies/overview.

National Institute of Mental Health. (2010). *Mental health medications.* Retrieved from http://www.nimh.nih.gov/health/publications/mental-health-medications/complete-index.shtml.

National Network to End Domestic Violence, National Census of Domestic Violence Services. (2009). *Domestic violence counts national summary.* Retrieved from http://www.nnedv.org/docs/Census/DVCounts2009/DVCounts09_ NatlSummary_Color.pdf.

New England Consortium. (2010). Retrieved from http://www.endpovertynew england.org.

New York Society for the Prevention of Cruelty to Children. (2000). *125th anniversary celebration booklet.* New York: Author.

Office of Juvenile Justice and Delinquency Prevention. (2008). *Juvenile offenders and victims: 2006 national report.* Washington, DC: U.S. Department of Justice.

Olfson, M., Marcus, S. C., Weissman, M. M., & Jensen, P. S. (2002). National trends in the use of psychotropic medications by children. *Journal of the American Academy of Child and Adolescent Psychiatry, 41*(5), 514–521.

Orfield, G., & Yun, J. T. (1999). *Resegregation of America's schools.* The Civil Rights Project, Harvard University. Retrieved from http://civilrightsproject .ucla.edu/research/k-12-education/integration-and-diversity/resegregation- in-american-schools/orfiled-resegregation-in-american-schools-1999.pdf.

Parry, J. (1997). *From prevention to wellness through group work.* Binghamton: Haworth Press.

Patterson, O. (2010). For African-Americans, a virtual depression—Why? *The Nation,* June 30, 2010. Retrieved from http://www.thenation.com/article/ 36882/african-americans-virtual-depression.

Payseur, C., & Raja, N. (2009). Desegregation in and around Prince Edward County: A look back. *Wake Forest Law Review,* Working Paper. Retrieved from http://lawreview.law.wfu.edu/issues/empirical/working/.

Podulka Coe, D., Pivarnik, J. M., Womack, C. J., Reeves, M. J., & Malina, R. M. (2006). Effect of physical education and activity levels on academic achievement in children. *Medicine & Science in Sports & Exercise, 38*(8), 1515–1519.

Popple, P. R., & Leighninger, L. (2011). *The policy-based profession: An introduction to social welfare policy analysis for social workers.* New York: Allyn & Bacon.

Powell, E. C., Ambardekar, E. J., & Sheehan, K. M. (2005). Poor neighborhoods: Safe playgrounds. *Journal of Urban Health, 82*(43), 403–410.

Pruitt, L. R. (2007). Missing the mark: Welfare reform and rural poverty. *Journal of Gender, Race & Justice, 10,* 440–477.

Pumariega, A. J., Glover, S., Holzer, C. E., & Nguyen, H. (1998). Utilization of mental health services in a tri-ethnic sample of adolescents. *Community Mental Health Journal, 34*(2), 145–156.

Ralston, K., Newman, C., Clauson, A., Guthrie, J., & Buzby, J. (2008). *The National School Lunch Program: Background, trends and issues.* United States Department of Agriculture, Economic Research Report # 61. Retrieved from http://www.ers.usda.gov/publications/err61/err61.pdf.

Roberts, D. E. (2002). *Racial disproportionality in the U.S. child welfare system: Documentation, research on causes, and promising practices.* Annie E. Casey Foundation. Retrieved from http://www.familyandchildwellbeing.com/images/Minority_Overrepresentation_in_Child_Welfare_-_Dorothy_Roberts_AECF_Paper.pdf.

Roberts, S. (2009). Westchester adds housing to desegregation pact. *New York Times,* August 11, 2009.

Robinson v. Cahill, 303 A. 2d 273, 62 NJ 473, 118 NJ Super. 223 (1973).

Rogers, C. C., & Dagata, E. (2000). Child poverty in non-metro areas in the 1990s. *Rural America, 15*(1), January 2000, 28–36. Retrieved from http://www.ers.usda.gov/publications/ruralamerica/ra151/ra151e.pdf.

Sedlak, A., & Broadhurst, D. D. (1996) *Executive summary of the third national incidence study of child abuse and neglect.* U.S. Department of Health and Human Services, Administration on Children, Youth and Families. Washington, DC: U.S. Government Printing Office.

Sedlak, A. J., McPherson, K., & Das, B. (2010). *Fourth national incidence study of child abuse and neglect (NIS-4): Supplementary analyses of race differences in child maltreatment rates in the NIS-4.* Office of Planning, Research and Evaluation and the Children's Bureau, Administration for Children and Families, U.S. Department of Health and Human Services, Washington, DC. Retrieved from http://www.acf.hhs.gov/sites/default/files/opre/nis4_supp_analysis_race_diff_mar2010.pdf.

Shaffer, D., Fisher, P., Dulcan, M. K., Davies, M., Piacentini, J., Schwab-Stone, M. E., & Regier, D. A. (1996). The NIMH diagnostic interview schedule for children version 2.3 (DISC-2.3): Description, acceptability, prevalence rates, and performance in the MECA study. *Journal of the American Academy of Child and Adolescent Psychiatry, 35*(7), 865–877.

Smith, C., & Thornberry, T. (1995). The relationship between childhood maltreatment and adolescent involvement in delinquency. *Criminology, 33*(4), 451–477.

Swanson, C. B. (2004). *Who graduates? Who doesn't? A statistical portrait of public high school graduation, 2001.* Education Policy Center, The Urban Institute. Retrieved from http://www.urban.org/uploadedPDF/410934_ WhoGraduates.pdf.

Tolman, R., & Raphael, J. (2000). A review of the research on welfare and domestic violence. *Journal of Social Issues, 56*(4), 655–682.

Trattner, W. I. (1999). *From poor law to welfare state: A history of social welfare in America* (6th ed.). New York: The Free Press.

U.S. Census Bureau. (2000). *2000 Decennial Census.* Retrieved from http://www .census.gov/main/www/cen2000.html.

U.S. Census Bureau. (2005). *Statistical abstract of the United States. Infant mortality rate.* Retrieved from http://www.census.gov/statab/ranks/rank17.html.

U.S. Census Bureau. (2010). *Current population survey.* Retrieved from http://www.census.gov/cps/.

U.S. Census Bureau. (2012). *American community survey.* Retrieved from http://www.census.gov/acs/www/.

U.S. Department of Agriculture. (2012a). *National School Lunch Program.* Retrieved from http://www.fns.usda.gov/cnd/Lunch/AboutLunch/NSLP FactSheet.pdf.

U.S. Department of Agriculture. (2012b). *The special supplemental nutrition program for women, infants and children.* Retrieved from http://www.fns.usda .gov/wic/WIC-Fact-Sheet.pdf.

U.S. Department of Agriculture. (2012c). *WIC Farmers' market nutrition program.* Retrieved from http://www.fns.usda.gov/wic/WIC-FMNP-Fact-Sheet.pdf.

U.S. Department of Agriculture. (2013a). *Farmers markets and local food marketing.* Retrieved from http://www.ams.usda.gov/AMSv1.0/ams.fetch TemplateData.do?template=TemplateC&navID=FarmersMarkets&right Nav1=FarmersMarkets&topNav=&leftNav=WholesaleandFarmersMarkets& page=WFMFarmersMarketsHome&description=Farmers%20Markets&acct= frmrdirmkt.

U.S. Department of Agriculture. (2013b). *Healthy Hunger-Free Kids Act of 2010.* Retrieved from http://www.fns.usda.gov/cnd/governance/legislation/ cnr_2010.htm.

U.S. Department of Agriculture. (2013c). *Supplemental Nutrition Assistance Program: Eligibility.* Retrieved from http://www.fns.usda.gov/snap/applicant_ recipients/Eligibility.htm#employment.

U.S. Department of Agriculture. (2013d). *Supplemental Nutrition Assistance Program: SNAP legislation.* Retrieved from http://www.fns.usda.gov/snap/ rules/Legislation/.

U.S. Department of Agriculture. (n.d.). *Child Nutrition Programs.* Retrieved from http://www.fns.usda.gov/cnd/.

U.S. Department of Education. (2010a). *Federal role in education.* Retrieved from http://www2.ed.gov/about/overview/fed/role.html.

U.S. Department of Education. (2010b). *Race to the top fund.* Retrieved from http://www2.ed.gov/programs/racetothetop/index.html.

U.S. Department of Education. (2010c). *21st century community learning centers.* Retrieved from http://www2.ed.gov/programs/21stcclc/index.html.

U.S. Department of Health and Human Services. (2010). *Health care.* Retrieved from http://HealthCare.gov.

U.S. Department of Health and Human Services, Administration on Children, Youth and Families. (2004). *Child maltreatment 2003.* Washington, DC: U.S. Government Printing Office.

U.S. Department of Health and Human Services, Administration on Children, Youth and Families. (2007). *Child maltreatment 2006.* Washington, DC: U.S. Government Printing Office.

U.S. Department of Health and Human Services, Administration on Children, Youth and Families. (2009). *Trends in foster care and adoption—FY 2002–FY2008.* Washington, DC: U.S. Government Printing Office.

U.S. Department of Health and Human Services, Administration on Children, Youth and Families, Administration for Children and Families, Office of Child Support Enforcement. (2013). *FY2010 annual report to Congress.* Retrieved from http://www.acf.hhs.gov/programs/css/resource/fy2010-annual-report.

U.S. Department of Health and Human Services, Centers for Medicare and Medicaid Services. (2010). *Medicaid.* Retrieved from https://www.cms.gov/home/medicaid.asp.

U.S. Department of Health and Human Services, Centers for Medicare and Medicaid Services, Statistical Enrollment Data System. (2009). *Annual statistical enrollment report FY2008.* Retrieved from http://www.cms.hhs.gov.

U.S. Department of Health and Human Services, Office of Head Start. (2010). *Office of Head Start.* Retrieved from http://www.acf.hhs.gov/programs/ohs/.

U.S. Department of Labor. (2009). Fact sheet # 28: The *Family Medical Leave Act of 1993.* Retrieved from http://www.dol.gov/whd/regs/compliance/whdfs28.pdf.

U.S. Environmental Protection Agency. (2013). *Lead: Learn about lead.* Retrieved from http://www2.epa.gov/lead/learn-about-lead#found.

U.S. Government Accountability Office. (1992). *Early intervention: Federal investments like WIC can produce savings.* Retrieved from http://archive.gao.gov/d32t10/146514.pdf.

U.S. Government Accountability Office. (2003). *Women's earnings: Work patterns partially explain difference between men's and women's earnings.* GAO 04-35. Retrieved from http://www.gao.gov/new.items/d0435.pdf.

Wang, C. T., & Holton, J. (2007). *Total estimated cost of child abuse and neglect in the United States*. Chicago: Prevent Child Abuse America.

Whitelaw Downs, S., Moore, E., & McFadden, J. (2009). *Child welfare and family services: Policies and practice* (8th ed). Boston: Pearson.

Wilson, D. (2009). Poor children likelier to get antipsychotics. *New York Times*. December 11, 2009.

6

Older Adults

Shannon Mathews

The aging of baby boomers has placed much attention on the growing population of older adults in the United States and across the world. Dictated by changing demographics, there is a great need for service providers to recognize the expanding, diverse aging population living in poverty.

The issue of poverty throughout this chapter seeks to provide readers with an understanding that poverty in the lives of aging Americans, "is more than a lack of financial resources; it is a serious threat to health, well-being, and dignity. Poverty isolates and marginalizes [older adults]" (Mayer, 2010, p. 108). Accordingly, poverty among older adults will be explored by identifying some of the social and structural factors defining the most economically vulnerable members of the aging population. This discussion is framed within a systems and life course perspective. This perspective connects later life circumstances to other life stages. The goal of this chapter is to address poverty among vulnerable subpopulations of older adults. Concurrently, it considers the issue of poverty by identifying and meeting the needs of the most vulnerable older adults within their communities. After completing this chapter, readers will describe the aging population, identify subgroups of older adults most at risk for living in poverty, explore programs and policies targeted at older adults, and consider strategies to assist older adults in need.

Demographics and Characteristics

The oldest-old subpopulation, meaning those individuals eighty-five years of age and older, is the fastest-growing segment. When compared to the young-old (those 65–74 years of age) or the old-old (those 75–84 years of age), it is revealed that a higher portion of the oldest-old live below or in poverty, which suggests there is an increase in economic vulnerability as one ages (Hooyman & Kiyak,

2011). The concept of economic vulnerability refers to a heightened insecurity or risk of multidimensional deprivation experienced by some older adults (Whelan & Maître 2008). In later life, economic vulnerability often relates to older adults' ability to financially cope with an emergency or crisis, a change in status, or changes in purchasing power, and these can be a key component of poverty (National Council on Aging, 2010). Over 3.9 million older adults do not have sufficient income to meet their basic expenses (U.S. Census Bureau, 2010b). As shown in figure 6.1, older adults when compared to other groups are at risk for living in poverty. The current economic downturn has only compounded this issue. Since the beginning of the economic recession in 2008, about 2.5 million people have fallen into poverty with individuals 65 years and older representing approximately 5 percent of this group. This chapter discusses how gender and other socio-demographic factors strongly determine the likelihood of living in poverty in old age.

Figure 6.1. Poverty Rates by Age: 1959 to 2011

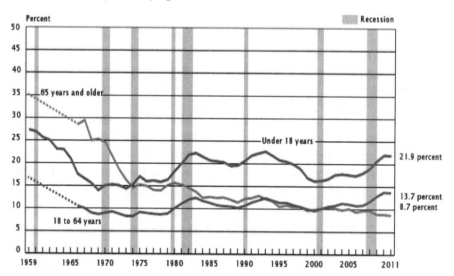

Note: The data points are placed at the midpoints of the respective years. For information on recessions, see Appendix A. Data for people aged 18 to 64 and 65 and older are not available from 1960 to 1965.

Source: U.S. Census Bureau, Current Population Survey, 1960 to 2012 Annual Social and Economic Supplements.

Source: U.S. Census Bureau (2011b), retrieved from www.census.gov/hhes/www/poverty/data/incpovhlth 2011/figure5.pdf.

According to U.S. Census Bureau (2010b) data, traditional poverty measures indicate that older adults are particularly affected by this social problem, with 9.0 percent of older adults (almost 3.9 million elderly) living below the poverty level. Older adults represented 5.8 percent (2.2 million) of those considered "near-poor" or economically vulnerable during this period (U.S. Census Bureau, 2010a). The number of older adults sixty-five years and older living in poverty would increase (to 16.1 percent) if out-of-pocket expenses, deductibles, and other medical costs are considered (Yen, 2010b).

Despite the current economic climate, the United States has made tremendous strides in addressing poverty in later life. In fact, poverty among older adults in the last four decades has fallen from 1 in 3 to 1 in 10 today (Mayer, 2010; Whitman & Purcell, 2006). In 2011, among those living in poverty, 11 percent of households were headed by older adults sixty-five years old and older, in comparison to 33 percent in 1967 (Fry, Cohn, Livingston, & Taylor, 2011). Unfortunately, despite antipoverty programs designed to address the overall economic status of older adults, there are still distinct subgroups among the aging population who are at great risk of living in or near poverty. A recent report, Spotlight on Poverty and Opportunity (2011) notes, "During the past decade, the overall poverty rate for Americans age 65 and older has held steady at about 10 percent. A closer look however, reveals drastically higher rates of poverty among older women, and racial and ethnic minorities" (para. 1).

Older women represent a higher proportion of those living in poverty in comparison to older men. In later life, a comparison of ethnic and racial minorities and their Caucasian counterparts suggests that ethnic and racial minorities are at greater risk of living in poverty. Additionally, rural-dwelling seniors are distinctly more impoverished than are their urban-dwelling counterparts. A review of the data on poverty among older adults strongly suggests that geographic location, marital status, gender, and ethnicity or racial backgrounds are significant factors associated with poverty status in later life. This chapter explores these factors in greater depth to provide readers with a better understanding of the context in which older adults find themselves.

Urban versus Rural Communities

When comparing poverty for all individuals in urban (metropolitan) communities (17 percent) to poverty in rural or small town (non-metropolitan) communities

(16.1 percent), the geographic distribution of poverty in the United States suggests that one's place of residence matters (Housing Assistance Council, 2012a, 2012b). For example, poverty rates are geographically concentrated in the following areas: Appalachia, the Lower Mississippi Delta, the Southern Black Belt, Rio Grande Valley, Native Americans lands, the Great Plains, and the Colonias along the U.S.-Mexico border (Housing Assistance Council, 2011; Rural Policy Research Institute [RUPRI], 2010). These clustered areas reveal persistent rates of poverty among ethnic and racial minorities, including older adults.

Geographic locality or one's area of residence can play a pivotal role in older adults' risk of living in poverty and the services available to support them. In 2010, adults sixty-five years and older accounted for 17.2 percent of those living in non-metropolitan communities and 12.8 percent of those living in metropolitan communities (Housing Assistance Council, 2011; U.S. Census Bureau, 2011a). Among the aging population, 10.4 percent of seniors living in poverty lived in non-metropolitan areas, in comparison to 8.7 percent who lived in metropolitan areas. About 26.2 percent of older adults in non-metropolitan areas were considered economically vulnerable or near poor, as opposed to 20.6 percent living in metropolitan areas (Housing Assistance Council, 2011; U.S. Census Bureau, 2011a). Clearly, seniors' area of residence makes a difference.

Higher-than-average poverty rates can be found for those living in the South and in rural areas as opposed to urban areas (Administration on Aging [AOA], 2013). Across the United States, rural poverty is clustered among specific regions with the South representing 19.7 percent, followed by the West at 17.3 percent and the Midwest and Northeast both at 13 percent (Housing Assistance Council, 2011). These geographically vulnerable regions have significantly large aging populations, in which older adults could be at particularly high risk for living in poverty.

Generally, when compared to individuals in urban or suburban areas, residents in rural areas tend to be older, receive Medicare or Medicaid, and/or public assistance. They are also likely to live further from health care resources. Historically, seniors living in rural areas in comparison to urban-dwelling older adults are at increased risk for poverty. There is a greater likelihood that rural older adults of color (especially those eighty-five years and older) are vulnerable because of limited resources, low wealth accumulation, and limited or no access to public assistance or resources (Rogers, 2005).

In 2010, 19.7 percent of those living in poverty resided in cities and 11.8 percent resided in suburban areas (U.S. Census Bureau, 2010b). In contrast to those in rural areas, urban-dwelling seniors may have greater access to services within heavily populated communities and include resources such as nutrition, home health care, broadband Internet, and transportation services (RUPRI, 2007). Older adults living in cities tend to be ethnic minorities, are economically limited, have low mobility, and live alone (Novak, 2012). Hispanic seniors, for instance, are nine times more likely, and African Americans are five times more likely compared to other seniors, to live in metropolitan areas. For these seniors, barriers such as language, poverty, and limited or unreliable public transportation may keep them from accessing necessary services. In some areas, a lack of door-to-door senior transit programs or discounted senior transportation options may lead to isolation among older adults, impact their health by minimizing their ability to stay active, and contribute to their dependency on others. Older adults living in inner cities may also experience barriers in relation to crime and safety. Ultimately, where a senior lives determines the types of programs, resources, and supports available to mitigate their risk of living in poverty.

Marital Status

Marriage typically provides protections across the life course from poverty, especially for women. Generally, this is known as the marital benefit or marital effect (Hillier & Barrow, 2011). This term denotes the wide range of benefits associated with marital status, including individuals' economic well-being and mental and physical health (Quadagno, 2011). Increased economic well-being among older married individuals is associated with higher earnings across the life course for men and less economic instability for older women.

Among older adults living in poverty, married people are least likely to be poor, and never married women are the most likely (American Association of Retired Persons [AARP], 2011). Married individuals sixty-five years of age and older who are living in poverty account for only 9 percent of impoverished older adults in comparison to never-married seniors who represent 39.2 percent (AARP, 2011). Also notable, in 2010, married couples had median incomes ($48,858 for men and $43,831 for women) that were about twice as high as people who were never married ($23,010 men, $22,038 women) (AARP, 2011).

Marriage additionally lowers seniors' risk for health-related issues such as depression or mortality. Married older adults report less depression, and greater life satisfaction than never-married and divorced individuals, who have twice the mortality rate than those who are married (Office of the Assistant Secretary for Planning and Evaluation [ASPE], 2007).

When compared to their single counterparts, married older adults are also more likely to own a home, have higher health status (especially older men), and have higher social support (ASPE, 2007). Although marital status can provide some buffer to becoming poor, particularly for women, a significant transition for women in later life can be widowhood (Novak, 2012). The loss of a spouse can radically alter later life resources, contributing to women's extreme economic vulnerability and susceptibility to poverty. The loss of income also creates a direct link to poverty. Thus, living alone and widowed older women are at particularly high risk of poverty due to lack of financial assistance, reduced social support, and a lack of compensatory resources (Gonyea & Hooyman, 2005). Older adults living alone (16.5 percent) are more likely to be impoverished than older adults living with families (5.0 percent), with Hispanic older women living alone (38.8 percent) at the greatest risk (AOA, 2013).

Ethnicity and Gender

Membership among certain racial or ethnic groups creates distinct disadvantages in later life. For example, older adults of color including African Americans, Native Americans, and Hispanics are at greater risk for living in poverty and have poverty rates 2.5 times higher than their Caucasian counterparts (Novak, 2012; Quadagno, 2011). Caucasians sixty-five years of age and older reflect 6.8 percent of those living in poverty, while African American and Hispanic older adults represent about 18 percent each (U.S. Census Bureau, 2010b). African Americans and Hispanics experience greater economic vulnerability and account for 10.5 percent and 9.8 percent respectively of those considered near poor, while Caucasians represent only 4.8 percent.

Among financially vulnerable seniors, a clear gender divide exists. Women constitute 16.2 percent of those living in poverty while men account for 14.9 percent. Six out of ten older women are economically vulnerable or already live in poverty (Alliance for Children and Families, 2010). The risk of poverty increases as women age, with women seventy-five years and older being three times more likely than men to live in poverty (Cawthorne, 2008). Women historically outlive men (though the gap is narrowing) and therefore are more likely than their male counterparts to be in jeopardy with respect to social and economic factors in their later years. The longer older adults live (especially women), the more they become susceptible to experiencing compounding life events, which may force them into poverty. Events such as widowhood, health decline, limited income, and shrinking social networks commonly are just some examples that influence the economic circumstances of older women and both genders among the oldest-old population.

Older women are distinctly disadvantaged in later life due to disparities in early adulthood work force participation and lower lifetime earnings (Folbre, Shaw, & Stark, 2005; Gillen & Kim, 2009). Often dictated by care-giving and family responsibilities, women experience greater lack of continuity in their work history. The connectedness of early life phases, labor participation, and gendered expectations clearly reveal how the feminization of poverty across the life course affects later life. This term describes the phenomenon in which women experience poverty at far greater rates than men (Thibos, Lavin-Loucks, & Martin, 2007). Women who often go in and out of the workforce due to factors such as family and other caregiver responsibilities are at risk of becoming economically vulnerable, since labor participation relates to individuals' payroll contributions into Social Security and employer-based pension plans (Gonyea & Hooyman, 2005). Consequently, women are less likely than men to accrue post-retirement or later life resources associated with their work histories. This is compounded by the reality that women's wages still lag behind men even when they are employed (Gonyea & Hooyman, 2005; Thibos et al., 2007).

The gendered difference in resources based on gender biases in the workplace, the complexity of women's roles, their longevity, lower pension coverage, and inadequate social insurance benefits distinctly shapes women's susceptibility to becoming poor as they age (Schulz & Binstock, 2011). Identifying factors related to the vulnerability of older women in later life requires addressing inequity across the life course.

Historical Perspective

This section provides a historical overview of aging issues to foster readers' understanding of historical factors that shape aging in the United States. Since much of the historical content is covered in depth later in the chapter within the discussion of government programs and policies, this section is abbreviated. Perspectives on aging and the responses developed to help those at risk of living in poverty have evolved. These historical elements help shape a collective understanding of the aging population through the years. Society views older adults as deserving help and entitled to benefits (Achenbaum, 2008). As such, society is willing to assist older adults living in poverty, particularly the oldest old. The development of pensions during the early twentieth century, for example, was based on the belief that the old and widowed should be cared for by society. Socially, age has long been correlated with poverty, sickness, and disability (Hudson, 2011). Specifically, the development of age-based policy beginning in colonial America was historically rooted in the view that older adults are deserving of help based on age-determined economic needs, inability to work, and illness. Older adults were not seen as the cause of their financial or medical problems, but instead were viewed as blameless and thus, were considered deserving of social assistance to cope with the conditions of old age (Achenbaum, 2008; Hudson, 2011; Schulz & Binstock, 2011).

Post-Depression-era social insurance programs were designed to provide income security for both the aged and unemployed and set the stage for the development of current policies and social programs intended to reduce poverty and economic vulnerability among older adults. The 1935 Social Security Act provided for unemployment insurance, old-age insurance, and means-tested welfare programs that still exist today (Martin & Weaver, 2005). In the 1930s, associated with the original Social Security Act, the needs of poor older adults received particular attention through Old Age Assistance, which provided benefits to destitute seniors. This became a cornerstone for current public social programs that assist many older adults (Amenta, Caren, & Olasky, 2005) and is discussed in more detail later in this chapter.

Throughout time, the provision of social programs and assistance has grown. During 1920–1970, later life issues were addressed from the perspective that old age was a distinct social problem (Quadagno, 2011). This perspective was largely defined by an increased need for institutional care involving a transition from almshouses to nursing home care. The 1946 Hill-Burton Act and 1954 amendments to the act, in response to the increased need for later life care, led to the rapid expansion of nursing homes constructed through federal funding with specific attention given to meeting the needs of frail older adults, and those living in poverty (Achenbaum, 2008). Expanded through the 1960 Kerr-Mills Act, nursing home care included custodial care in addition to skilled nursing care; however, skilled nursing care was not incorporated in the same magnitude as it is today. A lack of skilled nursing home care to meet the needs of frail and low-income seniors eventually led to increased funding of long-term care provided through the Medicaid program. Another expansion in nursing home care followed in 1965. Unlike the previous growth, the 1965 expansion represented an increased need to address the mental health of older adults due to deinstitutionalization occurring during that time (Quadagno, 2011).

During 1930–1970s, encouraged retirement and managed labor force participation strongly shaped economic issues for older adults. This meant that mandatory retirement or earlier retirement incentives removed older workers from the labor force. Involuntary retirement coupled with age discrimination created an economic disadvantage for older workers. In an effort to address the treatment of this population and potential economic issues that resulted in their removal from the labor market, the Age Discrimination in Employment Act (ADEA) was enacted in 1967 to provide protections for older workers (Hudson, 2011; Quadagno, 2011; U.S. Equal Employment Opportunity Commission, n.d.). Additional efforts to address potential economic issues affecting low-income individuals and older workers were evident in the creation of Supplemental Security Income (SSI) and enactment of the Employee Retirement Security Act.

The decade of 1960–1970 was characterized by modest efforts to address the economic needs of vulnerable older adults through employment and training efforts targeted specifically at older workers. The Senior Community Service Employment Program (SCSEP) designed to assist low-income older workers was implemented (Hudson & Gonyea, 2007). This program, currently under Title VI of the Older Americans Act, provides employment assistance to low-income workers fifty-five years old and older. Societal recognition of the economic plight and needs of vulnerable older adults at risk for living in poverty was a persistent focus. During the late 1970s and through the 1980s, a declining economy and the reality of an "aging of America" forced societal concern about the costs of an aging population and challenged America to help those most in need (Hudson, 2004). This period historically was marked by increases in cost containment measures, which included more restrictive eligibility requirements for those seeking help, funding cuts for social services, and concerns regarding Medicaid and Medicare spending, that put the needs of older adults in jeopardy. As a result, new efforts to partner educational institutions and the private sector emerged as a means of leveraging resources and opportunities to meet the needs of older adults. The Gray Lobby made up of organizations that represent the interests of the aged mobilized to protect services for this population (Achenbaum, 2008). Debates regarding an aging society, sustainability of entitlements, efforts to meet the needs of older adults in need, and the appropriate course of action began in the early 1990s and are still persistent today and have historically framed the twenty-first century debates on aging.

The original Social Security Act, discussed later in this chapter, addressed economic needs associated with later life, and assisted in the transition from work to retirement (Hudson, 2011; Quadagno, 2011). Recognition of economic need, the inability of some to work, and the susceptibility to illness in later life continue to frame policies and program developed to assist vulnerable older adults. This is most evident in recent protections for retirement income through the 2006 Pension Protection Act and the 2010 Affordable Care Act. Taken together, it is evident that concern for older adults and advocacy for aging issues is a consistent part of national discourse. Notably, however, the current focus of policy and program development seeks to balance individual responsibility, family obligation, private sector involvement, and government solutions as later life issues continue to be addressed, especially for those living in poverty (Hudson, 2011; Schulz & Binstock, 2011).

Key Issues

It is important that professionals working with older adults at risk of poverty become familiar with key issues that impact them. An enhanced understanding of this group's social and economic needs will enable practitioners to be more effective in their work. Although poverty among older adults has decreased with the advent of social insurance programs, many seniors still face an uncertain economic future.

Employment, Income, and Economic Vulnerability

Employment history and labor participation can significantly determine the likelihood of poverty as adults age. Factors that have a role in poverty status for older adults include "gainful employment" and sufficient earnings. In March 2010, adults fifty-five years and older accounted for 6.9 percent of those unemployed (AARP, 2010a). This percentage represents unemployment among over 2 million older workers. Although the unemployment rate among this group is less compared to younger workers, older adults who become unemployed spend more time seeking employment. Workers 55 and older have an average duration of joblessness of 35 weeks in comparison to about 26 weeks for younger workers (U.S. Department of Labor, 2010). Older adults seeking new employment opportunities are less likely to get a job when competing with younger workers. In fact, a younger worker is 40 percent more likely to be offered an interview than an older worker (Lahey, 2006).

Employment earnings are a key later life resource. Regardless of economic conditions, older workers generally suffer larger sustained earnings losses in comparison to their younger counterparts (Couch, Jolly, & Placzek, 2009). Earnings loss is a significant barrier for older adults living in poverty in rural areas who have a higher likelihood of earning lower incomes than do their metropolitan counterparts. Issues regarding change in the labor market often dictate the types of jobs available to older workers and are viewed as additional barriers to employment. Older adults who are now in their 60s and 70s may have dropped out of school when young to pursue manufacturing jobs that did not require high levels of education, but were generally considered "good jobs" at the time. Today, employment and earnings strongly correlate with educational attainment. Good-paying jobs that require little to no education are not the norm, and can leave very limited options for less educated workers. Older adults with restricted educational opportunities such as the oldest-old, older ethnic and racial minorities, as well as older women may find the labor market unfavorable. Members of these distinct groups at risk may have greater difficulty overcoming poverty and economic vulnerability based on an inability to find or maintain work.

Later life or post-retirement economic vulnerability is strongly associated with the types of income and resources that seniors accrue and rely on as they age. As shown in figure 6.2, sources of income available to older individuals can vary by marital status (AARP, 2011). Sources can also vary by factors such as gender, race, geographic locality, and living arrangements. Women, older adults of color, and rural seniors who may experience limited employment opportunities, restricted access to education, and lower wages across the life course typically have the fewest resources. Historically, older ethnic minorities had fewer opportunities to go to college, which forced many into low-paying service jobs as maids, janitors, and cooks, thus putting them at greater economic risk for poverty in later life than their more educated Caucasian counterparts who have had greater employment choices and earning opportunities.

Figure 6.2. Sources of Income for Married Couples and Nonmarried Persons Age 65 and Over, 2010

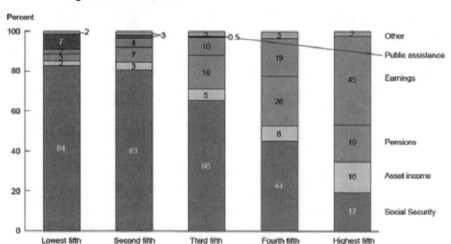

NOTE: A married couple is age 65 and over if the husband is age 65 and over or the husband is younger than age 55 and the wife is age 65 and over. The definition of "other" includes, but is not limited to, unemployment compensation, workers compensation, alimony, child support, and personal contributors. Quintile limits are $12,600, $20,683, $32,880, and $57,565 for all units; $24,634, $36,288, $53,000, and $86,310 for married couples; and $10,145, $14,966, $21,157, and $35,405 for nonmarried persons. Reference population: These data refer to the civilian noninstitutionalized population.
Source: Federal Interagency Forum on Aging-Related Statistics (2012, p. 15).

Housing

Economic vulnerability and poverty can impact housing conditions and households (Housing Assistance Council, 2011). Although rural housing conditions are among the worst in the nation, the most prominent housing issue in both rural and urban areas is affordability. Housing can be a significant portion of monthly spending for older adults living in or near poverty. More than 8.5 million households headed by individuals sixty-five years old and older are cost-burdened, which is defined as paying more than 30 percent of income on housing costs (AARP, 2010b). The quality of housing for community-dwelling older adults living on a fixed income is of great concern for many service practitioners.

Community Living Arrangements

Seniors living in poverty often live in substandard, poor-quality housing with limited alternatives. Living in substandard housing can negatively impact health and overall quality of life; therefore, living spaces must meet the needs of aging individuals (Robert Wood Johnson Foundation [RWJF] Commission to Build a Healthier America, 2008). For example, seniors living in poverty who are unable to afford heating oil in the winter may live in cold, unsafe conditions that can jeopardize their health, and even their lives in extreme cases. Many community-dwelling older adults living in poverty may also rent subsidized housing units within apartment complexes or as single-family homes. Approximately 6.6 percent of these renters are 65 years or older and 7.7 percent are 75 years and older (U.S. Census Bureau, 2010b). Notably, much public housing is heavily concentrated in low-income minority communities and is often in need of maintenance.

Although older adults with lowered income may be forced to rent, many older adults are more likely than are younger adults to be homeowners. In 2010, 14.3 percent of homeowners were seniors 65 years and older and 12.0 percent were 75 years and older (U.S. Census Bureau, 2010b). Many seniors become cost-burdened by homeownership. In fact, older adults are commonly house or equity rich and cash poor (Hillier & Barrow, 2011). This term is used to describe the phenomenon in which due to longevity in their homes, individuals may have accrued significant equity, but due to a fixed income have very little to no available cash resources. These cash-strapped seniors often live in poor housing conditions due to a physical inability to maintain their homes. Unfortunately, the design of many homes is not senior-friendly or designed in a way to promote aging in place, as they are ill equipped to meet changing physical needs. Aging in place is the term that refers to older adults' remaining in their homes or in familiar communities as long as possible, thereby decreasing the likelihood they will relocate in later life (AARP, 2010b). The inability to make repairs or needed modifications as older adults age considerably contributes to the ill fit of some homes. Although not all modifications have to be major (e.g., tacking down or removing throw rugs, changing lighting), modifications that can help older adults achieve a better person-in-environment fit may require additional financial resources. This can be a burden for older adults living in poverty with little to no financial reserves.

The house rich and cash poor phenomenon has led to the rise and development of reverse mortgages or home equity conversion mortgages (HECM) as an option for older adults in financial need. These are loans that allow seniors (who own their home free and clear) to convert their home equity into flexible cash advances while still living in their homes (Government Accountability Office [GAO], 2009). If taken, these loans do not affect Social Security or Medicare benefits (an advantage for some older adults), but may affect Supplemental Security Income (SSI) benefits for impoverished seniors (programs that will be discussed in more detail in the next section). Despite economic vulnerability, only 14 percent of older home-owners elect to obtain a reverse mortgage (MetLife Mature Market Institute, 2009). Although these loans can offer relief for some, it is important for older adults and families to pay close attention to the terms of the loan and to complete the manda-tory education required before taking out a loan.

Housing costs, the cost of living, and an ability to live independently can often dic-tate the conditions with which the impoverished live (Weber, Jensen, Miller, Mosley, & Fisher, 2005). Older adults living in poverty are nearly twice as likely as their non-poor counterparts to have limitations in their ability to live independ-ently (28.4 percent vs. 15.9 percent) (O'Brien, Wu, & Baer, 2010). Many older adults in need reside in board and care homes as an alternative to more expensive later life housing options (Quadagno, 2011). Board and care homes provide meals, assistance with activities of daily living, or ADLs (self-care activities such as bathing, toileting, and eating), and support for older adults who cannot live on their own. For low-income seniors these community-based residential settings are an affordable alternative living arrangement since they are about one-third the cost of nursing homes (Novak, 2012). Unlike more expensive assisted-living facilities or nursing homes, board and care homes do not provide extensive medical care. Cur-rently, much of the funding for board and care housing is provided through Sup-plemental Security Income (discussed later in this chapter).

Professionals working with older adults must continue to advocate for senior-friendly housing designs, improvements in quality of existing housing, and the availability of income support programs for seniors in the community. Another concern with regard to community-dwelling older adults is the likelihood of natu-rally occurring retirement communities, or NORCs. NORCs exist when a dispro-portionate number of older people live in an area, and vary by location, physical dimensions, population size, and demographics (Lun, 2010). In essence, a neigh-borhood or facility originally populated with members of all age groups evolves over time to contain a high proportion of older adults. Generally, as a NORC forms in a community, health and social services become distinct systematic challenges for those aging in place and living in poverty. This is largely related to an increased need for community-based services that meet the needs of individuals as they age. As a NORC evolves there may be a greater need to have community-based services respond to the aging population.

Institutional Living Arrangements

While the majority of older adults 65 years and older live within community settings, about 3.1 percent of those 65 years and older reside in skilled care facilities (U.S. Census Bureau, 2011a). Institutional living arrangements are associated with long-term care options. Today, institutional long-term care (LTC) is available within a continuum of care options that serve older adults with varied dependency levels and socioeconomic backgrounds. This continuum generally includes board and care homes, assisted-living facilities (ALFs), continuing care retirement communities (CCRCs), and nursing homes. As identified, the continuum reflects a gradient of care defined by a senior's need for assistance. Board and care is available for older adults requiring minimal assistance, while nursing home care is for those with the most extensive need for assistance. The cost of assisted-living facilities and continuing care retirement communities are cost-prohibitive for many impoverished seniors since these facilities require high monthly fees generally not affordable for those with limited income.

Board and care homes and nursing homes are primary options for older adults with limited economic resources such as those receiving assistance from government programs such as Medicaid and Supplemental Security Income. Individuals' financial situations further limit available options since many facilities do not accept clients on government assistance. Despite this practice, Medicaid and Medicare accounted for about two-thirds of the $143 billion spent on nursing homes in 2010 (Centers for Medicare and Medicaid Service [CMS], 2010c).

The chances of entering a nursing home at some point across the life course increases with age. Older adults living in poverty who have poor health are also more likely to enter a nursing home compared to healthier seniors. Not all nursing home placements are long-term stays; some older adults go into nursing homes for short rehabilitative services, usually after surgery (Novak, 2012). Whether long-term or short-term, seniors living in poverty are more likely in comparison to wealthier seniors to use this institutional housing option at some point in their lives.

Health

The connection between poverty and health status is complex. Financial barriers to accessing services, lack of health insurance, environmental conditions, and the lack of resources to maintain good health are illustrations of this (Panelli, Gallagher, &

Kearns, 2006). Impoverished older adults who have difficulty meeting the cost of daily living lack the ability to afford costs beyond food and shelter, making health costs a lower priority. As such, older adults living in poverty are significantly more likely than are those with higher income to have poorer health status (Louie & Ward, 2011; O'Brien et al., 2010).

Health status refers to the presence or absence of chronic or acute disease and the degree of inability in an older adult's level of functioning (Hooyman & Kiyak, 2011; Wacker & Roberto, 2008). Chronic diseases are long-term conditions (lasting more than three months) that are not curable, but are generally managed over time such as diabetes and arthritis. Acute (or temporary) diseases are short-term conditions that are curable and treated over a short period of time such as an infection or a common cold. Older individuals with poorer health and functional challenges associated with the normal aging process (universal changes that readily affect everyone as they age such as varying changes in visual acuity) or pathological age-related chronic illnesses become more vulnerable to health decline with advanced age. Living in poverty increases the likelihood of disease and physical or functional limitations in later life, which can result in work loss or earnings declines leading to higher levels of poverty (Louie & Ward, 2011).

Poverty may be associated with disability because of the possibility of cumulative unhealthy behaviors or untreated conditions due to prolonged hardship and inadequate resources (Louie & Ward, 2011). Poor health status, especially if coupled with disability, causes many older adults who are living in poverty to need assistance with activities of daily living (ADLs) in order to remain in the community. Depending on the specific impairment, some older adults may also require assistance with instrumental activities of daily living (IADLs) such as cooking, grocery shopping, and banking due to declines in ability (Adams, Dey, & Vickerie, 2007). Subsequently, chronic illness, and potentially related disability associated with later life may require social support that impoverished and already marginalized older adults may not have (Albert, 2006). Over time, the impact of progressive declines can intensify in degree and severity, placing the oldest segment of the aging population at the greatest risk of major health declines. Such declines can radically impact social, economic, and physical resources.

Among those living in poverty, people living with disabilities are generally among the poorest of the poor of any country; and among this group, women, ethnic minorities, and rural seniors with physical challenges are the most marginalized

(Albert, 2006; Housing Assistance Council, 2011). Nearly 26 percent of those 65 and older and 41 percent of those 75 years old and older have a disability of some kind (U.S. Census Bureau, 2010b). Among seniors living with a disability, 13 percent of those 65 years old and older live in poverty and 86 percent are economically vulnerable. Among those 75 years old and older 12 percent live in poverty and 88 percent are economically vulnerable. Approximately more than half of older people with severe disabilities are female (Johnson & Wiener, 2006). Older adults of color experience chronic illnesses and physical health declines at greater rates with advanced age than their Caucasian counterparts, which ultimately may result in greater disability (Reyes-Ortiz, Snih, Loera, Ray, & Kyriakos Markides, 2004).

Frequently speculated is whether having disabilities contributes to older adults becoming poor and living in poverty or whether being poor contributes to disability. It has been established that living in poverty increases the likelihood of poorer health status leading to disabilities. Additionally, older individuals with disabilities have higher rates of poverty and seniors living in poverty are more marginalized than are their wealthier and healthier peers (Lustig & Strauser, 2007). Disability in later life is associated with limitations in activities caused by physical, mental, and emotional problems (Centers for Disease Control and Prevention [CDC] and the Merck Company Foundation, 2007). Common disabilities among older adults affect hearing, vision, learning, movement, thinking, remembering, mental health, and social relationships (CDC, 2010). Health status and disability among older adults can significantly place individuals at risk for poverty.

The issues of health status and disability are far more extensive than the scope of this chapter can cover but will be addressed in chapter 7. However, the present chapter seeks to assist readers to recognize that being ill and belonging to one or more at-risk subgroups, such as older adults, increases individuals' risk of living in poverty. Additionally, readers should note that living in poverty is strongly linked to poor health. Furthermore, older adults of color and oldest-old women who experience greater disability or declines in physical health due to chronic illness across the life course are at the highest risk of being impoverished and in poor health.

Mental Health

Mental health is an integral component of health and wellness. Chronic health problems, disability, and financial worries in later life can increase the likelihood of mental health conditions among older adults living in poverty (Choi & McDougall, 2009). When compared to younger and middle-aged adults, older adults have a lower prevalence of mental health disorders; however, it is projected that the number of older adults coping with mental or behavioral conditions will increase to 15 million by 2030 (American Psychological Association, 2011; Zarit, 2009). Estimates reveal that 20 percent of older adults experience specific mental and cognitive disorders that are not part of the "normal" aging process (National Coalition on Mental Health and Aging, 2011, para. 4).

Living in poverty can often be linked to specific psychological stressors such as unemployment, financial worries, poor function or physical health, loneliness, social isolation, perceived overdependence, and family conflicts (Choi & McDougall, 2009). These psychological stressors correlate with the onset of mental disorders that may carry into later life (Saxena, Thornicroft, Knapp, & Whiteford, 2007). Most mental conditions experienced by older adults are chronic, recurring conditions across the life course (Zarit, 2009). Seniors who have low income and education are the most vulnerable among older adults living in poverty to develop mental health conditions.

Mental health disorders or conditions experienced by older adults commonly include anxiety and depression (Prina, Ferri, Guerra, Brayne, & Prince, 2011). These mental conditions may be experienced as primary conditions or as co-morbidities, which are coexisting conditions in addition to a primary condition. Unmet financial needs accompanied by a lack of social support or interaction can diminish quality of life and become depression or anxiety risk factors (Choi & McDougall, 2009). Older racial and ethnic minorities who live in rural or urban low-income neighborhoods or are homebound are more vulnerable to depression than are their financially affluent and less frail peers (Choi & Kimbell, 2009). Approximately 20 percent of community-dwelling older adults and 37 percent of older nursing home residents suffer from depression. Older adults also account for 20 percent of those who commit suicide, a mental health issue that has links to depression (American Psychological Association, 2011). Women are more likely than men to be diagnosed with both depression and anxiety. Stressors associated with poverty and economic vulnerability, and those accompanying later life transitions, such as the death of a loved one, caring for a relative with dementia, and coping with a disability, may especially contribute to depression and anxiety among older women. Depression in later life often goes undetected or is stereotypically misunderstood as a part of the aging process. As a result, the treatment of depression is often inadequate, especially among older adults of color and seniors living in poverty (Alliance for Children and Families, 2010).

Mental health services are consistently far more limited than any other health-related care. For instance, the lack of mental health parity in Medicare is a significant financial barrier to mental health treatment for older adults. Medicare reimbursement is only 50 percent of allowable charges for outpatient mental health treatment in comparison to 80 percent for general ambulatory services (Karlin, Duffy, & Gleaves, 2008). Two-thirds of older adults with a mental disorder do not receive needed services (National Coalition on Mental Health and Aging, 2011). Older adults of color and ethnic minorities living in rural areas are at particular risk. Barriers to low-income older adults accessing and continuing mental health treatment include lack of financial resources, availability of trained professionals, transportation, social support, accessible extended care options, alternatives, and availability of medication (Choi & Kimbell, 2009). Denial and stigma may be additional barriers. "Social policies and programs need to find ways to better serve these low-income older adults whose emotional well-being is negatively affected by continuing financial and other hardships" (Choi & Jun, 2009, p. 214).

Caregivers

The burden of care-giving for older adults with chronic disease or functional decline is often assumed by informal caregivers or unpaid caregivers (Schrag, Hovris, Morley, Quinn, & Marjan, 2006). Caregivers typically face competing responsibilities, and emotional or financial demands (including those acting as long-distance caregivers). Today, women account for the majority of the older adult population who receive care and represent two-thirds of informal caregivers (Johnson & Wiener, 2006). Adult daughters are most likely to provide care to aging parents in later life (Hooyman & Kiyak, 2011). Many of these caregivers are also caring for children under eighteen and are consequently labeled the "sandwich generation" (sandwiched between dual care responsibilities, simultaneously caring for two generations) (Pierret, 2006). Women in this position provide care for an aging relative about 18–20 hours per week. This average increases for older adults with progressive cognitive declines, particularly as the severity of illness intensifies (Etters, Goodall, & Harrison, 2008). The demands and accompanying financial strain of care-giving places informal caregivers at risk of living in poverty and developing a mental health condition (this is especially true for those caring for older adults with cognitive declines). Increased care-giving expenses, less ability to prepare for retirement, and difficulty paying bills are direct consequences associated with the care-giving role (Evercare & National Alliance for Caregiving, 2009).

Caregiver burden is the term used to describe the persistent physical, emotional, financial stress, and impaired psychosocial functioning of caregivers (Etters et al., 2008; Schrag et al., 2006). Caregiver burden is most prevalent among the nearly 15 million caregivers caring for someone with Alzheimer's disease (or AD) or other types of dementia, associated with progressive cognitive and functional declines. Approximately 5.2 million older adults (3.4 million women and 1.8 million men) sixty-five years and older live with Alzheimer's or other types of dementias (Alzheimer's Association, 2011). Among this group of caregivers, those who are older themselves and live in poverty are at the greatest risk of developing mental health issues associated with the strains of care-giving. Most caregivers caring for someone with Alzheimer's disease are fifty-five years old or older (56 percent) and possess less than a college degree (67 percent) (Alzheimer's Association, 2011). Among this group of caregivers, the majority are Caucasians (70 percent), with African Americans and Hispanics accounting for 15 percent and 12 percent respectively.

An older adult diagnosed with Alzheimer's at age 55 could live 10–15 years or more with the diagnosis, ultimately requiring increasingly more extensive care as the illness progresses. Alzheimer's caregivers compared to other caregivers typically care for the Alzheimer's patient 1–5 years longer. For older adults and families living in poverty, affording the average $5,000 per month to house an Alzheimer's patient in a memory care unit or to pay for around-the-clock care is impossible (Alliance for Children and Families, 2010). The current lack of resources for low-income or impoverished families with regard to respite care contributes to the burden felt by many caregivers. Respite care refers to planned or emergency short-term relief by someone other than the primary caregiver who provides ongoing care responsibilities or tasks (Etters et al., 2008). Respite care can include a wide range of services in or out of the home such as adult day care and overnight stays in a long-term care facility. Respite not only allows for relief of care duties, but it can also be a vital resource for maintaining mental health among older adults and aging caregivers.

Caregivers when compared to non-caregivers report poorer emotional well-being, poor health, and lowered utilization of health care services (Alzheimer's Association, 2011). Consequently, for those living in poverty, better interventions with regard to emotional, physical, and financial support are needed to mitigate the negative effect that care-giving may impose on both physical and mental health.

Pensions

Managing the economic risks associated with retirement can be a challenge for impoverished older adults. Many factors can influence the inability to accrue income for later life for individuals living in poverty. Chronic low earnings across the life course, poor health, and periods of unemployment may make the accumulation of economic resources very difficult or impossible (Schulz & Binstock, 2011). Social Security, private pensions, and personal savings are the three principal income sources for retirement in later life, sometimes referred to as the "three-legged stool" (Befort, 2007). Older adults who experience economic vulnerability and those living in poverty typically do not have a three-legged stool.

Pension income, a key component of the three-legged stool, may be a nonexistent or limited resource for an impoverished senior. Pensions help eliminate poverty and economic vulnerability and are designed to provide insurance by creating economic resources in the event of old age or disability, which may hinder the continuation of work (Hooyman & Kiyak, 2011; Schulz & Binstock, 2011). Pensions help older adults deal with economic risk experienced during later life. Over time, the term *pension* has described a variety of payment plans designed to provide retirement income. Employer-sponsored pension plans are widely expected in many industries today; however, these are voluntary and have become fragile benefits. Currently, a large percentage of workers do not have these types of private pensions. Approximately 52 percent of workers are not covered by a pension plan (Schulz & Binstock, 2011). Older adults living in poverty who typically have worked at low-paying or part-time jobs often do not have access to employer-based pension plans. Women and ethnic minority seniors are most at risk for not having private pension coverage.

In the current economic climate, employer-sponsored pension plans have high uncertainty, with many companies reducing, terminating, and radically changing pension programs. These actions can leave employees with nothing or very little economic resources, causing Social Security (discussed in the next section) to become a primary source of retirement income for an increasing number of older adults in later life. The uncertainty associated with current plans not only places older adults living in poverty in jeopardy, but may even add to the economic vulnerability of baby boomers. For the older population living in poverty who may be dependent on a public pension plan or low-wage workers who do not have jobs linked to contribution plans, the existence of a public pension system is crucial.

Government Policies and Programs

The current federal measures to assess poverty may not fully address later life challenges and economic vulnerability among the aging population. The current measures of older adult-headed households assumes lower food costs (calculations are based on projections of less consumption with age), and do not consider other expenses such as medication and transportation (Hillier & Barrow, 2011). For example, the sacrifice an older person might make to forfeit food in order to pay for medications or pay rent needs to be considered when defining poverty in later life (Richardson & Barusch, 2006).

Older adults caught in the position between means-tested eligibility and just outside eligibility for social programs, referred to as the "tweeners," are often more vulnerable than seniors receiving assistance and are not fully considered within the current assessment of poverty (Alliance for Children and Families, 2010; Richardson & Barusch, 2006). In this sense, the federal poverty measure does not assess the economic vulnerability of some older adults associated with a lack of health insurance or assets, when long-term care needs arise. Perhaps as suggested by current experimental measures to assess poverty, a more efficient tool is needed to more accurately assess poverty among older adults (Mayer, 2010; Yen, 2010a).

Despite some inadequacies associated with assessing poverty among older adults, there are many types of income support and health care programs available to assist vulnerable members of the aging population. The following is an illustration of the most common programs available to offer support in later life and to assist those living in poverty.

Social Security

As presented earlier, the three-legged stool referring to the typical three income sources for retirement income includes Social Security (Befort, 2007). Most economically vulnerable seniors have a one-legged stool consisting exclusively of Social Security benefits (see figure 6.2). A direct result of the 1935 Social Security Act, Social Security is one of several programs that impact older adults and those living in poverty. As an entitlement program for older adults, Social Security is recognized as the nation's most effective antipoverty program. Fundamental strengths of this program are the income assistance it offers older adults in later life, and the benefit compensation given to low-wage earners (Hudson, 2011). Social Security periodically provides for older adults' cost of living (through cost of living adjustments, COLAs), which benefits recipients. Table 6.1 shows the average benefit for

Table 6.1. Average 2011 Monthly Benefits for Social Security and Supplemental Security Income Recipients

Benefit Category	Social Security	Supplemental Security Income
Retired worker or individual	$1,174	$ 674*
Retired couple or couple	$1,907	$1,011*
Additional Categories		
Disabled worker	$1,067	
Disabled worker with a spouse and child	$1,813	
Widow or widower	$1,133	
Young widow or widower with two children	$2,409	

*Does not include state supplement.
Sources: Alliance for Retired Americans (2011); Social Security Administration (2011a) [Table 1 Average Monthly Benefit].

retired, disabled, and widowed workers. Almost 90 percent of people aged sixty-five or older receive some of their income from Social Security (Center on Budget and Policy Priorities, 2012). As a result of this program, only one-tenth of older adults (roughly 13 million older Americans) live in poverty. Without it, poverty would affect a significantly higher number of individuals.

The effectiveness of Social Security for women and minority older adults is significant. This program has generally improved the economic condition of older women of color and ethnic minorities who otherwise would not have retirement income. Social Security is an important source of income for minority groups who represent low earners with less opportunity to save and earn pensions (Center on Budget and Policy Priorities, 2012). Among beneficiaries aged sixty-five and older, Social Security represents 90 percent or more of income for 34 percent of African Americans and 33 percent of Hispanics.

There is much debate regarding the rising expenditures associated with Social Security related to the solvency or the ability of the program to sustain itself (Schulz & Binstock, 2011). In 2010, 37 million retired workers and dependents of retired workers, 6 million survivors of deceased workers, and 10 million disabled workers and dependents of disabled workers received Social Security benefits (Social Security Administration [SSA], 2011c). During this year, total expenditures for Social Security were $713 billion.

Current debates regarding the solvency of Social Security and proposals for reform suggest that adjustments to the structure of the Social Security program may be inevitable. Among the proposals is a key focus on the need to address the gendered aspects of entitlement programs. Determining how to provide women with credit for the types of obligations that remove them from the workforce is an important consideration for later life conditions. An example of a proposed reform measure offers caregiver credit to women for their withdrawal from the workforce to provide care-giving and meet family responsibilities (Richardson & Barusch, 2006). This credit would primarily help women, who tend to provide care-giving more often than men. If legislation such as this is passed women could be compensated when acting as informal caregivers, which as discussed previously, leads to this group incurring additional financial strain because of this added responsibility.

It is important to think critically about proposed reform that will change existing policies. Particularly those programs that historically provided antipoverty relief or economic support to vulnerable groups could potentially change, placing older adults in greater jeopardy of poverty. Therefore, in a policy climate dictated by a need to reduce spending and respond to economic challenges, professionals working with vulnerable populations must continue to advocate for groups such as older adults, women, and minorities.

Medicare

The Social Security Act of 1965 included the creation of Medicare. Medicare as a social insurance program was originally intended to provide older adults with income protection from catastrophic medical costs associated with later life (Hooyman & Kiyak, 2011; Novak, 2012). Financed by a portion of payroll taxes paid by workers and their employers, and in part by monthly premiums deducted from Social Security checks, Medicare provides universal health insurance coverage to adults sixty-five years and older without means-testing (Hudson, 2011). Medicare helps with the cost of health care, but it does not cover all medical expenses or the cost of most long-term care needs. The program is often criticized because Medicare covers only hospital and physician care services, and does not provide enough coverage for routine medical and mental health care, which is most needed during later life (Karlin, Duffy, & Gleaves, 2008).

Medicare consists of four parts: hospital insurance (Part A), medical insurance (Part B, requires a premium payment), Medicare Advantage plans (Part C, requires a premium payment), and prescription drug coverage (Part D) (SSA, 2010). Part A provides some assistance with inpatient care in a hospital or skilled nursing facility following a hospitalization, some home health care, and hospice care. Part B provides coverage for doctors' services (and many other medical services) and supplies that are not covered by the hospital insurance. Part C, Medicare Advantage plans, are medigap plans or supplemental insurance coverage that cover services not covered under Part B, bridging a gap in coverage. Prescription drug coverage (Part D) pays for medications doctors prescribe for treatment (SSA, 2010). Part D has been considered the most significant expansion of Medicare since its inception for it attempts to address a tremendous burden imposed by prescription drug costs among older adults (Hudson, 2011).

In order to receive coverage under Part C, older adults must have Medicare Part A and Part B, pay a monthly Medicare Part B premium to Medicare, and pay a monthly premium to the Medicare Advantage Plan for the extra benefits offered. The premiums associated with Medicare Part B can be a challenge for older adults with limited economic resources. Therefore, it is not difficult to conclude that the multiple premiums associated with joining a Medicare Advantage plan under Part C are cost-prohibitive for impoverished or economically vulnerable older adults. As a result, while Medicare provides several coverage options, these may not be affordable to an older adult living in poverty or near-poor senior.

As part of the 2003 Medicare Prescription Drug Improvement and Modernization Act (MMA), Medicare D (effective in 2006) was added to the program in an effort to address the burden of prescription drug costs experienced in later life (CMS, 2010a). However, this measure only created some assistance, since high deductibles continued to make medication costs a problem for many older adults. This has been referred to as the donut hole, a coverage gap between the difference between the initial coverage limit and the catastrophic threshold (Alliance for Children and Families, 2010). This results when total drug costs (including the deductible) reach $2,830, leaving older adults to pay full out-of-pocket prescription costs. Once out-of-pocket expenses reach $4,550 coverage resumes (Bihari, 2010). A component of the 2010 Patient Protection and Affordable Care Act signed into law by President Obama is an effort to address the burden of this gap, by allowing seniors who reach the donut hole to receive a $250 rebate. In 2011, those reaching the donut hole (about 4 million Medicare beneficiaries) were only required to pay half the cost for brand-name medications (Pavle, 2011). By 2020, incremental changes under the act are expected to completely eliminate the donut hole. Although Medicare beneficiaries receive some protections against medical care costs, the supplemental components of the program and associated copayments or out-of-pocket expenses still place some older adults in economic jeopardy.

Medicaid

Unlike Medicare, Medicaid is a means-tested state-operated social insurance program developed to help those considered medically indigent—including older adults. The program is jointly funded by the federal government and states, with the federal government paying states for a specified percentage of program expenditures. Medicaid provides coverage for more than 4.6 million low-income seniors (CMS, 2012b). Extremely impoverished older adults may qualify for both Medicaid and Medicare. This is referred to as dual eligibility (when a beneficiary is simultaneously eligible to receive assistance from more than one program). Generally, low-income seniors who cannot afford Medicare premiums or deductibles use Medicaid as a medigap program. For this group of older adults, Medicaid provides more comprehensive coverage for services related to needs in later life and includes nursing home and home health care, rural health clinics, prescription drugs, hearing aids, dental care, and prosthetic devices (CMS, 2010b).

Over the years there have been concerns regarding the number of older Medicaid recipients and expenditures for this group, some of which have been associated with abuses of the "spend down" (deliberate dumping of assets and resources for the purposes of qualifying for benefits) provisions to meet means-testing eligibility. While measures have been imposed to limit fraudulent use of the spend down policy, the increasing economic vulnerability of older adults suggests that many seniors are legitimately forced to use up all their assets and income in order to receive care in later life (Novak, 2012).

As a resource for low-income seniors, Medicaid provides some relief to those living in poverty who otherwise would go without medical care or who would experience large costs likely to strain their fixed or limited income (Hudson, 2011). Medicaid is currently the largest provider of long-term and nursing home care for the needy in the United States (Kaiser Family Foundation, 2013). This is largely based on the 1981 Omnibus Budget Reconciliation Act (OBRA) establishing the Home and Community-Based Services (HCBS) Medicaid Waiver Program allowing states to provide non-institutional services reimbursable by Medicaid to individuals who otherwise would be at risk of institutional placement. Older adults can receive assistance in their homes, thereby remaining in their communities. This effort to help older adults age in place has been strengthened by Medicaid and long-term care coverage provisions granted under the Affordable Care Act (Pavle, 2011).

In 2010, Medicaid spending was estimated at $354 billion (National Association of State Budget Officers, 2011). A fundamental problem of rising costs is the strain on states and the federal government to continue providing services to economically vulnerable older adults and those living in poverty without overtaxing budgets.

Supplemental Security Income

Supplemental Security Income (SSI) is a federal income program that makes monthly payments to low-income individuals with limited resources who are sixty-five and older, or permanently blind or living with disabilities. Approximately 1.1 million older adults receive SSI monthly benefits (SSA, 2011b). Some of these beneficiaries may receive a state supplement, which provides additional income in some states to improve benefit adequacy.

The Social Security Administration (SSA), the organization that administers this program excludes a portion of income and certain resources as part of the means-testing to determine an individual's eligibility. An older adult's house and car are usually not counted among means-tested resources (SSA, 2010). Traditionally, older adults with extremely limited income (such as a small Social Security check) and limited resources may still be eligible for SSI. Despite the existence of SSI, many older adults still live in poverty. This may suggest inadequate benefit levels and a low percentage of participation amongst older adults (Richardson & Barusch, 2006).

The Older Americans Act

The Older Americans Act (OAA) was enacted to provide universal non-means-tested programs for older adults through a network of federal, state, local, and other service agencies. Enacted in 1965, the OAA is one of the nation's largest sources of social service programs (Hooyman & Kiyak, 2011; Hudson, 2011). Historically, it has been reviewed for reauthorization every five years in order to extend the act's appropriations, with some allocations going toward program innovation and development (Napili & Colello, 2013). The reauthorization expected in 2011 did not occur as planned. The most recent reauthorization legislation, the Older

Americans Act Amendments of 2013, S. 1562 (introduced September 30, 2013), is under congressional committee review (Library of Congress, 2013; Napili & Colello, 2013). While reauthorization has not yet been enacted, Congress has appropriated funding for OAA authorized activities and other aging services through March 2013 as part of the Continuing Appropriations Resolution, 2013 (Napili & Colello, 2013). The lack of a five-year reauthorized period of funding puts many programs in jeopardy and has already resulted in unanticipated budget cuts for some services. Programs under the OAA are managed by the Administration of Aging (AOA), a branch of the Department of Health and Human Services, and fall within six general categories: nutrition services, preventative health services, supportive services, elder abuse prevention and protection services, the National Caregiver Family Support Program, and services for Native Americans (Novak, 2012). The OAA attempts to address the needs of older Americans by focusing on the provision of services that compensate for limited resources or increased vulnerability of loss (in a variety of areas) often experienced in later life (Hudson, 2011; Quadagno, 2011). Services are provided to all older adults but particular attention is given to assist those most vulnerable, including older adults living in poverty, experiencing isolation, and to those coping with severe health issues.

The OAA is the basis for the aging network, which is an array of public and private agencies and social services designed to help older adults remain independent and in the community (Hooyman & Kiyak, 2011; Novak, 2012). Currently, the aging network is made up of the Administration on Aging (AOA); 56 State Units on Aging (SUAs); 629 local Area Agencies (AAA) on Aging; 244 Native American and Tribal organizations; 2 Native Hawaiian organizations; over 30,000 service providers; and thousands of volunteers (AOA, 2010). A primary responsibility of the aging network is planning, care coordination, and research related to the needs of older adults. State Units on Aging (sometimes through the assistance of local Area Agencies on Aging) often administer the Home and Community Based Services Medicaid Waiver Program. The aging network is vital in the coordination of community-based services provided beyond just those associated with health care including areas such as senior centers, adult day care centers, transportation, Meals on Wheels, education, senior employment training, and research (Hillier & Barrow, 2011; Hudson, 2011). Early amendments throughout the 1970s added service areas to include mental health, planning, disease prevention, and criminal justice. A focus of the amendments during the 1980s–1990s was to increase attention given to the needs and services of older adults with chronic illnesses. In the last decade, amendments have helped to provide caregiver support with the enactment of the Family Caregiver Support Services Act, which provides some support to informal family caregivers and is part of the Older Americans Act (AOA, 2010).

The aging network has concentrated on care delivery and services that allow vulnerable seniors to stay in the community, a demand that is expected to continue. As Congress continues deliberations regarding reauthorization and the budget for current OAA services, it is notable that many advocates support continued funding for community-based programs that allow low-income and community-dwelling older adults to avoid the need for formal care or institutionalization. Entitlement programs and other social programs within the aging network are extremely vital to address the economic conditions of older adults. Such programs provide resources and support that can help economically vulnerable seniors and those living in poverty to maintain a basic standard of living.

Social Justice

The need for social justice and services may rise as economic vulnerability increases across the life course. As women continue to outlive men, it is important to address the gendered aspects of long-term care, employment, and race. Many of the current social programs such as Social Security, Medicare, Medicaid, and Supplemental Security Income have program limitations that without further accountability may increase the disadvantages experienced by vulnerable seniors. The current shift in today's political climate is placing greater responsibility on individuals, which can limit access to existing programs for older adults. The recent increase in the retirement age for full Social Security benefits from age 65 to age 67 places many who are unable to continue working in later life at a distinct disadvantage (Schulz & Binstock, 2011). The change in the retirement age ultimately affects Social Security and Medicare benefits, since eligibility for both are primarily determined by time and work credits. Therefore, older adults living with disabilities, chronic illnesses, and poorer health may need additional income assistance or access to supportive programs due to their inability to continue working to the increased retirement age. Social work professionals can be a vital asset in providing linkages and direct access to helpful services or programs for older adults facing this new challenge.

Since older impoverished women outlive their male counterparts, they make up a significant portion of SSI recipients. Addressing limitations in this program or advocating for higher benefit levels could help older women meet their expenses. SSI income and resource levels have been in place since the early 1980s; and adequate adjustments have not accounted for twenty years of inflation nor have benefits been adjusted for the cost of living (Hudson, 2011). Clearly, this benefit in its current form is inadequate in helping those most in need. Accordingly, social workers need to advocate for increases in benefit levels for programs such as SSI, to truly raise older adults out of poverty.

As expenditures for Medicare and Medicaid continue to increase, federal spending issues may place greater financial responsibility or what is often referred to as cost-sharing on an already vulnerable population of older adults. This may be evident through increases in individuals' out-of-pocket expenses (such as copayments, premiums, or deductibles) as a mechanism to counter escalating programs costs. However, it is important to note that for older adults already living in or near poverty, an increase in health care expenses will keep this group struggling and may ultimately push those who are near poverty over the line.

Another social justice concern relates to overextended caregivers. Providing caregivers, typically adult daughters, with access to social support and services may give families much-needed relief. As discussed previously, the burden of caring for aging family members sustained by informal caregivers will only increase as baby boomers age. Ultimately, this responsibility will take a toll on the mental and physical health of family caregivers. As a result, social workers and health care professionals should advocate for legislation that addresses the needs of this often forgotten group. Failure to assist caregivers can affect the entire family unit and places them at risk of poverty.

Elder abuse is a serious problem that should be included in a discussion regarding social justice. Elder abuse is a form of abuse, which can include physical, sexual, or emotional abuse and financial exploitation of an older adult (Hooyman & Kiyak, 2011; Novak, 2012). It also includes neglect, often by a person in a trusted relationship such as in a position of authority. Elder abuse also consists of abandonment, self-neglect, theft, or sexual assault of an adult sixty years or older (Brandl et al., 2007). Factors such as family structure, economic strain, and the dynamics of care may contribute to the abuse suffered by older adults (Tauriac & Scruggs, 2006).

It is estimated about 2 million Americans age sixty-five or older have been injured, exploited, or otherwise mistreated by someone whom they depended on for care or protection (National Center on Elder Abuse [NCEA], 2005). Older women are the majority of older people who experience abuse (Penhale, 2005), largely due to the longevity experienced by women. As the aging population increases and individuals live longer, the number of older adults susceptible to abuse is likely to increase.

Mistreatment or abuse can trigger a downward spiral leading to an older adult's loss of independence, serious illness, and even death (Burgess & Hanrahan, 2006). Cross-culturally, older adults along with children, women, and individuals living with disabilities are consistently vulnerable to victimization (Patterson & Malley-Morrison, 2006). Exploitation of older adults is a serious social justice issue. Caregivers may financially exploit individual older adults by depleting a senior's economic resources, leaving many seniors with no means of supporting themselves. Many dependent older adults may be aware of the caregiver's actions, but too often, nothing is said because of fear, denial, or loyalty to the caregiver who usually is a family member. Fraud can also cause the complete depletion of resources not just for an individual but also for an entire group of older adults. Older adults can lose money to licensed individuals selling lawful products in addition to con artists perpetrating criminal fraud (Schulz & Binstock, 2011). For example, the 2009 Bernie Madoff scandal defrauded older adults who invested their retirement savings. This kind of exploitation is devastating at a point in the life course when recouping losses is extremely unlikely. Older adults living in poverty may not have the means to invest, but may be equally susceptible to fraudulent practices by professionals and family members.

Elder abuse in any form is a social problem that must be addressed to ensure social justice, safety, and the well-being of all older adults. A key approach to social justice is advocacy for those in need. Social workers and other helping professionals can influence the types of policies, practices, and protections developed for older adults, through advocacy for stricter interventions to prevent elder abuse, and to promote additional services for older adults living in poverty.

Interventions

Social workers and other helping professionals impact the lives of impoverished seniors by employing intervention strategies across levels of practice (Zastrow, 2010). In order to comprehensively address issues among the aging population, professionals must utilize multilevel strategies that may include one-on-one approaches to assist individual seniors (micro level); work with small groups of older adults and their families (mezzo level); and collaborating with organizations in the aging network and advocating for change through social policy (macro level). Social workers and other professionals must readily understand that the path to living in poverty in later life is varied and many strategies are needed to meet the needs of an impoverished aging population.

Micro Interventions

Individual circumstances leading to economic hardship may be as diverse as the aging population itself. Therefore, social workers and other professionals working with seniors must use case-specific micro-level practices to address the financial circumstances and economic needs of individual older adults. As a result, individual counseling may be useful to assist older adults living in poverty. One-on-one efforts assist older clients with locating tangible resources within their communities and may include some element of empowerment.

> Empowerment is a process in which social workers work with [older/impoverished] clients to help them define their [economic] problems, make decisions to solve problems through individual and collective actions, and to build on clients' strengths in order to help clients access critical environmental resources. (Berkeman & Harootyan, 2003, p. 164)

Such empowerment can change the lives of older adults living in poverty and may require extended attention to community-based economic and social programs or services not only designed to educate the older client but to help avert any further economic hardship. A client-centered approach, which fosters shared decision-making, may be an effective practice. Allowing opportunities for an older adult, who may commonly be "spoken to" rather than "spoken with," to participate fully in the decision-making process can be beneficial to that older adult's self-esteem. Professionals may unwittingly perpetuate the powerlessness associated with living in poverty by how they talk to or interact with older clients. Establishing a one-on-one relationship and helping an older adult have a sense of autonomy can help build esteem and provide a sense of self-worth needed to overcome the challenges of financial hardship.

Professionals at the micro level can do far more than make referrals or identify services such as subsidized housing, mental health resources, and older adult-focused job training programs to meet older clients' needs. Social workers in particular, can create individual connections or build rapport with economically vulnerable older adults in ways that can remind them of their value and self-efficacy, despite their economic circumstances. Poverty can create social vulnerability, which impacts the older adult's ability to interact in their community. Through one-on-one strategies, social work professionals can help marginalized older adults reconnect.

Mezzo Interventions

A person-in-environment perspective suggests that poverty can limit older adults' integration into the physical and social contexts in which they live. Limited availability of social and economic resources and a lack of social capital may foster disadvantages for seniors living in poverty (Keating, 2008). Working with aging families and small groups, professionals can educate and mitigate the loss of social capital experienced when living in poverty. Diminished social capital is particularly problematic for the oldest-old and rural older adults who may need daily assistance, but lack appropriate social networks. Creating social support groups in rural or minority communities, which meet in church congregations or mobile facilities, can help restore lost community networks. Older women, older adults of color, rural seniors, and increasingly vulnerable suburban seniors with limited financial resources can manage when compensatory networks exist and services are made available (Keating, 2008). Addressing local concerns in a collective forum where families coping with economic hardship can learn about available resources and programs is essential in any community.

Professionals within the aging network working with small groups have been vital in creating social support groups such as caregiver support groups that can enable seniors to identify with others and provide socialization, while promoting a healthy activity not dependent on an individual's financial limits. Creating social support groups among seniors can provide opportunities for them to network with their peers and to share strategies for coping with aging, limited resources, or other aspects of life. This type of mezzo-level intervention can be beneficial and empowering to members of the aging population.

Macro Interventions

Social workers assisting older adults may need to develop collaborative relationships not used in the coordination of services to other population groups. Extending existing partnerships to include senior centers, Area Agencies on Aging, a network of nonprofits that create community-based services, religious communities, universities, social workers, and other entities that work with older adults may collaboratively create effective local solutions that meet the needs of clients living in poverty. For example, the Wisconsin Family Care Project founded in 1998 resulted from collaborative partnerships involving many agencies (both public and private) that serve older adults, including the Department of Health and Human Services (Alliance for Children and Families, 2010). This project resulted in a redesign of Wisconsin's long-term care services to create a more flexible and comprehensive "one-stop shop" wherein older adults could receive case management and referrals to multiple community-based services, all within one setting. The collaborative efforts eliminated traditional fragmentation in services for older adults that are often caused by agencies' retention of territorial lines and the duplication or inappropriateness of services. Working to centralize application processes, eligibility assessments, and making programs more senior-friendly can prove effective in meeting the needs of older adults.

There has been considerable emphasis on the construction of macro-level policy to combat poverty among older adults. On a national level, the refocusing of aging services across the country may be a crucial area for future collaborative efforts to more effectively meet the needs of economically vulnerable older adults (Judd & Moore, 2011). The implementation of a universal standardized comprehensive care management model supervised by independent intra-agency care managers (independent of collaborative agencies) may be more effective than current care models (Judd & Moore, 2011). The use of a care manager not employed or directly associated with agencies involved in services delivery could result in better care.

A refined model of service delivery could address the needs of economically vulnerable older adults by employing some of the best practices already used to meet the needs of at-risk older adults. Employing practices used by such programs as the Programs of All-Inclusive Care for the Elderly (PACE) within a more effective comprehensive care model may more efficiently help those living in poverty. PACE provides an alternative to institutional care for persons aged fifty-five or older who require a nursing facility level of care through an interdisciplinary team approach (CMS, 2012a). The care team provides health, medical, and social services and mobilization of other services as needed to provide preventive, rehabilitative, curative, and supportive care. This care is adaptable and can be provided in day health centers, homes, hospitals, and nursing homes, to help seniors maintain independence and quality of life. A similar more effective comprehensive care model nationally would reduce barriers to services and could provide greater access to help those living in and near poverty (Judd & Moore, 2011). Social workers and related health professionals should advocate for programs such as these at the macro level.

Collaboration across multiple organizations and among various communities to advocate for programs and policies such as those mentioned above or to increase Social Security benefits and long-term care reform are undoubtedly mechanisms to reduce poverty among older adults and are useful macro-level strategies. The lack of an adequate cost of living adjustment within both the Social Security and Supplemental Security Income programs is a vital advocacy area. These programs provide income to many economically vulnerable older adults, and the inability of such programs to account for inflation and changes in the economy is a critical shortcoming in meeting the needs of older adults, leaving many to live in poverty. Professionals who work day-to-day with this group can provide documentation of case examples that illustrate the difficulties experienced by clients who must live on their current monthly benefits, as shown in table 6.1. Such illustrations are valuable tools to educate policymakers about benefit shortfalls and the "real world" challenges faced by those trying to make ends meet. Advocacy from professionals working with impoverished adults can shed light on the importance of ending poverty among all older adults in a meaningful way, rather than simply reducing the number of welfare program recipients by reducing eligibility guidelines for social programs.

Concluding Comments

Nearly one in ten older adults sixty-five years and older live in households with incomes below the U.S. federal poverty line (O'Brien et al., 2010; U.S. Census Bureau, 2010b). Many older adults living in poverty may experience social isolation because of limited resources, which can influence their mental health status and exacerbate declines in their physical health (Keating, 2008). The current sociodemographic profile of older adults living in poverty strongly highlights the significance of factors such as gender, race, ethnicity, geographic locality (rural, urban, or suburban), and age (Hooyman & Kiyak, 2011; Novak, 2012). Poverty in later life is a complex reflection of life course opportunities or challenges, and in some instances societal failures with regard to distinct subgroups of older adults (Richardson & Barusch, 2006). Therefore, efforts to change later life circumstances may require efforts to improve economic stability across the entire life course for those at greatest risk for living in poverty during later life.

Case Studies
Micro Level

After thirty-five years of working for a local utilities company, Sheila Vann, a 69-year-old African American woman, has decided to retire. This decision was prompted by a decline in her health. Diagnosed with chronic obstructive pulmonary disease about twenty years ago, Mrs. Vann now seems to be experiencing increased difficulty maintaining activities and breathing throughout the day. Mrs. Vann had worked up to a very stressful mid-level information technology assistant position at the time of her retirement. Her company provided a defined contribution pension plan, which she expected to help provide for a good retirement. However, her retirement fund was invested in stocks and major declines in the market caused these funds to drastically decrease. Not really worried, trusting that God would provide, Mrs. Vann still expected to be able to have a decent retirement and had plans to visit her two daughters who lived out-of-state and enjoy her grandchildren.

Three years into her retirement, her husband, who been unemployed for about two years due to an injury from work in construction, suffered a major stroke, and needed extensive physical and speech therapy. After an initial short-term period in a local nursing home for rehabilitation, Mr. Vann came home to continue his recovery. Although the couple had Medicare coverage, due to coverage limitations and without supplemental insurance, they found themselves having to pay large out-of-pocket expenses to cover Mr. Vann's medical equipment costs and other fees. Additionally, Mrs. Vann needed help with primary care duties and initially hired a home health aide to assist her. However, she could not continue to pay for this help so she later took on all care duties herself despite her own health issues. Mrs. Vann was involved in a women's group at her local church prior to taking on her care-giving role and while she could no longer continue with this group, they did provide some assistance. The women occasionally brought over a meal or helped with light housekeeping, but many had care-giving responsibilities of their own and could only offer limited support.

Prior to Mr. Vann's original injury, the couple took out an equity line of credit on their home to make some necessary major repairs. As a result, they have struggled to maintain monthly payments in relation to the loan and fear they could eventually lose their home. They had some savings but these quickly diminished over the last few years. Mrs. Vann sought medical assistance through Medicaid but was denied. Overwhelmed by the escalating medical bills, she discussed the situation with her two daughters. However, they are both raising families with small children and have been unable to help their parents financially.

Socially isolated, unable to see her daughters, and burdened with care-giving, Mrs. Vann was diagnosed with depression. The financial insecurity and worry about being wiped out financially has begun to take a toll on Mrs. Vann's health. Approximately one year after his stroke, Mr. Vann died. The death of her husband only worsened Mrs. Vann's depression and her worry about her financial future. Her daughters suggested that their mother find some part-time work to both supplement her income and to give her something to do. However, Mrs. Vann has found it difficult to locate a job at her age. She recently heard from a neighbor about two local job-training programs for seniors through the Goodwill and the Urban League, but is not sure if it will be worth her time.

Questions

1. Kim is the social worker assigned to Mrs. Vann's case. What should she do first?

2. Should Kim set up a phone conference with her daughters and advise them of Mrs. Vann's health status and economic condition?

3. What values or beliefs does Mrs. Vann have that might relate to her needs?

4. Besides Mrs. Vann's needs, what might be the needs of her daughters?

5. How might sensitivity to gender and social roles be applicable in this case?

Mezzo Level

Karen Moore is a social worker at Peace Haven Center, a local adult day care center. She was recently asked by Mrs. Adams, the center director, to organize an event for their "regular" family caregivers. Over the course of working at Peace Haven, Karen has overheard several caregivers discussing the difficulties in managing care responsibilities and finding assistive services. She thinks the caregivers could benefit from workshops or support group sessions designed to educate them about local services and programs available to assist them. After some thought, Karen asks Mrs. Adams if she could organize a monthly support group for the caregivers rather than a one-time social. Mrs. Adams agrees that a support group might be more useful for the center's families.

At the suggestion of Mrs. Adams, Karen contacts a local university gerontology program to see if a student intern might be available to assist her with the new project. Mr. Jones, the program coordinator, agrees to assign a senior-level student intern to Peace Haven Center for the duration of the semester. He also offers to arrange a monthly reservation for one of the rooms at the university's conference center as a location for the meeting. Since the campus is only ten minutes away from the center, Karen thinks meeting at the conference center might be a good idea but decides to check with Mrs. Adams first. Upon approval from Mrs. Adams, she agrees to use the conference center room for the monthly meetings.

Karen initiated informal conservations with the regular caregivers over the course of two weeks regarding the start of the support group and their potential interest. Based on caregiver schedules, Karen and the intern decide on a Saturday morning for the group meeting times. She schedules the meetings for every fourth Saturday of the month and decides on calling them Care 4 Those Who Care. Karen has the student intern help create an electronic memo, which she sends out to local agencies in the aging services network. As a follow-up to the memo, Karen has the intern phone each agency about a week later. She also creates a hard-copy flyer to post at local area community recreation centers, senior centers, and churches. Once agency representatives have been notified and flyers posted in the community, Karen creates an invitation to send out to each family on the center's client list.

Several weeks before the initial meeting, in an effort to provide information on services useful to the caregivers, Karen places a suggestion box near the entrance of the center with a big sign indicating "Family Caregiver Support Group Starting, Your Suggestions Needed" and a short questionnaire asking for topics regarding services, workshops, and any other information caregivers might be interested in learning more about. Karen and her intern were happy to discover that a majority of the regular caregivers actually entered suggestions in the box. The topics of most interest related to free or low-cost services, respite care, and care management strategies. Karen made a list of local agencies that provided direct services related to the suggested topics. Representatives from these agencies were contacted and asked to conduct a short ten-minute presentation on information regarding their services at the support group meeting.

Fourteen regular caregivers attended the initial meeting and each attendee expressed enthusiasm about the meeting and indicated that they would be interested in attending the next one. The agency representatives also shared an enthusiasm about what they learned from hearing about caregivers' concerns. After meeting with caregivers for four months, Karen organized a light reception event where she asked the support group members to share with other families at the center about community programs they had learned about during the monthly meetings and may have actually used. Most of the support group members talked about local low-fee or volunteer-based services they had used, strategies for care they had tried, and friendships they had made as a result of attending the group. Many of the caregivers who had not attended the monthly meetings joined after hearing about the benefits of attending.

Questions

1. Why might caregivers using the center not attend the support group meetings?

2. What respite care services or programs might the caregivers benefit from learning about?

3. What local agencies other than those suggested might Karen engage to assist this group?

4. Based on the information provided, how might Karen more effectively work with the gerontology program to provide events for the caregivers?

5. What knowledge might Karen need to work with family caregivers caring for cognitively impaired older adults?

Macro Level

Many caregivers caring for someone with Alzheimer's disease have difficulty managing care as the illness progresses. Caregivers often find that the responsibility of care demands most of their time and energy. This can often create hardships with regard to physical health, mental well-being, employment status, financial stability, and family relationships.

In an effort to celebrate caregivers during National Caregiver Month, professionals in North Carolina organize a Caregiver Support Fair. This fair is organized to highlight services and resources available for Alzheimer's caregivers and families throughout the state. The annual location rotates throughout several of the largest counties and is traditionally held at the local fairgrounds. The Caregiver

Support Fair provides caregivers with information and services such as respite programs, meal preparation services, health screenings, and medication management products.

Representatives from a variety of agencies and organizations collaborate in the event. Federal, state, and local government representatives as well as nonprofit and private service providers participate each year. Organization representatives share information about social insurance programs such as Medicaid, Medicare, Social Security, Supplemental Security Income, and other programs offered under the Older Americans Act that might assist Alzheimer's caregivers. An Alzheimer Association Representative staffs a booth that is set up to demonstrate an Alzheimer's Toolkit or the latest news regarding treatment and care for individuals living with cognitive impairment. Researchers from universities across North Carolina discuss local ongoing Alzheimer's-related research projects and hand out information on participation criteria. The event is usually closed with a panel presentation of North Carolina family caregivers who share information regarding care-giving strategies, experiences, and concerns.

Volunteers provide activities and supervision for Alzheimer care recipients to allow caregivers an opportunity to freely explore the event. Caregivers are hosted at a "caregiver social hour" catered by local restaurants, which allows for some recreation and socialization with other caregivers. The annual event serves approximately 500 caregivers each year. The event connects caregivers to each other and engages them in the community.

Questions

1. What community-based agencies or services may be important to involve in this type of event?

2. How could service providers engage state and federal officials to better assist Alzheimer's caregivers?

3. Should government provide benefits such as cash assistance, Social Security caregiver credit, or other discounts for Alzheimer's caregivers?

4. If you could design legislation to respond to the needs of caregivers, what might you include? Also, who are the stakeholders you need to engage in order to pass your legislation?

Internet Resources

Aging-related agencies, resources, and statistical data, in addition to both state and federally based resources related to aging and poverty are widely accessible. The resources listed below are a sample of those available.

American Association of Retired Persons: http://www.aarp.org/

A nonprofit organization, advocating for people age fifty and over, which provides key resources such as antipoverty efforts to assist older adults. Resources include policy, health, and financial information.

Administration on Aging: http://www.aoa.gov

The Administration on Aging (AOA) is the newly established Administration for Community Living (ACL) within the U.S. Department of Health and Human Services (HHS) that provides resources and information on the latest key statistics regarding older adults.

Center for American Progress: http://www.americanprogress.org

An educational site that addresses economic growth and opportunity, immigration, education, health care, housing, and other resources related to poverty and aging.

Center for Law and Social Policy (CLASP): http://www.clasp.org

CLASP develops and advocates for federal, state, and local policies to strengthen families and create pathways to education and employment for low-income individuals. They provide the latest data regarding aging and poverty statistics.

Families in Society: http://alliance1.org

Families in Society disseminates innovative research and critical analysis to advance knowledge-based practice and social work education. The site has a new downloadable journal supplement with an overview on older adults trying to stay out of poverty.

Feeding America: http://feedingamerica.org

A domestic charity focused on hunger relief. They strive to serve America's hungry through a nationwide network of member food banks. The site also provides data regarding food security and poverty, which impacts older adults.

National Center on Elder Abuse (NCEA): http://www.ncea.aoa.gov/

The NCEA provides data, resources, and fact sheets about the national problem of elder abuse.

National Poverty Center (2006): Uhttp://www.npc.umich.edu/poverty/#2U

Research Center at the Gerald R. Ford School of Public Policy at the University of Michigan provides an overview of poverty-related statistics.

Office of Minority Health: http://minorityhealth.hhs.gov

This organization addresses issues related to health disparities among minority populations. It also offers resources on low-cost health programs and services.

Further Readings

Hudson, R. B. (2011). *The new politics of old age policy.* Baltimore, MD: Johns Hopkins University Press.

Iceland, J. (2006). *Poverty in America* (2nd ed.). Berkeley, CA: University of California Press.

Niles-Yokum, K., & Wagner, D. (2011). *The Aging Networks: A guide to programs and services* (7th ed.). New York: Springer Publishing Company.

Novak, M. (2012). *Issues of aging* (3rd ed.). New York: Pearson Higher Education.

Richardson, V. E., & Barusch, A. M. (2006). *Gerontological practice for the twenty-first century: A social work perspective.* New York: Columbia University Press.

Schulz, J., & Binstock, R. (2011). *Aging nation: The economics and politics of growing older in America.* Baltimore, MD: Johns Hopkins University Press.

Wacker, R., & Roberto, K. (2008). *Community resources for older adults: Programs and services in an era of change.* Thousand Oaks, CA: Sage Publication, Inc.

References

Achenbaum, W. A. (2008). The historical roles of states in shaping U.S. aging policies. *Generations, 32*(1), 10–15.

Adams, P., Dey, A., & Vickerie, J. (2007). Summary health statistics for the U.S. population: National Health Interview Survey. *Vital Health, 10*(233), 1–104.

Administration on Aging. (2010). *National aging network.* Retrieved from http://www.aoa.gov/AoARoot/AoA_Programs/OAA/Aging_Network/Index.aspx.

Administration on Aging. (2013). *A profile of older adults: 2012.* Retrieved from http://www.aoa.gov/Aging_Statistics/Profile/2012/docs/2012profile.pdf.

Albert, B. (2006). *Lessons from the disability knowledge and research KaR programme.* UK Department for International Development. Retrieved from http://www.dochas.ie/Pages/Resources/documents/kar_learn.pdf.

Alliance for Children and Families. (2010). *Aging in poverty: Call to action.* Milwaukee, WI: Families in Society.

Alliance for Retired Americans. (2011). *Fact sheet: Social Security & Medicare current facts and figures,* November 2011. Washington, DC: Alliance for Retired Americans. Retrieved from http://s3.amazonaws.com/zanran_storage/www.retiredamericans.org/ContentPages/2536577131.pdf.

Alzheimer's Association. (2011). *2011 Alzheimer's disease facts and figures.* Retrieved from http://www.alz.org/downloads/Facts_Figures_2011.pdf.

Amenta, E., Caren, N., & Olasky, S. (2005). Age for leisure? Political mediation and the impact of the pension movement on U.S. old-age policy. *American Sociological Review, 70*(3), 516–538.

American Association of Retired Persons. (2010a). *Fact sheet, The employment situation, March 2010: Unemployment rate for older adults dips slightly.* Washington, DC: AARP Public Policy Institute.

American Association of Retired Persons. (2010b). *Strategies to meet housing needs of older adults.* Washington, DC: AARP Public Policy Institute. Retrieved from http://www.aarp.org/home-garden/housing/info-03-2010/i38-strategies.html.

American Association of Retired Persons. (2011). *Income, poverty and health insurance coverage of older adults 2010.* Washington, DC: AARP Public Policy Institute.

American Psychological Association. (2011). *Psychology and aging: Addressing mental health needs of older adults.* Washington, DC: Retirement Research Foundation.

Befort, S. F. (2007). The perfect storm of retirement insecurity: Fixing the three-legged stool of Social Security, pensions, and personal savings. *Minnesota Law Review, 91*(4), 938–988.

Berkeman, B., & Harootyan, L. (2003). *Social work and health care in an aging society: Education, policy, practice and research.* New York: Springer Publishing Company.

Bihari, M. (2010). *Understanding the Medicare Part D donut hole: Learn about the Medicare Part D coverage gap.* Retrieved from http://healthinsurance .about.com/od/medicare/a/understanding_part_d.htm.

Brandl, B., Dyer, C., Heisler, C., Otto, J., Stiegel, L., & Thomas, R. (2007). *Elder abuse detection and intervention: A collaborative approach.* New York: Springer Publishing Company.

Burgess, A., & Hanrahan, N. (2006). *Identifying forensic markers in elderly sexual abuse.* Washington, DC: National Institute of Justice.

Cawthorne, A. (2008). *Elderly poverty: The challenge before us.* Washington, DC: Center for American Progress. Retrieved from http://www.americanprogress .org/issues/2008/07/pdf/elderly_poverty.pdf.

Center on Budget and Policy Priorities. (2012). *Policy basics: Top ten facts about Social Security.* Washington, DC: Center on Budget and Policy Priorities. Retrieved from http://www.cbpp.org/files/PolicyBasics_SocSec-TopTen.pdf.

Centers for Disease Control and Prevention. (2010). *Disability and health.* Retrieved from http://www.cdc.gov/ncbddd/disabilityandhealth/types.html.

Centers for Disease Control and Prevention and the Merck Company Foundation. (2007). *The state of aging and health in America 2007.* Whitehouse Station, NJ: Merck Company Foundation.

Centers for Medicare and Medicaid Services. (2010a). *Medicare.* Retrieved from http://www.cms.gov/Medicare/Medicare.html?redirect=/home/medicare.asp.

Centers for Medicare and Medicaid Services. (2010b). *Medicare-Medicaid coordination.* Retrieved from http://www.cms.gov/Medicare-Medicaid-Coordination/Medicare-MedicaidCoordination.html.

Centers for Medicare and Medicaid Services. (2010c). *National health expenditure projections 2009–2019.* Retrieved from http://www.cms.gov/Research-Statistics-Data-and-Systems/Statistics-Trends-and-Reports/NationalHealth ExpendData/downloads/proj2009.pdf.

Centers for Medicare & Medicaid Services. (2012a). *Program of All-Inclusive Care for the Elderly (PACE).* Retrieved from http://www.medicaid.gov/ Medicaid-CHIP-Program-Information/By-Topics/Long-Term-Services-and-Support/Integrating-Care/Program-of-All-Inclusive-Care-for-the-Elderly-PACE/Program-of-All-Inclusive-Care-for-the-Elderly-PACE.html.

Centers for Medicare & Medicaid Services. (2012b). *Seniors & Medicare and Medicaid enrollees.* Retrieved from http://www.medicaid.gov/Medicaid-CHIP-Program-Information/By-Population/Medicare-Medicaid-Enrollees-Dual-Eligibles/Seniors-and-Medicare-and-Medicaid-Enrollees.html.

Choi, N., & Jun, J. (2009) Life regrets and pride among low-income older adults: Relationships with depressive symptoms, current life stressors and coping resources. *Aging & Mental Health, 13*(2), 213–215.

Choi, N., & Kimbell, K. (2009). Depression care need among low-income older adults: Views from aging service providers and family caregivers. *Clinical Gerontologist, 32*(1), 60–76.

Choi, N., & McDougall, G. (2009). Low-income older adults. *Journal of Gerontological Social Work, 52*(6), 567–583.

Couch, K., Jolly, N., & Placzek, D. (2009). *Mass layoffs and their impact on earnings during recessions and expansions.* Connecticut Department of Labor, Office of Research Occasional Paper Series 2009. Wethersfield, CT: Connecticut Department of Labor, Office of Research.

Etters, L., Goodall, D., & Harrison, B. (2008). Caregiver burden among dementia patient caregivers: A review of the literature. *Journal of the American Academy of Nurse Practitioners, 20*(8), 423–428.

Evercare & National Alliance for Caregiving. (2009). *The Evercare survey of the economic downturn and its impact on family caregiving.* Minnetonka, MN: United Health Group.

Federal Interagency Forum on Aging-Related Statistics. (2012). *Profile of Older Americans 2012.* Retrieved from http://www.agingstats.gov/agingstatsdotnet/ Main_Site/Data/Data_2012.aspx.

Folbre, N., Shaw, L., & Stark, A. (2005, July). Introducing gender and aging. *Feminist Economics, 11*(2), 3–5.

Fry, R., Cohn, D., Livingston, G., & Taylor, P. (2011). *The rising age gap in economic well being: The old prosper relative to the young.* Washington, DC: Pew Research Center.

Gillen, M., & Kim, H. (2009). Older women and poverty consequences of income change from widowhood. *Journal of Applied Gerontology, 28*(3), 320–341.

Government Accountability Office. (2009). *Reverse mortgages: Product complexity and consumer protection issues underscore the need for improved controls over counseling for borrowers.* Highlights, GAO-09-606. Washington, DC.

Gonyea, J. G., & Hooyman, N. R. (2005). Reducing poverty among older women: Social Security reform and gender equity. *Families in Society, 86*(3), 338–346.

Hillier, S., & Barrow, G. (2011). *Aging, the individual and society* (9th ed.). New York: Wadsworth Publishing.

Hooyman, N., & Kiyak, H. (2011). *Social gerontology* (9th ed.). New York: Pearson Higher Education.

Housing Assistance Council. (2011). *Poverty in rural America.* Washington, DC: Housing Assistance Council. Retrieved from http://www.ruralhome.org/ storage/documents/info_sheets/povertyamerica.pdf.

Housing Assistance Council. (2012a). *Poverty in the United States–2012 map.* Washington, DC: Housing Assistance Council. Retrieved from http://www .ruralhome.org/information-and-publications/rural-rn/500-poverty-map-2012.

Housing Assistance Council. (2012b). *Research note June 2012: Poverty in rural America*. Washington, DC: Housing Assistance Council. Retrieved from http://www.ruralhome.org/information-and-publications/rural-rn/510-rrn-poverty.

Hudson, R. B. (2004). Advocacy and policy success in aging. *Generations, 28*(1), 17–24.

Hudson, R. B. (2011). *The new politics of old age policy*. Baltimore, MD: Johns Hopkins University Press.

Hudson, R. B., & Gonyea, J. G. (2007). The evolving role of public policy in promoting work and retirement. *Generations, 31*(1), 68–75.

Johnson, R., & Wiener, J. (2006) *A profile of frail older Americans and their caregivers*. Retrieved from http://www.urban.org/url.cfm?ID=311284.

Judd, R., & Moore, B. (2011). More comprehensive approach to care, aging in poverty: Making the case for comprehensive care management. *Journal of Gerontological Social Work, 54*(7), 647–658.

Kaiser Family Foundation. (2013). *The Kaiser Commission on Medicaid and the uninsured: The Medicaid program at a glance*. Retrieved from http://www.kff.org/medicaid/upload/7235-04.pdf.

Karlin, B., Duffy, M., & Gleaves, D. (2008). Patterns and predictors of mental health service use and mental illness among older and younger adults in the United States. *Psychological Services, 5*(3), 275–294.

Keating, N. (2008). *Rural ageing: A good place to grow old*. Bristol, UK: Policy Press.

Lahey, J. (2006, November). *Working Paper. Age, women, and hiring: An experimental study* (Number 2006-23). Center for Retirement Research. Boston: Boston College.

Library of Congress. (2013). *Older American Act Amendments of 2013. Bill summary 113th Congress (2013–2014), S. 1562*. Retrieved from http://beta.congress.gov/bill/113th/senate-bill/1562?q={"search":["S. 1562"]}.

Louie, G., & Ward, M. (2011). Socioeconomic and ethnic differences in disease burden and disparities in physical function in older adults. *American Journal of Public Health, 101*(7), 1322–1329.

Lun, M. W. A. (2010). Aging in place and urban social work: A case study of a NORC. *The New Social Worker,* Spring. Retrieved from http://www.social worker.com/home/Feature_Articles/General/Aging_in_Place_and_Urban_Social_Work%3A_A_Case_Study_of_a_NORC/.

Lustig, D., & Strauser, D. (2007). Causal relationships between poverty and disability. *Rehabilitation Counseling Bulletin, 50*(4), 194–202.

Martin, P., & Weaver, D. (2005). Social Security: A program and policy history. *Social Security Bulletin 66*(1). Washington, DC: Social Security Administration Office of Policy. Retrieved from http://www.ssa.gov/policy/docs/ssb/v66n1/v66n1p1.html.

Mayer, M. J. (2010). The impact of poverty on older persons. *Care Management Journals, 11*(2), 108–111.

MetLife Mature Market Institute. (2009). *Tapping in home equity in retirement.* Westport, CT: MetLife Mature Market Institute.

Napili, A., & Colello, K. J. (2013). *Funding for the Older Americans Act and other aging services.* Washington, DC: Congressional Research Service. Retrieved from http://www.fas.org/sgp/crs/misc/RL33880.pdf.

National Association of State Budget Officers. (2011). *Medicaid cost containment: Recent proposals and trends.* Washington, DC: National Association of State Budget Officers.

National Center on Elder Abuse. (2005). *Fact sheet: Older adults abuse prevalence and incidence.* Retrieved from http://www.ncea.aoa.gov/ncearoot/main_site/pdf/publication/FinalStatistics050331.pdfU.

National Coalition on Mental Health and Aging. (2011). *Resolution on mental health services and substance abuse interventions.* Retrieved from http://www.ncmha.org/index.php.

National Council on Aging. (2010). *Current economic status of older adults: A demographic analysis.* Washington, DC: National Council on Aging.

Novak, M. (2012). *Issues of aging* (3rd ed.). New York: Pearson Higher Education.

O'Brien, E., Wu, K., & Baer, D. (2010). *Older Americans in poverty: A snapshot.* Washington, DC: American Association of Retired Persons.

Office of the Assistant Secretary for Planning and Evaluation. (2007). *ASPE research brief: The effects of marriage on health.* Washington, DC: Office of the Secretary.

Panelli, R., Gallagher, L., & Kearns, R. (2006). Access to rural health services: Research as community action and policy critique. *Social Science & Medicine, 62,* 1103–1114.

Patterson, M., & Malley-Morrison, K. (2006). A cognitive-ecological approach to older adults abuse in five cultures: Human rights and education. *Educational Gerontology, 32*(1), 73–82.

Pavle, K. (2011). *National health reform: The Affordable Care Act includes great benefits for older adults.* Chicago: Chicago.org. Retrieved from http://www.thechicagobridge.org/national-health-reform-the-affordable-care-act-includes-great-benefits-for-older-adults/.

Penhale, B. (2005). Older women, domestic violence, and elder abuse: A review of commonalities, differences, and shared approaches. *Journal of Elder Abuse and Neglect, 15*(3), 163–183.

Pierret, C. (2006). The "sandwich generation": Women caring for parents and children. *Monthly Labor Review, 129*(9), 3–9.

Prina, A., Ferri, C., Guerra, M., Brayne, C., & Prince, M. (2011). Co-occurrence of anxiety and depression amongst older adults in low- and middle-income countries: Findings from the 10/66 study. *Psychological Medicine, 41*(10), 2047–2056.

Quadagno, J. (2011). *Aging and the life course: An introduction to social gerontology* (5th ed.). New York: McGraw-Hill.

Reyes-Ortiz, C., Snih, S., Loera, J., Ray, L., & Kyriakos Markides, A. (2004). Risk factors for falling in older Mexican Americans. *Ethnic and Disease, 14*(3), 417–422.

Richardson, V. E., & Barusch, A. M. (2006). *Gerontological practice for the twenty-first century.* New York: Columbia University Press.

Robert Wood Johnson Foundation Commission to Build a Healthier America. (2008). *Issue brief 2: Housing and health (September).* Washington, DC. Retrieved from Comissiononhealth.org.

Rogers, C. (2005). Older women and poverty in rural areas. *Amber Waves, 3*(4), 9–10.

Rural Policy Research Institute. (2007). Rural residence: Cause or effect of poverty. *Perspectives: On Policy, Poverty and Place 4*(2), 1–8. Retrieved from http://www.rupri.org/Forms/Perspectivesvol4n2.pdf.

Rural Policy Research Institute. (2010). *Poverty and human services.* Retrieved from http://www.rupri.org/povhumservices.phpU.

Saxena, S., Thornicroft, G., Knapp, M., & Whiteford, H. (2007). Resources for mental health: Scarcity, inequity and inefficiency. *Lancet, 370*(9590), 878–889.

Schrag, A., Hovris, A., Morley, D., Quinn, N., & Marjan, J. (2006). Caregiver-burden in Parkinson's disease is closely associated with psychiatric symptoms, falls, and disability. *Parkinsonism & Related Disorders, 12*(1), 35–41.

Schulz, J., & Binstock, R. (2011). *Aging nation: The economics and politics of growing older in America.* Baltimore, MD: Johns Hopkins University Press.

Social Security Administration. (2010). *Social Security, "A snapshot."* Washington, DC: Social Security Administration.

Social Security Administration. (2011a). *Office of Retirement and Disability Policy annual statistical supplement 2011.* Retrieved from http://www.ssa.gov/policy/docs/statcomps/supplement/2011/ssi.html.

Social Security Administration. (2011b). *2011 Annual report of the SSI program.* Washington, DC: Social Security Administration.

Social Security Administration. (2011c). *2011 Trustees report: Section II.A, highlights—Social Security.* Washington, DC: Social Security Administration.

Spotlight on Poverty and Opportunity. (2011). *Aging and poverty.* Retrieved from http://www.spotlightonpoverty.org/aging_and_poverty.aspx.

Tauriac, J. J., & Scruggs, N. (2006). Elder abuse among African Americans. *Educational Gerontology, 32*(1), 37–48.

Thibos, M., Lavin-Loucks, D., & Martin, M. (2007). *The feminization of poverty: Empowering women.* Joint Policy Forum on the Feminization of Poverty. Dallas, TX: Williams Institute and the YMCA. Retrieved from http://www.ywcadallas.org/documents/advocacy/FeminizationofPoverty.pdf.

U.S. Census Bureau. (2010a). *Income, poverty, and health insurance coverage in the United States: 2010.* Retrieved from http://www.census.gov/hhes/www/poverty/data/incpovhlth/2010/index.html.

U.S. Census Bureau. (2010b). *Poverty status in the last 12 months: 2010 American community survey 1-year estimates.* Retrieved from http://factfinder2.census.gov/faces/tableservices/jsf/pages/productview.xhtml?pid=ACS_10_1YR_S1701&prodType=table.

U.S. Census Bureau. (2011a). *The older population: 2010 census briefs.* Retrieved from http://www.census.gov/prod/cen2010/briefs/c2010br-09.pdf.

U.S. Census Bureau. (2011b). Poverty rates by age 1959–2011 figure 5. Retrieved from http://www.census.gov/hhes/www/poverty/data/incpovhlth/2011/figure5.pdf.

U.S. Department of Labor. (2008). *The Bureau of Labor Statistics: Economic news release displaced workers summary.* Retrieved from http://www.bls.gov/news.release/disp.nr0.htm.

U.S. Department of Labor. (2010). *Issues in labor statistics: Record unemployment among older workers does not keep them out of the job market.* Retrieved from http://www.bls.gov/opub/ils/pdf/opbils81.pdf.

U.S. Equal Employment Opportunity Commission. (n.d). *The Age Discrimination in Employment Act of 1967.* Retrieved from http://www.eeoc.gov/laws/statutes/adea.cfm.

Wacker, R., & Roberto, K. (2008). *Community resources for older adults: Programs and services in an era of change.* Thousand Oaks, CA: Sage Publication, Inc.

Weber, B., Jensen, L., Miller, K., Mosley, J., & Fisher, M. (2005). A critical review of the rural poverty literature: Is there truly a rural effect? *International Regional Science Review, 28*(4), 381–414.

Whelan, C., & Maître, B. (2008). Social class variations in risk: A comparative analysis of the dynamics of economic vulnerability. *British Journal of Sociology, 9*(4), 637–659.

Whitman, D., & Purcell, P. (2006). Income and poverty among older Americans. *Benefits Quarterly, 22*(4), 48–61.

Yen, H. (2010a, March 2). Government adopts formula that doubles the elderly poor. *The Boston Globe.* Retrieved from http://www.boston.com/news/nation/washington/articles/2010/03/02/govt_adopts_formula_that_doubles_elderly_poor/.

Yen, H. (2010b, October 7). Suburbs take hit as US poverty climbs in downturn. *Boston Globe.* Retrieved from http://www.memphisdailynews.com/news/2010/oct/8/suburbs-take-hit-as-us-poverty-climbs-in-downturn/.

Zarit, S. H. (2009). A good old age: Theories of mental health and aging. In *Handbook of Theories of Aging,* ed. V. Bengtson, M. Silverstein, N. Putney, & D. Gans (eds.) (pp. 675–692). New York: Springer.

Zastrow, C. (2010). *The practice of social work: A complete worktext* (9th ed.). New Belmont, CA: Cengage Learning.

7

People with Disabilities
Noam Ostrander

Intuitively, individuals understand the relationship between poverty and disability is complex and multifaceted. Throughout Western history, people with disabilities have been largely excluded from employment, education, and social inclusion at every level. The disabling attitudes that drive this exclusion remain largely intact today, despite significant civil rights gains made by members of disability communities over the past few decades. Still, people with disabilities often face mistreatment in society, which causes them to lag behind individuals without disabilities in several key economic and other related outcomes. For example, in 2011, the percentage of people with disabilities living below the federal poverty level was 28.8 percent compared to only 12.5 percent for people without disabilities (DeNavas-Walt, Proctor, & Smith, 2012). Of course, this statistic is only a sample of socioeconomic outcomes for people with disabilities, which will be explored in greater detail throughout this chapter.

The primary goal of this chapter is to expand readers' appreciation for the unique factors that contribute to the relationship between disability and poverty for a significant segment of individuals in the United States. Readers of this chapter will also gain a better understanding of how historical and contemporary disabling attitudes and policies contribute to inequality among people with disabilities. Finally, readers will explore ways that social workers and related health professionals can collaborate with others to work toward social justice at the micro, mezzo, and macro levels to meet individual needs, improve service provisions, and achieve social change.

Demographics and Characteristics

The term *disability* and the related phrase *people with disabilities* are important to understand, to help place the demographic profile of people with disabilities in context. The meaning of the term *disability* is extremely variable. The World Health Organization (WHO) (2012, para. 1) explains, "disabilities is an umbrella term, covering impairments, activity limitations, and participation restrictions." They also note that the notion of disability is "a complex phenomenon, reflecting an interaction between features of a person's body and features of the society in which he or she lives" (WHO, 2012, para. 2). Consequently, getting an accurate picture of the current demographic characteristics of people with disabilities in the United States is complicated. This is due to how the term *disability* is defined (addressed in the key issues section of this chapter) in addition to how data are collected about the population.

Data are largely compiled using three measures: the American Community Survey (conducted every year to explore how housing and communities across the country are changing), the Current Population Survey (conducted monthly to assess changes in the labor force), and the U.S. Census (conducted every ten years to understand changes in population and economy). While all of these surveys are administered by the U.S. Census Bureau, they all seek to collect different kinds of information and they measure disability differently. As a result, there is some confusion about official counts and demographics among the various communities of people with disabilities in the United States. Therefore, the demographic characteristics represented in this section may not provide a complete picture for this population, but it will provide a glimpse into the current figures and the historical trends.

The first glimpse of differences in disability statistics comes when attempting to count how many people have a disability in the United States. The 2010 U.S. Census indicated that 57.6 million people in the United States have a disability. This translates into approximately 19 percent of the U.S. population. However, the 2010 American Community Survey (ACS) lists that number much lower at 12.7 percent. The likely difference here is due to the ACS survey designers' decisions to limit their scope to non-institutionalized people with disabilities for the ACS versus all people with disabilities as measured by the 2010 U.S. Census. Based on these numbers we know that there are around 57 million people in the United States with a disability and of those people, approximately 46 million are not housed in institutions.

The 2010 American Community Survey data provide additional detail about the characteristics of this population by gender, Hispanic origin, and race. According to these data, approximately 52 percent of the people with disabilities are female and 48 percent are male. Among the various racial groups, Native Americans (15.8 percent) have the highest prevalence of disability, followed by Blacks/African Americans (13.5 percent), Whites/Caucasians (12.4 percent), and Asians (6.2 percent). Of all people with disabilities in the United States, 8.1 percent are Hispanic or Latino (U.S. Census Bureau, 2012). These figures mirror other health-related data and research that indicate an increased risk for chronic health conditions among members of minority communities.

Historical Perspective

Understanding the historical perspective of disability requires the reader to consider the ways in which society views the body and physical difference. For example, if one considers religious societies that view the human body as a gift from God, then physical differences and "abnormalities" must also originate from God as punishments or burdens given to individuals. Similarly, the history of disability is linked to the ways professional disciplines interpret these differences. Whether the professional discipline is the priesthood or medicine, people with disabilities have sometimes been viewed as "things" either to pity or heal. Indeed, these two models of disability—the moral model (disability as indication of sin) and the medical model (disability as indication of disease)—affect the entire history of people with disabilities—not only in American society, but also in global societies.

Well-written and researched histories of disability and persons with disabilities already exist. Readers should refer to the section on additional readings at the end of this chapter to find references for those histories. This section of the chapter summarizes the major legislative and policy developments related to disability history in the United States. Additionally, this section focuses most directly on legislation that reached across disability groups rather than impairment-specific legislation (e.g., the Randolph-Sheppard Act or the Ryan White CARE Act).

From the times of the English colonies through the founding of the United States, the Elizabethan Poor Laws gave families and local communities primary responsibilities for people with disabilities (Katz, 1996; Trattner, 1998). These Poor Laws, and many of the public welfare laws that would be developed throughout U.S. history, made a distinction between "worthy" and "unworthy" poor. The distinction, wrote Patterson (2000), identified "the deserving poor—those in need through no fault of their own—and the lazybones who would not work" (p. 19). People with disabilities, along with the aged and single mothers, are almost always grouped under the "worthy poor" category. During the colonial era and the early years of the United States, welfare laws assumed that people with disabilities and other worthy poor were a burden best dealt with in the private, family sphere or at the local level if the family was unavailable. The municipalities and town governments typically supported these efforts through a series of "outdoor" or home relief measures (e.g., food assistance, clothing, medical care, etc.) that allowed people with disabilities to stay in their dwellings and communities (Katz, 1996; Trattner, 1998). However, as immigration and industrialization increased across the United States, more institutions ("indoor relief") developed to house and "correct" the poor (Leiby, 1978; Trattner, 1998). Leiby (1978) referred to this movement during 1815–1845 as the "promise of the institution," where states and counties developed houses for delinquent children, schools for people who were deaf or blind, asylums for people with mental illnesses, and general hospitals. All of these moves alleviated crowding in the local almshouses and jails, while housing poor people away from the commercial areas that were developing in cities and other urban areas.

There is now an awareness of the terrible abuses that occurred in these institutions for all people housed in them, and particularly the abuses that occurred to people with physical and mental disabilities. For example, in the mid-nineteenth century, Dorothea Dix strenuously advocated for reform on behalf of people with mental illnesses after seeing the deplorable conditions in which they existed when incarcerated in prisons or jails. The shift toward asylums, at that time, marked an improvement in the living conditions for people with mental illness. Yet despite Dix's efforts to improve conditions for people with mental illness, she and her supporters also saw a serious defeat in 1854 when President Franklin Pierce vetoed a bill that would allow the federal government to grant land to the states to help finance the care of the "indigent insane" (Leiby, 1978; Trattner, 1998). President Pierce argued that allowing the bill to become law might enable the states to shift the care of all indigent people—insane or sane—to the federal government. Trattner (1998) noted that this veto slowed the federal government's involvement with social welfare for many years to come.

Federal Employers' Liability Act (FELA)

As people with disabilities and their families sought greater inclusion and protections, legislation began changing accordingly. Congress passed the Federal Employers' Liability Act (FELA) of 1908, which may mark the beginning of employment laws for people with disabilities. This legislation, the first of its kind, created protection for railroad workers who were injured while working on the railroads by establishing workers' compensation to pay their medical expenses. However, this law did not actually provide vocational rehabilitation services for workers with disabilities; rather, it protected workers who might receive a job-related injury by giving them an opportunity to sue their employers for financial recourse if the worker was injured on the job. This legislation overturned what Witt (2003) considered to be an unholy trinity of rules that prevented employees from suing their employers for damages. The unholy trinity consisted of (1) a rule that prevented workers from suing the company due to an injury they received at the hands of a negligent coworker, (2) a rule that workers assume certain risks when performing a job, and (3) a rule that if an employer's and employee's negligence contributed to a workplace injury, then the employer could not be sued given that the employee was also found negligent. As more people became injured, lawsuits increased, and public pressure increased to change the laws. Since passage of FELA, the U.S. government has developed similar industry-specific legislation to cover workplace disabilities (e.g., the Merchant Marine Act, Longshore and Harbor Workers' Compensation Act, Black Lung Benefit Act, etc.).

Smith-Fess Act

The push to provide vocational rehabilitation (VR) became more vigorous in 1920 with the Civilian Vocational Rehabilitation Act, otherwise known as the Smith-Fess Act. This act firmly established the concept of vocational rehabilitation and was funded as a 50/50 funding partnership between the federal and state governments. This act provided people with a disability the opportunity to meet with a counselor or case manager who could connect them with educational opportunities or medical services that might lead to employment opportunities (O'Brien, 2001). The services funded under this act included job training, job counseling, and job placement, and provided access to prosthetics or other adaptive equipment for people with physical disabilities. This act was particularly well-timed as the United States employment environment transitioned from agricultural-based to industrial-based, and greater numbers of individuals moved to cities. An interesting facet of vocational rehabilitation services under the Smith-Fess Act is that while approximately 250,000 people were becoming disabled on the job every year between 1920 and 1943, only 12,000 people in total were being served over that same time span (O'Brien, 2001). This means that out of the nearly 5.8 million people injured in the workplace during those 23 years, only 0.2 percent were served. O'Brien argued that this discrepancy might largely be due to the occurrence of VR counselors "creaming" from the people who sought services to distinctly focus on specific individuals who required fewer services and might be easier to place into jobs. Indeed, during the 1920s and 1930s, the typical recipient of VR services was white, male, and thirty-one years old (Berkowitz, 1980).

Federal Rehabilitation Acts

The vocational rehabilitation movement scored a major legislative victory in the 1950s with the passage of President Eisenhower's Vocational Rehabilitation Act of 1954. This act was largely steered by Mary Switzer, who was the director of the Office of Vocational Rehabilitation. Under the act several demonstration projects were funded to develop best practices for finding employment for people with specific disabilities (e.g., people who are deaf or people with epilepsy), as well as increased training for vocational rehabilitation counselors (O'Brien, 2001). Switzer argued that for vocational rehabilitation services to succeed a well-trained cadre of VR professionals was needed (O'Brien, 2001). Additionally, through the funding for the act, the Office of Vocational Rehabilitation developed more than 200 training facilities and workshops over six years for VR professionals (Walker as cited in O'Brien, 2001). Together with the Smith-Fess Act as a foundation, the Vocational Rehabilitation Act of 1954 firmly entrenched vocational rehabilitation as a major component of the disability services landscape for people with disabilities.

Also notable, the Rehabilitation Act of 1973 expanded and superseded these previous acts in terms of the employment and educational benefits provided to adults with disabilities. This act included important services and civil rights protections for people with disabilities who were involved in federally funded programs. Within this act, three sections deserve mentioning. Under Section 501, people with disabilities cannot be discriminated against in employment settings for federal offices. Section 501 required federal agencies and departments to institute affirmative action hiring policies to include people with disabilities. Agencies that received federal monies were required to develop a hiring plan with detailed goals on hiring qualified candidates with disabilities for federal jobs (Scotch, 2001). In this sense, the Rehabilitation Act provided an essential component for disability employment rights across the country, albeit only in the public sector and not yet in the private sector. Section 503 is similar in that it prohibits discrimination employment against people with disabilities by federal government contractors or subcontractors. Section 504 protects people with disabilities from discrimination in programs funded by the federal government. Under Section 504, people with disabilities gained more civil rights, as well as access to employment and education programs from which they had previously been denied. What is important to note about the Rehabilitation Act is that it established the protections for people with disabilities at the federal level. It would be another seventeen years before those protections were extended into the private sector.

Olmstead v. L.C.

Similarly in 1999, the U.S. Supreme Court in *Olmstead v. L.C.* held that people with disabilities—including people with mental illness—should not be isolated in institutions. The Court ruled that individuals with disabilities have a right to live in their communities and should not be segregated. Since the Olmstead ruling, states have implemented Olmstead commissions to assess and implement community living programs for people with disabilities. These living programs sought to increase community integration for people with disabilities in the least restrictive environments, such as group home settings. In this way, the Olmstead ruling continued the momentum for greater community inclusion for people with mental illnesses that began in the 1950s and 1960s in the United States.

Education Acts

The final piece of legislation to be addressed is the Individuals with Disability Education Act (IDEA), which was enacted in 1990 and reauthorized in 2004. This act, and its predecessor, the Education for All Handicapped Children Act of 1975, was designed to protect the rights of students with disabilities to ensure that everyone receives a "free appropriate public education" (IDEA, 2004). This legislation goes beyond the provision of equal access for students with disabilities to include additional special education services and accommodations. To determine these accommodations, children (ranging from birth to twenty-one years of age) who meet the definition of a "child with a disability" and who require special education because of the disability will be assessed by a multi-disciplinary team at no cost to the parents. Infants and toddlers up to thirty-six months of age with disabilities and their families receive early intervention services as part of IDEA Part C. Children and youth (ages 3–21) receive special education and related services under IDEA Part B. The IDEA legislation (2004, Section 602(3)(a)(i)) defined a child with a disability as a child with

> mental retardation, hearing impairments (including deafness), speech or language impairments, visual impairments (including blindness), serious emotional disturbance (referred to in this title as "emotional disturbance"), orthopedic impairments,

autism, traumatic brain injury, other health impairments, or specific learning disabilities; and . . . who, by reason thereof, needs special education and related services.

Through this assessment, students with disabilities receive an Individualized Education Plan (IEP) that is developed and implemented by a team that includes specific school personnel (e.g., teachers and resource teachers) and the child's parents or guardians. These plans are then reassessed every three years to ensure appropriate services are provided for the child.

Taken in concert, these pieces of legislation represent many historical movements where people with disabilities and their allies sought greater inclusion in society. Some of these battles will be touched on later in this chapter; however, Ruth O'Brien's *Crippled Justice* and Paul Longmore's *Why I Burned My Book* provide excellent, rich descriptions of these struggles that earned civil rights for people with disabilities.

Key Issues

To provide a snapshot of key issues for people with disabilities, three issues are outlined here. Readers also explore how disability is defined. This discussion is of great importance because how a disability is defined is crucial with regard to who gets access to services and benefits and who does not. After readers understand this salient issue, an examination of employment, income, and poverty rates is provided to demonstrate the current state of people with disabilities in terms of economic indicators. Educational attainment is additionally detailed in this section since educational attainment is generally a pathway out of poverty, yet people with disabilities still lag behind their able-bodied peers when it comes to enrollment and graduation. Finally, housing is discussed as a key issue for people with disabilities. The existing availability of accessible and affordable housing is typically limited for people with disabilities. As these issues coalesce for people with disabilities, individual opportunities for social and economic mobility are stymied. As a result, poverty and isolation become reinforced for many people with disabilities.

Defining Disability: Americans with Disabilities Act and Social Security Administration

Within the United States, there are at least two important definitions of the term *disability* to consider. One of these definitions emerged from the Americans with Disabilities Act (ADA) of 1990 and the revisions provided through the 2008 Amendments Act to the ADA. The other definition comes from the U.S. Social Security Administration (SSA).

With respect to civil rights issues as it relates to people with disabilities, the Americans with Disabilities Act (ADA) of 1990 is perhaps the most widely known disability rights act in the United States and one with which all helping professionals ought to be familiar. Essentially, the intent of the law is to protect the civil rights of people with disabilities. Notably, employers challenged this legislation, leading it to be revisited by the U.S. Congress in 2008 with the intent of providing greater clarity in defining "a person with a disability" and to explore the types of accessible accommodations that are viewed as reasonable for people with disabilities.

The ADA Amendments Act of 2008 went farther to clarify the definition of key items including the core definition of "disability," "major life activities," and people being "regarded as having such an impairment." As illustrated above, these clarifications came about partially due to employment-based lawsuits (e.g., *Sutton v. United Airlines Inc., Toyota Manufacturing Company, Kentucky, Inc. v. Williams,* etc.) that came before the U.S. Supreme Court. After passage of the ADA, the courts sought to clarify some ambiguity in the definitions of "disability" and "reasonable accommodations." As a result, Congress passed and President George W. Bush signed the ADA Amendments Act into law in 2008. Accordingly, the Amendments Act (ADA Amendments Act of 2008) states:

Rules of construction regarding the definition of disability:

(A) The definition of disability in this Act shall be construed in favor of broad coverage of individuals under this Act, to the maximum extent permitted by the terms of this Act.

(B) The term "substantially limits" shall be interpreted consistently with the findings and purposes of the ADA Amendments Act of 2008.

(C) An impairment that substantially limits one major life activity need not limit other major life activities in order to be considered a disability.

(D) An impairment that is episodic or in remission is a disability if it would substantially limit a major life activity when active.

(E)(i) The determination of whether an impairment substantially limits a major life activity shall be made without regard to the ameliorative effects of mitigating measures such as—

(I) medication, medical supplies, equipment, or appliances, low-vision devices (which do not include ordinary eyeglasses or contact lenses), prosthetics including limbs and devices, hearing aids and cochlear implants or other implantable hearing devices, mobility devices, or oxygen therapy equipment and supplies;

(II) use of assistive technology;

(III) reasonable accommodations or auxiliary aids or services; or

(IV) learned behavioral or adaptive neurological modifications.

(ii) The ameliorative effects of the mitigating measures of ordinary eyeglasses or contact lenses shall be considered in determining whether an impairment substantially limits a major life activity.

Additionally, the Amendment Act defined "major life activities" as:

(A) In general.—For purposes of paragraph (1), major life activities include, but are not limited to, caring for oneself, performing manual tasks, seeing, hearing, eating, sleeping, walking, standing, lifting, bending, speaking, breathing, learning, reading, concentrating, thinking, communicating, and working.

(B) Major bodily functions.—For purposes of paragraph (1), a major life activity also includes the operation of a major bodily function, including but not limited to, functions of the immune system, normal cell growth, digestive, bowel, bladder, neurological, brain, respiratory, circulatory, endocrine, and reproductive functions.

Finally, the Amendment Act determined that an individual is regarded as having an impairment if:

(A) An individual meets the requirement of "being regarded as having such an impairment" if the individual establishes that he or she has been subjected to an action prohibited under this Act because of an actual or perceived physical or mental impairment whether or not the impairment limits or is perceived to limit a major life activity.

These definitions from the ADA and the Amendments Act largely identify disabilities and impairments within the context of activities of daily living and the workplace environment. In this scenario, activities of daily living include dressing or feeding oneself, performing work or leisurely activities, and taking care of one's home.

In addition to clarifying who is to be categorized as disabled, the ADA prohibits discrimination of individuals with disabilities in employment (Title I), local government services (Title II), public accommodations and commercial facilities (e.g., restaurants, hotels, theaters, etc.) (Title III), and public transportation, and telecommunications (Title IV). As recognized in this law, individuals are covered under the ADA if they (1) have a physical or mental impairment that substantially limits one or more major life activities, (2) have a history or record of such an impairment, or (3) are perceived by others as having such an impairment. Within this context, a physical impairment is defined as "any physiological disorder, cosmetic disfigurement, or anatomical loss affecting one or more of the following body systems: neurological, musculoskeletal, special sense organs, respiratory (including speech organs), cardiovascular, reproductive, digestive, genitourinary, hemic and lymphatic, skin, and endocrine" (ADA, 1990). The ADA (1990) also defined mental impairments as "any mental or physiological disorder, such as mental retardation, organic brain syndrome, emotional or mental illness, and specific learning disorder" (902.2)(b)(2)). Notably too, the ADA also provided people with disabilities the latitude to participate in or access public spaces such as stores and restaurants, and offers more protections from discrimination in the workplace.

The clarifications offered by the ADA Amendments Act brought the ADA definition of disability closer to the U.S. Social Security Administration's (SSA) definition, which is focused more specifically on how an impairment impacts one's ability to work. For the SSA (2012a), a person is disabled if: (1) an individual cannot do work that he or she did before; (2) the U.S. Social Security Administration decides that the individual cannot adjust to other work because of a medical condition(s); and (3) the individual's disability has lasted or is expected to last at least one year or to result in death.

The SSA definition seems to apply best in situations where someone has acquired a disability through some sort of accident or an emergent chronic condition. Essentially, something has changed in individuals' lives so that they cannot work as they had before the accident or change in functioning has occurred.

Both the SSA definition and the ADA definition squarely focus on one's ability to perform work duties. In this sense, some have argued that the government definitions of disability view people for their value in the wage economy rather than their value as members of society (Michalko, 2002). Yet in reality, individuals' physical and mental differences may still drastically affect one's daily life, but still not rise to meet the threshold of "disability" according to the federal definitions identified above. Indeed, individuals who may have "sub-syndromal depression," which is a depression that does not meet the full criteria for a clinical diagnosis, could experience similar difficulties performing daily activities as people with clinical depression, but lack the protection that the ADA provides.

Rather than select one definition over the other, this chapter maintains the ambiguity of the definitions to underscore the shifting terrain of disability when it comes to federal, state, and local policies, legislation, and programs.

Employment, Income, and Poverty Rates

The American Community Survey (ACS) reports that 21.8 percent of people with disabilities were employed in 2010. This figure compares to 64.2 percent of people without disabilities for that same year (U.S. Census Bureau, 2012). The Disability Statistics Center in San Francisco examined employment numbers of these two populations from the 1990 U.S. Census and the 2000 U.S. Census. They found that from 1990 to 2000, people with disabilities made no statistically significant gains in employment despite the implementation of the Americans with Disabilities Act (Kaye, 2003). Meanwhile, people without disabilities increased their employment levels during this decade. Subsequently, it seems that people with disabilities actually lost ground in employment during the 1990s. This suggests that people with disabilities did not benefit economically from either the ADA implementation nor experience the increase in employment akin to their non-disabled counterparts. Indeed, even after the ADA was passed, poverty among people with disabilities in the United States remained higher than poverty for the same population in other so-called developed countries (Fremstad, 2009). A potential reason for this situation may revolve around policies that limit the amount of income and assets (e.g., savings, property, etc.) people with disabilities may have without losing federal and/or state-provided health insurance. As will be discussed later, people with disabilities often face the difficult task of finding jobs that offer affordable health care coverage that is comparable to the government-sponsored health care coverage they would lose once their income levels exceed thresholds for those government provisions.

For people with disabilities who do find jobs in the labor market, their income levels remain below their non-disabled counterparts. Based on the 2010 ACS, the median income for people with disabilities is $19,500 versus $29,997 for people without disabilities. (Note: this number combines people who work full-time and people who work part-time.) This disparity is even greater if we consider annual household income as a metric. The annual household income that includes someone between the ages of 21 and 64 with a disability is $39,600. This number is $21,600 below the annual household income of people without disabilities ($61,200) (Erikson, Lee, & von Schrader, 2010). Consequently, it appears that even if people with a disability are able to find a job, it is unlikely that they will earn a wage that is on a par with people without disabilities. If we turn to poverty rates for people with disabilities, the disparities are similarly vast. The percentage of people without disabilities who are living below the Federal Poverty Level (FPL) in the United States in 2010 was 12.3 percent. However, for people with disabilities this rate was 21 percent. Furthermore, when we consider subtypes of disabilities, this poverty level can balloon to 32.4 percent as in the case of individuals with cognitive disabilities (Erikson et al., 2010, p. 42), which is defined in the ACS by using this question: "Because of a physical, mental, or emotional condition, does this person have serious difficulty concentrating, remembering, or making decisions?" (U.S. Census Bureau, 2010, p. 1). Lastly, if the ability to find housing is an indicator of income attainment and poverty, it is important to consider that the U.S. Department of Housing and Urban Development noted that people with disabilities accounted for 43 percent of the total number of homeless people in the United States during a 2008 survey (U.S. Department of Housing and Urban Development, 2009).

Educational Attainment

Conventional wisdom suggests that the pathway to better employment is through education. This suggestion leads us to consider educational attainment trends for people with disabilities. According to data from the 2010 American Community Survey, 34.1 percent of people with a disability have only a high school education compared to 27.2 percent of people without a disability. While this difference may not be that pronounced, the disparity grows when considering the portion of both populations with completed bachelor's degree or higher. Using this metric, it is notable that while 31.2 percent of the able-bodied population possess a bachelor's degree or higher, only 13.3 percent of people with disabilities have attained that mark. This disparity increases for people with cognitive disabilities whereby only 8.8 percent have earned a bachelor's degree or higher. While these figures may seem like abstract numbers, the reality is that people with disabilities are not gaining access to the pathways for higher education and thus access to more gainful employment opportunities that might lift them out of poverty. Indeed, the U.S.

Department of Education (2010) figures indicate that the median income level of people with a bachelor's degree is more than $20,000 a year higher than that of the median income level of people with a high school degree. Given the differences between earnings for high school and college graduates, the inability of people with disabilities to gain access to pathways for higher education has a definite impact on their future economic mobility.

Housing

The U.S. Department of Housing and Urban Development (HUD) data indicate that the number of disability-related complaints under the Fair Housing Act (FHA) have now matched the number of complaints based on racial discrimination (Turner, Herbig, Kaye, Fenderson, & Levy, 2005). The FHA was initially passed in 1968 to expand on previous acts that prohibited housing discrimination against people based on race, religion, and national origin. Gradually, the FHA was extended to prohibit housing discrimination based on gender (1974) and disability (1988). In 2005 the Urban Institute released a report chronicling disability-related complaints stemming from demonstration projects they conducted in Chicago (Turner et al., 2005). Within the Chicago rental market, Turner et al. (2005) found that people with disabilities faced greater levels of mistreatment than did African Americans or Hispanics, two communities that historically have faced tremendous housing discrimination. The research also indicated that people with disabilities were frequently denied requests for reasonable accommodations for rental units, which is guaranteed under both the ADA and the Fair Housing Act. Furthermore, many of the advertised rental properties were not accessible enough to allow people with disabilities a chance to view the units even if the landlord would have been willing to make accommodations for the would-be renter. In this sense, people with disabilities face discrimination through landlords' attitudes about disability, in addition to the physical barriers that could be altered to accommodate them.

Government Policies and Programs

The federal government has begun to address potential discrimination that people with disabilities may experience through legislation such as the Americans with Disabilities Act (ADA) and the Fair Housing Act (FHA). The government also provides benefits for people with disabilities to meet their basic and medical needs through programs such as Social Security Disability, Supplemental Security Income, Medicaid, and Medicare. The following discussion will introduce some of these programs and policies.

Fair Housing Act

The Fair Housing Act (FHA), which is part of the Civil Rights Act of 1968, bans housing discrimination based on race, color, national origin, religion, sex, familial status, or disability. For people with disabilities, the FHA prohibits landlords from refusing to make reasonable accommodations to the dwelling or common area. These accommodations could range from having a grab-bar in the shower or a specified parking space for someone with a mobility impairment or waiving a "no pets" policy for someone who uses a service animal. For accommodations that come at a financial cost, however, the renter must pay for the alterations.

These pieces of legislation largely speak to structural components of the housing market. However, even if the rental units are accessible, they may not be affordable. This reality has spawned greater efforts across the country for accessible and affordable housing for people with disabilities and the elderly. In 2009, HUD pledged additional housing assistance for up to 4,000 families with disabilities to commemorate the ten-year anniversary of the Olmstead decision mentioned previously. The primary housing assistance the federal government provides, however, remains Housing Choice Vouchers for people with disabilities, very low-income families, and elderly persons. The Housing Choice Vouchers, formerly called Section 8 vouchers, allow participants to find housing in the private market (i.e., not public housing developments) that meets the program's safety and sanitary requirements. Through these vouchers, the tenant usually pays no more than 30 percent of their monthly income to the landlord for rent and utilities, with the remaining amount being subsidized by the government. The challenge continues to be finding accessible housing. To that end, Disability.gov now maintains a database of accessible housing for independent or assisted living across eighteen states. Hopefully, this database will increase in the coming years to assist people with disabilities who live in one of the other thirty-two states.

Medicaid and Medicare

People with certain disabilities, along with some low-income adults and children, typically receive health care coverage through Medicaid, which is a means-tested program jointly funded by the federal government and the state government. Each state implements and runs its Medicaid program. This program is in contrast to Medicare. Medicare, which is under Title XVIII of the Social Security Act, provides federally funded medical care for three types of individuals: (1) people sixty-five years and older, (2) people with disabilities who are entitled to Social Security benefits, and (3) people who have end-stage renal disease (Shi & Singh, 2004). Referring back to the U.S. Social Security Administration's definition of disability, someone can qualify for Medicare if (1) individuals cannot do work that they did before; (2) the Social Security Administration decides that individuals cannot adjust to other work because of a medical condition(s); and (3) individuals' disability have lasted or are expected to last at least one year or result in death (SSA, 2012a).

The primary difference between the two is that Medicaid serves people who have little or no income and Medicare serves people who are age sixty-five and older, as well as some people with disabilities. This distinction is important because people with disabilities must stay below an income level established by the state of residence to receive health care coverage, which may be especially necessary given the nature of their disability. One issue with the state Medicaid programs, however, is that there is greater variability in the state budgets to spend on Medicaid recipients. If one looks at two states with approximately the same number of people enrolled in the state Medicaid programs, one might see big differences. For example in 2010, Wyoming (87,433 Medicaid recipients) spent approximately $534 million on its program while North Dakota (82,762 Medicaid recipients) spent $708 million (Kaiser Family Foundation, 2011a, 2011b). North Dakota spent $174 million more than Wyoming yet Wyoming has 4,671 fewer Medicaid recipients. Disparities in state spending on Medicaid may further diverge in the future as states struggle to balance their budgets and deal with massive deficits. For individuals who earn slightly above the Medicaid threshold, most states employ a "spend-down" program that allows people with income levels that slightly exceed the Medicaid threshold to subtract medical bills during a six-month time period from their income to qualify for Medicaid. For example, if a person with a disability has an income level that is $100 greater than the Medicaid threshold, but has more than $100 in medical bills over a six-month period, then Medicaid would cover the rest of this person's medical bills once the initial $100 bill is paid.

The income means test for Medicaid might explain some of the employment level disparities discussed above between people with disabilities and people without disabilities. Indeed, if the choice for people with disabilities is between working at a job that might provide a decent wage, but mediocre health care coverage, and not working, to qualify for better health care coverage and receive a small living stipend from the government, in the form of Supplemental Security Income (discussed later in this chapter), then a sizable portion of the disability community might be forced out of the job market to maintain health coverage. Paul Longmore (2003), a noted scholar in disability history, provided his personal account of this false choice in *Why I Burned My Book*. This memoir detailed his time in graduate school when he had to turn down research and teaching assistant positions because they would have put him over the financial threshold, making him ineligible to receive health care coverage. However, by turning down these positions he was less attractive to future employers than his peers without disabilities who did not face the same dilemma and could work in these positions. In similar situations, people with disabilities may be faced with turning down entry-level employment opportunities that could lead to higher-paying jobs in the future because the beginning jobs do not offer them a livable wage that provides health care.

It is possible that the Patient Protection and Affordable Care Act (HR 3590) as modified by the Health Care and Education Reconciliation Act (HR 4872), which were both signed into law in 2010, might have a measurable impact on this health care dilemma. Specifically, the 2010 health care reform known as the Affordable Care Act carried at least four changes that are beneficial for people with disabilities. First, the legislation extended the threshold for Medicaid eligibility to 133 percent of the Federal Poverty Line. This move essentially expands Medicaid to cover more Americans than had previously qualified for the program. Second, the legislation eliminated insurance companies' ability to discriminate against applicants based on disabilities or other preexisting conditions. Prior to this legislation, insurance companies could reject an applicant if the applicant had a health condition that existed prior to their application for health insurance coverage. Effective 2014, this practice is no longer allowable. Third, the health care reform eliminated lifetime and annual benefits caps. By eliminating these caps, people with disabilities or other chronic illnesses cannot be dropped from their insurance once their medical bills reach a set threshold (typically $1 million). Finally, this legislation expands home and community-based service provisions that will enable people with disabilities and other chronic illnesses to remain in their homes and communities rather than live in an institution that may isolate them from their family and friends. The caveat to all of these items is that this legislation is being implemented in 2014. Given the Republican resurgence during the midterm elections in 2010, which worked to block these health care reforms, it is too soon to tell how these and other provisions of the Affordable Care Act will impact Americans.

Supplemental Security Income (SSI) and Social Security Disability Insurance (SSDI)

If people with disabilities are forced into this decision about health care over employment, what are their options for income? As established in the Social Security Act, the primary sources of income for people with disabilities who cannot work are Supplemental Security Income (SSI) and Social Security Disability Insurance (SSDI). Like Medicaid, SSI is a needs-based program. It is a cash assistance program that is based on an individual's financial need. Several factors are considered when determining the amount recipients receive. These factors typically include other income, living arrangements, the number of people in a residence, and other savings or assets owned by the individual (SSA, 2012c). Because this program is administered by the federal government and may have a state supplement, the benefit amounts may fluctuate from state to state. Social Security Disability Insurance, on the other hand, is a federally administered program that draws on contributions made from payroll taxes (SSA, 2012b). To qualify for SSDI, individuals must have a physical or mental condition that prevents them from working for at least twelve months. The difference between SSDI and SSI rests almost entirely in previous work experience. Because funding for SSDI is through taxes that employees, employers, and self-employed workers pay, the amount received per month depends on previous work that is "on the books" and is associated with the number of work credits earned (Shi & Singh, 2004). However, for SSI, it is provided to qualified individuals based on financial need.

Given the way the medical and supplemental income programs are designed, people with disabilities often face an unpleasant dilemma that may result in either poverty or poor health. Even with the spend-down flexibility that most states employ for Medicaid, the outlook is bleak. Add to this situation the trend among employer-based health care insurers to increase the cost-shifting strategies of employee contributions and larger deductibles (Enthoven & Fuchs, 2006). Recent research indicates that the cost for employees in the United States has increased by 5 percent from 2009 to 2010 for single coverage while wages rose only 2.2 percent (Claxton et al., 2010). Additionally, more employees entered into high deductible health plans that typically only provide coverage for a catastrophic medical matter after a high deductible is met (Claxton et al., 2010). This shift into high deductible plans is the primary significant shift in health plan enrollment during the past year. This development into the high deductible plans, however, would do very little for workers with disabilities that may need more regular access to health care services than the typical worker who enrolls in these health plans. These strategies especially hit heavy users of health care services such as people with disabilities, thus eroding more of their take-home pay.

Social Justice

"Social justice prevails when all members of a society share equally in the social order, secure an equitable consideration of resources and opportunities, and enjoy their full benefit of civil liberties" (DuBois & Miley, 2013, p. 16). This quote from DuBois and Miley underscores an approach to social justice that emphasizes individuals' right to have equal access to opportunities and resources within a society. However, the marginalization of groups of individuals within a society due to a categorical difference (e.g., race, ethnicity, gender, sexual orientation, disability, etc.) limits equal access to resources and results in discrimination. Accordingly, people with disabilities share a history of oppression that stretches across many cultures.

Societal Views of Disability

Within the United States, this history of oppression can be observed in policies ranging from eugenics movements, which sought to sterilize people with disabilities to prevent them from reproducing, to local "ugly laws," which criminalized people with disabilities or physical deformities for being out in public (Schweik, 2010). What is perhaps most shocking about laws such as these is that some of them existed in the legal system up until 1974 when Chicago finally repealed its last "ugly law" (Schweik, 2010). Mackelprang and Salsgiver (2009) noted, "the meaning of disability has been heavily influenced by society and by human service professionals" (p. 117). Paul Longmore (2003) wrote in an essay on the history of disability in the United States that "a 'cripple' on a public thoroughfare might have been seen as a divinely punished sinner in the 1830s, a potential rehabilitant in the 1950s, a political activist in the 1990s, and, in any era, a mendicant" [a beggar or someone relying on charity] (p. 57). Indeed, at different times in Western history and in different segments of society, people with disabilities have been labeled as immoral sinners and in need of a remedy, but they have always been viewed as deserving of people's charity and pity. These views of disability provide entry into a discussion about the key models of disability and the ways in which people with disabilities have pushed against oppressive interpretations of disability.

Twentieth-century society generally embraced medical perspectives of disability as an individual deficit that left them unable to fulfill social roles and duties. Given the common perception that people with disabilities were less than whole, an impairment was seen as a personal tragedy, marking individuals as living a subnormal, perhaps even subhuman, life. Barnes and Mercer (2003) argued that this perspective encompasses an individual and medicalized approach that interprets disability as (a) a problem for the individual, (b) a defect resulting in functional limitation, and (c) a situation that required medical treatment to normalize the individual. Thus, the societal view of disability is often one of dysfunction. This perspective guided social service interventions (e.g., institutionalization) and other charitable activities (e.g., Jerry's Kids) throughout the past century. In these interventions and activities, groups assume a deficit perspective of disability, rather than capitalizing on a strengths-based approach that could empower individuals with disabilities. Indeed, people with disabilities must often demonstrate creative problem-solving skills to accomplish tasks that able-bodied individuals take for granted. As Neil Marcus, a disability activist and artist remarked, "Disability is not a 'brave struggle' or 'courage in the face of adversity.' Disability is an art. It's an ingenious way to live" (1988, p.7).

Related to this medical model of disability is the perspective of disability and difference as a marker of social deviance. Talcott Parsons (1951) famously paralleled sickness and social deviance in noting that sickness threatens "normal" functioning. In this sense, society accepts an individual as temporarily sick. Society defines a sick role that individuals must follow. For example, a common belief in the United States is that individuals who are ill should remove themselves from society so as not to contaminate others. However, a challenge arises when an individual has a chronic illness or is permanently disabled. For these individuals, society determines that rehabilitation is unlikely to cure the condition or disability. Subsequently, one response to people with permanent disabilities was to develop a separate disability role. In this role, people with permanent disabilities should, according to society, be completely dependent on social services and agree to cooperate fully with medical and human service professionals to adapt to what society deems is some degree of normalcy. In this sense, most in society seem to believe that people with disabilities should become what Foucault (1995) referred to as "docile bodies." Specifically, people with disabilities become "better" when they comply with medical professionals to be transformed into an improved version of themselves. Individual experiences of this oppressive mindset permeate disability narratives such as Simi Linton's *My Body Politic* (2006), Robert Murphy's *The Body Silent* (1987), and Eli Clare's *Exile and Pride* (1999).

Organizing to Fight Social Injustice

In response to these perspectives of disability as an individual and medical problem that categorizes people with disabilities as ineligible for active roles in society, a movement developed among people with disabilities. While there are several points in time when people with disabilities have organized to challenge social injustices directed toward them, perhaps two examples best illustrate the quest for social justice in the United States for people with disabilities. The first example comes from the 1930s with the formation of the League of Physically Handicapped in New York City. This group appears to have been founded by young men and women with disabilities who mainly desired independence and dignity through employment, but who were shut out of the labor market due to the social perceptions of their impairments. Again, the theme of the worthy or deserving poor rises up. It seems that employers, lawmakers, and members of society did not believe people with disabilities should be included in employment assistance because of their impairments. As such, a perception existed that they deserved to be outside the job market and that available jobs should go to able-bodied workers. Stymied by the local job markets, these men and women looked to federal job programs that were emerging as part of President Roosevelt's New Deal. As a brief aside, one will remember that Roosevelt was also a person with a disability, affected by polio as a child. However, Roosevelt's Works Progress Administration (WPA) classified people with disabilities—along with older adults and mothers with dependent children—as unemployable. In response, members of the league and others started organizing. Indeed, they argued that they were not poor because of their impairments, rather they were poor because no one would hire them. Here they articulated an early version of the social model of disability that states people with disabilities are "disabled" not by their physical impairments, but by inaccessible environments and social attitudes about their impairments. The Union of Physically Impaired against Segregation (UPIAS) perhaps best articulated this social model almost forty years after the league formed. UPIAS wrote, "In our view it is society which disables physically impaired people. Disability is something imposed on top of our impairments by the way we are unnecessarily isolated and excluded from full participation in society. Disabled people are therefore an oppressed group in society" (UPIAS, 1976, p. 14).

The second example comes from the 1970s, beginning with President Nixon signing into law the Rehabilitation Act of 1973. Within the act, Section 504 provided a powerful tool to disability advocates. Section 504 states that "No otherwise qualified handicapped individual . . . shall . . . be excluded from participation in, be denied benefits of, or be subjected to discrimination under any program or activity receiving federal financial assistance." In many ways, this section established people with disabilities as a protected minority group akin to women and racial minorities. However, the federal Department of Health, Education and Welfare (HEW), which had the responsibility to enforce Section 504, did not make any attempt to do so in three years following Nixon's signature on the Rehabilitation Act of 1973. Finally, disability rights advocates applied pressure to HEW in the form of lobbying and eventually massive sit-ins at HEW offices in San Francisco and other major cities around the country. These efforts brought together people with disabilities across impairment groups and across organizations to demonstrate the power of people with disabilities and underscore the desires of people with disabilities to be included in society as active participants rather than the recipients of public aid and pity. Eventually, disability rights advocates prevailed and the secretary for HEW signed the implementation regulations that would make Section 504 an enforceable law. Through these efforts, disability rights activists and advocates defined people with disabilities as a protected minority group and created a new model of disability that identified society as the disabling entity and not an individual's impairment.

This social model of disability rests at the core of social justice and empowerment for people with disabilities. Jim Charlton's work, *Nothing about Us without Us* (1998), provided a clear vision of the ways that people with disabilities have become empowered through a shift froom thinking of themselves as being "docile bodies," to reference Foucault again, to becoming part of a powerful movement. Charlton's work, along with theorists like Ayesha Vernon, also remind us that "disability" as an identity category does not exist apart from other oppressed identity categories. Recall from the demographics section above that racial and ethnic minorities have higher rates of disabilities in the United States. The combination of oppressed identities adds to the level of oppression that some people with disabilities might face (Vernon, 1999). These identity intersections demand attention as social workers, policy makers, and advocates consider ways to alleviate poverty among people with disabilities. Indeed, these changes must combat not only oppression against people with disabilities, but also oppressions faced by racial and ethnic minorities; women; lesbian, gay, bisexual, transgender (LGBT) communities; and a host of other marginalized populations.

Interventions

The challenge for social workers and other helping professionals seeking to address social injustice such as discrimination toward people with disabilities and lift this population out of poverty is to know where interventions are needed and the methods that will be most effective. Certainly, a single approach will not be successful. The contextual factors and stakeholders should determine which methods might be most effective. To illustrate, three interventions at the micro, mezzo, and macro levels are explored below. These strategies explore interventions by disability advocates and human service professionals who are collaborating to create change in various situations in the lives of individuals with disabilities.

Micro Interventions

Micro-level interventions typically occur with individuals or families. This section considers a hospital-based program that works with individuals with recent disabilities. Critical Pathways to Education developed as part of Schwab Rehabilitation Hospital's Extended Service Program (Hayes, Balfanz-Vertiz, & Meldrum, 2005). Staff at Schwab created Critical Pathways in 1997 to assist people with disabilities who were returning to their communities following a serious injury or the development of a medical condition. A significant number of patients at the hospital were young and from minority ethnic and racial groups. Additionally, many of the patients had disabilities due to violent and traumatic injuries. Through years of serving this population, staff recognized that employment and education were two significant needs of this community. Many patients at Schwab had a desire to work and go to school, but encountered a variety of obstacles from limited work experience, to criminal backgrounds, to poor education, which prevented them from advancing.

To serve this population, the Critical Pathways staff developed a process called "Life Planning Coordination." Through this process, individual needs and aptitudes were assessed and an educational or vocational plan was tailored to meet individual patients where they were in their lives. The person at the center of this process is the life planning coordinator (LPC). The LPC has three specific tasks: (1) to work with the participant to set realistic educational and vocational goals; (2) to identify resources to help meet the participant's goals and needs; and (3) to provide instructional support (e.g., tutoring, teaching, etc.) for the participants in a one-on-one setting.

Upon assessment of the program, Critical Pathways staff learned some valuable lessons. First, they learned that many of the participants who enrolled in the program did so because they could not find similar programs that were accessible in their communities. Indeed, while many of their communities had GED programs or job readiness programs, few of the buildings were accessible to them. Second, 67 percent of the participants were able to enroll in educational programs while receiving services through Critical Pathways, and 33 percent of the participants were able to find employment while participating in the program (Hayes et al., 2005). These numbers are in stark contrast to the initial assessment figures that identified only 2 percent of the participants enrolled in educational programs and 10 percent of the participants were employed. While these two figures were promising for the staff, they also learned that they lacked tutors, computers, and transportation vouchers to meet the needs of the community. However, for the participants who could take advantage of the program, most believed the program provided tremendous support in helping them meet their individual needs.

Mezzo Interventions

Mezzo-level interventions typically involve changes with groups, organizations, and systems. To explore an intervention at the mezzo level, a program will be detailed that not only worked on an individual basis with people with disabilities, but also worked across systems such as the public schools, community colleges, and the Office of Vocational Rehabilitation. The College Connection to Career Development Opportunities Project (CCP) was a model demonstration project funded by the Rehabilitation Services Administration to support inner-city minority youth with disabilities as they transitioned from high school to college and other vocational training programs in the Chicago area. The program began as a means to address three issues. First, the path to a career is through post-secondary education. Second, as discussed previously, people with disabilities are unemployed at greater rates than people without disabilities. Finally, minorities living in the inner city face many obstacles that affect their opportunities for education and employment. CCP program staff partnered with workers at the Chicago public schools, the City Colleges of Chicago, and the Illinois Department of Human Services, Office of Rehabilitation Services to create a network of agencies committed to the success of this population.

On an individual level, the intervention approach for this program involved two primary components: intensive case management and skill development. Every participant in the project was assigned a case manager. The case manager initially worked with individuals one-on-one to identify their educational or vocational goals. Once these goals were established, case managers provided participants with guidance, emotional support, instrumental assistance, and other services, as needed. These additional services ranged from helping participants get a state identification card, to helping with registration for college courses, to accompanying them to appointments at state vocational rehabilitation offices. The primary task was to simultaneously support the participants as they worked toward their goals and teach them how to navigate and advocate within the various systems. These efforts helped provide scaffolding for the participants to build their skills for self-advocacy and self-determination.

The second component of the intervention entailed skill development. Like the case management component, skill development was also meant to promote self-advocacy and empowerment. The skill development component occurred in a classroom setting where participants learned through group exercises, one-on-one activities, and role-play simulations. These activities were designed to teach participants not only about their disability, but also about their rights; how to access resources, advocate for their needs, set goals, and develop plans for action; and how to recruit potential mentors and helpers to support attainment of their educational and vocational goals. To achieve these tasks, the case managers taught a course using a curriculum designed to be culturally sensitive for high school students with disabilities. The curriculum was developed and has been updated to reflect the specific goals of this project.

Perhaps the most significant piece of the CCP, however, was the cooperation that the project received from the various partners. They all recognized the importance of providing additional educational opportunities to minority youth with disabilities to advance their careers. The city colleges offered a variety of adult education programs that enhanced the employability of the participants to prepare them for competitive employment. The Office of Vocational Rehabilitation Services was very effective in supporting the tuition costs for the students as they enrolled in the college courses. More teachers from the Chicago public schools became aware of the program and began actively encouraging their students to participate. The families also realized that career development is in the best long-term interest of their children, even when they realized that they might lose some SSI dollars in the short term due to low-paying initial job opportunities.

Low-income, minority students with disabilities are not often encouraged or supported to pursue post-high school education and employment. They are often perceived as lifelong welfare recipients. These assumptions regarding the educational and vocational worth of this population speaks to the simultaneous oppression that minorities with disabilities encounter in society. Indeed, members of this population simultaneously face oppression based on skin color and ability status. This project demonstrated that with the appropriate supports, participants are not only capable of succeeding in their efforts, but are also willing to pursue careers and employment opportunities that could bring them the independence they desired.

Macro Interventions

To examine a macro-level intervention occurring at a state level, the University of Minnesota's Disability and Parental Rights Legislative Change Project offers a good example. This project is a collaboration between the School of Social Work and the Institute on Community Integration in the College of Education and Human Development. The project began in response to discriminatory legislation pertaining to child custody and parental rights for parents with disabilities. Legislation such as this continued the tradition of laws that sought to control the reproduction and parenting for people with disabilities. As of 2007, the project suggested that approximately two-thirds of states in the United States had laws that could be used to limit the parental rights of people with disabilities.

To address these issues, the Disability and Parental Rights Legislative Change Project convened a multi-disciplinary advisory group to develop suggested legislative language for other advocacy groups across the country to use. Additionally, they created other resources such as action guides and technical assistance for others to access. Overall, the project members developed six key principles (Lightfoot, LaLiberte, & Hill, 2007):

1. State statutes should be free of discriminatory language. For example, the statutes should not have discriminatory language in the areas of termination of parental rights, adoption, or child custody.

2. State statutes should affirm that no part of the statute should be used to discriminate against parents with disabilities.

3. State statutes should acknowledge that successful parenting can occur with proper accommodations and supports.

4. State statutes should require that parental assessments of people with disabilities focus on behaviors rather than impairments and chronic health conditions. Additionally, these assessments should be conducted by appropriate experts skilled in disability accommodations and parenting skills.

5. State statutes should require specialized protocols when family members with disabilities are investigated.

6. State statutes should require the inclusion of disability experts on multi-disciplinary teams.

The work at Minnesota further draws on the successful example of Fathers and Mothers Independently Living with Their Youth (FAMILY) in Idaho. FAMILY brought together participants from several stakeholder groups such as parents with disabilities, legislators, and other advocates to guarantee a consistent process that would prevent parents with disabilities from losing their children solely due to their disability. After four years of lobbying and advocacy, FAMILY's efforts remained unsuccessful. However, in 2002, a key Idaho legislative member saw the movie *I Am Sam*, which is about a father with a developmental disability who loses custody of his child through a child protection action. Moved by the story, the legislator became a key champion for FAMILY's cause, eventually helping usher in the group's legislation to have it passed in 2003. While the Idaho example may seem strange, seasoned policy and advocacy experts know that you can never doubt the power of a personal story or other relatable format to sway legislators.

Concluding Comments

This chapter sought to inform readers about the historical, social, and political context that keeps disability and poverty linked. As demonstrated throughout, social attitudes and poorly conceived policies often serve as disabling obstacles that prevent people with disabilities from becoming empowered and finding pathways out of poverty. Future policies must address the false choice for people with disabilities to either give up health care or seek a living wage. Indeed, the current structure keeps people with disabilities tied to health care and fails to provide a living wage through SSI or SSDI. For people with disabilities to advance economically, they cannot be forced into that dilemma. Real change in the United States that seeks to break the link between disability and poverty will address these sorts of issues.

Case Studies
Micro Level

Joseph is a 24-year-old African American man who was shot and paralyzed six months ago during a gang fight. He has lived all of his life in an inner-city neighborhood of Chicago and been involved in gang activities since he was eleven years old. As a result of his gang involvement, Joseph has been arrested several times for offenses ranging from drug trafficking to assault. This criminal record affects locations where Joseph can live. For example, many of the landlords in the city are hesitant to rent to someone with felony convictions. Furthermore, Joseph's Supplemental Security Income (SSI) only pays him $674 per month for all of his living expenses and he is ineligible for other government benefits beyond Medicaid and Food Stamps. Therefore, Joseph moved from the rehabilitation facility back to his girlfriend's apartment, which is in a three-story walk-up without an elevator. In order to exit and enter the building, Joseph must rely on his brother or friends to carry him out of the apartment and down the steps, then he must wait for them to return so he can reenter the building.

Joseph recently reported that his girlfriend has been abusive to him since he has returned. He says that she believes he was abusive to her before he was paralyzed and now that he has to rely on her for some of his needs, she is taking revenge. For example, if she is mad at him, she will take away his wheelchair so he cannot get around as easily within the apartment. Joseph is getting more depressed by this situation and "feels less like a man" since the injury because he has to rely on people to help him leave, his girlfriend is abusive, and he cannot do things that he believes makes one a man. As a result of these living conditions, Joseph wants to find new housing. Unfortunately, no one in his immediate or extended family has the space or accessibility to provide housing for Joseph. One alternative to this living situation is for Joseph to move to a nursing home or a skilled care unit, which would be accessible and provide him with some of the medical care that he still needs given that his injury is still recent. However, he would be living with people who are in their later stages of life while he is still a very young man. This living arrangement would likely not provide him with developmentally appropriate situations for his life course stage.

Questions

1. What are the essential characteristics of Joseph's situation?

2. What systems might be targets for advocacy on Joseph's behalf?

3. How would your advocacy strategies change based on which system you target?

4. What resources might you incorporate to advocate for Joseph?

5. What other concerns might you have about Joseph's current situation?

Mezzo Level

Tyler is a ten-year-old African American boy who was hit by a car while he was playing. The accident resulted in a traumatic brain injury and both his legs being crushed, leaving him unable to walk. Tyler returned home where he was being raised by his grandmother because his mother was battling substance abuse problems and his father was in prison. His grandmother had health concerns of her own with diabetes and a below-the-knee amputation as a result of poor management of the diabetes.

The hospital social worker met with Tyler before his release from the rehabilitation hospital and agreed to help the family navigate the public school system so that Tyler could receive a tutor while he continued to recover at home. Unfortunately, the social worker was unable to secure home-bound education from the public school system. The Office of Specialized Services at the school said that no one could go to the home because the neighborhood he lived in was dangerous. They suggested that Tyler would be fine to return to school; however, the school was not physically accessible. The grandmother did not know what to do to secure a public education for her grandson and the social worker felt stymied by the public school system as officials failed to return her phone calls, letters, and e-mails.

Concurrent with her own advocacy efforts, the social worker learned from many of her client families that "Tyler's story" is common. Often, her families explained, coping with a child's new disability while trying to navigate bureaucratic systems to obtain needed services is difficult. After speaking with her supervisor, the social worker began outreaching to the families on her caseload to explore the need to initiate a support group. After doing a needs assessment and determining that many families were interested in participating, the social worker developed a community-wide support group for family members of children with traumatic head injuries. She also arranged for a lending library, an Internet resource directory, and together with group members, planned several educational community forums.

Questions

1. What other group services do you think families such as Tyler's might need?

2. What other avenues could the social worker and the support group members have pursued to resolve issues such as Tyler's?

3. How would one go about identifying community resources to assist this population?

4. What type of knowledge and skills are needed to facilitate this type of group?

5. How important is it for helping professionals to understand the Americans with Disabilities Act as it pertains to public education requirements when working with this type of group?

Macro Level

Monica, a social worker and single mother of children with developmental disabilities, lives in a state that is transitioning its Medicaid program into a managed care model. The proposal will utilize a waiver to shift the state's medical services for low-income individuals and families to three for-profit companies. The state's governor and lieutenant governor claim that this shift will hold down long-term costs and streamline the system to be more effective. The proposal also includes services for people with developmental disabilities in the managed care plans. The new plan will focus on implementing a "medical model" that will leave all people with disabilities as individuals in need of a cure. Another concern with the program is that individuals will be randomly assigned into one of the three managed care organizations that are awarded the state's Medicaid contracts. With all of the managed care organizations being out of state, Medicaid recipients will likely need to be able to "meet" with representatives and case managers via telephone or a computer interface. Some people with developmental disabilities will struggle to navigate these technologies and may end up having their health compromised due to this barrier.

As a result of these changes Monica is concerned. She is concerned not only for her own children, but also for the clients with disabilities that she serves. A small coalition of people with disabilities, their family members, and other advocates have started gathering to challenge these changes to the state Medicaid system. Many of the parents involved expressed great concern over the dissolution of support networks they spent years developing. Specifically, the parents have renewed concerns about what will happen to their child with a developmental disability, should they, the parents, be injured or die. Who will take care of their children? Several provider groups, including social workers, have made this a top legislative issue for the upcoming year.

Questions

1. Why should people with disabilities and their allies be concerned with this change in the state's Medicaid plan?

2. Why would the new "medical model" be a problem for people with disabilities?

3. What strategies do you think the coalition should undertake to challenge the change in Medicaid provisions?

4. How might the state structure a Medicaid program that both controlled costs and considered the needs of people with disabilities?

5. How could other social workers in the state best assist this advocacy effort?

Internet Resources

Americans with Disabilities Act (ADA) Homepage: http://www.ada.gov/

Offers information, resources, and technical assistance on the ADA.

Center for Medicaid and Medicare Services: cms.hhs.gov

Provides current health care information for all Americans.

Cornell University, Disability Statistics: http://www.ilr.cornell.edu/edi/disability statistics/

Offers the most recent demographic and economic statistics on the non-institutionalized population with disabilities.

Disability Law Center: www.disabilitylawcenter.com

Offers national information regarding disability benefits, specifically disability benefit claims.

Equal Employment Opportunity Commission: www.eeoc.gov

Addresses national policies governing illegal employment discriminatory practices based on race, color, sex, nationality, age, and disability.

Housing and Urban Development for People with Disabilities: www.hud.gov/groups/disabilities.cfm

Offers content on housing rights of people with disabilities under federal law.

National Council on Disability: www.ncd.gov

An agency that advises the president, Congress, and other federal agencies regarding policies affecting people with disabilities.

National Institute on Disability and Rehabilitation Research (NIDRR): http://www2.ed.gov/about/offices/list/osers/nidrr/index.html?src=mr

Discusses current initiatives and online services focusing on improving the lives of individuals with disabilities through education and training.

Office of Special Education and Rehabilitation Services: http://www2.ed.gov/about/offices/list/osers/index.html

Offers resources that support persons with disabilities from infancy to adulthood, including their families.

Rehabilitation Services Administration: http://www2.ed.gov/about/offices/list/osers/rsa/index.html?src=mr

Oversees grant programs that give priority to significantly disabled individuals focusing on vocational rehabilitation, employment, and support services.

THOMAS: Legislation information from Library of Congress: http://thomas.loc.gov/

Provides federal legislative information to the public.

U.S. Census Bureau Data on Disability: http://www.census.gov/people/disability/

Provides a collection of disability data.

U.S. Website on Disability: http://www.disability.gov/

Offers information on disability programs and services in communities nationwide.

Further Readings

Albrecht, G., Seelman, K., & Bury, M. (2001). *The handbook of disability studies.* Thousand Oaks, CA: Sage Publications.

Burch, S. (2010). *Encyclopedia of American disability history.* New York City: Facts on File.

Charlton, J. (2000). *Nothing about us without us.* Berkeley: University of California Press.

DuBois, B., & Miley, K. (2008). *Social work: An empowering profession* (6th ed.). Boston: Allyn & Bacon.

Fleischer, D., & Zames, F. (2000). *Disability rights movement: From charity to confrontation.* Philadelphia: Temple University Press.

Johnson, M. (2003). *Make Them Go Away: Clint Eastwood, Christopher Reeve and the case against disability rights.* Louisville, KY: Avocado Press.

Longmore, P. (2003). *Why I burned my book.* Philadelphia: Temple University Press.

Longmore, P., & Umansky, L. (2001). *The new disability history: American perspectives.* New York: NYU Press.

Mackelprang, R., & Salsgiver, R. (2009). *Disability: A diversity model approach in human service practice.* Chicago: Lyceum Press.

Michalko, R. (2002). *The difference that disability makes.* Philadelphia: Temple University Press.

O'Brien, R. (2001). *Crippled justice: The history of modern disability in the workplace.* Chicago: University of Chicago Press.

O'Brien, R., & Smith, R. (2004). *Voice from the edge: Narratives about the Americans with Disabilities Act.* Oxford: Oxford University Press.

Schweik, S. (2009). *The ugly laws: Disability in public.* New York: New York University Press.

Scotch, R. (2001). *From good will to civil rights: Transforming federal disability policy.* Philadelphia: Temple University Press.

Shapiro, J. (1994). *No pity: People with disabilities forging a new civil rights movement.* New York: Three Rivers Press.

Stone, D. (1984). *The disabled state.* Philadelphia: Temple University Press.

References

Americans with Disabilities Act of 1990. (1990). Pub. L. No. 101-336.

Americans with Disabilities Amendments Act of 2008. (2008). Pub L. No. 110-325.

Barnes, C., & Mercer, G. (2003). *Disability.* Cambridge, UK: Polity Press.

Berkowitz, E. (1980). *Rehabilitation: The federal government's response to disability, 1935–1954.* New York City: Arno Press.

Charlton, J. (1998). *Nothing about us without us.* Berkeley: University of California Press.

Clare, E. (1999). *Exile and pride: Disability, queerness, and liberation.* Cambridge, MA: South End Press.

Claxton, G., DiJulio, B., Whitmore, H., Pickreign, J., McHugh, M., Osei-Anto, A., & Finder, B. (2010). Health benefits in 2010: Premiums rise modestly, workers pay more toward coverage. *Health Affairs, 29,* 1942–1950.

DeNavas-Walt, C., Proctor, B., & Smith, J. (2012). *Income, poverty, and health insurance coverage in the United States: 2011.* U.S. Census Bureau. Retrieved from http://www.census.gov/prod/2012pubs/p60-243.pdf.

DuBois, B., & Miley, K. (2013). *Social work: An empowering profession* (8th ed.). New York: Pearson.

Enthoven, A., & Fuchs, V. (2006). Employment-based health insurance: Past, present, and future. *Health Affairs, 25*(6), 1538–1547.

Erikson, W., Lee, C., & von Schrader, S. (2010). *2008 disability status report: The United States.* Ithaca, NY: University Rehabilitation and Training Center on Disability Demographics and Statistics.

Foucault, M. (1995). *Discipline and punish: The birth of the prison.* New York: Vintage Press.

Fremstad, S. (2009). *Half in ten: Why taking disability into account is essential to reducing income poverty and expanding economic inclusion.* Center for Economic and Policy Research. Retrieved from http://www.cepr.net/documents/publications/poverty-disability-2009-09.pdf.

Hayes, E., Balfanz-Vertiz, K., & Meldrum, R. (2005). Building critical pathways to education and employment among individuals with spinal cord injuries. *Psychosocial Process, 18*(1), 17–26.

Individuals with Disabilities Education Improvement Act of 2004. (2004). Pub. L. 108-446.

Kaiser Family Foundation. (2011a). *State health facts: Total Medicaid enrollment, FY 2010.* Retrieved from http://kff.org/medicaid/state-indicator/total-medicaid-enrollment-fy2009/.

Kaiser Family Foundation. (2011b). *State health facts: Total Medicaid spending.* Retrieved from http://kff.org/medicaid/state-indicator/total-medicaid-spending-fy2010/.

Katz, M. (1996). *In the shadow of the poorhouse: A social history of welfare in America.* New York: Basic Books.

Kaye, S. (2003). *Improved employment opportunities for people with disabilities.* San Francisco: Disability Statistics Center.

Leiby, J. (1978). *A history of social welfare and social work in the United States.* New York: Columbia University Press.

Lightfoot, E., LaLiberte, T., & Hill, K. (2007). *Guide for creating legislative change: Disability in the termination of parental rights and other child custody statutes.* Minneapolis: University of Minnesota.

Linton, S. (2006). *My body politic.* Ann Arbor: University of Michigan Press.

Longmore, P. (2003). *Why I burned my book and other essays on disability.* Philadelphia: Temple University Press.

Mackelprang, R., & Salsgiver, R. (2009). *Disability: A diversity model approach in human service practice.* Chicago: Lyceum Books.

Marcus, N. (1988). Storm Reading. Unpublished manuscript.

Michalko, R. (2002). *The difference that disability makes.* Philadelphia: Temple University Press.

Murphy, R. (1987). *The body silent.* New York: Henry Holt and Company.

O'Brien, R. (2001). *Crippled justice: The history of modern disability in the workplace.* Chicago: University of Chicago Press.

Parsons, T. (1951). Illness and the role of the physician: A sociological perspective. *American Journal of Orthopsychiatry, 21*(3), 452–460.

Patterson, J. (2000). *America's struggle against poverty in the twentieth century.* Cambridge, MA: Harvard University Press.

Rehabilitation Act of 1973. (1973). Pub L. No. 93-112.

Schweik, S. (2010). *The ugly laws: Disability in public.* New York: New York University Press.

Scotch, R. (2001). *From good will to civil rights: Transforming federal disability policy.* Philadelphia: Temple University Press.

Shi, L., & Singh, D. (2004). *Delivering health care in America: A systems approach.* Sudbury, MA: Jones and Bartlett Publishers.

Social Security Administration. (2012a). *Disability benefits.* Retrieved from http://www.socialsecurity.gov/pubs/EN-05-10029.pdf.

Social Security Administration. (2012b). *Disability planner: Social Security protection if you become disabled.* Retrieved from http://www.ssa.gov/dibplan/index.htm#a0=0.

Social Security Administration. (2012c). *A guide to Supplemental Security Income (SSI) for groups and organizations.* SSA Publication No. 05-11015, ICN 480300.

Trattner, W. (1998). *From poor law to welfare state: A history of social welfare in America.* New York City: Free Press

Turner, M., Herbig, C., Kaye, D., Fenderson, J., & Levy, D. (2005). *Discrimination against persons with disabilities: Barriers at every step.* Chicago: Urban Institute.

Union of the Physically Impaired Against Segregation. (1976). *Fundamental principles of disability.* Union of the Physically Impaired Against Segregation.

U.S. Census Bureau. (2010). *American community survey, 2010.* Retrieved from http://www.census.gov/acs/www/Downloads/QbyQfact/disability.pdf.

U.S. Census Bureau. (2012). *American factfinder fact sheet.*

U.S. Department of Education, National Center for Education Statistics. (2010). *The condition of education 2010.* NCES 2010–028.

U.S. Department of Housing and Urban Development. (2009). *The 2008 annual assessment report to Congress.* Retrieved from http://www.hudhre.info/documents/4thHomelessAssessmentReport.pdf.

Vernon, A. (1999). The dialectics of multiple identities and the disabled people's movement. *Disability and Society, 14*(3), 385–398.

Witt, J. F. (2003). *The accidental republic: Crippled workingmen, destitute widows, and the remaking of American law.* Cambridge, MA: Harvard University Press.

World Health Organization. (2012). *Disabilities.* Retrieved from http://www.who.int/topics/disabilities/en/.

8

Persons with Mental Illness and Co-Occurring Substance Use Disorders

Tim Devitt and Kristin Davis

Persons with severe mental illness constitute one subpopulation with whom social workers and related health professionals work. For those who do not know someone with a mental illness, popular media portrays the way one views people with a mental illness. Homicidal maniacs from horror movies or the "crazy" cartoon characters or the sight of people in public spaces who appear to be behaving inappropriately or asking for money are the typical images that may come to mind when one hears the term *mentally ill*. Persons with mental illness are often stigmatized, that is, treated differently because of being perceived as having a personal trait or attribute considered to be socially disadvantageous or scary. Alternatively, one may know a family member or acquaintance or coworker who has a severe mental illness. Research suggests that knowing someone with a mental illness is the most powerful means to combat stigma. Professional social workers and related helping professionals, who work in mental health, addictions, housing advocacy, employment, corrections, disabilities, or any other area of the field, are likely to come across people with a severe mental illness and a substance use disorder, sometimes referred to as a co-occurring disorder. Working well with people who have a mental illness and substance use disorder requires an understanding of their unique situation.

This chapter addresses common representations of mental illness. It also examines the complicated interaction among severe mental illness, substance use disorders, and social conditions, most notably poverty, in a way that aims to de-stigmatize those who suffer from these illnesses. The chapter provides a good foundation for readers to begin developing their understanding about individuals who suffer from a mental illness and the issues they face. It also reviews mental illnesses and co-occurring substance use disorders, how many people in the United States have a co-occurring disorder and live in poverty, the history of mental health and substance use treatment, and the relationship between mental illness, substance use disorder, poverty, policy, and treatment issues.

Demographics and Characteristics
Understanding Mental Illness

In the United States, several organizations weigh in on and guide the classification of mental illnesses for practitioners, advocates, and policy makers. The National Alliance on Mental Illness (NAMI), the nation's largest mental health advocacy organization, defines mental illness as a "disorder of the brain" that "disrupts a person's thinking, feeling, moods, and ability to relate to others . . . [and] often results in a diminished capacity for coping with the ordinary demands of life" (National Alliance on Mental Illness [NAMI], 2007, para. 1). NAMI is involved in the policy arena at both the state and federal levels and is an important resource for families who have children with severe mental illness, often providing them a voice in policy making.

The 1999 Surgeon General's Report on Mental Health defines mental illness as a set of "diagnosable mental disorders . . . characterized by alterations in thinking, mood, or behavior . . . associated with distress and/or impaired functioning" (U.S. Department of Health and Human Services, 1999, p. 57). According to the Surgeon General, "impairment in daily functioning" is what distinguishes mental illness from other, less severe problems. To be impaired in daily functioning one must not be able to deal with the typical tasks of life for long periods of time.

The *Diagnostic and Statistical Manual of Mental Disorders* (*DSM*) is a text published by the American Psychiatric Association (APA) that provides diagnostic criteria and classifies mental illnesses, some of which include neurocognitive disorders such as Alzheimer's disease, anxiety disorders, depression, bipolar disorder, schizophrenia and other psychotic disorders, and substance use disorders (APA, 2013). The manual was first published in 1952 and has been updated several times to reflect new understandings of the brain and mental illness. The fifth edition was published in May 2013. The *DSM* categorizes the various types of mental illness according to a range of criteria, including (a) characteristic symptoms, (b) impairment in social, occupational, or other important areas of functioning, (c) duration, and (d) making an assessment that the condition is not due to a medical condition or some other psychological or substance-related condition (APA,

2013). For instance, to be diagnosed with major depressive disorder, single episode, an individual would have experienced minimal problems from substance use, and at least five of nine specific symptoms, including sad mood, loss of interest in pleasurable activities, sleep disturbance, low energy, weight loss or a decrease or increase in appetite, difficulty concentrating, feelings of worthlessness or excessive guilt, and frequently thinking of death or self-harm over a consecutive two-week period (APA, 2013, pp. 160–161). Since public and private health insurers typically rely on current *DSM* diagnoses when considering insurance coverage for mental illness, this manual has come to play a critical role in mental health care policy.

The working definition of mental illness, derived from the above, used in the remainder of this chapter is as follows: mental illness is a bio-psycho-social brain disorder characterized by dysfunctional thoughts, feelings, and/or behaviors that meet *DSM* diagnostic criteria.

Severe Mental Illness

Severe courses of mental illness refer to periods of time when the psychiatric disorder impairs functioning across several life domains. More specifically, periods of severe illness course are characterized by long stretches of time of severe distress, pervasive debilitating symptoms, decreased quality of life, increased service use, and notably, loss of opportunities, including employment. Consequently, people with severe mental illness are often at risk of living in poverty. Schizophrenia, for example, is a mental illness characterized by delusions, hallucinations, cognitive deficits, and abnormal behavior (APA, 2013, p. 99). It is also characterized by what are referred to as negative symptoms: amotivation, social withdrawal, and diminished affect. The disorder involves experiencing a severe impairment in functioning across multiple life domains *at the period of initial onset,* and for some people, for prolonged periods of time throughout their lives. But the course of schizophrenia, like all mental illnesses, varies from person to person, and many adults with schizophrenia experience improvement in their psychotic symptoms as they age (Jeste & Maglione, 2013). Symptoms of schizophrenia can and do remit for some people, while others pursue a full and active life despite having the regular experience of symptoms from the disorder. The "Interventions" section of this chapter will expound more on the recovery factors and treatments that can help people with schizophrenia live meaningful lives.

Bipolar 1 disorder, also known as manic-depressive illness, is a brain disorder that causes unusual shifts in mood, energy, activity levels, and the ability to carry out day-to-day tasks. Symptoms of bipolar disorder can be severe as well. They are different from the normal ups and downs that everyone goes through from time to time. Severe symptoms of bipolar disorder can result in damaged relationships, poor job or school performance, suicidal ideation, and suicide.

Major depression, also known as clinical depression, can involve persistent sadness and inability to find pleasure in life that significantly interferes with daily functioning (APA, 2013, p. 160). It is characterized by a combination of symptoms that interfere with a person's ability to work, sleep, study, eat, and enjoy once-pleasurable activities. Severe symptoms of major depression can be disabling and prevent a person from functioning normally. An episode of major depression may occur only once in a person's lifetime, but more often, it recurs throughout a person's life.

Having a substance use disorder involves experiencing significant problems in cognitive, behavioral, and physical functioning related to the use of alcohol or drugs (APA, 2013). A partial listing of the criteria for having certain types of substance use disorders (e.g., alcohol, tobacco, cannabis, stimulant, opioid) include using more of a substance than was intended, not being able to cut down or stop using despite having the goal to do so, failure to live up to familial, occupational, or educational commitments because of the use, having strong cravings to use the substance, engaging in behaviors while using that puts one or others at risk of serious harm, increased tolerance that involves needing to use more of a substance over time to get the desired effect, and the experience of physical withdrawal when trying to decrease or stop using the substance (APA, 2013, pp. 483–484). A person is likely to experience severe impairments in functioning when several items on the substance use disorder list are met.

Understanding Mental Illness and Co-Occurring Substance Use Disorders

The term *co-occurring disorders* is often used interchangeably with dual disorders. The terms refer to people who have two disorders at the same time, such as a mental illness like the ones described in this section (e.g., schizophrenia, bipolar disorder, major depression), and a substance use disorder that could be mild, moderate, or severe, and which limits the person in his or her daily functioning or causes significant distress. For persons suffering from a mental illness, using substances can exacerbate symptoms and undermines attempts at being able to achieve one's full potential.

In this section, severe mental illness is defined by type and severity of symptoms, how disabling it is, and how long it lasts. People who have both a severe mental illness and a drug or alcohol problem are referred to as having a co-occurring disorder. Having both disorders can worsen mental illness and often leads to negative consequences, such as being homeless, jailed, and hospitalized. In the next section, the relationship between poverty and co-occurring disorders will be explained by introducing the bio-psycho-social model of behavior.

The Relationship between Co-Occurring Disorders and Poverty

As described above, mental illnesses vary in severity, length of time experienced, and the frequency with which someone experiences symptoms. This chapter focuses on the most debilitating mental illnesses and the role alcohol and drug use disorders play in their course. How the relationship among severe mental illness, substance use, and poverty is understood has implications for advocacy and the kinds of services provided, and how they are interpreted and understood.

The following section focuses on the bio-psycho-social perspectives (Engel, 1977; Zubin & Spring, 1977), which equally emphasizes the biological, psychological, and social realms of behavior. A bio-psycho-social perspective of co-occurring disorders shows how the biological factors of mental illness and substance use—genetic predispositions that are inherited and neurochemical or neurophysiological—interact with the psychological or personality of the person, and the social interaction between the person, others, and the world. Bio-psycho-social theory is good for understanding the relationship among poverty, mental illness, and substance use disorder.

Poverty as a Social Determinant of Mental Health

Social determinants of health are those socioeconomic conditions into which people are born and in which they live. Adequate housing, safe neighborhoods, access and money to buy healthy food, transportation to find employment, the ability to maintain a job, and social respect make up some of what determines people's health (Marmott, 2001a, 2001b). Social determinants account for health inequities across countries, and across subpopulations within countries. There is a consensus that social disadvantage correlates with increased *risk* of mental illness, physical illness, and substance use disorders (Williams & Jackson, 2005). The World Health Organization (WHO, 2003) states, "No group is immune to mental disorders, but the risk is higher among the poor, homeless, unemployed, persons with low education, victims of violence, migrants and refugees, indigenous populations, children and adolescents, abused women, and the neglected elderly" (p. 74). While the WHO is referring to more mild courses of mental illness, severe courses of mental illness have also been shown to be more prevalent among groups with high poverty rates, such as immigrants or racial minorities (Weiser et al., 2008). Recent work suggests that social disadvantage, broadly defined, puts one at risk of developing a mental illness that will result in periods of severe impairment (Van Os, Rutten, & Poulton, 2008).

Important to note, however, are the existence of studies that support the claim that mental illness leads to, rather than results from, poverty. This body of research coined the term "downward drift hypothesis" (Fox 1990; Hollingshead & Redlich, 1954). Simply stated, it suggests that individuals become so impaired because of their illness, and in many cases because of their co-occurring substance use disorder, that they cannot maintain their prior socioeconomic status because they are unable to work or to maintain housing. This hypothesis also holds that higher rates of mental illness that have been reported in areas of relative poverty are due to individuals migrating to these areas because housing is more affordable and discrepant behavior more acceptable (Faris & Dunham, 1939).

Recent work in social epidemiology suggests that a range of social and individual determinants interacting over time, or at key points in time, may contribute to the onset of a severe mental illness. For example, research suggests that both genetic predisposition and environmental factors, now known to include the prenatal environment and accumulated social disadvantage as one ages, increase the risk of schizophrenia (Brown & Susser, 2008). Indeed, studies suggest that a higher number of adverse social factors such as socioeconomic disadvantage and social exclusion present in childhood correlate with an increased risk of developing a severe mental illness in later life (Mueser & McGurk 2004; Wicks, Hjern, Gunnell, Lewis, & Dalman, 2005). Significantly, personal or recent family history of migration, which is linked to socially adverse factors such as racial discrimination, unemployment, and poor housing conditions, and overall relative poverty, has been found to be a considerable risk factor (Cantor-Graae & Selten 2005; Selten, Cantor-Graae, &

Kahn, 2007). Childhood experiences of abuse and trauma have likewise been found to be linked with an increased risk of developing severe mental illness in later life (Janssen et al., 2004; MacMillan et al., 2001). Finally, evidence supports the relationship between being born in an urban environment and psychosis. While such research remains in the early phases, some studies link urban environments to multiple risk factors for schizophrenia, including malnutrition, exposure to viruses, and stress, which is believed to be more prevalent in cities (Van Os, Hannsen, Bijl, & Vollebergh, 2001). Work is continuing to determine if social isolation or other factors related to urban environments might explain the high incidence of mental illness among urban dwellers. At present, exposure to risk factors provides provisional understanding of the relationship between mental disorders and poverty.

Research also shows that mental illness and substance use often occur together, and that together, they are often linked to poverty. Living in poverty tends to be associated with a host of chronic stressors, including housing instability, social exclusion, and feelings of general hopelessness. Similarly, co-occurring disorders often result in people losing housing, employment, and social supports.

Epidemiology of Mental Illness and Co-Occurring Substance Use Disorders

Epidemiology refers to the estimated prevalence, incidence, and distribution of a certain condition in the general population. The numbers reported in this section describe the prevalence. Prevalence refers to the current number of people suffering from an illness in a given year, while incidence refers to the number of new cases in any given year. Recent epidemiological studies estimate that 5.8 percent of the United States population reports having a mental illness that qualifies as severe (National Institute of Mental Health [NIMH], 2011). Two and half million adults or 1.1 percent of the U.S. population report having schizophrenia. Over 5 million adults or 2.6 percent of the U.S. population have been diagnosed with a bipolar disorder, while 7 million suffer from severe depression (NIMH, 2011).

Two large epidemiological studies in the 1980s and early 1990s were the first to report the prevalence of co-occurring mental illness and substance use disorders in the United States. Both surveys used the most current versions of *DSM* criteria at the time they were administered and employed research assistants to call people to ask them about their mental health (Kessler et al., 1997; Regier et al., 1990; Regier et al., 1984). The surveys, which together sampled approximately 30,000 people, estimated lifetime prevalence rates to be 23 to 25 percent for drug use disorder (Regier et al., 1990). Among those with a mental illness, the survey showed that 29 to 51 percent also met the criteria for a lifetime of a substance use disorder (Kessler et al., 1994; Regier et al., 1990). At the time of the second survey, five percent of respondents met criteria for a severe mental illness, as defined above (Kessler et al., 1997).

More recent estimates suggest that approximately 27.3 percent of persons with a severe course of mental illness, or 9.6 million adults, suffer from a co-occurring mental health and substance use disorder (Substance Abuse and Mental Health Services Administration, 2013). Individuals with disorders such as schizophrenia or bipolar disorder, in particular, are more likely than the general population to have a substance use disorder. Reports indicate nearly 50 percent of individuals suffering from schizophrenia have a substance use disorder (Greene, Drake, Brunette, & Noordsy, 2007). Similarly, 40 percent of people with bipolar disorder and 30 percent of people with major depression also have a substance use disorder (Grant et al., 2005; Merikangas et al., 2007). The National Comorbidity Survey Replication Study reported that patients with bipolar I disorder are approximately nine times more likely than other psychiatric patients to have lifetime substance use disorders (Merikangas et al., 2007). Twenty-six percent of individuals who met criteria for bipolar disorder experienced a substance use disorder in their lifetime. Nineteen percent of those suffering from major depression also had a substance use disorder.

Reasons for high rates of co-occurring substance use disorders among those suffering from severe mental illness vary. Some theorists rely on a bio-psycho-social model, invoking social determinants described above—which posits accumulated stressors and environmental factors, making one more vulnerable to using substances. It suggests that if someone has a biological vulnerability and lives in poverty, experiencing chronic stressors such as housing instability and social exclusion, this may lead to a mental illness as well as a substance use disorder. Other theorists suggest that persons with severe mental illness self-medicate in order to alleviate psychiatric symptoms or to reduce medication side effects (Potvin, Stip, & Roy, 2003). More recent research shows that persons suffering from schizophrenia may suffer from reward circuitry dysfunction, which means that they do not experience the same degree of pleasure or rewards in response to experiences and events that most people find enjoyable. Drugs and alcohol are hypothesized to improve this circuitry deficit during active substance use and lead to an increase in good feelings (Green, Zimmet, Strous, & Schildkraut, 1999; Green, Drake, Brunette, & Noordsy, 2007).

Prevalence of Poverty for Those with Co-Occurring Disorders

Poverty, unemployment, and homelessness are inextricably linked. It is estimated that 744,000 people in the United States are homeless at any given point, and that one-third or up to 200,000 have a severe mental illness (Treatment Advocacy Center, 2011). It is estimated that up to 38 percent of homeless people have an alcohol use disorder and 26 percent have a drug use disorder, with alcohol use disorders being more prevalent in older people and drug use disorders being more common with youth and young adults (Didenko & Pandratz, 2007, as cited in the National Coalition for the Homeless, 2009). Addiction increases the likelihood of being precariously housed, and once on the streets, it becomes incredibly difficult to find housing. Moreover, among the homeless population in the United States in 2000, it is estimated that up to 37 percent of women and 32 percent of men have a mental illness and co-occurring substance use disorder (North, Eyrich, Pollio, & Spitznagel, 2001, as cited in Center for Substance Abuse Ttreament [CSAT], 2007a). Among persons with severe mental illness, unemployment rates have been reported to be between 80 percent and 90 percent (Pandiani, Simon, Tracy, & Banks, 2004; Sturm, Gresenz, Pacula, & Wells, 1999). From these numbers, one can estimate that the majority of persons with the most severe mental illnesses live in absolute or relative poverty.

Historical Perspectives

How mental illness was viewed throughout different eras suggests that the definition and level of understanding about mental illness has changed over time. This includes the types of interventions provided and how this population lived. For instance, seven thousand years ago during the Stone Age, beliefs that evil spirits were inside the heads of people with mental illness led to an intervention called trephining, or drilling holes in the head to let the spirits out (Dworetzky, 1982). Similarly, in the Middle Ages, people who exhibited symptoms of mental illness were labeled witches and burned alive (Dworetzky, 1982).

Examining the history of how mental illness has been conceptualized is a useful way to understand the variability of the words *sanity* and *normality*. A historical perspective also shows how different definitions and origins of mental illness result in different treatments for mental illness, and characterize those who are said to suffer from the disorder. The focus addresses the history of the United States' response to mental illness and eventually to the historical forces that led to the term *co-occurring disorders*. This section also shows how the foundation of what is referred to as the United States "de facto" mental health system (to be described more fully) was established early in the country's history, quite separate from the addictions system. Like most overviews of the history of mental illness treatments, this discussion is divided into six periods: (a) the colonial period (eighteenth century–early nineteenth century), (b) era of the asylum period (1840–1900), (c) mental hygiene movement period (1900s–early 1940s), (d) the post-World War II era (1945–1960), (e) Community Mental Health Act implementation era (1960s–1970s), and (f) the fragmented system of care era (1980s–present).

Colonial Period (Eighteenth Century to Early Nineteenth Century)

Individuals with mental illness were primarily cared for at home during colonial times, unless the family was too poor to recruit a family member to care for another, or if care at home became too overwhelming. In those cases, persons suffering from mental illness (MI) typically would be put out and often would end up in jails or almshouses. Originating in Britain, almshouses were privately financed houses for the poor. Indeed, the colonists relied on the English Poor Law system that mandated local responsibility for suffering community members. There were so few people living in the United States and the density of these living areas was so sparse that such persons did not present a problem until the turn of the century (early nineteenth century), as rapid socioeconomic change swept the United States (Grob, 1983, 1994).

Mental illness was not viewed as a public problem to be solved but rather as a natural part of the human condition. As Grob suggests, in colonial times, persons with mental illness were viewed as a problem, as they might pose an economic burden on family, or if they had no family, on the perceived safety of the community (1994). In fact, individuals exhibiting "distracted" behavior who could work, most often continued to do so (Grob, 1994). At this time, severe mental illness was understood and accounted for by a mix of religious and secular beliefs. It was not until the country became more populous and city centers denser, that persons with mental illness began to be seen as in need of special care. Addiction treatment was similarly unknown despite "alcohol use and occasional drunkenness (being) pervasive in colonial America" (White, 1998, p. 2). But, like severe mental illness, these levels of consumption were not considered a problem deserving or needing a social response. It was not until the mid-nineteenth century that treatment began to emerge in the form of asylum care.

Era of the Asylum (1840s to 1900s)

To this point, mental illness had been understood through a hodgepodge of natural law and secular and religious beliefs and had not been viewed as a social problem. By the middle of the nineteenth century, urbanization, increased immigration, and separation of the home and workplace led to more people migrating to the United States, resulting in cities' populations rising with a greater number of people lacking family supports, and a larger number of individuals living in squalid, impoverished conditions. Subsequently, more persons could become mentally ill, and live in conditions that might precipitate such illnesses. Thus, informal methods of care were no longer adequate.

New systems of care emerged at this time. The first "hospital" for the insane opened in 1773 in Williamsburg, Virginia. It did not become, however, a model for other hospitals. At the impetus of Dorothea Dix, an influential figure in mental health advocacy and reform, many more such hospitals were built. People who were not housed with family and those who were housed in local almshouses and jails were slowly moved to these larger institutions. Importantly, individuals suffering from alcoholism were also admitted to these hospitals. The prevailing thought during this time was that persons with mental illness must be separated from others, including family, to avoid stresses of any kind. Living in a peaceful environment separated from the vagaries of daily life was seen as a treatment that could lead to a cure. The asylum was not designed for those suffering from addictions, which were people largely unwanted and merely tolerated. Special institutions would later be created to treat alcoholism and other addictions (White, 1998).

When hospitals admitted only a small number of people, allowing for personal attention and close interpersonal relationships, they were successful. As hospital admissions increased, administrative asylums often perpetuated injustices in the name of keeping institutional order. Important to note, however, is that hospitals varied in size, quality of care, and organization (Grob, 1994). Hospitals were run and overseen by state boards, with names such as the State Lunacy Commission. At first, local communities paid for hospital care despite states being responsible for oversight and day-to-day operations. Eventually financing of the hospitals was centralized in the state. While the hospitals' goal was restorative, in reality they were designed and operated to constrain one's personal behavior and liberties.

Progressive Reform: Mental Hygiene Movement (Early Twentieth Century to 1945)

During the Progressive era the shameful asylum conditions were best documented by Clifford Beers in his autobiography, *A Mind that Found Itself*. Beers sought to protest on "behalf of thousands of outraged patients in private and state hospitals whose mute submission to such indignities has never been recorded" (1907, p. 36). Beers commandeered a small group of influential men with whom he set out to improve asylum care. The movement, however, quickly came to include the prevention of mental illness and subsequently lost its focus on asylum care. With his leadership and the support of a handful of influential figures, including William James, a noted social scientist and philosopher, and Adolph Meyer, a preeminent psychiatrist, Beers organized the National Committee on Mental Health Hygiene, which evolved into the National Institute of Mental Health.

It was during this period that special institutions, called "inebriate asylums," were created for those with addictions (White, 1998). Psychiatric asylums welcomed this development as it meant fewer addicts for them to house. While the inebriate asylums were public and available to anyone in need, a second system of private sanitariums emerged for persons who could afford them (White, 1998). The early twentieth century broadened discussions and treatments of mental illness to include prevention. Some also integrated the current environmental view into their understanding of alcoholism and argued that an important cause of alcoholism was the early family environment. As a result, treatments or environmental interventions were developed, especially for mental illness, which were thought to stop mental illnesses from developing. Interventions moved from the hospital to places in which preventative treatments could work. Children, families, and schools became the focus for therapeutic care and intentional communities created environments to ensure family dynamics were conducive to strong mental health.

In 1930, the U.S. Public Health Service established the Narcotics Division, later named the Department of Mental Hygiene. Despite the name, the term *co-occurring disorder* did not exist and persons with severe mental illness suffering from a substance use disorder were not considered a group for whom services needed to be specially tailored. The National Committee on Mental Health Hygiene eventually became the National Institute of Mental Health. Also important to note is the book *Alcoholics Anonymous* (AA), published in 1939, sparking the creation of Alcoholics Anonymous groups across the United States. AA groups were not adapted for persons with a severe mental illness. Recently, however, specific groups were created to meet the needs of people with co-existing disorders. For example, Dual Disorders Anonymous and Schizophrenia Anonymous are specific mutual aid groups, which allow individuals with severe mental illness and substance abuse disorders to receive appropriate services. These types of groups frequently maintain the same twelve-step ideology as AA groups.

The fate of public mental health services and the experience of mental illness in the United States for individuals, particularly those individuals without a family who can care for them, are tied to the fiscal health of the state. As Grob (1983) describes the status of institutions in the 1930s,

> The depression of the 1930s and ensuing global conflict discouraged investment in the public sector as a whole. A decade and a half of fiscal neglect would lead to a deterioration of a mental hospital system responsible for an inpatient population that by 1940 approached nearly half a million, the majority of whom were in the chronic category. (p. 165)

Overcrowding and neglect were rampant and the physical plant of the hospitals deteriorated.

Post-World War II (1945 to 1960)

Veterans returning from World War II, the exposé of institutional life, the reorganization of American psychiatry, a spirit of anti-authoritarianism, and new treatments for mental illness led to a number of improvements to the physical plant of hospitals and to the quality and culture of care within them (Fox, 1990; Grob, 1994). Most importantly, these events precipitated a radical reevaluation of the need and value of institutional care, which set the stage for the current system. Many events occurred in close enough succession to either lead to change or to put into motion radical adjustments to how mental health services would be offered. Each variable will be discussed in turn.

First, the number of veterans returning from war with a mental disorder and in need of care made mental health care a national issue. In some cases, treatment developing during the war was introduced to hospitals. Maxwell Jones, a revolutionary British psychiatrist in postwar England, for example, began to treat impaired service members by creating what he termed a "therapeutic culture." U.S. hospitals followed suit and began to think of how the hospital environment could be actively involved in treatment.

Second, a series of exposés on the state of dilapidated, understaffed, and overcrowded hospitals were published. The exposé had been used earlier to advocate for changes in institutional care. While there were few specific recommendations on how to fund improvements, and what kinds of improvements were necessary, the exposés put the issue of how to care for persons with MI on the national political agenda for many years. A short-term solution was the creation of the Central Inspection Board. This board was important in reducing the staff-patient ratio in hospitals and in reducing overcrowding conditions.

Third, the reorganization of psychiatry and the anti-authoritarian spirit of the late 1950s and 1960s had an impact on how hospitals provided care. The late 1950s were a time of ferment for many of the social movements that became so influential in the 1960s. Psychiatry and hospitals were not immune. While the authoritarian structure of the hospital had been critiqued before, it was not until the 1950s that the idea of democratic participation on the part of patients in the hospital became a viable idea. At the same time, the psychiatric profession was changing and new medications emerged that reduced patients' symptoms.

At the same time, novel treatments became available, and hospitals began to take dramatic measures to contain escalating costs (Grob, 1973; Johnson, 1990). Such interventions included electroconvulsive therapy (ECT), neurosurgery, and psychotropic medication. Although tranquilizer or sedative medications had been used for decades, it was in the 1950s that medications such as chlorpromazine and thioridazine were introduced. These medications helped manage the debilitating symptoms of severe mental illness, including psychosis and mania. Also, the medications reduced agitation, which could stem from living with symptoms of a mental illness, and be exacerbated by the coercive and overcrowded conditions that were prevalent in institutional care at that time. More people were discharged as more medications became available that improved functioning (Grob, 1973). As Fox (1990) argues, these treatments supported the decision to find community-based alternatives to treatment rather than being the reason for deinstitutionalization, sometimes a precursor to poverty.

Implementation of the Community Mental Health Centers Act (1960s to 1970s)

The single greatest change to mental health services, and arguably the key for recognizing co-occurring disorders, was the Community Mental Health Centers Act of 1963 (Rochefort, 1984). This act called for the creation of a federal system of 2,000 community health centers to meet the needs of persons with mental illness. By 1980, however, of the 2,000 centers proposed, only 754 existed (Grob, 1994). In addition, definitional ambiguity allowed the centers to open and operate with different purposes, often with the centers choosing to serve those with less severe symptoms rather than those experiencing significant impairments in functioning.

Given the very public displays of drug use and increasing use of drugs, federal policy shifted in the late 1960s to add and fund substance use services for those who had one disorder and were, overall, less impaired. As a result, there were often fewer community services available to those with severe mental illness.

While some people were released from long-term care starting after 1955, it was in the 1970s that, for the first time, dramatically fewer people were hospitalized, and if they were hospitalized, it was for shorter periods of time. Between 1970 and 1986, the number of hospital beds shrank from 413,000 to 119,000 (Grob, 1994). The length of stay dropped as well, with the median stay being twenty-eight days (Grob, 1994). In lieu of state hospitals offering long-term care, there was a loose and uncoordinated set of services in the community. A very large number of young adults were coming of age during this time period. Indeed, more than 59 million individuals came of age at the riskiest time for developing a severe mental illness (Grob, 1994). Those who developed a mental illness at this time were the first to do so within the system of community care.

Important too, is that these youth came of age at a time of increased recreational drug use and cultural acceptance of its use. As suggested by the Super-Sensitivity Model (Mueser, Noordsy, Drake, & Fox, 2003), even small amounts of substance use for persons with a mental illness can lead to deleterious effects, including homelessness. While having a co-occurring disorder is not sufficient to cause homelessness and poverty, as mentioned above, it is a significant risk factor. Once homeless, it is difficult to access treatment.

Grob (1994) suggests the move to community treatment rested on five assumptions that quickly proved untrue and would impact the available treatments and services for persons with co-occurring disorders. These are (1) families or significant others existed who could take people in; (2) families were financially and emotionally strong enough to care for a relative; (3) in lieu of family, affordable housing was available for people who did not have an income coming out of the hospital; (4) community mental health centers would provide treatment targeting persons with more severe mental illnesses; and (5) continuity of care would exist between the new centers and the existing state hospitals.

Fragmented Systems of Care (1980s to Present)

The 1980s experienced an increase in poverty in the United States, and with it increased rates of homelessness, unemployment, and substance use. Urban areas saw alarming rates of drug use, including crack cocaine, and the mental health and substance abuse treatment systems experienced an influx of people with co-occurring disorders. The mental health and substance abuse treatment systems of care were funded separately and operated in a parallel manner at that time. There was little if any integration of the two service types. People with co-occurring disorders tended to be viewed by both systems of care as difficult to engage in treatment because this population tends to experience more severe problems, including more severe symptoms, and higher rates of homelessness, incarceration, and institutionalization (Drake, Mercer-McFadden, Mueser, McHugo, & Bond, 1998; Drake et al., 2001).

People with co-occurring disorders often were labeled by both mental health and substance abuse treatment professionals as not ready, in denial, and as poor candidates for treatment. Often they were met with treatment approaches that included confrontation, rejection, and extrusion from services. These tended to be very stressful and often led to the exacerbation of psychiatric symptoms among persons served. For example, it was commonplace for a person with a co-occurring disorder who had symptoms of psychosis to be denied services from drug and alcohol treatment programs for being "too mentally ill." Similarly, showing up intoxicated at a mental health program seeking help for housing or employment would likely elicit a response such as "you need to first get sober and show that you are ready for housing or a job." In both cases, the programs and larger systems sent the message that their failure to provide adequate services was due to an inherent quality in the person with the co-occurring disorder, which for many, further stigmatized this population. The failure of the treatment system to provide needed services to people with co-occurring disorders has been referred to as "falling between the cracks in the system of care," and often perpetuates their experience of homelessness, unemployment, incarceration, and poverty.

Research studies in the 1990s began to show that people with co-occurring disorders had improved outcomes when mental health and substance abuse treatments were provided in an integrated manner (Drake et al., 1998). Subsequent sections of this chapter will provide information on evidence-based integrated mental health and substance abuse treatment, and the continued need for systems of care to be reconfigured to best meet the needs of persons with co-occurring disorders.

Mental illness treatments have often been unfair and undermined the dignity and rights of those subjected to them. Until the mid-1990s, there were few, if any, treatments or services designed to help people who had both a mental illness and a substance use disorder, despite the large number of people who suffered from both.

Key Issues

Two key issues face persons with mental illness and co-occurring disorders: (1) the onset of the disorder often moves them into poverty if they are not already there, and (2) the system of care tends to keep them stuck in poverty, primarily focusing on access to psychotropic medications while providing inconsistent attention to integrated treatment, including sporadic opportunities for employment and affordable housing.

Age of Onset

Although the age of onset for developing a mental illness can vary from person to person, the first experience of symptoms for most people occurs during the late teen and young adult years. People who have a later age of onset tend to have a better prognosis than people with an onset at an earlier age. This is, in part, because they are more likely to have achieved developmental and economic milestones that mark the transition into adulthood. Consider the stressors impinging on a person as they achieve typical milestones during young adulthood—separating from parents and family of origin, leaving one's home and possibly neighborhood or city, starting college or entering the workforce, having an intimate relationship with a partner, becoming a parent, and serving in the military and perhaps a war. Even with support from family and close friends, young adulthood can be a very challenging time. Moreover, working through hardships during young adulthood prepares one for meeting even greater challenges in adulthood. Indeed, the extent to which developmental milestones are achieved can shape the course of individuals' lives, the type of job they have and how much income they earn, where and how they live, and with whom they share their lives.

For people with a neurobiological and genetic predisposition for mental illness, the onset of psychotic or depressive symptoms during early adulthood can interrupt their ability to achieve developmental milestones. Imagine not finishing school because of a series of psychiatric hospitalizations, which may limit access to certain jobs and career opportunities. Envision experiencing symptoms of paranoia that lead to erratic or bizarre behavior, and cause estrangement from family, friends, and perhaps intimate partners. Experiences such as these can be very confusing and can contribute to a sense of great loss and despair, and may become life-threatening in cases where one experiences suicidal ideation. Alcohol and drug use may offer some relief, but at the same time can further impair one's functioning and forward movement. Not achieving developmental milestones can limit individuals' capacity to become employed and self-sufficient, putting them at greater risk for living in poverty. In this regard, the experience of mental illness, substance use problems, and poverty becomes intertwined.

In addition, as discussed in the "Demographics and Characteristics" section of this chapter, many people are already living in poverty before the onset of a mental illness or co-occurring disorder. Some may have experienced symptoms in childhood, making it difficult to do well in school. As a result, they may not have finished high school nor learned skills that better-paying jobs require.

It is important to note that *some* people with mental illness and co-occurring disorders do show tremendous resiliency in their recovery from both disorders and regularly overcome setbacks brought on by the onset of mental illness and living in poverty. The integrated treatment model, combined with supported employment and permanent supportive housing services, will be discussed in subsequent sections as approaches that can assist people in moving out of poverty. However, the fragmented system of care in most of the United States poses a primary barrier to the implementation of these treatment models.

Medically Oriented Treatment Approach

One treatment approach widely used for people with serious mental illnesses throughout treatment centers such as inpatient units, community mental health centers, and jails is psychotropic medications. Psychotropic medications address treatment for the biological component of mental illness, and can be remarkably effective at facilitating symptom reduction and remission. However, they do not work for everyone. Nor does their use come without some risk. Even newer antipsychotic medications have negative side effects, ranging from weight gain to life-threatening conditions, such as diabetes.

There are political reasons for attributing mental illness and co-occurring disorders to biological factors, rather than to the environment (Perry, 1996). Only looking at the biological factors places the responsibility for getting well and overcoming deficits in functioning on the individual (Perry, 1996) rather than the system of care. Medicaid, the public medical insurance for people living in poverty, paid for 80 percent of all psychotropic medications sold in the United States in 2003 (Duggan, 2004; Frank, Conti, & Goldman, 2005). This expenditure is indicative of the role policy makers have in identifying and meeting the treatment needs of low-income people with mental illness. Medication alone cannot combat the continued stress of living in poverty, nor can it create new social ties, or improve self-esteem because of life circumstances. Unlike psychotropic medications, environmental interventions require access to affordable housing and finding employers who are willing to hire someone with a severe mental illness and co-occurring substance use disorder.

In sum, the key issues faced by people with severe mental illness and co-occurring disorders include the interrelationship between illness onset and poverty and the need for policy makers to support treatment interventions in addition to psychotropic medications. This includes enabling access to a well-funded and designed public mental health system that addresses poverty and its correlates, including decent, safe, affordable housing and jobs. Unlike medications alone, environmental interventions cannot be easily delivered in a mental health center. They require changing attitudes on micro, mezzo, and macro levels, along with advocacy efforts that are committed to social justice.

Government Policies and Programs

The "Historical Perspectives" and "Key Issues" sections introduced readers to the current U.S. system of care for people with mental illnesses, a system of care notoriously described by the New Freedom Commission on Mental Health (2003), which was charged with evaluating and providing recommendations for the nation's public mental health system, as "a patchwork relic." This characterization is a result of the incremental nature of change in the U.S. political system.

De Facto Mental Health Service System

People with severe mental illness and co-occurring disorders tend to have multiple mental and physical health needs, which are often treated by caregivers or care managers who work in diverse, relatively independent, and loosely coordinated facilities and programs. These are referred to as the de facto mental health service system (Luhrmann, 2007, 2008; Regier, Goldberg, Carl, & Taube, 1978). People with severe mental illness have multiple needs and coordinating care between providers has not typically been part of standard practice. A lack of coordinated care often creates a *gap* or *crack* in the delivery of services, which can have a deleterious effect on mental and physical health functioning.

Other government agencies have become ad hoc or default treatment centers. Many government agencies, such as jails and county emergency rooms, not intended to treat persons with co-occurring disorders, end up providing services nonetheless, and given the limited housing and treatment resources, discharge patients to homeless shelters or temporary transitional living programs in local communities. Indeed, for many persons with co-occurring disorders, being passed along between jails, shelters, hospitals, transitional housing, and for short periods of time, treatment, is best described as the "Institutional Circuit" (Hopper, 2003). This care-as-usual routine undermines the chances for persons with co-occurring disorders to find jobs and housing that may pull them out of this cycle.

Periods of economic downturn can have a detrimental impact on the availability of community mental health services, jobs, and affordable housing. While finding jobs, housing, and adequate mental health services is difficult for the general population, it is especially difficult for persons who have a mental illness or co-occurring disorder. There are fewer service providers who are able to oversee the coordination of services, in part because funding levels neither support this practice nor allot sufficient time to provide them.

Eligibility for Public Entitlements

Persons with limitations on their functioning because of a severe mental illness, and who have limited financial resources, can apply for public entitlements, including Supplemental Security Income (SSI), Social Security Disability Income (SSDI), Medicaid, and Medicare. These entitlements are typically not enough to raise people above the poverty line. The rate of SSI in 2011 was $674 per month or $8,088 per year. The poverty threshold for a single person under age sixty-five in the United States that same year was $11,702 (University of Wisconsin-Madison, Institute for Research Policy, 2011). People earning SSDI usually paid into Social Security when employed, and typically have a higher income because of it. Becoming eligible for health insurance typically hinges on first being approved for SSI or SSDI.

People with severe mental illness typically experience prolonged symptoms of their illness prior to becoming eligible for SSI or SSDI. Symptom exacerbation, including cognitive deficits, sudden and frequent shifting in mood, and substance use can lead to difficulty following through on the application process. It typically takes a family member or paid professional to advocate and assist in seeing the process through. Denials are common, especially for persons that have a severe mental illness and a co-occurring substance use disorder.

Currently, there is very little policy work being done to change the SSI/SSDI rate or to remake mental health services so that these public benefits are less necessary. Mental health policies that promote employment may allow more states to offer employment services to persons with co-occurring disorders, which in turn may lead to fewer people needing public entitlements to support themselves.

Affordable Care Act and Medicaid

The Patient Protection and Affordable Care Act (PPACA) (2010) impacted *behavioral* health care—the care targeting mental illness and substance use—by expanding eligibility for Medicaid to those who were uninsured, mandating coordination among providers on the behavioral health care continuum, and by making prevention of illness and wellness promotion as important as managing existing conditions. Individuals living 133 percent below the poverty line became eligible for Medicaid, resulting in 46 million previously uninsured gaining access to behavioral health services, and because of the earlier passed Mental Health Parity Law, received services equal to physical health services (Henry J Kaiser Family Foundation, 2010). In addition, approximately 1.2 million individuals who were homeless at the time the act was upheld became eligible for insurance (Henry J Kaiser Family Foundation, 2010). Of these 1.2 million homeless people, 110,000 were estimated to be chronically homeless—living in poverty for at least twenty-four months—and presenting with the most complex chronic health care needs (Wilkins, Burch, & Mauch, 2012).

The PPACA placed a premium on care coordination as a way to improve health outcomes, ensure safety, and reduce costs. The act incentivized care coordination by tying how much a doctor or agency received from an insurer to patient outcomes. If the majority of patients or clients being seen by a provider stay healthy or became healthier, the more money the provider would receive. In so doing, the act encouraged providers to proactively work together to prevent illness, or in the case of persons with severe mental illness and co-occurring substance use disorders, prevent psychiatric and substance use relapses. Also, ensuring a person's well-being helps maintain general health, especially for some subgroups of people. This allows partners to share responsibility and the cost for care. Since community health providers are often the first point of contact with the health care system, they are designed to serve not only as treatment providers but as treatment coordinators.

The act laid the groundwork for expanding the health care continuum to include non-traditional health services, especially for people who have severe mental illness and co-occurring disorders. Primarily concerned with physical health, the act has the potential to broaden covered mental health services to include substance use treatment, supported employment, and care management in supported living services (Henry J Kaiser Family Foundation, 2010). Some states have taken advantage of this provision and have created funding mechanisms to provide case management in supportive housing and to fund supported employment services. The act was the first step in conceptualizing health as more than just seeing a provider and taking medications, but also in terms of social determinants such as having a job and appropriate housing.

This reform alone does not solve the problem of uncoordinated care. The expansion of Medicaid coverage to include services such as substance use treatment, supportive housing, and employment, however, will increase the number of people receiving assistance. Greater accessibility of these services, particularly housing, may help to engage and maintain individuals in mental health treatment.

The Fair Housing Act

The Fair Housing Act of 1968 addressed the need for public and private entities to provide equal access to housing, and not discriminate based on race, color, gender, and national origin. The Fair Housing Amendments Act of 1988 extended this law to people with disabilities, and included the following three objectives: (1) to end segregation of housing available to people with disabilities; (2) to give people with disabilities the right to choose where they will live; and (3) to require reasonable accommodations for securing and living successfully in the housing they so desire (as cited in Milstein, Pepper, & Rubenstein, 1989). Notably, people with severe mental illness and substance disorders are protected under this act as these conditions are presently viewed as disabling medical conditions.

Housing

Social service agencies began providing housing for people with severe mental illness in the 1970s because they could not afford market-rate apartments and there was a paucity of affordable housing available (Allen, 2004). This housing, which is professionally staffed, was set up to ensure treatment compliance, including abstinence for those with co-occurring disorders. Often rules were put in place to make managing the property easier, at the cost of the residents having little say how they spend their day. For example, meal times, chore schedules, shopping trips, and group times have to be worked into one's schedule and followed accordingly. Decisions regarding admission and readiness for moving into more independent housing were made by the staff working at the housing programs. Examples of "readiness" often included being abstinent from substances or adhering to mental health and substance abuse treatments (e.g., taking medications as prescribed, keeping appointments, and following group home rules and schedules).

Congregate group home housing is still offered today. Many persons with co-occurring disorders either end up "stuck" in this type of housing for years, or *choose* not to be subjected to these rules and fail to engage in treatment. Others leave on their own or are forced out. The latter groups are those who end up back on the streets and reenter the "institutional cycle." Unfortunately, few alternative housing resources exist, and practices that support and encourage individuals' housing preferences remain unevenly implemented, despite surveys that reveal the majority want to live in their own apartments (Carling, 1990, 1993).

In the past decade, community mental health providers focused on accessing housing subsidies through the U.S. Department of Housing and Urban Development (HUD) and local housing authorities. Services are also focused on helping people secure apartments and offer support once they take occupancy. The Housing First model (Tsemberis, Gulcur, & Nakae, 2004) has been successful at helping those who are homeless with co-occurring disorders move from the streets to subsidized apartments. Under this model, comprehensive case management support is provided to help maintain housing. Recipients are not expected to show readiness in terms of adherence to treatment expectations or sobriety before accessing housing as has historically been the case.

The American with Disabilities Act (ADA) of 1990 and Amendments Act of 2008

The Americans with Disabilities Act (ADA) (1990) requires the federal government to oversee state and local laws, which mandates that people with disabilities have equal access to employment, housing, public accommodation, education, public transportation, recreation, health services, voting, telecommunications, and access to other public services (Americans with Disabilities Act [ADA], 1990). The ADA defines disability as follows: "a) a physical or mental impairment that substantially limits one or more major life activities of such individual; b) a record of such an impairment; or c) being regarded as having such an impairment" (ADA, 1990, Section 12102.1, p. 11). The law requires that the United States federal government play a central role in enforcing that states and local governments adhere to the standards of the ADA.

The ADA has a direct impact on the lives of people with mental illness, as it protects the rights of all people with disabilities, including people with severe mental illness and co-occurring disorders. The law serves to deter discrimination and provides due process when it occurs. The ADA makes it illegal for an employer with fifteen or more employees to deny hiring or advancing a person on the basis of mental illness or a landlord to deny renting an apartment to a person on the basis of mental illness (ADA, 1990). In regard to employing people with substance use disorders, the ADA does not protect people who have active substance use disorders, but does protect those who have a history of having one but are no longer using substances (ADA, 1990).

Olmstead v. L.C., 1999

In *Olmstead v. L.C.* (1999), the U.S. Supreme Court upheld the community integration mandate of the ADA, and found the State Mental Health authority of Georgia was negligent for not creating housing opportunities when none existed for two people living in a psychiatric institution, who were assessed to be ready for discharge (Bazelon Center for Mental Health Law, 1999). More recently, as a result of a class action lawsuit involving 4,300 plaintiffs living in state-funded privately owned institutions for mental illness, the state of Illinois consented to conduct assessments to determine their need and desire for that level of care, and facilitate their integration into community-based mental health treatment and housing of their choosing, including permanent supportive housing (Consent decree, *Williams v. Quinn*, 2010). By March 2013, a quarter of the residents had been contacted and by July 2013, over 600 were projected to have moved out of nursing homes and into their own apartments, with the help of community-based coordinated mental health and medical care.

In sum, over the course of fifty years, the Affordable Care Act, the Americans with Disabilities Act, public entitlements, the Fair Housing Act, and the Olmstead Act were legislated or mandated in response to problems with either the existing system of care or the safety net designed to support persons with disabilities. The passage of laws advocating for the provision of adequate mental health services and equal opportunities for education, employment, and housing does not provide a quick fix, however. It takes time, funding, and committed leadership at every level of the service delivery system.

Social Justice

This section emphasizes recurring social justice issues such as the chance to form one's own life plan, and to enjoy the same political and civil rights of other citizens. Individuals suffering from psychiatric disabilities and co-occurring disorders must have access to mental health services and equal opportunities for housing and employment in order to live productive lives.

Understanding the experiences of persons with severe mental illness is important insofar as social workers and related helping professionals will likely encounter and work with people who suffer from a severe mental illness and co-occurring substance use disorder. This understanding is also important for citizens concerned with social justice to advocate for those who have not been granted the same rights and opportunities as others. For example, historically the United States has not provided sufficient resources for mental health care for people with the most severe forms of mental illness. Unfortunately, the current situation is no different. Mental health services continue to be one of the first services cut as states struggle to balance their budgets. A review of the literature over the past twenty years shows that people who have mental illness and co-occurring substance use disorders experience a worse illness course, including higher rates of institutionalization, including inpatient hospitalization, jail time, and nursing home placements, than those with just one disorder (Drake et al., 2001). Persons with co-occurring disorders are at increased risk of (a) relapse (Swofford, Kasckow, Scheller-Gilkey, & Inderbitzen, 1996), (b) hospitalization (Haywood, Kravitz, Grossman, & Cavanaugh 1995), (c) violence (Cuffel, Shumway, & Chouljian, 1994), (d) incarceration (Abram & Teplin, 1991), (e) homelessness (Caton et al., 1994), and (f) rates of infectious disease such as HIV and hepatitis (Rosenberg et al., 2001).

A number of laws have been passed over the past fifty years that have had the potential to help persons with severe mental illness. For example, as noted in the prior "Historical Perspectives" section of this chapter, the early 1960s saw the passing of the Community Mental Health Act of 1963, which was intended to shift the focus of mental health care from psychiatric institutions to community-based care. The creation of community mental health centers allowed people who have mental illness to receive treatment in the community, where they could see a psychiatrist, receive psychotropic medications, and connect with peers and helping professionals.

Unfortunately, the level of funding needed to build an adequate community mental health system did not follow the legislative intent of the Community Mental Health Act of 1963. The states have not been consistent in following through on the allocation of funds for community mental health, and federal oversight and enforcement have been poor.

Although the laws discussed in the section on government programs and policies, such as the Fair Housing Act, the Americans with Disabilities Act (ADA), and the Olmstead Act, are designed to secure the civil rights of individuals with severe mental illness and co-occurring disorders by providing equal access to jobs and independent housing, poverty still presents barriers for pursuing a better life. The lines of discrimination may not always be so clear, as the system itself makes it difficult for people to move ahead.

Recovery and the Right to Self-Determination

This chapter, thus far, has discussed how the mental health delivery system needs to be transformed to better serve people with severe mental illness and co-occurring disorders. Moreover, the chapter has emphasized how the history of mental health services has often assumed that people with severe mental illness could not determine the kinds of treatment they were offered, where they were treated, or what kinds of lives they wanted to live. Over the past twenty years, people in recovery from severe mental illness, including those with co-occurring disorders, have joined together to raise awareness of the injustices that have taken place. Additionally they are striving to articulate a vision of mental illness as something individuals can "recover" from, as defined by the individuals themselves, not by psychiatrists or other experts who most often equate recovery with symptom remission.

Recovery

This movement is both personal and political. It calls for reclaiming one's life in whatever form one chooses and for exercising basic human rights to make this possible. Recovery, according to Anthony (2000), is "a deeply personal, unique process of changing one's attitudes, values, feelings, goals, skills, and/or roles. It is a way of living a satisfying, hopeful, and contributing life" (p. 159). It may be a life different than what was originally planned, but it can be meaningful, and lived according to and based on one's own choices (Anthony, 2000). Although the concept of recovery varies across stakeholders, the recovery movement, overall, is about being able to exercise basic civil rights (Jacobson, 2004).

The concept of recovery, articulated by the movement, has advanced as an expectation and practice in many mental health centers. This is largely due to the role of people with mental illness who receive services from the system of care (Anthony, 2000). Through their involvement in clinical practice, research, political action, and authorship, they have significantly advanced recovery, which in turn has helped move along the system of care (Anthony, 2000). Recovery practices are now seen as being those practices that value people with mental illness and their individualized preferences, goals, and dreams, in a manner that fosters hope and empowerment. Although this has likely been the experience of people seeking mental health services from professionals in the private sector, the public mental health system has for years not followed this dictum.

Empowerment and Self-Determination

This new understanding of recovery is perhaps what helps empower people with severe mental illness, including those with co-occurring disorders, to be participants in transforming the current mental health system, to one that can assist them in moving beyond the confines of poverty. Social justice advocacy can advance anti-discrimination laws, by making it a legal right for people with severe mental illness and co-occurring disorders to access a model of care that provides for their comprehensive needs including housing, health care, education, employment, and social supports (Anthony, 2000). This will require coordination between multiple providers and the mental health system, with persons served as taking a lead role in deciding how it will impact their lives (Anthony, 2000). Housing, for example, provides a sense of stability and a place to come from and return to each day. Likewise, job and educational pursuits provide individuals with income, ongoing structure, and a sense of purpose, all of which are needed for life choices and to fully participate in society. Consider what it might be like to be without housing, employment or school, and to not have any money. Where might one turn for a place to stay or receive money to get basic necessities? Family? Friends? Government or charity groups? Having adequate housing, a job, meaningful activity to do most days, and money to meet one's basic needs are normalizing. It empowers individuals to have free and full participation in society.

Interventions
Micro Interventions

As was discussed in the "Historical Perspectives" section, research studies in the 1980s and 1990s showed that people with co-occurring disorders responded well to integrated mental health and substance abuse treatments. An integrated treatment approach enables individuals to work with the same clinician or group of clinicians that provides both mental health and substance abuse services. The key micro components of the integrated model include building a therapeutic relationship, conducting an ongoing integrated assessment, setting goals based on the client's (patient's) preferences, and collaborating on clinical interventions and case management activities, such as securing housing, health care, and employment. A person with a co-occurring disorder often exhibits severe symptoms of mental illness and a substance use disorder. Severe symptoms can include delusions, hallucinations, depression, mania, and compulsive thoughts to use substances. Symptoms can be made worse if the person actively uses drugs or alcohol.

The integrated approach tailors interventions based on the person's stage of readiness to address substance use reduction (Prochaska, DiClemente, & Norcross, 1992). Throughout the integrated model process, a primary task for helping professionals is to develop a therapeutic alliance based on mutual trust. One way to start the process of building a therapeutic relationship is to envision what it might be like to walk in the person's shoes—to empathize with their struggles and concerns and reflect back what they may be thinking and feeling in order to convey an accurate understanding (Miller & Rollnick, 2012). The goal-oriented work and interventions need to be collaborative and undertaken with respect for the person's autonomy and right to choose the course of treatment.

Often the task of identifying and setting goals with a person who has a co-occurring disorder involves asking what it is they want or need. However, given the hardships and poverty that people with co-occurring disorders often endure, some may lack confidence in their ability to set and work toward achieving ambitious goals, such as getting a job, pursuing an education, or reunifying with family. The internalization of stigma can contribute to a sense of despair and hopelessness.

Another key component of the integrated treatment model includes supporting people with mental illness and co-occurring substance use disorders in finding and maintaining employment, even in cases where the person does not want to stop using substances. A job provides income that can further one's self-esteem, provide a sense of belonging and connectedness to society, and improve one's financial situation, thereby reducing the stigma of being poor. A job can also provide structure to one's day, contact with people who do not have problems with alcohol and drugs that can be supportive and accepting, and enjoyable experiences that lead to reducing or stopping substance usage over time (Alverson, Alverson, & Drake, 2000).

Social workers and helping professionals can play a vital role in assisting people with mental illness and substance abuse access affordable housing and employment. As discussed in the history section of this chapter, housing services have evolved over the past 100 years from institutionalization to varying levels of independence in the community. The Permanent Supportive Housing model is a set of best housing practices designed to help people who are living in poverty, are homeless, and have disabilities, including mental illness and co-occurring disorders, achieve success in housing (Corporation for Supportive Housing [CSH], 2013a). Permanent Supportive Housing is rooted in a number of criteria to ensure quality programming, some of which include (a) housing is a right that one does not need to show they are ready for or deserve, and is not restricted by unnecessary program rules or requirements (CSH, 2013a), (b) housing is affordable, and does not ideally account for more than 30 percent of a person's income (CSH, 2013a), and (c) choice of housing is based on the preferences of the person served and one has choice in terms of type of housing, and level and type of supportive services, including the right to refuse any services at all (CSH, 2013a).

Social workers and helping professionals practice tenets of the Permanent Supportive Housing model when they (a) offer an array of housing choices related to housing type (e.g., private apartment, shared housing, group home), (b) provide linkages and increased access to affordable housing (e.g., 30 percent of a person's income); and (c) provide comprehensive supports as needed to help the person maintain housing (e.g., case management assistance to reconcile problems with landlords, provide assistance with budgeting to ensure rent is paid, and provide integrated mental health and substance abuse treatment to address severe mental illness and co-occurring disorders).

Supported Employment is a model that can help people with co-occurring disorders secure competitive jobs. Supported Employment is defined in the Rehabilitation Act Amendments of 1986 as "competitive work in integrated work settings with follow-along supports for people with the most severe disabilities" (Becker, Drake, & Naughton, 2005, p. 333). Supported Employment represents a major change from first requiring lengthy periods of pre-vocational training and support and then helping people secure jobs, sometimes in sheltered workshops or group placements. The only requirement for involvement in Supported Employment is a desire to work (Mueser et al., 2003). A social worker providing Supported Employment on a multidisciplinary team conducts a vocational assessment that explores preferences, past work, and educational history, and then assists the person with deciding on realistic steps for attaining their employment goal. The search for a job begins rapidly, with the practitioner seeking out jobs that match the person's expressed preference. Ideally, services are individually tailored to meet the person's needs and preferences, including help with résumé development, interviewing, role-play rehearsal, and helping troubleshoot barriers to securing a job. On the job support and coaching, as needed, can be provided for individuals who become gainfully employed and disclose to their employer they are receiving mental health services.

Having access to integrated treatment, affordable housing, and supportive employment is an important prevention measure against poverty for people with co-occurring disorders. Social workers and other helping professionals can play an important role on the micro level when working with people with mental illness and co-occurring disorders by providing support and advocacy, and emphasizing that opportunities for pursuing meaningful goals are realistic and important for recovery.

Mezzo Interventions

Organizational and community service delivery systems can do a number of things to support the implementation of the evidence-based practices described above. This mezzo intervention section focuses specifically on what organizations and communities can do to help promote access to evidence-based practices for people with severe mental illness and co-occurring disorders. To assist organizations with implementing evidence-based practices, several of the models discussed in this chapter have accompanying implementation guides that organizations can use (e.g., General Organizational Index, [Center for Mental Health Services [CMS], 2003a], Supported Employment—Evaluating Your Program [CMS, 2009], and Supportive Housing Quality Toolkit, [CSH, 2013b]). The implementation guides provide evaluation criteria for measuring baseline and subsequent adherence to the specific model's practices. Repeated evaluations at 6 and/or 12-month intervals can help steer and monitor the implementation process. Attention to program outcomes is also an important part of the implementation process, to ensure that the practices are helping persons with severe mental illness and co-occurring disorders achieve short-term and long-term goals and attain affirmative changes in areas such as substance use reduction, securing appropriate housing, and employment.

For most organizations, the implementation of innovative practices involves reviewing and often changing programmatic policies and structures. The need for change is often a barrier to evidence-based practice implementation. One barrier, for example, at the organizational level is that supervisors and other leaders may not have direct experience doing or implementing the practice. Training sessions in an office or classroom setting typically teach social workers and other helping professionals about an intervention model; however, it takes ongoing practice with supervision to develop proficiency in clinical skills. Agencies need to create infrastructures, which support supervisory and front-line staff learning and utilize evidence-based practices. Such practices involve supervisors, trainers, and consultants modeling the practice, facilitating role-playing before meeting with clients, providing coaching to help work through early practice, and later shadowing (e.g., follow along and observe for the purpose of providing feedback) as they develop competency in skills (Fixsen, Naoom, Blase, Friedman, & Wallace, 2005).

It is best to get support and buy-in from organizational leaders as a first step in implementing evidence-based practices (Fixsen et al., 2005). Also, the literature suggests that it is best to (a) start with those staff members who want to learn the practice, (b) help them understand how learning the practice can potentially affect their ability to be more effective in their work with clients, and (c) help them make the connection that the practice can potentially lead to better outcomes for their clients (Fixsen et al., 2005; Torrey et al., 2001).

This "Mezzo Interventions" section stresses the importance of organizations to take steps to implement evidence-based practices that focus on empowering the individual to participate fully in society. The mental health evidence-based practices discussed in this chapter place great importance on community integration, and getting individuals to participate as equal members within their communities. The remainder of the "Mezzo Interventions" section addresses how the greater community can play an important role in helping people with co-occurring disorders have a sober support network for moving ahead in life. Specific attention should be given to creating opportunities for jobs and decent, safe, and affordable housing, as well as providing access to peer support networks through the community mental health system and mutual aid groups.

The Permanent Supportive Housing and Supported Employment models involve landlords and employers opening their buildings and businesses to people with severe mental illness and co-occurring disorders. Social workers and other helping professionals can assist by providing housing location and job development services. Additionally, professionals can educate the community about people with mental illness and co-occurring disorders in a manner that lowers stigma, and creates opportunities for this population to access decent housing and steady employment.

Early recovery from mental illness and co-occurring disorders is often met with challenges and setbacks that can be very trying. Having a relationship with someone in recovery for a severe mental illness or co-occurring disorder, who has worked through similar challenges can be very empowering and help one believe that they can regain control of their life. Two examples of peer support include relationships that develop between clients and mental health and co-occurring disorder service providers who self-identify as being in recovery, and attending twelve-step and/or mutual aid groups within the community.

Over the past two decades, more and more mental health organizations have hired people who self-identify as being in recovery from a mental illness and co-occurring disorders. Peer-run programming and integrated treatment teams are examples where special efforts are made to recruit and train people with severe mental illness and co-occurring disorders. The benefit is that people in recovery who are working in the field of mental health and substance abuse treatment can convey a sense of hope and optimism that recovery from severe mental illness and co-occurring disorders is possible. Also, people in recovery for severe mental illness and co-occurring disorders often have experienced stigma firsthand. Through their own advocacy, resiliency, and belief that recovery is possible, they can have a powerful impact helping colleagues who do not have a mental illness overcome their own biases and attitudes.

In addition to participating and receiving services from peers recovering from severe mental illness and co-occurring disorders, sober peer support can be accessed through twelve-step and mutual aid groups in the community. Starting with Alcoholics Anonymous (AA) in the 1930s, twelve-step mutual aid groups were initiated by people recovering from substance abuse problems as a way to provide mutual support and guidance in a confidential and anonymous format. There are now twelve-step groups for a number of different types of issues, including Narcotics Anonymous, Cocaine Anonymous, Marijuana Anonymous, and Dual Disorders Anonymous or Double Trouble for people with mental illness and co-occurring substance use disorders.

Twelve-step groups are for people who have a desire to not use substances. Meetings take place in most communities, with large urban areas having one an hour during most times of the day. The 2007 Membership Services Survey reports that year there were 113,000 AA groups throughout the world (Alcoholics Anonymous

World Services Inc., 2007). One can learn about meeting locations by calling the local number in a phone book, or using the meeting locator on the website for the group they are seeking to join. Open meetings can be attended by anyone, and closed meetings are for people who self-identify as having an alcohol or drug problem and have a desire to stop using substances.

The twelve-step groups reference the need for one to accept powerlessness over problems with substance use and turning over or surrendering that power and control to one's own understanding of a Higher Power or God (AA World Services, 1980). Importantly, not everyone with a mental illness and co-occurring substance use disorder is comfortable giving up their power and control over problems related to substance use, especially if they are intertwined with a trauma history, experiencing discrimination, or living in poverty. The evidence-based model of integrated mental health and substance abuse treatment, Integrated Dual Disorders Treatment, encourages helping professionals to provide education about the groups, help those with interest access the groups, and accompany them to open meetings (CMS, 2003b).

In summary, providing integrated treatment often involves organizational change on both the staff and management levels. Addressing these changes in philosophy and practice organizationally is key to mezzo-level interventions being implemented successfully.

Macro Interventions

On the macro level, social workers and other helping professionals can advocate for evidence-based practice for people with severe mental illness and co-occurring disorders. The field of research that studies evidence-based practice implementation has recommendations concerning what state mental health authorities can do to implement evidence-based practices such as Integrated Treatment, and shorten the science to service gap, which is the length of time it typically takes for "practices" to become implemented after the "evidence" is generated through randomized controlled research studies (Goldman et al., 2001). Specifically, implementation requires (a) continuity of leadership to guide the infrastructure changes needed for system-wide implementation, (b) financial incentives and sufficient reimbursement to pay for the delivery of evidence-based practices, and (c) holding organizations accountable for providing quality evidence-based practices with a focus on program outcomes, and monitoring the quality through fidelity measures.

The New Freedom Commission on Mental Health (2003) vision statement speaks to "a future where everyone with a mental illness will at any stage of life have access to effective treatments and supports—essentials for living, working, learning, and participating fully in the community" (p. 1). The commission under former President George W. Bush also concluded the mental health system in the United States was ill-prepared to serve those with severe mental illness and that all stakeholders needed to work together in bringing about a transformation in a manner that includes implementing more evidence-based practices (Gold, Glynn, & Mueser, 2006). There is no mandate or legislation requiring that states institute the New Freedom Commission. It is up to each of the states to plan and implement.

It takes more than legislation and policy to make changes and implement evidence-based practices. As in the case of *Olmstead v. L.C.,* 1999, the law is intended to provide people with mental illness with housing and services in the least restrictive environment (Bazelon Center for Mental Health Law, 1999). The evidence-based practices are established to provide people with mental illness and co-occurring substance use disorders with a high likelihood for success. However, implementation of evidence-based practices requires funding, and funding is often not available. States are often in a financial shortfall. Implementing Integrated Treatment models, Supported Employment and Permanent Supportive Housing comes at a great financial cost for federal, state, and in some cases, local governments. During periods of economic downturn and hardship, states tend to pull back on spending for social services programs, including mental health spending. In the most recent economic downturn (2008–2010), states across the United States cut more than $1.8 billion for services to children and adults with mental illness (National Alliance on Mental Illness, 2011, p. 3). These budgetary cuts come at a catastrophic cost to both society and people with mental illness, and often put into motion a series of events leading to "frequent visits to emergency rooms, hospitalizations, homelessness, entanglement with juvenile and criminal justice systems, the loss of critical developmental years, premature deaths and suicides" (National Alliance on Mental Illness, 2011, p. 4). At the same time, significant cuts had been made to other public agencies, such as law enforcement and housing (Merrick, 2010).

Part of providing quality services at the organization level involves having funding for technical assistance, so supervisors and line staff can learn the evidence-based practices, and presumably provide higher-quality services. It requires that clinicians receive supervision and consultation while learning clinical practices (Brunette et al., 2008; Fixsen et al., 2005). This also requires that supervisors and others knowledgeable in the practice work closely with practitioners while they conduct meaningful integrated assessments, develop person-driven goals, assist with securing housing and employment at every stage of treatment, and practice motivational interventions and substance abuse counseling. As stated, technical assistance requires funding, and the harsh reality is that this important piece of implementing evidence-based practices is not typically factored into the rates organizations receive for providing the services. One strategy is to seek being part of early adoption evidence-based practice implementation and demonstration projects, where the funding for technical assistance comes from federal implementation grants, such as the 53 cities in 8 states that were part of the National Evidence Based Practice Implementation Project (McHugo et al., 2007).

Perhaps the most important macro strategy is the need to provide access to housing that people with severe mental illness and co-occurring substance use disorders can afford. As reviewed in the "Micro Interventions" section, Permanent Supportive Housing aims to be affordable and sustainable, with rent and utilities ideally costing no more than 30 percent of a person's income and overall housing expenses costing no more than 50 percent, with a rental subsidy picking up the balance of the market rate rent (CSH, 2013a).

The majority of people with severe mental illness and co-occurring disorders live in poverty and have incomes that make securing clean and safe apartments impossible to achieve. Significantly, costly apartments in urban areas where the majority of people with co-occurring disorders tend to live pose a barrier to full integration in society. Organizations seeking to provide Permanent Supportive Housing often contract with federal rental subsidy programs through the Housing and Urban Development (HUD) department and other state and local groups. In cases where there is more than one funding resource, there may be multiple funding regulations requiring adherence to each one. This comes at a financial cost for organizations, but assures a level of accountability for the use of public money. Positively, the regulations for continued funding currently include components of the Permanent Supportive Housing model.

Despite evidence showing that work is a significant factor in recovery and people who secure jobs tend to attain periods of abstinence at higher rates than people who are unemployed (Alverson, Alverson, & Drake, 2000), many state mental health authorities will not pay for non-direct service hours needed for successful job development for Supported Employment services. Also notable is that the direct service hours they do pay for are often at a rate much lower than what is needed to provide the service with fidelity to the model.

Social workers and helping professionals can make a difference by becoming knowledgeable about the government policies and legislation that affect funding and services for people with mental illness and co-occurring substance disorders. Specific macro interventions include advocacy at the political level and interfacing with state legislators and mental health authorities, and engaging lobbyists, state and national trade associations, and advocacy organizations such as the National Alliance on Mental Illness to fund the housing, employment, and integrated treatments for people with mental illness and co-occurring substance use disorders. When approaching state legislators and mental health authorities, it is important to also collaborate with people in recovery and support their self-advocacy efforts to become informed of key issues. Inviting legislators to special activities and celebrations at programs, helping to organize self-advocacy groups, and attending events sponsored in the community are other important steps. Talking with political and community leaders about recovery from mental illness and co-occurring substance use disorders, and the extent to which policies and pending legislation have the potential to help people move out of poverty, can ultimately help improve service delivery.

Summary

The integrated approach to treatment involves working with a person in the community to secure the supports and services necessary for leading a full and active life. Assessing needs, setting goals, and providing practical assistance to meet the goals are paramount. The next steps are assisting with harm reduction and motivational approaches to address substance abuse, followed by skill building once motivation is enhanced. Employment and housing are critical areas to explore and require important interventions, even for people who are still using substances, and not interested in stopping.

Despite the federal government endorsing the Integrated Dual Disorders Treatment, Supported Employment, and Permanent Supportive Housing models, the implementation of these practices has been relatively scarce at state and local levels. Implementing change comes at a great cost and most public mental health systems of care are financially strapped. Social workers and helping professionals can play an important role advocating on a political level with local and state legislators to secure dedicated funding, and working to ensure that mental health authorities remain accountable to promulgating the implementation of evidence-based practices.

Evidence-based practice models can transform the service delivery system so that people with mental illness and co-occurring disorders are more likely to secure jobs (Supported Employment) and affordable, decent, and safe housing (e.g., Permanent Supportive Housing). It takes all levels of the system working together— micro, mezzo, and macro—for these to be truly implemented in a manner that helps people with severe mental illness and co-occurring disorders have the best opportunity for overcoming impoverished conditions.

Concluding Comments

This chapter explores the relationship between poverty, mental illness, and co-occurring substance use disorders. It reviewed (a) definitions of mental disorders, focusing on co-occurring severe mental and substance abuse disorders, (b) the biological, psychological, and social factors to understand the relationship between poverty and mental illness and co-occurring disorders, (c) the epidemiology and etiology of mental illness and co-occurring disorders, (d) the history of U.S. policy regarding persons with mental illness and the systems of care for them, (e) key issues that both are impacted and guided by various systems, (f) social justice factors that impede and promote positive change, and finally (g) interventions at the micro, mezzo, and macro levels.

In so doing, this chapter offered an interdisciplinary perspective on how public health policy, housing and health policy, agency-level systems of care, restricted employment opportunities, and untreated symptoms of the illnesses contribute to the large numbers of persons with mental illness and co-occurring disorders living in poverty. Persons with mental illness and co-occurring disorders who seek treatment do so at the nexus of several interrelated systems—the community mental health system, the public welfare system, and the array of affordable housing. These systems have unintentionally resulted in a *de facto system of care* for persons who do engage in treatment. This system of care has existed for decades and has made it almost impossible for persons with mental illness and co-occurring disorders to create or reclaim lives marked by economic achievement, an achievement that possibly could be (and should be thought of as) a condition for recovery rather than a consequence of it.

Finally, the chapter has reviewed evidence for treatments that assist people with mental illness and co-occurring disorders move beyond poverty. Integrated mental health and substance abuse treatment, underpinned by harm reduction, motivational counseling approaches, and the Permanent Supportive Housing and Supported Employment models can lead to improved outcomes for people with severe mental illness and co-occurring disorders. Evidence-based practices are available and practitioners, administrators, researchers, funders, and policy makers need to be strong advocates for making transformative change occur.

What does it all mean for social workers and related helping professionals going forward? It means that improving the lives of persons with psychiatric disabilities, and those who also have co-occurring substance use disorders, requires advocating at the micro, mezzo, and macro levels for improved options for housing, employment, and integrated treatment for mental illness and co-occurring substance use disorders. Right now, at the very minimum, it means viewing the issue of disabilities in terms of civil and political rights.

Case Studies
Micro Level

Louis is a 46-year-old African American man. He was raised in an impoverished neighborhood in an urban area, in a family that consisted of a mother, an older brother, and two younger half-sisters. His biological father was absent during Louis's childhood. His mother vacillated from working cleaning jobs to being unemployed and receiving public assistance. He reports she drank alcohol in excess when unemployed. Louis started using marijuana and alcohol at age fourteen and stopped attending school before completing the tenth grade. He describes making money after quitting school by "hustling" on the streets, noting that some days he brought in over a $100 a day in the mid-1980s.

His older brother was tragically killed in a street fight when Louis was sixteen years old. This event had a profound effect on him and he became increasingly vigilant about others, including his family members' whereabouts and their lives in general. Louis's substance use picked up at this time, with marijuana, crack cocaine, and alcohol consumption taking over his day-to-day life. His first psychiatric hospital-ization occurred when he was arrested on multiple drug charges and became psy-chotic while in jail.

Over the next several years, Louis had a number of incarcerations for drug posses-sion charges and psychiatric hospitalizations. He only took the psychotropic med-ication for brief periods when in treatment and preferred the calming effect from alcohol and marijuana. He also used crack cocaine and marijuana when it was available from cousins. He was eligible for SSI because he had functional impair-ments related to having a mental illness, and was able to secure an apartment.

His use of crack cocaine continued through his twenties, which tended to exacer-bate his intense belief that others wanted to harm him and those close to him. He tried drug treatment several times as a condition of probation but was often dis-charged prematurely for not being able to follow the program structure. One time he applied to a group home owned by a mental health center and was denied because he had an active substance use problem. Despite wanting to work, employ-ment services were not available to him at the mental health center because he was actively using drugs.

The following cycle played out repeatedly for Louis during the 1990s: jail—psychi-atric hospitalization while in jail—discharge to either a mental health or substance abuse treatment program—extruded because of not following program rules or substance use—return to grandmother or a homeless shelter. The message he heard from each treatment system upon discharge—get help for the other disorder and then we can better help you.

In the early 2000s, Louis was referred to an outreach team serving people who had a mental illness and co-occurring substance use disorders. The team began engag-ing with him while in jail and met him outside the jail the day of his release to take him to a single-room occupancy hotel where he lived for a few months. The work-ers on the outreach team visited him three times a week and provided practical assistance with navigating the social welfare system, including connecting with the state human services office to apply for medical benefits and Food Stamps, and securing the necessary documents to apply for these benefits, such as a birth cer-tificate, Social Security Card, and state identification card. Also, the team accompa-nied him to the Social Security Administration (SSA) office to reinstate his SSI, and offered to become his representative payee when the SSA told him he needed to have one due to his co-occurring substance use disorder. A representative payee is someone who helps a person to manage the SSA benefit to ensure the money is used to meet basic needs (e.g., pay the monthly rent and use the remaining funds for personal hygiene items and transportation expenses).

He expressed interest in working at a janitorial job and was referred to an employment specialist who had experience using the Supported Employment model to help people with co-occurring disorders. The employment specialist helped him identify job preferences, including job location and work hours, and steps for finding available jobs by filling out applications and scheduling interviews. Over time, the employment specialist was able to help Louis get an interview with a janitorial company that serviced large office buildings, and he secured the job.

During the subsequent months, Louis continued using crack when he was paid every Friday. The drug use would last that night and into the next day. He tended to get increasingly paranoid during these periods, but was always ready for work by Monday afternoon, and he refrained from using substances during the week. He was still getting SSI, albeit at a lower rate because of his work income, but it was enough to pay rent. He continued talking with the outreach team about his substance use, noting that he still enjoyed it but was beginning to realize it was coming at a price. He did not like himself for using. Other downsides were he used up his paycheck, spent time with people while using who only wanted him around while he had money to spend on drugs, and believed they would try and break into his apartment when he was not home and take some new things he had recently acquired, such as a television and stereo.

The outreach team offered to link Louis with a psychiatrist who worked for their agency. Louis was reluctant to take psychotropic medications because they caused him to feel restless. In collaboration with this psychiatrist, he tried several medications, including a newer psychotropic medication, which had side effects such as weight gain and early stage diabetes. He opted to go on an older antipsychotic medication and cope with the restlessness, which he manages with behavioral relaxation strategies he learned from the employment specialist.

Upon talking to the team, he agreed to check out a peer-run drop-in center on Saturday mornings, the day he cashed his paycheck. He reported liking the peer staff that worked there, began to trust their input, and reported feeling similar to them and hopeful at the same time. Other members who attended often went out afterward for coffee and Louis joined them and found the time enjoyable. Several months later when meeting with a member on his outreach team, Louis shared that staying busy and doing something enjoyable on Saturdays helped him not use so much of his money on drugs and alcohol.

As Louis began showing greater interest in cutting down his substance use, the outreach team began reviewing with him the possible benefits of attending a twelve-step group such as Alcoholics Anonymous or Narcotics Anonymous. He did not want to go at first, reporting that listening to others talk about alcohol and drugs would lead to him wanting to use. The outreach team backed off. One morning several months later, Louis was flipping through the television channels and found a show on the founding of Alcoholics Anonymous. He liked the story and when he told his worker, she offered to accompany him to an open meeting. The outreach worker introduced herself as someone there to learn about twelve-step groups and to support Louis and others who might benefit from the program. After the meeting, the chairperson asked Louis if he was coming back and when he said yes, she asked if he could come a half hour early to help set up chairs. He agreed and went to subsequent meetings on his own.

Louis continued to slowly reduce his substance use, and began saving his money for items in his apartment. Of importance, his substance use reduction occurred slowly over time as he engaged in developing a more positive life. He is now in the relapse prevention stage of substance abuse treatment (Mueser et al., 2003), which is defined as six or more months of not meeting the current *DSM* criteria for a substance use disorder. The outreach team continues to help him learn sober lifestyle skills to further his recovery, including anticipating and avoiding situations where substance use is likely to occur, refusing offers to use, finding alternative activities when wanting to use, and having places to go and sober people to see.

Questions
1. What impact did poverty have on Louis developing a mental illness and substance use disorder?

2. What are examples of integration in the provision of services for Louis?

3. At what point did his life during adulthood begin to improve? What were the factors that accounted for this?

Mezzo Level

A well-established agency with a commitment to best practices identified the need to provide integrated services to persons with co-occurring disorders while facing barriers, including lack of support and leadership from the state, including ongoing funding difficulties. This agency was a vanguard in collecting and using data to improve services and detect trends. Without doing this, they may not have identified the need to serve those with co-occurring disorders early on. Although most large hospitals collected data, public-funded outpatient behavioral health agencies of any size typically did not. The data showed an agency-wide increase in psychiatric hospitalizations in the late 1980s. Further analysis revealed that active substance use was contributing to the increase.

These data prompted the agency to convene the first of what would be two task forces devoted to serving people with co-occurring disorders. The first task force report concluded that specialized services were needed for people with co-occurring disorders. At the same time as senior level management was grappling with how to provide better services, the homeless population was growing at such a rate that state funding was made available to mental health agencies and others to address the problem. This agency received funding to form two new outreach teams to bring those living on the streets into treatment. Doing so brought staff into regular contact with a large number of people suffering from both a severe mental illness and a substance use disorder. At that time, the majority of mental health and substance abuse treatment providers operated in two vastly different systems of care with conflicting treatment philosophies and funding and regulatory compliance. Sadly, for two decades many people with dual disorders were not well served by the disorganized service system. The sheer number of individuals who suffered from both disorders meant that it was difficult to refer all of them to other substance use treatment providers, as had been the common practice. Treating them within the mental health agency was difficult because staff were not trained in substance abuse treatment counseling strategies.

Now, with the numbers of homeless viewed as a significant target population, staff were offered substance abuse counseling classes through a local community college, which led to qualifying for the Certified Alcohol and Drug Counseling (CADC) exam. This agency, unlike other agencies, had an internal training department, and therefore did not have to pay for external trainings. Through its internal training department, the agency provided training on the role of substance use in the course of mental illness through quarterly trainings. In early 2000, a mental health practice specifically targeting persons with co-occurring disorders became available on a limited basis. Called Integrated Dual Disorder Treatment (IDDT), this practice was a more systematic approach to what the agency had been trying to do. This is when the agency hired a director of IDDT.

This agency contacted the lead developer to consult with them pro bono about how to implement this practice. The consultant primarily worked with senior-level staff members who were left to educate front-line staff. The emerging best practice required the agencies to screen, diagnose, and assess substance use on a regular basis as well as hire an IDDT specialist.

At this point, however, the quarterly trainings regarding evidence-based practices were the only part that could be implemented. Trainings on how to engage and motivate individuals who did not want to reduce their use were utilized. The training focused on helping people with co-occurring disorders pursue high-priority goals, but staff still had difficulty accessing the resources necessary to help them work on important goals such as securing jobs and affordable housing. Also, the dual disorder groups and housing programming for people with co-occurring disorders tended to target those who were already committed to reducing their substance use. While all staff were required to monitor use through the assessments, only a few did so. There was no money or commitment from the state to funnel funds to the agency for training and oversight of these requirements. What these trainings did do, however, was to raise awareness and emphasize the importance of people with co-occurring disorders to staff. The agency's implementation of co-occurring disorders treatment evolved non-linearly as the organization worked without funding or implementation guidelines.

Training all staff systematically and ensuring that they were following best practices was beyond what the agency could afford to do. The agency could be paid for providing most of the IDDT services, including assertive outreach and engagement, individual and group counseling, and pharmacological interventions to persons with co-occurring disorders. However, without adequate funding, the agency could not afford to provide oversight, reduce treatment drift, or assure standardization across all of its programs.

The agency opened two residential treatment programs, in 1997 and 1999 respectively, and in 2000 appointed a director of Integrated Dual Disorders Treatment (IDDT). The first residential program required people with co-occurring mental illness and substance use disorders to adhere to a fairly restrictive program designed to address abstinence from the onset of treatment. The second program had an assertive "inreach" focus, and attempted to implement aspects of harm reduction, including responding to substance use relapses with motivational approaches aimed at understanding the factors that precipitated the substance use, and recovery plan enhancement. Both programs initially had zero-tolerance for on-site substance use, but later rescinded policies that extruded people for using substances on-site. Over time, the program staff learned that people tended to do much worse when extruded from housing for using substances on site. The rule was revised a few years later, with on-site substance abuse reviewed on a case-by-case basis, and a focus on assisting people with maintaining their housing to the greatest extent possible. With the appointment of an IDDT director in 2000, the agency began to implement IDDT in earnest, using standardized measures to track substance use, to provide ongoing oversight of the practice through biannual fidelity measures, and offering systematic feedback to teams based on fidelity.

Unfortunately, public mental health agencies are subject to abrupt changes in how services are funded and offered. In 2006, the State Department of Mental Health moved all public mental health agencies to a fee-for-service model of payment with concurrent changes to how and what kinds of services could be offered. Most agencies had to reorganize and devote time to maximizing "productivity." The financial/productivity system is difficult to reconcile with providing evidence-based practices.

Just as the agency was getting used to the new way of billing and providing services, the state financial crisis reduced their funding by $20 million. As a result, agency overhead decreased and many staff that were conducting fidelity assessments and doing ongoing training were let go. Many clinical staff were let go too, which meant that there were fewer staff available to work with the same number of people. Such a situation made it difficult to implement evidence-based practices, as before.

In summary, a large highly regarded agency with a wide and deep network of social and institutional capital, including a reliable cadre of private donors and connections with advocacy groups, has an easier time weathering funding extremes. Put differently, the agency has been successful in tapping outside funding to continue to do what needs to be done. Size and status, though, do not ensure successful implementation of an evidence-based practice. It is only top-down buy-in and commitment to providing the best possible care that can make that happen.

Questions

1. What were the barriers this organization experienced in its effort to implement evidence-based practices?

2. What were the lessons learned by this organization as they worked to implement Integrated Dual Disorders Treatment?

3. What did the agency do and then modify to achieve better success with their implementation effort?

Macro Level

Mary was born in New York City into a family who had a history of substance misuse, and into a neighborhood that was ridden with unemployment and crime. Mary's family often felt unsafe and struggled with a number of daily hassles, ranging from having to walk through drug dealers on their way to the corner store to regularly having their landlord not turn on the hot water heater. Mary's parents were uninsured and had difficulty accessing health care. Despite this, Mary's mother found a free city clinic to which she took Mary for all her vaccinations and well baby visits. After five years of struggling, the clinic had lost too much of its public funding and shut down. The closest clinic for Mary's mother to use was two hours away.

She was not able to access free preschool as there were no Head Start programs in the neighborhood, so when both of Mary's parents were working, she shuttled between neighbors. Mary's parents were also saddled with so much debt that they were unable to afford a car that would allow them to take a job outside of New York City, where job prospects were better. Bad credit would not allow them to take out a car loan. After years of fighting with her husband about having too little money and him drinking too much, Mary's mother left her father, when Mary was six. She and her mother moved many times after this, as her mother, who had only a high school degree, tried to find a well-paying job. Her mother's stress during this time distracted her from Mary's needs, including her erratic moods and school attendance. Not knowing how to help her daughter was painful, but much of the time, she believed Mary was just a particularly intense and difficult adolescent. She watched helplessly as Mary struggled in school with periods of intense depression, during which Mary could not get out of bed to go to school, alternating with periods of intense energy and focus, during which Mary would concentrate on her writing, which was her favorite subject in school and after school activity.

In her junior year of high school, Mary's school counselor hospitalized her at the public psychiatric hospital, which was understaffed and underfunded. There, she was put on and taken off a number of anti-psychotic medications, finally being prescribed a set of medications that were not supported by the newest evidence on bipolar treatment. The medication combination resulted in a number of intolerable side effects that made it impossible for her to get out of bed in the morning. She dropped out of high school shortly after the hospitalization, and at sixteen, Mary got a job as a waitress.

She also decided to go off her medication because of the caustic side effects. Her mood swings became more frequent and more severe. Her mother, who had never been contacted by the psychiatrist or any staff at the hospital to coordinate care such as educating her on her daughter's illness or medications, thought her daughter might be better off living with friends because she felt helpless that she could not make sense of Mary's erratic behavior. Unfortunately, the first family with whom Mary lived had different expectations of what having another young adult in the house would be like. They soon asked Mary to leave.

On her own, Mary started a cycle of moving between her mom's apartment, various friends, shelters, and with short periods of homelessness. She had trouble maintaining stable housing because she could no longer afford to pay the rent after losing yet another job. When she started to stay with family or friends, many times they would ask her to leave because of her substance use or mania or both. After almost three years of housing instability, Mary finally decided to seek treatment for her substance use disorder. She went to a community-based substance use provider because she did not have any insurance. In the intake interview, the substance use provider asked her about her mental health and Mary told him that she suffered from a bipolar illness that was easy for her to control if she had social support, was not drinking, and was taking her medications. The intake worker indicated that due to government funding being limited, they could not help her with her substance use problem because they did not provide housing to people with severe mental illnesses. Instead, she should go to a local shelter.

Her only recourse was to go to the shelter the intake worker had recommended, one very similar to others she had been to previously. The shelter was a place to sleep but offered no services and required her to be out from 9:00 a.m. to 5:00 p.m., leaving a large part of the day free. In addition to having nowhere to go during the day, the shelter was a place where she could not admit her mental illness, as the residents were always referring to people like her as "the crazies." On the first day at the shelter, during the time that residents are not permitted to be in the shelter, a social worker, who tries to link individuals who are homeless to care, happened to come across Mary, who was out on the street drinking again. The social worker informed Mary there was a program that would enable her to enter housing and receive treatment for both her mental illness and substance use disorder.

After some discussion, Mary finally assented to receive help, in large part because the social worker told her that she could receive mental health treatment without having to be sober and there was a chance she could be housed immediately or at least put on a waiting list. Unfortunately the state had just changed their policies and the social worker was not aware that the state funding for residential treatment such as group homes, congregate housing, and treatment residences were cut, thereby depleting the agency's housing vouchers, which subsidized apartments. The only housing the mental health agency could offer was a single-room occupancy motel, which meant that Mary's only option was to move into the small room in a neighborhood where drugs and alcohol were easily accessible. Despite asking regularly about moving to a better neighborhood, the agency did not have enough housing vouchers to move her into a better setting. After some time, the state began considering reinstating capacity dollars, which would allow the agency to reopen its residential treatment home; however, this was still in the discussion phase.

Using Mary's situation as an example of the increasing number of people with mental health and co-occurring disorders not having appropriate housing due to severe budget cuts, advocates began appealing to local and state lawmakers to reinstate money to assist this at-risk population. Advocates began making appointments to meet with state legislators and the state commissioner of mental health to address the service cuts, highlighting that the cuts were not cost-effective. They emphasized that the cost of housing someone in a motel could be as much as $67 per day or $2,010 per month through public assistance funds, which was significantly greater than providing housing through supplemental vouchers. Additionally, people suffering from mental illness and co-occurring disorders who lacked stable housing were more likely to visit emergency rooms, which are far more expensive than providing routine substance abuse and mental health care.

Advocates also reached out to community leaders asking their assistance in circulating petitions. The petitions stated that it was far better for government to provide funding to assist people with mental illness and co-occurring disorders secure adequate housing than having them living on the streets, which potentially creates additional issues (such as increased police and court intervention). Through outreach and community advocacy, the state reinstated capacity dollars so agencies could reopen residential treatment homes to assist this population.

Questions

1. How is the institutional cycle evident in this vignette?

2. Describe how this cycle is a structural phenomenon.

3. On a policy level, what additional interventions could be utilized to effect change?

Internet Resources

Addiction Technology Transfer Centers (ATTC): http://www.attcnetwork.org/

ATTC provides resource information for professionals working with people who have substance use disorders. The website provides free publications specific to alcohol and drug prevention and treatment.

Corporation for Supportive Housing (CSH): http://www.csh.org/

The CSH is a nonprofit organization committed to helping communities house those most in need. The website provides free downloads to written resources, including implementation toolkits on the Permanent Supported Housing model.

National Alliance on Mental Illness (NAMI): http://www.nami.org/

NAMI is a mental health advocacy organization that provides information on mental illness, evidence-based treatments, and peer and family support.

National Institute on Drug Abuse—Research Dissemination Center (NIDA): http://drugpubs.drugabuse.gov/

NIDA funds research and disseminates knowledge specific to drug prevention and intervention. This website provides publications on drug prevention and treatment.

The Substance Abuse and Mental Health Services Administration (SAMHSA): http://www.samhsa.gov/

SAMHSA funds research and disseminates information on evidence-based practices for treating mental illness and substance use disorders. This website provides publications on integrated mental health and substance abuse treaments, including Supported Employment.

Mutual Aid Group Resources for Specific Substances. These websites provide information about each specific mutual aid group, including national meeting times and locations.

Search the following group titles and URL Internet addresses:

Alcoholics Anonymous: http://www.aa.org

Cocaine Anonymous: http://www.ca.org/

Dual (Mental Illness and Substance Use Disorder) Recovery Anonymous: http://www.draonline.org/

Marijuana Anonymous: http://www.marijuana-anonymous.org/

Narcotics Anonymous: http://www.na.org/

Nicotine Anonymous: http://www.nicotine-anonymous.org/

Smart Recovery: http://www.smartrecovery.org/

Further Readings

AA World Services. (1980). *Alcoholics Anonymous.* New York: Author.

Corrigan, P. W., Mueser, K. T., Bond, G. R., Drake, R. E., & Solomon, P. (2007). *Principles and practices of psychiatric rehabilitation: An empirical approach.* New York: Guilford Press.

Hopper, K. (2003). *Reckoning with homelessness.* Ithaca, NY: Cornell University Press.

Marlatt, A. G., Larimer, M. E., & Witkiewitz, K. (eds.) (2011). *Harm reduction, second edition: Pragmatic strategies for managing high-risk behaviors.* New York: Guilford Press.

Miller, W. R., & Rollnick, S. (2012). *Motivational interviewing, third edition: Helping people change.* New York: Guilford Press.

Mueser, K. T., Noordsy, D. L., Drake, R. E., & Fox L. (2003). *Integrated treatment for dual disorders: A guide to effective practice.* New York: Guilford Press.

White, W. L. (1998). *Slaying the dragon: The history of addiction treatment and recovery in America.* Normal, IL: Chestnut Health Systems.

References

Abram, K. M., & Teplin, L. A. (1991). Co-occurring disorders among mentally ill jail detainees: Implications for public policy. *American Psychologist, 46,* 1036–1045.

Alcoholics Anonymous World Services. (1980). *Alcoholics Anonymous.* New York: Author.

Alcoholics Anonymous World Services. (2007). *Alcoholics Anonymous 2007 membership survey.* New York: Author. Retrieved from http://www.aa.org/pdf/products/p-48_07survey.pdf.

Allen, M. (2004). *Just like where you and I live: Integrated housing options for people with mental illness.* Bazelon Center for Mental Health Law: Washington, DC. Retrieved from www.bazelon.org/LinkClick.aspx?fileticket=4sZjOa313oI%3D.

Alverson, H., Alverson, M., & Drake, R. E. (2000). An ethnographic study of the longitudinal course of substance abuse among people with severe mental illness. *Community Mental Health Journal, 36*(3), 557–569.

American Psychiatric Association. (2013). *Diagnostic and statistical manual of mental disorders, fifth edition (DSM-5).* Washington, DC: Author.

Americans with Disabilities Act of 1990. (1990). Pub. L. No. 101-336, 104 Stat. 327.

Anthony, W. A. (2000). A recovery-oriented service system: Setting some system level standards. *Psychiatric Rehabilitation Journal, 24*(2), 159–168.

Bazelon Center for Mental Health Law. (1999). Under court order: The Supreme Court ruling in *Olmsted v. L.C.* Washington, DC: Author. Retrieved from http://www.bazelon.org/LinkClick.aspx?fileticket=aaFpHtscPWU%3d&tabid=104.

Becker, D. R., Drake, R. E., & Naughton, W. J. (2005). Supported employment for people with co-occurring disorders. *Psychiatric Rehabilitation Journal, 28,* 332–338.

Beers, C. (1907). *A mind that found itself.* New York: Longman, Greens, and Company.

Brown, A. S., & Susser, E. S. (2008). Prenatal nutritional deficiency and risk of adult schizophrenia. *Schizophrenia Bulletin, 34*(6), 1054–1063.

Brunette, M. F., Asher, D., Whitley, R., Lutz, W. J., Wieder, B. L., Jones, A. M., & McHugo, G. J. (2008). Implementation of integrated dual disorders treatment: A qualitative analysis of facilitators and barriers. *Psychiatric Services, 59,* 989–995.

Cantor-Graae, E., & Selten, J. P. (2005). Schizophrenia and migration: A meta-analysis and review. *American Journal of Psychiatry, 162*(1), 12–24.

Carling, P. J. (1990). Major mental illness, housing, and supports: The promise of community integration. *American Psychologist, 45*(8), 969–975.

Carling, P. J. (1993). Housing and supports for persons with mental illness: Emerging approaches to research and practice. *Hospital & Community Psychiatry, 44*(5), 439–449.

Caton, C. L., Shrout, P. E., Eagle, P. F., Opler, L. A., Felix, A. F., & Dominguez, B. (1994). Risk factors for homelessness among schizophrenic men: A case-control study. *American Journal of Public Health, 84,* 265–270.

Center for Mental Health Services. (2003a). *The general organizational index (GOI)* (draft version 2003). Rockville MD: Center for Mental Health Services, Substance Abuse and Mental Health Services Administration.

Center for Mental Health Services. (2003b). Integrated dual disorders treatment fidelity scale. *Co-occurring disorders: Integrated dual disorders treatment implementation resource kit* (draft version 2003). Rockville MD: Center for Mental Health Services, Substance Abuse and Mental Health Services Administration.

Center for Mental Health Services. (2009). *Supported employment: Evaluating your program.* DHHS Pub. No. SMA-08-4364, Rockville, MD: Center for Mental Health Services, Substance Abuse and Mental Health Services Administration, U.S. Department of Health and Human Services.

Center for Substance Abuse Treatment. (2007a). *Addressing co-occurring disorders in non-traditional service settings. COCE overview paper 4.* DHHS Publication No. (SMA) 07-4277. Rockville, MD: Substance Abuse and Mental Health Services Administration, and Center for Mental Health Services. Retrieved from store.samhsa.gov/shin/content/SMA07-4277/SMA07-4277.pdf.

Center for Substance Abuse Treatment. (2007b). *The epidemiology of co-occurring substance use and mental disorders. COCE overview paper 8.* DHHS Publication No. (SMA) 07-4308. Rockville, MD: Substance Abuse and Mental Health Services Administration, and Center for Mental Health Services. Retrieved from www.samhsa.gov/co-occurring/topics/.../OP8Epidemiology 10-03-07.pdf.

Consent Decree, *Williams v. Quinn.* (2010). No. 1:05-cv-4673, N.D. IL, 2010.

Corporation for Supportive Housing. (2013a). *Dimensions of quality supportive housing.* Dimensions of Quality Guidebook. Retrieved from www.csh.org/DimensionsofQuality (full document posted on CSH website, www.csh.org).

Corporation for Supportive Housing. (2013b). *Supportive housing quality toolkit.* Retrieved from http://www.csh.org/qualitytoolkit_TOC (full document posted on CSH website, www.csh.org).

Cuffel, B., Shumway, M., & Chouljian, T. (1994). A longitudinal study of substance use and community violence in schizophrenia. *Journal of Nervous and Mental Disease, 182,* 704–708.

Drake, R. E., Essock, S. M., Shaner, A., Carey, K. B., Minkoff, K., Kola, L., . . . Richards, L. (2001). Implementing dual diagnosis services for clients with mental illness. *Psychiatric Services, 52,* 469–476.

Drake, R. E., Mercer-McFadden, C., Mueser, K. M, McHugo, G. J., & Bond, G. R. (1998). Review of integrated mental health and substance abuse treatment for patients with dual disorders. *Schizophrenia Bulletin, 24,* 589–608.

Duggan, M. (2004). Do new prescription drugs pay for themselves? The case of second-generation antipsychotics. *Journal of Health Economics, 24*(1), 1–31.

Dworetzky, J. P. (1982). *Psychology,* (pp. 500–501). St. Paul: West Publishing Company.

Engel, G. L. (1977). The need for a new medical model: A challenge for biomedicine. *Science, 196,* 129–136.

Faris, R. E., & Dunham, H. W. (1939). *Mental disorders in urban areas.* Chicago: University of Chicago Press.

Fixsen, D. L., Naoom, S. F., Blase, K. A., Friedman, R. M., & Wallace, F. (2005). *Implementation research: A synthesis of the literature.* Tampa, FL: University of South Florida, Louis de la Parte Florida Mental Health Institute, National Implementation Research Network. Retrieved from http://cfs.cbcs.usf.edu/_docs/publications/NIRN_Monograph_Full.pdf.

Fox, J. W. (1990). Social class, mental illness, and social selection drift hypothesis. *Journal of Health and Social Behavior, 31,* 343–353.

Frank, R. G., Conti, R. M., & Goldman, H. H. (2005). Mental health policy and psychotropic drugs. *Milbank Quarterly, 83*(2), 271–298.

Gold, P. B., Glynn, S. M., & Mueser, K. T. (2006). Challenges to implementing and sustaining comprehensive mental health service programs. *Evaluation and the Health Professions, 29,* 195–218.

Goldman, H. H., Ganju, V., Drake, R. E., Gorman, P., Hogan, M., Hyde, P. S., & Morgan, O. (2001). Policy implications for implementing evidence-based practices. *Psychiatric Services, 52,* 1591–1597.

Grant, B. F., Stinson, F. S., Hasin, D. S., Dawson, D. A., Chou, P., Ruan, W. J., & Huang, B. (2005). Prevalence, correlates, and comorbidity of bipolar I disorder and axis I and II disorders: Results from the National Epidemiologic Survey on Alcohol and Related Conditions. *Journal of Clinical Psychiatry, 66,* 1205–1215.

Green, A. I., Drake, R. E., Brunette, M. F., & Noordsy, D. L. (2007). Schizophrenia and co-occurring substance use disorder. *American Journal of Psychiatry, 164,* 402–408.

Green, A. I., Zimmet, S. V., Strous, R. D., & Schildkraut, J. J. (1999). Clozapine for comorbid substance use disorder and schizophrenia: Do patients with schizophrenia have a reward deficiency syndrome that can be ameliorated by clozapine? *Harvard Review of Psychiatry, 6*(6), 87–296.

Grob, G. (1973). *Mental illness in America: Social policy to 1875.* New York: Free Press.

Grob, G. (1983). *Mental illness and American society: 1875–1940.* Princeton, NJ: Princeton University Press.

Grob, G. (1994). *The mad among us: A history of care of America's mentally ill.* New York: Free Press.

Haywood, T. W., Kravitz, H. M., Grossman, L. S., & Cavanaugh, D. L. (1995). Predicting the "revolving door" phenomenon among patients with schizophrenic, schizoaffective, and affective disorders. *American Journal of Psychiatry, 152,* 856–861.

Henry J Kaiser Family Foundation. (2010). *Expanding Medicaid under health reform: A look at adults at or below 133% of poverty.* Author: Washington, DC. Retrieved from http://kff.org/health-reform/issue-brief/expanding-medicaid-under-health-reform-a-look/ (Brief Report selection).

Hollingshead, A. B., & Redlich, F. (1954). Social stratification and schizophrenia. *American Sociological Review, 19,* 302–307.

Hopper, K. (2003). *Reckoning with homelessness.* Ithaca, NY: Cornell University Press.

Hopper, K. (2010). Taking inequality's measure: Poverty, displacement, unemployment and mental health. In *Principles of Social Psychiatry* (2nd ed.), ed. C. Morgan and D. Bhugra. Chichester, UK: John Wiley & Sons, Ltd.

Jacobson, N. (2004). *In Recovery: The making of mental health policy.* Nashville: Vanderbilt University Press.

Janssen, I., Krabbendam, L., Bak, M., Hanssen, M., Vollebergh, W., de Graaf, R., & van Os, J. (2004). Childhood abuse as a risk factor for psychotic experiences. *Acta Psychiatrica Scandinavica, 109,* 38–45.

Jeste, D. V., & Maglione, D. (2013). Treating older adults with schizophrenia: Challenges and opportunities. *Schizophrenia Bulletin, 43*(1), 90–96.

Johnson, A. B. (1990). *Out of bedlam: The truth about deinstitutionalization.* New York: Basic Books.

Kessler, R. C., Crum, R. M., Warner, L. A., Nelson, C. B., Schulenberg, J., & Anthony, J. C. (1997). Lifetime co-occurrence of *DSM-III, R* alcohol abuse and dependence with other psychiatric disorders in the National Co-Morbidity Survey. *Archives of General Psychiatry, 54*(4), 313–321.

Kessler, R. C., McGonagle, K. A., Zhao, S., Nelson, C. B., Hughes, M., Eshleman, S., . . . Kendler, K. (1994). Lifetime and 12-month prevalence of DSM-III-R psychiatric disorders in the United States. *Archives of General Psychiatry, 51,* 8–19.

Kessler, R. C., Nelson, C. B., McGonagle, K. A., Edlund, M. J., Frank, R. G., & Leaf, P. L. (1996). The epidemiology of co-occurring addictive and mental disorders: Implications for prevention and service utilization. *American Journal of Orthopsychiatry, 66*(1), 17–31.

Laudet, A. B., Magura, S., Cleland, C. M., Vogel, H. S., Knight, E. L., & Rosenblum, A. (2004). The effect of 12-step based fellowship participation on abstinence among dually diagnosed persons: A two-year longitudinal study. *Journal of Psychoactive Drugs, 36,* 207–216.

Luhrmann, T. (2007). Social defeat and the culture of chronicity: Or, why schizophrenia does so well over there and so badly here. *Culture, Medicine and Psychiatry, 31,* 135–172.

Luhrmann, T. (2008). "The street will drive you crazy:" Why homeless psychotic women in the institutional circuit in the United States often say no to offers of help. *American Journal of Psychiatry, 15,* 15–20.

Marmot, M. (2001a). Inequalities in health. *New England Journal of Medicine, 345*(2), 134–136.

Marmot, M. (2001b). Economic and social determinants of disease. *Bulletin of the World Health Organization, 79*(10), 988–989.

McHugo, G. J., Drake, R. E., Burton, H. L., & Ackerson, T. H. (1995). A scale for assessing the stage of substance abuse treatment in persons with severe mental illness. *Journal of Nervous and Mental Disease, 183,* 762–767.

MacMillan H. L., Fleming J. E., Streiner D. L., Lin, E., Boyle, M. H., Jamieson, E., . . . Beardslee, W. R., et al. (2001). Childhood abuse and lifetime psychopathology in a community sample. *American Journal of Psychiatry, 158*(11), 1878–1883.

McHugo, G. J., Drake, R. E., Whitley, R., Bond, G. R., Campbell, K., Rapp, C.A., . . . Finnerty, M. (2007). Fidelity outcomes in the National Implementing Evidence-Based Practices Project. *Psychiatric Services, 58*, 1279–1284.

Merikangas, K. R., Ames, M., Cui, L., Stang, P. E., Uston, T. B., Von Korf, M., & Kessler, R. C. (2007). The impact of comorbidity of physical and mental conditions on role disability in the U.S. adult household population. *Archives of General Psychiatry, 64*(10), 1180–1188.

Merrick, A. (2010). Big State, big cuts, little room: Illinois Agency has to pare hundreds of millions, but mandates restrict fall of the ax. *Wall Street Journal.* Retrieved from http://online.wsj.com/article/SB10001424052748704312104 575298632860515858.html.

Miller, W. R., & Rollnick, S. (2012). *Motivational interviewing, third edition: Helping people change.* New York: Guilford Press.

Milstein, B., Pepper, B., & Rubenstein, L. (1989). The Fair Housing Amendments Act of 1988: What it means for people with mental disabilities. *Clearinghouse Review, 23*, 128–140.

Mueser, K. T., & McGurk, S. R. (2004). Schizophrenia. *The Lancet, 363*(9426), 2063–2072.

Mueser, K. T., Noordsy, D. L., Drake, R. E., & Fox, L. (2003). *Integrated treatment for dual disorders: A guide to effective practice.* New York: Guilford Press.

National Alliance on Mental Illness. (2007). *What is mental illness: Mental illness facts.* Retrieved from http://www.nami.org/Content/Microsites181/NAMI_ Mid-Carolina/Home168/Education20/MentalIllnessFactSheet_2007.pdf.

National Coalition for the Homeless. (2009). *Substance abuse and homelessness.* Washington, DC: Author. Retrieved from www.nationalhomeless.org/ factsheets/addiction.pdf.

National Institute of Mental Health. (2011). *Statistics.* Rockville, MD: Author. Retrieved from http://www.nimh.nih.gov/statistics/index.shtml.

New Freedom Commission on Mental Health. (2003). *Achieving the promise: Transforming mental health care in America. Final report.* DHHS Pub. No. SMA-03-3832. Rockville, MD.

Pandiani, J. A., Simon, M. M., Tracy, B. J., & Banks, S. M. (2004). Impact of multi-agency employment services on employment rates. *Community Mental Health Journal, 40,* 333–345.

Patient Protection and Affordable Care Act. (2010). Pub. L. No. 111–148, 124 Stat. 119 through 124 Stat. 1025.

Perry, M. (1996). Relationship of social class and mental illness. *Journal of Primary Prevention, 17*(1), 17–30.

Potvin, S., Stip, E., & Roy, J. Y. (2003). Schizophrenia and addiction: An evaluation of the self-medication hypothesis. *Encephale, 29*(3, pt. 1), 193–203.

Prochaska, J. O., DiClemente, C. C., & Norcross, J. C. (1992). In search of how people change: Applications of addictive behaviors. *American Psychologist, 47,* 1102–1114.

Regier, D. A., Farmer, M. E., Rae D. S., Locke, B. Z., Keith, S. J., Judd, L. L., & Goodwin, F. K. (1990). Co-morbidity of mental disorders with alcohol and other drug abuse. Results from the Epidemiologic Catchment Area (ECA) study. *Journal of the American Medical Association, 264,* 2511–2518.

Regier, D. A., Goldberg, I. D., Carl A., & Taube, C. A. (1978). The de facto US mental health services system: A public health perspective. *Archives of General Psychiatry, 35*(6), 685–693.

Regier, D. A., Myers, J. K., Kramer, M., Robins, L. N., Blazer, D. G., Hough, R. L., . . . Locke, B. Z. (1984). The NIMH Epidemiologic Catchment Area program: Historical context, major objectives, and study population characteristics. *Archives of General Psychiatry, 41,* 934–941.

Rochefort, D. A. (1984). Origins of the "third psychiatric revolution": The Community Mental Health Centers Act of 1963. *Journal of Health Politics, Policy and Law, 9*(1), 1–30.

Rosenberg, S. D., Goodman, L. A., Osher, F. C., Swartz, M. S., Essock, S. M., Butterfield, M. I., . . . Salyers, M. P. (2001). Prevalence of HIV, hepatitis B, and hepatitis C in people with severe mental illness. *American Journal of Public Health, 91,* 31–37.

Selten, J. P., Cantor-Graae, E., & Kahn, R. S. (2007). Migration and schizophrenia. *Current Opinion in Psychiatry, 20*(2), 111–115.

Sturm, R., Gresenz, C. R., Pacula, R. L., & Wells, K. B. (1999). Datapoints: Labor force participation by persons with mental illness. *Psychiatric Services, 50,* 1407.

Substance Abuse and Mental Health Services Administration. (2009). *Supported employment: Evaluating your program.* DHHS Pub. No. SMA-08-4364, Rockville, MD: Center for Mental Health Services, Substance Abuse and Mental Health Services Administration, U.S. Department of Health and Human Services.

Substance Abuse and Mental Health Services Administration. (2013). *Results from the 2012 national survey on drug use and health: Mental health findings,* NSDUH Series H-47, HHS Publication No. (SMA) 13-4805. Rockville, MD: Substance Abuse and Mental Health Services Administration.

Swofford, C. D., Kasckow, J. W., Scheller-Gilkey, G., & Inderbitzen, L. B. (1996). Substance use: A powerful predictor of relapse in schizophrenia. *Schizophrenia Research, 20,* 145–151.

Torrey, W. C., Drake, R. E., Dixon, L., Burns, B. J., Flynn, L., Rush, A. J., . . . Klatzker, D. (2001). Implementing evidence-based practices for persons with severe mental illnesses. *Psychiatric Services, 52,* 45–50.

Treatment Advocacy Center. (2011). *Homelessness: One of failing individuals with severe mental illness—backgrounder.* Author: Arlington, VA. Retrieved from http://www.treatmentadvocacycenter.org/index.php?option=com_content&task=view&id=1379&Itemid=217.

Tsemberis, S., Gulcur, L., & Nakae, M. (2004). Housing first, consumer choice, and harm reduction for individuals with dual diagnosis. *American Journal of Public Health, 94,* 651–656.

U.S. Department of Health and Human Services. (1999). *Mental health: A report of the Surgeon General—executive summary.* Rockville, MD: U.S. Department of Health and Human Services, Substance Abuse and Mental Health Services Administration, Center for Mental Health Services, National Institutes of Health, National Institute of Mental Health.

University of Wisconsin-Madison, Institute for Research on Poverty. (2011). *What are poverty thresholds and poverty guidelines?* Madison, WI: Author. Retrieved from http://www.irp.wisc.edu/faqs/faq1.htm#whatis.

Van Os, J., Hanssen, M., Bijl, R. V., & Vollebergh, W. (2001). Prevalence of psychotic disorder and community level of psychotic symptoms: An urban-rural comparison. *Archives of General Psychiatry, 58*(7), 663–668.

Van Os, J., Rutten, B. P., & Poulton, R. (2008). Gene-environment interactions in schizophrenia: Review of epidemiological findings and future directions. *Schizophrenia Bulletin, 34,* 1066–1082.

Weiser, M., Werbeloff, N., Vishna, T., Yoffe, R., Lubin, G., Shmushkevitch, M., & Davidson, M. (2008). Elaboration on immigration and risk for schizophrenia. *Psychological Medicine, 38*(8), 1113–1120.

White, W. L. (1998). *Slaying the dragon: The history of addiction treatment and recovery in America.* Normal, IL: Chestnut Health Systems.

Wicks S., Hjern, A., Gunnell, D., Lewis, G., & Dalman, C. (2005). Social adversity in childhood and the risk of developing psychosis: A national cohort study. *American Journal of Psychiatry, 162*(9), 1652–1657.

Wilkins, C., Burt, M. R., & Mauch, D. (2012). *Medicaid financing for services in supportive housing for chronically homeless people: Current practices and opportunities.* Prepared for Office of Disability, Aging and Long-Term Care Policy, Office of the Assistant Secretary for Planning and Evaluation, U.S. Department of Health and Human Services.

Williams, D. R., & Jackson, P. B. (2005). Social sources of racial disparities in health. *Health Affairs, 24*(2), 325–334.

World Health Organization. (2001). *The world health report 2001—Mental health: New understanding, new hope.* Geneva, Switzerland: Authors. Retrieved from http://www.who.int/whr/2001/en/.

World Health Organization, Department of Mental Health and Substance Dependence, & Noncommunicable Diseases and Mental Health. (2003). *Investing in mental health.* Geneva, Switzerland: World Health Organization.

Zubin, J., & Spring, B. (1977). Vulnerability: A new view of schizophrenia. *Journal of Abnormal Psychology, 86,* 103–126.

9

Poverty among Immigrants and Refugees

David Becerra, Cecilia Ayón, Maria Gurrola,
David K. Androff, and Elizabeth A. Segal

The United States is a country of immigrants, from the earliest settlers who found their way from Europe over the oceans to land on the eastern shores. For most immigrants, the reason for their journey centers on the opportunity to better their economic fortunes. However, the history of immigration to the United States was not always linked to economic opportunity. The taking of land and resources from indigenous people, the enslavement of Africans to create pools of cheap labor, and low wages and poor working conditions for recent immigrants were efforts to achieve economic gain by early immigrant groups with significant power, at a cost to those with less power. In this chapter, readers will explore the link between immigration and poverty, from (1) the standpoint of people's hopes to immigrate for better economic fortune, and (2) efforts to produce economic prosperity. Often the latter was built on the availability of immigrant labor and the vulnerability of immigrant populations. Readers will also explore the historical aspects of immigration and key issues that demonstrate the important connections between immigrant status and living in poverty in the United States. This chapter also addresses dimensions of immigration in terms of pursuing economic opportunities, connected with the prevalence of poverty faced by those relocating to the United States. Finally, limited programs available to impoverished immigrants are explained, and readers explore issues associated with social justice and various interventions designed to assist this population.

Immigrants are among those groups in our population who have higher concentrations of people living in poverty. Some of the reasons are obvious—lack of fluency in English; fleeing poor economic conditions in their countries of origin; lower education; and they tend to be younger and lacking strong work history. History has proven that given time, immigrant groups assimilate and future generations gain the skills that their parents and grandparents lacked (Aizenman, 2008). One common concern today is that immigrants bring poverty, but research has not supported that supposition. Analysis of the trends during the 1990s reveals that although immigrants are disproportionately among lower income groups, poverty rates are primarily due to economic factors (Chapman & Bernstein, 2003). Although recent immigrants are typically less educated and lower skilled than the native-born population, it is not true that they swell the poverty rates nor that they reduce employment opportunities for native-born workers (Hoynes, Page, & Stevens, 2005). Thus, the long-standing relationship between poverty and immigration in the United States is characterized by the arrival of poor immigrants. However, the causes of poverty among this population are complex and common to our economic system, rather than linked to immigration. It should be noted, that over time, immigrant groups have moved up within the U.S. economy with varying degrees of success, similar to native-born populations.

Demographics and Characteristics

Migration and living as an immigrant are a worldwide phenomenon. The United Nations (2008) estimates that there are 214 million migrants around the world. An increasing share of the world's population is migrating across political borders, primarily seeking improved economic opportunities (Bacon, 2008). Immigrants face severe challenges, most significant of which is poverty. This is especially true in the United States where immigrants have been economically vulnerable and are disproportionately affected by poverty (Migration Policy Institute, 2013).

The United States did not record statistics on immigration until 1850. This is because the earliest immigrants were regarded as settlers, thereby ignoring the indigenous peoples' nativity. The differentiation between foreign-born and native populations did not arise until an American identity was firmly rooted. Based on decennial census counts, in each decade between 1850 and 2000, the percent of foreign-born population ranged from a low of 4.7 percent to a high of 14.8 percent, averaging 10.6 percent over the 150 years (Gibson & Jung, 2006). Of course, immigrants of one generation often become the parents and grandparents to native-born or new generations. This indicates that the roots of immigration within the U.S. population are deep and complex.

Defining Immigrants and Refugees

The United States population is made up of immigrants, with only one percent of more than 300 million people counted as Native American. In 2010, 12.9 percent, or almost 40 million people, were counted as foreign-born (U.S. Census Bureau, 2012). The term *immigrant* is far-reaching, including any person who comes to a new country to become a permanent resident. There are several categories of immigrants in the United States.

For most immigrants, their entrance to the United States begins legally through a variety of classifications for admissions. Most are temporary in nature, such as visas for visits, business purposes, or academic studies. When visitors choose to stay past their visa, they either must apply to stay, which may or may not be granted, or stay past the legal time limit and remain in the country illegally. This action then moves people into the category commonly referred to as undocumented. Some people cross the border illegally never having received any visa, and they too fall into the category of undocumented.

Immigrants who have been granted lawful permanent residence in the United States are considered "legal permanent residents" (LPRs). Often referred to as "green card" recipients (based on the green color of early permit cards), these are people who have received permanent residence in the United States. LPRs are free to live and work anywhere in the United States, own property, join some branches of the armed forces, and apply to become U.S. citizens.

Policies have been enacted to control the number of immigrants to the United States over the decades. The Immigration Act of 1990 set an annual limit of 416,000 to 675,000 immigrants to be awarded LPR status (U.S. Department of Homeland Security, 2008). Over one million people were granted LPR status in 2009, while 36 million non-resident admissions to the country were recorded in the same year (U.S. Department of Homeland Security, 2010).

Refugees are immigrants who fall under a very specific category. They are people who leave their native countries to escape persecution. Refugees, those who apply for admission while outside the United States, and asylum-seekers, those who apply when entering or after entering, are small in number. In 2009, about 75,000 people were admitted, most of whom were from Asia and Africa (U.S. Department of Homeland Security, 2010). Refugee status is a legal classification set by the U.S. government to cover countries officially recognized by the U.S. government as oppressive of certain groups of people. For example, people leaving Cuba are considered refugees. Thousands of Southeast Asians who fled Vietnam after the end of the Vietnam War were also considered refugees. Passage of the Refugee Act of 1980 gave legal status to refugees and provided additional social services for the resettlement of refugees. On the other hand, people coming from Mexico are not considered refugees and, hence, are not entitled to special services and assistance in resettlement.

In recent years, the focus has been on people who are illegally living in the United States. In 2008, it was estimated that 11.9 million people were unauthorized or undocumented immigrants in the United States (Passel & Cohn, 2009). Although it can be difficult to accurately track undocumented immigrants, well-regarded analyses by the Pew Hispanic Center have estimated that about three-fourths of the 11.9 million are Hispanics, while approximately 11 percent are Asian, 4 percent Caribbean, and less than 2 percent from the Middle East. Household composition is significantly centered around young families, with almost half of undocumented adults living with their children, compared to only 21 percent of U.S-born adult residents. Most children of undocumented immigrants (73 percent in 2008) were born in the United States and are therefore citizens. This creates a legal split among many immigrant families with one or both parents illegally living in the United States who have children that are U.S. citizens.

Immigrants Are Disproportionately Impoverished

Regardless of nation of origin, most immigrants are economically at the lower end of the educational and labor systems. Data reveal that the likelihood of being poor and uneducated is higher for immigrants than for those who are native-born. Since the 1970s, the poverty rates for immigrant households have been higher than the rates for native households, with an average of 12–13 percent of native households living in poverty compared to 16–17 percent of immigrant households in poverty (Hoynes et al., 2005). The recent recession was hard on all low-income families, but immigrants were hit harder. The 2009 poverty rate for those who were native-born was 13.7 percent while the rate for foreign-born persons was 19 percent. Closer examination reveals even greater differences. Of those who were foreign-born and for those who were naturalized citizens, the poverty rate was lower, at 10.8 percent, while for immigrants who were not naturalized citizens, the rate was 25.1 percent (DeNavas-Walt, Proctor, & Smith, 2010). More than a third of all those who are foreign-born lack health insurance, and the rate is greater, almost half, for those people who are not U.S. citizens (DeNavas-Walt et al., 2010).

This is especially true for undocumented immigrants. Passel and Cohn (2009) documented these disparities. Adults who are undocumented are six times more likely than United States-born residents to have less than a high school education

(47 percent compared to 8 percent). Their median household income was significantly lower, with double the poverty rate of native-born adults and children. Thus, their precarious state of living illegally in the United States is linked to the lowest income and social service levels.

The connection between economic conditions and immigration is complex. There is a disproportionate level of poverty among immigrants despite the U.S. dependence on foreign labor. Most of the growth in the American workforce since 1990 has been as a result of immigration (Marshall, 2009). The bottom line is that immigrants come to the United States for economic opportunities. The workplace encourages the hiring of immigrants for many jobs, primarily low-wage positions, and the outcome is that the economic situation for immigrants is well below that of the native-born population.

Historical Perspectives

Despite the recent outcry, immigration to North America is not a new phenomenon. Although millions of indigenous people were already living in North America, people from northern and western Europe traveled to the Americas to settle and start a new life for themselves and their families. European settlers decimated the indigenous population and way of life and established cities based on the political, social, and economic structures of Europe. In order to maintain their political and economic dominance in the region, European countries recruited and encouraged immigration to the Americas to increase the European population and provide labor, including the importation of African slaves, for the ever expanding cities, towns, and plantations in the Americas, thereby increasing the property value and wealth of European landowners (Bernard, 1998). In an effort to further restrict opportunities for non-white immigrants, Congress passed the Naturalization Act of 1790, which allowed only white male immigrants to become citizens of the United States, thereby excluding not only African slaves from citizenship, but non-white immigrants and American Indians as well (Johnson, 2003; Takati, 1993). Non-white immigrants therefore did not have the opportunities that came with citizenship such as voting, serving on juries, holding public office, and in some cases they were even restricted from owning land. These restrictions limited the upward social and economic mobility of non-white immigrants and perpetuated the high rates of poverty among this population. By the late eighteenth century, almost 600,000 Europeans had migrated to the American colonies. With the descendants of the earlier immigrants, the population grew to almost 3 million, which did not include 300,000 African slaves and over 100,000 indentured servants (Daniels, 1998; Fogleman, 1998). The importation of African slaves to the United States ended in the 1860s (Segal, 2013).

As immigration from Europe to the American colonies (and after independence to the United States) continued, settlement and acquisition of land to the west began. The growth in U.S. immigrants living in the then Mexican territory of Texas eventually led to the Texas Revolution of 1846 and the eventual annexation of Texas by the United States. Conflicts over the location of the newly created border between the United States and Mexico led to the Mexican-American War. In 1848, the Treaty of Guadalupe Hidalgo officially ended the war and granted the United States possession of California, New Mexico, Texas, and parts of Colorado, Utah, and Arizona. With the purchase of the southern portion of Arizona in 1853, the modern border between the United States and Mexico was formed (Massey, Durand, & Malone, 2003). Although the last major wave of immigration from Europe to the United States ended in the 1920s, the hope of economic prosperity and freedom from persecution continued to lure people from all over the world to the United States (Eltis, 1983).

Throughout the twentieth century, various factors have led to policies that have either encouraged or restricted immigration to the United States. In the early twentieth century, laws were established that restricted immigration and established quotas based on the percentage of each ethnic group already living in the United States; this would ensure that ethnic composition in the United States would not be altered by new immigrants. With the population and geographic growth of the nation and involvement in World War I, U.S. employers actively recruited Mexican workers between 1900 and 1929 (Massey et al., 2003). However, the mass unemployment of the Great Depression changed attitudes toward Mexican immigrants and as a result, thousands of Mexican immigrants, including U.S. citizens of Mexican descent, were deported (Day, 2008).

World War II created a shortage of agricultural workers in the United States and agricultural growers lobbied Congress and President Roosevelt for assistance with the shortage. This led to the Bracero program that ran from 1942 to 1965 and granted temporary work visas to Mexican workers (Becerra et al., 2010). Although the Bracero Program ended, the U.S. demand for workers did not and despite the need for workers, Congress reduced the number of visas granted to Mexican workers from 450,000 to 20,000 per year (Andreas, 2000; Massey et al., 2003). Demands for labor, coupled with the inability of workers to access legal means to immigrate to the United States have led to the rise of undocumented immigration (Cerrutti & Massey, 2004; Martin, 2003).

In 1965, the Immigration and Nationality Act (INA) of 1965 replaced the quota system and allowed for increased immigration from Latin America, Asia, and eastern and southern Europe. Since that time there has been a significant increase in immigration from those regions and as a result, those populations in the United States have had the fastest growth, with the Latino population surpassing African-Americans to become the second largest population in the U.S. (Humes, Jones, & Ramirez, 2011).

Border Development

The history of immigration from Mexico to the United States is unique and different from the relocation of Europeans, as well as the border formation in the north with Canada. In truth, "the Mexico-U.S. border has not always existed as a practical reality. On the contrary, it was defined slowly but steadily through a process of social construction" (Massey et al., 2003, p. 25). Unlike immigration from other countries, passage across the border between Mexico and the United States has been very different. There are families whose roots have been consistently located in the southwest, but shifted from living in Mexico to living in the United States without actually moving.

Porous and vague definitions of the southern borders of the United States, coupled with economic factors, have resulted in varying responses—including ignoring the separation, encouraging Mexican laborers to work in the United States, enforcement of the border with military personnel, and enactment of harsh state policy initiatives. Most of these efforts have resulted from shifting economic conditions here and in Latin America, and the desire of those migrating to achieve economic opportunity.

The northern border with Canada has reflected very different social and economic conditions. Until the events of September 11, 2001, the border with Canada was of minimal concern to U.S. authorities. The primary interest revolved around commerce across the border, not persons. Although attention to who crosses between the United States and Canada has increased, it is not as great a concern as it is on the southern border. Those who typically traverse the southern border are of Latin American descent, contributing to the racialization of border policies. The results of this bifurcation are different border concerns and politics in the north and the south. Although public policies on immigration and border security are managed as one set of policies for the entire country, there are different needs on the southern border, particularly in terms of traffic from undocumented persons and the smuggling of drugs from Latin American countries. These are the concerns that have informed most public debate regarding immigration today.

Key Issues

The circumstances that accompany each immigrant to the United States vary by numerous characteristics of the person and his or her country of origin. There are the shared concerns about adapting to a new land, acquiring new language skills, and balancing the values and customs of one's homeland and those of the new land. But there are structural elements that are endemic to the social, political, and economic landscape of the United States that impact the immigrant experience.

Anti-Immigrant Sentiment

Although immigrants from other countries founded the United States, there has been a historical anti-immigrant sentiment toward non-English speaking or non-Protestant immigrant groups. In the nineteenth century, there were concerns over Irish and German immigrants because of their language and religion. Even Benjamin Franklin worried that the population of non-English-speaking German immigrants would become too large and that they would cause the English language to be replaced with German (Schrag, 2010). Franklin was not alone in his fears of immigrants; many people worried about immigrants' ability to integrate into the developing American society. In 1844 an angry group of 3,000 Protestants in Philadelphia protested against Irish Catholic immigrants who were not forcing their children to read the King James Bible in school and who feared that Irish Catholic immigrants were trying to make the United States dependent on the pope. Those protests erupted into violence that lasted for several weeks and became known as the "Bible Riots" (Sekulow & Tedesco, 2005). Subsequent waves of immigration have provoked the same fears about the loss of the English language and U.S. culture (Portes & Rumbaut, 2001).

Anti-immigrant sentiment in the United States toward Latino immigrants has existed since 1848 and the signing of the Treaty of Guadalupe Hidalgo, but has become more pronounced during periods of economic turmoil. Recent anti-immigrant sentiments can be traced back to the 1990s. For instance, a fear of the loss of American culture and identity led to the passage of Proposition 187 in California in 1994, which ended public social services to undocumented immigrants in California, including schooling for children, food assistance, and medical care (Michelson & Pallares, 2001). In 1996, the Illegal Immigration Reform and Immigrant Responsibility Act (IIRIRA) and the Personal Responsibility and Work Opportunity Reconciliation Act (PRWORA) imposed federal limits on documented and undocumented immigrants' eligibility for Social Security and most other social services (Massey et al., 2003). As a result of these acts, states were allowed to restrict or completely deny legal immigrants from both federal and state programs (Androff et al., 2011). With the federal and state governments pushing to restrict or eliminate immigrants' eligibility for various social programs, public discourse emerged regarding what immigrants do and do not deserve because of their documentation status, their time in the United States, and their lack of contributions to social programs through taxes. The subsequent policy changes that decreased social services have worsened the economic and social well-being of immigrants.

Political and public reactions after the attacks of September 11, 2001 exacerbated already heightened anti-immigrant sentiments in the United States, particularly toward Muslims and those of Middle Eastern descent. Enforcement of existing immigration laws increased, which led to an increase in deportations of undocumented immigrants. Immigration and law enforcement authorities raided businesses and even churches to capture and deport undocumented immigrants (González, 2008; Hensley & Kiefer, 2009a).

The U.S. economic recession, which started in 2007, contributed to a rise in the unemployment rate. One of the unfortunate outcomes of national economic instability has been that undocumented immigrants have become the scapegoats for the high unemployment rate and for the lack of funding for social programs (Becerra, Androff, Ayón, & Castillo, 2012; Hanson, 2007; U.S. Chamber of Commerce, n.d.). Immigrants working in the United States do not take away jobs from U.S. citizens and they provide a needed pool of unskilled labor (U.S. Chamber of Commerce, n.d.). While this is a sentiment often expressed in debates about immigrants, the jobs that most immigrants find are low-level jobs that often are undesirable to U.S.

citizens or legal resident workers due to low wages or lack of benefits. Studies have also found that undocumented immigrants actually contribute more in tax revenue than they consume in social services (Camarota, 2004; National Council of La Raza, 2008; Strayhorn, 2006). Despite studies that demonstrate the positive impact that immigrants have on the U.S. economy, the anti-immigrant sentiments displayed in public policies and in the media have led to the rise of border vigilante groups such as the Minutemen that only serve to perpetuate the anti-immigrant discourse in the U.S. (Becerra et al., 2010).

Recent state legislation has demonstrated that anti-immigrant sentiments have become more institutionalized. In 2010, the state legislature of Arizona passed SB 1070, which gained national attention. SB 1070 required that state and local police officers check the immigration status of anyone they arrest or suspect is illegally in the country (Pew Hispanic Center, 2010). Parts of the law were not upheld in circuit court, thus police officers are not as strictly bound to check immigration status, but the threat of that is still in place. Arizona's law was widely accepted— almost two-thirds of Americans supported Arizona's immigration law (Pew Research Center, 2011) and other states, such as Alabama, Indiana, Utah, and Georgia enacted similar legislation. The state of Alabama went the farthest, and included barring undocumented children from attending public schools and criminalized an undocumented person's solicitation to work, transporting an undocumented person, or even housing an undocumented person. There were additional stringent punishments placed on businesses that hire undocumented workers or take tax deductions related to wages paid to those workers. This law was also immediately appealed, and the federal appeals court blocked the most stringent provisions, allowing children to attend public schools regardless of their legal status. In 2012, the U.S. Supreme Court struck down three of the major provisions in SB 1070, but the court upheld the "show me your papers requirement" that allows police officers to question people's immigration status if reasonable suspicion is present.

Poverty, Immigration, and Employment

The demand for low-wage workers in the United States as well as the low wages and high rates of poverty in Latin America have impacted migration from Latin American countries, primarily Mexico and Central America, to the United States. Immigrants from Latin America can make significantly more money working in the United States than they can in their home countries. Although poverty in other countries does influence migration to the United States, studies have also found that because of the costs associated with migration, areas with the highest poverty rates often have lower rates of migration to the United States than other regions (Zenteno, 2006). Recent immigrants, especially undocumented immigrants, often have to work in dirty, dangerous, and physically demanding jobs with low pay and no health benefits (Androff et al., 2011). Poverty and a lack of opportunities for individuals with high levels of education in Asian countries (such as India, Pakistan, and China), combined with U.S. policies that promote immigration of highly skilled and highly educated populations have led to an increase in Asians migrating into the United States (Kerr & Lincoln, 2010). Immigrants fill a demand for labor in the U.S., but in order to deter undocumented immigration, some states have passed employer sanction laws that are intended to punish employers for hiring undocumented immigrants. The enforcement of those policies, however, illustrates the anti-immigrant sentiment behind them. The employer sanction policies are intended to punish employers, but despite the increased number of workplace raids, few businesses actually get sanctioned for hiring undocumented workers (Hensley & Kiefer, 2009b).

Another program intended to deter undocumented immigration that has impacted businesses and employment in the United States is E-Verify—an automated Internet-based verification system that allows employers to voluntarily check the work eligibility of potential new employees (U.S. Citizenship and Immigration Services, 2013). Government efforts to ensure all employees are documented immigrants or U.S. citizens do not decrease the demand for labor. Increased government regulations may lead businesses and employees to choose a cash payment system in order to circumvent the new regulations. This choice would have a negative impact on tax revenue collected by state and federal governments. The Congressional Budget Office (CBO) estimated that if the E-Verify program were mandated across the United States, the number of workers leaving the formal economy for an untaxed cash system would decrease federal revenues by $17.3 billion between the years 2009 and 2018 (Orszag, 2008).

Geographic and Social Isolation of Immigrants

Historically, new immigrant groups in the United States have settled in blighted urban areas or in rural areas where housing is less expensive (Baily, 1983; Wallace et al., 2007). Particularly with the last wave of European immigrants to the United

States in the early twentieth century, new immigrant groups formed geographically concentrated ethnic communities based on their country of origin. New York City, for example, has a section called "Little Italy" which attracted Italian immigrants beginning in the late nineteenth century when unemployment and poverty in Italy was high. Little Italy itself was divided geographically to reflect the specific neighborhoods in the homeland (Little Italy, 2011). Although many ethnic immigrant communities were located in large cities in the East Coast or Midwest, these ethnic communities often had little contact with mainstream U.S. culture, and as a result had few opportunities to acquire the English language. Over time, family and social networks developed from these communities to their home countries, which attracted friends, relatives, and others to these ethnic immigrant communities in the United States (Massey, 1995). New immigrant communities, which often included other immigrants from the same country of origin, also had limited access to schools, health care, and other social services (Baily, 1983; Wallace et al., 2007).

Employment opportunities in the ethnic immigrant communities were often limited to physically demanding jobs such as day laborer, miner, or factory worker, and even when immigrants worked in the same factory as native-born U.S. workers, immigrant workers were segregated from native workers (Pagnini & Morgan, 1990). The xenophobia of native U.S. whites in the early twentieth century led to prejudice and discrimination toward immigrants because native U.S. whites perceived immigrants as a threat to American culture and as competitors for jobs. Experiences of discrimination served to further unite ethnic immigrant communities and delayed their full integration into U.S. society. Recent legislation and increased enforcement of immigration policies have led to greater criminalization of immigrants, particularly those who are undocumented, further ostracizing them from established communities and the care of social service providers (Cleaveland, 2010).

Race and Ethnicity

Although each immigrant group faces unique challenges and hardships when arriving in the United States, current immigrant groups may have additional challenges that earlier generations of immigrants did not face. European immigrants in the early twentieth century were originally classified as separate racial and ethnic groups and faced intense racism and discrimination. In that era, integration and acceptance of European immigrants into U.S. society was facilitated through the process of English language acquisition, acculturation, and interethnic marriages, and their phenotypes made them difficult to distinguish from native populations (Pagnini & Morgan, 1990; Portes & Rumbaut, 2001). In the twenty-first century, race and ethnicity continue to be factors in today's society. The darker the skin color of a particular group, the more difficult it may be to gain acceptance into the majority culture regardless of the person's education, socioeconomic status, or language (Portes & Rumbaut, 2001). More recent immigrants from Southeast Asia, Latin America, Africa, or the Middle East may have a more difficult time gaining full acceptance into U.S. society regardless of their ability to speak English or the adoption of U.S. culture because they have phenotypes that distinguish them from native white populations (Portes & Rumbaut, 2001). Although their reasons for immigrating parallel previous generations of immigrants, their race and ethnicity further reinforce their outsider status.

Today, the majority of immigrants to the United States are from Latin America. The 2010 census reported that 53 percent of the foreign-born population was from Latin America compared to 28 percent from Asia, 13 percent from Europe, and 4 percent from Africa (U.S. Census Bureau, 2012). This has been a major shift since 1970 when 19 percent were from Latin America and 60 percent were from Europe (Gibson & Jung, 2006). There has been a continuous flow of immigrants from Latin America since the end of the Mexican-American War in 1848, but major waves began after 1910, during World War II, and the most recent wave starting in the 1970s (Massey, 1995). Immigrants from Latin America followed similar patterns of ethnic immigrant community development as European immigrants of the early twentieth century, but immigrants from mainland Latin American countries tended to settle in the West, while Latino immigrants from the Caribbean countries settled in Florida and New York. These Latino immigrant communities are also similar to ethnic immigrant populations of previous generations as immigration patterns favor moving to established Latino immigrant communities. Other factors such as housing costs often lead to de facto segregation from mainstream U.S. society and result in limited access to health and social services, as well as quality schools (Cutler, Glaeser, & Vigdor, 2008).

Although most of the Latino immigrant communities are located in or near urban areas in the U.S., some Latino immigrants live in extremely isolated communities known as colonias. Colonias are rural unincorporated subdivisions usually located along the Texas-Mexico border and are among the poorest areas in the United States. There are an estimated 1,800 colonias along the Texas-Mexico border that are located outside of the official boundaries of border cities and towns. These communities are composed of primarily Mexican immigrants and their children, and collectively these colonias have an estimated 500,000 residents. Colonias are even more isolated from mainstream U.S. society than other Latino immigrant communities and often lack potable water, sewer systems, electricity, and paved roads, and have limited access to health and social services. Residents of colonias work primarily in agriculture either locally or as migrant workers in various parts of the United States (Ortiz, Arizmendi, & Cornelius, 2006).

Despite the higher proportion of educated and highly skilled workers, many Asian immigrants, especially Southeast Asian immigrants, must also deal with multiple issues related to the immigrant and acculturation experiences such as language barriers, limited resources, discrimination, and social isolation (Bui, 2003; Kim, Lau, & Chang, 2007; Lee & Hadeed, 2009). The stress of acculturation, for example, increases the risk for intimate partner violence among some Asian immigrant populations (Lee & Hadeed, 2009). As an illustration, Kim and Sung (2000) found that Korean immigrant husbands who experienced high levels of acculturation stress were more likely to assault their wives compared to those with lower acculturation stress. Many Asian populations also form isolated immigrant communities such as the Chinatowns that exist in many large U.S. cities. The Chinatown in San Francisco, for example, has the highest concentration of immigrants in the San Francisco Bay area (Dube, 2003). The geographic or social isolation of those Asian immigrant communities may impede their acculturation process to mainstream U.S. culture, which can negatively impact U.S.-born Asian immigrant children living in those communities (Huang, Appel, & Ai, 2011).

Foreign-born blacks are a diverse group, with different cultures and overlapping languages. In 2005, two-thirds of the 2.8 million foreign-born blacks were born in the Caribbean or another Latin American country, typically speaking Spanish as their native language, while about one-third were born in Africa. A small amount (about 4 percent) were born in Europe, Canada, or elsewhere (Kent, 2007). Although smaller in number, one of the newest and fastest-growing groups among immigrants are African immigrants. Of the approximately one million African immigrants, over half immigrated since the 1990s, with the biggest proportion coming between 2000 and 2005, and primarily settling in the major metropolitan areas of New York, Washington, DC, Miami, and Atlanta (Kent, 2007; Venters & Gany, 2011). Being black in America has a long history of discrimination and poverty. For black newcomers, their immigrant experience is compounded by racial discrimination. Race dictates place of residence and economic opportunities, with black immigrants more highly segregated than other immigrant groups (Freeman, 2002).

Employment

Unfortunately for many low-skilled immigrants, the available jobs, such as in agriculture or the service industry, do not pay well and provide little opportunity for advancement compared to jobs available during the immigrant waves of the early twentieth century. This change in employment and industry makes it difficult for many low-skilled immigrants to emerge from poverty. In addition, agricultural and service industry jobs further perpetuate the social isolation of certain immigrant groups such as Latinos, Africans, and Asians from mainstream U.S. society (Kent 2007; Kwong, 1998; Ortiz, Arizmendi, & Cornelius, 2006). One of the factors contributing to immigration to the United States from Europe during the early twentieth century was the availability of industrial jobs. These jobs required a certain skill set that was acquired with time and experience. For European immigrants, time and experience in industrial employment provided an opportunity for upward mobility through increased wages and other job opportunities. Second-generation European immigrants could expect to make decent wages working industrial jobs without the need for higher education (Hirschman, 1996; Portes & Rumbaut, 2001). Since the end of World War II, the percentage of industrial and manufacturing jobs declined from over a third of all employment in the United States to less than 15 percent by 1996. In 2010 manufacturing jobs accounted for 8.1 percent of all employment in the United States and the Bureau of Labor Statistics estimates that this percentage will decline to 7 percent by 2020 (Henderson, 2012). These jobs were replaced by service employment positions that are typically low-paying jobs with little opportunity for advancement (Portes & Rumbaut, 2001).

Unlike in previous generations, when immigrants or succeeding generations could obtain a well-paying job with little education or at most a high school diploma, a college degree is now the only way individuals can enter many mid-range jobs (Haveman & Sneeding, 2006; Pew Hispanic Center, 2004). It is more difficult for the current generations of Latino and Southeast Asian immigrants and children of immigrants to achieve middle-class status because they cannot gradually improve on their parents' skill or educational level over time (Ngo & Lee, 2007; Portes & Rumbaut, 2001). To parallel the gains of earlier immigrant groups, often they must dramatically improve on their parents' education by obtaining a college degree in order to achieve middle class status (Portes & Rumbaut, 2001).

Language and Education

As mentioned previously, communities of recent immigrants tend to be socially, culturally, and often geographically isolated from mainstream American culture. As a result, there are few opportunities for adults living in those communities to interact with English speakers and learn to speak English. These linguistically isolated neighborhoods are lower socioeconomic status ethnic immigrant enclaves where newly arrived immigrants have created social structures and businesses within the community that reinforce their language, culture, and religion (Vega, Ang, Rodriguez, & Finch, 2011). Although linguistically isolated communities tend to be of lower socioeconomic status and often lack adequate health and social services, these communities provide new immigrants with support that may help the transition in settling in a new country and learning a new language and customs. Linguistically isolated communities with a high percentage of undocumented immigrants may choose to have fewer contacts with mainstream American culture for fear of detection and deportation, which serves to further isolate the community. While linguistically isolated communities may provide some protective factors such as the retention of the language, culture, and religion of recent immigrants, their social, geographic, and linguistic isolation may inhibit the education and acculturation process, which can negatively impact their ability to improve their socioeconomic status (Vega et al., 2011).

Children living in socially, geographically, or linguistically isolated communities are also at a disadvantage when it comes to education. Portes and Rumbaut (2001) argue that new immigrants tend to be of low socioeconomic status and therefore must live in urban, low socioeconomic status neighborhoods, and low socioeconomic status has been identified as a barrier to K–12 academic achievement, enrollment in college, and the completion of a degree. A lack of understanding of the K–12 and higher education systems in the United States among parents and children has also been shown to be a barrier. Immigrant parents may not fully

understand teachers' and school administrators' expectations of parental involvement with the school and teachers may not have the cultural competence and language ability to communicate with immigrant parents. The lack of communication
between teachers and parents may hinder students' academic progress (Becerra,
2012; Bohon, Macpherson, & Atiles, 2005; Ngo & Lee, 2007).

English may not be the first language for many Southeast Asian, African,
Caribbean, and Latino students, including those born in the United States (Capps,
Fix, Murray, Ost, Passel, & Herwantoro, 2005; Kent 2007; Ngo & Lee, 2007). There
were 5.3 million students in pre-K–12 public schools classified as English language
learners (ELLs) during the 2008–2009 academic school year, which is a 51 percent
increase from 1997–1998 (Becerra, 2012; U.S. Department of Education, 2011).
Forty-five percent of all Latino students in U.S. public schools are classified as ELLs
and 79 percent of ELLs in elementary schools are Latino (Lazarin, 2006; National
Clearinghouse for English Language Acquisition and Language Instruction Educational Programs [NCELA], 2011). Portes and Rumbaut (2001) and Bohon et al.
(2005) found that language affects ELLs because the elimination of bilingual education has forced ELLs into English immersion programs where students do not
truly learn the complexities of the English language well enough to compete with
native English speakers. These negative effects persist throughout a child's K–12
education and lead to lower grades, lower educational aspirations, and can eventually lead to dropout (Bohon et al., 2005; Kerper Mora, 2002; Portes & Rumbaut,
2001). Language may also indirectly affect the academic achievement of Latino
students through their parents' limited English skills. Non-English-speaking or
limited English-speaking parents may be interested in their children's education,
but lack the English skills to assist with their children's homework (McLaughlin,
Liljestrom, Lim, & Meyers, 2002; Ngo & Lee, 2007; Sandefur, 1998) or may find it
difficult or embarrassing to communicate with teachers or school administrators
(Bohon et al., 2005). Even immigrants who speak English report difficulties in
school performance and employment. For example, African immigrants who are
fluent in English reported experiencing major problems being understood because
of their accents (Shabaya, 2006).

Acculturation

Acculturation is the process of changing attitudes, norms, behaviors, and identity
in order to adapt to a new culture (Berry, 2007). Acculturation is a complex
process, and not all individuals acculturate at the same rate and some may choose

to maintain connections with their cultural heritage (Marsiglia & Kulis, 2009). Nevertheless, due to the increased contact with majority culture systems and English speakers in school, children tend to acculturate at faster rates than adults.

Traditional views of acculturation and assimilation argue that higher academic and socioeconomic outcomes occur with each succeeding generation, and it has been argued that the immigrant waves of the early twentieth century followed this pattern of acculturation and assimilation (Gordon, 1964; Lieberson, 1980; Waldinger & Feliciano, 2004). As immigrants spent more time in the United States and were exposed to the majority culture, they would eventually fully acculturate into society and as a result, their children would benefit because they tended to have higher levels of acculturation and would be able to more effectively use the resources available in schools and the community (Waldinger & Feliciano, 2004). This pattern of children having higher levels of education and income than their parents would continue with each generation (Oropesa & Landale, 1997; Waldinger & Feliciano, 2004). Unfortunately, changes in the U.S. economy as well as different countries of origin of newer immigrants may limit economic opportunities for new immigrants and make it difficult to follow previous patterns of acculturation and economic progress. The race, ethnicity, or country of origin of specific immigrant groups, as well as the economic opportunities available in the United States, may have facilitated the acculturation process for the immigrants of the early twentieth century. That pattern is not as strong today.

The Impact of Immigration and Poverty on Children

Immigrant children are the fastest growing segment of the population (Tienda & Haskins, 2011). In fact, six out of seven immigrants arrive as children with their young adult parents or during their early adult years (Rumbaut & Komaie, 2010). Notably, the most vulnerable group to experience poverty is the children of immigrants. There are approximately 17.2 million children in the United States who have foreign-born parents, and among these children it is estimated that 4.2 million are poor (Wight, Thampi, & Chau, 2011). Although immigrant children tend to live in two-parent families with at least one full-time working parent, their immigrant parents tend to encounter lower wages as a result of limited proficiency in English (Capps, Fix, Ost, Reardon-Anderson, & Passel, 2004). Additionally, children with immigrant parents fare worse on most social indicators, including education, physical and mental health, and economic security than do native-born children (Tienda & Haskins, 2011).

According to the National Center for Children in Poverty, there is much diversity among children born with foreign parents. Accordingly, poverty may depend on length of residency, and whether children live in mixed immigration households, where there is one native parent and one immigrant parent, or one is an established immigrant and one a recent immigrant parent. Most children of immigrants have parents who have resided in the United States for more than ten years (12.2 percent), whereas 3.8 percent have parents who are recent immigrants, and 7.6 percent have parents with mixed immigration experiences (Wight, Thampi, & Chau, 2011). Children with parents who are recent immigrants have the highest poverty rates (38.5 percent), and the rate of established immigrants is lower (27.2 percent), while the poverty rate is lowest for children with native-born parents (18.2 percent) (Wight et al., 2011). Poverty levels for children with foreign-born parents also varied by parents' documentation status, with a high rate among children with legal non-citizen parents and a higher rate for children living with undocumented parents. This illustrates the economic precariousness of immigrant families, the most vulnerable of whom are undocumented. Today, the vast majority of children of immigrants, both established and recent, are of Latino origin (Wight et al., 2011).

The poverty rate and other material hardships found among immigrant children and children of immigrants can have deleterious effects on the children's long-term health and well-being (Wight et al., 2011). For example, many children lack proper nutrition and access to health and other support services, which place them at risk for poor health and impaired development. Many children who have immigrant parents are U.S. citizens themselves and are eligible to receive public support. However, many do not access such services (Skinner, 2011; Wight et al., 2011). Kersey, Geppert, and Cutts (2006) found that Latino children in immigrant families were less likely to participate in the Supplemental Nutrition Assistance Program (SNAP), formerly known as Food Stamps, and Temporary Assistance for Needy Families (TANF) compared to non-Latinos, but more likely to participate in the Women, Infants, and Children (WIC) supplemental food program. Consequently, Latino families were found to have higher rates of child hunger and household food insecurity than non-Latino families. Even after controlling for socio-economic and demographic variables, Latino immigrant children were more likely to be hungry compared to non-immigrant children (Kersey et al., 2006).

These needs are compounded by the fact that children in immigrant families lack health insurance coverage. Based on a national sample, Zhihuan, Yu, and Ledsky

(2006) examined the health status and service access among children in immigrant families. The results indicate that children of foreign-born parents, regardless of parental citizenship, were significantly more likely to not have health insurance. Children of foreign-born non-citizen parents were also more likely than children from U.S.-born parents to not have visited a doctor, dentist, or mental health specialist in the previous year. Comparing children from native-born low-income families living 200 percent below the poverty line to children from foreign-born non-citizen parents, children of foreign-born non-citizen parents were five times more likely to lack health insurance.

With the emergence of several anti-immigrant policies, children of immigrants are placed at greater risks due to increased rates of parental deportation. Parent-child separation, due to deportation, poses serious risks to children's immediate safety, economic security, well-being, and long-term development, as children who are separated from their parents experience many challenges during critical developmental stages (Chaudry et al., 2010). Such families experience financial hardships as often the sole provider is detained for long periods of time, deported, or released without job prospects. On average, families in these situations will lose $650 per week, and as a result, experience housing instability and food insecurity (Chaudry et al., 2010). In addition, children experience a wide range of changes in their behavior, including changes in eating and sleeping patterns, excessive crying, clinging to parents (among young children), and aggressive and withdrawn behaviors among older children (Chaudry et al., 2010).

Overall, the economic, social, and political situation for immigrant children today is different than those of previous generations. Some of the increase in immigrant child poverty from that of fifty years ago is due to increases in risks related to immigrant status, such as lower educational attainment, low wage employment, and the non-working status of immigrant mothers (Van Hook, Brown, & Kwenda, 2004).

Changing Role of Women among Immigrant Families

Although immigrant women work at a lower rate than native-born women, the role of immigrant women within their families changes with relocation. Immigrant women and girls in the United States accounted for 18.9 million in 2008. Women come to this country from all around the world, although Mexico is the country with the largest number, representing more than one quarter (27 percent) of all foreign-born women, followed by China and the Philippines (both with 5 percent), and India (4 percent). Some of the key characteristics that influence the immigration experience for women include education, socioeconomic status, and language. Education is a predictor of success in this country. More than 60 percent of women from Mexico do not have a high school diploma, compared with women immigrants from countries such as India, Philippines, Korea, and Canada with higher levels of formal education. In 2008, only 5.6 percent of women from Mexico had obtained a bachelor degree compared with women from India who had the highest college completion rate (68.2 percent). Among all immigrant women, 9.5 percent of women from India had graduate degrees compared to 9.6 percent of U.S.-born women. Immigrant women from Mexico have the highest poverty rate (28.5 percent) compared with the Philippines (5 percent) and U.S.-born women (14 percent). Immigrant women from Mexico also had the lowest percentage of women speaking English (44.7 percent) followed by El Salvador (47.7 percent), compared to the highest from India (86.1 percent), the Philippines (92.7 percent), and Canada (98.5 percent) (Immigration Policy Center, 2010).

The relationship between gender and migration has been a topic rarely mentioned in scholarly writing. Living in a patriarchal society where laws and research are done by men has meant that women often have been put aside (Hondagneu-Sotelo, 2000). Additionally, patriarchy and capitalism set the guidelines for discrimination toward women of color (Collins, 2004). Frequently, immigrant women must navigate their status not only within their family, but within institutions, workplaces, and labor demand. Discrimination against immigrant women can lead to ignoring the intersection of race and class (Pessar, 1999). Thus, in addition to being foreign-born and experiencing all the barriers that immigration status brings, women immigrants must often contend with the issues that confront all women due to their gender, race, and class.

Migration to the United States began with men arriving to discover and colonize a new land, and women came later. Historically among most immigrant groups, the migration trajectory continued with men from other countries looking for jobs and opportunities and then later bringing their families (Massey et al., 2003). Migration from Latin America and Asia has changed this pattern. This is attributed to changes in technology and the economy (Martin, 2007).

Many societies now need women working outside the home to be able to financially support their families. These social changes have shifted gender roles to a more egalitarian relationship. However, this shift has created conflict with women continuing to be responsible for their children's upbringing and the home environment while taking on new responsibilities outside the home. Furthermore, this egalitarian shift in roles can create additional conflict, particularly if women earn more than men, which can create a hostile family environment (Hirsch, 1999). Compounding this issue, immigrant women in the United States who are responsible for their families and are in need of government assistance are at higher risk of being ignored by social services due to their gender, language, and race (Pearce, 2006).

Society views women who are employed outside the home as more reliable than men due to their responsibility to their family and their need to work. Thus, women cannot be ignored in the immigration and labor force any longer. An emerging way that immigrant women are making an impact is through the remittances they send to family back home (Martin, 2007). Women sending money to their country of origin go through different and more complicated conditions than men. They send approximately the same amount of money, yet they have more difficulty finding jobs and get paid less for the same work (Martin, 2007). Thus, immigrant women face greater opportunities to work outside the home and their paid employment becomes increasingly more important to the well-being of their families in the United States. However, this new change in role presents challenges because working outside the home conflicts with traditional female gender roles and creates difficulties in finding adequate child care.

Other factors that contribute to changes in migration patterns include divorce and/or single families in which women are the main breadwinners (Martin, 2007; Tuiran, 1993). Also, women are often forced to migrate to get out of an abusive relationship or to survive financial hardships (Pearce, 2006). Frequently, women migrating to the United States have opportunities not available in their country of origin that can dramatically improve their emotional and physical health and financial status.

When discussing immigrant women working outside the home, it is important to recognize that some cultures regard this in a negative way. Gender and migration in the United States also intersect with domestic violence. Due to gender differences and power struggles, men use violence to maintain power and control in a relationship. New immigrant women are not aware of their rights and often do not realize that the abuse from their husbands is against the law in the United States. Often men threaten women with deportation or children's custody to continue the abuse and maintain the control (Pearce, 2006). The Violence against Women Act (VAWA), began in 1994 and amended in 1996, 2000, 2005, and 2013, addresses this problem. VAWA permits women involved in a domestic violence relationship to request permanent residency in the United States, allowing the victims to safely leave the abusive relationship and denounce their abusers (Carothers Graham, 2008). This act empowers women by providing a venue for undocumented women to safely and legally obtain permanent residency, which could not be obtained otherwise. Unfortunately, VAWA was allowed expire in 2012 due to a lack of consensus between Senate and House versions of the bill. However, in January 2013 the bill was reintroduced in and passed by Congress with bipartisan support and signed by President Obama. Those who work with undocumented women need to be aware of the protections under VAWA and advocate that abused immigrant women receive legal permanent resident status.

Immigrant Women and Their Relationships with Their Children

The earlier circular migration patterns where many immigrants would migrate to the United States for work and go back to their country of origin have changed (Massey et al., 2003). The difficulty of maintaining previous circular migration patterns, fueled by financial need in their countries of origin, has led to growth in the migration of women and a decrease in family reunification (Palloni, Massey, Ceballos, Espinosa, & Spittel, 2001). This shift in migration has created growing social conflict due to the future composition of the United States population. According to the Current Population Report, the Hispanic population is the fastest growing population in the United States as a result of immigration and fertility (Dye, 2010). Immigrant women, particularly Latinas, have been the target of attention and criticism due to their fertility rate (Gonzales, 2008; Romero, 2011), as their U.S.-citizen children will have citizen's rights in this country while potentially adhering to their native culture (Romero, 2011). Immigrants are appreciated as workers, but not as citizens, as demonstrated by policies such as Proposition 187 in California, which would have required that schools request documentation to prove U.S. citizenship or legal residency, thereby prohibiting undocumented immigrant children from attending public schools, and withholding all non-emergency medical care from undocumented immigrants. Similarly, the most recent immigration bill in Alabama also sought to prohibit undocumented children from attending public schools (Calavita, 1996; De Genova, 2005). Although the courts negated this edict, variations of these efforts to limit access to education, particularly recognition of in-state status to attend state-funded universities, has passed successfully, such as Proposition 300 in Arizona in 2006.

Sometimes immigrant women leave their children behind to be taken care of by their own mothers or immediate family members (Hewett, 2009). This creates transnational mothers. These mothers continue their mother/child relationship from afar, thereby creating a different bond with their children. Transnational mothers, besides being targeted for potential discrimination due to their race, gender, and immigration status, are also seen as bad mothers. The perception is women are the pillars of strength in their home, and responsible for their children's well-being (Pedone, 2006). Mothers who are forced to migrate and leave their children behind are ostracized for not meeting society's expectations.

Social Networks

By migrating to the United States, women develop their own social networks that allow them to contest domestic patriarchal authority. Transnational mothers build social relationships and networks regardless of everyday life and struggles they face (De Genova, 2005). Women in the United States have more opportunities than in their country of origin to work outside their homes and participate in other activities that could provide income to their family (Ricourt & Danta, 2003). Women are able to get in contact with other women in similar circumstances, allowing them to work together for a better future. The interactions with other women that often occur in the workplace help them to unite and organize to change their neighborhoods, their children's schools, or their communities (De Genova, 2005). These interactions also provide opportunities to learn how other women have overcome personal issues such as abuse at home or work. Besides the opportunity for building community networks and meeting financial needs at home, this facilitates immigrant women's empowerment and independence that they previously lacked in their countries of origin (Hirsch, 1999; Hondagneu-Sotelo, 2000).

Role Conflict

New generations of American women or adolescent women who grow up in environments with two cultures often experience double standards (Gonzalez-Lopez, 2004). Adolescent and young adult women participate in community activities, such as in churches or schools, whereas at home they are mothers, godmothers, *comadres*, and sisters, indicating the multi-dimensionality of their many roles. Following the familism value, family is highly valued as the first line of support for its members; they live by the ideal that if everything fails, family will be available. Motherhood is also highly valued because it is conceptualized as the continuance of a legacy. In many situations, parents encourage women to succeed and avoid struggles and poverty, while overcoming the cultural tradition in which women must adhere to a submissive role, have children, and tend to their family (Gomez et al., 2001).

As stated earlier in the "Changing Role of Women among Immigrant Families" section, women's migration has increased and this has shifted family relationships, creating new challenges for gender roles, education, and economics (Pedone, 2006). Historically, mothers and younger daughters were the last ones to migrate (Massey, Durand, & Malone, 2003). Overall, women's migration to the United States has increased since the 1960s and is likely to continue. The subsequent change in women's roles when they migrate contributes to social and economic shifts within their families. Even when the changes bring additional resources and can help lift immigrant families out of poverty, there are accompanying social and familial changes that can have significant impact on families and communities. These shifts need to be considered by social workers and social service providers. Transnational families and globalization have given a new meaning to migration in which women are playing a key role.

Government Policies and Programs

Public policies and social welfare programs related to immigration have changed over the years, in response to changes in the immigration population, and the state of the economy. Numerous policy changes have reflected public sentiments, such as anti-immigrant feelings as previously discussed, and changes in economic conditions. Current political debate surrounds the issue of immigration, with a lack of consensus on what is the best course for public policy. The result is variation in policies and programs at the state level and barriers to services and support for many immigrants.

Language-appropriate services are not only part of providing culturally competent services—they are a legal right. "Under the provisions of Title VI of the Civil Rights Act of 1964 ... individuals with limited English proficiency (LEP) are guaranteed language access as a civil right and have protection from discrimination in federally funded human services" (Suleiman, 2003, p. 186).

Communication is critical to receiving appropriate and effective needed services. Suleiman (2003) highlights several components to communication that are necessary to ensure equal access to benefits and services for LEP children and families. These include families' abilities to "(a) understand information about the services and process, (b) understand the resources and services available to address the particular situation, and (c) communicate with the service provider" (p. 190). Studies have found several limitations to the use of interpreters. A systematic review of the literature on the use of interpreters finds numerous negative outcomes. Quality of care is compromised when LEP patients need, but do not get, interpreters. The quality of care is inferior and interpreter errors are common among untrained, ad hoc interpreters (Flores, 2005). Moreover, Suleiman (2003) indicates that in accordance with Title VI guidelines, interpreters should meet certain competencies including "(a) proficiency in both English and the other language, (b) training on the ethics of interpreting, and (c) knowledge in both languages of any specialized terms and concepts in the particular field" (p. 191). With the economic downturn of recent years, service providers and government agencies are less likely to have the resources for adequate interpreter services.

Public Policies Impact Immigrants' Well-Being

Immigrant communities experience barriers to services at a policy level as well. As stated previously, United States policies on immigration have denied or limited entry to the United States by immigrants and have also led to anti-immigrant sentiment influencing policies that guide access to care. In recent years, access to care for immigrant communities has been severely limited and curtailed (Kullgren, 2003). The Personal Responsibility and Work Opportunity Reconciliation Act of 1996 restricted federal, state, and local publicly funded services to undocumented immigrants (Kullgren, 2003). Undocumented immigrants and recently documented individuals are ineligible for many services including "retirement, welfare, health, disability, or other similar benefit for . . . which payments or assistance are provided . . . by an agency of the State or local government" (p. 1630). These restrictions exclude access to health care in case of an emergency; non-cash, short-term, in-kind emergency disaster relief; and immunizations or testing related to communicable diseases (Personal Responsibility and Work Opportunity Reconciliation Act [PRWORA], 1996). Even with legal residence, immigrants have restricted access to services. Individuals who became legal residents after the enactment of PRWORA are subject to a five-year waiting period before they can access publicly funded benefits (Loue, Faust, and Bunce, 2000; PRWORA, 1996). PRWORA, a federal policy, prohibits access to care. An example of growing anti-immigrant sentiment is that although already established through federal law, states have also passed laws that prohibit access to care, and in some cases have added stringent conditions. In 2004, Proposition 200 was passed in Arizona. Proposition 200 requires state and local agencies to verify the immigration status of service applicants and to report any immigrant that is not documented to immigration authorities (Immigration Omnibus, S.B. 1611, 2011). Failure to file a report is a class 2 misdemeanor for the employee and employee's supervisor if he or she knew about the failure to report. Following the passage of Proposition 200, the media reported that many immigrants and their U.S. citizen children were deterred from seeking services for which they remain eligible, including literacy training, nutrition assistance, health programs, and domestic violence shelters. Additionally, parents were confused about whether or not children could attend school (Slattery, 2004). Many undocumented immigrants refrain from seeking needed health services for fear of deportation. This policy has led to increased fear among documented immigrants and has restrained many from seeking public services (Slattery, 2004).

In 2012, President Obama initiated two key executive actions that impact immigrants, primarily those who are undocumented. The first provision was the Deferred Action for Childhood Arrivals (DACA). DACA allows undocumented immigrants to apply for a two-year temporary work permit if they arrived in the United States before sixteen years of age, are in school, a high school graduate, or honorably discharged from the U.S. armed forces, have not been convicted of a felony or serious misdemeanor, and are younger than thirty-one years as of June 15, 2012 (Batalova & Mittelstadt, 2012). While this program can potentially benefit hundreds of thousands of undocumented immigrants living in the United States, many politicians oppose the DACA program and have initiated steps to reduce DACA's impact. For example, Jan Brewer, the governor of Arizona, signed an executive order that prohibits individuals who received work permits through DACA from receiving state benefits, in-state tuition, or even drivers' licenses. The inconsistent and often contradictory policies from the federal and state levels leave families in a state of fear and confusion. As a result, undocumented immigrants may avoid not only applying for DACA, but those with U.S.-born children may also avoid applying for services their children are eligible to receive for fear of being apprehended by immigration authorities. The second executive provision, which went into effect in March 2013, allows undocumented immigrants who are married to U.S. citizens to apply for a special waiver to remain in the country while they are awaiting the documentation process. This is a major change from the previous policy that mandated returning to their country of origin to apply for papers to join their U.S. citizen spouse and wait for ten years as punishment for living illegally in the United States. These two changes in policy have significant implications for the economic well-being of undocumented individuals and their families because the waivers allow them to seek employment and legally participate in the economic system while waiting for immigration reform or resolution of their cases.

Global Policies Affecting Immigrants

Internationally, Article 13 of the Universal Declaration of Human Rights (1948) holds that everyone has the right to freedom of movement (United Nations [UN], 1948). The International Labour Organization (ILO) has promoted international conventions for protecting the rights of migrants (ILO, 2006). The 1949 ILO Migration for Employment Convention (No. 97) called for equal wages, social security, and unionization between national and migrant workers. The 1975 ILO Migrant Workers Convention (No. 143) goes further to protect the human rights of migrant workers by promoting anti-smuggling and anti-trafficking measures. Furthermore, the United Nations (1990) has recognized the increasing numbers of international migrants by adopting the International Convention on the Protection of the Rights of All Migrant Workers and Members of Their Families, which calls attention to the dehumanization and human rights violations of migrant workers and their families. This convention aims to foster respect for migrants and their families and to protect them against discrimination. The United States has not ratified or signed any of these international conventions. Some argue that the reason the United States does not ratify many international treaties is due to the constitutional requirements requiring congressional support, while others cite political conservatism and an attitude of American exceptionalism that views America as a distinct nation, which does not have the same human rights issues as the rest of the globe. As noted previously, however, public policies and discrimination in the United States deprive immigrants of many human rights, including health care, welfare, and economic opportunities.

Social Justice

The National Association of Social Workers (NASW) Code of Ethics identifies social justice as one of the six core values of the social work profession. Social justice is a complex term with a meaning that has long been debated and often depends upon one's ideological perspective. For social workers, social justice means striving to secure basic rights, legal protections, and social and economic opportunities for all people. Social justice commonly involves related concepts of fairness, equality, and sometimes economic redistribution among individual members of a group or society. One approach to advancing social justice is the promotion and protection of human rights. Through the protection of all people's human rights to freedom, peace, opportunity, and development, society can be made more just. The goal of establishing and protecting human rights is a key framework to guide advocacy for the welfare of immigrants.

As noted in this chapter, immigrants face many challenges, including disparities in income and disproportionate rates of poverty. Immigrant families face significant challenges related to obtaining and maintaining adequate employment, educational barriers, poor health outcomes, and discrimination (Androff et al., 2011). These inequalities coupled with a history of exclusionary policies and many contemporary stereotypes and discrimination in our culture make immigrants particularly vulnerable to injustice and human rights violations. Treating people differently because of where they come from is unjust and a form of discrimination.

Social workers are ethically obligated to protect the human rights of migrants and their family members. The NASW Code of Ethics (2008) calls for social workers to advocate for non-citizens regardless of immigration status [6.04 Social and Political Action (d)]. This means that social workers are ethically bound, by professional standards, to advocate for the well-being of immigrants regardless of their legal status in the country. Social work's commitment to ethical action is considered a core aspect of the profession.

The 2006 NASW Immigration Policy Toolkit expresses that the social work profession's commitment to serve immigrant populations should be based upon their needs, as opposed to ideology or foreign policy. This means that social workers should reject language, ideology, policies, and practices that are discriminatory and anti-immigrant. When people choose to migrate, particularly for economic reasons to improve their well-being, professionals have an obligation to serve immigrant populations, keeping social justice and human rights at the forefront. This is particularly challenging in light of historical and recent events.

In the post 9-11 world, immigration has been reframed as a security issue rather than a human rights issue. Immigration policy has been shaped in the United States by policies related to the War on Terror, and the federal immigration agency has been reorganized under the Department of Homeland Security. This has contributed to an increased use of a law enforcement approach to the issue of immigration, resulting in what has been called the "criminalization of immigration" (Androff & Tavassoli, 2012). A law enforcement or criminal justice approach to immigration may serve to protect the United States from those foreigners who bear ill will and harbor terrorist intentions, but it often conflicts with other goals such as economic development and the welfare of immigrant families and communities. It is social workers' ethical responsibility to prioritize the welfare and dignity of immigrants.

Factors Influencing Service Delivery and Access to Care

Evidence suggests that immigrants are less likely to utilize medical/social services than native-born individuals (Kullgren, 2003; Vega, Kolody, Aguilar-Gaxiola, & Catalano, 1999). In order to have their service needs met and obtain appropriate health services, including access to medical, mental health, and substance abuse programs, immigrants have to overcome many personal, structural, financial, and policy-related barriers (Ayón, 2009; Cooper, Hill, & Powe, 2002).

Personal barriers include conceptualization of problems, stigma, lack of familiarity with systems of care and preference for alternative services, and mistrust of services providers. It is likely that immigrants conceptualize or label problems differently (Bridges, de Arellano, Rhingold, Kmett Danielson, & Silcott, 2010). For example, studies have found that Latinos tend to conceptualize mental health symptoms as somatic (Peifer, Hu, & Vega, 2000). How families define their needs and problems influence where they seek services. For example, Bridges et al. (2010) commented that families who are more assimilated may define needs in terms of having psychiatric, behavioral, or substance abuse problems, compared to families who have retained their native culture. Assimilated families may seek services from behavioral health clinics or mental health services. Alternatively, families who have maintained their native culture may seek services consistent with the definition of their needs, including folk healers or herbalists commonly known as *curanderos,* priests, or respected elders in their community (Delgado, 1998; Vega, Kolody, & Aguilar-Gaxiola, 2001). On the same note, if families are not familiar with the type of services available or where services can be obtained, they are likely to not seek services.

In 2009, the foreign-born population without health insurance was about 2.5 times greater than the native-born population in the United States (DeNavas-Walt, Proctor, & Smith, 2010). Latinos have the lowest level of health insurance coverage in the United States with 31 percent of Latinos lacking health coverage. Among foreign-born Mexicans and Central Americans, insurance coverage is lower with 57 percent and 55 percent lacking health insurance, respectively (Saenz, 2010). Several factors impact the access to health care among Latino children in immigrant families (Rodriguez, Elliott, Vestal, Suttorp, & Schuster, 2008). Multivariate analysis revealed that older parents (older than thirty), lower levels of education among parents (less than sixth grade), less time in the United States, being a migrant worker, and living in the Southwest or Southeast regions of the United States were significant factors associated with having uninsured children. Overall, among children who were immigrants, it was more common to find that they lacked a usual source of care, physician visits, emergency visits, and well-child visits compared to natives and foreign-born citizen children (Perez, Fang, Inkelas, Kuo, & Ortega, 2009).

Similarly, the Asian population, who represent one third of all immigrants in the United States, lags behind non-Hispanic whites on various aspects of access to health care (Huang & Carrasquillo, 2008). In a study examining differences in types of health insurance among the six largest Asian groups (i.e., Chinese, Filipino, Indian, Korean, Vietnamese, and Japanese), Huang and Carrasquillo (2008) found that Koreans had the highest rate of non-coverage, followed by Vietnamese and Chinese. Among non-citizens, 27 percent of Chinese participants were uninsured, with Koreans and Vietnamese experiencing higher rates of non-coverage at 41 percent and 31 percent, respectively. The authors attributed this disparity in health care coverage to employment in both the service industry and blue collar occupations, which are less likely to provide coverage.

Mistrust of service providers is often due to the lack of cultural competence found among service providers (Snowden & Yamada, 2005). Service providers who approach practice from a Western medicine model may prevent immigrant families from engaging in service delivery if immigrants and their families expect a more holistic approach to care where medicine, religion, and cultural practices are inter-twined. Immigrants often report feeling discriminated against by physicians due to their race/ethnicity, health care insurance status, and inability to speak English (Friedman et al., 2005; Keller, Silbergerg, Hartmann, & Michener, 2010; Smedley, Stith, & Nelson, 2003). Furthermore, Keller and colleagues found that perceived discrimination was associated with increased likelihood of going without needed health care.

Cultural competence includes linguistic-appropriate services. Language is a strong barrier to accessing care. Language barriers can result in misdiagnosis and poor quality of care (Ku & Flores, 2005; Ku & Matani, 2001; Viladrich, 2006), exclusion from programs, and delay or denial in services (Suleiman, 2003). In addition, language barriers also prohibit immigrants from negotiating cheaper health care and charitable services (Viladrich, 2003).

Additionally, immigrants are sometimes treated in society as throwaways. Migrant communities in the United States have been described in different settings and environments as a "disposable community"—the members can be used or recruited when needed and discarded when no longer required, which increases the odds of violence, discrimination, and vulnerability (Chang, 2000; De Genova, 2005; Romero, 2002).

As stated previously, immigrants face many challenges. Immigrants who experience the highest rate of poverty often do not qualify for services. New welfare policy indirectly restricts access to services for American children or second generation of immigrants who qualify for services. Some non-documented parents of U.S. born children do not seek services because they are afraid they are going to get deported or that this will impede their ability to qualify for permanent legal status. Overall, policies and programs have become more limited or unavailable for this population in part due to the current anti-immigrant sentiment making the transition from their countries of origin to the United States more difficult.

Interventions

Immigration remains a basic pattern of human life around the world. As the process of economic globalization continues to shape both societies in the global north as well as the global south, immigration patterns will continue and grow. For effective practice with immigrants, social workers and other helping professionals must be able to apply a global perspective to their local context. This includes education about and awareness of global social conditions, and fostering an understanding and appreciation for immigrants' cultural backgrounds and experiences.

Micro Interventions

Social work practitioners who work with immigrants face a complicated task. The central tenet for social workers is to begin where the client is, which is simple to say but can be a very difficult task to achieve when working with people who come from different cultures, backgrounds, and countries of origin. In addition, immigrants can have different legal statuses, making them eligible for different services, or not eligible at all. For example, refugees can receive subsidies depending on their country of origin while immigrants cannot.

Informal services can be vital for immigrants. The immigration transition can be less frustrating when there is someone who can guide the immigrant through his or her settling in this country and acculturating to living in the United States. Typically this role is taken by a relative or a friend. Social work practitioners can adopt this approach for intervention while working with immigrants, designing social services to help with acculturation while at the same time acknowledging the person's culture of origin. This service delivery approach is unique to working with immigrants, and should be developed as part of specialized social work training.

As stated previously, immigrants without appropriate documentation who live in this country encounter numerous barriers to obtain social services. Again, agencies and helping professionals need to become aware of the vulnerability of people lacking documentation, and in need of services. Many social service agencies located in immigrant areas have developed policies that do not involve asking for documentation or citizenship status. In the case of federal and state services that are linked to legal status, agencies have begun to separate services that are under those funding sources to ensure compliance, and move services for possibly undocumented people to other parts of the agency through funds that are local or privately donated. This creates an administrative barrier to the provision of services and requires specialized training and awareness by social workers and helping professionals in each agency.

There is also the prospect of discrimination based on race and ethnicity. For many immigrants, in spite of discrimination, their new lifestyle and opportunities are better than in their countries of origin. This does not negate the impact of discrimination, particularly for the children of immigrants. Helping professionals need to consider the impact and consequences of facing discrimination.

Overall, social workers and other helping professionals must be aware of their own culture and values to help clients effectively. Additionally, they must learn about other cultures and develop effective skills to engage different groups from various cultures without bias from their own backgrounds (Williams, 2006).

Another important issue in working directly with immigrants is language. In the United States there are more than 300 spoken languages. The United States recognizes 39 individual languages; seven of these have more than one million speakers. Spanish is the language most commonly spoken after English, then Chinese, French, Tagalog, Vietnamese, German, and Korean. Although today it is becoming more likely to find a social worker or helping professional who speaks another language in addition to English, it is still very difficult to find professionals who speak the primary languages of many immigrants. Large cities with high concentrations of immigrants have translation services, but services can take longer while arranging for interpreters. Also, the relationship and rapport with the client will be affected by having someone interpret, potentially losing some of the conversation's meaning.

A barrier when working with immigrants is access to appropriate services. Because immigrants come from many different countries and cultures, appropriate services and interventions often are not available. Cultures are so diverse that an intervention that works with a specific immigrant group might not work with another one. Individualized services are essential to be able to have positive outcomes. Most important is that social workers and other helping professionals are aware of the barriers and difficulties immigrants have within their families and their surrounding environment.

Mezzo Interventions

Mezzo practice typically refers to practice with groups and organizations, such as community-based organizations. Social work practice with groups has its origins in the settlement house movement of the Progressive Era. Perhaps the most famous settlement house in the United States was Jane Addams' Hull House in Chicago, which served a predominantly immigrant population. Therefore, social work mezzo practice is historically rooted in practice with immigrants.

Unfortunately, in recent decades schools of social work in the United States have deemphasized community practice and development (Specht & Courtney, 1994; Stoesz, Karger, & Carrilio, 2010). Although all schools of social work discuss the importance of cultural competency, few schools actually teach effective intervention strategies to work with various immigrant communities. As the immigrant population in the United States continues to grow, it is important for schools of social work to adequately prepare students for the realities immigrant communities face, and develop effective intervention strategies that go beyond the individual and family level and allow immigrants to successfully transition to their new environment while maintaining their cultural strengths.

Social work practice interventions at the mezzo level can be informed by theories of human capital, the capabilities approach, and micro-enterprise. Briefly, human capital is measured by educational and economic attainment. Social welfare programs designed to increase immigrants' human capital include English-language education, job training, employment placement and job referrals, and educational programs. By stressing the building of human capital, social workers and other helping professionals reinforce the capabilities approach, which involves immigrants in programs that are designed to enhance their capabilities. One approach that has been used in immigrant communities is to encourage the development of micro-enterprise programs and asset-building interventions (Robles, 2005). Fronting resources for individuals and small groups from immigrant communities to develop small businesses can provide the first step in building economic autonomy.

Social workers and other helping professionals engaged in mezzo practice can also work to raise the public's awareness regarding immigrant issues through community education. Through social networking, education campaigns, and public service announcements, professionals can educate people and raise public awareness about the economic and cultural benefits of immigration.

Immigration can be linked to economic development, both for individuals and communities. Increasing the well-being and success of immigrants can result in the revitalization of communities. This has been the historical path for immigrants' acclimation and economic success in the United States for generations.

Macro Interventions

The well-being of immigrants, their families, and communities is affected by the larger social and political context of the United States. As seen during the recent economic recession, the social environment can have a severe effect upon immigrants. Unemployment has increased over the last several years in the United States, as with other destination countries (United Nations Development Program, 2009). When natives of the United States face economic challenges and insecurity, some look for others to blame for their difficulties and often focus that blame on immigrants. Throughout history, economic difficulties in the United States have been tied to anti-immigrant sentiment and anti-immigrant policies. As a contemporary example, the 2008 Troubled Asset Relief Program restricts companies receiving stimulus money from hiring foreign workers (Kalita, 2009). Despite the prevalence of negative stereotypes, there are many positive effects of immigration, such as boosting economic development and reducing crime (Becerra et al., 2012; United Nations Development Program, 2009). Historically, immigrants have contributed much to the United States, adding to rich cultural traditions as well as to the American ideal of a pluralistic, multicultural society that honors and respects diversity.

Many interventions work to effect change on the macro level of society. Community organizing is based on the idea that when ordinary people join together, they can accomplish positive change in their communities and improve the quality of their lives. The work of community organizing involves identifying local leaders, choosing and framing an issue, developing strategies, and engaging in tactics, in addition to widespread community outreach and recruitment. Because immigrants tend to live with and near other immigrants, community organizing is particularly well suited when working with immigrants.

The concepts of empowerment and consciousness raising, influenced by the work of Paolo Freire (1990), are central to macro work with communities. Freire stressed "conscientization" or critical consciousness, which is developed through efforts at consciousness raising. Consciousness raising is the process of those who have been affected by oppression discovering the nature of their oppression and their ability to influence and improve their lives. Organizers can include consciousness raising when working with immigrant communities. Another relevant concept is social capital, which builds on the development of human capital, as discussed in the section on mezzo practice. Social capital refers to the strength of relationships and networks within communities. Working with social service agencies, as well as indigenous groups such as churches and informal groups can help build social capital and mobilize community members to access societal resources.

Macro social work practice also includes political action. Social workers and other helping professionals engaged in macro practice can advocate for human and socially just immigration reform. Professionals can organize people and communities to take action by introducing and influencing legislation, as well as lobby political leaders and legislators who are responsible for passing laws. Focusing on lobbying and influencing the policy process is a key part of social work intervention. Focusing on supporting public leaders who favor immigration reform and working to change leaders who do not is known as electoral advocacy. Immigrant populations and their children represent future voters and hence a growing political force in the United States, especially among Latinos. Electoral advocacy can take the form of registering new voters and supporting participation in elections and the democratic process.

Some concrete strategies for social workers and helping professionals on the macro level may include working with communities with refugee and immigrant populations to facilitate educational forums to discuss the fears and issues surrounding the new refugee and immigrant populations. Inviting community members, local politicians, and the media to these education forums can help dispel fears or misunderstandings about refugee and immigrant populations. Social workers and helping professionals can hold similar educational forums to dispel the misunderstandings and misinformation about the economic impact of undocumented immigrants and demonstrate the overall positive impact that undocumented immigrants have on the U.S. economy. Social work agencies providing services to refugee and immigrant communities can create coalitions with other social service and health organizations that lobby politicians and advocate for policy change, which is more effective in addressing the needs of immgrants and refugees, thereby helping them transition to the United States.

Concluding Comments

The vast majority of Americans can trace their ancestry to another country of origin. The Statue of Liberty, built to be the first sight for immigrants who arrived at U.S. shores, symbolized the nation's commitment to freedom for all. The words engraved on the base of the Statue of Liberty were written to welcome those who are searching for a better life:

Give me your tired, your poor,
Your huddled masses yearning to breathe free,
The wretched refuse of your teeming shore.
Send these, the homeless, tempest-tost to me,
I lift my lamp beside the golden door! (Lazarus, 1888)

The quest for a better economic, social, and political life for immigrants continues today, and the United States still symbolizes those hopes and dreams. However, the experience of being an immigrant is often linked to poverty, which contributes to a precarious living situation. While this has been the case for many immigrant groups historically, it is particularly true today as opportunities and attitudes toward immigrants are closely linked to race and country of origin. As has been the case throughout history, immigrants will continue to arrive. Our professional commitment to social and economic justice means that social workers and other helping professionals will be involved in supporting immigrants on their journey.

Case Studies

What is it like to be an immigrant to the United States today?

Micro Level—The Osman Family

Abdi Osman, the first-born child in his family, has been in the United States for fifteen years. He came when he was a 25-year-old man with his younger sisters and parents as refugees fleeing civil war in Somalia, Africa. One of his brothers, also in his twenties, lost his life while fighting in the civil war. Two of Abdi's brothers and all of their extended family remained in Somalia. While still living in Somalia, Abdi had a chance to study medicine in Turkey, and trained to be a doctor. He had returned to Somalia and worked, but the civil war made that impossible. He and his family were able to come to the United States as refugees—a protected group due to the strife in their homeland. While the United States was a haven from the violence at home, it was not always the Osman family's plan to leave Somalia. In fact, they had a small successful grocery in the capital city of Mogadishu, and were able to afford to send their son Abdi to school.

Upon arrival in the United States, Abdi was able to find employment in a nursing home, initially at the lowest caregiver level, cleaning rooms and taking the least desirable hours at night and on the weekends. As his English improved, his medical knowledge emerged, and over several years, he rose to the position of a medical technician. While this role paid more than his starting position and gave him some seniority to work better hours, it was far below what his medical training had prepared him for. He was still struggling financially as his salary went toward the household expenses. During his off hours, he studied English so he could take the medical exams that would place him for consideration of transferring his medical degrees. So far he had twice failed the parts of the exams that required the most reading and comprehension of English. Abdi feared that he would never be able to practice medicine as he had in Somalia, because coming to the United States as an adult made learning English much more difficult for him. He took great pride in the progress of his younger sisters who were able to learn English and attend college, but worried that his own hopes of practicing medicine in the United States would never come to be. As the oldest son, he was expected to financially support his family.

Questions

1. How might you as a helping professional be of assistance to Abdi?

2. When working with this family, what would you want to know in order to be culturally competent?

3. What resources are available to the Osman family and others like them to transition to living in the United States?

4. What mental health issues can you imagine might need attention for refugees such as Abdi and his family?

5. Do you think resources for refugees such as the Osman family differ from resources for other immigrants to the United States? Why?

Mezzo Level—The Community of Center Pointe

Center Pointe is a former southern and eastern European immigrant community located in an urban area in the western United States. It is located in a relatively densely populated city of 5,500 residents per square mile. The poverty rate is 62 percent with an unemployment rate of 8.7 percent. The community is 83 percent Latino and 17 percent Southeast Asian; 68 percent are foreign-born. Most of the Latino population is of Mexican descent, with the remainder from a variety of

Central American countries. Almost half of the community is estimated to be undocumented residents, and the majority of Latino adult residents are monolingual Spanish speakers. Forty-two percent of the residents are under the age of twenty-five. With respect to insurance coverage, more than half of the adults ages 18 to 65 have no health insurance. The nearest hospital is over ten miles away, and the one urgent care center in the area is often overcrowded with long waiting times. There are several social service agencies in the area with a history of working with Latino immigrants and have some bilingual staff, but undocumented immigrants do not qualify for services at these agencies. Most of the residents identify as Catholic, but there are several other religious services offered in the community, which are well attended weekly.

The majority of the residents have low levels of education. Two-thirds of the adults age twenty-five and older have not graduated from high school and almost half had less than a ninth-grade education. The high-density dwellings and low property values of the area mean that the public schools (2 elementary schools, 1 middle school, and 1 high school) are not funded well enough to meet the needs of the students (89 percent qualify for free and reduced lunch and 70 percent are classified as English language learners). The teachers are primarily white and do not speak Spanish. Bilingual staff or students are often used to interpret communication between school staff and monolingual Spanish-speaking parents. Although interpreters are provided by the district for school board and individual school meetings, most monolingual Spanish-speaking parents do not attend.

There are no major chain grocery stores in the area, but there is one grocery store that caters to the Asian residents, and three that are targeted to Latinos. Most businesses, including the ones targeted to Asian residents, have Spanish-speaking employees. Businesses, including apartment housing, rely on the patronage of all the residents, including undocumented immigrants in the community, and the city and state governments also rely on the revenue generated by sales tax paid by these residents.

Recently a series of new laws were passed aimed at deterring undocumented immigration to the state. The first law mandates that all schools and health and social service providers report undocumented immigrants to authorities. The second law requires local police officers to verify the documentation status of individuals they suspect of being involved in criminal activity or of being undocumented.

Questions

1. How do you think these new laws would impact Center Pointe?

2. If you worked as a helping professional in a social service agency in Center Pointe, what would you do to address the new laws designed to restrict services to undocumented immigrants?

3. What issues do you think need to be addressed between the different immigrant groups living in Center Pointe?

4. What might be available resources for the schools and hospitals in Center Pointe?

5. What are the major community issues affecting Center Pointe? What community strengths could you use to work with the residents in order to address some of the issues affecting the community?

Macro Level—The Impact of Anti-Immigrant Legislation

Daniel, Martha, and Francisco work, cleaning the public library during the night while the building is closed to the public. One night police officers and a SWAT team entered the building and several individuals were arrested as it was suspected that they were using forged identifications. This workplace raid was prompted by passage of the Legal Arizona Workers Act (LAWA, 2007) in the state of Arizona. LAWA requires all employers in the state to use the E-Verify system to check the immigration status of new employees. Violators risk having their business licenses revoked with multiple infractions. To date this policy has been implemented through more than thirty workplace raids.

Daniel had been employed at the public library for over ten years. He and his wife have a junior in high school and two children at a state university. They are very proud of their children as they are the first in their family to go to college and are one step closer to obtaining the American dream. Martha has two daughters, four and five years old. She is married but her undocumented husband was recently deported to Mexico. These last few months have been very difficult on her and the children. Martha is now the sole provider for her children and it is very difficult for her daughters to understand why their father is no longer with them. Francisco has three U.S.-born children ages one, three, and five, although he was not born in the United States. He works the night shift at the public library and has a part-time job during the day as he is the sole provider for his family. Francisco, without legal documents, worries what will happen to his family if he is deported. Will his wife and children have enough money to keep up with the bills and buy food while he is detained? Will they need to follow him to Mexico if he is deported?

Daniel and Martha's concerns are different as they are a permanent resident and U.S. citizen, respectively. After insisting that their paper work was authentic, they were still arrested. Daniel migrated to the United States in his late teens and became a permanent resident through the federal government's amnesty program of 1986. Martha was born in the United States but her family lived in Mexico most of her life. She moved to the United States in her early twenties and speaks very little English. Daniel and Martha wonder why this is happening to them when all they want to do is work to provide for their families. In the ride to the police department they wonder what challenges their children will face when assumptions are made about their immigration status based on the color of their skin, particularly as states are passing laws and implementing policies that further restrict undocumented immigrants from receiving benefits guaranteed to others. Martha and Daniel will eventually be released but what will happen to Francisco and his family?

Questions

1. What can social workers and helping professionals do to change policies surrounding immigration?

2. As described, is the law in Arizona discriminatory? If so, how?

3. How can social workers or other helping professionals work with police and other law enforcement agencies to reduce the negative impact that immigration enforcement strategies have on families?

4. What other macro-level interventions do you think would be appropriate to address issues caused by immigration enforcement?

5. Are there ethical dilemmas that arise among the social work mission and NASW Code of Ethics when assisting undocumented immigrants?

Internet Resources

The Advocates for Human Rights: http://www.theadvocatesforhumanrights.org

A nonprofit organization dedicated to research, education, and advocacy for human rights movements, including immigrant rights.

American Civil Liberties Union: http://www.aclu.org/

A non-governmental organization engaged in legal advocacy to protect individual rights and liberty.

American Immigration Council: http://www.americanimmigrationcouncil.org

A nonprofit organization working to promote American's diversity and recognition of immigrants through education and policy reform.

American Immigration Lawyers Association: http://www.aila.org

The professional bar association for immigration lawyers provides legal information and resources for legislation, cases, and advocacy on behalf of immigration reform.

Amnesty International USA: http://www.amnestyusa.org

An international nonprofit working to expose and prevent human rights abuses, including refugee and migrant rights.

Center for Immigration Studies: http://www.cis.org

A nonprofit research organization working to provide information about the consequences of immigration for policymakers, researchers, and media, advocating for reducing immigration while supporting those who are admitted.

Global Campaign for Ratification of the Convention on Rights of Migrants: http://www.migrantsrights.org/

Contains information on the campaign to have the International Convention on the Protection of the Rights of All Migrant Workers and Members of Their Families ratified.

Immigration Policy Center: http://www.immigrationpolicy.org

This is the research and policy arm of the American Immigration Council that conducts research for policymakers, the media, and the public.

Leadership Conference on Civil and Human Rights: http://www.civilrights.org

A coalition of civil and human rights organizations focusing on outreach and legislative advocacy.

Migration Policy Institute: http://www.migrationpolicy.org/

A nonprofit think tank studying all aspects of the movement of people around the globe.

Further Readings

Bacon, D. (2008). *Illegal people: How globalization creates migration and criminalizes immigrants.* Boston: Beacon Press.

Brotherton, D. C., & Kretsedemas, P. (eds.) (2008). *Keeping out the other: A critical introduction to immigration enforcement today.* New York: Columbia University Press.

Carens, J. H. (2010). *Immigrants and the right to stay.* Cambridge, MA: MIT Press.

Daniels, R. (2002). *Coming to America: A history of immigration and ethnicity in American life* (2nd ed.). New York: HarperCollins Publisher.

Ganster, P., & Lorey, D. E. (2007). *The U.S.-Mexican border into the twenty-first century.* Lanham, MD: Rowman & Littlefield Publishing.

Johnson, K. R. (2009). *Opening the floodgates: Why America needs to rethink its borders and immigration laws.* New York: NYU Press.

Takati, R. (2008). *A different mirror: A history of multicultural America.* (Rev. ed.). New York: Back Bay Books, Little, Brown and Company.

References

Aizenman, N. C. (2008, May 19–25). Newcomers to the U.S. assimilate rapidly. *Washington Post National Weekly Edition, 25*(31), 33–34.

Andreas, P. (2000). *Border games: Policing the U.S.-Mexico divide.* Ithaca, NY: Cornell University Press.

Androff, D., Ayon, C., Becerra, D., Gurrola, M., Salas, L., Krysik, J., . . . Segal, E. (2011). U.S. immigration policy and immigrant children's well-being: The impact of policy shifts. *Journal of Sociology & Social Welfare, 38*(1), 77–98.

Androff, D., & Tavassoli, K. (2012). Deaths in the desert: The human rights crisis on the U.S.-Mexico border. *Social Work, 57*(2), 165–173.

Ayón, C. (2009). Shorter time-lines, yet higher hurdles: Mexican families' access to child welfare mandated services. *Children and Youth Services Review, 31,* 609–616.

Bacon, D. (2008). *Illegal people: How globalization creates migration and criminalizes immigrants.* Boston: Beacon Press.

Baily, S. L. (1983). The adjustment of Italian immigrants in Buenos Aires and New York, 1870–1914. *American Historical Review, 88*(2), 281–305.

Batalova, J., & Mittelstadt, M. (2012). *Relief from deportation: Demographic profile of the DREAMers potentially eligible under the deferred action policy.* Migration Policy Institute.

Becerra, D. (2012). Perceptions of educational barriers impacting the academic achievement of Latino K–12 students. *Children & Schools, 43*(3), 167–177.

Becerra, D., Androff, D., Ayón, C., & Castillo, J. (2012). Fear vs. facts: The economic impact of undocumented immigrants in the U.S. *Journal of Sociology & Social Welfare, 39*(4), 111–134.

Becerra, D., Gurrola, M., Ayón, C., Androff, D., Krysik, J., Gerdes, K., . . . Segal, E. (2010). Poverty and other factors affecting migration intentions among adolescents in Mexico. *Journal of Poverty, 14*(1), 1–16.

Bernard, W. S. (1998). Immigration: History of U.S. policy. In *The immigration reader: America in a multidisciplinary perspective,* ed. D. Jacobson (pp. 48–71). New York: Wiley.

Berry, J. W. (2007). Acculturation strategies and adaptation. In *Immigrant families in contemporary society,* ed. J. E. Lansford (pp. 69–82). New York: Guilford Press.

Bohon, S. A., Macpherson, H., & Atiles, J. H. (2005). Educational barriers for new Latinos in Georgia. *Journal of Latinos and Education, 4*(1), 43–58.

Bridges, A. J., de Arellano, M. A., Rheingold, A. A., Kmett Danielson, C., & Silcott, L. (2010). Trauma exposure, mental health, and service utilization rates among immigrant and United States-born Hispanic youth: Results from the Hispanic Family Study. *Psychological Trauma: Theory, Research, Practice, & Policy, 2*(1), 40–48.

Bui, H. N. (2003). Help-seeking behavior among abused immigrant women: A case of Vietnamese American women. *Violence against Women, 2,* 207–239.

Calavita, K. (1996). The new politics of immigration: "Balanced budget conservatism" and the symbolism of Proposition 187. *Social Problems, 43*(3), 284–305.

Camarota, S. (2004). *The high cost of cheap labor: Illegal immigration and the federal budget* Washington, DC: Center for Immigration Studies.

Capps, R., Fix, M., Murray, J., Ost, J., Passel, J. S., & Herwantoro, S. (2005). *The new demography of America's schools: Immigration and the No Child Left Behind Act.* Washington, DC: Urban Institute.

Capps, R., Fix, M., Ost, J., Reardon-Anderson, J., & Passel, J. S. (2004). *The health and well-being of young children of immigrants.* Washington, DC: Urban Institute.

Carothers Graham, L. (2008). Relief for battered immigrants under the Violence Against Women Act. *Delaware Law Review,* 10 Del. L. Rev. 263, 1–13.

Cerruti, M., & Massey, D. (2004). Trends in Mexican migration to the United States, 1965 to 1995. In *Crossing the border: Research from the Mexican migration project,* ed. J. Durand & D. Massey (pp. 17–44). New York: Russell Sage Foundation.

Chang, G. (2000). *Disposable domestics: Immigrant women workers in the global economy.* Cambridge, MA: South End Press.

Chapman, J., & Bernstein, J. (2003). Immigration and poverty: How are they linked? *Monthly Labor Review,* April, 10–15.

Chaudry, A., Capps, R., Pedroza, J. M., Castañeda, R. M., Santos, R., & Scott, M. M. (2010). *Facing our future: Children in the aftermath of immigration enforcement.* Urban Institute. Retrieved from http://www.urban.org/UploadedPDF/412020_FacingOurFuture_final.pdf.

Civil Rights Act of 1964. (1964). Pub. L. 88–352, 78 Stat. 241.

Cleaveland, C. (2010). "We are not criminals": Social work advocacy and unauthorized migrants. *Social Work, 55*(1), 74–81.

Collins, P. H. (2004). Comments on Hekman's "Truth and method: Feminist standpoint theory revisited": Where's the power? In *The feminist standpoint theory reader: Intellectual and political controversies,* ed. S. Harding (pp. 247–254). New York: Routledge.

Cooper, L. A., Hill, M. N., & Powe, N. R. (2002). Designing and evaluating interventions to eliminate racial and ethnic disparities in health care. *Journal of General Internal Medicine, 17,* 477–486.

Cutler, D. M., Glaeser, E. L., & Vigdor, J. L. (2008). When are ghettos bad? Lessons from immigrant segregation in the United States. *Journal of Urban Economics, 63,* 759–774.

Daniels, R. (1998). What is an American? Ethnicity, race, the constitution and the immigrant in early American history. In *The immigration reader: America in a multidisciplinary perspective,* ed. D. Jacobson (pp. 29–47). New York: Wiley.

Day, P. (2008). *A new history of social welfare.* Boston: Pearson Education.

De Genova, N. (2005). *Working the boundaries. Race, space, and "illegality" in Mexican Chicago.* Durham, NC: Duke University Press.

Delgado, M. (1998). *Social services in Latino communities: Research and strategies.* Binghamton, NY: Haworth Press.

DeNavas-Walt, C., Proctor, B. D., & Smith, J. C. (2010). *Income, poverty and health insurance coverage in the United States: 2009.* P60-238. Washington, DC: U.S. Census Bureau.

Dube, A. (2003). *San Francisco restaurant industry analysis.* Berkeley: Center for Labor Research and Education, University of California.

Dye, J. L. (2010). *Fertility of American women: 2008.* U.S. Department of Commerce, Economics and Statistic Administration. U.S. Census Bureau.

Eltis, D. (1983). Free and coerced transatlantic migrations: Some comparisons. *Historical Review, 88*(2), 251–280.

Flores, G. (2005) The impact of medical interpreter services on the quality of health care: A systematic review. *Medical Care Research and Review, 62*(3), 255–299.

Fogleman, A. S. (1998). From slave, convicts, and servants to free passengers: The transformation of immigration in the era of the American Revolution. *Journal of American History, 85*(1), 43–76.

Freeman, L. (2002). Does spatial assimilation work for black immigrants in the US? *Urban Studies, 39*(11), 1983–2003.

Freire, P. (1990). *Pedagogy of the oppressed.* New York: Continuum Publishing.

Friedman, J. Y., Anstrom, K. J., Weinfurt, K. P., McIntosh, M., Bosworth, H. B., Oddone, E. Z., . . . Schulman, K. A. (2005). Perceived racial/ethnic bias in health care in Durham County, North Carolina: A comparison of community and national samples. *North Carolina Medical Journal, 66*(4), 267–275.

Gibson, C., & Jung, K. (2006). *Historical census statistics on the foreign-born population of the United States: 1850 to 2000.* Working Paper No. 81. Washington, DC: U.S. Census Bureau.

Gomez, M. J., Fassinger, R. E., Prosser, J., Cooke, K., Mejia, B., & Luna, J. (2001). Voces abriendo caminos (Voices forging paths): A qualitative study of the career development of notable Latinas. *Journal of Counseling Psychology, 48,* 286–300.

Gonzales, F. (2008). *Fact sheet: Hispanic women in the United States, 2007.* Pew Hispanic Center.

González, D. (2008, May 8). Migrant crackdowns have churches on edge. *Arizona Republic,* A1, A10.

Gonzalez-Lopez, G. (2004). Fathering Latina sexualities: Mexican men and the virginity of their daughters. *Journal of Marriage and Family, 66,* 1118–1130.

Gordon, M. M. (1964). *Assimilation in American life.* New York: Oxford University Press.

Graham, C. L. (2008). Relief for battered immigrants under the Violence Against Women Act. *Delaware Law Review,* 10 Del. L. Rev. 263, 1–13.

Hanson, G. H. (2007). *The economic logic of illegal immigration.* Council on Foreign Relations.

Haveman, R., & Sneeding, T. (2006). The role of higher education in social mobility. *The Future of Children, 16*(2), 125–150.

Henderson, R. (2012). *Employment outlook 2010–2020: Industry employment and the output projections to 2020.* Washington, DC: Bureau of Labor Statistics, United States Department of Labor.

Hensley, J. J., & Kiefer, M. (2009a, November 19). Employer sanctions law yields first case. *Arizona Republic,* A1, A13.

Hensley, J. J., & Kiefer, M. (2009b, December 18). First firm punished under Arizona hiring law. *Arizona Republic,* B1, B8.

Hewett, H. (2009). Mothering across borders: Narratives of immigrant mothers in the United States. *Women's Studies Quarterly, 37,* 121–139.

Hirsch, J. S. (1999). En el norte la mujer manda: Gender, generation, and geography in a Mexican transnational community. *American Behavioral Scientist, 42,* 1332–1349.

Hirschman, C. (1996). Studying immigrant adaptation from the 1990 population census: From generational comparisons to the process of "becoming American." In *The new second generation,* ed. A. Portes (pp. 54–81). New York: Russell Sage Foundation.

Hondagneu-Sotelo, P. (2000). Feminism and migration. *Annals of the American Academy of Political and Social Science, 571,* 107–120.

Hoynes, H., Page, M., & Stevens, A. (2005). *Poverty in America: Trends and explanations.* Working Paper 11681. Cambridge, MA: National Bureau of Economic Research.

Huang, B., Appel, H., & Ai, A. L. (2011). The effects of discrimination and acculturation to service seeking satisfaction for Latina and Asian American women: Implications for mental health professions. *Social Work in Public Health, 26*(1), 46–59.

Huang, K., & Carrasquillo, O. (2008). The role of citizenship, employment, and socioeconomic characteristics in health insurance coverage among Asian subgroups in the United States. *Medical Care, 46*(10), 1093–1098.

Humes, K., Jones, N., & Ramirez, R. (2011). *Overview of race and Hispanic origin: 2010. Census Briefs.* U.S. Department of Commerce, Economics and Statistics Administration. U.S. Census Bureau. Retrieved from http://www.census.gov/prod/cen2010/briefs/c2010br-02.pdf.

Immigration Act of 1990. (1990). Pub. L. No. 101–649, 104 Stat. 4978.

Immigration and Nationality Act of 1965. (1965). Pub. L. No. 89-236, 79 Stat. 911.

Immigration Omnibus. (2011). S.B. 1611, A.R.S. § 1-501, 1-502. Retrieved from http://www.azleg.gov/legtext/50leg/1r/bills/sb1611p.pdf.

Immigration Policy Center. (2010). *Immigrant women in the United States: A portrait of demographic diversity.* American Immigration Council. Retrieved from http://www.immigrationpolicy.org/just-facts/immigrant-women-united-states-portrait-demographic-diversity.

International Labour Organization. (2006). *ILO multilateral framework on labour migration: Non-binding principles and guidelines for a rights-based approach to labour migration.* Geneva: International Labour Organization.

Johnson, L. (2003). Multicultural policy as social activism: Redefining who "counts" in multicultural education. *Race Ethnicity and Education, 6*(2), 107–121.

Kalita, M. (2009). U.S. deters hiring of foreigners as joblessness grows. *Wall Street Journal,* March 27.

Keller, S. C., Silbergerg, M., Hartmann, K. E., & Michener, J. L. (2010). Perceived discrimination and use of health care services in a North Carolina population of Latino immigrants. *Hispanic Health Care International, 8*(1), 4–13.

Kent, M. M. (2007). Immigration and America's black population. *Population Bulletin, 62*(4), 1–18.

Kerper Mora, J. (2002). Caught in a policy web: The impact of education reform on Latino education. *Journal of Latinos and Education, 1*(1), 29–44.

Kerr, W. R., & Lincoln, W. F. (2010). The supply side of innovation: H-1B visa reforms and U.S. ethnic invention. *Journal of Labor Economics, 28*(3), 473–508.

Kersey, M., Geppert, J., & Cutts, D. B. (2006). Hunger in young children of Mexican immigrant families. *Public Health Nutrition, 10*(4), 390–395.

Kim, I. J., Lau, A. S., & Chang, D. F. (2007). Family violence among Asian Americans. In *Handbook of Asian American psychology*, ed. F. Leong, A. G. Inman, A. Ebreo, L. Yang, L. M. Kinoshita, & M. Fu (pp. 363–378). Thousand Oaks, CA: Sage.

Kim, J. Y., & Sung, K. (2000). Conjugal violence in Korean American families: A residue of the cultural tradition. *Journal of Family Violence, 15*, 331–345.

Ku, L., & Flores, G. (2005). Pay now or pay later: Providing interpreter services in health care. *Health Affairs, 24*(2), 435–444.

Ku, L., & Matani, S. (2001). Left out: Immigrants' access to health care and insurance. *Health Affairs, 20*(1), 247–256.

Kullgren, J. T. (2003). Restrictions on undocumented immigrants' access to health services: The public health implications of welfare reform. *American Journal of Public Health, 93*(10), 1630–1633.

Kwong, P. (1998). *Forbidden workers: Illegal Chinese immigrants and American labor.* New York: New Press.

Lazarín, M. (2006). *Improving assessment and accountability for English language learners in the No Child Left Behind Act.* Washington, DC: National Council of La Raza.

Lazarus, E. (1888). *The poems of Emma Lazarus, Volume 1: The new colossus,* p. 202. Boston: Houghton, Mifflin and Co. Also available at http://www.libertystatepark.com/emma.htm.

Lee, Y. S., & Hadeed, L. (2009). Intimate partner violence among Asian immigrant communities: Health/mental health consequences, health seeking behaviors, and service utilization. *Trauma Violence Abuse, 10*(2), 143–170.

Legal Arizona Workers Act. (2007). Ariz. Rev. Stat. § 23-2114.

Lieberson, S. (1980). *A piece of the pie: Blacks and white immigrants since 1880.* Berkeley: University of California Press.

Little Italy. (2011). Retrieved from http://www.nyc.com/visitor_guide/little_italy.75857/editorial_review.aspx.

Loue, S., Faust, M., & Bunce, A. (2000). The effects of immigration and welfare reform legislation on immigrants' access to health care, Cuyahoga, and Lorain Counties. *Journal of Immigrant Health, 2*(1), 23–30.

Marshall, R. (2009). *Immigration for a shared prosperity.* Washington, DC: Economic Policy Institute.

Marsiglia, F. F., & Kulis, S. (2009). *Diversity, oppression, and change.* Chicago, IL: Lyceum Books, Inc.

Martin, P. (2003). *Mexico–US Migration.* Washington, DC: Institute for International Economics.

Martin, S. (2007). *Women, migration, and development.* Institute for the Study of International Migration, Walsh School of Foreign Service, Georgetown University. Retrieved from http://www.biblioteca.cij.gob.mx/Archivos/Materiales_de_consulta/Migracion/Articulos/ingles9.pdf.

Massey, D. S. (1995). The new immigration and ethnicity in the United States. *Population and Development Review, 21*(3), 631–652.

Massey, D. S., Durand, J., & Malone, N. J. (2003). *Beyond smoke and mirrors: Mexican immigration in an era of economic integration.* New York: Russell Sage Foundation.

McLaughlin, H. J., Liljestrom, A., Lim, J. H., & Meyers, D. (2002). LEARN: A community study about Latino immigrants and education. *Education and Urban Society, 34*(2), 212–232.

Michelson, M. R., & Pallares, A. (2001). The politicization of Chicago Mexican Americans: Naturalization, the vote, and perceptions of discrimination. *Aztlán, 26*(2), 63–86.

Migration Policy Institute. (2013). *2011 American community survey and census data on the foreign born by state.* Retrieved from http://www.migrationinformation.org/datahub/acscensus.cfm#.

National Association of Social Workers. (2006). *Immigration policy toolkit.* Retrieved from http://www.naswdc.org/diversity/ImmigrationToolkit.pdf.

National Association of Social Workers. (2008). *Code of ethics.* Retrieved from http://www.naswdc.org/pubs/code/code.asp.

National Clearinghouse for English Language Acquisition and Language Instruction Educational Programs. (2011). *What language do English learners speak?* Washington, DC. Retrieved from http://www.ncela.gwu.edu/files/uploads/NCELAFactsheets/EL_Languages_2011.pdf.

National Council of La Raza. (2008). *Five facts about undocumented workers in the U.S.* Retrieved from http://www.nclr.org/index.php/publications/five_facts_about_undocumented_workers_in_the_united_states/.

Ngo, B., & Lee, S. J. (2007). Complicating the image of model minority success: A review of Southeast Asian American education. *Review of Educational Research, 77*(4), 415–453.

Oropesa, R. S., & Landale, N. S. (1997). Immigrant legacies: Ethnicity, generation and children's familial and economic lives. *Social Science Quarterly, 78*(2), 399–416.

Orszag, P. R. (2008). *Congressional Budget Office letter.* Retrieved from http://www.cbo.gov/ftpdocs/91xx/doc9100/hr4088ltr.pdf.

Ortiz, L., Arizmendi, L., & Cornelius, L. J. (2006). Access to health care among Latinos of Mexican descent in colonias in two Texas counties. *Journal of Rural Health, 20*(3), 246–252.

Pagnini, D. L., & Morgan, S. P. (1990). Intermarriage and social distance among U.S. immigrants at the turn of the century. *American Journal of Sociology, 96*(2), 405–432.

Palloni, A., Massey, D. S., Ceballos, M., Espinosa, K., & Spittel, M. (2001). Social capital and international migration: A test using information on family networks. *American Journal of Sociology, 106*, 1262–1298.

Passel, J. S., & Cohn, D. (2009). *A portrait of unauthorized immigrants in the United States.* Washington, DC: Pew Hispanic Center.

Pearce, S. (2006). *Immigrant women in the United States: A demographic portrait.* Immigration Policy Center, American Immigration Law Foundation.

Pedone, C. (2006). Changes in education and family life in current Ecuadorian migration: A transatlantic perspective. *Athenea Digital, 10*, 154–171.

Peifer, K. L., Hu, T., & Vega, W. A. (2000). Help seeking by persons of Mexican origin with functional impairments. *Psychiatric Services, 51*, 1293–1298.

Perez, V. H., Fang, H., Inkelas, M., Kuo, A. A., & Ortega, A. N. (2009). Access to and utilization of Elath care by subgroups of Latino children. *Medical Care, 47*, 695–699.

Personal Responsibility and Work Opportunity Reconciliation Act of 1996. (1997). U.S. Pub. L. 104–193.

Pessar, P. (1999). The role of gender, households, and social networks in the migration process: A review and appraisal. In *The handbook of international migration,* ed. C. Hirschman, P. Kasinitz, & J. DeWind (pp. 53–70). New York: Russell Sage Foundation.

Pew Hispanic Center. (2004). *Latino youth and the pathway to college.* Washington, DC: Author.

Pew Hispanic Center. (2010). *Hispanics and Arizona's new immigration law.* Washington, DC: Author.

Pew Research Center. (2011). *Public favors tougher border controls and path to citizenship.* Washington, DC: Author.

Portes, A., & Rumbaut, R. (2001). *Legacies: The story of the immigrant second generation.* Berkeley, CA: University of California Press.

Refugee Act of 1980. (1980). Pub. L. No. 96-212, 94 Stat. 102.

Ricourt, M., & Danta, R. (2003). *Hispanas de Queens: Latino panethnicity in a New York city neighborhood.* Ithaca, NY: Cornell University Press.

Robles, B. J. (2005). *Wealth building in the borderlands: Linking tax refunds to asset building.* Tempe, AZ: Arizona State University.

Rodriguez, R. L., Elliot, M. N., Vestal, K. D., Suttorp, M., & Schuster, M. A. (2008). Determinants of health insurance status for children of Latino immigrant and other US farm workers. *Archives of Pediatrics and Adolescent Medicine, 162*(12), 1175–1118.

Romero, M. (2002). *Maid in the U.S.A. tenth anniversary edition with new introduction and afterword by Dorothy Smith.* New York: Routledge, Taylor & Francis Group.

Romero, M. (2011). Constructing Mexican immigrant women as a threat to American families. *International Journal of Sociology of the Family, 37*, 49–68.

Rumbaut, R. G., & Komaie, G. (2010). Immigration and adult transitions. *The Future of Children, 20*(1), 43–66.

Saenz, R. (2010). *Latinos in the United States 2010: Population bulletin update.* Retrieved from http://www.prb.org/pdf10/latinos-update2010.pdf.

Sandefur, G. D. (1998). Race, ethnicity, families, and education. In *Resiliency in Native American and immigrant families,* ed. H. I. McCubbin & E. A. Thompson. *Resiliency in families series* (vol. 2, pp. 49–70). Thousand Oaks, CA: Sage.

Schrag, P. (2010). *Not fit for our society: Nativism in America.* Berkeley, CA: University of California Press.

Segal, E. (2013). *Social welfare policy and social programs: A values perspective* (3rd ed.). Belmont, CA: Brooks/Cole.

Sekulow, J. A., & Tedesco, J. (2005). The story behind *Vidal v. Girard's* executors: Joseph Story, the Philadelphia Bible Riots, and religious liberty. *Pepperdine Law Review, 32*, 605–646.

Shabaya, J. (2006). English language acquisition and some pedagogical issues affecting the adaptation of African immigrant children. In *The New African Diaspora in North America,* ed. K. Konadu-Agyemang, B. K. Takyi, & J. A. Arthur (pp. 257–272). New York: Lexington Books.

Skinner, C. (2011). *SNAP take-up among immigrant families with children.* National Center for Children in Poverty. Retrieved from http://www.nccp.org/publications/pdf/text_1002.pdf.

Slattery, I. (2004). *Latino groups poised to challenge anti-immigrant Proposition 200.* The Leadership Conference on Civil and Human Rights/The Leadership Conference Education Fund. Retrieved from http://www.civilrights.org/immigration/arizona/latino-groups-poised-to-challenge-anti-immigrant-proposition-200.html.

Smedley, B. D., Stith, A. Y., & Nelson, A. R., eds. (2003). *Unequal treatment: Confronting racial and ethnic disparities in health care.* Washington, DC: National Academies Press.

Snowden, L. R., & Yamada, A. M. (2005). Cultural differences in access to care. *Annual Review of Clinical Psychology, 1,* 143–166.

Specht, H., & Courtney, M. (1994). *Unfaithful angels: How social work has abandoned its mission.* New York: The Free Press.

Stoesz, D., Karger, H. J., & Carrilio, T. (2010). *A dream deferred: How social work education lost its way and what can be done.* New Brunswick, NJ: Transaction Publishers.

Strayhorn, C. (2006). *Undocumented immigrants in Texas: A financial analysis of the impact to the state budget and economy.* Office of the Comptroller, Texas. Retrieved from http://www.window.state.tx.us/specialrpt/undocumented/.

Suleiman, L. P. (2003) Beyond cultural competence: Language access and Latino civil rights. *Child Welfare, 82*(2), 185–200.

Takati, R. (1993). *A different mirror: A history of multicultural America.* Boston, MA: Little, Brown.

Tienda, M., & Haskins, R. (2011). Immigrant children: Introducing the issue. *The Future of Children, 21*(1), 3–18.

Tuiran, R. (1993). Familia: Estructura familiar: Continuidad y cambio. *Demos, 7,* 20–22.

United Nations. (1948). *Universal declaration of human rights.* Retrieved from http://www.un.org/en/documents/udhr/index.shtml.

United Nations. (1990). *International convention on the protection of the rights of all migrant workers and members of their families.* Retrieved from http://www.unesco.org/most/lnlaw21.htm.

United Nations. (2008). *International migrant stock: The 2008 revision.* Retrieved from http://esa.un.org/migration/.

United Nations Development Program. (2009). *Human development report 2009: Overcoming barriers: Human mobility and development.* New York: United Nations Development Program. Retrieved from http://hdr.undp.org/en/media/HDR_2009_EN_Complete.pdf.

U.S. Census Bureau. (2012). *The foreign-born population in the United States: 2010.* Washington, DC: U.S. Department of Commerce.

U.S. Chamber of Commerce. (n.d.). *Immigration myths and the facts: Behind the fallacies.* Washington, DC: Labor, Immigration, and Employee Benefits Division, U.S. Chamber of Commerce.

U.S. Citizenship and Immigration Services. (2013). *History and milestones.* Retrieved from http://www.uscis.gov/portal/site/uscis/menuitem .eb1d4c2a3e5b9ac89243c6a7543f6d1a/?vgnextoid=84979589cdb76210 VgnVCM100000b92ca60aRCRD&vgnextchannel=84979589cdb76210 VgnVCM100000b92ca60aRCRD.

U.S. Department of Education. (2011). *The growing number of English learner students: 1998–99/2008–09* (Table 1). Retrieved from http://www.ncela.gwu .edu/files/uploads/9/growingLEP_0809.pdf.

U.S. Department of Homeland Security. (2008). *U.S. legal permanent residents: 2007, annual flow report (March, 2008).* Washington, DC: Department of Homeland Security, Office of Immigration Statistics.

U.S. Department of Homeland Security. (2010). *2009 yearbook of immigration statistics.* Washington, DC: Department of Homeland Security, Office of Immigration Statistics.

Van Hook, J., Brown, S. L., & Kwenda, M. N. (2004). A decomposition of trends in poverty among children of immigrants. *Demography, 41*(4), 649–670.

Vega, W. A., Ang, A., Rodriguez, M. A., & Finch, B. K. (2011). Neighborhood protective effects on depression in Latinos. *American Journal of Community Psychology, 47,* 114–126.

Vega, W. A., Kolody, B., & Aguilar-Gaxiola, S. A. (2001). Help-seeking for mental health problems among Mexican-Americans. *Journal of Immigrant Health, 3*(3), 133–140.

Vega, W. A., Kolody, B., Aguilar-Gaxiola, S., & Catalano, R. (1999). Gaps in service utilization by Mexican Americans with mental health problems. *American Journal of Psychiatry, 156*(6), 928–934.

Venters, H., & Gany, F. (2011). African immigrant health. *Journal of Immigrant Minority Health, 13,* 333–344.

Viladrich, A. (2003). *Social careers, social capital, and immigrants' access barriers to health care: The case of the Argentine minority in New York City (NYC).* Ph.D. thesis. New York: Graduate School of Arts and Sciences, Columbia University.

Viladrich, A. (2006). Latino immigrant health in the US: A growing field amidst unraveling challenges. *Journal of Latino-Latin American Studies, 2*(2), 125–139.

Waldinger, R., & Feliciano, C. (2004). Will the new second generation experience "downward assimilation"? Segmented assimilation re-assessed. *Ethnic and Racial Studies, 27*(3), 376–402.

Wallace, S. P., Castaneda, X., Guendelman, S., Padilla-Frausto, D. I., Felt, E., & Lee, J. (2007). *Immigration, health, & work: The facts behind the myths.* Los Angeles: UCLA Center for Health Policy Research.

Wight, V. R., Thampi, K., & Chau, M. (2011). *Poor children by parents' nativity: What do we know?* New York: National Center for Children in Poverty.

Williams, C. C. (2006). The epistemology of cultural competence. *Families in Society, 87*(2), 209–220.

Zenteno, R. (2006). Pobreza, marginación, y migración Mexicana a Estados Unidos. [Poverty, marginalization and Mexican migration to the United States]. In *Panorama actual de las migraciones en América Latina,* ed. A. I. Canales (pp. 161–196). Asociación Latinoamericana de Población, Universidad de Guadalajara.

Zhihuan, J. H., Yu, S. M., & Ledsky, R. (2006). Health status and health service access and use among children of U.S. immigrant families. *American Journal of Public Health, 96*(4), 634–640.

10

Poverty and Its Impact on the Military Family and the American Veteran

John Uriarte

Have you ever found yourself sitting in your car at some street corner, looking at some man or woman dressed in ragged clothes looking unkempt, and holding a sign that read either, "Will work for food," or "Homeless vet, Please help?" Perhaps your first instinct may be to lock your door, or avert your gaze out of fear that he or she will ask for money. Where does this stereotype of homelessness come from? Why are we so quick to say, "If you just would go out and get a job, then maybe you wouldn't be homeless?" Now let's add another layer to the mix and say that the man or woman is a veteran. They have served their country. Many have seen combat, received an honorable discharge, and had money for their education. So how on earth did they end up homeless or living in poverty?

In this chapter, readers will be able to identify and recognize how veterans and military families end up living in poverty. It also addresses the transition military families face when entering civilian life, recognizing the historical significance that poverty has on the military family and how this legacy impacts veterans today. Additionally, readers will explore how socioeconomic factors contribute to poverty, examine U.S. Department of Veterans Affairs programs and policies that combat poverty, and assess if enough is being done in the military to end poverty among military families and veterans.

Demographics and Characteristics

According to the U.S. Department of Veterans Affairs (2011a), a veteran is someone who has served the country in the armed forces, and is eligible for Veterans Administration (VA) benefits earned upon discharge from active military service. Notably upon discharge, many veterans come home with disabling physical injuries, but almost 600,000 of this population also come home with some form of post-traumatic stress disorder (PTSD), a disabling condition caused by witnessing or being involved in a horrifying trauma (Murdoch, van Ryn, Hodges, & Cowper, 2005).

Poverty among Families in the Military

Advocates for military families and veterans who are living in poverty or are homeless stress that low wages or PTSD are root causes for these situations. All veterans deal with visible and invisible wounds of war, and these wounds should be viewed as temporary barriers to individuals' higher level of functioning. In regards to the military family, these wounds, despite whether they are physical or mental, are intensified by the lack of family and social supports (National Coalition for Homeless Veterans [NCHV], 2010).

In order to understand poverty among families in the military, it is important to first look at poverty from a national perspective. According to Kiviat (2011), there is no single archetype of America's poor. Being poor is not about material deprivation, owning a car, or subscribing to cable TV. People who live in poverty ". . . are low-wage workers, single mothers, disabled veterans, the elderly, immigrants, marginalized factory workers, the severely mentally ill, the formerly incarcerated, the undereducated and the fallen middle class" (Kiviat, 2011, p. 34). For the military, most service members are not poor, but some young enlisted soldiers who have large families struggle to make ends meet.

Government benefits may be available to struggling military personnel who qualify under the federal guidelines; some of these programs specific to veterans and their family members are discussed later in this chapter (i.e., "Veterans' Pensions"). General types of assistance are discussed earlier in this book. For example, the U.S. Department of Agriculture uses income and family size to determine eligibility for the Supplemental Nutrition Assistance Program (SNAP), formerly known as Food Stamps. With respect to military personnel, cash given to those who live off base is counted as income, however, housing provided by the military (albeit on or off base) is not. Accordingly, it is possible that service members with low income who live in military housing, with an unemployed spouse, and a large family, may qualify for SNAP (Webb, 2011, p. 44). The last U.S. Department of Defense (DOD) estimate was that 5,100 service members receive assistance for food through SNAP. However, many of these service members who are in line for a pay raise will most likely not stay on SNAP for long (Webb, 2011).

Throughout the history of the military, enlisted soldiers could not marry unless they were non-commissioned officers (NCOs) and had their commanding officer's approval. This practice prevented the problem of destitute families headed by young enlistees. According to Webb (2011), the military never had any official directives that warned soldiers against spending within one's limits or prematurely taking on family responsibilities before one was ready. Any admonitions or guidance came after an individual had gotten in over his or her head. Service members were not encouraged to go out and immediately spend their whole paychecks or to get married, but they were likewise not cautioned against doing so, which remains a problem.

Today, as in the past, many soldiers get married right before they go to war to get the benefits. Those who get into financial trouble are most often young people away from home for the first time, earning more than ever before. It is no wonder so many of the barracks-bound live from paycheck to paycheck, go on spending binges immediately after payday, then live on mess hall food and the free on-base recreation for two weeks until the cycle repeats itself. Similarly, it is no wonder junior enlistees living off base with families find themselves cash-strapped most of the time (Webb, 2011).

The strength of personal and familial relationships is thought to serve as a buffer between family members and the stressors commonly found in military life. Any combination of these factors may be associated with a deterioration of functioning for family members of military personnel (McCubbin, 1980).

Socioeconomics and Military Families

According to recent studies, military recruits came from households with an average annual income of $43,122, slightly above the national average of $41,994 (U.S. Census Bureau, 2007). As a percentage of the 18- to 24-year-old population from which most recruits are drawn, average household incomes fell into two economic groups: $35,000–$79,999, and $85,000–$94,999 (U.S. Census Bureau, 2007). These socioeconomic groups were overrepresented among recruits while families in the highest and lowest socioeconomic groups were underrepresented. Interestingly, the percentage of recruits from high-income households has increased since 9/11 while the percentage from low-income households declined (Perl, 2009).

In 2005, 22.8 percent of recruits came from the richest quintile, while only 13.7 percent came from the poorest. Thus, the average enlistee is drawn from the middle class, not the urban poor (Lowther, 2010). Two other groups yet to be mentioned are women veterans and young, single vets between the ages of 18 and 30. Although small in number, these two groups are growing within the overall veteran population.

Also notable is that soldiers returning home from Iraq and Afghanistan face a new set of readjustment hurdles than veterans in previous times. While problems such as PTSD, major depression, traumatic brain injury (TBI), anxiety, stress, and anger management continue to plague veterans, mental health services have expanded throughout the VA to address these problems. However, veterans are increasingly facing poverty and homelessness when they return stateside. According to the National Center on Family Homelessness [NCFH] (2009), the number of homeless vets in New York alone jumped more than 60 percent between 2005 and 2008.

Historical Perspectives
The Revolutionary War to Mid-Twentieth Century

Poverty among U.S. veterans is not a new problem. The issue of lack of resources to support military families was first realized during the Revolutionary War. At that time, army regulations did not address issues with military families in any way because these families were "viewed as a hindrance to mission accomplishment" (Albano, 1994, p. 284). Also, army regulations avoided any references to families and did not provide financially for soldiers' dependents either while they were on active duty or in the event of their death. Soldiers were offered incentives and land grants to enlist, but no provisions were made for their families if they were married. Most of the Revolutionary War veterans died before receiving pensions that were ultimately issued more than forty years after the war ended. Furthermore, only indigent veterans were eligible.

In 1794, the army first formally acknowledged fiscal responsibility for family members by providing cash payments to widows and orphans of officers who were killed in battle. By the early nineteenth century, these benefits were extended to noncommissioned officers. From the 1850s to the 1880s many army wives and children accompanied their soldier husbands as they moved westward into the new frontier (Albano, 1994). They encountered domestic concerns such as problems with food, laundry, child rearing, rough travel, weather, and contact with American Indians (Baker, 2005). Baker (2005, p. 22) points out that although army wives found life difficult at times, army wives did not spend their lives as "uncomplaining, pious, and submissive" but rather "embraced the masculine and martial values of that institution: self-sacrifice, duty and honor, toughness and stoicism, courage and a love of adventure" (Baker, 2005, p. 23).

For the next 150 years, army policy changed very little and the idea of a soldier or officer, up to the rank of captain, getting married was strongly discouraged. Little by little the army began addressing family policy issues. At the time, the policy was not to feed a soldier's family. It was the responsibility of a married soldier to take care of his own family. However, when there were children to support, the government would allow the family to receive the equivalent of one-half of the soldier's food rations and quarter rations for marching with the troops and providing certain services. These included cooking, sewing, knitting, assembling food baskets, providing forage for horses, cleaning barracks, providing medic services, supervising field hospitals, and even loading and firing muskets. The term *camp followers* was coined to describe any woman who followed military units and provided these services. They were paid employees of the federal government (Albano, 1994).

1940s to Present

The army spouses of today are not that different from army wives of previous generations. Life in today's army is significantly better than in 1850; however, every army family still has to deal with financial hardships, travel to foreign countries, setting up a household, having personal property lost while in transit, traveling alone, or with children and pets, and without the soldier being present to help.

In support of veterans returning home from World War II, Congress passed the Servicemen's Readjustment Act of 1944, commonly known as the GI Bill (Serow, 2004). It gave veterans two years of unemployment compensation, no questions asked. The idea was to remove millions of veterans from the labor force and put them into schools, while the economy reverted to civilian-driven production. The GI Bill helped many veterans of World War II avoid homelessness. This was not the case in the Vietnam War, where large numbers of men returned home and for some, ended up homeless after failing to reintegrate back into everyday life.

Throughout the history of warfare, all combat veterans had to deal with the intensity, duration, and frequency of combat exposure. Despite repeated traumatic events, these experiences are not predictors of homelessness or poverty. Rather, the reasons veterans become homeless or end up living in poverty have little to do with their military service but much to do with their backgrounds.

Today U.S. soldiers are recruited from a greater cross-section of society and represent the country's diversity. Those individuals entering the military could have pre-existing problems, such as poor finances, or newly married with small children. While deploying to a combat zone might temporarily relieve the soldier from the issues, they will still face these problems once they return home. The big difference is that war will only exacerbate these problems when compounded with PTSD, TBI, and depression. The challenges of readjustment can be overwhelming for any vet. Every veteran who has left the service will have a transition into civilian life, but it is ultimately up to the individual how smooth or rough that transition will be. Those who have a support system at home and who take advantage of the programs and resources offered by the military will have an easier time with their transition than those who do not (Lowther, 2010).

Key Issues

There are several questions to think about when addressing the problem of poverty among military families and veterans. Many agree that poverty among veterans is a societal problem, but was it society that created it? Whose fault is it? Do homeless veterans or any veteran living in poverty bear any personal responsibility for being in their situation?

Socioeconomic Factors of Poverty

Giving the military family more money will not get them out of poverty. Furthermore, when service members transition out of the military to become civilians, they may bring with them a great deal of financial debt (Greendlinger & Spadoni, 2010). Soldiers who decide to leave the military may suffer financially when the country undergoes hard economic times, making it difficult to find work. For those without any kind of support system, finding a place to live becomes even more difficult. Other notable issues include the risk of family violence, which increases with unresolved PTSD, especially in families with dual-military spouses. Finally, problems related to mental health may be more closely related to a lack of access to medication and proper medical care.

Homelessness and Poverty among Veterans

In July 2011, the Veterans Administration estimated that 9,000 veterans of the Iraq and Afghan wars have been homeless or living in poverty at some point in time since they returned home (Kiviat, 2011). Furthermore, the wars in Iraq and

Afghanistan have created a new generation of veterans with mental health issues. More than 300,000 of the estimated 2 million Iraq and Afghanistan war veterans have requested mental health services from the Veterans Administration because of head trauma from roadside bombs and psychological trauma such as PTSD, in part due to a greater number of repeat deployments (NCFH, 2009).

Veterans are at a greater risk of becoming homeless or experiencing poverty due to a number of factors including unique military skills not needed in the civilian sector, combat-related health issues, minimal income due to unemployment, and a shortage of safe, affordable housing. Some fall victim to drug and alcohol abuse and others are unable to maintain jobs.

According to a University of Virginia study conducted in 2008, an estimated 1.1 million American veterans were living in poverty, though the poverty rate for veterans was lower than the overall rate of poverty in the United States (U.S. Census Bureau, 2007). Household factors also increase the likelihood that a family will enter poverty. Some of these factors may include having children, teen parenthood, marital status, and female-headed households. Many female-headed households are divorced. Divorce erodes the economic well-being of both parents and their children. Studies have shown that while the female's income declines, the income for divorced men remains stable or even increases (Teachman & Paasch, 1994). A father leaving the family increases the likelihood that families with children will be impoverished.

Family Life and Divorce

The strength of personal and familial relationships is thought to serve as a buffer between family members and the stressors commonly found in military life. The spouses or significant others of service members have often been left to manage difficult tasks alone, such as during deployment or absences during trainings for possible military action, and potential relocation of the family to a new military post, which often creates or increases stressors associated with military life (Albano, 1994). Any combination of these factors may be associated with a deterioration of functioning for family members of military personnel (McCubbin, 1980). The Associated Press (2008) reported that in 2008, 3.2 percent of all army married families got divorced. This percentage represents 8,748 out of 275,000 army families.

Divorce in the military can be difficult. If living on the military installation, housing will be taken away. The soldier can return to the barracks to live. However, the dependent spouse (more often female), and their children will be forced to move off base or return home to her family. In those cases where the family support system is no longer available, the non-military spouse and children are forced to manage with child support and maintenance payments. The only difference between divorced military spouses and their civilian counterparts is that the military children maintain their status as military dependents and are eligible for free medical care.

For Reserve and National Guard units, veterans' family, social, and professional networks may be strained due to extensive mobility while in military service or lengthy periods away from their hometowns and civilian jobs. Oftentimes these problems are directly traceable to their military service or to their return to civilian society without appropriate transitional support.

Employment/Unemployment

Veterans from Iraq and Afghanistan face a number of challenges. Many return home with a different view of themselves, their family, community, and society. Others will come home to broken families, divorce, or financial ruin. Some will have limited or no support system or will face unemployment and serious competition for the few jobs that exist.

Veterans hold one of the highest unemployment rates in the nation. In the past ten years, veteran unemployment stood at 13.3 percent, more than 4 percent higher than the overall unemployment rate of 9.2 percent (NCFH, 2009). Encouraging however, in 2009 nearly 200,000 returning veterans entered the labor force after completing their service (NCHV, 2010).

In general, if a veteran is unemployed, the cause may be a severe form of PTSD or TBI. Research conducted by the VA shows no link between PTSD/TBI and homelessness (U.S. Department of Housing and Urban Development/Veterans Affairs Report [HUD/VA], 2009). Many homeless veterans do have jobs, but keeping these jobs may be difficult for them. The question then becomes, if homeless veterans have jobs, then why are they homeless? For those veterans who are working, many of them earn minimum wage. These jobs do not provide enough pay for basic living expenses in many parts of the country. Also, many of these veterans are not working enough hours to pay the bills. When hours are cut even further, they go from being one of the "working poor" to becoming homeless.

Incarceration and Mental Health

In May 2007, the Bureau of Justice Statistics released a special report on incarcerated veterans estimating there were 140,000 veterans held in state and federal prisons (Noonan & Mumola, 2007). The median age (45) of veterans in state prison was 12 years older than that of non-veterans (33). Non-veteran inmates (55 percent) were nearly four times more likely than veterans (14 percent) to be under the age of 35. Veterans were much better educated than other prisoners. Ninety-one percent of all veterans in state prison had their high school diploma or General Educational Development (GED). Forty percent of non-veterans lacked either (NCHV, 2010).

Regarding mental health, incarcerated veterans self-reported that mental health problems had nothing to do with their imprisonment. Further, veterans who saw combat reported their service had nothing to do with any recent mental health problems (NCHV, 2010). Over a third reported they had sought emergency care in the first three months of 2009. Fifty-one percent of this group reported they visited the emergency room once, 27 percent visited twice, 11 percent visited three times, and 12 percent visited four or more times. Veterans identified through the survey are disproportionally African American (84 percent) and are frequent inmates of correctional institutions: 69 percent have been jailed (incarcerated one year or less), while 32 percent reported having spent time in prison (incarcerated one year or more) (Greendlinger & Spadoni, 2010).

Domestic and Family Violence

There is an increased risk of domestic violence in military families, but it was not until the start of the Afghanistan and Iraq invasions that the issue of domestic violence and military families began showing up on the nightly news. Along with all the anxiety that goes along with nuclear family life, military families suffer additional stresses specific to their situations. While life in the armed forces is not responsible for every episode of military domestic violence, an increase in stress and anxiety may trigger undesirable behavior in men or women who already are at risk for aggression. This type of aggression can manifest itself in peacetime, but is most prevalent before shipping out to war, as well as after returning from combat. The following risk factors may contribute to problems with domestic violence and military families: prior history of violence within the family, witnessing domestic violence during childhood, isolation from family and support systems, weapon accessibility, stress factors such as family separation and reunification, post-traumatic stress disorder or battle fatigue, and living conditions and poverty (Martin, Gibbs, Johnson, Rentz, Clinton-Sherrod, & Hardison, 2007).

Throughout the American military's history, domestic violence has often plagued families with enlisted members. In 2000, the U.S. military responded to the growing problem by forming the Defense Task Force on Domestic Violence to assess the situation and formulate appropriate military responses. Data have been collected since the inception of the program.

In 2001, the U.S. Department of Defense Family Advocacy Program reported over 18,000 episodes of spousal abuse. Eighty-four percent of reported abuse in 2001 was physical in nature and women were 66 percent more likely than men to experience domestic violence in a military family. For women that have been enlisted in the armed forces, both past and present, 30 percent reported lifetime intimate partner abuse, and 22 percent reported intimate partner abuse during active duty only (Forgey & Badger, 2006).

Mental Health

Notably, a large number of veterans who served during conflicts and are at risk of homelessness have suffered from post-traumatic stress disorder. The NCHV (2010) states that at least 45 percent of homeless veterans suffer from mental illness, while over 50 percent may have some form of substance abuse problem. According to Tanielian and Jaycox (2008), nearly 20 percent of military service members who have returned from Iraq and Afghanistan report symptoms of post-traumatic stress disorder or major depression, yet only slightly more than half have sought treatment. This new generation of Iraq and Afghanistan combat veterans, both men and women, also suffer from other war-related conditions including traumatic brain injuries, which also put them at risk of homelessness and poverty.

Women and Children

The gender mix of the military is evolving. Women presently represent 15 percent of the military population, which poses new challenges for the nation's support system for returning veterans and their families (NCHV, 2010). Women veterans report serious trauma histories and episodes of physical harassment or sexual assault while in the military. The VA and homeless veteran service providers are also seeing increased numbers of veterans with children seeking their assistance because they are living at or below the poverty level.

The Government Accountability Office (GAO) reported that in 2004, more than 15 percent of female respondents said they had been sexually assaulted in military academies (National Women's Law Center, Women's Research and Education Institute, & Alliance for National Defense, 2008). In a related U.S. Department of Defense (DOD) report from 2012, it was revealed there were 3,192 reported sexual assaults against military women during fiscal year 2011 (DOD, 2012).

For more than a decade, women have walked combat patrols, staffed machine guns on convoys, flown combat aircraft, and served on naval ships and submarines. However, they have not been allowed to serve in combat units that have historically been filled by men. In January 2013 that changed when the Pentagon lifted the ban on women serving in combat units. This new role for women in military operations brings some physical and mental health concerns. All branches of the armed services have until 2016 to complete plans for integrating women into the combat arms, and according to Baldor (2013), the Pentagon intends to open approximately 230,000 positions to women by that same year.

While the United States has lifted the combat exclusion rule, the military is trying to redefine the role of women in combat, and it is noteworthy very few are looking at the potential increase in PTSD among female service members. Females facing combat is a relatively new phenomenon and thus far, little is known about the specific needs and issues facing female service members and other women with combat-related PTSD (Bumiller & Shanker, 2013). Unique stressors may impact their mental health such as feelings of isolation and lack of support from colleagues, friends, and family. Women also bear the stress of often being the primary caregiver for family members—not only for their children, but also for their aging parents (Society for Women's Health Research [SWHR], 2008). The stress of extended deployments for this group of women soldiers is compounded by the demands of caring for their families back home. According to SWHR (2008), 35 percent of women combat veterans studied reported more depressive symptoms than did males, while males reported more irritability, anger, nightmares, and flashbacks. It was also noted that female patients were more receptive to psychotherapy, while men expressed a stronger preference for medication. Another important gender difference relates to PTSD among combat troops. Professionals treating women with PTSD stated that almost 65 percent of the females reported that sexual trauma (either childhood or in the combat zone) was the cause. For men, the traumatic event was related to killing or seeing people killed or injured.

It is critical that the U.S. Department of Veterans Affairs (VA) and private sector providers are preparing to identify and care for the unique needs of female service members, veterans, and contractors suffering from PTSD. Likewise at this point, it is too early to speculate what impact the new law will have on military children. Practitioners should be aware that family care plans are in place for single-parent military families. The purpose of these plans is to ensure that children of the deployed parent will be cared for in the event that the parent does not return home. Finally, it should be expected that as women are exposed to greater frequency, duration, and intensity of combat, there will be a corresponding rise in PTSD and secondary PTSD within the family.

Government Policies and Programs

According to a congressional staff analysis of 2000 U.S. Census data conducted in 2005, 1.5 million veterans, nearly 6.3 percent of the nation's veteran population, have incomes that fall below the federal poverty level, including 634,000 with incomes below 50 percent of the poverty level (NCHV, 2010). Neither the Veterans Administration nor its state and county equivalents are adequately funded to respond to this group of veterans' health, housing, and supportive service needs. Moreover, community-based and faith-based service providers also lack sufficient resources. As discussed in the section on history, the federal government has made minimal attempts to address poverty among military families throughout U.S. history. This appears to be changing.

Supportive Services for Veteran Families (SSVF) Program

In 2008, Public Law 110-387, the Veterans' Mental Health and Other Care Improvements Act, Title VI, Section 604 (2008), authorized the VA to develop the Supportive Services for Veteran Families (SSVF) Program. Under this program, the VA will award grants to private nonprofit organizations and consumer cooperatives who will provide supportive services to very low-income veteran families residing in or transitioning to permanent housing. The grantees will provide a range of supportive services designed to promote housing stability to eligible very low-income veteran families.

HUD-VASH Housing

The HUD-VASH Program is a collaborative partnership between the U.S. Department of Housing and Urban Development (HUD) and the U.S. Department of

Veterans Affairs (VA) Supported Housing (VASH). In this partnership, HUD provides housing choice vouchers for permanent shelter to homeless veterans, while VA provides veterans with case management and supportive services that promote and sustain recovery and housing. VA case management services are designed to improve veteran physical and mental health, and to enhance the veteran's ability to remain stable, housed, and community-integrated. The ultimate goal is to move veterans and their families out of homelessness.

HUD-VASH case managers visit community agencies that provide services to homeless veterans, educate the agency about the HUD-VASH program, and meet with potential program candidates. HUD-VASH case managers work with VA homeless programs to assist veterans who are involved in the VA homeless continuum of care. In addition, they determine if the veteran is an appropriate candidate for the program.

VetSuccess

The goal of the VetSuccess in Transition program is to assist veterans in exploring the options available to them to ensure their seamless transition from military to civilian life. VetSuccess equips veterans with the tools necessary to acquire that "perfect" job to match their abilities and ambitions. Veterans find military skills translators (who assist military members to match their experience and skills to employment), job skills preparation, along with federal and other civilian job search assistance that help in attaining their career goals. In order to bridge the gap from military to civilian employment, it is sometimes necessary for veterans to augment their already numerous and strong transferable skills with higher education. VetSuccess on Campus will assist veterans with choosing the right VA program, school, and degree program that yields the "right" career for their future goals (U.S. Department of Veterans Affairs, 2011a).

The Work Study Program is another popular VetSuccess benefit. Veterans training at the three-quarter or full-time rate may participate in VA's work-study program and provide VA outreach services, prepare/process VA paperwork, work at a VA medical facility or Vet Center, or perform other VA-approved activities. This program allows students to work up to twenty hours per week (U.S. Department of Veterans Affairs, 2011a, p. 31).

Veterans Pension

VA Pension "veterans with low incomes who are either permanently and totally disabled, or age 65 and older, may be eligible for monetary support, referred to as Veterans Pension or VA Pension if they have 90 days or more of active military service; at least one day of which was during a period of war. The 90-day active service requirement does not apply to veterans with a service-connected disability justifying discharge from the military. The veteran's discharge must have been under conditions other than dishonorable and the disability must be for reasons other than the veteran's own willful misconduct" (U.S. Department of Veterans Affairs, 2011a, p. 37). Veterans who are awarded the Medal of Honor receive a monthly pension of $1,194.

Disability Compensation

Disability compensation provides monetary payments that are not subject to state or federal income tax to veterans with injuries, illnesses, or disabilities, incurred or aggravated during active military service. These disabilities are called "service-connected" (U.S. Department of Veterans Affairs, 2011a, p. 25). The monthly amount of money a veteran receives is measured as a percentage and therefore will vary depending on the degree of disability. Notably, additional disability compensation may be provided if the veteran has a severe service-connected disability (i.e., loss of limb[s]), or if the veteran has a spouse, child(ren), or dependent parent(s) (U.S. Department of Veterans Affairs, 2011b).

The U.S. Department of Veterans Affairs (2008) also considers individual unemployability as part of their disability compensation program. This distinction allows the "VA to pay certain veterans compensation at the 100% rate, even though VA has not rated their service-connected disabilities" at the total (100 percent) level (U.S. Department of Veterans Affairs, 2008, p. 1). To be eligible for this compensation, veterans must be unable to maintain what the VA refers to as "substantially gainful employment" because of the veteran's service-connected disabilities. Additionally, the veteran must meet a service-connected ratability. Accordingly, the veteran must have one service-connected disability ratable at 60 percent or more, *or* two or more service-connected disabilities. If the veteran falls into the latter category, the veteran must have one disability ratable at least 40 percent or more and with two or more disabilities that have a combined rating of 70 percent or more (U.S. Department of Veterans Affairs, 2008). Special consideration is given to veterans if they are considered unemployable due to one or more service-connected disabilities, but who do not "meet the minimum percentage standards, or if there is evidence of *exceptional* or *unusual* circumstances to impairment of earning capacity due to disabilities (for example, interference with *employment or frequent periods of hospitalization*)" (U.S. Department of Veterans Affairs, 2008, p. 1).

Additional Benefits for Veterans

"The payment of military retirement pay, disability severance pay and separation incentive payments, known as SSB (Special Separation Benefits) and VSI (Voluntary Separation Incentives) affects the amount of VA compensation paid to disabled veterans" (U.S. Department of Veterans Affairs, 2011a, p. 25). To be eligible, the service of the veteran must have been terminated through separation or discharge under conditions other than dishonorable.

Other programs that provide special benefits under disability compensation include the following categories: prisoners of war, veterans exposed to Agent Orange and other herbicides, veterans exposed to radiation (also known as atomic veterans), Gulf War veterans with chronic disabilities, and the combat-related special compensation (CRSC) program. Under the CRSC, eligible retired veterans with combat-related injuries can receive tax-free monthly payments. CRSC veterans can receive both their full military retirement pay and their VA disability compensation if the injury is combat-related (U.S. Department of Veterans Affairs, 2011a).

Dependents and Survivors Benefits

A death gratuity is a military service benefit that pays $100,000 to the next of kin for service members who die while on active duty as a result of service-connected injury or illness. If there is no surviving spouse or child, then parents or siblings designated as next of kin by the service member may be entitled to the payment. An application may be submitted to the VA if the beneficiary is not automatically paid (U.S. Department of Veterans Affairs, 2011a, p.103).

Dependency and Indemnity Compensation

For a survivor to be eligible for Dependency and Indemnity Compensation (DIC), the veteran's death must have resulted from a disease or injury incurred in the line of duty while on active duty or active duty for training (U.S. Department of Veterans Affairs, 2011a, p. 103). The death can be a result of a "heart attack, cardiac arrest, or stroke incurred or aggravated in the line of duty while on inactive duty for training or a service-connected disability or a condition directly related to a service-connected disability" (U.S. Department of Veterans Affairs, 2011a, p. 103).

Death Pension

U.S. Department of Veterans Affairs (2011a, p. 105) explains the VA provides death pensions "to low-income surviving spouses and unmarried children of deceased veterans with wartime service." Eligibility guidelines require that spouses must not remarry and that "children must be under age 18, or under age 23 if attending a VA approved school, or have become permanently incapable of self-support because of disability before age 18" (U.S. Department of Veterans Affairs, 2011a, p.105). Designed to provide a monthly payment to eligible persons, the death pension brings the income of dependents (surviving spouses and unmarried children) up to a specified level. Notably, this payment is reduced if recipients have annual income from other sources (i.e., Social Security). Payment may be increased, however, if recipients have "unreimbursed medical expenses that can be deducted from countable income" (U.S. Department of Veterans Affairs, 2011a, p.106).

Survivors' and Dependents' Educational Assistance

Educational assistance is available to spouses and dependents if the service member or veteran died of a service-connected disability. Eligibility for this program expires ten years from either the date the veteran's spouse applies or the date of the veteran's death. Eligibility for spouses of service members who died while on active duty expires twenty years from the date of death (U.S. Department of Veterans Affairs, 2011a).

Educational assistance can provide family members with higher education opportunities including associate, bachelor, or graduate degrees. It also covers technical and vocational training, including "on-the-job training programs; farm cooperative courses; and preparatory courses for tests required or used for admission to an institution of higher learning or graduate school" (U.S. Department of Veterans Affairs, 2011a, p. 108).

VA Health Care Benefits

The VA operates the nation's largest integrated health care system with over 1,400 hospitals, community clinics, community living centers, domiciliary, readjustment counseling centers, and various other facilities. Anyone who served in active duty and who was discharged under conditions other than dishonorable qualifies for health care benefits. After enrollment, a veteran is placed into one of four categories: having a (1) service-connected disability of 50 percent or more; (2) a disability the military determined was incurred or aggravated in the line of duty; (3) a service-connected disability only; or (4) registry examinations (ionizing radiation, Agent Orange, Gulf War/Operation Iraqi Freedom, and depleted uranium) (U.S. Department of Veterans Affairs, 2011a, p. 2).

Veterans who are more than 50 percent disabled receive priority in scheduling of hospital or outpatient medical appointments. Woman veterans are eligible for the same VA benefits as male veterans. They receive comprehensive health services that include primary care, specialty care, mental health care, and reproductive health care. Military sexual trauma counseling is available for both male and female veterans.

Eligible veterans have the opportunity to enroll in several health registry programs. The Veteran Health Registry is a program in which veterans can receive free medical examinations, including laboratory and other diagnostic tests deemed necessary by an examining clinician. The Gulf War Registry is for veterans who served on active military duty in Southwest Asia during the Gulf War, which began in 1990 and continues to the present, including Operation Iraqi Freedom. This program was established to identify possible diseases resulting from U.S. military personnel service in certain areas of Southwest Asia (U.S. Department of Veterans Affairs, 2011a, p. 9).

Additional programs include the Depleted Uranium Registry, which was established to identify soldiers who were exposed to harmful doses of radiation from exposure from nuclear power plants and depleted uranium that was in various military weapons. The Agent Orange Registry was established to identify Vietnam veterans who were possibly exposed to "dioxin or other toxic substances in herbicides used during the Vietnam War between 1962 and 1975, regardless of length of service, or while serving in or near the Korean demilitarized zone (DMZ) between April 1, 1968 through August 31, 1971, or as a result of testing, transporting, or spraying herbicides for military purposes" (U.S. Department of Veterans Affairs, 2011a, p. 10). The Ionizing Radiation Registry is for veterans who were exposed to the adverse effects of their atomic exposure either from World War II or who participated in various nuclear testing programs.

Other health care benefits include mental health treatment at VA medical centers and outpatient clinics; Vet Centers provide readjustment counseling to combat veterans and their dependents; there are also PTSD and drug and alcohol inpatient treatment programs and video teleconferencing to veterans located in rural areas who do not have access to their primary care provider. Specialized services for veterans include prosthetic and sensory aids; services for blind and visually impaired; outpatient dental treatment; nursing home care; foreign medical program; online health services; and caregiver support programs (U.S. Department of Veterans Affairs, 2011a).

Social Justice

Social justice is the view that everyone deserves equal economic, political, and social rights and opportunities, particularly for the service men and women who protect the United States and help ensure the democracy of the country. For many advocates, it is disheartening that more federal, state, and local programs are not available to both current and former military and their families. The role of social workers and other helping professionals is to provide access to services for everyone, particularly those in greatest need (Flynn, 1995). With veterans who are living in poverty, for example, social workers and other related professionals can make sure their clients have access to SNAP (commonly known as Food Stamps), and health care. In addition to their work with individual clients, social workers should also apply social justice principles to structural problems within the agencies in which they work and the communities within which they practice.

Armed with the long-term goal of empowering clients, social workers and other helping professionals should use their knowledge and organizational skills to advocate for and assist their clients who are often powerless and underserved. For example, social workers ensure staff treat clients respectfully and they may examine the organization's policies on personal client information to make sure it is held in confidence.

Historically, the vast majority of patients who receive health care through the VA have been men. As of September 2009, there were more than 1.8 million women veterans in the United States. More than 102,000 of these women were veterans of the military operations in Afghanistan and Iraq. Today, women veterans are younger than their male counterparts and almost all are under the age of forty. The VA is estimating that while the total number of veterans will decline 37 percent by

2033, the number of women veterans will increase by more than 17 percent over the same period (GAO, 2010). Medical facilities throughout the VA are expanding their services for female veterans to ensure that they get the same quality service their male counterparts receive.

In an effort to attack poverty and to prevent homelessness, the VA requires its staff to give homeless veterans a referral for shelter or short-term housing while they await placement in veteran housing. According to the GAO (2010), female veterans waited an average of four months before securing HUD-VASH housing.

Without referrals for shelter or temporary housing during these waits, homeless and poverty-stricken women veterans may be at risk of physical harm and further trauma on the streets or in other unsafe places. Lack of housing for women with children is a significant barrier to accessing veteran housing and is considered a major problem because it puts women and their children at a greater risk of remaining homeless and in poverty.

While the VA is taking steps, such as launching an outreach campaign to end homelessness among all veterans, it does not have sufficient data about the population and needs of women veterans to plan effectively for increases in their numbers as service members return from Iraq and Afghanistan. Further, without improved services, women including those with children and those who have experienced military sexual trauma remain at risk for living in poverty and being homeless (Zinzow, Grubaugh, Monnier, Suffoletta-Malerie, & Freuh, 2007).

Likewise, if the trend toward reducing the number of homeless veterans is to continue, more funding is needed for supportive services, employment, and housing options to ensure that veterans who served prior to the Iraq and Afghanistan wars can live independently and with dignity. Additionally, increased appropriations to VA homeless veteran assistance programs will help prevent homelessness among the newest generation of combat veterans from Iraq and Afghanistan (NCHV, 2010). Through a coordinated effort, Congress, the VA, and other federal, state, and local agencies will be able to develop an approach to reduce, eliminate, and ultimately prevent homelessness among all of America's veterans (Perl, 2009).

Interventions

For social workers and other helping professionals, it is the point of entry of the homeless or impoverished veteran that will dictate the intervention strategy. The type and focus of intervention will vary depending on the agency. At the micro level, where counseling services are provided to individual clients, the focus of intervention may be more on information and referral. Mezzo-level intervention would take the form of a "stand down" where the focus is on "seek and safety" programs and helping vets who are at risk of homelessness or facing poverty. Intervention at the macro level may provide community-wide counselor education on the military culture and homeless veterans.

Micro Interventions

Within the VA there is an organization called the Readjustment Counseling Service (RCS). This service has approximately 300 outpatient counseling centers across the country, otherwise known as "Vet Centers." Staffed primarily with licensed clinical social workers and licensed professional counselors, these vet centers provide individual, group, couple, and marital counseling services to any combat veteran.

When homeless vets present to a Vet Center, they are assessed and a determination is made on how to best help. A social worker would most likely evaluate the veteran for basic needs: shelter, food, and warm clothes. Second, the veteran may need to see a primary care doctor if there are any health care issues. In addition, for veterans living in a homeless shelter, an immediate referral to the VA social worker/case manager would be done and transportation would be arranged to get the veteran from the shelter to the VA for services.

Beyond completing a needs assessment, the initial contact may not be the best time to start formal counseling. The goal for the Vet Center counselor is to get the veteran a place to sleep and some food. Although supportive counseling and case management services are provided at the shelter for the veteran, the Vet Center counselor can still make themselves available to discuss any readjustment issues resulting from deployment.

Mezzo Interventions

In times of war, exhausted combat units requiring time to rest and recover were removed from the battlefields to a place of relative safety. At secure base camp areas, troops were able to take care of personal hygiene, get clean uniforms, enjoy warm meals, receive medical and dental care, mail and receive letters, and enjoy the camaraderie of friends in a protected environment. This "stand down," as it was called, afforded battle-weary soldiers the opportunity to renew their spirit, health, and overall sense of well-being.

Today, Stand Down refers to a grassroots, community-based intervention program designed to help the nation's estimated 107,000 homeless veterans survive any given "night combat" life on the streets. The first Stand Down was organized in 1988 and since then has been used as an effective tool in reaching more than 200,000 veterans and their family members between 1994 and 2000. They are collaborative events, coordinated between local VA centers, other government agencies, and community agencies who serve veterans who are at risk of homelessness or facing poverty. They are held at one central location for one to three days and provide comprehensive services, which encourages homeless veterans and those at risk of poverty to overcome their feelings of distrust and isolation. Veterans receive assistance with food, shelter, clothing, health screenings, legal or mental health assistance, job counseling, and referrals. Community resources, such as VA and Social Security benefits counseling, and referrals to a variety of other essential services, such as housing, employment, and substance abuse treatment, are also provided to assist veterans in rebuilding their lives. It provides a safe environment in which veterans can connect with others who have shared similar experiences and cultivates hope for the future.

Macro Interventions

Social workers or other helping professionals can work on a macro level in many ways. For example, they can provide a series of trainings to the mental health and counseling communities of a city in order to educate the larger community on how to work with veterans who are homeless. Training such as this could last a week and include presentations on understanding military culture, where veterans get their strength, and how to restore resilience, self-worth, and self-esteem. The social worker can increase awareness in cities and municipalities, advocating for changes in legislative policies and developing programs to better meet the needs of veterans. For instance, they may develop vocational rehabilitation programs, thereby providing veterans with marketable skills. Veterans want to continue to be productive members of society and go back to work. As a group, homeless veterans do not want a handout; they want to get their life back. By working at the macro level, social workers and other professionals can go beyond helping individuals to helping an entire population.

Concluding Comments

This chapter offers a glimpse into the many issues involving veterans who are experiencing homelessness or are impoverished. The sheer number of veterans who are currently leaving the service and readjusting to civilian life creates challenges for social workers and helping professionals who may be unfamiliar with the issues they are facing. Recognizing that veterans and military families encounter many unique challenges is important for practitioners to consider when engaging with this population or developing policies or programs that respond to their needs. A "band-aid approach" will have little impact on creating positive long-term change. In order to sustain lasting positive change for this population, advocates must identify and address the causes of homelessness and poverty. For instance, it is essential to design effective programs that specifically meet the needs of mentally ill and medically disabled veterans. For veterans who demonstrate repeated patterns of behavior resulting in homelessness or poverty, interventions in addition to social services may be necessary. For social workers and helping professionals engaged with this population, developing skills to assist those who have served this country is vital in order to make a difference for individuals and their family members. The sheer number of veterans who are leaving the service and who will be struggling with their own readjustment issues are likely to present challenges to social workers and to the organizations in which they work.

This chapter aimed to provide readers with an introduction to poverty and homelessness among veterans and military families. Historically there were few programs that benefited this population. Now, because of the work of committed advocates, the difficulties that face this population are becoming more recognized and are addressed at micro, mezzo, and macro levels of practice. There is certainly more that needs to be done, particularly when considering concepts such as social justice as it relates to this group, but programs and policies that benefit veterans and their families are growing.

Case Studies
Micro Level

Bill is a 36-year-old white male veteran who became homeless eleven years ago. He grew up in a very strict home, with occasional physical abuse. Bill began drinking in ninth grade, and drank heavily during high school. He was expelled from school after the eleventh grade and his parents helped him obtain his GED. Shortly after, Bill was arrested on a burglary charge and was sentenced to ten years of probation. While on probation, he married and had a daughter. In order to support his family, Bill studied to be an electrician. One day while at a job site, his friend and coworker was electrocuted in front of him.

Following the death of his friend, Bill decided to join the army. He reported to basic training and enjoyed the structure it offered. While attending Advanced Individual Training (AIT) to be a helicopter mechanic, he fought with several fellow soldiers. These fights resulted in Bill's elimination from helicopter mechanic school and being sent to field artillery training. Upon completion, he reported to his permanent duty station, where his wife and daughter joined him. The relationship was strained due to their separation during basic training and AIT. Once they were reunited, Bill's wife had multiple affairs while he participated in training exercises. During this stressful time, Bill's mother died, and he began drinking excessively and using drugs. Bill reported that he tried to ask for help from the military, but received a general discharge due to drug use.

After his discharge from the military and separating from his family, he moved around, sleeping on friends' couches. He tried several times to access drug and alcohol programs through the VA, but he would inevitably relapse while waiting for a program start date and eventually become homeless. He encountered a group of displaced veterans who taught him how to survive on the streets and steal to support his addictions. Bill was arrested for theft and spent several months in jail. After his recent release, Bill is trying to remain alcohol and drug-free. Currently unemployed, he stated he does not have any real experience or even understand how to fill out a job application. He has received a housing voucher from the VA, but he is having a difficult time locating quarters. Presently, he is living with a friend, but can stay for only two weeks.

Questions

1. As Bill's social worker, how might you engage Bill to develop a list of issues to begin addressing? What do you feel are the top three issues and explain your reasoning.

2. What strategies would you use to effect positive change? How would you use the concept of empowerment to bring about change?

3. What type of service delivery method would you use when working with Bill and why?

Mezzo Level

For many veterans, whether recently returning from active duty or those who have served in the military decades ago, reentry into society can be challenging. Many find that they have changed and have a difficult time adjusting. Reentry into one's community often creates hardships such as maintaining relationships, coping with mental health issues, securing jobs, and becoming financially secure.

Recognizing that reentry can be difficult, a county located near New York City began sponsoring a Veterans Stand Down, which is aimed at assisting vets with personal matters and integrating back into the community. The Stand Downs, which are held twice a year, provide veterans with concrete services such as clothing, food, and housing. Representatives from federal, state, and local government are on hand to discuss services and entitlement programs such as Medicaid, Medicare, SNAP (formerly called Food Stamps), Home Energy Assistance Program (HEAP), Social Security, and Supplemental Security Income (SSI). Nonprofit agencies and service providers including mental health counseling are also on-site to help returning veterans. Free haircuts, eye exams, and medicals are additional services available. At the Stand Down, a volunteer escorts veterans to each service provider in order that they can gather useful information. Once veterans have had an opportunity to hear about the programs and services, they can obtain items such as non-perishable food and clothing. The biannual Stand Downs draw in over 150 veterans and offers them an opportunity to receive services tailored for their specific needs. One county employee who served in the Air Force and now is employed at the local Department of Social Services reports that veterans who attend the Stand Down also come for the socialization. At the Stand Down they feel connected and not isolated. Additionally, the inclusiveness of the Stand Down allows veterans who would typically not seek services to hear about programs. All interventions are done in a respectful way to maintain their pride and dignity. Mental health counselors specializing in PTSD and sexual assaults, in addition to drug and alcohol addiction specialists are on site to assist this group.

Questions

1. What are the benefits to working with veterans as a group?

2. How might you encourage participation in a group activity such as this?

3. What is the role of the helping professional at the mezzo level of practice?

4. Are there alternative types of groups that might be helpful to this population?

Macro Level

A large suburban community in a Midwest state has recently experienced an increase in the number of veterans returning from the Middle East. These veterans are having difficulty locating employment given the current economic climate and cannot afford their housing, placing themselves and their families at risk of homelessness. Recognizing this as a growing issue, community advocates began soliciting local and state elected officials asking for assistance. Specifically, through petitions, letter writing, and visiting their local and state government officials, the advocates requested legislation pass to give returning veterans and their families safe, subsidized housing. The advocates recommended taking abandoned military bases and refurbishing the residences, making them safe. Community-based agencies found willing volunteers to undertake these repairs at no cost. In addition to providing housing, advocates hoped the community would be revitalized and attract local businesses to the area. Some retired social workers agreed to provide supportive services to the residents.

The outpouring of support for this initiative impressed the legislators. They were also encouraged that an abandoned military base could be used for this purpose. Their staff worked with community-based attorneys to draft a bill, which was later introduced to the legislators who unanimously voted on this legislation. This was the first time in decades that there was bipartisan support for a community initiative.

Questions
1. How could service providers engage with government officials to improve services to veterans and their families in your community?

2. Should services to veterans be provided by volunteers, nonprofit agencies, or by the state and federal government?

3. In the United States, certain housing is available to older adults with limited income. Should similar benefits be given to veterans for protecting the country?

Internet Resources

U.S. Department of Housing and Urban Development and the Department of Veterans Affairs HUD-VASH Program: www.hud.gov/offices/pih/programs/hcv/vash/#1

Provides program information about housing vouchers for eligible homeless veterans and families.

Grace After Fire: www.graceafterfire.org

Provides resource and referral information for women veterans.

Make the Connection: http://maketheconnection.net/

Shared Experiences and Support for Veterans provides resource, referral, and support information for returning veterans with medical/economic problems.

SAMHSA's Service Members, Veterans, and Their Families Technical Assistance Center (SMVF TA Center): http://www.samhsa.gov/MilitaryFamilies/tacenter/

Helps develop responsive behavioral health systems for service members, veterans, and their families.

Service Women's Action Network (SWAN): www.servicewomen.org

SWAN works to ensure high-quality health care and benefits for women veterans and their families.

United States Department of Housing and Urban Development, Office of Community Planning and Development Resources for Homeless Veterans: https://www.onecpd.info/homelessness-assistance/resources-for-homeless-veterans/

One-stop spot for veterans, and those who help veterans find housing.

U.S. Department of Veterans Affairs, Center for Women Veterans: www.va.gov/womenvet

Provides information and referral on benefits, housing, education, and financial assistance for women veterans.

U.S. Department of Veterans Affairs, National Center for PTSD: www.ptsd.va.gov

Provides resource and referral information on a variety of PTSD issues for veterans and their families.

United States Department of Veterans Affairs, National Center for Veterans Analysis and Statistics: www.va.gov/vetdata

Provides information on reports, surveys, and statistics regarding the veteran population.

Further Readings

American Psychological Association. (2007). *The psychological needs of U.S. military members and their families: A preliminary report.* Presidential Task Force on Military Deployment Services for Youth, Families and Service Members. www.apa.org/about/governance/council/policy/military-deployment-services.pdf.

Bassuk, E. L., Dawson, R., Perloff, J., & Weinreb, L. (2009). Posttraumatic stress disorder in extremely poor women: Implications for health care clinicians. *Journal of the American Medical Women's Association, 56,* 79–85.

Bassuk, E. L., Weinreb, L., Buckner, J., Browne, A., Solomon, A., & Bassuk, S. S. (1996). The characteristics and needs of sheltered homeless and low-income housed mothers. *Journal of the American Medical Association, 276*(8), 640–646.

Center for Deployment Psychology, Course 101: Military Culture and Terminology. www.deploymentpsych.org/training/training-catalog/military-culture-and-terminology.

Foster, L., & Vince, S. (2009). *California's Women Veterans: The challenges and needs of those who served.* California Research Bureau, California State Library. Available at www.library.ca.gov/crb/09/09-009.pdf.

Mulhall, E. (2009). *Women warriors: Supporting she "who has borne the battle."* (Issue Report). Iraq and Afghanistan Veterans of America. http://media.iava.org/IAVA_WomensReport_2009.pdf.

National Center for Veterans Analysis and Statistics. (2011). *Profile of veterans: 2009.* Data from the American Community Survey. U.S. Department of Veterans Affairs. http://www.va.gov/vetdata/docs/SpecialReports/Profile_of_Veterans_2009_FINAL.pdf.

U.S. Department of Labor, Bureau of Labor Statistics. (2012). *Employment situation of veterans.* Retrieved from www.bls.gov/spotlight/2010/Veterans/ and www.bls.gov/spotlight/2010/Veterans/ and www.bls.gov/news.release/pdf/vet.pdf.

U.S. Department of Veterans Affairs, Center for Women Veterans. (2010). *Women veterans—A proud tradition of service.* Advisory Committee on Women Veterans Report. Available at www.va.gov/WOMENVET/docs/ACWV_Report_2010.pdf.

Watson, P. (2009). *PTSD 101.* National Center for PTSD. United States Department of Veteran Affairs. Retrieved from http://www.ptsd.va.gov/professional/ptsd101/presenters/patricia_watson_phd.asp.

References

Albano, S. (1994). Military recognition of family concerns: Revolutionary War to 1993. *Armed Forces and Society, 20*(2), 283–302.

Associated Press. (2008, March 1). *U.S. military divorce rates still at 3.3 percent.* Retrieved from http://abclocal.go.com/kabc/story?section=news/national_world&id=5992673.

Baker, A. (2005). Daughters of Mars: Army officers' wives and military culture on the American frontier. *The Historian, 67*(1), 20–42.

Baldor, L. (2013, January 23). Women in combat: Leon Panetta removes military ban, opening front-line positions. *Huffington Post.* Retrieved from http://www.huffingtonpost.com/2013/01/23/women-in-combat_n_2535954.html.

Bumiller, E., & Shanker, T. (2013, January 23). Pentagon is set to lift combat ban for women. *New York Times.* Retrieved from http://www.nytimes.com/2013/01/24/us/pentagon-says-it-is-lifting-ban-on-women-in-combat.html?pagewanted=all.

Department of Defense. (2012). *Fact sheet on Department of Defense annual report on sexual assault in the military for fiscal 2011.* Retrieved from http://www.defense.gov/news/sexualassaultannualreportfactsheet.pdf.

Flynn, J. P. (1995). Social justice in social agencies. In *Encyclopedia of Social Work,* ed. R. L. Edwards (19th ed., vol. 1, pp. 95–100). Washington, DC: NASW Press.

Forgey, M., & Badger, L. (2006). Patterns of intimate partner violence among married women in the military: Type, level, directionality and consequences. *Journal of Family Violence, 21*(6), 369–380.

Greendlinger, R., & Spadoni, P. (2010). *The toolkit for effectively engaging and delivering services to America's veterans and their families.* The National Center on Family Homelessness.

Kiviat, B. (2011). Below the line. *Time, 178*(21), 34–41.

Lowther, A. B. (2010). The post-9/11 American serviceman. *JFQ: Joint Force Quarterly* no. 58, 75–81.

Martin, S., Gibbs, D., Johnson, R., Rentz, E., Clinton-Sherrod, M., & Hardison, J. (2007). Spouse abuse and child abuse by army soldiers. *Journal of Family Violence, 22*(7), 587–595.

McCubbin, H. (1980, Winter). Coping with separation and reunion. *Military Chaplains' Review*, DA Pamphlet 165-124, pp. 49–58.

Murdoch, M., van Ryn, M., Hodges, J., & Cowper, D. (2005). Mitigating effect of Department of Veterans Affairs disability benefits for post-traumatic stress disorder on low income. *Military Medicine, 170*(2), 137–140.

National Center on Family Homelessness. (2009). *Understanding the experience of military families and their returning war fighters: Military literature and resource review.* Retrieved from www.familyhomelessness.org.

National Coalition for Homeless Veterans. (2010). *Background and Statistics: FAQs about homeless veterans.* Retrieved from http://nchv.org/index.php/news/media/background_and_statistics/.

National Women's Law Center, The Women's Research and Education Institute, & Alliance for National Defense. (2008). *Eliminating sexual assault should be a top priority of the Department of Defense.* Retrieved from http://www.nwlc.org/sites/default/files/pdfs/elimsexualassault.pdf.

Noonan, M., & Mumola, C. (2007, May). Veterans in state and federal prison, 2004. *Bureau of Justice Statistics: Special Report.* Retrieved from http://www.bjs.gov/content/pub/pdf/vsfp04.pdf.

Perl, L. (2009, June 26). *Veterans and homelessness.* Washington, DC: Congressional Research Service.

Serow, R. C. (2004). Policy as symbol: Title II of the 1944 G.I. Bill. *Review of Higher Education, 27*(4), 481–499.

Society for Women's Health Research. (2008). *PTSD in women returning from combat: Future directions in research and service delivery. A Report by the Society of Women's Health Research.* Retrieved from http://www.womens healthresearch.org/site/DocServer/PTSD_in_Women_Returning_From_ Combat—reduced_file_size.pdf.

Tanielian, T., & Jaycox, L. (2008, April 17). Stop loss: A nation weighs the tangible consequences of invisible combat wounds. *Rand Review.* Retrieved from http://www.rand.org/pubs/periodicals/rand-review/issues/summer2008/ wounds1.html.

Teachman, J. D., & Paasch, K. M. (1994). Financial impact of divorce on children and their families. *The Future of Children, 4*(1), 63–83.

U.S. Census Bureau, Current Population Survey. (2007, August). *Annual social and economic supplement, microdata.* Calculation conducted by the Mid-American Institute on Poverty of Heartland Alliance.

U.S. Department of Housing and Urban Development and U.S. Department of Veterans Affairs. (2009). *Veteran homelessness: A supplemental report to the 2009 homelessness report to Congress.* Retrieved from www.hudhre.info/ documents/2009AHARVeteransReport.pdf.

U.S. Department of Labor, Bureau of Labor Statistics. (2012). *Employment situation of veterans.* Available at www.bls.gov/spotlight/2010/Veterans/ and www.bls.gov/spotlight/2010/Veterans/ and www.bls.gov/news.release/ pdf/vet.pdf.

U.S. Department of Veterans Affairs. (2008). *Individual unemployability fact sheet.* Retrieved from www.vba.va.gov/VBA/benefits/factsheets/service connected/iu.doc.

U.S. Department of Veterans Affairs. (2011a). *Federal benefits for veterans, dependents & survivors.* (VA Pamphlet #80-11-01). Washington, DC: U.S. Government Printing Office.

U.S. Department of Veterans Affairs. (2011b). *VA disability compensation.* Retrieved from http://www.vba.va.gov/bln/21/compensation/index.htm.

U.S. Government Accountability Office. (2010). *VA health care: VA has taken steps to make services available to women veterans, but needs to revise key policies and improve oversight processes* (report to Congressional addresses). Retrieved from www.gao.gov/new.items/d10287.pdf.

Veterans' Mental Health and Other Care Improvements Act. (2001). Pub. L. No. 110-387, § 4, 604, Stat. 4133 (2008).

Webb, A. (2011). The myth of military poverty. *Washington Monthly, 33*(4), 44.

Zinzow, H., Grubaugh, A., Monnier, J., Suffoletta-Malerie, S., & Freuh, A. (2007). Trauma among female veterans: A critical review. *Trauma, Violence & Abuse, 8,* 384–400.

11

Poverty: What You Can Do

Elissa D. Giffords and Karen R. Garber

This chapter focuses on the things you can do to reduce poverty. By now, you have read about the multidimensional term, *poverty*. You have also learned about the contemporary public and private sector approaches used to address poverty, and the importance of meaningful employment policies. Finally, you explored how poverty affects specific at-risk populations such as older adults, people with disabilities, families, children, and those with co-occurring disorders. Throughout your reading, you have also learned how value-based beliefs and political ideologies influence social welfare policies. Social workers and other helping professionals must be aware of social welfare history as well as the contemporary approaches for addressing policy. Trends shift over time, which have a monumental impact on people in need and human service workers.

Chapters 4–10 of this book address specific populations at risk. This chapter briefly highlights some of the main points of these chapters and provides ways in which you can get involved in your community to help individuals and families who are facing poverty. Some suggestions include activities that focus on individuals. Others address groups and families. Additional activities offer community-based and legislative approaches. Taken together, antipoverty advocates may find these suggestions useful when working to decrease poverty.

Being Aware of the Impact of Social Welfare Policies

It is essential for anyone interested in reducing poverty to be committed to understanding general concepts as well as ongoing trends that influence the social welfare system. This is especially true for people entering or already working within a helping profession, such as social work. It is crucial for workers to understand the impact of social policies and programs on the lives of the people with which they work. Social workers, for example, must know what benefits are available for their clients as well as the related eligibility and procedural criteria. For example, Jennifer is a social worker at a soup kitchen. One day she notices there is a new family there—a single mother with two small children. Jennifer explains her role within the organization and offers to meet with the mother. After thinking about it briefly, the mother shares with Jennifer that she recently lost her job and that she is finding it difficult to feed her family. To help this family effectively, Jennifer must know what resources are available to assist this mother and her children. For instance, in the short-run is the mother eligible for Food Stamps and other public assistance? Is she entitled to unemployment insurance? Can Jennifer help her complete the complicated paperwork for child support collection from the local Department of Social Services? What about child care for her children so she can go on a job interview a friend told her about? If the mother is eligible for any benefits, are there time limits on this assistance? Assuming the mother is eligible, will the amount she receives be adequate to meet the family's needs? Is there a local parish outreach center or other community resource available to assist this family with groceries? If so, will the mother qualify? How often can she go there for groceries? Is there a specified time when she needs to go? Does she have transportation to this food pantry or live nearby? Longer-term assistance may require that Jennifer be knowledgeable regarding the existence of job training or educational programs. In addition, she must consider whether the existing programs adequately meet her client's needs. If not, what can she do to promote social change? Readers may note that the possibilities are plentiful. However, Jennifer must be aware of the various programs available to help her client, as well as having knowledge regarding the adequacy of the assistance. In addition, Jennifer may need to work with other social workers to develop a network or coalition with enough power to educate not only this family, but other families, practitioners, and the larger community so that they may learn about specific needs, such as hunger. Jennifer may develop a system that works to facilitate legislative change. Notably too, it is important for workers to have a sense of how social welfare policies and programs affect them as well. Social welfare does not only impact clients but also social workers. For instance, readers learned that historically, during difficult financial times, or when society is going through a conservative era, the budget for social programs is often reduced. Beyond the devastating impact that a reduction of funding may have on clients, workers may also find they have less money and resources to meet client needs. Typically there are also fewer workers to deal with increasing problems, as more people are seeking services. During economic downturns, the number of people applying for benefits increases, which places a further drain on local departments of social services. Local social service staff must review applicants' paperwork within mandated time frames in order to make eligibility determinations according to social services law. With a reduction in staff and an increase in applications, the timeliness of reviewing paperwork delays case openings. Delayed case openings can cause a number of issues for people in need, such as loss of housing, inadequate medical care, delays in obtaining medication, and insufficient food.

While some may enter the human service field to become private practitioners, therapists, or counselors, opportunities still exist to make meaningful social change. As discussed in chapter 1, social workers and other related professionals are taught to promote awareness of issues that lead to social injustice and disparities likely to result in some populations experiencing poverty or not attaining the social minimum. Helping professionals must use their skills as advocates, to fight for equality and the rights of people to gain access to necessary resources. These efforts take place at the micro, mezzo, and macro levels of practice. Case advocacy finds the practitioner engaging in strategies to help individuals attain social and economic justice while cause advocacy seeks the same outcome for a group of people or community. Ideally, practitioners will take on both case and cause advocacy approaches to helping, which is enhanced by the practitioner's knowledge about social trends. Social workers and other helping professionals must also work toward empowering people to help themselves. By using a person-in-environment approach (discussed in chapter 1), social workers consider the various aspects of clients' lives, to work to ensure individual well-being and social betterment for individuals, families, and communities. Often strategies to fight poverty involve creative thinking and plans. Examples of some ideas are discussed after the review of chapter highlights.

A Review: Populations at Risk of Poverty

In the first ten chapters of this book, readers learned there are circumstances that exist disproportionately among populations at risk. Groups such as those discussed here often experience poverty for reasons beyond their control. The following underscores some of the issues correlating with poverty that authors emphasized in their specific chapters. These chapter summaries are not intended to be a comprehensive review; rather, the purpose is to offer readers a synopsis of some key factors that make certain populations more at risk of experiencing poverty than others. Also included are some intervention strategies that are discussed in detail throughout the book.

Employment

In chapter 3, Goldberg explained the United States has never adopted a full employment policy, making it impossible for millions of Americans to find suitable work at livable wages, thereby increasing the risk of poverty. As we observed in the first three chapters of the book, TANF mandates work as a condition of benefits. Even marginal employment is preferred over welfare (Altman & Goldberg, 2008; Edin & Lein, 1997). Social and cultural factors can influence employability, such as skills, attitude, and economic booms (Wilson, 2009). Additionally, education has a direct relationship to economic mobility. When the labor market decreases, more people look for employment, which results in stagnated wages that can limit access to benefits such as employment-based health care. Conversely, when the job market is at its peak, wages and benefits rise. This is also true for people at the low end of the labor market (Pollin, 2007). Disparities occur regarding employment. Single mothers, for example, are less likely to be hired because employers perceive they have limited availability due to factors such as child care, and when hired, they are more likely to have lower starting salaries (Correll & Bernard, 2007; Waldfogel, 1998).

Homelessness and Housing

In chapter 4 Hanesworth explained the stereotypical view of the homeless is that they are dirty, dress in worn-out clothing, smell of alcohol, and are mentally unstable, but homelessness affects all populations. The recent economic crisis, for instance, has threatened the stability of housing for the working poor and middle class, thereby putting a new face on homelessness throughout the country. The middle class in particular, has fallen victim to foreclosure as a result of the housing market collapse. Personal difficulties such as unemployment, underemployment, mental health issues, and drug or alcohol dependency have also significantly contributed to homelessness. In order to combat this social problem, efforts have been made by many communities to create ten-year plans to end homelessness and bring awareness to the structural, political, and economic issues. Homelessness impacts every population discussed throughout this book. Ensuring affordable and safe housing is one crucial step in meeting the needs of vulnerable populations.

Families, Women, and Children

As we have read in Krase's chapter on "Families, Women, and Children," who raises a child and the size of the family unit can influence the risk of living in poverty. Likewise, geographic location can impact economic and social factors, which directly correlate to child poverty. For instance, families living in rural settings may lack job opportunities, transportation, and affordable child care. Likewise, a disproportionate number of children live in poverty as a result of their social environment. They are more likely to have health issues (Aligne, Auinger, Byrd, & Weitzman, 2000; Centers for Disease Control and Prevention [CDC], 1995, 2009), lower education attainment (Swanson, 2004), a higher chance of juvenile justice involvement (Office of Juvenile Justice and Delinquency Prevention, 2006), increased risk of mental health issues (Howell, 2004), greater risk of witnessing domestic violence (Davies, n.d.), as well as experiencing child abuse, neglect, or maltreatment (Garbarino & Collins, 1999).

Older Adults

The aging population in the United States is growing, and many older adults do not have the income they need to meet their basic needs. While social insurance programs such as Social Security and Medicare have helped to decrease financial hardship, and improve routine medical care, many older adults still face poverty. As we have read in Mathews's chapter on "Older Adults," poverty has social and physical consequences. Many elderly, for instance, may find themselves residing in naturally occurring retirement communities (NORC), as they cannot afford to leave, and many are unable to afford the upkeep and maintenance of their homes. Employment earnings, therefore, are a key post-retirement resource. If you earn more while working, you will have substantially more at retirement. Those lacking financial resources often choose to continue working or look for part-time employment to supplement their Social Security. Finding employment can be challenging as ageism exists. For example, younger workers are more likely to be hired than older adults.

People with Disabilities

Ostrander explains in chapter 7 that while people with disabilities have some federal protections under the Americans with Disabilities Act (ADA), there are noticeable limitations. While the ADA and Fair Housing Act require reasonable accommodations, suitable and appropriate housing is limited, which can result in homelessness. Additionally, people with disabilities are at risk of poverty, as they often experience discrimination with employment, and typically earn less than individuals without physical or mental challenges. Furthermore, there are noticeable disparities with educational levels, such as attainment of advanced degrees. Since they do not have the same access to higher education, this impacts the ability that people with disabilities have to be gainfully employed, thereby preventing many in this group from earning a livable wage. Traditionally, interventions that benefit this population focus on a deficit model rather than a strength-based model. For this reason, in addition to advocacy for legislative change, empowering people with disabilities through a shift in thinking is a critical intervention strategy.

Mental Illness and Co-Occurring Disorders

In chapter 8, Devitt and Davis discuss the term *co-occurring disorders*, which refers to people who are mentally ill and have a co-occurring substance abuse disorder that limits their daily functioning. Many individuals with co-occurring disorders are caught in a vicious cycle of exacerbating symptoms or increased substance use or both. As stressors intensify, the risk of living in poverty likewise increases. During these times, services are particularly critical. Given the current recession however, the availability of community resources, coordinated care services, nonprofit community mental health centers, and other treatment programs has been cut, resulting in service shortages. Social workers and health care professionals can assist individuals with co-occurring disorders by locating suitable programs and navigating systems, which otherwise are difficult to access. They can also educate the public about laws and policies that may benefit this population at risk. For example, advocating for inmates to participate in inpatient substance abuse programs is cost-effective as it provides an alternative to incarceration and reduces recidivism.

Immigrants and Refugees

Becerra, Ayón, Gurrola, Androff, and Segal explain the plight of immigrants and refugees living in poverty in chapter 9. They report that immigrants experience poverty more than other groups since they tend to have lower wages, limited proficiency in English, and lower education (Capps, Fix, Ost, Reardon-Anderson, & Passel, 2004). Poor health and discrimination are other factors that often contribute to poverty (Androff et al., 2011). Given the legal status of undocumented immigrants, many find work in dirty, dangerous, and physically demanding jobs with low pay and no health benefits (Androff et al., 2011). This group of immigrants often is socially isolated, living in their own communities, and do not always integrate into American culture. Moreover, like other groups, female immigrants and refugees find work outside the home to help lift families out of poverty. This is a change to their culture, traditions, and values, and is an important aspect for professionals to understand when working with families of immigrants. These changes can have significant consequences for the family and community as it creates new challenges to gender roles and economics (Pedone, 2006). The protection of human rights is critical with regard to all immigrants regardless of their legal status.

Military Families and American Veterans

In chapter 10, Uriarte discusses the plight of veterans leaving active service and readjusting to civilian life. Veterans are at an increased risk of experiencing mental health issues such as post-traumatic stress disorder, depression, traumatic brain injury, anxiety, stress, and anger management after returning from active duty. Mental health issues can lead to problems such as homelessness, poverty, and substance abuse. Likewise, military families face significant challenges, as the breadwinner typically enlists in the armed forces, leaving the other parent to manage the household and handle daily family matters. Women are increasingly participating in military service, which may pose additional challenges for military families. Upon return home, the readjustment for the entire family can be stressful as roles and expectations often change. While the United States has begun to invest more in its veterans by providing additional services and programs, Uriarte explains that the increasing number of veterans presently leaving the service and readjusting to civilian life is creating challenges for social workers and helping professionals who may be unfamiliar with the unique issues this group faces.

Working toward Social and Economic Justice

Social workers and related health and human services professionals should challenge social and economic injustice whenever possible. This is true for every population discussed in this book and other vulnerable groups as well. Social workers and other professionals need to provide a voice for those at risk of poverty in order to help make a difference. Helping professionals should also be cognizant of things they can do to empower individual clients and communities to advocate for themselves. Each chapter discusses this in greater detail as it relates to specific populations addressed throughout this book.

Individuals do not usually believe that they have the power to make a difference in the lives of individuals—but you do. You can learn more about poverty including feasible strategies for decreasing disparities. Below are suggestions that will deepen your understanding of this social problem, and facilitate community activities that may help to reduce poverty in your community.

21 Things You Can Do
Volunteer at a Parish Outreach

Contact a local parish and ask if they have a community center that provides services to parishioners. Offer to take applications for public assistance to the parish office and offer to help parishioners (who may be eligible for benefits such as public assistance, Medicaid, or SNAP/Food Stamps) fill out the applications. Applications can be obtained by contacting the local Department of Social Services (applications may also be available online). Also, offer to take a parishioner who is in need of services to the local Department of Social Services.

Volunteer at a Soup Kitchen

Make an appointment to visit a local soup kitchen to find out what services they provide and to volunteer. In addition to serving meals and cooking, the organization may run a boutique, which provides clothing to the guests. You can also volunteer to read books to children who come to the soup kitchen with their parents.

Mentor a Child at Risk of Poverty

Many times parents living at or near poverty face challenges and may not be able to meet the emotional needs of their children. Children have better outcomes when their emotional needs are met and they have positive role models in their lives. Mentoring provides one-on-one emotional support by matching a child with a positive role model referred to as a mentor. Mentors engage with children through activities such as playing sports, board games, helping with career decisions, or simply spending time together. Contact a mentoring program such as Big Brothers/Big Sisters about becoming a mentor for a child at risk. Mentoring programs usually require a one-year commitment. In addition, completing an application, participating in an interview, and taking an introductory course are typically required prior to being matched with a young person, referred to as a mentee.

Donate Professional Clothing to an Organization, Arrange a Clothing Drive, or Hold a Prom Boutique

Donate professional clothing to an organization (such as Dress for Success) that helps people get back into the workforce. You can also solicit donations from local dry cleaners who have unclaimed clothing. In addition to donated clothing, consider approaching a dry cleaner to clean the clothes for free before they are distributed.

You can also consider organizing a "Prom Boutique." Many young women cannot attend their proms because they do not have dresses or gowns, nor can they afford to purchase one. You may want to reach out to local universities and approach the sororities on campus to request gently worn gowns, dresses, and accessories (e.g., shoes and a purse). After getting donations, find a location to hold the Prom Boutique and advertise the event. The best time to hold a Prom Boutique is in the early spring, a few months before prom season begins.

Volunteer to Teach Someone How to Read

There are some adults who cannot read, yet they have completed elementary and junior high schools. They may have dropped out of high school and found jobs in landscaping or construction, for example, which do not require significant reading skills. Often they are ashamed of being illiterate and find it difficult asking for help. Contact a literacy program in your community and explore how to get involved in teaching an adult how to read. The program may require that you participate in a few seminars before you can begin teaching. Once you have completed the required training, you should be ready to begin tutoring. It is recommended that you meet in a local library where you have access to books for all reading levels.

Volunteer to Teach English as a Second Language

Many immigrants, particularly from Spanish-speaking countries, come to the United States with limited education. They may not have completed high school and may or may not be literate in their native language. Contact agencies in your community that provide services to people from different countries and ask how you can get involved in teaching English as a second language (ESL). Local schools that provide adult education classes may also offer ESL. Contact the program's director asking how you may volunteer.

Sponsor a Food Drive

After partnering with a nonprofit agency or local parish, sponsor a food drive in your community. Distribute flyers to local businesses and groups requesting donations. You can also solicit donations from local supermarkets or manufacturers of non-perishable items such as pasta, rice, and canned goods. Once you collect the non-perishable items, come up with a plan for how you will distribute the food to individuals and families in need within your community. You may want to reach out to shelters in addition to contacting food pantries that may have low food reserves.

Prepare and Deliver Meals to the Homeless

Collaborate with an established organization, such as the Coalition for the Homeless or another group such as a social work club, religious organization, fraternity, or sorority to prepare and deliver food to the homeless. Make sandwiches and distribute them at bus or train stations in the late evenings or early mornings. Also, when the weather is inclement, go to areas where homeless congregate, for instance under bridges, in the woods, and in parks, and provide soup or hot coffee. To all the locations, bring literature including phone numbers for local programs including food pantries and the Department of Social Services. It is suggested to give this information in small wallet-size cards to make it easier to put in a pocket for safekeeping.

Sponsor a Toy or Children's Book Drive

Sponsor a toy or children's book drive and bring the donations to a family shelter. Contact local youth groups that work with children to ask if they would be interested in working jointly on this project. Frequently youth groups are interested in community-sponsored events. Local Girl Scout chapters often participate in gathering items to be distributed to people in need. Your local Department of Social Services' housing division will accept your donations or refer you to a shelter where you can make your donation directly to the recipients.

Organize a Blanket Blitz

Contact local knitting stores and ask if there are any knitting groups that would be interested in making and donating blankets for people who are homeless, living on the streets or in shelters. During Hurricane Katrina, some knitting groups made blankets for survivors who were displaced as a result of this natural disaster. For children who are homeless, a knitted blanket can literally keep them warm and may become their security blanket since they are easy enough to take from place to place. Other types of blankets such as fleece and wool are also useful for many people living on the streets. Providing them with blankets can help them stay warm in the winter.

Organize a SNAP (Food Stamp) Challenge

Ask your friends, family, classmates, legislators, reporters, and others to live on the average amount of food stamps for one week, which according to the Kaiser Family Foundation (Kaiser Family Foundation, 2013) for 2012 was approximately $133.42 per month in the United States. This is $4.45 per person per day for all food and beverages (each state is different). To complete this challenge, go to a supermarket that is near public transportation, and try to plan and eat a balanced nutritious menu for one week that will not exceed $31.13. Or to obtain the exact monthly SNAP benefit in your state go to the U.S. Department of Agriculture (USDA) Food and Nutrition Service (2013) SNAP data report located at http://www.fns.usda .gov/pd/snapmain.htm. Then go to the Food Research and Action Center (FRAC) for a link to a short instructional guide for organizing this challenge in your own community: http://frac.org/pdf/snap_challenge_toolkit_frac.pdf.

Sponsor a Veterans Stand Down

Contact your local veterans office and community-based organizations who work with veterans to sponsor a stand down, which is aimed at assisting veterans. The veterans include those returning to the community from active duty, any veteran in need of services, and any veteran who is homeless. Services can be tangible, such as clothing and medical care, to intangible such as counseling referrals. Start with identifying a central location to hold the stand down. Following that, arrange for federal, state, and local departments (such as Health and Human Services) to participate. Also be sure to include community-based agencies. Government agencies can provide information and applications for services including Medicaid, SNAP (formerly called Food Stamps), Home Energy Assistance Program (HEAP), Public Assistance, Social Security, and SSI. Community-based agencies such as mental health counseling centers and drug and alcohol treatment programs can bring literature explaining their programs. Also, reach out to local business owners, such as barbers, who can provide free haircuts. Some businesses may have open positions they wish to fill. Encourage them to participate, emphasizing they can interview candidates at the stand down, which eliminates the need to set up appointment interviews in the future. Suggest to veterans that they bring their resumes to the stand down. In addition, contact local hospitals asking that they participate and provide free health screenings, including eye and dental exams.

Job Fairs

Contact the Department of Labor (DOL) in your community about holding a job fair. They will have lists of local employers who may be interested in participating. Work with DOL to reach out to other agencies and local departments to set up tables at the fair. Also, contact your local small business owners' association inviting them to participate. Through advertisements, invite the public to attend the job fair, encouraging participants to bring their resumes. For people involved with DOL or social services, provide job readiness classes in advance of the job fair. Job readiness can include how to appropriately dress for an interview, how to respond to questions regarding skill sets, and resume writing.

Collecting Data

Explore the number of individuals who are poor in your local and state community and their demographics (age, gender, and ethnic or racial characteristics). Some techniques to do this involve conducting online research to obtain statistics. Good places to start include http://www.fedstats.gov, which is a website that contains links to statistics from more than 100 agencies, and the Census Bureau located at http://www.census.gov/hhes/www/poverty.html. The census is where you will find official national poverty estimates. Another census-sponsored resource is http://factfinder2.census.gov/, which will enable you to search for specific data using your own terms. They explain, for example, to find data about grandparents in Indiana, users simply type "grandparents" in the topic field and "Indiana" in the geography field.

Once you gather these data, you will be able to create a custom economic profile of your community. In addition to demonstrating the overall number and percentage of people who are poor or near poor, you can describe this population by characteristics such as race, ethnicity, age, and housing.

Compiling Stories

To gain a deeper understanding of what it is like to live in poverty in your own community, you can work with a local human service organization with a predominant population of at-risk clientele, to solicit clients' individual stories or to share their own perceptions of what it is like to be poor. By collecting stories such as these, you may strengthen your own understanding of what life is like for people with limited income and resources. In addition, the individuals' struggles may be used to inform lawmakers, and to strengthen the legislation to support people living in poverty, and the working poor. Personal anecdotes help to personalize statistics.

Contact Your Member of Congress

Do you know the names of your congressional representative and senators? If not, go to http://www.govtrack.us/congress/findyourreps.xpd to find out. Once there, you will select a state, or enter your zip code, or street address. After you enter the information, you will see the names of your members of Congress as well as a district map. This website also enables you to find the status of United States federal legislation, voting records for the Senate and House of Representatives, information on members of Congress, congressional committees, and the *Congressional Record*. After you know who represents you, consider visiting their website to read about where they stand on various issues, including poverty. You will also have the opportunity to sign up to receive their e-newsletter, and to obtain their address, phone, and fax information.

There are many ways to contact your legislator. You can consider calling, e-mailing, sending a traditional letter through the post office, or even visiting face-to-face. This is referred to as "constituent communication." Written letters, either through e-mail or traditional mail, are an effective means to let your representatives know your opinion on issues or to share information. Letters are particularly successful in large volumes, so it is a good idea to get like-minded friends, family members, or colleagues to write to their legislators too, especially about an issue such as poverty. You want to keep your letters brief (about one page). When writing, mention that you are a constituent, and identify reasons why your representative should support or intensify his or her support regarding the issue. It is also beneficial to include relevant data, and to share stories about how individuals are affected by the problem to illustrate or personalize the issue. In the letter, ask your legislator for a response. It is important to be courteous and refrain from including vulgar language or anything that can be construed as a threat. There are sample letters and tips for writing them online. A simple search should yield many. To help you ascertain specific detail about his or her position, consider following up with your legislator's office through a phone call or visit.

Contact Your Local Newspaper

Contact your local newspaper and suggest they feature a family in need of assistance, on a weekly basis, and ask the community to donate needed items such as food, school supplies, and clothing. Local community-based agencies or parish outreach centers can provide the names of families in need.

Another useful thing you can do that utilizes your local newspaper is by responding to a recent news article or an editorial by writing a letter to the editor or an Op-Ed piece. This type of letter, if published, enables you to share your opinion with the community. Similar to what you do when writing to a legislator, this correspondence should be to the point, and free from sarcasm and vulgar language. All newspapers have guidelines for types of letters, but generally, they are brief (250–300 words), while Op-Ed pieces may be longer. Successful letters usually contain relevant data, which help present a strong argument regarding the issue.

Volunteer for a Candidate or Run for Office

Another way to assist various populations at risk is to volunteer to work for a political candidate or consider running for office yourself. A legislator has the ability to enhance public policy, and to shape government's role in establishing meaningful antipoverty legislation. Social workers and related human service providers can make ideal legislators or political advisors by integrating a social work perspective into their work. While there are many offices available for which individuals can run, if you wish to hold office, you should consider starting at the local level and working your way up to state and federal office.

Visit Your State Capital

Investigate the names of your local congress people and senators. Through the Internet you can determine their office days and hours at the state capital. It is suggested you read their profiles on the Internet to understand their platform positions. Once you know their platform, you can frame your discussion accordingly. For instance, some politicians are members of special committees, which focus on different topics such as health and welfare. By gathering information related to their position on health and welfare, you can get a better sense of their priorities and issues. At the meeting with your local politicians, you can present your findings and suggest ways to improve service delivery to their constituents. This type of advocacy can be very effective as politicians are committed to fulfill promises they make to their constituents in order to be reelected.

Interview Your Local Social Services Commissioner

Contact your local social services office and ask for an appointment to interview the commissioner. Prior to the appointment, come up with a list of questions you would like to ask such as: How are services provided in your community? What are the funding streams for the entitlement programs? Do the federal, state, and local government all contribute equally? What is the role of caseworkers and welfare examiners? What are the educational requirements for these jobs? What qualifications do the caseworkers and welfare examiners need to perform their jobs? How are services delivered? Ask the commissioner if there are any unmet needs in the department with which you can help. Many times, there are volunteer opportunities at the local Department of Social Services office such as collecting toiletries for clients or soliciting donations for pens that clients can use to complete their applications.

Reach Out to Your Local Bar Association

Contact your local bar association and discuss the idea of holding a pro bono clinic for low-income individuals who need help navigating public benefit programs. People may be unfamiliar with entitlement programs, eligibility criteria, and their right to apply for services. Additionally, negotiating public benefits can be confusing and overwhelming. Attorneys familiar with public benefits law could sponsor a pro bono clinic to advise people of programs available in their community. Likewise, attorneys familiar with public benefits law could offer continuing legal education seminars to other attorneys and then hold larger pro bono clinics for individuals seeking legal assistance with government programs.

Internet Resources

AmeriCorps: http://www.americorps.gov/

AmeriCorps offers opportunities for adults to serve their communities through local and national nonprofit groups. It offers education awards to pay for college or to pay back student loans.

Corporation for National and Community Service: http://www.nationalservice.gov/

The Corporation for National and Community Service engages Americans in service and leads the President's national call to service initiative.

Feeding America: http://feedingamerica.org/how-we-fight-hunger.aspx

This group provides food bank information nationwide to help feed the hungry.

Food Research and Action Center (FRAC): http://frac.org/

FRAC is a nonprofit organization working to improve public policies and public-private partnerships to eradicate hunger and under-nutrition in the United States.

Kids Count: http://datacenter.kidscount.org/databook/2011/familystories.aspx

Five families from Atlanta, Georgia; Baltimore, Maryland; Los Angeles County, California; Rochester, New Hampshire; and San Antonio, Texas share their personal struggles and stories about the help they received.

Live Below the Line: http://www.livebelowtheline.com

Live Below the Line is a formal initiative where participants *Live Below the Line* for five days and are challenged to eat only as much per day as can be purchased for $1.50.

Martin Luther King Day of Service: http://mlkday.gov/

Martin Luther King Day of Service calls for Americans from all walks of life to work together to provide solutions to our most pressing national problems.

MENTOR: The National Mentoring Partnership: http://mentoring.org

MENTOR provides information on mentoring programs in your community.

The National Alliance to End Homelessness: http://www.endhomelessness.org/

This organization is a nonprofit, nonpartisan organization committed to preventing and ending homelessness in the United States.

National Coalition for Homeless Veterans: http://www.nchv.org/

The NCHV offers resources and technical assistance to a national network of community-based service providers and local, state, and federal agencies that provide services for homeless veterans. It also serves as the primary liaison between the care providers, Congress, and the executive branch.

Senior Corps: http://www.seniorcorps.gov/

Senior Corps offers adults over fifty-five years old opportunities to volunteer in their communities as mentors, coaches, or companions to people in need, or by donating job skills and expertise to benefit community projects and organizations.

Further Readings

Gerlach, B. (2010, November 12). Take action: 10 things you can do to improve your community today. *The New Pursuit.* Retrieved from http://www.thenewpursuit.com/2010/11/12/take-action-10-things-you-can-do-to-improve-your-community-today/.

Homan, M. (2008). *Promoting community change: Making it happen in the real world* (4th ed.). Belmont, CA: Thomson Brooks/Cole.

Hoose, P. (1993). *It's our world, too!: Young people who are making a difference: How they do it—how you can, too!* Boston: Joy Street Books.

Singer, J. (2006). *Stirring up justice: Writing and reading to change the world.* Portsmouth, NH: Heinemann, Reed Elsevier Inc.

References

Aligne, C. A., Auinger, P., Byrd, R. S., & Weitzman, M. (2000), Risk factors for pediatric asthma: Contributions of poverty, race and urban residence. *American Journal of Critical Care and Respiratory Medicine, 162*(3), 873–877.

Altman, J. C., & Goldberg, G. S. (2008). Rethinking social work's role in public assistance. *Journal of Sociology and Social Welfare, 35*(4), 71–94. Retrieved from http://heinonline.org/HOL/LandingPage?collection=journals&handle=hein.journals/jrlsasw35&div=44&id=&page=.

Androff, D., Ayon, C., Becerra, D., Gurrola, M., Salas, L., Krysik, J., . . . Segal, E. (2011). U.S. immigration policy and immigrant children's well-being: The impact of policy shifts. *Journal of Sociology & Social Welfare, 38*(1), 77–98.

Capps, R., Fix, M., Ost, J., Reardon-Anderson, J., & Passel, J. S. (2004). *The health and well-being of young children of immigrants.* Washington, DC: Urban Institute.

Centers for Disease Control and Prevention. (1995). *Poverty and infant mortality.* Retrieved from http://www.cdc.gov/mmwr/preview/mmwrhtml/ 00039818.htm.

Centers for Disease Control and Prevention, Morbidity and Mortality Report. (2009). *Obesity prevalence among low-income, preschool-aged children: United States 1998–2008.* Retrieved from http://www.cdc.gov/mmwr/preview/ mmwrhtml/mm5828a1.htm.

Correll, S. J., & Bernard, S. (2007). Getting a job: Is there a motherhood penalty? *American Journal of Sociology, 112*(5), 1297–1338.

Davies, J. (n.d.). Policy blueprint on domestic violence and poverty. National Resource Center on Domestic Violence, University of Iowa School of Social Work, and Greater Hartford Legal Assistance. *Building comprehensive solutions to domestic violence,* Publication #15. Retrieved from http://new .vawnet.org/Assoc_Files_VAWnet/BCS15_BP.pdf.

Edin, K., & Lein, L. (1997). *Making ends meet: How single mothers survive welfare and low-wage work.* New York: Russell Sage.

Garbarino, J., & Collins, C. C. (1999). Child neglect: The family with a hole in the middle. In *Neglected children: Research, practice and policy,* ed. H. Dubowitz (pp. 1–23). Thousand Oaks, CA: SAGE Publications.

Howell, E. (2004). *Access to children's mental health services under Medicaid and SCHIP.* Washington, DC: Urban Institute. Retrieved from http://www.urban .org/uploadedPDF/311053_B-60.pdf.

Kaiser Family Foundation. (2013). *Average monthly food stamp benefits per person, FY2012.* Retrieved from http://kff.org/other/state-indicator/avg-monthly- food-stamp-benefits/.

Office of Juvenile Justice and Delinquency Prevention. (2006). *Juvenile offenders and victims: 2006 national report.* Washington, DC: U.S. Department of Justice.

Pedone, C. (2006). Changes in education and family life in current Ecuadorian migration: A transatlantic perspective. *Athenea Digital, 10,* 154–171.

Pollin, R. (2007). A people's economy is possible. *New Labor Forum, 16*(3/4), 8–17.

Swanson, C. B. (2004). *Who graduates? Who doesn't? A statistical portrait of public high school graduation, 2001.* Education Policy Center, Urban Institute. Retrieved from http://www.urban.org/UploadedPDF/410934_WhoGraduates.pdf.

USDA Food and Nutrition Service. (2013). *Program data Supplemental Nutrition Assistance Program (SNAP).* Retrieved from http://www.fns.usda.gov/pd/snapmain.htm.

Waldfogel, J. (1998). Understanding the "family gap" in pay for women with children. *Journal of Economic Perspectives, 12*(1), 137–156.

Wilson, H. (2009). President Eisenhower and the development of active labor market policy in the United States: A revisionist view. *Presidential Studies Quarterly, 39*(3), 519–554.

Glossary

Absolute Poverty A fixed measure of poverty, which describes the minimum amount of money necessary for individuals and families to meet their basic needs (food, shelter, and clothing). An example of an absolute measure is the poverty line.

Acculturation A complex process of changing attitudes, norms, behaviors, and identity in order to adapt to a new culture.

Active Labor Market Policy Government provides paid employment, training, and other measures to promote employment in contrast to unemployment insurance, which offers only income support. Like unemployment insurance, it can be available for unemployed workers in "normal" times as well as during periods of high unemployment. In the United States it has only been offered during some periods of very high unemployment.

Activities of Daily Living (ADLs) The simple activities or tasks associated with daily living and self-care such as bathing, toileting, and eating.

Affirmative Action A government policy for overcoming segregation in employment. It includes active efforts to recruit, train, hire, and promote groups that have historically been disadvantaged by segregation and discrimination—especially racial and ethnic minorities, women, and persons with disabilities.

Affordable Housing Defined by the U.S. Department of Housing and Urban Development (HUD) as housing that costs no more than 30 percent of a household's income.

Aging in Place The phenomenon of older adults remaining in their homes or in familiar communities as long as possible, thereby decreasing the likelihood they will relocate in later life.

Aging Network An array of public and private agencies and social services designed to help older adults remain independent and in the community.

Aging Out Children in foster care who are too old to remain in the child welfare system. In some states, children age out of foster care at 18 years of age, while in other states the age can go to 21.

Aid to Dependent Children (ADC) ADC was a federal program offered to the states under the Social Security Act of 1935 to provide an income subsidy to households with children with fathers who were deceased, absent, or unable to work. This program was later expanded to Aid to Families with Dependent Children (AFDC), which permitted assistance to also go to unemployed male parents with a work history. It was later replaced by Temporary Assistance to Needy Families (TANF) under the Personal Responsibility Work Opportunity Reconciliation Act of 1996 (PRWORA).

Alzheimer's Disease (AD) A type of dementia, associated with progressive cognitive and functional declines.

Americans with Disabilities Act (ADA) The ADA first passed in 1990 under President George H. W. Bush, creating civil rights legislation for people with disabilities. The ADA banned discrimination based on disability in a number of domains, including employment, public transportation, and public accommodations.

Bipolar Disorder Also known as manic-depressive illness, it is a brain disorder that causes unusual shifts in mood, energy, activity levels, and the ability to carry out day-to-day tasks. Symptoms can be severe. Bipolar disorder symptoms can result in damaged relationships, poor job or school performance, and even suicide. The disorder is treatable and people with this illness can lead full and productive lives.

Block Grants A specific amount of federal money, which is allocated to states and local governments to be used at their discretion for specific programs. This provides states and local governments more freedom over how they administer their allocated funds because there is less federal oversight; however, once the funding runs out, it limits a program's ability to respond to increased need.

Caregiver Burden The persistent physical, emotional, and financial stress and impaired psychosocial functioning of caregivers. Caregiver burden is most prevalent among caregivers caring for someone with Alzheimer's disease or other types of dementia.

Cash Assistance Provides eligible recipients with money in the form of cash or a check. An example of a cash assistance program is Supplemental Security Income, or TANF (welfare) cash assistance.

Charity Organization Societies (COS) Created in the later part of the nineteenth century, these non-governmental agencies sought to coordinate philanthropic giving and promoted a scientific approach to avoid duplication of assistance. Initially COS workers offered moral guidance to those in need and later provided financial assistance and social casework to help individuals and families.

Child Abuse and Neglect Under current law child abuse and neglect refers to a failure of a parent or caretaker to act on behalf of a child, which results in death, serious physical or emotional harm, sexual abuse or exploitation; or whose actions cause imminent risk of serious harm to a child. The term *child neglect*, the most common type of maltreatment, considers the failure of parents or guardians to provide for a child's basic needs, including medical, educational, emotional, and physical care.

Child Poverty A term that reflects the measurement of the number of children living in poverty, whereby each child is counted separately.

Colonias These communities are unincorporated rural areas located outside of the official boundaries of cities along the U.S.-Mexico border. These communities are often without electricity, paved roads, sewer systems, potable water, and lack access to quality education and health services.

Comprehensive Employment and Training Act (CETA) CETA was enacted in the 1970s when unemployment was at its highest post-Depression level. It resembled the Works Progress Administration (WPA) in that it was a temporary program that provided jobs in the service of the public to unemployed workers, but it differed by having a training component.

Co-Occurring Disorders A term used to describe the existence of suffering from two disorders or illnesses simultaneously. In mental health, it most often refers to having a mental illness and a substance use disorder.

Defense Task Force on Domestic Violence A Department of Defense Task Force that identifies ways to prevent and curb domestic abuse in the military and provide more timely and effective aid to victims.

Deferred Action for Childhood Arrivals (DACA) This allows undocumented immigrants who arrived in the United States prior to the age of sixteen to apply for a two-year temporary work permit if they meet certain requirements.

Deinstitutionalization A sociopolitical movement beginning in the mid-1960s whereby psychiatric patients were removed from inpatient settings with the intent of transitioning them to private homes and community outpatient clinics.

Deserving Poor Individuals and groups thought to be poor through no fault of their own, due to conditions such as old age, illness, or lack of available work.

Diagnostic and Statistical Manual of Mental Disorders (*DSM*) The standard classification of mental disorders used by mental health professionals in the United States (developed by the American Psychiatric Association). It is intended to be applicable in a wide array of contexts and used by clinicians and researchers of many different orientations (e.g., biological, psychodynamic, cognitive, behavioral, interpersonal, family/systems).

Disability A physical or mental impairment that substantially limits one or more of an individual's major life activities (as defined by the Americans with Disabilities Act).

Disability Compensation This may be provided to military veterans with a service-related disability that was incurred in or aggravated by their active military service. If eligible, the Veterans Administration (VA) pays the veteran a monthly tax-free payment. The amount is determined by the degree or percentage of disability.

Disproportionate Minority Representation (**DMR**) reflects the over-representation of a particular minority group involved with a service system. An example is the significantly higher representation of children of color in the foster care system.

Domestic Violence (DV)/Intimate Partner Violence (IPV) DV or IPV are terms used to describe physical, sexual, psychological, economic, or other abusive behavior by a spouse or intimate partner against the other.

Donut Hole Under Medicare prescription drug coverage, recipients exceeding the amount of money covered for prescription drugs must pay out-of-pocket for their medication. This gap is referred to as the Donut Hole.

Doubled Up A circumstance in which a person or family is living in housing designed for less occupants. For example, two families each with four people living in a two-bedroom apartment. Doubled ups are not officially counted among the homeless because they are not visible.

Early Intervention (EI) This federal program assists families with children from birth through three years who have been classified with special needs such as developmental disabilities. Children who are classified are eligible for a host of services. By providing child-specific interventions at an early age such as speech or physical therapy, children have a greater chance of needing less services in later years, thereby improving long-term outcomes.

Earned Income Tax Credit (EITC) Government income support to supplement the wages of employed workers with low earnings. Workers file claims for the benefit through the Internal Revenue Service (IRS). Called a "tax credit," it is largely provided to workers who pay no federal income taxes and is therefore a form of public assistance but is differently perceived because it supplements earned income.

Economic Bill of Rights In his 1944 Message to Congress, President Franklin Roosevelt observed that the constitutional guarantee of political rights had proven insufficient to guarantee economic security. Roosevelt proposed a second bill of rights that would guarantee rights to employment and a decent living, health care, protection against sickness, unemployment, and insecurity in old age and decent housing. Paramount among these, he later stated, was the guarantee of employment.

Economic Vulnerability A heightened insecurity or risk of multidimensional deprivation experienced by some individuals or at-risk groups, such as older adults, which is often related to the degree to which people have the capacity to cope financially with an emergency or crisis or perhaps due to a change in their marital status, or other relevant life changes that impact individuals' purchasing power.

Elder Abuse A form of abuse, which can include physical, sexual, or emotional abuse or financial exploitation of an older adult. Elder abuse is a serious growing problem that is often hidden from public view.

Emergency Shelter Housing for the purpose of providing temporary housing, usually 30–90 days, for individuals or families who have become homeless.

Employer Sanction Laws Laws that are intended to punish employers for hiring undocumented immigrants.

Entitlement Programs A type of assistance that provides individuals with financial benefits, goods, or services by virtue of citizenship. Eligible families and individuals have a legal right to receive this assistance whenever they meet eligibility guidelines specified by law. Individuals and families cannot be denied benefits regardless of the fiscal climate of the state or federal government. An example of an entitlement program at the federal level in the U.S. is Social Security Retirement benefits.

Eugenics Movement Beginning in the late nineteenth century, this movement advocated for social measures to eliminate the procreation of people deemed to have undesirable traits (e.g., disabilities). Measures under this movement included sterilization, euthanasia, and laws forbidding people with disabilities to marry.

E-Verify An automated system for employers to verify the work eligibility of potential employees in order to ensure that undocumented immigrants do not work in the United States.

Fair Housing Act, which is part of the Civil Rights Act of 1968, bans housing discrimination based on race, color, national origin, religion, sex, familial status, or disability.

Familism A concept to describe the high value and attachment placed on the immediate and extended family among Latinos.

Family Advocacy Program This federal program focuses on military service members and their families. The Family Advocacy Program raises awareness to prevent intimate partner violence and child abuse by improving family functioning and creating a community that is supportive of families. Services include specialized support to new parents, victim advocacy, sexual assault prevention, and a program that identifies special medical needs of adult and child family members.

Family Care Plan This written plan is a requirement for all soldiers in active duty and in the reserves that have dependents. It outlines who will take responsibility for the care of the soldier's minor children in the event of deployment.

Family Medical Leave Act (FMLA) This federal act provides employees the opportunity to take off from work for medical-related reasons (such as the birth of a baby or caring for an ill family member) without the risk of losing their jobs.

Family Poverty A term that refers to family households where children are present and household income falls below the poverty line. In the family poverty measure the entire family unit is measured once regardless of the number of children residing in the household.

Foster Care A temporary living arrangement designed to meet abused, neglected, and dependent children's needs while their parents or guardians are unable to care for them.

Full Employment The British economist Sir William Beveridge defined full employment as more available jobs than job seekers. Notably, however, there is no universally accepted definition among economists. For some, it refers to a market where there are more jobs than job seekers. For others it refers to a very low unemployment rate or the availability of living-wage jobs for all who want to work.

Great Society A term for the many social welfare programs established under President Lyndon Johnson to end poverty, promote equality, improve education, and enhance community programs. Programs of this era included Food Stamps, Medicare, Medicaid, job training, and community development initiatives. It also established several federal departments such as the Department of Housing and Urban Development (HUD).

Hidden Unemployment This includes two types of jobless workers who are not officially counted as unemployed: (1) those working part-time (less than thirty-five hours a week) who want a full-time job but cannot find one; and (2) those who are jobless, would take a job if it were available, but are not actively looking, in some cases because they have become discouraged.

House (or Equity) Rich and Cash Poor The phenomenon in which due to longevity in their homes, individuals may have accrued significant equity, but due to a fixed income have very little to no available cash resources.

HUD-VASH Program The Department of Housing and Urban Development–VA Supportive Housing (HUD-VASH) Program is a joint effort between HUD and the Veterans Administration to move veterans and their families out of homelessness and into permanent housing.

Human Service Organizations Many human service organizations focus on the prevention and remediation of problems, and seek to improve the quality of life of their clients. Generally, these agencies assist a specified client population with an identified social need such as individuals, groups, and/or communities who are poor or at risk of living in poverty.

Individuals with Disabilities Education Act (IDEA) Passed in 1990, this act worked to ensure that children with disabilities receive appropriate public education that would be paid for through public funding.

Informal Caregivers Unpaid caregivers face competing responsibilities, and emotional and/or financial demands (including long-distance care-giving). Today, women account for the majority of informal caregivers providing care to older adults.

In-Kind Assistance Help provided to eligible recipients in the form of goods or services. In-kind services include health benefits and child care.

Institutional Circuit The frequent and circular pattern of use of shelters and other custodial institutions that, by default, have acquired hybrid functions that effectively substitute for more stable and appropriate housing for some persons with severe mental illness.

Institutional View of Social Welfare A belief that government social programs should assist all socioeconomic groups to meet their basic needs (e.g., food, education, shelter, income, employment) as a right of citizenship, through programs such as Social Security retirement benefits. This view takes a universal approach to social welfare rather than just helping those in poverty. There is not usually a stigma associated with this type of assistance.

Instrumental Activities of Daily Living (IADLs) The complex tasks or activities associated with day-to-day living such as cooking, grocery shopping, and banking that are rendered difficult due to declines in ability.

Integrated Dual Disorder Treatment A treatment model for treating co-occurring mental illness and substance use disorders simultaneously. The model is comprised of organizational requirements and specific clinical interventions, while being underpinned by a harm-reduction philosophy. Organizations must have staff that understand the interaction of both disorders and are trained to treat them simultaneously. Choices of clinical interventions are determined based on readiness to work on reducing substance use. Clinical interventions include motivational interviewing and cognitive behavioral therapy.

Laissez-Faire A popular conservative philosophy from the nineteenth century that reflects opposition to governmental interference in economic and social affairs of society beyond the minimum required to maintain order.

Life Course Perspective A perspective that connects later life circumstances to other life stages experienced throughout one's life.

Long-Term Care (LTC) A continuum of care options that serve older adults with varied dependency levels and socioeconomic backgrounds. This continuum generally includes a stepwise level of care options including board and care homes, assisted-living facilities (ALFs), continuing care retirement communities (CCRCs), and nursing homes.

Macro Intervention Community organization, administration of social agencies, and other related macro-level practice approaches that seek to intervene on behalf of, or with clients through changes in policies, planning, or administration.

Major Depression A mental disorder characterized by persistent sadness and an inability to find pleasure in life. Major depression is a combination of symptoms that interfere with a person's ability to work, sleep, study, eat, and enjoy once-pleasurable activities. Major depression is disabling and prevents a person from functioning normally. Some people may experience only a single episode within their lifetime, but more often a person may have multiple episodes.

Marital Benefit (or **Marital Effect**) The wide range of benefits associated with marital status, including individuals' economic well-being and mental and physical health.

McKinney Vento Act Originally known as the "McKinney Act," a federal law enacted in 1987 providing funding to fifteen different types of interventions to address homelessness, including Continuum of Care and the Emergency Shelter Grant Program. Later, the law was renamed "McKinney Vento" after legislators adapted it to include protections to homeless children, with emphasis on their rights to access education.

Medicaid Included in the Social Security Act of 1965, this federal program provides publicly funded health care for individuals and families with low income and resources. It also provides health care to qualified elderly and people with disabilities.

Medical Model of Disability Disability is defined as the result of a physical condition that can be cured or managed to minimize the limitations of a person with a disability.

Medicare As part of the Social Security Act of 1965, this federal program provides health insurance for older adults, people with disabilities, and individuals with specific health conditions such as end stage renal disease.

Mezzo Intervention Mezzo practice seeks to intervene at the group level or to work with families. This involves working with many individuals simultaneously through a group process rather than one-on-one.

Micro Intervention Micro practice seeks to intervene on a one-on-one basis to help individuals with the goal of helping them adapt to or make changes in the environment to better meet their needs. Casework is an example of a micro-level intervention.

Moral Model of Disability Disability is viewed as the result of sin or moral defect.

Mutual Assistance or Mutual Aid This approach to helping is often thought of as friends, neighbors, and peers helping each other. A classic example of a self-help group is Alcoholics Anonymous (AA); another is the National Alliance for the Mentally Ill (for families and friends of people with a serious mental illness).

Naturally Occurring Retirement Communities (NORCs) The phenomenon exists when a disproportionate number of older people live in an area, varied by location, physical dimensions, population size, and demographics. A neighborhood or facility originally populated with members of all age groups evolves over time to contain a high proportion of older adults.

Nonsectarian Organization An organization without a religious affiliation or not oriented toward a specified religious cohort.

Normal Aging Process The universal changes that readily affect everyone as they age such as varying changes in visual acuity. These changes are associated to time and use rather than disease-related processes.

Official Unemployment As counted by the U.S. government, it includes those persons who do not have a job, have actively looked for work in the prior four weeks, and are currently available for work. Actively looking for work includes such activities as contacting an employer or employment agencies, looking at job-wanted ads, sending out résumés, or filling out employment applications.

Orphan Train Movement A controversial initiative that lasted from 1853 to the early twentieth century, the Orphan Train Movement removed children from impoverished and neglectful homes in crowded cities and sent them by train to live and work on farms in the West. It is said to be the precursor of the current U.S. foster care system.

Outreach Seeks to locate individuals and families in order to provide supportive services. Outreach is often used with populations that are isolated and experiencing barriers to accessing resources.

Pay Equity A policy for equalizing the rewards of a segregated workforce by determining the "comparable worth" of the jobs held by historically advantaged and disadvantaged workers (for example, male and female prison guards and adjusting the pay of the latter accordingly).

Personal Responsibility and Work Opportunity Reconciliation Act (PRWORA) Signed into law by President Bill Clinton in 1996, PRWORA legislation drastically changed the U.S. welfare system. It ended the entitlement programs Aid to Families with Dependent Children (ADFC), Job Opportunities and

Basic Skills Training (JOBS), and the Emergency Assistance (EA) program and replaced them with the block grant known as Temporary Assistance for Needy Families (TANF). This ended several guaranteed safety-net programs for many vulnerable Americans.

Populations at Risk Specific groups of people such as older adults, people with disabilities, women, and people who are culturally diverse who are at risk of experiencing poverty more than other groups (e.g., Caucasian males). Often vulnerable populations are more at risk because of social and economic conditions, which are beyond their control due to factors such as prejudice and discrimination that lead to members of these groups being denied equal opportunities to enhance their quality of life.

Poverty Line The minimum level by which the federal government determines an individual or family can financially manage before they are classified as poor.

Preventive Service Programs These aim to prevent child maltreatment and to reduce the risk of children entering foster care.

Progressive Era An era that began in the late nineteenth century and reflects a time of change when Americans thought about and responded to poverty and social conditions differently than they did previously. Progressives were responsible for numerous social and legislative reforms, placing an emphasis on social and economic justice.

Public Assistance The social welfare expenditure called public assistance includes all types of noncontributory, tax-financed assistance to people living in poverty. Examples include TANF (commonly referred to as welfare), Supplemental Nutrition Assistance Program benefits (SNAP, previously referred to as Food Stamps), and Medicaid.

Reduced Work Time A proposal to reduce the standard work week that would help prevent employees from being overworked and provide more time for family life and leisure. Since additional workers would be needed for some of the uncovered hours, it is promoted as a means of reducing unemployment.

Rehabilitation Act of 1973 Following numerous struggles for the social inclusion of people with disabilities, this act included provisions for services and civil rights for people with disabilities involved in federally funded programs.

Relative Poverty A felt measure of poverty where poverty is defined subjectively in relation to other members of society.

Residual View of Social Welfare A concept that suggests the individual, the family, and the market should be the first line of assistance for individuals and that the government should only help when all other systems have failed. When breakdowns in these systems occur, it is believed that any assistance provided should be offered temporarily through safety-net programs that have strict eligibility criteria. Residual programs often have a stigma attached.

Reverse Mortgages (or **Home Equity Conversion Mortgages, HECM**) An option for older adults in financial need. These are loans that allow seniors (who own their home free and clear) to convert their home equity into flexible cash advances while still living in their homes.

Sandwich Generation The group of caregivers sandwiched between dual care responsibilities, simultaneously caring for two generations, often children under eighteen years old and older adults. Women represent the majority of this group.

SB 1070 An Arizona law passed in 2010 that requires that state and local police officers check the immigration status of anyone they arrest or suspect is illegally in the country. This law became the model for similar laws in other states in the United States.

Schizophrenia Spectrum Disorders A group of mental disorders in which people experience hallucinations, delusions, and difficulty interacting with others and participating in many activities of daily life. People with the disorder may hear voices other people do not hear. They may believe other people are reading their minds, controlling their thoughts, or plotting to harm them. Treatment helps relieve many symptoms of schizophrenia, but most people who have the disorder cope with symptoms throughout their lives, and many manage to lead rewarding and meaningful lives. Researchers are developing more effective medications and using new research tools to understand the causes of schizophrenia. In the years to come, this work may help prevent and better treat the illness.

Sectarian Organization Also referred to as a faith-based agency, this is an organization that has a religious affiliation and an orientation toward a specified religious cohort.

Service Member Someone who is currently serving on active duty. This title is also used to denote soldiers, sailors, and airmen who are serving in National Guard and Reserve units.

Servicemen's Readjustment Act of 1944 This act was passed by Congress to support veterans returning home from World War II. Commonly known as the GI Bill, this act gave veterans two years of unemployment compensation. The idea was to remove millions of veterans from the labor force and put them into schools, colleges, and universities.

Settlement Houses Institutions formed around the late nineteenth century to address the effects of industrialization, urbanization, and immigration. Settlement houses are sometimes referred to as neighborhood or community centers. Settlement house workers utilize a self-help or mutual aid model to assist those in need, and their programs and services are often developed collaboratively with community members. Early settlement houses focused on establishing communities and organizing members and sought reforms to address the real causes of poverty. The social work methods of group work (mezzo) and community organization (macro) are associated with this movement.

Skid Row Originally a path used by loggers to skid or drag logs out of the woods to lumber yards in the Pacific Northwest. Later, it became a slang term for any area of town that was dilapidated or run down and populated by vagrants and alcoholics.

Social Darwinism The application of Charles Darwin's theory of evolution applied to social conditions. This view is rooted in the idea that social conditions reflected the survival and prosperity of those fittest to survive. In order not to interfere with this process, the government should not regulate the economy, thereby enabling the market to regulate itself.

Social Determinants of Health The circumstances in which people are born, grow up, live, and age, and the systems put in place to deal with illness. These circumstances are in turn shaped by a wider set of forces: economics, social policies, and politics.

Social Gradient A phenomenon found around the world in which those individuals who are on the lower end of the income gradient or scale have worse health than those who are on the higher gradient.

Social Insurance The social welfare expenditure called social insurance comprises collectively funded federal programs that cover workers and their dependents, provided individuals contributed to the system while they worked. Examples include Social Security retirement benefits, unemployment benefits, and Medicare.

Social Justice It is rooted in the belief that all people should have equal access to the same opportunities to freely and fully participate in society. For example, all children should receive quality education, regardless of their community.

Social Minimum A general standard of well-being in society beneath which no one should be permitted to fall.

Social Model of Disability Disability is considered to be a socially constructed category where personal and environmental discrimination creates the disability for people with physical or mental impairments.

Social Security Act (SSA) Following the Great Depression in 1935, the Social Security Act became law. This legislation established the role of the federal government in helping to meet the social and economic needs of its citizens. The act provided federal funds and established programs for older adults, children, the unemployed, and people with disabilities to reduce the likelihood that vulnerable groups will experience poverty.

Spend Down Intentionally reducing assets and resources for the purposes of qualifying for benefits and/or to meet means-testing eligibility for social programs.

State Children's Health Insurance Program (SCHIP) Enacted in 1997 and financed by the federal and state governments, SCHIP, sometimes referred to as the Children's Health Insurance Program (CHIP), is designed and administered by the states to provide health coverage to children who are uninsured and ineligible for Medicaid.

Stigma Making judgments of others based on factors such as personal traits, appearance, behavior, mental illness, sexual orientation, race, or religion.

Stress Diathesis Model This posits a relationship between non-biological or genetic predisposition (diathesis) with the environment and life events (stressors), explaining the origins of mental illnesses. It is a general framework for understanding more recent work on complex gene and environment interactions.

Subprime Lending "Subprime" refers to the status of a borrower whose income and credit history place them at risk for defaulting on a loan. These borrowers are often targets of scams as they are charged high interest rates and thought of as vulnerable and desperate.

Substandard Housing Housing with conditions posing a risk to the health, safety, and welfare of the occupants. Each state defines "substandard" with a set of codes setting minimum guidelines for sanitation, structure, and safety.

Supplemental Nutrition Assistance Program (SNAP) The new name for the program commonly known as Food Stamps is a residual means-tested federal program (administered by the United States Department of Agriculture) that provides resources for individuals and families to purchase food.

Supplemental Security Income (SSI) Enacted in 1974 under Title XVI (Supplemental Security Income for the Aged, Blind, and Disabled) of the Social Security Act, Supplemental Security Income (SSI) provides minimal financial assistance to U.S. citizens with limited income and resources who are sixty-five years of age or older, disabled, or blind at any age.

Supportive Services for Veterans Families Program (SSVF) The SSVF is a community-based program that provides a range of supportive services to very low-income veteran families in or transitioning to permanent housing to promote housing stability. The primary goals are to assist families transitioning from homelessness to permanent housing and prevent at-risk families from becoming homeless.

Survival of the Fittest A term that reflects the harsh belief of the mid- to late nineteenth century that individuals with limited income and resources must survive on their own or perish.

Temporary Assistance for Needy Families (TANF) This replaced Aid to Families with Dependent Children (AFDC) as part of the Personal Responsibility Work Opportunity Reconciliation Act of 1996 (PRWORA). This federal block grant program places an emphasis on stringent work participation requirements and changed welfare into a time-limited assistance program.

Transitional Housing Housing designed to provide a bridge between emergency shelter and permanent housing. Transitional housing may provide 1–2 years of residence and supportive services for the purpose of aiding individuals and families in becoming self-sufficient.

Treaty of Guadalupe Hidalgo The treaty that officially ended the U.S.-Mexico War and granted the United States possession of California, New Mexico, Texas, and parts of Colorado, Utah, and Arizona.

Tri-Morbid This is a term given to some people who are homeless with multiple problems involving medical, psychiatric, and drug and/or alcohol addictions.

Undeserving Poor A term that reflects the belief that individuals and populations living in poverty are poor due to laziness or an unwillingness to work, and thus they are not deserving of public assistance.

Undocumented Immigrant Term used to described individuals who cross the border without a passport, without receiving any type of visa, or who stay in the United States after their visas have expired.

Unemployment Insurance A federal income support program initiated by the Social Security Act of 1935 that replaces part of the wages of unemployed workers, usually for twenty-six weeks, but can be extended for longer periods during times of high unemployment.

Universal Declaration of Human Rights In 1948, the United Nations General Assembly adopted and proclaimed the Universal Declaration of Human Rights, which comprises thirty articles that seek to promote respect for human rights and related freedoms among all member nations.

Vagrant A term used to describe a person who is "idle," although capable of work, and who lives off the charity of others. The term was used to create vagrancy laws in the early nineteenth century to persecute individuals without housing or work.

Vet Centers Congress established the Vet Center Program in 1979 out of recognition that a significant number of Vietnam veterans were still experiencing readjustment problems. Vet Centers are community-based agencies that are staffed primarily by social workers, counselors, and psychologists. In April 1991, in response to the Persian Gulf War, Congress extended the eligibility to veterans who served during armed hostilities in World War II, Korea, Lebanon, Grenada, Panama, the Persian Gulf, Somalia, and Iraq.

Veteran Someone who has served in the armed forces of the United States and is eligible for Veterans Administration (VA) benefits earned upon discharge from active military service.

Veteran Health Registry Certain veterans can participate in a Veterans Administration (VA) health registry and receive free medical examinations, including laboratory and other diagnostic tests deemed necessary by an examining clinician. The VA maintains health registries to provide special health examinations and health-related information. Current registries include Ionizing Radiation, Agent Orange, Gulf War, and Depleted Uranium.

VetSuccess The Department of Veterans Affairs' Vocational Rehabilitation and Employment (VR&E) VetSuccess program—also known as Voc-Rehab or Chapter 31—offers disabled vets counseling, training, education, and other services needed to prepare for, find, and maintain suitable jobs.

Violence Against Women Act (VAWA) Federal legislation that requires intervention from the law enforcement community in situations involving domestic violence, dating violence, stalking, and sexual assaults against women. This act also allows women from other countries involved in a domestic violence relationship to request permanent residency in the United States, allowing the victim to safely leave the abusive relationship and denounce their abusers.

War on Poverty During the 1964 State of the Union address, President Lyndon B. Johnson declared a war on poverty and subsequently he tried to make poverty a national concern through a series of antipoverty initiatives.

Widow's Pension The original widow benefits provided economic security to widows by replacing income lost when a spouse died at a point when the widow herself, because of age or family responsibilities, could not participate in the labor market. The program continues today with some changes such as offering the benefit to both women and men and is presently considered a social insurance program, which is administered by the Social Security Administration.

Women, Infants, and Children (WIC) Established in 1972, WIC is a food, health, and nutrition program that benefits pregnant women and children up to age five for families with limited income and resources.

Working Poor Employed persons whose earnings fall below a given poverty line. One definition includes those who work full-time, year-round but earn less than the U.S. poverty standard for a family of four ($23,550 in 2013).

Works Progress Administration (WPA) The WPA was one of the best known of Depression-era government employment programs. It had the dual purpose of providing jobs to unemployed workers, and at the same time their work contributed significantly to the nation's physical, educational, and cultural resources.

About the Contributors

David K. Androff, MSW, PhD, is an assistant professor in the School of Social Work at Arizona State University. He earned his MSW and PhD in social welfare from the University of California at Berkeley. His work examines the intersection of human rights and social work, and has focused on immigration policy, human trafficking, and Truth and Reconciliation Commissions. He won the Emerging Scholar Award of 2011 from the Association of Community Organization and Social Administration, and the Frank Turner Prize for the best article in *International Social Work* in 2011. He currently serves on the Council of External Relations for the Council on Social Work Education. He teaches in the areas of international social work and community practice.

Cecilia Ayón, MSW, PhD, is an assistant professor at the School of Social Work at Arizona State University. Her research focuses on Latino family well-being, including their experiences and interactions with the public child welfare system and the impact of public policies on immigrant families.

David Becerra, MSW, PhD, is an assistant professor in the School of Social Work at Arizona State University. His research focuses on the adverse effects of poverty among Latinos, particularly in the areas of migration and immigration, health, and academic achievement.

Kristin Davis, PhD, is director of evaluation in the Thresholds-Dartmouth Research and Evaluation Center. She has worked in the center for ten years, and during this time has conducted health services research on the Integrated Dual Disorder Treatment (IDDT) model and its key components. She has also trained on IDDT and conducted fidelity reviews of the practice. Her research has sought to understand how persons who typically do not spontaneously seek treatment are engaged in treatment and/or change negative behaviors. Finally, she is interested in the role social determinants play in shaping motivation and aspiration to change.

Tim Devitt, PsyD, has worked with community mental health programs for over twenty-five years as a case manager, homeless outreach worker, team leader, therapist, program director, researcher, trainer, and consultant. His current position as the director of Integrated Dual Disorders Treatment at Thresholds, a large psychiatric rehabilitation agency in Chicago, involves providing training and consultation on the implementation of evidence-based mental health and co-occurring nicotine and other substance use treatments. He has presented nationally on topics related to the integration of mental health and substance use practices, is an adjunct instructor at the University of Chicago, School of Social Services Administration, and a member of the Motivational Interviewing Network of Trainers.

Gertrude Schaffner Goldberg, DSW, is professor emerita of social policy and former director of the PhD program in social work at Adelphi University. Her areas of study are full employment, public assistance, the feminization of poverty, and comparative social welfare systems. She has written numerous articles in refereed journals, chapters in edited books, and coauthored or edited six books. With Sheila Collins Goldberg she coauthored *Washington's New Poor Law*, which studied employment and social welfare policy from the Great Depression to the early twenty-first century. Goldberg was the editor and author of several chapters in *Poor Women in Rich Countries* (2010), the first work to study the feminization of poverty over the life course. Goldberg is co-founder and chair of the National Jobs for All Coalition.

Maria A. Gurrola, MSW, PhD, is an associate professor in the School of Social Work at New Mexico State University. She teaches human behavior and macro practice and her research involves social justice and inequality issues. Her research includes the impact of migration policy and family separation by international borders. She also examines gender relations within the family and social environment and the impact of globalization in transnational families. Her work is based around the U.S.-Mexico border states including Arizona, California, and New Mexico and looks at mental health, the impact of immigration law, and future goals for children's education. Her future research will examine community involvement and the access to bilingual and bicultural services in border cities.

Carolyn J. Hanesworth, LCSW, is an assistant professor of social work at Mercy College in Dobbs Ferry, New York. Prior to entering academia, Hanesworth worked for thirteen years as both a clinician and administrator serving homeless families in Dallas, Texas, and New York City. Her expertise and interests are in the area of chronic poverty and its impact on child development, parenting, and family life. In addition, Hanesworth has a strong interest in the education, training, and support of social workers working with homeless families, and continues this work as a consultant to organizations working to end homelessness. Currently, Hanesworth is working with the Partnership for the Homeless to develop a best practice model of service for families experiencing homelessness in East New York, Brooklyn.

Kathryn Krase, MSW, JD, PhD, is a social worker, lawyer, and social work educator. She is currently an assistant professor of social work at Long Island University-Brooklyn. She is an expert in the reporting of suspected child maltreatment. She coauthored a book, entitled *Mandated Reporting of Child Abuse and Neglect: A Practical Guide for Social Workers,* and serves as a mandated reporter trainer for professionals across the country. Krase previously served as a law guardian and guardian-ad-litem representing children in New York City Family Court for the New York Society for the Prevention of Cruelty to Children. She also served as the associate director of Fordham University's Interdisciplinary Center for Family and Child Advocacy and was the clinical social work supervisor for the Family Defense Clinic at New York University Law School.

Shannon Mathews, PhD, is currently an associate professor of gerontology and gerontology program coordinator at Winston-Salem State University, in North Carolina. She received her PhD degree in gerontology and an MA degree in medical anthropology from the University of Kentucky, Lexington. Mathews has served as assistant professor in the Gerontology Program at Towson University, Towson, Maryland, and as an instructor at Eastern Kentucky University, teaching sociology courses. She has conducted workshops, seminars, and presentations in a variety of venues on diverse aging topics. Her research interests include care-giving, issues of diversity within an aging population, developing an aging workforce, and meeting the needs of at-risk groups among the aging population. As an educator, she is very active in curriculum development, pedagogy, and service learning.

Noam Ostrander, PhD, LCSW, is the director for the Master of Social Work Program at DePaul University and the co-editor of *Disability Studies Quarterly.* He received his AM from the School of Social Service Administration at the University of Chicago and his PhD in disability studies at the University of Illinois at Chicago. Ostrander's research interests include the intersections of disability, violence, and masculinity, community health interventions, and social work pedagogy. He has published in journals spanning the fields of disability studies and social work. He has also coedited a book with Bruce Henderson entitled *Understanding Disability Studies and Performance Studies* (2010). His previous work in the field included both clinical and policy positions at social service agencies.

Elizabeth A. Segal, MSW, PhD, a professor in the School of Social Work at Arizona State University, is a social policy analyst with a background in professional social work. Her scholarship has focused on the impact of public policies and programs on disenfranchised populations and others who suffer from social inequities. Segal was a cofounder of the *Journal of Poverty*. She has coedited books on poverty and inequality and authored several social work textbooks. Her current research is on social empathy, the application of empathic insights to create social welfare policies and programs. She has completed work on an instrument to measure people's inclination toward social empathy. The instrument can be used as a tool to gauge the effectiveness of methods to teach social empathy.

John Uriarte, MSW, LCSW, BCD US Army Ret, is currently an adjunct instructor in the Department of Social Work and teaches online in the Department of eLearning and Distance Education at the University of Alaska, Fairbanks. He taught as a senior clinical lecturer at Texas State University and served for twenty-four years as a social work officer in the U.S. Army and retired as a lieutenant colonel. He has held assignments in Europe, Iraq, Cuba, and South Korea. He currently works for the Department of Veterans Affairs where he is a clinical supervisor of a counseling center for combat veterans. He is a graduate of the Social Work Fellowship Program at Walter Reed Army Medical Center, where he earned a subspecialty in child and family practice. He earned his MSW from the University of California, Berkeley.

Index

About the Editors

Elissa D. Giffords, DSW, LCSW, is a professor in the Social Work Department at Long Island University (LIU) Post. Her responsibilities include oversight of the LIU MSW Programs policy sequence and the child welfare concentration. She is also currently active in the community. Her present activities include her service as the chairperson of the Nassau County Department of Social Services Commissioner's Advisory Council and the program co-chair of the Nassau County Executive's Family Violence Task Force.

Giffords previously served as a child protective services caseworker, homeless prevention coordinator, policy advocate, direct service, and outreach coordinator. Her publications address chronic illness, health policy, child welfare, administration, ethics, and technology. She previously coauthored the workbook *Challenging the Myths and Stereotypes about the Poor*. She received the National Association of Social Workers' NYS Social Worker of the Year Award in 2008.

Karen R. Garber, LMSW, JD, is a social worker, attorney, and adjunct professor. Currently, she manages the Office of Consumer and Public Information and is the administrator for Adult Protective Services, Family and Children's Services, and Child Protective Services at the Nassau County Department of Social Services. Prior to her current administrative position, she worked exclusively in child welfare, directly overseeing programs including foster care, adoption, persons in need of supervision, juvenile delinquents, mentoring, and independent living. She is also an adjunct professor at Long Island University (LIU) Post, teaching child welfare in the BSW and MSW programs. She also facilitates a women's cancer support group and volunteers for two national nonprofit organizations.